Hoover's War on Gays

ALSO BY DOUGLAS M. CHARLES

The FBI's Obscene File: J. Edgar Hoover and the Bureau's Crusade against Smut

J. Edgar Hoover and the Anti-interventionists: FBI Political Surveillance and the Rise of the Domestic Security State, 1939–1945

Hoover's War on Gays

Exposing the FBI's "Sex Deviates" Program

Douglas M. Charles

University Press of Kansas

© 2015 by the
University Press
of Kansas
All rights reserved

Published by the
University Press of
Kansas (Lawrence,
Kansas 66045),
which was organized
by the Kansas Board
of Regents and is
operated and funded
by Emporia State
University, Fort Hays
State University,
Kansas State
University, Pittsburg
State University, the
University of Kansas,
and Wichita State
University

Library of Congress Cataloging-in-Publication Data

Charles, Douglas M.
    Hoover's war on gays : exposing the FBI's "sex deviates"
program / Douglas M. Charles.
        pages cm
    Includes bibliographical references and index.
    ISBN 978-0-7006-2119-4 (hardback)
    ISBN 978-0-7006-2150-7 (ebook)
 1. United States. Federal Bureau of Investigation—History.
 2. Homosexuality—Government policy—United States—
History—20th century. 3. Gays—United States—History—
20th century. 4. Intelligence service—United States—History—
20th century. 5. Internal security—United States—History—
20th century. 6. United States—History—20th century. I. Title.
    HV8144.F43C4285 2015
    363.25'9536—dc23

                                              2015014447

British Library Cataloguing-in-Publication Data is available.

Printed in the United States of America
10 9 8 7 6 5 4 3 2 1

The paper used in this publication is recycled and contains
30 percent postconsumer waste. It is acid free and meets the
minimum requirements of the American National Standard for
Permanence of Paper for Printed Library Materials Z39.48-1992.

For those who have fought and continue to fight for simple equality

Contents

Acknowledgments, ix
Prologue, xi

Chapter 1. Was J. Edgar Hoover Gay? Does It Matter?, 1

Chapter 2. "The Victim of a Degenerate": The Origins of FBI
Surveillance of Gays, 1937, 22

Chapter 3. "Sex Perverts in Government Service": Second World War
Gay Baiting and the FBI Investigations of Sumner Welles, David
Walsh, and Philip Faymonville, 36

Chapter 4. "Sex Deviates in Government Service": The Lavender Scare
and the FBI Sex Deviates Program and File, 69

Chapter 5. "Take This Crowd On and Make Them 'Put Up or Shut
Up'": The FBI; the Mattachine Society; ONE, Inc.; and the
Daughters of Bilitis, 153

Chapter 6. "Something Uniquely Nasty": The FBI; the Mattachine
Societies of New York and Washington, DC; Donald Webster
Cory; and ECHO, 216

Chapter 7. "It's a Thing That You Just Can't Tell": The FBI and the
Johnson and Nixon Administrations, 269

Chapter 8. "I'm Ready to Die for the Cause!": The FBI Confronts Gay
Liberation, 302

Epilogue, 343
Notes, 369
Bibliography, 425
Index, 439

Photo gallery follows page 199.

Acknowledgments

Writing a book of this size and scope cannot be accomplished single-handedly, and it is a pleasure to thank those who offered their kind and crucial assistance. These include the director of academic affairs on my Penn State campus, Margaret Signorella, who graciously offered a course release to complete Chapter 5, which allowed me to finish this book on time. Our reference librarian, Andrew Marshall, deftly located much material for me; the head librarian, Courtney Young, was instrumental in getting me an FBI file central to this book. Our faculty secretary, Nancy Lucas, helped me to print the big manuscript. Steve Rosswurm kindly shared with me a much-needed document. The staff of the ONE Institute Archive and Library kindly photocopied what they had of the FBI Daughters of Bilitis (DoB) file after I had departed without it. Marjorie Bryer of the GLBT Historical Society helped me get access to a differently redacted copy of the FBI DoB file. Genny Beemyn was ever so kind in sharing information with me that pointed me in valuable directions. Matthew Cecil not only helped with his expertise on the FBI and the media and FBI personnel files but he kindly shared with me FBI files and photos to which he won access (and vice versa); one of those files turned out to be crucial to this story. *New York Times* reporter Matt Apuzzo graciously connected me with Charles Francis and shared vitally important documents. J. Louis Campbell III, at Penn State Altoona, was kind enough to share obscure information he knew about Jack Nichols. Aaron Stockham graciously shared with me a document he ran across that turned out to be part of a larger story in Chapter 4. C. Todd White was ever so helpful with detailed information he knew about the early homophile activists. My onetime research assistant Karl Sokalski helped me locate photos, and Sabina Medilovic, a research assistant early in this project, helped me gather biographical data and foil redactions. John O'Brien and John Lauritsen shared some of their experiences in the Gay Liberation Front and Lauritsen a useful photo. I must also thank the two readers of the manuscript for the University Press of Kansas (UPK), who offered excellent advice and encouragement. My editor at UPK, Michael Briggs, and the entire staff there are unparalleled; I have never worked with any publisher as good as they are.

The staffs of the FDR and Truman Presidential Libraries were helpful and kind, and this project would not have developed as it did without generous research funding from the Truman Library Institute. The staff at the Eisenhower Library quickly and generously responded to my mandatory review requests. The staff at the Minnesota Historical Society was quite helpful. Phil Runkle, at the Marquette University Archives, kindly and promptly responded to my various requests from afar. The FBI Freedom of Information Act (FOIA) staff was helpful in narrowing some of my larger requests and promptly responded to my inquiries, even if getting hold of the actual FBI files is a slow process.

It cannot be articulated how fortunate I have been to have access to Athan Theoharis's encyclopedic knowledge about the FBI. His always helpful and insightful responses to my many inquiries were invaluable. The same goes for my dissertation director, Rhodri Jeffreys-Jones, whose support and advice have remained unparalleled since 1998.

Prologue

For decades in the United States, particularly dating from the mid-twentieth century, gay men and women feared law enforcement of every stripe. Being arrested at a private gathering or party, in a gay bar, or soliciting sex in a seemingly remote location meant being publicly outed, losing their jobs, and an end to life as they knew it. Being arrested on a "morals charge" meant social stigmatization, including possible incarceration or commitment to a mental institution, and being ostracized by family and friends. Topping the list of law-enforcement agencies gays and lesbians feared most was the Federal Bureau of Investigation (FBI). Unlike local police, FBI agents had not only inexhaustible federal resources and connections but a carefully crafted public image as scientific investigators who never failed in their efforts. To be discovered, then outed, by J. Edgar Hoover's FBI was one of the worst possible scenarios any gay man or woman could face.

Until now, the history of the FBI investigations, monitoring, filing of information, and deep obsession with gays and lesbians has only been documented sporadically and its origins unknown. There are reasons for this lacuna. Sophisticated and documented histories of the FBI have existed only since the mid-1970s, after FBI abuses became public through congressional investigations and a newly invigorated Freedom of Information Act (FOIA) permitted scholars access to FBI files as primary sources. Contemporaneous to this, also for the first time, historians began to develop gay and lesbian history. Necessarily, then, it took time before an effort to reconstruct a comprehensive history of the FBI and gays was even possible. The first FBI histories focused, naturally, on documenting bureau investigative abuses, civil liberties violations, and the creation of specialized files used to insulate sensitive or illegal FBI activity. Biographies of the long-serving FBI director then began to appear, followed by a variety of "FBI and . . ." books covering everything from racial minorities to student activists to anthropologists to obscenity; the list is now extensive. Few FBI historians have touched upon FBI interest in gays and lesbians, and those who have did so in a limited or focused fashion.

Historians of the gay and lesbian past have not examined in detail, or comprehensively, FBI interest in those with same-sex attraction. This is a function of the difficulty in accessing source material on a wide range of subjects using the FOIA. It is time-consuming and costly. Released files are often heavily redacted, sometimes the FBI resists researchers' efforts, and the bureau still routinely destroys files it deems nonhistorical and will not release anything if the subject is still living—limiting what we can know about the FBI and more recent gay and lesbian history. Gay and lesbian historians have also typically lacked a sophisticated understanding of both the complicated nature of the long history of the FBI and its byzantine filing procedures. Without an appreciation for both, any examination of FBI files relating to gays and lesbians often will make no sense and reveal little. FBI files are not stamped "Sex Deviates File," for example. The FBI document file number alone, a cryptic series of numbers—105-34074-104—reveals FBI agents' use of the Sex Deviates File, type of case, and size of the file. Knowing this first is key to FBI research.

There have been occasional and episodic histories of FBI interest in gays, lesbians, and their respective advocacy groups, however. FBI historian Athan Theoharis offered the best when he wrote his book *Chasing Spies* (2002), an examination of FBI failures to stem foreign counterintelligence but success in promoting the politics of McCarthyism. Theoharis devoted a chapter to the FBI and gays, "The Politics of Morality," that detailed J. Edgar Hoover's promotion of both a politics of counterintelligence (gays as liable to blackmail) and a politics of morality (gays as a moral peril). Theoharis examined briefly, and only as part of his larger study, the 1950s congressional committees investigating the gay threat; the start of the more formal Sex Deviates Program and File; and the FBI in relation to Adlai Stevenson, Arthur Vandenberg, and Joseph Alsop.[1]

Other FBI historians offered less on the FBI and gays, a function of writing comprehensive single-volume histories of the bureau. Richard Gid Powers restricted his coverage only to the rumors surrounding Hoover's sexuality in his FBI history *Broken* (2004). Rhodri Jeffreys-Jones briefly touched upon FBI interest in gays at different points in *The FBI: A History* (2007). Journalist Tim Weiner also only briefly touched upon the FBI and gays as they related to the Central Intelligence Agency (CIA), Stevenson, and the Dwight Eisenhower and Lyndon B. Johnson administrations in *Enemies: A History of the FBI* (2012).[2]

The first significant notation of the FBI in a history of the gay and lesbian past was in John D'Emilio's *Sexual Politics, Sexual Communities* (1983). As both lesbian, gay, bisexual, and transgender (LGBT) and FBI studies then were young, D'Emilio was necessarily restricted to simply noting the varied

FBI interest and footnoting some FBI files related to gays and lesbians. As part of a larger study examining gender—specifically the "ideology of masculinity"—and the US descent into Vietnam, Robert Dean dissected FBI targeting of Charles Thayer, Charles Bohlen, and others in the foreign policy establishment during the 1950s Lavender Scare in his *Imperial Brotherhood* (2001). (During the 1950s the color red denoted communists, pink signified sympathizers, and lavender was reserved for gays.) As Dean saw it, bucolic conservatives such as J. Edgar Hoover, Joseph McCarthy, and others found it expedient to attack members of the elite, entrenched, foreign policy establishment who had propagated the containment policy by questioning their sexuality (the "effete" elite), their associations with gays, and their level of anticommunist resoluteness (being "soft" on communism). Without a doubt, perceptions of gender were an important ingredient in FBI efforts, but they were not *the* driving force. Dean's thesis, moreover, is convincing only when looking narrowly at the temporal confines of the 1950s public Lavender Scare and the eastern elite. When one considers more broadly FBI targeting of gays over five decades (dating from the mid-1930s) and well beyond elites, it becomes clear there were multifaceted influences at different times driving FBI targeting of gays.[3]

Marcia Gallo's otherwise excellent history of the lesbian group Daughters of Bilitis (DoB), *Different Daughters* (2006), only briefly noted FBI interest in the group. Unsurprisingly, Gallo also mischaracterized FBI interest as part of its illegal COINTELPRO disruption program. Her inexact and brief treatment of FBI interest in that organization represents the typical problem with LGBT histories: an incomplete understanding of the FBI and, especially in the case of the DoB, the spotty nature of extant FBI records. In his important book *The Lavender Scare* (2004), David K. Johnson deftly documented the public and political Lavender Scare, in which Hoover's FBI played a major role, but only briefly noted Hoover's interest in Bohlen, Stevenson, Thayer, and the like. The FBI itself was not indexed in the book. As with Gallo's study, this is an unsurprising function of the difficulty and lengthy time it takes to access sometimes incomplete FBI files along with Johnson's not being a specialist in FBI history.[4]

Other limited scholarly examinations that have touched upon both the FBI and gays are either those that stand alone without any broader FBI contextualization or those that are part of altogether different studies. These include Alexander Stephan's book *"Communazis": FBI Surveillance of German Émigré Writers* (2000) and Adrea Weiss's article "Communism, Perversion,

and Other Crimes against the State: The FBI Files of Klaus and Erika Mann"
(2001). Also in this category are Lawrence R. Murphy's article about the
gay baiting of Senator David Walsh, "The House on Pacific Street: Homosexuality, Intrigue, and Politics during World War II" (1985), and Irwin F.
Gellman's first exposé of Undersecretary of State Sumner Welles's peccadilloes in *Secret Affairs: Franklin Roosevelt, Cordell Hull, and Sumner Welles*
(1995). The FBI involvement in gay baiting General Philip Faymonville was
briefly recounted in Mary Glantz's article "An Officer and a Diplomat? The
Ambiguous Position of Philip R. Faymonville and United States–Soviet Relations, 1941–1943" (2008).[5] No one has ever contextualized or examined
together the FBI's concurrent investigations of Welles, Walsh, and Faymonville, however.

Hoover's War on Gays presents the first comprehensive history of FBI
interest in, obsession with, and politics surrounding gays, lesbians, and their
respective organizations. As such, it attempts to merge FBI scholarship with
the scholarship of gay and lesbian history to reach a more comprehensive
understanding and contextualization of the broader history. This book is
therefore predominantly original research and, in part, historical synthe-
sis, revisiting different areas previously, but often separately, researched and
examined by other historians. To understand better FBI interest in some
of these once-trod subjects, I have returned to the primary sources to construct my own understanding of them in light of broader FBI history and
to suss out details others have overlooked.

This book, therefore, revisits the Second World War–era FBI interest in
Welles, Walsh, and Faymonville but examines them together as part of a
greater whole. It also revisits, including with new material, FBI investigations of Thayer and Bohlen (and others), subjects of interest to Dean and
(with Bohlen) Theoharis. It further revisits and contextualizes, again with
new detail, the FBI and Stevenson, Vandenberg, Alsop, and Senator Henry
Cabot Lodge Jr., all subjects Theoharis has previous discussed. Significantly,
this study also builds on Theoharis's discovery of the FBI Sex Deviates Program and File. Theoharis learned about it from FBI documents that indirectly described its general purpose and methods. This book offers, for
the first time, analysis using the previously unreleased and original FBI Sex
Deviates Program policy document. It offers previously unknown details
about the program and, with other documents, dates the program's implementation to earlier than we had previously thought.

The pages that follow make clear that there was no single causal factor, gender or otherwise, to explain the fifty-plus-year FBI interest in gays, lesbians, and the politics surrounding them. A confluence of forces at particular moments—starting in 1937 and ending in the 1990s—including gender, perceptions of morality, politics, bureaucracy, personality, economics, culture, the construction and intensity of homophobia in the United States, and changing perceptions of homosexuality helped shape the ways in which the FBI responded to gays, lesbians, and their respective organizations. Yet even with all this, there was always one common, persistent thread ever present since 1937: an overarching and intense fear and loathing of gays. Although FBI officials and others always had an official rationale for targeting gay citizens—characterizing them as criminals or vulnerable to blackmail and influence, for example—always underneath it all was an irrepressible animus. One Civil Service Commission (CSC) bureaucrat, incredibly, even admitted as much in a policy memo in the mid-1960s. The construction and intensity of homophobia changed over time and was/is something influenced by shifts in US society and culture. The FBI responded with this homophobia, influenced by contemporaneous forces and events of many types. FBI agents, throughout, were able to marshal a seemingly inexhaustible supply of willing informants and use their liaisons with police departments, government agencies, and others in targeting gays and lesbians. Their efforts both frightened and intimidated countless gay citizens and energized still others to organize and fight for equality. In the long run the FBI was unable to resist forces demanding change from it and other more conservative institutions, yet none of those efforts in any way were easy. In fact, going up against the FBI was singularly difficult as well as dangerous.

Hoover's War on Gays

CHAPTER I

Was J. Edgar Hoover Gay?
Does It Matter?

To address the questions posed in this chapter's title simply and directly: we do not, and cannot, know; and no.

For decades, even during his own directorship, J. Edgar Hoover's sexuality was the subject of rumors. These rumors were largely based on gay stereotypes and potent US sociocultural influences that dictated gender roles during Hoover's lifetime. For much of US history—particularly in the post–Second World War period—a paternalistic, hypermasculinized, dominant, heterosexual culture defined expectations in US society. A man was presupposed one day to marry, have several children, and be the breadwinning king of his suburban castle. He further was expected to dominate his demure wife, whose only jobs were to raise the kids, buy the groceries, haul them home in a station wagon, cook the meals, and clean the home. Hoover defied all of this. He remained a lifelong bachelor and a man particularly close to his mother. He lived with her until she died in 1938, by which time Hoover was forty-three years old, and only then did he buy his own house. Hoover also maintained a long and close friendship with another bachelor, the number two man at the Federal Bureau of Investigation (FBI), Clyde Tolson, with whom he regularly dined and took vacations. All the while Hoover touted a strict, Victorian value system and castigated those forces in US society he believed were decaying it from within. He dispatched FBI agents to intimidate anyone who suggested he was gay.

A couple of examples illustrate this last point. During 1943, FBI agents learned that District of Columbia businessman John Monroe had claimed Hoover was a "fairy." This was not all. Monroe also claimed to have proof, which, he bragged, protected him from the FBI. This information was developed by the New York Field Office of the FBI but not reported to headquarters until January 1944. When Hoover learned about it, he responded instantly in two ways. First, FBI officials officially admonished the special agent in charge (SAC) in New York for not forwarding the information promptly. Second, FBI Assistant Director Louis Nichols paid a visit to Monroe to make him, in Hoover's oft-uttered refrain, "put up or shut up." Monroe was sufficiently intimidated, which was the goal, and he signed a statement affirming he had never made the claim about Hoover.[1]

FBI harassment of those spreading homosexual allegations about Hoover was not restricted to prominent individuals. After FBI agents learned a woman had made disparaging comments about the FBI director's sexuality at her bridge club in Cleveland, the SAC in that city paid her a visit. He admonished her about the claim and convinced her to tell her bridge partners at the next meeting that she was wrong and sorry for having made the comments. Similarly, after a beautician in Washington, DC, gossiped about Hoover's sexuality, she was visited by two FBI officials who similarly intimidated her.[2]

It is not a surprise that many people—then as well as now—recognized something peculiar about Hoover and his unbending social orthodoxy and just assumed he was gay. Over the decades, moreover, there appeared a multitude of stories purporting to prove Hoover's homosexuality or other seemingly related aspects or quirks about him, but it all came to a head at a precipitous moment. With the cold war and its attendant anxieties over by 1993—at the same time a fired gay FBI agent daringly sued the FBI to win back his job—these stories about Hoover received a significant boost after conspiracy-theory novelist Anthony Summers published his sensational biography of the FBI director. Summers resurrected the old rumors to claim not only that Hoover was gay but that he wore dresses and failed to target organized crime rings for prosecution because they had blackmailed him with a compromising sexual photo.[3]

In a world more driven by media than ever before, that boost accelerated to become a cultural phenomenon, the effects of which continue even today. The magazine *Vanity Fair* published excerpts from Summers's book, the normally discriminating PBS series *Frontline* aired a documentary on Hoover using Summers as somehow an expert on the FBI director, and then the media frenzy multiplied exponentially. Various news outlets carried unverified stories about Hoover's sexuality and related topics, including a 1993 *New York Post* piece that claimed Hoover had been caught up in a 1960s extortion investigation involving somebody using young men to target prominent gays by placing them in compromising positions and then extorting from them sums as large as $150,000. This particular rumor contained a kernel of truth, however. In fact, a 1960s FBI investigation captioned "Compromise and Extortion of Homosexuals," code-named HOMEX, investigated famed pianist and performer Liberace among others (see Chapter 7), but it never involved Hoover as a subject. The media hype then extended to lowbrow jokes on Jay Leno's *Tonight Show* about the FBI director's presumed sexuality, and jokes were even offered by opposing prominent national politicians—notably President Bill Clinton and Republican Bob Dole—about Hoover's alleged cross-dressing.[4] The media hype then evolved to become a common and instantly recognizable cultural meme as reflected in the Hollywood spoof film *Naked Gun 33 1/3: The Final Insult* (1994), in which Detective Frank Drebin is retiring and shown his exalted spot on the retirees' wall of fame. The wall included not portraits but Drebin's carefully framed handcuffs and detective's suit situated among others, including J. Edgar Hoover's carefully framed handcuffs and pink, frilly, froufrou dress.[5]

The indomitable Hoover meme, and the seemingly uncritical public acceptance of the "fact" of Hoover's homosexuality and cross-dressing, prompted Athan Theoharis—the dean of FBI historians and no defender of Hoover—to respond with a book examining the evidence Summers used in his biography. In short, Theoharis deflated that evidence by showing none of it was verifiable, convincing, or from credible sources—the bread and butter of academic historians. He also pointed out that many in the gay community, perhaps unsurprisingly, happily anointed Hoover homosexual because they had a vested political interest either in exposing "his hypocritical homophobia" or in holding him up as an example that gays, in fact, had long held sensitive and important government positions.[6]

There is no need to recount in detail here every single example of Summers's so-called evidence, but the now culturally popular stories about Hoover and the most significant of Summers's evidence should nevertheless briefly be surveyed. One of Summers's sources, Susan Rosenstiel, claimed to have seen Hoover at two separate gay parties, one in 1958 and the other in 1959, at the Plaza Hotel in New York City. These were parties hosted by Roy Cohn (former aide to Senator Joseph McCarthy and himself reputedly a gay man), at which Hoover was alleged to have been wearing women's clothing while having gay sex. A skeptical Theoharis asked the question: why would Rosenstiel be attending gay orgies? Why, moreover, would she be attending them with her wealthy, conservative-minded husband who was so worried about his public image that he hired former FBI official Nichols—Hoover's skilled public relations man in charge of the FBI Crime Records

Division—to protect that image? Rosenstiel, moreover, was divorced from her husband by the time she told these tales, and Summers had paid her for them.[7]

Theoharis argued convincingly the details of Rosenstiel's claims were so outlandish that they defied credulity. In the midst of the Lavender Scare, when even an allusion to homosexuality would wreck someone's career and forever ruin his or her life, the director of the FBI supposedly not only allowed himself to be seen at two gay orgies but wore a "fluffy black dress, very fluffy, with flounces, and lace stockings and high heels, and a black curly wig . . . makeup on and false eyelashes, . . . sitting there in the living room of the suite with his legs crossed." Hoover was introduced to Rosenstiel, moreover, as "Mary"—a common gay euphemism—and openly had sex with two teenagers dressed in leather while one of them read from a Bible.[8] "Nothing is missing" in this account, Theoharis perceptively noted, while concluding it best represented a stereotypical "homophobic account" from a motivated woman seeking to "defame her second husband, with whom she had been involved in a bitterly contested divorce which lasted ten years in the courts."[9]

Theoharis also critically examined another source Summers used to suggest Hoover sought professional treatment for his homosexuality. Again this raises the issue of even the slightest allusion to homosexuality ruining one's career, which should lead any discriminating historian to question the source's authenticity. Theoharis pointed out, moreover, that the source was not the psychiatrist himself, who supposedly treated Hoover, but his widowed wife. Raising even more flags was her assertion that the medical records that would prove the contention had been destroyed, leaving nothing backing the claim but hearsay. More fantastical yet was Summers's claim that Democratic Senator William Fulbright was the individual who had recommended this particular doctor to Hoover. In short, using hearsay evidence, Summers asks us to believe that Hoover, again, in the middle of the Lavender Scare, unhesitatingly sought a recommendation from a prominent politician—whose political views he did not share—so that he could place himself in the vulnerable position of seeking psychotherapeutic treatment to cure his homosexuality. Even worse, Hoover was willing to do this when he knew therapists' confidentially was not inviolable. His own FBI agents, as this book demonstrates, used therapists as willing sources of information about gays.[10]

Summers's third source on Hoover's homosexuality involved the claim that a photo existed of Hoover having gay sex with Tolson, that members of the Mafia had it, and that they were blackmailing the FBI director to avoid investigation. Just as with the previous evidence, this allegation is loaded with red flags. As Theoharis pointed out, nobody has ever produced the photo; people have merely claimed to have seen it. Even more fantastical, the photo was supposedly taken by Office of Strategic Services (OSS) officers in 1946 to be used as bureaucratic leverage against Hoover's FBI. At the time, federal agencies were entangled in a bureaucratic fight over who would be responsible for foreign intelligence after the Second World War. The photo then somehow supposedly found its way into the hands of organized crime rings. One glaring problem with this account, Theoharis observed, was that the OSS had dissolved a year prior to the photo having been taken. Theoharis also keenly pointed out that if the OSS, indeed, had a compromising photo of Hoover, the agency would not have used it as mere leverage but would have used it to purge Hoover from the FBI. Hoover would have been regarded as a security risk, and it would have been an unprecedented opportunity to forever remove a perennial, manipulative bureaucrat. It is true enough Hoover and other bureaucrats wrangled over who would control postwar foreign intelligence—I have written about it myself—but the photograph story simply defies credulity.[11]

There have been various responses to the renewed, post-1993 suggestions about Hoover's sexuality and supposed cross-dressing in which authors have typically come down on one side or the other. Several former FBI officials have offered their views, including Ray Wannall, who long served as a top bureau official at headquarters—ultimately rising to be assistant director of the FBI Intelligence Division. Wannall dismissed Summers's allegation in his memoir, arguing that the best journalists in the country had covered Hoover for almost fifty years and "developed nothing to confirm rumors of this nature, which cropped up occasionally during Hoover's lifetime, usually tied to his status as an avowed bachelor." He even cited the fact that journalist Jack Anderson, who famously and publicly questioned Hoover's sexuality in the 1970s, decided by the 1990s he did not believe either the cross-dressing story or that Hoover was gay given the FBI director's history of "venomous" comments about homosexuality.[12]

Cartha DeLoach, once head of the FBI Crime Records Division (where the Sex Deviates File was kept) before rising to the number three position in the FBI, similarly commented on the homosexual allegations in his memoir and elsewhere. DeLoach referred to Summers's conclusions as nothing but a "string of opinions, rumors, and undocumented charges" that the biographer presented as fact. Revealing his own homophobia (and no doubt that institutionalized in Hoover's FBI), DeLoach wrote that the allegations "so disgusted me that I simply put it out of my mind" until he was so commonly asked about it that he devoted a chapter of his memoir to the issue.[13]

To DeLoach, the idea that Hoover and Tolson could be gay was unbelievable. "You can't work side by side with two men for the better part of twenty years," he argued, and "fail to recognize signs of such affections." He also refuted Summers's claims that Hoover and Tolson had effeminate characteristics. DeLoach said, employing typically gendered language of his era, both "were tough and manly. Hoover was a bulldog." As for Tolson, "there wasn't the slightest sign of weakness or 'prettiness' in his face." Then, taking a dig at Summers personally, DeLoach observed that Tolson "was certainly more of a man then Mr. Summers, and I've seen both at close quarters."[14]

Besides relying on his own bigotry and stereotypes to refute Summers, DeLoach recognized that Summers's evidence was flimsy at best. He characterized that evidence as the "testimony of corpses. They are convenient witnesses because they can't be cross-examined." DeLoach even castigated the media for seemingly excusing Summers's homophobic and stereotypical characterization of Hoover, especially "given the current fashion to approve of and promote homosexuality."[15]

The rumors about Hoover remained alive and strong, however, leading DeLoach to continue his defense of the FBI director. In 2003 he commented online, "Many of us who knew Director Hoover for many years know he was not a cross-dresser and homosexual. As one of his top assistants (Deputy Director), I traveled with him, saw him frequently each day and often under trying circumstances while working on major cases. He was a deeply religious, old-fashioned, twofisted type, who believed in firm discipline. Under no circumstances would he have risked his reputation and that of the FBI by such habits unbecoming to his way of life. He was tough and recognized that to gain the cooperation of the public he had to win respect."[16]

William W. Turner, a former FBI agent who served the bureau for a decade, in 1970 wrote a memoir (updated and republished in 1993) about his experiences, characterizing himself as the Ralph Nader of the FBI—a man who "gradually became disabused of my illusions about the Bureau" and decided the US public needed to know what it was funding. Turner, a man who was fired from the FBI in 1961, obviously had a bone to pick and was no defender of the bureau or Hoover. He, in fact, believed Hoover devoted too much time to anticommunism at the expense of organized crime. Turner decided to accept the notion that Hoover was gay and claimed that agents, having no evidence of Hoover's sexuality, often referred to his closeness with Tolson as "unwholesome." He wrote that Hoover's sexuality, to him, "really didn't matter except for the fact that Hoover not only preached family values, he bashed homosexuality with a vengeance."[17]

The impact and persistence of these popular notions about Hoover's supposed homosexuality have, indeed, been profound. Those writing popular history have, perhaps unsurprisingly, accepted the cultural meme blindly or with little skepticism. To cite just one example, writer Charles Kaiser published a well-written popular history of the gay movement, *The Gay Metropolis* (1997), in which he described Hoover's relationship with Tolson as "homoerotic" regardless of whether we know the answer to the "mystery of whether the relationship was actually consummated."[18]

Even some academic historians have accepted the story with qualification or seemingly at face value. Hoover biographer and FBI scholar Richard Gid Powers noted in his 1987 biography, *Secrecy and Power,* that the work routine and friendship between Hoover and Tolson "was so close, so enduring, and so affectionate that it took the place of marriage for both bachelors." He also cited the only suggestive evidence he found about their relationship, intimate photos Hoover took of Tolson asleep. Powers did not fully discount the notion that Hoover and Tolson might have had a sexual relationship, and he purposefully called it "spousal" because it was so unclear, but in the end he was forced to conclude, perceptively, "There is no compelling evidence for a definitive judgment in either direction."[19]

Craig Loftin argued in his otherwise excellent study of ordinary gays who wrote to *ONE* magazine that a "strong case can be made that Hoover and Tolson should be considered a gay married couple." Loftin arrived at this conclusion after having examined the ways in which everyday gay couples lived their lives at midcentury: masking their relationships in different ways, often living separately but otherwise doing everything else together, including jointly owning a business, which gave them both financial independence and an officially "partnered" relationship. To him, because Hoover and Tolson were seemingly inseparable but especially because they worked as the top two FBI officials, vacationed together, and dined together constantly, because Hoover willed most of his estate to Tolson, because their life together as heterosexuals "makes no sense" and evidence of their heterosexuality "is nonexistent," and because Hoover's targeting of gays is evidence of his passing as straight, Loftin concluded Hoover and Tolson fit

the typical pattern of other gay couples of the time.[20] To arrive at this conclusion, one must first accept the notion that Hoover and Tolson were gay—
and evidence of that is based on nothing but conjecture and stereotyping.
Second, none of Hoover's and Tolson's behavior as described by Loftin is
evidence of sexuality unless one accepts stereotyped behavior somehow
as valid historical evidence. For that matter, why does anyone's relationship—especially when there is an inexhaustible supply of widely divergent,
nontraditional relationships in humankind—have to "make sense"? That a
relationship somehow "makes sense" really means that it fits dominant cultural expectations. As for Hoover targeting gays to cover, or mask, his sexuality, as we shall see in this book, there were specific and larger forces behind
the fact that Hoover's FBI targeted gays originating in 1937 and escalating in
1950–1951. The events transpiring in these periods had nothing whatsoever
to do with masking. Besides, Hoover was not the only bureaucrat targeting
gays; a multitude of others also targeted gays ruthlessly in an effort to purge
them from federal employment. Masking is an unconvincing and simplistic
explanation for gay targeting.

In a byzantine essay, Claire Bond Potter pondered proof of sexuality and
the issue of rumor in history. She asked, "How ought historians to treat evidence about events that may be not factual, partially factual, or impossible
to prove? And in the absence of proof, how do we account for the capacity of unfactual stories to tell otherwise unspeakable truths about political
culture?"[21]

Making use of queer theory, Potter on one level made a valid point
about historians' attempts either to prove or disprove Hoover's sexuality.
She keenly observed, "Whether J. Edgar Hoover was a homosexual or not is
not the point." She noted that whichever way one examined it, Hoover did
not fit the mold of what would have been considered a "normal" man in
his era—not that he was necessarily gay but that he was peculiar, or queer,
for what would be expected in the midcentury United States.[22] This is fair
enough because dwelling on whether Hoover was gay (or straight), I think,
misses the point about what all the various Hoover stories tell us about the
homophobia of his era and the paramount power of conformist heterosexual culture (i.e., Hoover's sexuality was questioned precisely because he
did not fit culturally imposed expectations).

Potter also called for a "queer narrative in which gossip is critical historical evidence about the tension between public political culture and private
citizenship, [which] would suggest that both things [Hoover as closeted gay

man and Hoover as confirmed bachelor] may be true and yet neither factual." She asserted, "We do not have facts about Hoover's sex life, but we
do have evidence in the gossip about Hoover's sex life." She then called for
reading evidence "from the vantage point of dissonance, repression, stigma,
perversion, and inversion" for an "intervention in political history." Her
point seems to be that lack of proof of Hoover's homosexuality is also not
proof of his heterosexuality, especially given popular recognized traits of
the closet in Hoover's life. Strangely, she suggested not holding "researchers'
feet to the fire over the quality of their evidence."[23] Instead, she proposed
historians examine what Hoover desired, "whether sexually or politically."[24]

I contend that the discourse over whether Hoover was gay or straight
might be tempting and something interesting about which to speculate
(provided one admits to speculation), but in the end is not particularly
helpful in advancing our understanding of what Hoover's FBI did when
investigating or monitoring gays for more than half a century. We simply do
not know—and, indeed, cannot know—what Hoover's sexual preference
(whether gay, straight, bisexual, asexual, or repressed), was and whether it
played any discernible role in what he and his FBI did. It seems no longer
worth expending the energy to prove, factually, his sexuality one way or the
other. It is already illuminating that Hoover's not fitting cultural expectations of masculinity inspired curiosity about his sexuality (and he always
quickly and quietly, but unsurprisingly, had such speculation quashed).
Additionally, drawing theoretical conclusions using gossip as historical
evidence over Hoover's sexuality seemingly just complicates the matter at
hand. I will leave that task to historians immersed in queer theory.

Many people, though, seem to thrive on the question of whether a gay
or straight Hoover explains what his FBI did vis-à-vis gay citizens. We can
easily dismiss this proposition, I think, by employing an historical coun-
terfactual—a what-if question. What if we knew—as a concrete fact—that
Hoover was, as they say, straight as an arrow? What if he had married, had
several children, had the typical 1950s wife as a homemaker, and so forth?
Would, then, FBI Director Hoover have done anything markedly different
vis-à-vis gays over the decades? It seems logically consistent that he would
have done nothing different. Hoover's treatment and targeting of gays
would still make sense to us given the era and the larger historical, political,
social, and cultural forces at play. Therefore, and to reiterate, dwelling on
Hoover's sexuality is not helpful to our comprehension of the FBI's relationship with gays. It should also be remembered that not only did Hoover's

FBI go after gays but virtually every part of government was targeting or somehow attempting to regulate gays dating from the federal government's mid-1930s "discovery" of homosexuality. Far more helpful to understanding the FBI role in targeting gays is comprehending how their place as a unique group of human beings in US society unfolded and changed over time as public and cultural attitudes about them evolved from the late nineteenth century and rapid US industrialization and urbanization to the advent of the Great Depression.

The recognition of a unique group of human beings, singled out and known for their same-sex attraction, did not exist until the latter third of the nineteenth century. The German medical community, or more specifically the neuropsychiatric medical community, first recognized gays in a clinical fashion. It started with the German medical professor Karl Westphal, who in 1869 published a medical treatise about a woman with same-sex attraction and a man who was effeminate. Westphal used the (translated) phrase "contrary sexual sensation" to describe their apparent condition. Later as other European sexologists such as Vienna-based Richard von Krafft-Ebing further researched the topic, the notion evolved, in German, into the term *homosexualität*—medical terminology crafted by combining the Greek *homos*, or "same," with the Latin *sexualis*. By 1892, as German medical texts were being translated, the term migrated into the English language as "homosexuality." Even before the 1880s, however, US medical professionals were making use of Teutonic-inspired same-sex concepts. Intriguingly, medical professionals and others did not, and could not, recognize a specific group of "heterosexuals" until they recognized "homosexuals." Heterosexual (from the Greek *hetero*, or "different") as a term thereby came into existence only by 1900.[25]

As medical professionals began to recognize and observe what they styled homosexuals, ordinary people with same-sex attraction began to realize their own unique status as a minority group. This phenomenon was a function in the United States of rapid industrialization and urbanization during the last three decades of the nineteenth century. Prior to this, same-sex copulation—sodomy, or buggery—was regarded merely as an individual, sinful act, grouped together with other sexual transgressions such as adultery, fornication, incest, and even bestiality.[26]

As US culture shifted from its traditional, rural, agricultural roots to an urban, industrial, and interconnected life, society and culture dramatically changed. Land was no longer the basis of wealth. New and varied technological developments shifted the basis of wealth, which now became a function of technological innovation. Power-driven machines fueled by coal after 1830 replaced water, animals, and human beings as sources of energy; technology increased productivity; factories rather than cottages became the locus of production of goods; and developments in transportation made the movement of those goods and people more rapid. Innovations in communications technology, such as the telegraph, led to instant communications and a now-functional (and smaller) national economy rather than a collected assortment of local markets. Using railroads as a guide, big businesses began to organize in cities and on a national level, leading to urban development and exploding municipal populations. In these urban populations, teeming with factory workers, the gay identity would form.

Cheap human labor was central to keeping these urban, industrial factories operating without pause. This attracted not only immigrants from Eastern and Southern Europe—fleeing desperation and bringing with them new languages, customs, religions, and ideas—to US industrial centers after 1880 but also a large number of rural US citizens. Those who had previously lived in close-knit farm villages or towns, where they were constantly under the watchful eyes of their families and religious authorities, now found themselves living among thousands of strangers. They realized, for the first time, they were living largely autonomous and anonymous personal lives free from the yoke of moral overseers. Many of those who moved to the cities in search of work, moreover, were single. They lived in boarding houses or tenements rather than with their nuclear or extended families. Living largely isolated lives, they craved social interaction, which they were forced to seek out among the businesses in cities that catered to hospitality.

As they began to socialize, those with same-sex attractions—that is, those the medical community was starting to recognize as members of a distinct group—suddenly realized they were not alone. They were not aberrations or individuals driven into sin by moral lapses or plotting supernatural beings. There were others like themselves, and they began to meet. Because their sexual activity was still regarded as sinful, they met in the least respectable parts of town, in bars where people like themselves would be tolerated and where they could meet freely and interact. Places such as New York City's Paresis Hall became notorious in the view of middle-class denizens not only for their apparent degeneracy but their working-class dominance. Yet even places such as these fascinated well-to-do citizens, who occasionally visited them to take in the spectacle and gawk at these strange and different people. This form of entertainment came to be known as "slumming."[27]

Quite naturally a new vernacular evolved beside the one invented by the medical community to describe these people with same-sex attraction. These terms had varied meanings and were applied in different ways and in different circumstances. They are important to note because they were used at different historical times covered in this book. At the turn of the twentieth century, because most people identified men interested in same-sex relations as either acting in an effeminate manner or assuming the female sexual role, they commonly and popularly referred to these people in society euphemistically as "fairies." This gendered descriptor, used to differentiate the *other* from the "normal," dominated until the mid-twentieth century.[28]

Law enforcement, along with medical and moral regulators, typically used the terms *degenerate* and *pervert*, or—again viewing same-sex attraction as essentially a reversal of men's and women's gender-specific roles—as *invert*. In the 1920s and even more so by the 1930s, "deviate" or "sex deviate" became common to describe somebody not perceived as "normal." As historian George Chauncey has pointed out, our contemporary term, *homosexual*, did not really catch on as common parlance until the mid-twentieth century.[29]

During the 1920s and later, gay men were still commonly perceived as effeminate (despite the fact that how individuals carried themselves ran the spectrum), and some compared them to flowers: pansy, daisy, or buttercup. Some were called *nance* or *nancy boy*. Lesbians could be called, crudely, *she-men* or, at least in New York, *bull daggers*—again, based on a gendered view. Some homosexual men referred to themselves as *faggots* or *queens*, but these also had more specific meanings alluding to one's uniquely effeminate manner. Men who were otherwise considered heterosexual but would consent to sex with gay men provided they played the dominant, assertive, or "male" role, were called *trade*. In other words, they were willing to trade something in exchange for sex. In the 1910s and 1920s, some homosexual men did not want to be identified by effeminate traits and thus chose *queer* (as in not the usual) as a more neutral term that, itself, would evolve to become derogatory. Finally, by the 1930s and 1940s, *gay* came into usage by a younger generation who perceived the popular terms *fairy* and *queer* as unpalatable.[30]

To be sure, from the late nineteenth century through the 1920s, there were common negative perceptions or even hatred of those with same-sex attraction, but it was never dominant. Historian Jay Hatheway has located the origin of US homophobia as having two roots. One origin was the concept of American exceptionalism—that US citizens were special, uniquely different, and morally superior to the corruption, depravity, and debased values of the Old World. In one sense, dating to the Founding Generation and the Enlightenment, the concept of liberty—so essential to the new nation—was rooted in the laws of nature, which if followed resulted in harmony. It therefore did not take much for US educators, moral champions, politicians, and others to focus on the regulation of sex as a moral, and perhaps unique to this nation, political obsession.[31]

Hatheway found the second origin of US homophobia in the concept of essentialism. Dating from the late nineteenth century, the idea that men and women had firm and concrete *essential* characteristics that defined them was powerful and unchallenged. In what we would today consider social stereotypes, women were regarded as weak, subordinate, docile, and demure—the feminine; men were regarded as strong, aggressive, dominant, and tough—the masculine. Hatheway observed that both American exceptionalism and essentialism coalesced "in early antebellum America to forge a very conservative national ideology that resisted inclusion," so that when a group of citizens emerged in the late nineteenth century identified by their same-sex attraction—perceived through a gendered lens—it is easy to understand how the dominant, heterosexual culture came to view them so negatively (to whatever degree) given perceptions of themselves and the world.[32]

Those negative perceptions came to a head in 1919 after the conclusion of the First World War, at the US Naval Base in Newport, Rhode Island. Besides the base, Newport was also home to the Naval War College and a military hospital, making it a significant location for the navy in the immediate postwar period. The scandal's origins can, in one sense, be dated to the arrival at the base in early 1919 of Chief Machinist's Mate Ervin Arnold, a patient suffering from rheumatism transferred from San Francisco.[33]

Prior to joining the navy well over a decade before, Arnold had been a trooper with the Connecticut State Police. Perhaps as a result of his policing duties—he regularly pursued and arrested "perverts"—Arnold was a confirmed homophobe. He said in official testimony, "I can take you up on Riverside Drive [in New York City] at night and show them [homosexuals] to you, and if you follow them up, nine times out of ten you will find it is true." He even claimed he could identify them by how they carried themselves and how they looked. In the hospital, Chief Arnold, a self-anointed gay expert, saw navy personnel and patients, all male, referring to one another using female nicknames, discussing sex, acting in an effeminate manner, and even apparently sometimes wearing makeup—all violating proscribed gender roles.[34]

Chief Arnold took detailed notes of his observations and discussed the situation with others who held similar views. His discussions led to his learning that the local Army-Navy Young Men's Christian Association (YMCA) was a popular meeting place for gay men, who were known there as the "gang." Perhaps believing enough was enough, Arnold approached the hospital welfare officer, Dr. Erastus Hudson, who also held views similar to Arnold's. The information was then passed up to the commander of the naval station, who then traveled to Washington, DC, to discuss the matter with senior Navy Department officials: Secretary of the Navy Josephus Daniels and Assistant Secretary of the Navy Franklin D. Roosevelt. Daniels was not available, and it was the job anyway of the assistant secretary to run the day-to-day affairs of the navy, so Roosevelt was receptive to and authorized an investigation that extended into 1920.[35]

We can understand the navy's broad interest in these matters by recognizing its context. Around the same time the Newport matter was unfolding, the Red Scare of 1919–1920 was also under way. In the aftermath of a seemingly endless number of labor strikes in 1919, followed by a series of mail and house bombings at the hands of anarchists, all happening after the Bolshevik Revolution in Russia, Attorney General A. Mitchell Palmer decided to purge the United States of its apparent foreign radical threat. The Bureau of Investigation (the "Federal" was not added until 1935) worked in collusion with the Immigration Bureau of the Department of Labor to round up foreign radicals via dragnet raids and mass arrests to have them deported. The end result was widespread civil liberties violations. In Newport, as nationally, the navy was looking for threats.

In Newport, a court of inquiry was formed to investigate further beyond the observations of Chief Arnold. Initially, Navy Department officials wanted the Bureau of Investigation to investigate, but a request was hastily prepared and a preoccupied bureau was lackadaisical in responding. In the end the bureau was not interested, no doubt having its hands full with the Red Scare. The navy therefore continued its own investigation and, given his background, made use of Chief Arnold. Arnold suggested employing an undercover operation to trap gay men at the YMCA. The base commander authorized Chief Arnold and Dr. Hudson to focus on three matters: drug and alcohol use, "perverts," and female prostitution. In their efforts, Arnold and Hudson ignored the first and third matters to focus almost exclusively on the prevalence of homosexuality at the navy base.[36]

Over March and April 1919 the two men recruited investigators—willing decoys, really—to catch gay men red-handed. They sought out reliable but not overly intelligent, good-looking, young sailors in their late teens or early twenties who were willing to place themselves in awkward positions as sex decoys. Once recruited, these young men combed the city making friends with suspects, attending their parties, taking them to dinner, and returning with them to their rooms.[37]

To catch their prey, the decoys were quite willing—despite self-identifying as heterosexual—to have sex with them and unhesitatingly report the lurid details to their superiors. This included taking their clothes off with the suspects and having oral and anal sex all the way to climax. This, along with other circumstantial and hearsay evidence, was then compiled by the court of inquiry, which then authorized arrests to drag targeted men for questioning before the court. Over the next three weeks, twenty-four sailors were questioned or had witnesses offer evidence against them. The arrested men never knew about the decoys until after being found guilty, but some of them, upon facing interrogation, decided to inform on their colleagues.[38]

In the end, the court of inquiry recommended that seventeen men be court-marshaled on charges of sodomy, scandalous behavior, or both. Few had lawyers; none were permitted to confront their accusers (the decoys). Two men were dishonorably discharged from the navy, and two others were released for lack of evidence, but most were found guilty and received jail terms of between five and twenty years. The investigation, however, was not finished. It quickly expanded beyond the military to focus next on civilians.[39] At the time, military authorities and the federal government had jurisdiction for the region adjacent to military bases.

The navy investigators resented the fact that the YMCA was being used as a gay meeting place, and they disliked equally the fact that this was all happening under the nose of the Reverend Samuel Kent, who worked at the YMCA. Because this all happened on his watch, because he seemed to allow gays to use the YMCA, because he showed excessive sympathy for hospitalized sailors, and because he was perceived as effeminate, Reverend Kent himself was suspected of being gay. Kent and others were arrested and charged with lewd conduct under state law.[40]

Because of lack of evidence against him, Kent was found innocent in court. Navy investigators then promptly charged him with violation of federal law—there was a wartime law aimed at reducing "moral contamination" in the area of a military base. After his first trial Kent had left New England for Michigan and had to be forced to return for trial. This time, however, Kent had the backing of clergy and other influential supporters. The prosecution then backfired on the navy, and Kent was again found innocent of all charges.[41] The now-embarrassing event led to a larger navy investigation of the Newport affair, which, unsurprisingly, promptly exonerated the investigators.

Secretary Daniels wrote to Roosevelt in March 1921, during the last days of the Wilson administration, that he had been "sweating blood over the Newport case" but believed the "conclusion reached is just to all concerned."[42] The navy investigation was, of course, really a whitewash. That, in turn, led to a highly politicized US Senate investigation, the report of which was not released until 1921 (after the presidential election in which Roosevelt was the Democratic vice-presidential nominee), making the political lives of both Secretary Daniels and Assistant Secretary Roosevelt markedly uncomfortable.[43]

When released in the summer of 1921, the Senate report condemned the decisions of both Daniels and Roosevelt. The Senate, of course, was firmly in the hands of Republicans after the 1920 election, so their conclusions, though with some merit, nevertheless had a strong political tinge. The Senate found that Daniels and Roosevelt both knowingly used sailors "as participants in immoral practices for the purpose of obtaining evidence on which to dismiss offenders from the navy." To Republicans this was dismissive "of every American boy who enlisted in the navy to fight for his country."[44]

The Democratic leader on the Senate committee investigating Newport, Senator William King of Utah, found the Senate report "in many particulars unjust and unfair." He castigated Republicans for making unjust deductions and writing a report designed to "confuse the reader and compel unjust and false judgments." He asserted that neither Daniels nor Roosevelt were aware of the methods employed at Newport until it was too late. He cited the fact that even the navy court noted Roosevelt's ignorance until he had been approached by clergy defending Reverend Kent in September 1919.[45]

Roosevelt also issued his own public statement regarding the Senate findings. He said he bemoaned the "bad faith and a conscious perversion of facts" by the majority of senators using the Newport incident "as the vehicle for cheap ward politics." He also claimed it amused him that they "consider me worthwhile attacking so maliciously and savagely." Roosevelt admitted that he asked for help from the Justice Department rather than leaving it to the navy, but that it did not work out. He also admitted to assenting to the "formation of an investigating squad" led by Hudson and Arnold, who, he said, had been "recommended to me by all concerned and by the Red Cross Officer at Newport." He categorically denied, however, that he had ever supervised their work or knew any of the details as they investigated. He said that as assistant secretary of the navy, he was far too busy with other matters to deal with something so small and involving a relative handful of people. When by September 1919 he learned of the investigative methods employed, Roosevelt claimed to have issued orders immediately that they be stopped.[46]

The Newport incident is significant in a couple of ways. As historian Chauncey has pointed out, despite the furor over "moral" conditions at Newport and the employment of young sailors engaging in "immoral practices"—as the *New York Times* reported—to trap gay sailors, the decoys themselves were never considered homosexual, deviant, or perverted. Provided they played the masculine, dominant sex role—the penetrative role, or, in the case of oral sex, the receptive role—they were not regarded as homosexual and, thereby, not a (or the) problem. This tells us much about cultural perceptions and construction of homosexuality (based on perceived and preferred gender roles) during the New Era of the 1920s and prior to the Great Depression.[47]

Newport is also significant, it seems to me, for the role played by Assistant Secretary of the Navy Roosevelt. Although he might not have been intimately involved with the tactics employed to trap gay men in Newport, Roosevelt nevertheless authorized the investigation and in that sense was a significant player in the first major federal investigation of gays in US history. It is terribly ironic, then, that he would later, and for a second time, play a significant role—this time as president—when he decided to involve the presidency in another investigation. This one involved the kidnapping and murder of ten-year-old Charles Mattson in 1937 and prompted J. Edgar Hoover's FBI to begin a systematic and widespread collection of information about "sex offenders" that would only continue to grow and evolve over the following five decades. This made Roosevelt central to the first significant federal investigation of gays and to the start of the most significant federal targeting of gays.

One final event preceding the Great Depression sheds significant light on the origins of the FBI surveillance of gays: the brutal 1924 murder of fourteen-year-old Bobby Franks at the hands of nineteen-year-old Nathan Leopold and eighteen-year-old Richard Loeb. Products of well-to-do, prominent families in Chicago and highly intelligent (in fact, arrogantly so), Leopold was a University of Chicago law student in the process of transferring to Harvard and Loeb was a graduate of the University of Michigan. The two gay lovers, clearly sociopaths, decided to commit murder to see if they could get away with it. The case engrossed the US public and illustrates the perceptions of gays in the 1920s and how those views would change within only twelve years.

In the fall of 1923, Leopold and Loeb decided to commit murder. Knowing something about criminal forensic techniques, they used a portable Underwood typewriter stolen from a University of Michigan student on which to write the ransom note. Through the fall and spring they planned the murder, believing if they did it carefully and deliberately enough they would never be discovered and thereby demonstrate (to themselves) their superior intelligence. Knowing they could not use their own automobile, under an assumed named Leopold rented a car from the Rent-a-Car business on Michigan Avenue in Chicago while Loeb waited by the phone to confirm Leopold's fake identity for the car rental agent when he called.[48]

According to the prosecution, Leopold and Loeb had no particular victim in mind other than some boy with wealthy parents. They wanted a ransom of $10,000 that, they instructed in their prewritten note, should be thrown from a train at a specific point. They proceeded with their plan on 21 May 1924. Leopold attended classes at the University of Chicago while Loeb made preparations for the murder. Their premeditated plan included using ether to render their victim unconscious, rope to bind him, a metal chisel to bludgeon him to death, and hydrochloric acid to burn away his identifying features.[49]

They drove to the Harvard School in Chicago, the same private school both Leopold and Loeb once attended, to find and choose a victim. They parked their rental car at a distance and used binoculars to spot their target. Initially targeting young Johnnie Levinson because he had wealthy parents, their plan was foiled when Levinson failed to walk in their direction. It was then that fourteen-year-old Franks, who was an acquaintance of Loeb's, walked by the car. They offered him a ride home and convinced him to climb into the front passenger seat, which he did. They then pulled the car around a corner to avoid undue scrutiny. Immediately after parking, one of them savagely and repeatedly bludgeoned the boy in the head with the chisel, then pulled him into the rear seat and shoved a rag in his mouth while using his hand to clasp his mouth shut until the boy expired.[50]

According to the prosecution, immediately after killing Franks, Leopold and Loeb "took his shoes and stockings and trousers off"—the prosecution argued they raped the boy. They then wrapped the "bleeding, mangled, and dead" body in a blanket and, armed with revolvers in case they were stopped, drove it to a remote area with which Leopold was familiar from ornithology class. Before dumping the body, however, they coldly stopped to eat their packed dinner.[51] Only after they arrived at their disposal location did they remove the remainder of the boy's clothes before pouring acid on his face and submerging the body, face first, in a drain. The water ended up washing away most of the acid, foiling that aspect of their plan. It was here that Leopold, unbeknownst to him, accidentally dropped his eyeglasses. They then returned to the Leopold family home to burn the boy's clothes and dispose of the other evidence, including tossing the chisel from the car and burying those items that would not burn. They then washed the rental car, returned it, phoned the Franks house to inform his parents about the kidnapping, and mailed the ransom note.[52]

After finding the body and Leopold's glasses, the police managed to trace them to the teenager. They were uncommon glasses, made in New York City and sold by only one company in Chicago. By measuring the prescription, the police were able to narrow the glasses down to three suspects, including Leopold. Brought in for questioning, Leopold made up a lie about bird-watching in the area and having tripped and fallen, thus explaining losing his glasses. The police only dug deeper, gathering more evidence incriminating Leopold and Loeb until they finally confessed on 31 May.[53]

Coming from well-to-do families, Leopold and Loeb ended up hiring as their lawyer Clarence Darrow, the famous attorney noted for taking on unusual cases. (It would be the following year that Darrow defended biology teacher John T. Scopes in the famous so-called monkey trial.) Recognizing the hopelessness of their case given their confession and the mountain of evidence against them, Darrow convinced them to change their plea to guilty. His goal, as he explained to them, was to save them from execution. Darrow believed a jury would never find the pair innocent and would not likely be convinced to spare them from the noose. If they pleaded guilty, however, Darrow believed he could convince a single judge schooled in

the law, as opposed to a biased jury, to spare the teenagers from death—
especially because Illinois had never in its history executed a teenager who
confessed to murder.[54]

Leopold and Loeb pled guilty and threw themselves on the mercy of the
court, necessitating a hearing to determine their final punishment. Darrow, long an opponent of capital punishment, noted the state's execution
history and argued that the two were mentally deranged and, as such, deserved incarceration rather than execution. The state argued for execution
using the defendants' homosexuality against them. The prosecutor argued,
"These two defendants had had a quarrel and made it up—and I will not
go into the nature of that quarrel; there is a lot of evidence in this case that
has not come out and I do not intend to repeat it, to shock any person who
may be listening" and then referred to Leopold and Loeb as "perverts." He
argued that, sexually, Leopold was the "aggressor" and Loeb the "victim"
and that they "entered into a childish compact" of murder so that Leopold
would continue "these unnatural crimes" with Loeb. In other words, Leopold convinced Loeb to help him get away with murder in return for sexual
favors. The prosecutor exclaimed that he himself "was a grown man before
I knew of such depravity."[55]

The Leopold and Loeb trial was followed intently in the press and as a
state crime did not involve the Bureau of Investigation—an organization,
in any event, that only evolved into a true national police force with a scientific crime lab during the Great Depression. Given the New Era's preoccupation with sex, it is little wonder that a trial using psychological theories
about sex as evidence was so closely scrutinized. The theories of Sigmund
Freud were popular among members of the US public in the 1920s, even if
they did not truly understand them. Sex was discussed openly like never
before, a function of the so-called New Morality. Followers of the case were
fascinated by the legal spectacle, and when the judge decided to spare the
murderers' lives, it was reported in newspapers from coast to coast.[56] Yet
the significance of the Leopold and Loeb case, ironically enough, lies not
so much in what happened as in what *did not* happen. The case, with all its
vivid detail reported in the press and consumed nationally, did *not* lead to
a sex-crime panic or a widespread national clampdown on gays, nor did it
spark a systematic federal effort to target apparently dangerous homosexuals as a threat to children.

On the contrary, it was regarded as a curiosity and an aberration. Frederick Lewis Allen, for example, merely listed Leopold and Loeb in his iconic

and near-contemporaneous retrospective *Only Yesterday* (1931) as one example among many of something merely interesting to the "casual newspaper reader in 1924." Historian of the 1920s Michael Parrish noted that critics
of the Leopold and Loeb case saw in the teens the "moral wasteland created
by families with too much money, young men with too much education and
not enough simple morality grounded in religion." In other words, members of the public did not perceive an overarching flaw in US society that
would lead them to see a dangerous threat in gays and reevaluate gender
roles, as they would during the Great Depression. Instead, the Leopold and
Loeb case was perceived as a function of the material excesses and moral
drift of the 1920s, not among the larger society necessarily but a specific
segment and particular example. After the economy crashed in 1929 and
the Depression started in 1930, however, US citizens would make profound
social and cultural reevaluations so that when an eerily similar kidnapping
and murder of another young boy transpired a decade later, the ramifications would be profound for the FBI's relationship with gays.[57]

CHAPTER 2

"The Victim of a Degenerate"

The Origins of FBI Surveillance of Gays, 1937

Two days after Christmas 1936, in a well-to-do neighborhood of Tacoma, Washington, ten-year-old Charles Mattson, the son of a prominent surgeon who lost most of his wealth in the 1929 stock-market crash, sat in his family's living room Sunday evening after having listened to Jack Benny's radio program, drinking root beer and eating popcorn with his two siblings and a friend. His parents were not home at the time. Unexpectedly, a stranger appeared outside, beyond the French doors that led to a rear courtyard. The stranger, later described as a "swarthy, middle-aged man with a heavy growth of beard" who wore a blue jacket and light-colored cap and carried a pistol, demanded that the children let him into the house, a residence that gave the impression that the family still had substantial wealth. When the children refused, the stranger smashed the glass in the door and opened it himself. Searching the children for money but not finding any, he turned to Charles—a small, towheaded boy with blue eyes—and said, "I want you to come with me right away. You're worth money." He grabbed Charles by the arm, dropped a ransom note on the floor, and fled from the house. Young Charles Mattson was never seen alive again.[1]

Almost immediately the press got hold of the story, and it engrossed the US public from coast to coast for many months. One of the reasons it was so scrutinized, besides being reminiscent of the popular Lindbergh kidnapping of 1932, which itself led to the first federal kidnapping law, was that there had not been a major case of this kind in the country since the spring of 1935. At that time, ironically enough, another boy from Tacoma—George Weyerhaeuser—was kidnapped, but he had been returned unharmed, and the perpetrators were apprehended and incarcerated. Federal Bureau of Investigation (FBI) Director J. Edgar Hoover, who had previously referred to the Weyerhaeuser case as the last of its kind, now faced a frightened public and the dubiousness of his own misplaced claim. His FBI immediately took over the case, and Hoover dispatched eight agents from various western FBI field offices to Tacoma, including an FBI laboratory technician with "complete laboratory equipment."[2]

In a second ransom note written by Charles Mattson (the handwriting was confirmed by the FBI laboratory) mailed to the family and received on 30 December, the abductor demanded a cash payment of $28,000 for the boy's safe return. Mattson's parents, meanwhile, over several days tried to communicate with the kidnapper. They did so by placing messages to a "Mabel-Ann" in the *Seattle Times.* This was eerily similar to the way the Lindberghs had communicated with the abductor of their child. While the parents desperately waited to hear something, FBI Assistant Director for Investigations Harold Nathan, who had successfully overseen the Weyerhaeuser case, was placed in charge and led forty-five agents in pursuing any and all leads. Included in their investigative arsenal, according to rumors reported in the press that FBI records confirm as true, was the use of wiretaps and phone traces. (The reason it was only reported as a rumor was because dating from 1934 and the Federal Communications Act, wiretapping was an illegal activity, so FBI officials would have been hesitant to admit its use.) Technicians in the FBI laboratory also attempted to identify a possible suspect by comparing latent fingerprints lifted from the ransom note, by comparing samples of handwriting, and by undertaking a "general appearance search" of the bureau's general appearance file of criminals. Despite these efforts, however, no clear suspect was found.[3]

As the ransom deadline approached and passed, the family heard nothing from the kidnapper. FBI agents then found their job increasingly more difficult as desperate imposters, claiming to be the kidnapper, tried to swindle the ransom money from the Mattson family.[4] The agents were also frustrated by incessant leaks to the newspapers, leading FBI Assistant Director Edward Tamm to order a "stamp down on the police department or the family with both feet [to] shut them off because the newspapers are getting too much information." On 10 January 1937, the weather took a turn for the worse, and it became bitterly cold and then began to snow. This led FBI agents to conclude the kidnapper would wait before releasing the boy and collecting the ransom so as to avoid being easily tracked. FBI agents, in the meantime, searched an uninhabited island in Puget Sound after someone reported seeing two men and a boy there. They found nothing.[5]

On Monday, 11 January 1937, all hopes for the safe return of the boy evaporated when a teenager hunting rabbits about fifty miles from Tacoma and six miles from the town of Everett discovered Mattson's body lying about 600 feet from a road. The body was found naked and frozen in the snow, with obvious signs it had been terribly brutalized. The boy's skull had been crushed, his teeth knocked out, and his torso and face bruised badly. Forensic evidence indicated Charles had suffered a nonfatal, but torso piercing, stab wound in his back. The boy's hands were tightly bound. An FBI memorandum further reported that the coroner believed Charles could have died as late as Saturday night, but most likely on 6 January. Further evidence indicated he was murdered suddenly and unexpectedly while eating an orange because remnants of such were found in his mouth and stomach. Many of these gruesome details were reported without redaction in the *New York Times*, as were some presumed details about the kidnapper.[6]

Given how the body appeared when it was found—naked and bound— the news reporting seemed to suggest what investigators believed but seemingly hesitated to state bluntly or forthrightly: that Charles Mattson was the victim of a sexual predator. The *Times* reported that investigators had determined the kidnapper, in his behavior, to be "somewhat childish," "incoherent," and "demented." (The only witnesses to the kidnapping and thus the only source of information about the kidnapper were children.) The *Times* also described Charles the day he was snatched as a "blonde-haired boy rather small for his age." Because the kidnapper had his choice over which child to abduct and the fact that he chose small Charles over the other children, this reporting seemed to suggest some kind of peculiar attraction on the part of the abductor. Investigators even speculated about the "personality factors" that were "apparent" from the kidnapper's modus operandi: he was "bold," cowardly, childish, and "eccentric." All of these descriptors were traits commonly and popularly associated, at the time, with gays. In the midcentury United States, society stereotyped gays and unhesitatingly categorized them alongside, or with no distinction from, genuine "sex offenders." A significant aspect of this was the notion that gay men targeted children. Given these popular and culturally ingrained assumptions, FBI agents searched hospital records hoping to locate a mentally ill perpetrator, and Hoover promised that the FBI would "use all the resources at our command to apprehend . . . the kidnapper and slayer of the Mattson boy."[7]

Vivid and suggestive news reporting notwithstanding, the Charles Mattson murder was elevated from a local crime to the status of a national cause célèbre after President Franklin D. Roosevelt (FDR) commented on it. On 12 January 1937, the president publicly referred to the crime as "ghastly" and recognized how it had "shocked the nation." The president then offered his personal promise that FBI agents would pursue the case "relentlessly" and that it "will not be terminated" until the perpetrator was captured. "A crime of this kind," the president said, "is renewed evidence of the need of sustained effort in dealing with the criminal menace." FBI Director Hoover thereafter personally took charge of the case and even sent the Mattson family a floral piece for the boy's funeral. Hoover's third in command at the FBI, Assistant Director Tamm, personally kept abreast of all developments, twenty-four hours a day, even from home and by telephone, rather than assigning that duty to an FBI supervisor at headquarters during nights. Tamm believed this arrangement preferable to enable him to make on-the-spot decisions rather than having to rely on third-hand summaries of current developments.[8]

The day after FDR's comments, the Associated Press released a story that FBI agents were on the lookout for a California ex-convict named Fred Orrin Haynes, a repeat offender. Haynes not only bore a resemblance to the kidnapper but had served two prison terms for receiving stolen property and burglary. (FBI files show that agents listed many named suspects, but none of them panned out.) That investigators immediately focused their efforts on an ex-convict in 1937 is not surprising. During that time, it was a common belief, but especially among public authorities, that homosexuality was a typical trait among criminals. One judge publicly suggested as much in 1937 when commenting on the Civilian Conservation Corp's (CCC) accidental admission of a paroled criminal into its ranks of impressionable young men authorities wanted to keep from transiency and protected from perceived immorality. The judge observed, "It is a well-known fact that sexual perversion is frequently found among ex-convicts."[9] The Associated Press also suggested in its reporting on the murder that the kidnapper was "desperate" and "almost insane with fear," descriptions that jibe with FBI reports. Significantly, the Associated Press reported that FBI agents, who rarely revealed anything to reporters, would not "say definitively" whether Charles "was the victim of a degenerate," but this was the assumption everyone, including FBI agents, made.[10]

Investigators then located a shack, referred to in the press as the kidnapper's "lair," where he had kept the boy. In the shack, they found Charles's bloodstained clothes, including, according to newspapers, his underwear. Such a discovery, in a ramshackle yet typical Depression-era example of transient housing, confirmed the type of suspect FBI agents sought, leading them to raid hobo encampments and to detain thousands of suspects in cities across the West. It was even reported in the press that FBI agents "were seeking a degenerate for the kidnap-murder but did not know his identity." (The Haynes lead turned out to be a dead end.)[11]

The most visible sign of the Great Depression and reflection of mass unemployment and homelessness was the tramp, or hobo. Popularized in literature and film, moving from place to place typically by jumping trains, the hobo ultimately became the iconic image of hard times in the United States. Almost forgotten today, at the time the transient was also widely believed to be a member of a group heavily populated by sexual perverts, a belief not restricted to the Depression era but with a storied past dating at latest to the turn of the century. Yet with many men in such desperate straits, it was not unusual for transients either in search of food or money to trade sexual favors to sustain their mercurial lives. It was even commonly believed that the desperate hobo—referred to as a "wolf" in hobo vernacular (who stayed in a "lair")—would target a destitute and homeless youth—called a "lamb" or "chicken" in their parlance—in search of sexual pleasure and in the process corrupt and recruit him into his own deviant lifestyle. As pointed out by historian Margot Canaday, this was, in fact, one reason New Dealers created the CCC, as an effort to prevent transiency and therefore degeneracy among US youth. The federal government even tried to deal with the transient via its Federal Transient Program but failed. Indeed, Canaday quotes one authority on transiency as commenting in 1937, "Most fags are floaters."[12]

FBI officials and agents, indeed, focused their investigative efforts on those they perceived to be degenerates. Shortly after the murder, FBI officials sought the opinions of experts who might be able to profile the kidnapper. One such expert, a physician FBI officials consulted but then decided could not provide enough "tangible" and workable information, suggested that the "kidnapper is a mental case." The doctor was "also . . . of the opinion that the kidnapper is a sexual pervert," not insane but someone with "sexual abnormalities." He suggested monitoring closely local arrests and asylums. This information was not particularly useful to FBI agents, though, because they were already doing these things. The chief of police in Eldora, Iowa, even suggested fingerprinting all hobos in order to find a suspect. He related that his office jailed all hobos rather than "letting them sleep in the boxcars."[13]

With assumptions such as these being common, FBI agents were drawn particularly toward suspects who fit this specific profile. In one example,

FBI Assistant Director Tamm developed information out of New York City about a man named Tim Lazero, who except for his age fit the description of the kidnapper, including the name "Tim," signed on the Mattson ransom note. Lazero, furthermore, was known to be "engaging in various criminal activities out there [in Tacoma], he was a pervert, and had a cabin in a very isolated place where he used to take young boys on whom he practiced his perversion." What is more, Lazero had even been previously arrested in Tacoma for child abuse. Despite FBI agents investigating him, the Lazero lead went nowhere. In a second example, an FBI informer provided agents the name of his former jail cellmate, Charles Foggee, as the possible murderer because "Foggee was a sexual pervert" and because "he believes the perpetrator of the Mattson kidnapping to be likewise a pervert; therefore, Foggee must have committed the crime." This lead also went nowhere because the FBI informant was "very elderly" and "in advanced stages of senility."[14]

The popular view that a "deviate" had committed the Mattson crime inevitably led others to perpetuate specific views on the case despite investigators, in truth, knowing little to nothing about the perpetrator. A New York minister, Reverend Christian Relsner, commented that with this crime US citizens now realized the "possible bestiality of man." He said that men's "habits and methods have made life cheap and pleasure sensual," and the murder illustrated "our bad moral state." He remarked, "If done by degenerates, remember that degenerates are born to drunkards and sexual sinners." Relsner even had a solution and dire warning: "Unless America repents her sins, then, like Nineveh of old, further destruction will come." Unlike the Leopold and Loeb case of 1924, Relsner was blaming the nation itself and not just the excesses of New Era wealth.[15]

The Mattson case was intently pursued by investigators and reported regularly in the press. None of the leads or suspects detained—FBI agents had eliminated a staggering 24,000 suspects (no doubt mostly hobos, convicts, and mental patients)—revealed a solution to the crime and, in fact, the murderer was never located. The Mattson case, moreover, became a national media sensation that inaugurated what became a long sex-crime panic during the second half of the 1930s as the country sank deeper into the Great Depression. Following the Mattson murder, the public and press between 1937 and 1940 began to focus on the perceived threat to children from "sexual degenerates." This, in fact, as pointed out by historian Estelle Freedman, led the *New York Times* in 1937 to create a separate news category for its index: "Sex Crimes." In 1937, the *New York Times* published 143 articles on the topic, and, although most of the victims were girls, nobody really made any fine differentiations about the work of people they regarded as degenerates. Although not contemporaneous with 1937, a view from 1950 and another sex-crime panic illustrate this perception. *Coronet* magazine writer Ralph Major in September 1950 described the "homosexual" as "an inveterate seducer of the young of both sexes." Another example, printed in the *Washington Times,* related the story of a thirty-two-year-old man who in September 1937 admitted to murdering two ten-year-old boys in New Hampshire. He was unsurprisingly described in the article as a "degenerate." One concerned citizen from Iowa, also reflecting these concerns as well as the larger sex-crime panic, wrote the FBI director to demand "protection against the known Morons who are roaming the streets as well as the paroled convicts who are daily killing people. . . . They should be taken care of—burn them alive."[16]

FBI Director Hoover responded, but he only sustained the public's new obsession and contributed to public biases when he spoke in September 1937 calling for a "War on the Sex Criminal." In Hoover's view the "sex fiend, most loathsome of all the vast army of crime, has become a sinister threat to the safety of American childhood and womanhood." Hoover warned the public that the sex criminal was not mythic or an innovation of modernity but someone who fed on public "apathy and indifference in the handling of out-of-the-ordinary offenders." A previously "ordinary offender," Hoover continued, was turned into a "dangerous, predatory animal . . . because he has been taught he can get away with it." The FBI director then listed the deviate's teachers as "parental indifference, parole, abuses, political protection, and other factors." Warning US citizens what to watch for, Hoover wrote that the "sex fiend is a progressive criminal" who starts "with annoyances," then moves on to engaging in "obscene letters" and exhibitionism, until he graduates to murder.[17]

Hoover then told US citizens that only they could summon the government to effect a "new approach" to this specific problem. He called on the public to demand special laws to deal with sex criminals. Hoover also asked for studies to be made of the influence of marijuana and hashish in promoting sex crimes, as well as examinations into the psychological underpinnings of perversion. In this, Hoover demanded in-depth investigations into the "history of every offender" across the country. "The present apathy of the public toward known perverts generally regarded as 'harmless,'" Hoover warned, "should be changed to one of suspicious scrutiny."[18]

Although the sex-crime stories made for good copy, the increases in crime rates were not significantly different from any other period except for the intense public interest. What fed the panic though, according to Freedman, was the convergence of three phenomena during the mid-1930s: the rise of forensic psychiatry to explain crime, the Great Depression having left many destitute, and the new prominence of a sexual theory of crime.[19] It was, therefore, the confluence of these and—in the matter of the origins of the obsessive FBI interest in gays—*other* events that ultimately led FBI Director Hoover to initiate the systematic FBI collection of information on gays, who, given 1930s perceptions of sexuality, were categorically regarded as and automatically labeled "sex offenders."

For full appreciation of their significance, it is necessary to review the totality and impact of these events. First, the sensational effects of the Mattson case were overarching. The abuse and murder of a small boy made for emotional news particularly given the popular issue of crime, particularly child kidnappings, during the Great Depression, especially in the context of Hoover's previous comment that such kidnappings were a thing of the past. Many people remembered both the Lindbergh kidnapping/murder and the Leopold and Loeb case. With the perceived increase in the incidence of crime, the Justice Department in the years preceding the Mattson case took advantage of the publicity to convince Congress to grant the FBI increased crime-control powers and jurisdiction in areas such as kidnapping that previously had been the responsibility only of local and state police. The Mattson case, however, was especially sensitive and crucial to Hoover given the embarrassment of his previous claims about the end of child kidnappings, and this motivated him in relentlessly pursuing sex crimes and monitoring a target contemporary public authorities found obvious: gay men, or, as they would put it, "sex offenders."

The dogged FBI pursuit of the perpetrator and "sex offenders" in general was amplified when FDR stepped in to promise publicly that the FBI would not stop until the murderer was located. Why would the president of the United States so publicly comment on a local crime? He was likely taking advantage of the intense popularity of the case to advance his federal crime-control program, and he called for a "sustained effort" to eliminate this particular type of "criminal menace." This is particularly significant because at the time Hoover—a holdover political appointee of the conservative Republican Calvin Coolidge and Herbert Hoover administrations—was actively catering to the liberal Democrat FDR's particular political and policy interests in an effort to preserve his position as FBI director while endeavoring to expand his bureau. Always acutely sensitive to FDR's desires and always seeking any opportunity to ingratiate himself with the chief executive, Hoover had little choice but to intently follow up on the president's concerns, especially because the president made his views so public. (Suggesting how seriously Hoover and later FBI officials took the case, they, in fact, investigated it relentlessly until 1985 but never solved it.) Indeed, one newspaper, the *Washington Herald,* even picked up on Hoover's relationship with the president when it reported on the death of the Mattson boy with the headline: "Spurred by President, Hoover Flies Here to Push Hunt."[20]

Hoover, of course, had good reason to do this. When FDR entered office in 1933, the first Democratic president in more than a decade, he announced as his choice for attorney general Senator Thomas Walsh of Montana. Walsh was a man with a previous history with the FBI and Hoover. He had investigated popular FBI abuses and intended to undertake a complete reorganization of the Justice Department. As a Republican political appointee, Hoover's future as FBI director was seriously threatened, and it was commonly believed he would soon go. However, Hoover never lost his job because, fortuitously for him, Walsh unexpectedly died of a massive heart attack before taking office. His replacement, New Dealer Homer Cummings, unlike Walsh, was not particularly interested in Hoover's past and decided it was simpler to retain him as FBI director. Hoover, thereafter, would be a lone conservative bureaucrat among New Dealers, and as such, he worked diligently to preserve his position and expand FBI authority, especially after Cummings sought an unprecedented increase in the federal law-enforcement role. This was not all. Hoover even developed a close personal relationship with the president—something he would do with most subsequent presidents—by providing him detailed reports he thought FDR would find interesting and, eventually, reports detailing the activities of his political opponents. The relationship developed to the degree that Hoover dealt directly with the president and often completely bypassed his nominal boss, the attorney general.

Also contributing to the new focus on gays was the onset of the Great Depression and its widespread and cataclysmic effects. These developments led to a societal reexamination of gender roles in the United States because the former breadwinning man, whether husband or father, was now at best desperately struggling to fulfill his assigned role. Indeed, men across the country suddenly and dramatically receded from valued, wage-earning, upright citizens to jobless, even homeless, destitute men unable to support their families.[21] So traumatic was this development that many families often had to send their children away to live with relatives because they could not afford to care for them. Amid this social crisis and concurrent sex-crime panic, gays like never before during robust economic periods stood out as one obvious and seemingly serious and dangerous social problem necessitating action amid cataclysmic economic disaster.

Indeed, as historian Canaday revealed in her groundbreaking book *The Straight State* (2009), the federal government came to "discover" homosexuality more broadly the more the bureaucracy of the federal government expanded, particularly with the New Deal. Because for the first time government bureaucrats were dealing directly with citizens, New Dealers (who always held a family-values focus), she argued, were forced to regulate homosexuality when attempting to manage larger social problems such as crime, poverty, and homelessness. As she described it, her analysis is of the "*bureaucratization* of homosexuality—something forged, in short, through legal and administrative processes."[22] Although she did not address the FBI in her book, it is nevertheless obvious this was precisely what was happening under Hoover's watch in 1937.

Finally, dating from August 1936, with rising concerns that a subversive Fifth Column was operating in the country as the Second World War developed, FDR had authorized the FBI to ascertain the extent of the influence of fascism and communism on the US domestic economic and political scene.[23] Given widespread and popular fears that a subversive minority could radically influence the country during economic disaster, as reflected in the activities of both groups during the contemporaneous Spanish Civil War of 1936–1939, it required only a small leap of presumptive logic, given the totality of recent experiences, for members of the US public and government bureaucrats to regard men with same-sex attraction, too, as a serious domestic and subversive threat. For Hoover and the FBI, gays not only threatened the safety of children, but, if war developed, gays in prominent positions could be blackmailed by foreign agents into betraying their country's secrets and security. All of this, together, led Hoover in 1937 to begin systematic collection of information on gays under the rubric of "sex offenders."

We know, in fact, that FBI officials began to collect information on gays in a systematic fashion dating from 1937 from documents detailing the destruction of the FBI's Sex Deviates Program and File. FBI Director Hoover created the Sex Deviates Program and File in 1950–1951 to ensure the firing of gays from government employment (and beyond) by quietly disseminating information about them to trusted recipients across the federal government and even beyond that. Although the formal Sex Deviates Program was created in 1950 and augmented in 1951, it was, as the FBI's 1977 requisition seeking National Archives approval for its destruction tells us, created by combining several separate FBI files. One of those was FBI File 105-34074, spanning the years 1937–1977 and described as containing information dating to the 1937 sex-crime panic that "relates to the subject of 'sex offenders.'"[24] The "105" in the FBI file number means "foreign counterintelligence" and reflects less the FBI starting to collect information on gays in 1937 and more the Sex Deviates File's underlying cold war–era purpose: to prevent a presumed breach of security via blackmail of gays by foreign agents.

FBI officials also maintained a research file captioned "Sex Degenerates and Sex Offenders," numbered file 94-4-980, that, if not a formal part of the 1951 Sex Deviates File, was clearly related to the collection and dissemination of information about gays.[25] (The number 94 indicates a research file.) FBI Director Hoover approved the creation of research files to assist him in disseminating information to the public to shape opinion, including information he used in his speeches and writings. The best example of this vis-à-vis gays from the period of the Mattson kidnapping and murder was Hoover's 1937 article "War on the Sex Criminal." We know the FBI Sex Offenders File was used for this purpose given FBI documents detailing the creation in 1959 of a special research file on pornography that "would be of benefit to the Director, in the event he would like to inform the American people on this subject, as he has in the past." An FBI official wrote that maintaining this pornography file would be easy because similar "research" information is "presently kept under the subjects of Parole and Probation and Sex Offender material," and the same people managing this information could manage the pornography file. Those people belonged to the Special Projects Unit of the Crime Research Section of the Crimes Records Division, the section of the FBI whose responsibility it was to disseminate information to the media and Congress. Heading the Crime Records Division was Assistant Director Louis Nichols, who served as the FBI liaison in these matters.[26]

Another constituent part of the 1951 Sex Deviates File, FBI File 105-12198, was created in 1942 during the Second World War—"Sex Perverts in Government Service." The creation of this file reflected wartime domestic security concerns that gays could be blackmailed by the enemy into betraying government secrets given contemporary negative public views of homosexuality.[27] As a Second World War–era creation, this portion of the file reflected an evolutionary stage in the systematic FBI collection of information from one involving a sex-crime panic—and the urgency to solve it while educating the public about the danger of this particular "criminal menace," as FDR put it—to one in which gays were elevated in the government's view to a wartime security threat.

The FBI's 94 file classification originated in 1938. The 105 file classification—though it was originally called Internal Security, Foreign Intelligence before being dubbed Foreign Counterintelligence—also appears to have originated in that same year.[28] That particular year, then, appears to have been a nexus point for the future development of the Sex Deviates File. As international events were becoming increasingly perilous by 1938, and as FDR's attention shifted away from the New Deal and toward dealing with foreign affairs, Hoover's FBI was already well into the process of transitioning from a primary focus on criminal investigations to (noncriminal) intelligence gathering as its raison d'être. Concerned with the threats of domestic communism and fascism in 1936, FDR had already verbally authorized Hoover to conduct intelligence investigations. In 1938 the president increased counterespionage funding for the FBI and the military intelligence agencies, thus explaining FBI officials' creation of their 105 file during the precipitous year 1938.[29]

In terms of the 94 research matters file, the year 1938 is central. By that point, as the bureau shifted away from a priority of criminal law enforcement, it was also shifting in terms of its public relations efforts away from a focus on celebrity gangsters and the glories of scientific crime detection. Hoover, instead, began using the noncriminal intelligence he was gathering not only to keep the president informed about domestic subversive groups but also to educate (and influence) the public as to the perils of communism and fascism and other subversive forces (such as sex offenders). Thus the creation of the 94 research matters file in 1938 is central to the new FBI interest in gays. Quite naturally, then, as FBI agents were gathering more and more information about "sex offenders" after the 1937 Mattson kidnapping, that information—while filed in the Mattson case under file classification 7 (kidnapping)—invariably found its way, probably first, into a 94 file so that FBI agents in the bureau's public relations arm, the Crime Records Section (which itself was only created in 1935), could write articles and speeches under Hoover's byline on the perils to youth of sex criminals, fascists, or communists. Later (as will be illustrated in Chapter 3), as FBI agents began to investigate the seeming threat of gays holding sensitive governmental positions during the Second World War, information about "sex perverts in government" would be filed under FBI file classification 105. The final evolutionary step (discussed in Chapter 4) would be the creation of a formal FBI program and file to disseminate information about gays using and combining these disparate files.

The origin of FBI surveillance of gays was a significant development in both gay and lesbian history and FBI history. In addition to revealing the origins of the long FBI interest in homosexuality, it also reflected a larger development, as described in the Canaday thesis, that during the Great Depression and New Deal the federal government "discovered" the homosexual by way of other pressing national issues. This discovery resulted in a decades-long adversarial relationship that would profoundly change the ways in which gays conducted themselves and even organized in search of equality. In this case, the FBI discovery of homosexual people was part of a larger and evolving federal effort to deal with crime. The FBI during the New Deal developed into a truly national law-enforcement agency, then an intelligence-gathering security agency after 1936, then a much larger and more complex bureaucracy than ever before, and in short order found itself, more or less, regulating homosexuality. The nature of the bureau's original concern was in dealing with a criminal issue and seeming threat to US youth from transient sexual deviants who Hoover believed were "progressive criminal[s]" whose abnormal nature inevitably led them to murder.

This view in and of itself, although a significant development, was not enough to lead FBI officials to collect in a systemic fashion information about gays for a research file. What is further significant here is the FBI director's relationship with the president. As the bureaucracy of the FBI (and federal government) was growing, so too was Hoover's relationship with FDR. By 1937, that relationship had advanced not only in terms of the FBI's federal criminal mission but also (since 1936) in collecting noncriminal intelligence in a systematic fashion about "subversive" threats. Gay men, in particular, by this time could easily be regarded as both a criminal menace and subversive threat to the nation's values. It would therefore have seemed only natural that at this particular moment, when FBI officials were compiling intelligence by way of a presidential directive on the domestic communist and fascist threats, they should also maintain a research file on homosexual activities.

The FBI interest in homosexuality was an evolutionary phenomenon. It began during the New Deal when the federal government's bureaucracy expanded dramatically in its efforts to deal with the Great Depression. The new and expanded federal responsibilities of the FBI in regulating crime such as kidnapping led its leaders—given contemporary beliefs about homosexuals and transients—to target gay men in an effort to protect children and society at large during economic collapse, with Hoover's desire to inform and educate the public about this threat. Over time, as the bureau's national security responsibilities grew with the onset of the Second World War, FBI officials, albeit in a limited way, began to target gays in government as a security threat. This evolutionary step is the subject of the following chapter.

CHAPTER 3

"Sex Perverts in Government Service"

Second World War Gay Baiting and the FBI
Investigations of Sumner Welles, David Walsh,
and Philip Faymonville

Following the Charles Mattson kidnapping and murder in early 1937, J. Edgar Hoover's Federal Bureau of Investigation (FBI) began to systematically collect information about gays. Five years later, its interest in them evolved. If during the 1930s gays were regarded as threats to home, family, and society at large amid the Great Depression and advent of the New Deal, that perceived threat was refocused and magnified during the 1940s and wartime. Gays were no longer perceived as simply a criminal or societal threat but now a national security threat, and concerns mounted that enemies of the United States were working to disrupt the country from within. Given the dominant perception of gays as repulsive, immoral, criminal, and even medically deviant, if an enemy agent identified a gay person in government—especially someone in a sensitive or influential government position—given the intensity of negative public attitudes toward homosexuality, that person, or so the thinking went, could be blackmailed into betraying government secrets. According to 1940s thinking, then, if such blackmail took place and wartime secrets were revealed, not only would the Allied war effort be jeopardized but countless young lives could be lost. It mattered not that no evidence existed to lend credence to these suppositions. The evolving cultural biases of the time about gays almost guaranteed they would be targeted.

Three extant cases the FBI investigated involving prominent individuals serving in government illustrate this evolution during the Second World War. Hoover's FBI was probably involved in many more cases at that time, but historians' reliance on the Freedom of Information Act (FOIA) to acquire FBI files dictates identifying subjects, proving they are deceased, and only then gaining access to their redacted FBI files if even extant. There no longer exists a central index identifying for researchers everyone who fell under FBI interest, so we must rely upon what is known—often through difficult research or through happenstance—and available to researchers. What is available for that period are the records of prominent individuals (and some lesser-known individuals associated with them) FBI agents investigated for their questionable sexual proclivities or who were gay baited by political or bureaucratic enemies, rather than nameless lower-level government bureaucrats and military personnel. These three extant examples are Undersecretary of State Sumner Welles, Senator David I. Walsh, and lend-lease official Brigadier General Philip Faymonville.[1]

Undersecretary of State Welles, until late 1943, was the most important foreign policy advisor of the Franklin D. Roosevelt (FDR) administration. Although Cordell Hull of Tennessee held the position of secretary of state, and as such formally led the State Department, he was, nevertheless, chosen for that position for political reasons. As a southerner, he satisfied a major Democratic constituency in Congress upon which the Roosevelt administration relied to ensure the passage of New Deal legislation. Though a man unusually interested in reciprocal trade agreements, he was not an expert in foreign affairs. The expert and man the president relied upon most was Welles, who, from the position of undersecretary of state, also happened to run the day-to-day operations of the State Department. Related to Civil War–era radical Republican Senator Charles Sumner, Welles was born to a wealthy New York family. Given his social status, home state, and familial connections, it is probably not surprising he happened to be a close friend of FDR's. When first hired, Welles rose rapidly in the State Department, ultimately serving as chief of the State Department's Latin American Affairs Division, before he resigned to become a banker. Later he was foreign policy advisor to FDR's presidential campaign, was made an assistant secretary of state upon FDR's election, devised FDR's Good Neighbor Policy, served as ambassador to Cuba, helped draft the Atlantic Charter of 1941, and was a valued member of Roosevelt's inner circle. Welles was so important to FDR, in fact, that not even revelations of his apparent homosexuality persuaded the president immediately to fire him. It was only by 1943, after a jealous and resentful Secretary of State Hull learned the full details of Welles's peccadilloes, that he and others used the information to force the undersecretary to resign, forever removing from the State Department Hull's bureaucratic nemesis. Central to the exposure of Welles's sexual activities, and thereby his firing, was FBI Director Hoover, who led an in-depth investigation to document Welles's activities and who deftly leaked information about Welles and directed persons interested in ruining the undersecretary to sources of information. If Hull forced the resignation, Hoover was the one who made it possible.

The sexual improprieties that would undermine Welles's government position occurred in 1940. On 18 September of that year, Welles attended the funeral of House Speaker William Bankhead in Jasper, Alabama, after which he boarded the presidential train to return to Washington, DC. While onboard he drank numerous cocktails—scotch and soda was his drink of choice—to build up enough drunken nerve to solicit sex from the train's male, African American porters. The undersecretary, renowned for his drinking problem, first solicited a waiter who had brought dinner to him. After the waiter entered Welles's passenger compartment, according to official accounts, the undersecretary locked the door and without invitation began to loosen the man's tie and unbutton his coat while directing him to remove his clothes. When the waiter objected, Welles offered him $20 to sleep with him but to no avail. Welles then raised the amount to $100, but still failed. Later, Welles apparently tried "several times" to convince this man to return to his compartment, which led the man to report the incident to his superiors.[2]

Having failed in his solicitations, Welles then rang for a Pullman porter. When the porter arrived, Welles—still drunk—began to speak to him in French and, finding this going nowhere, asked the man to have the previous waiter return to the compartment. When the porter refused Welles rang him several more times and, at one point, apparently asked the porter if he would "go down on him."[3]

Having failed in this attempt, Welles called for yet another porter, who also rebuffed the undersecretary's advances, and when later interviewed by an FBI agent the porter described Welles as having a "feminine accent."[4] Welles then solicited still another porter who passed by his compartment, offering him $20 for an unspecified purpose, which the porter refused. Finally Welles propositioned two other porters who both rebuffed his advances.[5]

This was not an isolated incident. Ten days later, while en route to Cleveland to deliver a speech, Welles engaged in further drunken solicitations. On this particular voyage, again after having drunk a significant amount of alcohol, Welles propositioned a bartender and several train porters. One of them, whom Welles wanted for "screwing purposes," later informed the conductor of the incident.[6]

About four months later, word of these incidents reached the president via the Secret Service. Concerned by Welles's activity and curious about the details, FDR assigned his trusted aide and appointments secretary, General Edwin Watson, to look into the matter. Watson summoned FBI Director Hoover to the White House for a meeting with himself, Rudolph Forster (another presidential secretary), and Secret Service Agent Dale Whiteside— an agent who was assigned to the presidential detail when the first incident with Welles occurred.[7]

Agent Whiteside related to Hoover the story about Welles, which he had learned from a railroad executive onboard the train. He and Watson also informed Hoover they had convinced railroad executives and those involved "never to speak a word about it" and to "not go any further" with an internal railroad complaint. Watson then told Hoover that the president wanted a "full and thorough investigation" and report from the FBI. Forster added that he had heard Welles might have engaged in similar behavior as a young man during the Theodore Roosevelt (TR) administration, which supposedly had led TR to ban him from the White House.[8]

Hoover immediately went forward with an investigation. FBI agents interviewed all of the porters involved in the two trips, both train conductors, and other railroad employees who had been involved or learned of Welles's activities. Each of these individuals signed affidavits attesting to what they had experienced or learned that day. Significantly, however, FBI agents never interviewed Welles himself, highlighting the fact that Hoover was conducting this probe quietly and strictly at the behest of the president. This is not surprising because over the previous few years Hoover had been offering FDR political intelligence reports on his foreign policy opponents and other information Hoover thought he would find useful. FDR, who had an innate love of cloak and dagger, valued these reports, which Hoover well knew, leading the FBI director to cater proactively to the president's political interests time and again. Because Hoover was a Republican political appointee, he was careful to do everything at his disposal for the president to ensure his continued tenure as FBI director.[9]

The bureau's investigation was completed by the end of January, at which time Hoover called on General Watson at the White House with the results. Arriving at the White House, Hoover met with Watson, Forster, and Postmaster General Frank Walker. After verbally briefing the assembled men, they all agreed Hoover should personally relate the FBI findings to the president. Hoover offered the president the details of all of the various incidents and handed him the various affidavits, a summary of them, and a brief memorandum outlining the larger FBI report. Hoover also informed FDR he had learned through Senator Burton Wheeler that William Bullitt—former ambassador to the Soviet Union and France, enemy of Welles, and a man with ambitions for higher diplomatic office—had learned about the Welles incident. The FBI director told FDR that Welles and Bullitt did not see eye to eye, and Welles had learned Bullitt was spreading rumors about his sexual peccadilloes. This had led Welles, according to Hoover, to speak to the attorney general, to whom he denied the incident but did claim to have been drunk as well as ill that night. Welles also claimed, said Hoover, to have no memory of the events ascribed to him, two excuses not uncommon in this area (see Chapter 7 and the Walter Jenkins episode).[10]

After Hoover briefed FDR, the president asked the FBI director for his thoughts. Hoover replied that there was "no question" in his mind Welles had made "improper advances and propositions" to the various individuals on the train "while he was drunk." FDR, according to Hoover's account, concurred. The president, seemingly making an excuse for his valued foreign policy advisor and friend, said it indeed appeared that Welles was inebriated, and, therefore, "without knowing what he was really doing," had propositioned the men. Hoover then advised FDR that Bullitt and Wheeler, an anti-interventionist critic of the president's the FBI was monitoring, would likely spread the story—but, Hoover pointed out, it was not unusual for public figures, in any event, to be charged with "indulging in immoral acts and acts of degeneracy." (Because Hoover, a lifelong bachelor, was regularly accused of being gay, he, indeed, had a unique perspective on the matter!) Reflecting the assumptions of the time, Hoover also claimed that, in Welles's case, his problem "was more of a mental condition than anything else," which, he said, meant there was no guarantee that it would not happen again.[11]

FDR then asked for Hoover's advice on how to handle the situation. The FBI director, again catering to FDR's wishes, advised the president that if he wanted to retain Welles while not tipping his hand regarding Welles's sexual advances, he should assign Welles a "mature" travel companion to prevent him from either becoming intoxicated or, if he did drink, to keep the undersecretary from seeking "immoral relations." Hoover then suggested FDR have a friend of Welles's confront him about acquiring a travel partner to "prevent any frame up or the circulation of any story that would reflect upon his character." FDR, according to Hoover, did just this.[12]

On 23 April 1941, while soliciting FDR for a new diplomatic assignment, Ambassador Bullitt gave the president an affidavit he had somehow acquired from the Welles investigation. Seeking a promotion, he hoped to discredit Welles and place himself in the good graces of the president. Bullitt did not realize, however, that not only was FDR well acquainted with the Welles investigation but also of Bullitt's petty efforts to destroy the undersecretary and advance his own interests. (Hoover had briefed FDR, for example, on Bullitt's initial worry about bringing the homosexual charges to the president because, in Bullitt's view, anybody giving the president bad news "would get his own legs cut off."[13]) FDR told Bullitt he already knew of the charges, and, more importantly, he was not fearful of Welles being a liability or blackmailed by foreign powers. FDR told Bullitt that Welles would be escorted when he traveled to ensure his moral rectitude. Bullitt probably did not realize it at the time, but his machinations for higher office had ended that day.[14]

Hoover's reporting to FDR, however, did not end the FBI interest in Welles's sexual life. A year and a half after Hoover's report to the president, FBI Assistant Director Louis Nichols, at the time head of the FBI Administrative Division and, as such, supervisor of the Crime Records Section, learned that in 1941 Welles had allegedly "got in bad in his last trip to South America." Welles was supposed to have had a "boy" in Brazil with whom he had "unnatural relations." According to Nichols's source, the boy "broke down and told the South American authorities," which resulted in Welles being "compromised" by an unnamed South American government. To FBI officials this was a grave concern given their firm belief, by this juncture, that gays were security risks precisely because they could be blackmailed into revealing state secrets, and to Nichols, in this instance, Welles had clearly been "compromised."[15]

Yet because of the sensitivity involved, Welles being a friend of FDR's and a powerful State Department official, and because of Hoover's unique relationship with the president—Hoover hesitated to begin a formal FBI investigation of this most recent charge. Instead, Nichols informed Associate Director Clyde Tolson that a well-connected lawyer from New York City and former assistant secretary of state, Francis White, who knew of the incident, was supposed to volunteer the information to Hoover. This way, Hoover would not have to ask for it, and more importantly, he would "not be placed in the position of making an investigation" but still get the information.[16]

Two months later, FBI officials developed further information that, in their view, demonstrated how Welles's homosexuality had compromised his ability to serve as undersecretary of state. FBI agents learned that Welles was the friend and former Harvard roommate of a man who had become the focus of an FBI "Internal Security case." Welles's friend, a retired architect and First World War army veteran named Harden de Valson Pratt, had reportedly acted "in a suspicious manner" when contacting army officers. FBI agents subsequently learned that Pratt had contacted these officers because he "was a sexual pervert." In their view, this was further evidence that the undersecretary was a weak link precisely because Pratt had maintained a relationship with Welles during 1942.[17]

Despite FDR's attempt to keep stories about Welles's sexuality quiet, there were multiple rumors being circulated about him. By October 1942, Secretary of State Hull learned of the incidents from his wife—who had learned of them as gossip from the wives of various senators—which prompted him to arrange a meeting with Hoover. The secretary had, undoubtedly, already been aware of stories about the FBI investigation, but because these stories about Welles were "becoming more wide-spread," he now asked Hoover for a copy of the FBI report. Because the investigation had been requested directly by the president, Hoover essentially told Hull he could not provide him a copy. Hoover also claimed he did not have a "copy of the report available." Having therefore insulated himself from being responsible for providing Hull an FBI report, Hoover then directed Hull to FDR's secretary, Marvin McIntyre, to "obtain access to the report [in his possession]."[18]

Hoover and Hull did not confine their discussion of gays simply to Welles when the FBI director visited the secretary in his Wardman Park apartment. Hoover also revealed to Hull some information about the "immoral activities" of General Philip Faymonville, the lend-lease administrator in Moscow, an investigation the FBI had only recently begun at the request of the War Department (discussed in detail later in this chapter). The discussion about Faymonville then moved on to one about the "prevalences [*sic*] of degeneracy in the American Embassy at Moscow," about which Hoover had learned a year before after an FBI agent was assigned to investigate security procedures at the embassy. Upon learning of this (for the first time) Hull was "shocked" and whereas he had previously dismissed stories about homosexuals in the diplomatic corps, he was, according to Hoover, "now greatly concerned about them."[19]

The following month, an FBI agent learned of a further incident that suggested, to him, the vulnerability of Welles. Samuel Klaus, a Treasury Department official, told the agent that a jailed Philadelphia "racketeer" named Moe Annenberg had learned of the Welles incident and attempted to use it to leverage a pardon. Annenberg allegedly had the information brought to the attention of the White House and threatened to make it public if FDR failed to grant him amnesty. Because Annenberg died shortly thereafter the issue was moot, but, according to Klaus, his advocates were intent upon continuing with their efforts. Significantly, this was one further piece of evidence indicating to FBI officials the vulnerability of Welles. Rationalizing this perceived threat, Hoover carefully worked to expose the undersecretary (as he had done in leading Hull to information), leaving the president with no option but to fire his friend Welles.[20]

FBI officials were not restricted to investigating the sexual peccadilloes of only FDR's primary advisors during this period. They also looked into the alleged homosexuality of one of FDR's foreign policy critics. Dating from 1939, FDR fought a bitter political battle over extending aid short of war to the beleaguered Allied nations that faced the expansionist regime of Adolf Hitler. As the war in Europe and Asia intensified, so too did the foreign policy debate within the United States. Catering to the president's political and policy interests, primarily to ensure the continuation of his own tenure as FBI director, Hoover provided FDR political intelligence on his mostly conservative foreign policy opposition and helped develop information to discredit some of them. The president did not initiate this activity, but he also did not question the ethics of receiving political intelligence reports from Hoover. In fact, he thanked the FBI director for them.[21]

One influential anti-interventionist who fell under FBI scrutiny during the foreign policy debate, and who interested FBI agents in terms of their surveillance of gays, was Senator David I. Walsh. A Democrat from Massachusetts, Walsh was also the powerful chair of the Senate Committee on Naval Affairs between 1937 and 1947. Despite being a Democrat, Walsh was not, in the words of Attorney General Francis Biddle, "sympathetic with" or a "friend of the President's."[22] He fought hard, as did the aviator Charles Lindbergh, to convince US citizens they faced no threat of invasion from a foreign power provided the country's air and sea approaches were adequately defended. Making such an argument, he claimed there was no need for the United States to become involved in the Second World War, which, he believed, would be disastrous for the country.

On 4 May 1942, in an effort to discredit Walsh, FDR ally, attorney, and cofounder of the American Civil Liberties Union (ACLU) Morris Ernst contacted the special agent in charge (SAC) of the FBI New York office with information he had obtained about the senator. Ernst claimed Walsh was involved in a scheme to use his Senate position to award a $16 million naval contract to a friend. Walsh's friend, however, turned out to be under indictment for a crime, which made him ineligible to receive the government contract directly. The contract, therefore, was allegedly awarded in an indirect manner to a corporation Walsh's friend effectively controlled.[23]

Learning of the charge from Ernst, who regularly maintained contact with FBI officials and often proffered advice to the president on how to discredit his critics, Hoover received authorization from the attorney general to initiate a preliminary criminal investigation. This was not the first time, however, Walsh was subject to FBI interest. In January 1942, as part of the bureau's extensive efforts to monitor and discredit FDR's anti-interventionist foreign policy critics, FBI agents also had (wrongly) suspected Walsh of leaking a War Department contingency plan to the *Chicago Tribune*. This time, Hoover scrawled on the memo outlining the charges directing his subordinates to begin an "immediate investigation with vigor" and to "report to me further after preliminary investigation." FBI agents pursued the matter for the remainder of 1942, but no evidence was ever developed to indicate any criminal behavior on the part of Senator Walsh. Nevertheless, given his relationship with the president, Hoover was more than willing to investigate the activities of a prominent and powerful Senate chair who was also a foreign policy critic of the White House.[24]

This was not the only charge Ernst had leveled against Senator Walsh. Just prior to the other charge, on 24 April 1942, in one of his regular "tidbits" reports to the president, Ernst informed FDR that Walsh was about to be connected with a "scandalous criminal case in Brooklyn." He advised him, moreover, to monitor this "shocking story" because it "may be of great help to you." FDR thanked Ernst on 27 April and asked him to "follow up" on the revelation. He even thanked Ernst for his tidbits reports because "they give me a real relaxation from the high ether of naval and military strategy." Three days later, Ernst indeed followed up. Making use of his contacts with

FBI officials, Ernst informed them that one Gustave Herman Beekman, the operator of a "house of degradation" on Pacific Street in Brooklyn, had recently been found guilty of violating a sodomy law and, more importantly, "had identified a picture of Senator Walsh as that of an individual who had frequented Beekman's house." The "house of degradation" was, more specifically, a "male brothel" frequented by soldiers and sailors seeking homosexual encounters. With this particular accusation, Ernst was gay baiting Senator Walsh in an effort to discredit him. Ernst undoubtedly pursued this avenue of attack because the senator's life did not fit the gender stereotypes and expectations of the era's dominant hypermasculine culture. Walsh was not only a lifelong bachelor but was known to have had only platonic relationships with women. Most damning of the stories about Walsh, though, was that he had a Filipino houseboy, with whom, according to rumor, he enjoyed a close relationship.[25]

On 1 May 1942, in the first of a series of articles, the pro-Roosevelt *New York Post* broke the Walsh story while adding that the brothel was a German "Spy Nest." Nazi espionage agents allegedly had frequented the brothel to question its navy patrons about the "comings and goings of their ships." The *Post* also published an affidavit Beekman had signed on 30 April testifying to the veracity of his story, in which he claimed that Walsh had kissed and sodomized two sailors. Other newspapers then picked up the story, which made for good copy over a two-week period.[26]

So popular were the sensational charges that a limerick about the incident began to be heard across Washington, DC. It went:

> Said Senator David I. Walsh,
> These charges against me are false.
> Though I did go to Brooklyn
> For sooklyn and fooklyn,
> Not a gob laid his hands on my balsh.[27]

The same day the story went public, rumors about it began to circulate in Washington. Attorney General Biddle got wind of a rumor that naval intelligence officers, in an effort to identify Senator Walsh, were bringing witnesses to the capital. After Hoover disabused Biddle of the rumor, the attorney general advised the FBI to look into the Walsh matter quietly by telling Hoover to "just make the investigation and say nothing." He also informed Hoover that he would ask Senator Alben Barkley, the Senate majority leader, if he wanted a "private investigation."[28]

On 2 May, FBI agents accompanied by an assistant district attorney and naval intelligence officer interviewed Beekman. He confirmed that for the past five years he had operated "houses which are frequented by homosexuals" and that he had been arrested four times. Twice he was arrested for sodomy, once for "operating a degenerate house," and once for violating local liquor laws. Beekman claimed, moreover, that Senator Walsh had visited his brothel about fourteen times, where he had sexual relations with sailors. When presented with a spread of photographs, Beekman identified the photo of Walsh as a "very good likeness" of the man he knew.[29]

Two days later, Hoover advised the president's personal secretary, McIntyre, that the bureau's interest in the Walsh matter was "only insofar as it pertains to possible espionage, and that we are not interested in any personal aspects." McIntyre replied that the FBI was "absolutely right" to investigate the case for espionage reasons. Regardless of what Hoover told McIntyre, the FBI was very much interested—if not mostly interested—in the "personal aspects" of the Walsh case.[30]

Two pieces of evidence highlight this. The first can be found in the bureau's 2 May questioning of Beekman. In eight paragraphs that reiterated the content of the interview, in which details of Walsh's alleged sexual activities were thoroughly discussed, only the last sentence touched upon whether Beekman knew of any espionage activities. Second, dating from 1937 FBI officials had begun systematic collection of information on the personal activities of gays, and this surveillance only escalated over time, from the examples discussed in this chapter to a massive FBI file and program by 1951 to ensure that gays lost their federal jobs. The Walsh matter, as it was, clearly fell within FBI interest in foreign espionage but even more so in homosexuality.[31]

On the same day Hoover told McIntyre that the bureau's only interest was the espionage angle, Oscar Cox, a senior Justice Department official, asked Hoover for a complete report on the Walsh matter. Cox wanted to share it with Senator Barkley, who sought to be "fully informed in case any Senator wished to discuss the matter on the floor of the Senate." Hoover complied and forwarded reports to the attorney general.[32]

Three days later, on 7 May, Beekman submitted another affidavit to a Brooklyn district attorney reiterating his previous claims about Walsh. On 16 May, however, after intensive interviewing again by FBI agents, Beekman recanted his claims. Specifically, Beekman said he knew an individual named "Doc," who, while bearing a striking resemblance to Senator Walsh, was nevertheless not him. Clarifying his previous error about Walsh, Beekman said he had too freely substituted Walsh's name for "Doc," and he blamed the district attorney and his own lawyer for leaving him with the impression that Doc was Walsh.[33]

FBI agents not only reinterviewed Beekman in an attempt to get to the heart of the Walsh case but also interviewed at least eighteen others involved in the Beekman "house of degeneration." Many of them signed statements or affidavits, but all denied that Walsh had been a visitor to the brothel. They all testified that the ubiquitous "Doc," indeed, closely resembled the senator. As for espionage activity, FBI agents were unable to develop any information to support that charge.[34]

Then, on 20 May 1942, from the well of the Senate, Majority Leader Barkley publicly revealed the FBI investigation results as conclusive evidence Walsh was innocent of the charges leveled against him. Anti-interventionist senators then rallied behind Walsh and referred to the homosexual charge as nothing but a "diabolical" smear campaign initiated by the pro-Roosevelt press to discredit every anti-interventionist senator. Given the three-year-long bitter political fight over FDR's increasingly interventionist foreign policy, members of the president's political opposition stuck closely together in the face of what they perceived as a smear campaign linked to the foreign policy debate. Relieved, Senator Walsh wrote a thank-you letter to Hoover for "seeking the truth" in the "recent unpleasantness and disagreeable incident." Hoover replied that it was the FBI's job to investigate facts and he "was happy indeed to render every possible assistance in establishing the facts which have so thoroughly disproved the unjust allegations which were made against you."[35]

Shocked by Barkley's revelation that the FBI had cleared Walsh, the *New York Post* published that same day another affidavit Beekman had signed only two days before. In this affidavit, coming shortly after he had signed an FBI statement recanting his former statement, Beekman claimed FBI agents had pressured him into recanting and "to identify someone else as Mr. Walsh." Beekman claimed the agents wanted him to identify "Doc" as the man he had thought was the senator. He further claimed to have been questioned at "great length," during which time he was "very nervous." Beekman said he was questioned so intensively that FBI agents were forced to bring in a physician to treat him. When presented with the typed-up statement, Beekman said, "Even though I knew it was untrue, I signed it."[36]

In explaining why the *Post* had decided to print Beekman's most recent affidavit, the editor said he did not believe in the "use of the Department of Justice as a private detective agency, even in behalf of the Senators." On 21 May, he then published an open letter to Attorney General Biddle chastising him for permitting the FBI to be used "as though it were the counterpart of the secret political police of Communist Russia or Nazi Germany." He added that the US public had been "denied" all of the evidence and that the bureau's conclusions were based upon a limited set of facts. To FBI officials, the *Post*'s reply was merely part of a "scheme to discredit the Bureau." Hoover, therefore, advised the attorney general to start "legal action" against the *New York Post,* a paper with a history of criticizing the FBI.[37]

Hoover then ordered FBI agents to forensically trace the *Post*'s investigation. Following the newspaper's journalistic footprints, FBI agents interviewed a number of people sought by the *Post*'s reporters. One person FBI agents interviewed was George Boden, a Chicago lawyer and friend of the *Post*'s legal team, who by June 1942 was an employee of the Office of the Coordinator of Information, forerunner to the Office of Strategic Services (OSS), the US wartime intelligence apparatus. Boden told FBI agents the *Post* had taken affidavits from seven people who claimed to be able to "place Senator Walsh in Beekman's house." He also claimed that Walsh's attorney tried to persuade the newspaper to drop its story and that he questioned the number of times Walsh had visited Beekman's brothel; Walsh's lawyer supposedly conceded to four visits rather than fourteen. Finally, Boden claimed the *Post* had "obtained a photograph of Senator Walsh having unnatural relations with a page boy of the Senate in the Riggs Bath House in Washington."[38]

In their investigative effort, interestingly enough, FBI agents found "no indication" that any of Boden's claims were true. Yet they observed that the "activities of the *New York Post* in this matter would seem to show otherwise." Apparently, on one level at least, FBI officials were not wholly convinced that Walsh was, indeed, innocent. As agents continued to follow up with the *Post*'s sources, however, they failed to verify the newspaper's version of the story. They even confirmed that "Doc"—Dr. Harry Stone—was, in fact, the individual who committed the various acts in the brothel that had been ascribed to Senator Walsh.[39]

During 1943, rumors about Welles continued to spread, and FBI agents continued to monitor their development. In late April, Senator Ralph Brewster, a Republican from Maine and member of Senator Harry Truman's committee investigating irregularities and corruption in war production, met with Hoover after he learned of the FBI investigation of Welles. The details of Welles's activities were so "shocking" to Senator Brewster that he immediately sought to talk with Hoover to confirm the allegations. Because the senator had "obviously" received his information from sources interviewed by FBI agents, Hoover confirmed the FBI investigation and told Brewster he had submitted a report to the president. Hoover then advised Brewster that because "of the seriousness with which he [Brewster] viewed the matter," he should talk with Secretary of State Hull, who Hoover knew was aware of the Welles situation. In other words, Hoover directed Senator Brewster, who was not a political ally of FDR's, to a source of information, Hull.[40]

Several days later, after Brewster's meetings with the FBI director and then Hull, Attorney General Biddle advised Hoover that Brewster had also called on him. Biddle told Hoover that Senator Brewster had plans to raise the Welles incident with the Truman Committee. Given this development, and with Hoover's concurrence, Biddle decided to inform FDR. The president, it appears, was able to quash any senate investigation into Welles, but the cost of it appears to have been the ouster of Welles.[41]

On 15 August 1943, with rumors of Welles's homosexuality spreading, Secretary Hull decided to make a move to remove his nemesis, the undersecretary. Hull had long sought to terminate the career of Welles, whom the secretary resented for his closeness to FDR and whom he truly came to detest because he undermined what Hull regarded as his lead position in foreign policy. Since mid-July 1943, Hull had coordinated with others, such as Senator Brewster and Ambassador Bullitt, who also viscerally disliked Welles while wanting a better diplomatic position within the administration. When lunching with the president that midday in August, Hull demanded that he fire Welles. With the stories of Welles's homosexuality about to become the subject of senate debate, and Hull demanding his ouster, Roosevelt, who had long protected Welles, was now politically forced into a corner and had no other choice but to accede to his secretary of state's demand.[42]

Following Welles's resignation, there was wide speculation as to why the undersecretary had resigned. Given the FBI probe, Hoover took interest in any idle talk that Welles's sexual habits were behind his firing. In September, the FBI Los Angeles office reported that several employees of Warner Brothers Studios, described as either "Communist sympathizers or Communist

Party members," had claimed the undersecretary had resigned because of his "sexual affairs with young Negro boys." The employees, moreover, claimed to have gotten their information from Los Angeles Police Commissioner Al Cohn. What concerned Hoover, however, was the men's claim that Cohn had learned about Welles from his contacts with the FBI director. Hoover's FBI maintained contacts with a plethora of police organizations and private ones, so the director was always concerned if any of them violated his demands for confidentiality.[43]

Because the FBI investigation of Welles was initiated at the behest of the president, any talk that Hoover was sharing the fruits of this investigation without White House authorization was a serious concern for the FBI director. Hoover, therefore, ordered FBI agents to interview Cohn to get to the bottom of his comments. When confronted, Cohn denied saying Hoover had provided him the information about Welles. He claimed, rather, that while on a trip to Washington, DC, a senator, whom he refused to name to agents, had given him the details and let him read the FBI report. Cohn, in fact, had met with Senator Brewster. Brewster was the same senator to whom Hoover confirmed the FBI investigation and the senator Hoover had directed to Secretary Hull for details on Welles (Hull presumably obtained a copy of the FBI report from the White House, as per Hoover's advice).[44]

Hoover was incensed that his name had been made public in relation to the Welles matter, especially since it *was* Hoover, in fact, who had freely confirmed the Welles allegations to Senator Brewster, who subsequently passed this information on to others. Given Hoover's role in disseminating information about Welles to Brewster (and indirectly to Hull), he therefore sought to cover his tracks to defuse any potentially damaging gossip that could threaten his carefully cultivated relationship with FDR. To his subordinates, Hoover damned Cohn as a "scoundrel and a malicious liar" and ordered them to draft memos on the man and his claims to both Presidential Secretary Watson and Attorney General Biddle.[45]

In the memoranda to Watson and Biddle, the FBI director outlined Cohn's claims and called them an "absolute falsehood." Labeling Cohn an "unsavory character" who had no reliability, Hoover advised both men that Cohn had passed on the Welles story to a Hollywood filmmaker along with actress Irene Dunne. In closing his report, Hoover claimed to have halted "further circulation of the story," and he used the incident, ironically, as an example to point out "how vicious rumors can be circulated." Hoover never mentioned, of course, that he had led Senator Brewster to a source of information on Welles and that Brewster had told Cohn.[46]

In a latent effort to justify the firing of Undersecretary Welles, on 3 September 1943, Hoover forwarded a report to FDR reiterating the comments of a Communist Party member. According to Hoover, a member of the party's national committee commented, "I think Welles' resigning is one of the biggest blows we've had. It really hurts the Movement." Hoover also reported that communists in Chicago wanted to protest Welles's firing and demand an explanation for it, and, he claimed, communist leaders believed Welles to be the "most 'pro-Russian'" member of the State Department. Finally, Hoover forwarded an article from the *Daily Worker* that defended Welles. In Hoover's eyes, this information seemingly confirmed the danger Welles posed, and, to Hoover, Welles's termination seemingly prevented communists from gaining a toehold in the State Department because they had no weak link to target.[47]

A third prominent government official targeted for alleged sexual impropriety during the Second World War, and thus a major subject of FBI investigation, was the US lend-lease coordinator in Moscow, General Faymonville. On the evening of 19 September 1942, Major General George Strong, deputy chief of staff for intelligence—in other words, the head of US Army intelligence—telephoned the FBI intelligence liaison, Assistant to the Director Edward Tamm, about an urgent matter. He explained to Tamm they had a "mess" among the personnel at the US Embassy in Moscow that "has to be cleaned up." Admitting to Tamm that he knew little, General Strong explained there was no way to unearth the facts except "by sending over a man who knows how to investigate and who is of the highest integrity." Both army and State Department personnel, he said, were ill equipped for the mission. The problems in Moscow, moreover, were so sensitive that this FBI agent would need to be undercover, "of the highest qualifications," and speak Russian. Finally, General Strong hoped the matter could be cleared up promptly and he hoped to brief Hoover about it in person.[48]

Two days later, because Hoover was busy, Tamm met with General Strong. Strong said he was concerned with rumors surrounding General Faymonville. Strong explained Faymonville allegedly had "transformed the lend-lease office in Russia into virtually a house of prostitution." Even worse, Strong said, Faymonville himself was rumored to be "engaging in sexually perverted practices and is consorting with sexual perverts." Explaining why the army wanted the help of an FBI agent, General Strong said the "allegations are of such a nebulous nature" that he did not believe the War Department adequately suited to "take action upon them." Possibly aware of the extensive FBI work and expertise in homosexual investigations, Strong emphasized, the "War Department is interested in obtaining a comprehensive report prepared in a completely unbiased manner as to exactly what Faymonville's conduct and activities are."[49]

Hoover was amenable to lending General Strong FBI assistance, but because it was "outside the Bureau's sphere of activity" and a matter that "should be handled by the War Department," he demanded a written request from Army Chief of Staff General Marshall. Hoover's concern was a bureaucratic one. In 1940 and 1942, the heads of the FBI, army, and naval intelligence concluded delimitation agreements to define precisely which jurisdictions each agency oversaw. An FBI agent investigating an army matter outside of the Western Hemisphere would violate those agreements and step on many bureaucratic toes. (Hoover's FBI had responsibility for US domestic security, except on military bases, and foreign intelligence in Latin America.)[50]

General Strong, therefore, arranged for General Marshall's letter, dated 21 September 1942. Marshall formally requested the assignment of a "qualified FBI man to conduct an investigation in regard to certain American Army personnel in Europe." Conceding the request was "somewhat unusual," Marshall assured Hoover that the "urgency of the matter makes any other course impractical." With bureaucratic bases covered, FBI officials located the most qualified G-man to undertake the mission, Special Agent Louis C. Beck.[51]

Because of his experience level, it is easy to understand why FBI officials chose Beck. During the summer of 1940, State Department officials, in coordination with military intelligence, initiated an undercover inspection of overseas diplomatic posts. Their concern rested on a recent international espionage incident at the US Embassy in London involving cipher clerk Tyler Kent. Kent had stolen thousands of secret documents and delivered them to Nazi Germany, leading State Department officials to ensure the security of other US diplomatic posts from any future Kents. Because they were too well known, the State Department could not use its own personnel, and army intelligence had no one qualified for this particular type of mission.

The one federal agency with both the investigative and international exper-tise—having already coordinated with foreign intelligence organizations and having assumed a prominent counterintelligence role—was Hoover's FBI. State Department officials, therefore, reached out to Hoover for a qual-ified investigator.[52]

FBI officials chose and sent several men to London, Rome, Madrid, Lisbon, Berlin, and Moscow, including Beck. Beck, in fact, was specifically assigned to the US Embassy in Moscow. A product of the University of Southern California Law School, Beck spoke German, Spanish, and Russian all to varying degrees. To disguise his mission and offer him complete inves-tigative access, Beck was given the cover of an embassy messenger. In Beck's assessment, embassy security was seriously lacking. He not only believed foreign intelligence organizations had easy access to secret information, he found embassy personnel engaged in scandalous sexual activity, whether of the hetero- or homosexual variety, and even involving prostitutes.[53]

When FBI officials needed an agent to investigate new and sensitive con-cerns at the US Embassy in Moscow, Beck was the logical choice. Between his first and second missions to Moscow, Beck had been reassigned to the FBI Special Intelligence Service (SIS). The SIS was Hoover's foreign intelligence apparatus with responsibility for collecting economic and political intelli-gence in Latin America, an effort General Strong's successor, General Sher-man Miles, described as "encyclopedic in scope."[54] Recruited again, Beck spent two weeks studying and prepping himself for Moscow. He met with military intelligence personnel, including General Strong, who briefed him on Faymonville and the situation at the embassy. Early on, Beck learned, and reported, that "all of the accusations in this case appear to have origi-nated with [deleted but General Joseph A. Michela]," the military attaché in Moscow.[55] Beck also told Hoover and Tamm that Michela had singled out "rumors" that "Faymonville engaged in homosexual practices," which Beck related to his previous investigation in Moscow. According to Agent Beck, during his previous mission "at least one employee of the Military Attache's office was blackmailed by the GPU [Soviet secret police] and by Soviets with whom he had carried on homosexual activities." Furthermore, Beck explained, "Charge d'Affaires Alexander Kirk was commonly regarded as a homosexual. However, while in Moscow I never heard anyone accuse Gen-eral Faymonville, and [deleted but Michela] makes no specific allegations in this regard." Kirk, in fact, despite the charge, would escape scrutiny.[56]

Beck then learned that General Michela further described Faymonville as a communist sympathizer. According to Michela, Faymonville was re-called as the Moscow military attaché in 1939 "because of 'known Red tendencies,'" and he claimed the General Staff regarded him as a "pink," and someone suspected of spying for the Russians. The latter charge, Michela suggested, was probably the result of Soviet blackmail. Beck also explained that Michela had forwarded a report to the Pentagon claiming "that General Faymonville is 'again' involved in sexual abnormalities" while condemning the "immoral conditions existing in the US Embassy building."[57]

Embassy rumor had it, Beck explained, that every noon Faymonville and his staff "go to the Bolshoi Opera House, where they occupy the first two rows in the orchestra." This happened so often, Beck wrote, that the Russians referred to it as the "Second Front." Afterward and all night the men would drink themselves into a stupor and "associate with persons of low character." Faymonville, Beck continued, was known for entertaining "lavishly, serving excessive amounts of wine and vodka." His extensive entertaining, indulged in by embassy personnel, was supposed to be the reason nobody ever reported Faymonville.[58]

Rumors about Faymonville were not restricted to 1942. Faymonville was also supposed to have regularly engaged in homosexual activity with a young Russian while he was the US military attaché in Moscow from 1934 to 1939. After Faymonville was recalled as attaché, his young lover was supposedly arrested and the "GPU placed him in a concentration camp where he supposedly still is." What is more, after Faymonville returned to Moscow as the lend-lease coordinator, he was supposed to have initiated efforts to have the young man released.[59]

After briefing Hoover and Tamm about Faymonville, Beck outlined his proposed investigation. In consultation with army intelligence, Beck decided not to reuse his old cover (as a messenger) because he would be required to live with embassy staff at an inconvenient location. Instead, Beck would now be a "cryptographic expert, carrying special documents from the American Government to the Soviet Government," and attaché. This particular cover, moreover, would be believable to embassy staff who remembered Beck. They would assume he had been transferred to the military given his prior experience in the Soviet Union. Given Michela's central role in the allegations, Beck also believed he would have to reveal to him the real reason behind his mission.[60]

As part of his cover, Beck was made a captain in the army. He was then handed all the necessary diplomatic visas, passport, endorsement from the

Soviet Embassy, and transportation to Moscow (flying via bomber from London to the Soviet capital). Interestingly, however, and probably to ensure secrecy, Beck emphasized to army officials arranging his particulars "that the State Department was not to be advised of my identity." Because of red tape, moreover, Beck explained to his FBI superiors that they would have to finance his trip and provide money to pay potential informants. No other sources of funding were easily or readily available.[61]

Beck's preliminary conclusion about the mission, he reported to Hoover and Tamm, was that the "allegations against General Faymonville are very general and not supported by any specific evidence." Beck said if he uncovered no evidence of misconduct, he could wrap up his investigation within weeks, but if he unearthed evidence of malfeasance, it could linger on for months. "I have the impression," Beck elaborated, "that what the Army wants is not mere dismissal, but the court martial of General Faymonville, if he is guilty of the charges made."[62]

In early October 1942, as Agent Beck was studying military intelligence codes and ciphers and brushing up on his Russian at the Pentagon, Admiral William Standley, the US ambassador to the Soviet Union, urgently requested permission to return to Washington, DC. Beck reported this to Tamm for two reasons. First, after being told of Beck's pending arrival, Standley suspected Beck "was in the employ of another agency of the government." Unsure of precisely how Standley knew this, but with several educated guesses, Beck discussed the matter with General Strong, who said Beck's mission had to proceed regardless. Second, Beck told Tamm that Standley, Michela, and Naval Attaché Admiral Jack Duncan all, in fact, were returning to Washington, DC, "because of a major political crisis." Little did Beck know at the time but Standley and company's voyage was related to Beck's investigation of Faymonville. The so-called political crisis involved political and bureaucratic differences between the men, and this, in fact, was at the root of the "morals charges" leveled against Faymonville.[63]

To fully appreciate the intrigue and intricacies surrounding Faymonville's presumed sexuality, we must examine his background and how he became lend-lease coordinator in Moscow. Faymonville originally was the US military attaché in Moscow between 1934 and 1939. Historian Mary Glantz has pointed out that Faymonville was different from the garden-variety US diplomats and military personnel in Russia whose perspectives commonly were Eurocentric and virulently anticommunist. Faymonville, who spoke fluent Russian and Japanese, was not only a Russian expert but also one in

Japanese and Asian affairs. He therefore interpreted US-Russian interests, unlike his colleagues, through the broader lens of Asia and larger US global interests. Additionally, and in line with the FDR administration, Faymonville firmly believed the United States needed good economic and political relations with the Soviet Union (in part as a bulwark against Japan), relations the United States had pointedly avoided ever since the Bolshevik Revolution of 1917.[64]

Faymonville's positive reports about the Russian military, even after Josef Stalin's murderous 1930s purge of the Russian army officer corps and others, stood in stark contrast to those of other US observers in Russia. This disparity, in fact, was the origin of the all-too-common view that Faymonville was somehow dangerously sympathetic to the Soviets. As Glantz pointed out, Faymonville's continued willingness to work with the Russians along with his positive reports about them, while earning him respect and access among Soviet officials, simultaneously alienated him from his US colleagues. As a black sheep among US Soviet experts because the White House at the time relied upon more traditional-minded Soviet experts for advice, this ideological clash led to Faymonville's recall in 1939.[65]

After Nazi Germany invaded the Soviet Union in June of 1941, initiating Hitler's plan to create *lebensraum* for the Third Reich, the United States extended to the Soviets unqualified access to US lend-lease materiel. As a ready expert, Faymonville soon found himself in charge of this lend-lease in Washington, DC, and in September 1941 he returned to Moscow as part of a conference to work out formalities in extending aid. Because Faymonville worked so well with the Soviets, he remained in Moscow to better coordinate lend-lease needs. Unfortunately, this assignment again brought him into irreparable conflict with other embassy personnel, but especially with the new US military attaché, General Michela, and the new US ambassador in Moscow, Admiral Standley.[66]

Underlying this conflict were not only disparate views about the Soviets but a bureaucratic and jurisdictional problem. As lend-lease coordinator, Faymonville's job was to offer the Soviets, without restriction, whatever military supplies they might need. This flew in the face of the traditional, if biased, view among military and diplomatic advisors who adamantly opposed cooperating with, let alone trusting, the Soviets. Faymonville's position, moreover, was unique. Despite being a general he did not report to the Pentagon, and despite playing a significant role in US-Russian diplomatic relations he did not report to the US Embassy or State Department. Instead, as was often typical in the Roosevelt administration, Faymonville bypassed traditional lines of authority to be accountable only to the White House. In fact, Faymonville's position evolved to become more influential than those of the military attachés and the ambassador. The primary reason for this was his direct line to the White House and his access with the Soviets—a function of his long-standing, nonhostile, good relations. This created a plethora of resentments from Michela, Duncan, and Standley, but especially Michela.[67]

This then explains the message Standley sent to Washington, DC, that FBI Agent Beck reported to Hoover. The "major political crisis" Beck described in fact, was rooted in Standley's, Michela's, and Duncan's resentment of Faymonville's access. Beck wrote, "The Soviets continue to be successful in keeping our representatives ignorant of their condition and of their plans." He characterized Michela's job as one of "voluntary imprisonment." Beck told Tamm the Soviets revealed nothing about their own or enemy operations, equipment, counterintelligence, air-raid safeguards, weapons production, or losses and refused to give embassy personnel access to evaluate any of this. Beck even wrote, "No attache has been permitted to visit the front."[68] This last example perfectly captured the bureaucratic and personal impasse between Faymonville, Michela, Duncan, and Standley. In the spring of 1943 while Faymonville's lend-lease superior, Major General James Burns, visited Moscow, Russian authorities granted Faymonville access to the Russian front. Faymonville, moreover, only told the embassy about it after the fact. This elicited from an exasperated Standley an angry telegram to the State Department decrying Faymonville's failure to cooperate with the embassy.[69]

When Standley was in Washington in October 1942 he complained about Faymonville's independent position and his own inability to control the lend-lease coordinator. Standley, in fact, wanted to bring Faymonville under his authority. General Burns did not like that idea and proposed a compromise solution to Standley: placing Faymonville under general embassy supervision with the exception of lend-lease issues. Standley stood firm, however, threatening to resign unless he got his way. Standley won, but, as Glantz has pointed out, the arrangement under which Faymonville was to report to Standley remained ambiguous.[70] Over time, the personal animosities between Faymonville, Standley, Duncan, and particularly Michela became so bitter that Michela even tried to destroy Faymonville's career. As Glantz so aptly put it:

Michela despised the Soviet Union and the Roosevelt administration's Soviet policy. Powerless to change the unconditional aid policy of the United States, Michela turned on its representative in Moscow. Michela's struggle with Faymonville became so bitter and so personal that Michela was unsatisfied with anything less than the destruction of Faymonville's career. This struggle became so public that it threatened the continuation of Roosevelt's policy.[71]

In his vendetta against Faymonville, Michela conveniently used the recent issue over the security of US embassies following the Kent episode. Those investigations, which involved FBI Agent Beck, had exposed apparent homosexual scandals in Moscow. Because Faymonville was attaché in Moscow between 1934 and 1939, departing just before Beck's first investigation in 1940, and because Faymonville did not fit the expected and stereotypical gender role of the period (to be discussed as part of the FBI investigation below), he was an ideal candidate for Michela to gay bait.

By January 1943, FBI Agent Beck finally arrived in Moscow posing as a cipher clerk. Given the embassy's problem with Faymonville's access to the Soviets, Beck assumed a second undercover role as Soviet liaison officer,[72] while revealing his true identity to General Michela. Michela, according to FBI Assistant Director D. Milton Ladd, then "suggested numerous leads, [and] urged that a physical and technical surveillance be employed" against Faymonville, unavoidably extending Beck's mission.[73] Technical surveillance was an FBI term describing either wiretaps or microphones, and in this case, upon the urging of Michela, Beck had FBI officials send him via military attaché airmail pouch "complete wall microphone equipment." This kind of microphone was placed inside or along the wall of an adjoining room permitting FBI agents to record sounds (i.e., voices). In this instance, Beck and Michela asked Ambassador Standley to rearrange apartment space so Beck could listen in on Faymonville's private activities. The goal, at least on Michela's part, was to secure evidence proving the general's allegations. There were delays both in rearranging apartment space and in the delivery of the surveillance equipment, and in the end Beck developed no incriminating evidence.[74]

Beck, in fact, by his own account was unable to uncover any evidence whatsoever to "substantiate any of the accusations" made against Faymonville. He even noted for his FBI superiors the "almost insurmountable obstacles" his investigation faced because of the friction between Michela and

Faymonville and because Faymonville suspected he was under investigation. Beck even reiterated his previous suspicion that the "entire case [is] a political one." Nevertheless, because Michela insisted his allegations were true and because Beck had the "secret interest and cooperation of [the] two highest officials" at the embassy, he continued the investigation.[75]

By May 1943, Beck pursued several investigative avenues. One stemmed from a woman who claimed to know a "Soviet man with whom . . . [Faymonville] had engaged in homosexual acts." Beck also requested FBI agents in San Francisco conduct a background investigation of Faymonville because he "still maintains his residence" in that city. Yet Beck still characterized the investigation as "all political except for [the] morals charge," but even regarding that he had "not succeeded in uncovering anything specific." In a later message to his FBI superiors, Beck elaborated that the situation at the embassy was "based on almost complete failure of the Soviets to cooperate with all U.S. representatives here other than Lend-Lease [coordinator Faymonville, who] . . . has been using [the situation] to advance his own interests by ignoring [the] ambassador and attaches."[76]

In the meantime, a "well-qualified and experienced" FBI agent in San Francisco conducted an investigation "of utmost discreetness so that no embarrassment would result to the Bureau." He interviewed people who knew Faymonville, including army officers with whom he served, business contacts, and one of his high-school classmates. The agent described all of these individuals as "highly reliable and responsible." In his report, the agent used loaded language and described Faymonville as a "splendid man of high character, an excellent musician, and a highly cultured person with a delightful personality." The FBI agent also noted, according to these sources, that Faymonville was "rather reticent" and a "man who, throughout his entire life, has shown a complete disinterest in women."[77]

The descriptive language this agent employed throughout his report is illuminating. Although he ultimately concluded that "no derogatory information as to General Faymonville's moral character was uncovered," the way he described Faymonville suggested he did not fit the masculine ideal. For example, the agent reported that while a "schoolboy, General Faymonville had the reputation of being a 'sissy.'" He explained that the reason this reputation continued was his "love for music and his aversion to sports, such as football and baseball." The agent explained that Faymonville "preferred to remain alone with his music and studies." What is more, Faymonville's friends were "surprised" when he decided upon a military career because they felt "his quiet nature and shyness" made him not "mentally equipped for life in the Army."[78]

Faymonville's fellow army officers said that while he was stationed in Manila in 1917 he never had "any particular circle of friends" and "appeared very reserved and never made a confidant of anyone." He also never visited any nightclubs, socialized with his fellow officers, or had "any affairs with women." According to these officers, in fact, Faymonville "never interested himself in members of the opposite sex and remained very cool and indifferent toward them."[79]

Officers who served with Faymonville in Vladivostok between 1918 and 1919 reported that he lived in a private apartment separate from the other officers. This fact, apparently, suggested to them that he might have engaged in questionable private behavior, but his fellow officers reported "there was absolutely nothing ever said or done to indicate that there were any irregularities committed in those quarters." The officers believed, moreover, that Faymonville had secured the private quarters to afford himself the space and privacy to play his piano. The FBI source characterized this as "normal" behavior.[80]

The FBI agent in San Francisco finally summarized his informants' views. He wrote that they had attributed Faymonville's "lack of interest in women to a low sex interest." They insisted, though, that Faymonville was "not sexually perverted." They attributed his personality to "his emotional interest" being "concentrated in his love for music." One even described it as being "incomprehensible" that "Faymonville would ever engage in an improper action," and he was "definitely certain that General Faymonville is not perverted in any manner." Two years later, FBI Assistant Director Ladd summarized the content of this report by reminding Hoover that "two officers who had been closely associated with Faymonville stated they regarded him as 'queer' but not necessarily homosexual," and that he "did not associate with women . . . but did continually associate with some 'rosy-cheeked boys' who were clerks and subordinates in his office."[81]

By June 1943, FBI Agent Beck had returned to the United States and submitted his reports on Faymonville.[82] On 6 July 1943, Hoover forwarded to General Strong several memoranda Beck submitted. Two memos detailed Faymonville and his influence on US-Soviet military relations, and a third described the "morals charges" Michela and company leveled against Faymonville. Beck concluded that "no evidence has been uncovered which would prove the charges in this case." He said he had been "present at many frank conversations engaged in by members of Faymonville's staff and members of the other missions there, at which times Faymonville and every type of sex subject were discussed, but at no time have I heard any specific reference made to any immoral conduct by General Faymonville." In fact, Beck continued, "if he had ever engaged in such conduct and it were known to persons who are now on the Embassy staff in Moscow, I feel positive that I would have heard it." Beck concluded with the observation that given the bad relationship between Faymonville and Michela and the fact that Faymonville suspected he was being investigated, "it is of course unlikely that he would jeopardize his position by engaging in activity such . . . [as] has been suspected."[83]

Shortly after forwarding Beck's memoranda to General Strong, the animosities between Faymonville, Michela, and Duncan erupted in public. Because it happened so soon after Beck's return, and because it involved political intrigue connected indirectly to FDR, FBI Director Hoover wanted the full details. FBI Agent Beck, being in a good position to acquire this information, used his sources and submitted to Hoover a memo.[84]

The incident involved former ambassador to Russia and FDR confidant Joseph Davies, whom the president sent to Moscow to hand deliver a letter to Stalin. The president hoped to improve US-Soviet relations. Given the fact that Faymonville was the president's primary source of information in Moscow, FDR was fully informed about difficulties there involving his ambassador and military attachés. Davies was also close to Faymonville; the general had served as military attaché when Davies was US ambassador to Moscow. Upon arriving in Moscow, Davies (and by extension Faymonville) fell into a trap set by Michela and Duncan, who had conspired to embarrass Faymonville (and by extension FDR about his pro-Russian policies) at a public news conference. According to Beck, prior to the news conference, Michela and Duncan met with reporters who "are said to be on the side of the Ambassador and his aides." Michela's and Duncan's plan, with the direct support of Ambassador Standley, was to give Faymonville the "most difficult hour . . . [he] has ever had."[85]

When the news conference started, according to Beck, "Davies did not know that they [the reporters] had been primed for the occasion." One of the reporters began by asking Davies why the Soviets refused to cooperate with US diplomats in Moscow. Davies, who knew all about Faymonville's troubles, replied that the Russians were "under no obligation" to cooperate.

According to Beck, Davies then said if he "were in the position of the Russians he would not give these 'underlings' any information." By "underlings" Davies meant the US military and naval attachés. Davies also explained that FDR was kept well informed about Russian affairs, by which he meant from Faymonville. One reporter questioned this assertion and, according to Beck, "not wishing to mention Michela's name" claimed to have talked with other military officers who said the Russians were not, in fact, cooperating. Davies disagreed. A reporter then asked why the military attachés in Moscow wanted "greater cooperation and more information." Davies is supposed to have answered (Beck pointed out that this information originated with Michela) "that the reporters and anyone else who tries to secure information concerning the Soviets are 'traitors.'"[86]

According to Beck, Ambassador Standley was present and "is said to have enjoyed it thoroughly, 'chuckling and winking' at the reporters from time to time." Beck also said other members of the press were stunned by the news conference and that Standley told Michela it was "'the most amazing press conference' he had ever heard." Furthermore, some of the reporters met with Naval Attaché Duncan afterward to "secure additional ammunition for a second [news] conference." But at that conference, a careful Davies moderated his words and retracted his statement that the Soviets were cooperating with the United States, claiming he had been misinformed.[87]

Several days later Beck reported to Hoover that the positions of Ambassador Standley and General Michela have "been greatly weakened by a report which someone has submitted." According to Beck's source, "higher officials feel that Michela 'went too far' in some matter," and the source "indicated that Admiral Standley and General Michela may be recalled." Beck feared "this probably refers to the report which the Bureau submitted to General Strong."[88] The FBI report on the Faymonville investigation no doubt played a role in ending Standley's and Michela's careers as ambassador and military attaché, respectively. Given their tense and dysfunctional relationships in Moscow, their days in any event were numbered. Additionally, there were other reports on problems in Moscow, and these no doubt also contributed to Standley's and Michela's downfall. One came from lend-lease official Sidney Spalding, who recommended that Michela and Faymonville be replaced, and another from General Burns, who argued the FBI report was based on nothing but Michela's "gossip."[89] What FBI Agent Beck did not know was that Standley had already submitted his resignation to FDR on 3 May 1943, citing his desire not to spend another winter in Russia, but clearly he must have been pressured by higher authorities into resigning.[90] Two months after Beck's memo, Michela, Duncan, and Faymonville also were recalled with newspaper accounts citing the "friction" among US personnel in Moscow. An FBI memo from 1945, moreover, reported the "Bureau file indicates that possibly Michela was removed for spreading false information concerning the former head of the American Lend Lease Mission in Moscow, the then Brigadier General Philip R. Faymonville." Indeed he was.[91]

FBI officials' interest in Faymonville's activities did not end with Beck's final report. Having been the subject of a top-level inquiry, he occasionally drew their interest over subsequent years, especially given his alleged pro-Russian sympathies. Not long after having been recalled from Moscow, while Faymonville was serving as a supply officer in Atlanta, an informant provided the FBI with a private letter of his. Faymonville had written to journalist Ella Winter, widow of noted muckraker Lincoln Steffens, to congratulate her on the publication by Little, Brown in Boston of her book *I Saw the Russian People* (1945), a sympathetic examination of the common lives of Russian citizens. Faymonville told Winter the "book is exactly what we need at this moment" because it helped to offer US readers a true understanding of who, exactly, the Russian people were especially now that the war was over. What interested the FBI SAC in Boston, who obtained a copy of the letter from an informant either at Faymonville's military base or from the publisher, was Faymonville's line about how the book "gives us the exact truth about our friends over there" and the fact that even some procommunist bookstores in Washington, DC, and New York had returned copies to the publisher. In the view of the SAC, this was revealing because those bookstores believed Winter's book "so obviously propaganda" that it would never sell. Additionally, Faymonville hinted that he would allow Winter to quote him to help publicize the book, but he later reconsidered that decision. In the end, Hoover simply filed this information in Faymonville's FBI file.[92]

Another FBI informant in the spring of 1949 offered the bureau his opinion as to why Faymonville was sympathetic to the communists. He claimed that both Davies and Faymonville had purchased Russian rubles on the black market to fund the "ordinary necessities of life, which were priced very highly by the Russian Government." Afterward, the Soviets confronted both men, blackmailed them to "speak well of Russia," and got Faymonville to write articles praising "Russian military strength." This opinion, of course, was nothing but speculation. Nevertheless, FBI officials placed it in Faymonville's FBI file.[93]

Perhaps the most concerning postwar Faymonville story to cross FBI officials' desks was a 29 April 1953 article by Westbrook Pegler that appeared in the *Washington Times-Herald*. In his article, Pegler claimed to "have a report by an agent of the FBI who was sent into Soviet Russia in 1943 to investigate backbiting among the American representatives." Pegler then quoted extensively and precisely from FBI Agent Beck's report but only concerning the political infighting at the embassy. An FBI official noted to his superiors that "no mention of Faymonville's alleged sexual deviation [appeared] in Pegler's column." Hoover's FBI was famous for leaking select information to sympathetic reporters and journalists whose views were in sync with Hoover's to advance the FBI director's political agenda. Despite the fact that Pegler and Hoover were ideological allies, Hoover thought Pegler was too much of a loose cannon who could never be relied upon to adhere to Hoover's line. So what concerned Hoover about Pegler in this incident was exactly how the rabble-rousing journalist had gained access to a sensitive FBI report.[94]

Hoover demanded an investigation. FBI Assistant Director Nichols, Hoover's liaison to Congress and the media, pointed out that Pegler had mentioned Admiral Standley in the article, and Nichols noted that Pegler "is very close to Admiral Standley." It was, therefore, Nichols's "guess that Standley got access in some way to [Beck's] reports on Faymonville and in this manner made them available to Pegler."[95]

FBI agents investigated the matter with army intelligence to determine if Pegler had somehow gotten access to the FBI report forwarded to General Strong. After a thorough investigation, army investigators determined that Beck's three memoranda, including the one detailing the morals charges against Faymonville, and even Hoover's cover letter, were all missing from army archives. They were never able to determine who was responsible.[96]

The FBI began its systematic monitoring of gays during the Roosevelt administration in 1937. The economic and social effects of the Great Depression had led to a backlash against gays, who conducted themselves with relatively few impediments during the 1920s. With the end of Prohibition in 1933, stepped up regulation of bars and social clubs, and the threat perceived to masculinity with the onset of the Great Depression, the US public reassessed the danger posed by people holding same-sex attraction. In the middle of the decade, therefore, the advent of a sex-crime panic, energized by FDR's comments, led FBI Director Hoover to begin systematic monitoring of gays.

With growing concern that subversive elements operated in the US population in the late 1930s, which many believed had led to the successes of fascism and communism during the economic collapse of the 1930s, the president stepped up FBI intelligence-gathering work in August of 1936. To protect the country from Fifth Columnists, FBI officials began systematic monitoring of groups they considered threats. Add to this the fact that gays, who from the perspective of the dominant, hypermasculine culture appeared a potent subversive threat, were now being singled out and considered vulnerable to blackmail, especially during a sex-crime panic. To bureaucrats such as Hoover, there could be nothing more concerning than a compromised homosexual in an influential government position while Fifth Columnists operated in the country.

Given this belief, it is not surprising Hoover responded with vigor to FDR's personal request that FBI agents look into the allegations of sexual impropriety on the part of Undersecretary of State Welles—the most important individual in the State Department during the Second World War. Despite FDR's desire to look the other way and retain his valuable undersecretary, the FBI director privately disagreed. He warned FDR there was no guarantee that Welles would not place himself in a compromising position, and FBI agents continually developed unsubstantiated information to suggest that Welles, in fact, had been compromised, whether by South American governments or racketeers.

This led Hoover, very carefully and selectively, to provide information about Welles to individuals who *had* an interest in undermining the undersecretary. Hoover knew he was in no position to publicly reveal the FBI report on Welles. The president was the one who had requested the investigation, and if he learned that Hoover had leaked the report to Welles's enemies, the FBI director's close relationship with the president—the basis for his being kept on as FBI director—would have been irreparably damaged. But Hoover could and did verbally confirm for others that the FBI, in fact, had investigated Welles's activities, not only confirming their suspicions about Welles but encouraging them to respond. Hoover then directed these people to others who legitimately had and could without repercussion share authorized copies of the FBI report, such as White House aides or, in the case of Senator Brewster, Secretary of State Hull. By doing this Hoover sustained the concerted efforts of Hull, Bullitt, and Brewster to have Welles—an FDR confidant—ousted from office. Hoover undoubtedly believed he was protecting the country from subversive elements even if he was undermining the president's desire to retain Welles. Hoover's reports to FDR on various communists and their opinions of Welles's resignation confirms Hoover's negative opinion of him and the righteousness of his own actions and of Roosevelt's firing him. Never mind, of course, that no evidence existed that foreign agents were blackmailing Welles.

The FBI interest in Senator Walsh is equally telling. Some people at the time of the Walsh incident and later have suggested that the FBI whitewashed the Walsh incident to protect the influential naval affairs committee chair. This view does not stand up to scrutiny. Walsh was no friend of FDR's and was, in fact, a vocal anti-interventionist foreign policy critic. FDR, moreover, even questioned the efficacy of giving FBI information to Senator Barkley to share with the president's anti-interventionist critics in the Senate. FDR viewed these critics with enmity, and given extensive FBI political surveillance and reporting on their activities, it is inconceivable that the president would use the bureau to clear from wrongdoing this particular type of political opponent. It is paradoxical, in fact, because during the first half of 1942 FDR, in a petty bid for revenge, had urged his Justice Department to prosecute various vocal critics under the sedition, foreign-agents registration, or conspiracy statutes.[97]

Although the preponderance of evidence in the Walsh investigation suggests the senator was innocent of the charges leveled against him—and that, in fact, he was gay baited—it is evident from the FBI reports that FBI officials were not, themselves, convinced of the senator's innocence. From their perspective, there could be no greater danger than a vulnerable and careless homosexual serving as chair of an important Senate committee during wartime. Even a careful reading of the correspondence between Hoover and Walsh shows that although the FBI director claimed to be happy to have cleared the senator, he was also careful to make certain to Walsh that his bureau was only interested in the facts—Hoover's standard line to conceal his real interests. But the fact of the matter is that vocal opponents of Walsh—namely FDR ally Morris Ernst—in April of 1942 gay baited the senator in an effort to discredit one of FDR's foreign policy critics. Ernst knew full well of FDR's close relationship with FBI Director Hoover; in fact, Ernst maintained a close relationship with FBI officials (undoubtedly because of his own known close relationship with the president), feeding them information on anti-interventionist critics. By suggesting to FDR that Walsh was involved in a sexual scandal, which prompted FDR to have Ernst "follow up" with the FBI, Ernst initiated the gay baiting of Walsh. It was, in fact, a particularly vicious way to discredit a political opponent and a method that predated a common occurrence of the Lavender Scare of the 1950s.

Faymonville was similarly gay baited. As individuals, both Walsh and Faymonville did not fit the expected masculine gender roles of the period, leading some to question their sexual propriety and leading to their being gay baited, the purpose being, of course, to destroy their careers. In Faymonville's case, as lend-lease coordinator in Moscow, he enjoyed special access to the Soviets, was favored by the White House, and supported its policy toward the Soviet Union, all of which earned him the bitter enmity of the US ambassador and military and naval attachés in Moscow. Given past allegations about sexual, and homosexual, improprieties at the US Embassy in Moscow and the fact that Faymonville was present during that period, the ambassador and attachés, particularly General Michela, found it expedient to discredit Faymonville and destroy his career by gay baiting him. As experts in investigating gays systematically, Hoover's FBI naturally played a prominent role in all of these incidents.

All three of these FBI investigations—of Sumner Welles, David Walsh, and Philip Faymonville—reflect the evolving FBI interest in monitoring and investigating gays. What started in 1937 as a response to FDR's demand and public promise that the killer of 10-year-old Charles Mattson be found had evolved into a systematic collection of information about "sex offenders" for educational and law-enforcement purposes. This was a function of Hoover's embarrassing comment that child kidnappings were a thing of the past and his efforts to cater to the president's every wish while ingratiating himself with FDR at every opportunity, all at the very moment the New Deal–era federal government had "discovered" homosexual people. It was with little surprise, then, that by the Second World War a new perception about gays evolved. They were elevated from dangerous, predatory criminals to security risks.

We know the FBI began its systematic collection of information about "sex offenders" in 1937 from records documenting the destruction of the Sex Deviates File in 1977 and 1978. Those same records note that the second major file constituting the Sex Deviates File contained records dating from 1942 and that related to the "subject of 'sex perverts in Government service.'" It is clear the 1942 start of FBI collection of information about "sex perverts in Government service" involved Welles, Walsh, and Faymonville, three prominent government officials who, despite lack of evidence, were viewed as liable to blackmail by foreign agents and whose careers were irreparably damaged by both the allegations and FBI investigations. It also seems logical that there must have been many other lower-level officials who found themselves subject to questions about their sexuality and then separated from their government jobs. Yet given realities in acquiring FBI records it is impossible to know the true extent of FBI efforts. It seems possible, though, that during this period the FBI might, in any event, have restricted itself to prominent targets, as it had not yet become the all-encompassing agency engaged in seemingly endless name-checks it would become during the cold war, McCarthy, and Lavender Scare periods, but we shall never know the full extent of FBI efforts in this era. This gay issue, however, would certainly skyrocket after the Second World War and the advent of the Lavender Scare.

"Sex Deviates in Government Service"

The Lavender Scare and the FBI Sex Deviates Program and File

Official concern over a gay man in the State Department who potentially could be blackmailed did not remain isolated to the Second World War and Sumner Welles. Following the conclusion of that war, the United States shifted from wartime ally of the Soviet Union to engaging the Russians in a long-lasting cold war characterized by fears not only of communist but gay subversion. Central to how this developed was the evolution of foreign and domestic events after 1945 and how a new president dealt with them. With the death of the urbane Franklin D. Roosevelt (FDR), a less-experienced and more provincial man became chief executive, Harry S. Truman. As had long been tradition, FDR had kept Vice President Truman at arm's length. Truman was not informed about important programs or developments— such as the development of the atomic bomb—nor was Truman gifted with FDR's charisma, which had enabled him, over the long run, to bring people around to his side of an issue. Instead, Truman was rigid, stubborn, and quick to act. He was also a hardline anticommunist apt to listen to those advisors who, like himself, saw in Soviet Premier Josef Stalin and communists not people with whom to work but adversaries with whom to compete.

Tension between the two superpowers was evident immediately in how the new president dealt with the Yalta Accords. At Yalta, FDR and Allied leaders drafted purposefully vague agreements on the future of postwar Poland and Germany. To avoid internal conflict, the president purposefully avoided making already controversial issues worse by pushing hard for conclusive agreements during wartime. Instead, as was classic FDR style, he preferred to delay them and rely on his grand and magnetic personality, hopefully, to win Stalin over at a later date.

As president, Truman, who was not privy to any of FDR's reasoning, saw things differently. To him, the Allied nations concluded firm agreements at Yalta, and his worry was how to persuade the Russians to adhere to their side of the bargain. He therefore berated Soviet Foreign Minister Molotov "with words of one syllable," and after the Russian complained about the president's undiplomatic language, Truman famously responded: "Carry out your agreements and you won't get talked to like that."[1] Thus began a confrontational foreign policy that would evolve by 1947 into the Containment Doctrine, characterizing decades of cold war.[2]

FDR's death and international events not only changed the way US postwar foreign policy evolved but also changed the nature of US domestic politics. In 1945 the House Un-American Activities Committee (HUAC) became a permanent fixture in Congress. Formed in 1938 under the chairmanship of Texan Martin Dies, HUAC was repeatedly used by conservatives to attack FDR and the New Deal by investigating the loyalty of administration staffers. With the rise of cold war tensions and a new, confrontational, and anticommunist president leading the country, HUAC took on new significance, particularly in terms of domestic politics and growing fears of communist subversion.[3]

Several events helped to ignite US fears of subversives. Early in 1945, after the leftist journal *Amerasia* published an article that copied, almost verbatim, a classified Office of Strategic Services (OSS) report on Thailand, FBI agents broke into *Amerasia*'s office, bugged it, and wiretapped its telephone lines. Then, in November 1945, former Soviet spy Elizabeth Bentley approached the FBI. After her Russian handler/lover died, Soviet intelligence cut all ties with her, leading to resentment on her part. She offered the bureau more than a hundred names of purported Soviet espionage agents but, in part because the Soviets had shut down their spy ring, FBI agents were unable to corroborate Bentley's story. Around the same time, Igor Gouzenko, a Soviet consular official in Canada, defected and claimed to have knowledge of Soviet espionage operations in both Canada and the United States, including the existence of a spy serving as an assistant to the secretary of state. US anticommunists, notably J. Edgar Hoover, would later single out Alger Hiss as this assistant and pursue him relentlessly as an alleged spy.

Concerned with the seeming infestation of Soviet agents and the ignorant or apathetic public response, in February 1946 FBI officials created a special program to inform public opinion about the communist threat. FBI officials dubbed their program an "educational campaign" whereby they leaked derogatory information culled from FBI files to sympathetic news reporters and government officials. Within a year, Hoover also established a secretive relationship with HUAC to sustain its anticommunist campaign, and dating from March 1951, FBI officials provided information to the other anticommunist body on the Hill, the Senate Internal Security Subcommittee (SISS). Over time, Hoover used others to promote "the cause" of anticommunism, or antisubversion, while obsequiously working to discredit the Truman administration's policies. Hoover was not close with Truman like he was with FDR.

In response to perceptions of a national security problem, some members of Congress began to demand tighter loyalty and security procedures. On 16 August 1946, Senator Patrick McCarran sponsored a rider to a State Department appropriations bill that authorized the secretary of state to dismiss any employee he regarded as a security risk. Moving beyond the issue of communist infiltration, State Department officials focused, significantly, on those they thought could be blackmailed into betraying state secrets, including adulterers, drunks, and especially gays. Concern over gays in the State Department was nothing new, but, in the context of the early cold war, bureaucrats began to feel an urgent need to purge them from federal employment. Known historically as the Lavender Scare, the McCarran rider, in fact, was an early example of it.[4]

The momentum created by these labyrinthine events led President Truman, in an effort to undercut criticism he was "soft" on communism, to institute on 22 March 1947 the Federal Employee Loyalty Program. FBI agents were to screen federal employees and prospective job applicants by looking into their past beliefs and present activities, and, if the agents deemed them disloyal, they would be fired or denied employment. Significantly, those targeted were not permitted to confront their accusers. They were further denied access to evidence that implicated them, whether it was witnesses or information from FBI files. The insularity of FBI files and investigations, moreover, gave FBI officials wide latitude in manipulating the screening process.

Also in the year 1947, the State Department began to remove from its ranks, albeit quietly, anyone suspected of being homosexual. The department's assistant secretary for administration, John Peurifoy, led the effort, which resulted in thirty-one suspected gays being dismissed, followed by fifty-nine over the next two years.[5] Yet it was not only the State Department ferreting out suspected gay and lesbian employees. FBI agents were also developing information on them using their already established (1937) Sex Offenders File, Second World War–era Sex Perverts in Government Service

File, and Obscene File. They used the Obscene File, created to identify and shut down interstate pornography rings, as a means to collect and file information to purge gays from government or military service. In one instance during September 1947, after receiving complaints about it, military intelligence officers in San Antonio, Texas, snapped photos of a local gay bar—Angie's Place—and gave the photos to an FBI agent. The agent then submitted the photos to headquarters, where officials incorporated them as part of the Obscene File. Because the gay bar had nothing to do with an obscenity ring, the only possible purpose of the photos was to identify an establishment specific members of the military might frequent. This was not a stand-alone event. In 1964, an Oak Park, Michigan, police detective forwarded fourteen "obscene" photos, two of which depicted gays, to the FBI laboratory. Unable to identify the subjects in the photos, FBI officials added the same-sex photos to the Obscene File and filed an unrecorded copy of the memo about them in the FBI's Sex Deviates File (the development of which will be discussed below).[6]

If the Great Depression had helped to stimulate a sex-crime panic in 1937, the effects of the Second World War followed by the rise of the Soviet Union as a superpower, the threat of nuclear annihilation, and fears of domestic subversion had a similar impact. US citizens were genuinely frightened but overreacted to perceived threats at home. What emerged between 1947 and the mid-1950s was a second sex-crime panic that, in the very least, fueled the Lavender Scare in 1950. It was, moreover, another series of highly publicized murders of children at this time that focused public scrutiny, again, on the broad category of "sex offenders" but made no distinction between gays and true predators. Nationwide, advocacy groups and the press demanded that authorities act to protect children, leading Congress and fifteen state governments to create special investigatory commissions. Several states and municipalities enacted sexual psychopath laws that remanded those arrested—many simply gay men—either to prisons or mental institutions. The best example, perhaps, was Washington, DC's, own "Pervert Elimination Campaign," which targeted popular gay cruising areas such as Lafayette Park, next to the White House.[7]

FBI Director Hoover only amplified public fears when in July 1947 he published an article in *American Magazine* titled "How Safe Is Your Daughter?" (Actually it was ghostwritten by the FBI Crime Records Division using information culled from its Sex Offenders File.) Citing an increase in sex crimes, Hoover recommended some solutions. As he once did in 1937, Hoover again asserted parole and probation were dangerous because released criminals would only strike again; and he offered his readers examples of repeat offenders attacking children. He also claimed, "The seriousness of sex crimes is either not recognized by some authorities" or sex criminals received minimal punishments. He therefore argued that only aroused public opinion could force local and state authorities out of their "laxity." Hoover claimed the "time was long overdue" for "*every* sex criminal" to be "accorded specialized treatment." If mental defects could not be repaired, he wrote, then these people needed to be isolated from the public.[8]

The Lavender Scare predated McCarthyism, as is evident with the 1947 purge of gays from the State Department, and outlasted it by decades. Yet by 1950 the Lavender Scare also took on a vociferous, influential, and decidedly public dimension that captured the attention of the US public nationwide and significantly expanded a once-demure hunt for gays in government.[9]

Exemplifying this, in September 1950 Ralph H. Major Jr., a popular author for *Coronet* magazine (a periodical owned by *Esquire*), decided to tackle the gay issue. His article vividly captured growing fears over gays and lesbians in the public and the strength and dominance in US culture of gay stereotypes, visceral hatred of gays, and widespread homophobia. When prefacing the piece, the editors of *Coronet*, in fact, claimed to be offering readers a "frank and factual discussion of homosexuality." They claimed the article violated all the taboos and was based on six months of in-depth research. Readers needed to know these details, they claimed, because it was in the public interest given the "sinister threat to American youth [that] is fast developing." The author even purported to offer a "sober attempt to analyze the nature of these men."[10]

Major began his piece with the observation that, prior to the Lavender Scare, gays had only caught press attention when involved in crime. Even then, he claimed, medical professionals dismissed it as only happening "in extreme cases." He bizarrely characterized this minimal press coverage as the result of "prejudice and prudery"—not prejudice unfairly aimed at gays but an overarching and robust moral condemnation that precluded people from talking about gays. Major therefore claimed to offer previously unknown information about the "danger" of gays, especially given that their numbers were "rapidly increasing throughout America today."[11]

Major observed that although homosexuality sometimes, but rightly, elicited "fury" among heterosexual men, most brushed it off with "disgust and gutter humor." Many others, he wrote, regarded a "sex pervert merely as a 'queer' who never harms anyone but himself." Major called this attitude "dangerous and shortsighted" and cited a California prosecutor who specialized in sex crimes. "All too often," the California official stated, "we lose sight of the fact that the homosexual is an inveterate seducer of the young of both sexes and that he presents a social problem because he is not content with being degenerate himself; *he must have degenerate companions, and is ever seeking younger victims.*" To Major, this was the "hidden danger of homosexuality," drawing in thousands of victims annually.[12]

Major then described "pathetic cases" of young boys who succumbed to the devilish sex deviate. He warned, moreover, harkening back to Hoover's 1937 and 1947 prophesies, "Irreparable mental and psychological damage is only one side of the story. The other is even more reprehensible. Some male sex deviants do not stop with infecting their often-innocent partners: they descend through perversions to other forms of depravity, such as drug addiction, burglary, sadism, and even murder." Explaining this, Major wrote, "Once a man assumes the role of homosexual, he often throws off all moral restraints." Major concluded, "Homosexuality may be a disease, a condition, a criminal offense, or a moral sin. Nevertheless, steps must be taken now to protect American youth from an ever growing peril." If done properly, the "sinister shadow of sexual perversion can be removed from the pathway of America's youth."[13]

Two other authors specializing in crime and criminals, Charles C. Thomas in 1950, then supplemented by physician J. Paul De River in 1965, wrote a book that over the 1950s and 1960s served as guide to sex criminals. They wrote that because "acts of sadism and masochism are practiced among both the homosexual male and female," it was "not unusual to find sadistic homicide, particularly among the male homosexuals." The authors cited the root causes of these murders: "jealousy, envy, hatred, robbery, or blackmail." Because gays were closeted and society deemed them outcasts, being outed was a prime motivation for murder. Another motivation was found in the jilting of a homosexual partner. Moreover, they claimed, the "homosexual will murder his victim during an act of sexual frenzy, and afterwards rob him."[14]

Underlying all of these fears was a cultural tendency to see in frightening and unfolding events a threat to masculinity, similar to that in the mid-1930s, that evolved as part of cold war US culture. If godless communists were the epitome of subversion—which anticommunists often defined rhetorically in terms of weakness, effeminacy, or softness—then the perception of gays in the United States of the 1950s perfectly fit this definition as a threat to manliness in hypermasculinized, patriarchal US culture. The irony is that this depiction belied notions of a threat to security, and in terms of crime, even society. A perfect contemporary example was the description of gays offered by Jack Lait and Lee Mortimer in their sensational exposé series of *Confidential* books (1948–1951). Throughout the series, the authors with no reserve whatsoever referred to gays and lesbians as "psychopaths," "fags," "dull, dumb deviates," "perverts," "homos," "female homos," or "mannish women." Gays stood out, moreover, largely because of the effectiveness of the Second World War in bringing that minority together. The mass mobilization of millions of men and women across the country who suddenly found themselves in same-sex living environments enabled many gays and lesbians to realize they were not alone but were, in fact, a widely scattered minority. It was no coincidence, then, that the first gay rights groups formed—and the homophile movement emerged—soon after the demobilization of the US military in 1945. It was also no coincidence that gays and lesbians were quickly singled out by government bureaucrats and the public at large as a dangerous threat.[15]

One early but significant target in FBI officials' postwar but pre-1950s Lavender Scare, the hunt for gays in government, was State Department employee Charles W. Thayer. On 26 January 1949, an agent advised Associate FBI Director Clyde Tolson about the results of a Senate inquiry into Voice of America (VOA). The subcommittee concluded that time-consuming FBI background checks of VOA employees had created understaffing issues. Always concerned with any public criticisms of the FBI, Tolson and Hoover ordered an inquiry, believing the FBI "ought to nail this if it is incorrect."[16]

In his report, FBI Assistant Director Alex Rosen, taking a moderate approach, noted the subcommittee had not necessarily criticized the FBI but the vast State Department bureaucracy that required the background reports. Rosen further pointed out that there was, in fact, no delay on the FBI's part, and as proof he cited the number of successful FBI checks that year. Rosen, however, recognized one worrisome source of criticism, and it was from the head of the VOA in New York, Thayer.[17]

In May 1948, Thayer started criticizing the FBI for "hamstringing" the

VOA by not completing its investigations within thirty days. This led Thayer to state publicly in the *New York Herald Tribune* that the State Department International Broadcasting Division (IBD) had been "handicapped" by not having qualified employees knowledgeable about Eastern Europe and Russia. To Rosen, Thayer was "prejudiced against the Bureau," leading FBI officials to file a complaint with Peurifoy, who promised no further trouble from the IBD.[18]

To contextualize the tone of Thayer's comment, Rosen explained that VOA employees had a reputation as "the most disreputable group of individuals" FBI agents had ever investigated. He said the bureau's files were "replete" with evidence showing they "were totally unfit for employment, either for loyalty, security, or moral reasons." His last description, "moral reasons," was, of course, a common euphemism for homosexuality. Rosen then singled out Thayer because he fathered an illegitimate child and because the State Department never asked that Thayer receive an FBI background check. This prompted Hoover, a product of the Progressive Era and champion of puritanical and Victorian values, to ask whether the law required all VOA employees to be investigated. He then ordered his subordinates to look into it with a curt, "Keep on top of this. Make a most thorough investigation of Thayer."[19]

Peurifoy assigned Donald Nicholson, chief of the State Department Security Division, to ascertain why the FBI never checked Thayer's background. In short order he reported that, according to the VOA law, anybody appointed by the president and confirmed by the Senate was exempt from an FBI background check. The State Department granted Thayer this exemption because FDR had appointed him to the Foreign Service, and the Senate had confirmed it. Nicholson, however, informed FBI officials that Thayer's exemption was a "mere technicality," and Thayer's superiors did not want the issue pressed. Nicholson also advised FBI officials that, for reasons unknown to him, Thayer's loyalty form had never been forwarded to the FBI. He promised to forward it. In Nicholson's opinion, to bypass the State Department's exemption of Thayer, if FBI agents could locate any "derogatory information" about him, then they could "open a full field loyalty case."[20]

In a related case, FBI officials learned that State Department official Lloyd Lehrbas had testified before Congress claiming FBI investigations were slow and, therefore, restricting VOA operations. When asked, Lehrbas said he never intended to criticize the FBI. Instead, he only wanted to impress upon Congress how cumbersome the process really was. This further bit of perceived criticism was too much for Hoover, who dismissed, for a second time, a State Department official's rational explanation with a curt "Usual State Dept. double talk." A master bureaucrat, Hoover always defended his carefully crafted FBI image like a pit bull, knowing it was often the key to bureaucratic success. Regarding Thayer, Hoover ordered an investigation but not under the Loyalty Program or VOA screening. Instead, it was to be a domestic security investigation. An impatient FBI director believed he had enough information "as regards Thayer [to] proceed with a Security investigation. We have enough without Loyalty form receipt to warrant a thorough investigation."[21]

With a convenient justification in hand, Hoover directed the FBI New York City Field Office to begin a "thorough but discreet investigation." Hoover warned the special agent in charge (SAC) of the New York office that Thayer was a critic of the FBI and father of an illegitimate daughter and that his office should conduct a "full background" investigation focusing on Thayer's "character, loyalty, and activities." In short order, the New York office supplied some information to Hoover, but none of it was derogatory.[22]

On 8 April 1949, Guy Hottel, the SAC of the FBI Washington, DC, Field Office (WFO) and bureau liaison with the State Department, reported far more useful information. Hottel acquired from State Department Security Division officer John Finlator a report on Thayer dated 22 July 1948 "not to be found in the official files of the State Department." Finlator handed over the "unofficial" report provided the FBI never "embarrass or compromise the source from which it was received." The report revealed to FBI officials, for the first time, the allegation that Thayer was homosexual, the original basis for the State Department investigation. It also listed several of his associates who were gay or rumored to be gay, including Carmel Offie, Ambassador Alexander Kirk (see Chapter 3), Colonel Ira W. Porter, Nicholas Nabokoff, and Jacques Brosse, among others. Given the value placed on this document, Hoover ordered Hottel not to ask Senator Karl Mundt—former member of HUAC—"for information concerning Thayer" as had previously been planned.[23]

Despite the fact that Hoover had learned of Thayer's alleged homosexuality—information that if leaked, whether true or not, could have ended Thayer's career on the spot—the FBI director could not use it. If FBI officials disseminated the information, it would have been obvious where the information originated and who offered it to Hoover. Hoover's hesitation here also illustrates the value to which he assigned collecting derogatory information that did not compromise FBI sources and, even more so, the fact that the FBI had not yet developed the intimate and secure working relationship with State Department Security Division it later would. At this point, Hoover did not want Finlator to be a onetime source, nor did he want to "ruin an excellent source of information for the Washington Field Office." Ironically, Hoover found this constraint irritating because it prevented him from easily dispatching Thayer, who, Hoover learned, had used his connections to quash the State Department probe of his personal life. Thayer's brother-in-law was State Department Counsel Charles "Chip" Bohlen, who asked Undersecretary of State Robert Lovett to terminate the probe. Regardless of Hoover's predicament, he concluded that Thayer "as a matter of fact . . . should have no place in govt." Hamstrung for the moment, Hoover nevertheless awarded Hottel at the WFO a letter of commendation for being "most discreet and circumspect" for not "revealing the Bureau's interest in Thayer." The case, moreover, illustrates for us the early problems Hoover's FBI had in collecting, collating, and disseminating information about alleged homosexuals *prior* to the formulation of its Sex Deviates Program.[24]

With the Thayer security investigation hitting roadblocks, Hoover eventually shifted gears and ordered FBI agents to begin a loyalty investigation. Hoover based the loyalty probe on unsubstantiated information purporting that Thayer, while an OSS officer in Italy during the Second World War, was sympathetic to communism. Hoover had hoped a loyalty investigation "would permit a more open type of investigation," through which certain leads could be followed up unlike those in a "more discreet security investigation." Yet because Thayer was related to Bohlen, Hoover demanded the investigation be made carefully and sources be questioned indirectly.[25]

In April 1949, Hoover learned—again from his confidential State Department source—that Thayer had the previous December telephoned the State Department New York security office and had spoken with agent Edwin Lennerts. Using the pseudonym "Mr. B." and with assurance his call would be revealed to none but the chief of the Security Division, Nicholson, Thayer admitted to having fathered an illegitimate child. Thayer was attempting to end an investigation that alleged he was homosexual by freely admitting to the less-damning charge (at the time) of having a daughter out of wedlock. By admitting to this particular charge, Thayer hoped to continue his career unabated, albeit with a black mark, whereas the stigma of a homosexual charge regardless of its veracity surely would have ended it.[26]

That same month, using the information obtained from Finlator, SAC Hottel wrote a twenty-five-page FBI summary report on Thayer, detailing various allegations against him, particularly those alleging that he was homosexual. Not intended for dissemination outside of the FBI, the report was to be used "only for the Bureau's information and guidance" because many of the report's sources were interviewed not by FBI agents but by State Department Security Division officers.[27] Hoover hoped FBI agents would develop their own information they *could* then use to ensure Thayer's termination. This is evident in an FBI memo dated 22 April 1949 reporting the fact that Thayer had resigned from VOA and was looking to move into diplomatic work. This raised Hoover's ire, evident from his scrawl on the memo ordering subordinates to move forward "promptly" with their investigation because the State Department "will probably give Thayer another assignment unless we come up with something."[28]

Hoover authorized FBI agents to interview Thayer's neighbors and colleagues—just as agents would do in any loyalty investigation—but to do so discreetly so as to "avoid any criticism of the Bureau by Thayer," who, Hoover noted, already held negative views of the FBI and made them publicly known. Hoover also arranged for the State Department and US Army to conduct investigations outside of the United States, a requirement of the loyalty investigation given Thayer's international work.[29]

By May 1949, FBI agents had begun to interview some of the State Department's sources. One witness, Eric Prindonoff, of San Marino, California, accused Thayer of holding views sympathetic toward communism, failing to help US citizens when stationed in Belgrade during the summer of 1945, and having worked in the black market (similar to charges made in the past against Faymonville). According to Prindonoff, Thayer had bought diamonds and cameras in Yugoslavia and then sold them in Egypt for "huge profits." He also accused Thayer of selling US military mission foodstuffs, motorized equipment, and even stocks and securities. Prindonoff estimated Thayer had amassed about $500,000 working through the black market.[30]

The FBI investigation of Thayer and many others presumed to be gay received—to put it mildly—a significant boost after February 1950, when the junior senator from Wisconsin, Joseph McCarthy, entered the limelight to inaugurate a public anticommunist witch hunt that would grip US government and society. Yet it was not the senator, per se, or the anticommunist campaign that assumed his name, by which Thayer and company found themselves targeted. Instead, paralleling the hunt for communists inside and outside of government was a companion effort—though actually distinct—to ferret out gays and lesbians from all manner of government and nongovernment positions. It is significant that McCarthyism—and the partisan politics surrounding it—although not an inextricable part of the Lavender Scare, nevertheless fed and energized it.

On 9 February 1950, in a speech before a small Republican women's group in Wheeling, West Virginia, Senator McCarthy offered his audience a convincing explanation for why the United States was seemingly "losing" the cold war. Significant to his success, McCarthy spoke after a series of events had stunned the public. In a very public trial during 1948, twelve American Communist Party members were prosecuted for violating the Smith Act—advocating the violent overthrow of the US government. Then, during 1949, the Soviets detonated an atomic weapon, and China, a valued Second World War ally, was "lost" to communism. US citizens were further shocked by revelations of apparent communist espionage at home, such as the cases involving Hiss and Judith Coplon—a Justice Department employee who secretly worked as a Soviet intelligence courier. In an effort to explain all of this, McCarthy claimed communists had infiltrated the State Department.

That communists allegedly worked in the State Department was nothing new. What was new, however, was the senator's claim to have a list of 205 "known Communists." He delivered the speech several more times, and in each instance his phony number of "known Communists" changed, alternating variously from 205 communists to 57 communists to 81. To McCarthy and other right-wing conservatives with an agenda aimed at discrediting the Roosevelt-Truman administrations and the New Deal, US security problems originated in FDR's appeasement policies at Yalta and Truman's refusal to change course. Those administrations, by kowtowing to communists, according to McCarthy and his sympathizers, permitted reds, over time, apparently to infest the US government and influence policy.

In addition to these cases, on 20 February 1950 in the Senate, McCarthy singled out two specific cases not of political subversion but "sexual deviance." One of them, McCarthy's case No. 14, involved the State Department hiring a translator in 1945 who was a "bad security risk" and should be fired because "another Government investigating agency" determined he "was flagrantly homosexual." Even worse, after this man was, in fact, fired in February 1946, he was rehired two months later. McCarthy's other case of sexual deviance was a man he believed vulnerable to blackmail; he described him as having "peculiar mental twists."[31] By singling out these two cases, as historian David Johnson has pointed out, McCarthy had unwittingly focused public attention on a topic previously only simmering under the political surface for years—gays in government—and linked it to the now-exploding issue of communists in government.[32]

Today we know the identities of the two individuals McCarthy singled out for their alleged sexual perversion. We know because McCarthy was using a list compiled in 1947 by House Appropriations Committee investigators led by staffer and former FBI agent Robert Emmet Lee. Assisted by two other former FBI agents—Eugene Rinta and Harris Huston—Lee surveyed 108 State Department personnel files and created a list. Later called the "Lee list," it referenced subversives in the State Department by number, just as McCarthy had done in his Senate speech. In March 1950, moreover, McCarthy offered the Tydings Committee the names associated with the numbers. In April 2007, Library of Congress archivist and historian John Earl Haynes made the list and associated names public, so we know McCarthy's case No. 14 was Ernest Theodore Arndt and case No. 62 was Isham W. Perkins.[33]

In the Lavender Scare of 1950, Arndt and Perkins were, essentially, the first publicly identified alleged gays in government. As such, they were both subject to FBI investigation. The FBI released to this author, however, only eight pages of material regarding Arndt. One document briefly summarized the FBI investigation. It indicated Arndt was subject to an FBI loyalty investigation in 1949—this, of course, was prior to the creation of the Sex Deviates Program. In FBI interviews with Arndt's friends and acquaintances, some apparently questioned his loyalty, thought he was "pro-Nazi," and generally described him as a "bad egg" and a "troublemaker." FBI agents also learned Arndt had been discharged from the Marine Corps "by reason of habits and traits of character," which he had somehow managed to have changed to an honorable discharge "for the convenience of the Government." The FBI agent who wrote the summary added that the "above investigation revealed subject was investigated as a homosexual as he was suspected of being homosexually inclined." I submitted a second Freedom of Information Act (FOIA) request for the remainder of Arndt's file not released to me, but the FBI responded that these records "were destroyed between October 1961 and August 30, 1982," thereby precluding us from knowing the extent of FBI agents' investigative efforts.[34]

Perkins was also subject to FBI investigation. The FBI released to this author twenty-nine pages on Perkins dating from 1940. These records constituted Perkins's original background check prior to employment with the State Department, a background check he passed with flying colors. I was further informed by the FOIA staff at the FBI that records possibly relating to Perkins from two FBI headquarters files—one concerning the Motor Vehicle Theft Act and the other laboratory examinations—were destroyed on 1 May 1993. Unlike in Arndt's extant FBI file, however, there is no indication FBI agents looked into Perkins's sexuality, but this destruction now precludes the possibility of finding out that it may well have happened.[35]

Because concern with gays in the State Department was nothing new—but now reinvigorated after McCarthy's Wheeling speech and subsequent Senate speeches—State Department officials tried to avoid falling into McCarthy's red-baiting trap. Given cultural stereotypes, they thought gays were easier to identify than communists, and if they purged them perhaps McCarthy would be mollified. This was easier as well because the State Department had in any event already been focusing on this issue, albeit quietly, since 1947. The State Department, therefore, announced in 1950 that it had dismissed from its ranks some 202 "security risks." Instead of deflating McCarthy's claims, however, the revelation only piqued people's curiosity. When pressed on exactly what was meant by 202 security risks, Deputy Undersecretary of State Peurifoy admitted that 91 of the 202 dismissals were homosexuals. Republicans who had rallied behind McCarthy because his claims resonated with the public and could readily discredit the Truman administration quickly embraced the 91 to illustrate the "infiltration" into the State Department of "sexual perverts" who could be blackmailed by Soviet agents. In light of the recent espionage cases that headlined the news, regardless of the fact that there existed no known case of a compromised gay civil servant, the charge worked well for conservatives.[36]

With little recourse, the State Department then began a systematic purge of gays while the now national political issue of the Lavender Scare quickly expanded both in scope and in intensity. In April 1950, for example, the national chair of the Republican Party, Guy Gabrielson, further inflamed the gays-in-government issue by asserting homosexuals were at least "as dangerous as the actual Communists."[37] While political tensions and a sense of urgency surrounding the gay issue steadily grew, inflamed by the parallel communists-in-government issue, probably to demonstrate to the administration his bureau was on top of the issue, FBI Director Hoover on 10 April 1950 forwarded to the White House a list of 393 people arrested in Washington, DC, "on charges of sexual irregularities" since 1947 who claimed to be federal employees. Hoover had obtained the list from Lieutenant Roy Blick, chief of the Metropolitan Police Department's Morals Division (the four officers of which, according to him, "give their full time to detecting and arresting homosexuals"), and it offered names, job positions, and dates of arrest. Hoover advised the White House he had also forwarded the list to the Civil Service Commission (CSC) and the various branches of the armed services.[38]

Hoover did not restrict himself only to forwarding the information to the Truman White House. After receiving Blick's list, Hoover implemented the first, albeit limited, incarnation of the FBI Sex Deviates Program. This early version of the program relied on fingerprint and arrest records only and was therefore housed in the FBI Identification Division (later it would be Crime Records). Whenever Blick's morals squad arrested someone "for a sex offense," the police-generated fingerprint card was forwarded to the FBI. Bureau personnel in the Identification Division then took the name of the person arrested and cross-checked it with the card indexes of "both the criminal and noncriminal files." FBI agents then conducted a second search "against the fingerprints in the criminal file" but not those in the noncriminal file. The information culled from bureau records was then provided to the CSC or the employing federal agencies, and, according to the head of the Identification Division, FBI Assistant Director Stanley J. Tracy, "the first report was prepared on April 14, 1950." That report, using the FBI fingerprint files, identified 363 federal employees between 1947 and 1950.[39]

About a month after Hoover forwarded his list to the White House, Lawson Moyer, executive director of the CSC, having also received Hoover's list, reported to the White House the commission's procedures and policies regarding federal employees arrested "for sex offenses." Moyer described the CSC's general policy as including three components: first, sending a copy of the arrest record to a particular agency or department; second, determining if and where the CSC had jurisdiction; and third, asking agencies with jurisdiction to report to the CSC whatever action they took. Moyer then explained to White House officials his commission's response to the various lists of gays it had recently received from Hoover and others.[40]

In addition to Hoover's list, the State Department had forwarded its list of the ninety-one so-called security risks "separated from the State Department because of alleged sex deviation." Moyer reported that the CSC had "promptly" compared the list to its service records and identified fourteen of the ninety-one as being employed in the executive branch. Nine of those fourteen fell under CSC jurisdiction, and five were under the jurisdiction of whatever specific agency employed them. One of the nine, Moyer wrote, had resigned while the CSC sent letters to six agencies requesting separation for their respective listed employees. The remaining two of the nine, Moyer noted, were currently under investigation, and of the five names remaining of the identified fourteen, the CSC had learned that one had resigned and the CSC did not yet know the disposition of the last four. The commission, moreover, had also "flagged in its Master Index [the ninety-one individuals] in order that they may be identified if they seek re-entry into the Federal service."[41]

Significantly, Moyer also reported to the White House the disposition of Hoover's list. The CSC actually received from Hoover multiple lists over several days—12, 17, and 28 April and 4 May 1950, respectively—of people arrested "for alleged sex offenses, or investigation [*sic*] for alleged sex offenses." CSC officials compared Hoover's "original group of persons" (from 12 and 17 April) with the one he forwarded on 12 April (in other words, the one he had sent to the White House) and found names from the original list included in Hoover's new list, but no arrest records were included or received from the FBI director. Even more alarming, some of the departments and agencies associated with people on Hoover's list were inaccurate. The CSC learned that some of the people were either never federal employees or not presently employees. This led Moyer to conclude that had the CSC forwarded to the respective agencies Hoover's list and arrest records, "much unwarranted confusion and embarrassment to individuals and agencies would have resulted." Hoover's initials were typed on this CSC memo, indicating that a copy was forwarded to him.[42]

This can only be described as a terribly embarrassing episode for Hoover regarding gays in government, and it was quickly followed in May 1950 with Senate hearings on the topic chaired by Nebraska Republican Kenneth

Wherry. Framing himself a longtime expert on gays in government—dating from the State Department's initial 1947 purge, for which he took full credit—Wherry formed a subcommittee of two senators (himself and Senator J. Lister Hill of Alabama) to study the issue. Stating that "there has been dereliction to duty in the executive branch in permitting these moral perverts to obtain employment by the Government," Wherry and Hill avidly investigated. Together they questioned officials from the State Department, Defense Department, and CSC about the revelations of Blick and Sergeant James Hunter of the Morals Division, who had previously testified before the full appropriations subcommittee, where they offered startling testimony. Blick, as leader of the morals squad, offered testimony on the number of gays in the State Department, which he put at between 300 and 400. Attempting to highlight the larger problem in the capital, Blick estimated that there were "5,000 homosexuals in the District of Columbia and that three-fourths of them, 3,750, work for the Government." Hunter estimated that there were "1,000 bad security risks now walking the streets of Washington, DC," an estimate military intelligence officials believed was "conservative." As historian Athan Theoharis has pointed out, these numbers were just as fabricated as McCarthy's "known Communists" in the State Department. Yet, clearly, they lent a sense of urgency to the issue and helped to fan homophobic flames.[43]

Blick later explained to State Department Security Division personnel how he came to his 300–400 figure. First, however, he admitted his reasoning was "not based upon factual knowledge." Blick explained that he started with the US Public Health Bureau's estimate that of people with venereal disease, only one in ten reported their affliction to health officials. Therefore, in his mind, "since 86 known perverts have been discharged from the Department of State ten times that number would be 800." For inexplicable reasons, Blick thought dividing this number by two would give him a reasonable estimation of how many gays worked in the Department of State![44]

Blick explained in testimony why so many gays escaped notice. He testified that when arrested for solicitation, most men simply posted $25 collateral and then forfeited it, hence only taking a disorderly conduct charge rather than facing in open court more serious and damaging charges of moral perversion. A disorderly conduct conviction was common, imprecise, and survivable; the other charge would lead to public exposure, unemployment, and the end of one's life as he or she knew it. Because they were only misdemeanor charges, moreover, Blick said people were legally permitted to post and forfeit collateral and therefore avoid trial. A stunned Wherry called this a "scant deterrent to the eradication of this loathsome vice."[45]

Blick further testified that "prior to 2 years ago" he had maintained a liaison with the State Department Security Division. The Morals Division chief said he had forwarded to that bureau "many names" of homosexuals but was never informed what, if anything, the State Department did about them. The Wherry Committee then requested access to the State Department list of alleged gay employees, hoping to compare it with Blick's list, but the department promptly denied the request, citing Truman's executive order preventing congressional committees' access to personnel files. Highlighting the extent of the FBI liaison efforts at the time, Blick also revealed to the committee the fact that "he furnishes to the Federal Bureau of Investigation the names and fingerprints of every person arrested in the District of Columbia for moral perversion."[46]

Given this testimony, Senator Wherry concluded that current efforts at keeping gays out of government were inadequate. "Wherever they may be employed in a department handling defense secrets," he argued, "moral perverts are a security risk, because of their proximity to persons having security secrets and documents containing such information." He argued, in agreement with military authorities but with absolutely no supporting evidence, that the "blackmailing of moral perverts . . . is a long-established weapon among nations plotting aggression."[47]

Senator Wherry therefore recommended a larger Senate committee look into the broader issue of gays in government, conduct a "thorough investigation," and offer recommendations on "eliminating moral perverts from employment by the Government." He also suggested, significantly, establishing liaison arrangements between departments and agencies of the federal government "for the exchange of information on alleged homosexuals and teamwork in ridding them from the Government rolls." The upshot of the Wherry hearings, as historian Johnson has perceptively concluded, was that it had linked the previously isolated issue of "moral perverts" to government bureaucracy, ensuring the continuation of the Lavender Scare. It would also significantly influence future developments at the FBI.[48]

It did not take long before a Senate committee formed, as recommended in the Wherry Report, to examine the issue. Chaired reluctantly by Democrat Clyde Hoey of North Carolina, it held hearings that summer and, after some delay, issued its report in December 1950. An old-school, conservative, southern Democrat, Hoey was so reticent about being associated with such a controversial topic, and fearful that it could become hyperbolic like the communists-in-government issue had become with McCarthy, he demanded the committee conduct all of its work in private. Even more, Hoey left it to the committee's chief counsel, former FBI agent Francis "Frip" Flanagan, to manage all of the investigating, witness calling, and final report writing. Flanagan, therefore, was the most influential force on the committee.[49]

As the target of McCarthyite charges of being soft on communists and, even worse, being responsible for the State Department harboring homosexuals, the Truman administration was keenly interested in the Hoey Committee. The White House, in fact, sought to defuse the gays-in-government issue by trying to nudge Hoey toward focusing on the medical aspects of homosexuality rather than the controversial issue of security. The effort failed, and the committee, led by Flanagan, plunged forward investigating gays directly as security risks. To the dismay of White House officials, Flanagan even wanted executive departments to give him lists of homosexuals in their employ. Although the Truman administration flatly refused to cooperate in this regard, Flanagan's efforts nevertheless clued him in to the fact that different federal departments, indeed, maintained such lists.[50]

With little doubt, as an agency of the federal government deeply involved in monitoring gays since 1937, regarding them as security risks since the Second World War, and having already started a limited Sex Deviates Program in April 1950, Hoover's FBI must have cooperated with the Hoey Committee. Historically, the FBI director repeatedly played a central role when individual members of Congress or congressional committees pursued issues that also happened to be in Hoover's own interest. Hoover, for example, secretly provided US Representative Richard Nixon information about Hiss in 1948 by passing it to him indirectly through anticommunist priest Father John Cronin. Hoover also helped McCarthy with information and political advice until the senator could no longer be trusted to keep Hoover's role confidential. Likewise, Hoover provided confidential assistance to both HUAC and SISS, again provided they remain silent about it. He even offered, dating from February 1951, information on potential communist subversives to governors and municipal authorities through the bureau's Responsibilities Program and worked with the House Appropriations Committee by feeding it information that boosted its interests and built political capital with those who determined FBI funding.[51]

So did Hoover's FBI similarly work with the Hoey Committee?

To date, the FBI Records/Information Dissemination Section has responded to FOIA requests for information about Senator Hoey and his committee that the FBI holds no records about either. It seems inconceivable that the FBI would not have maintained a file, of whatever type, on either Hoey or his committee. In the very least it would have indirectly documented information about the activities of both through individual FBI agent reports, compiled unsolicited information from committee members or those associated with committee members, or compiled documentation from the lone FBI official who testified before the committee or through compiling newspaper clippings (as it so often had done). If such records did exist, and it seems likely they did, they probably were destroyed according to routine FBI record destruction policies or were maintained in Hoover's secret office file and destroyed after his death.

We know that Hoey Committee Chief Counsel Flanagan had requested that the Truman administration provide him "names and files from the agencies" so he could create a master index of gay employees to disseminate across government to eliminate these "security risks." He claimed when the committee finished its work, he would turn the index over to either the FBI or the CSC. Flanagan even argued he could "not see how the Subcommittee could determine whether the existing method of handling this problem was adequate unless they could look at some files on a sampling basis." Citing previous White House denials of Loyalty Program records to congressional committees, the Truman administration quashed Flanagan's idea and only permitted the release of statistical data.[52] This would have made FBI cooperative efforts a sensitive matter and documentation about said cooperation something Hoover might have wanted destroyed. FBI personnel may have even destroyed such material more recently because the FBI has continued wantonly to destroy files it somehow deems of no historical value. Other extant records, however, indicate the FBI was, in fact, interested in cooperating with the Hoey Committee and did so, *at minimum*, on a limited basis. Yet even with these documents we are still precluded from gaining a full understanding of FBI officials' cooperation with this committee.

What we know is that on 18 July 1950, ten days after Flanagan discussed with presidential assistant Stephen Spingarn the issue of gaining access to "names and files," he telephoned FBI Assistant to the Director D. Milton Ladd—the number three man at the FBI, the previous head of the bureau's Domestic Intelligence Division, and the man once in charge of FBI counterintelligence—requesting permission to visit the FBI and "talk to someone with reference to the handling of fingerprints and criminal records on perverts in the Government." He told Ladd the committee was "groping trying to find out how information concerning this matter was handled and what, if anything further, should be done." He added that he was "interested at this time in the mechanics of handling the arrest cards and the criminal records."[53]

Ladd recommended to Hoover that Flanagan be allowed to see FBI Assistant Director Tracy, head of the bureau's Identification Division, where the Sex Deviates Program as it was then configured was housed. FBI Associate Director Tolson, who regularly read memos going to Hoover and added his own advice, concurred but wanted Ladd as well as Tracy to talk with Flanagan. Hoover agreed and wrote on the memo, "Yes. Be most circumspect."[54]

Flanagan met with Tracy and Ladd at FBI headquarters on the morning of 20 July 1950. Tracy and Ladd told Flanagan that on 2 April the FBI had received from Blick "on a confidential basis" the list of those arrested on morals charges who claimed federal employment (the list Hoover sent to the White House). They also told him FBI officials had "checked" the list "through the Identification Division" and forwarded the list, with "a copy of the actual arrest record," to the CSC. Tracy and Ladd also told Flanagan that in the past police departments had sent fingerprint records to the FBI but neglected to indicate on them whether the subject was a federal employee. Given current efforts at targeting gay federal employees, Ladd and Tracy told Flanagan that in April 1950 FBI agents contacted regional police departments to urge them to add to their fingerprint records whether those arrested were federal employees. If this were done, they said, FBI efforts in providing the CSC information about gays would be expedited.[55]

Flanagan asked Tracy and Ladd whether they thought the FBI should have the responsibility of "following up on cases of this kind." They responded that "at the present time" the CSC held the authority to investigate federal employees. They also told Flanagan that through the Loyalty Program the CSC had initiated a "post-audit program" to check with federal agencies to "be sure what appropriate action was being taken" in each case. Tracy and Ladd added, reflecting the limited nature of the early version of the FBI Sex Deviates Program, that it was "logical for such a post-audit program to be placed in the Civil Service Commission; that the job of policing the Federal Service should not be placed in the FBI."[56]

Several hours after the meeting, Flanagan telephoned Ladd requesting information about those on the list Hoover sent to the White House. Flanagan wanted to know if the FBI received from Blick fingerprints for each name listed, in how many cases a fingerprint card denoted federal employment, and whether the fingerprint card indicated "an arrest for a sex offense or did it merely show disorderly conduct?" Flanagan said he wanted this information so he "might use it in talking with the police department." He wanted to persuade them to do all the preceding in all fingerprint cases. Flanagan claimed he "was not interested in the identity of any individuals as such, but merely in the cost figures."[57]

Ladd recommended that Hoover "furnish it to the Committee." A cautious Hoover replied, "O.K. but I don't want to go to too much work on this. We have so many other pressing matters; Flanagan is always likely to turn something we give him to our detriment as he so often tried to do in the K.C. case."[58] Like an elephant that never forgets, Hoover was referencing Flanagan's previous work as assistant chief counsel for the Second World War–era Truman Committee when, in Hoover's view, he had "manifested a hostile attitude toward the Bureau"[59] by making "derogatory remarks concerning the Bureau's activities in several investigations." At the time Flanagan denied all of this, but Hoover was nevertheless moved to note in 1948, "This is the man who Assistant AG [Attorney General T. Vincent] Quinn indicated is manifesting a hostile attitude toward the FBI in the current Kansas City Election Inquiry—be most alert in all dealings with him."[60] Evidentially, this fit a particular pattern with "Frip" Flanagan. Ever since training to become an FBI agent, and as an FBI agent, Flanagan developed a reputation for "curtness in attitude . . . [that] might be taken for a lack of tact and courtesy."[61]

What is significant here was Hoover's willingness to cooperate with Flanagan even though he did not like him. Hoover concluded as early as April 1948, after Flanagan began working for the Truman Committee, that he "has been hostile to [the] FBI since he went to committee."[62] However, because Flanagan as of July 1950 was in a position to promote the interests of the FBI, Hoover approved working with him. Flanagan, in fact, had a particular interest in gays and, according to Spingarn, he "seems strongly committed to the position that the homosexual is the most serious security threat of all, and he seems to regard the fact that there is scant documentation of this as an unfortunate accident."[63] Hoover's views were not significantly different from Flanagan's. When Hoover testified before the Senate Appropriations

Committee on 7 September 1950, Senator John McClellan of Arkansas was struck by just how emphatically the FBI director asserted gays "were a definite security risk."[64] To date we do not know the full extent of FBI assistance to the Hoey Committee, whether through Flanagan or others—FBI denial of having records about it precludes us from knowing—but it is clear nevertheless that by 1953, long after the Hoey Committee dissolved, Flanagan had found himself out of favor with Hoover. By that time, Hoover was describing Flanagan as "persona non grata,"[65] and three years later he placed Flanagan's name on the FBI do-not-contact list.[66]

Ex-FBI agents, although often beneficial to Hoover in advancing his agenda, indeed, sometimes were a concern for him. Perhaps the best example was Hoover's falling out with Senator McCarthy. Hoover had funneled McCarthy information and political advice ever since he became famous after his 1950 Wheeling speech, but in July 1953, against Hoover's advice, McCarthy lured a *current* FBI agent, Frank Carr, away from the bureau to become his staff director. Because the move could easily be construed as Hoover directly helping McCarthy and his committee and was thus too risky, Hoover terminated his long assistance.[67]

By February of the following year, as McCarthy was increasing his focus on the issue of communists in the US Army, McCarthy's chief counsel, Roy Cohn, discussed with FBI Assistant Director Louis Nichols a matter that raised the issue of ex-FBI agents. Nichols told Cohn the FBI was "getting sick and tired" of ex-FBI agents being hired because of their inside FBI knowledge. Associate FBI Director Tolson wrote on the memo, "The main difficultly is that Cohn, if he hires enough ex-agents, will get access to our complete security setup as well as knowledge of individual cases and informants." Hoover agreed, scrawling on the memo, "That is exactly the point & that is the reason I originally opposed Carr's appointment both to McCarthy & Cohn. Ex-agents trying to make good on the committee job are not going to drop an iron curtain on their past knowledge of Bureau cases, informants, etc."[68]

By the middle of July 1950, the Hoey Committee began to hold executive session hearings on the issue of "sex perverts" in government. (It would take more than four decades before the hearing transcripts were made public.) In these hearings, FBI Assistant to the Director Ladd, who six days later would meet with Flanagan and provide him FBI information, testified as a witness. His testimony revealed not only politicians' perceptions of gays at the time, as reflected in their questions, but what probably motivated

Hoover, later, to augment his Sex Deviates Program and assume a central role in eliminating gays from government.

Ladd began his testimony with a typical Hoover-era statement in which he emphasized that the FBI only investigated and collected facts. It did not, he pointedly asserted, make policy. In response to the committee request for the FBI's "views on the relationships between sex deviates and security," Ladd explained, "the FBI, however, does have certain definite observations to make based upon its experience." He said to ensure security one must have officials who take practical steps to guarantee it, and there must never be officials in sensitive positions who could jeopardize that security. He then borrowed an old Roman proverb: "They, like Caesar's wife, should be above reproach."[69]

Ladd then cited the FBI itself as an example. He explained FBI policy was such that "even a suspect sex deviate" would never be hired. Even then, if FBI officials were to learn an agent had "developed such an affliction, or such an affliction be undetected at the time of appointment," then that employee would immediately be fired. He then turned to examine the "general relationship between sex deviates and security." Ladd asserted one of the oldest human crimes was blackmail, and a "blackmailer always seeks a weakness in the life of his victim and then sets a course of action to capitalize upon that weakness."[70]

The assistant to the FBI director then pointed out what he regarded as a fundamental fact. In our society, Ladd said, there were transgressions that could be forgiven after appropriate punishment. He cited robbery, as an example, where a perpetrator could "reform himself." He questioned, though, in a comparative sense, "whether a sex deviate can be cured." Ladd cited an age-old "fear of sex expression . . . instilled" in people's minds since childhood. Because homosexuality was not "accepted as normal," he explained, it was the "subject of social condemnation," and because a homosexual then kept his sexuality a secret from "normal men," it became a weakness for subversive predators, like spies, to exploit.[71]

Ladd then cited several examples, yet never offered any evidence whatsoever of their veracity. He noted a newspaper editor who had focused his efforts on exposing municipal corruption, but then the "underworld" had acquired photos of this man "in an unnatural act" and forced him from his job because he was a "sex deviate." He also claimed (ironically given later stories about Hoover) there was an example of a government employee—he did not elaborate on which level or branch of government—whose colleagues discovered "his unnatural tendencies," then blackmailed him. Even worse, this information then fell into the hands of a "foreign intelligence service" that acquired compromising photographs of this individual engaged in a "perverted act and then sought to blackmail him." Ladd provided no corroborating evidence whatsoever but stressed that the Nazis "were notorious" for doing this and that Russian agents had been specifically tasked to locate weaknesses in the lives of US officials. He even noted that both the Nazis and Soviets respectively purged and expelled gays from their ranks. Later in the hearing, in answering a senator's question, Ladd claimed, "Perverts would be more subject to blackmail than any other group."[72]

The first question posed to Ladd, though, concerned what, exactly, FBI officials did with information they had acquired about gays. Ladd said for "most Government agencies" the bureau gave it to the CSC, but if it was regarding members of the armed forces then such information was forwarded to those services through "direct liaison."[73]

When Hoey asked about FBI Loyalty Program investigations, there was some confusion. Ladd explained that in a Federal Loyalty Program check, if FBI agents uncovered information indicating a person was gay, it would be reported. With the Loyalty Program, however, Ladd elaborated that information about one's sexuality would not directly "be sought out because the loyalty directive does not include an investigation for that purpose." Ladd then explained that the investigation "goes merely to the loyalty [issue] and not the security." There was some back and forth, then, between Ladd and the senators because some of them did not understand the difference between a loyalty case and a security case. In the end, however, Ladd succeeded in differentiating the two for the legislators; that is, how gays were a security risk, not a loyalty risk.[74]

After this discussion Senator John McClellan of Arkansas asked the clarifying question, "At least, now, you have no directive, your agency has no directive or responsibility for seeking out and undertaking to develop information with respect to homosexuals, but if incidentally you happen to come upon it, you simply report it; is that correct?" Ladd responded "with reference to the loyalty program" in the affirmative. He made no effort to explain the existence of the Sex Deviates Program.[75]

Chief Counsel Flanagan then asked if while FBI agents were conducting a nonloyalty investigation, would they "look to any defect in his character?" Ladd answered yes and added that FBI agents would then undertake a "complete and full investigation . . . with reference to all phases of his background." He then offered examples of agencies for whom FBI agents made background checks, including the Central Intelligence Agency (CIA), the Economic Cooperation Administration, VOA, and the State Department. He noted, however, that in the case of the State Department, the check was made only upon specific request.[76]

Ladd further explained the FBI relationship with the Metropolitan Police Department and how as of April 1950 FBI officials asked local police departments to include in their fingerprint submissions to the bureau information about arrested men's department or agency of employment in the federal government. Senator McClellan followed up by asking if the FBI effort was initiated only "after some publicity had been given to this state of affairs that we are now investigating?" Ladd replied, "Yes, that is correct."[77]

To clarify, Senator McClellan asked if prior to the April 1950 effort any FBI liaison arrangements regarding gays other than special investigations occurred. Ladd replied, interestingly, "No liaison for that particular purpose, because the FBI has no responsibility specifically to seek out perverts in Government employment." After that, the senator asked Ladd his final question: "In other words, there is no agency that now has that definite responsibility?" "That is correct, Senator," Ladd replied. Ladd was not being wholly disingenuous here because the FBI Sex Deviates Program at that point was quite limited.[78]

Hoey Committee hearings were held between July and September 1950, and the committee did not release its final report—written by Flanagan, the true driving force behind the committee—until mid-December 1950. The committee concluded there was "no place in the United States Government for persons who violate the laws or the accepted standards of morality," especially those who "bring disrepute to the Federal service by infamous or scandalous personal conduct." The committee had also deemed gays "unsuitable" for federal employment because they were "security risks" as well as people engaged in illegal and immoral activities.[79]

The committee concluded that in the past the federal government "failed to take a realistic view of the problem of sex perversion," and officials failed directly to confront and stop the issue. It was only after the committee began its work, the report observed, that federal officials began to take the issue seriously. Flanagan cited in the report the fact that in the past seven months 382 cases of "sex perversion" were processed, whereas in the past three years only 192 cases were adjudicated. According to Flanagan, the Metropolitan Police Department had arrested hundreds of men over the previous four years, but this fact was only reported to the CSC in April 1950 (via the FBI). The committee concluded this was the result of a "lack of proper liaison between the law-enforcement agencies and the departments of Government." To adequately protect the "public interest," Flanagan wrote, the federal government must "adopt and maintain a realistic and vigilant attitude toward the problem of sex perverts in the Government." "To pussyfoot or to take half measures," he continued, only "will allow some known perverts to remain in Government and can result in the dismissal of innocent persons."[80] The committee's conclusions, Johnson keenly observed, directly helped the Lavender Scare to "move beyond partisan rhetoric to enjoy bipartisan support and become part of standard, government-wide policy." Most significantly, it had an effect on FBI policy regarding gays in government.[81]

The combination of the Wherry and Hoey Committees' conclusions, the surge in public and political interest in actively purging gays from government, and recognized deficiencies in FBI efforts prompted Director Hoover to expand dramatically the FBI Sex Deviates Program by the summer of 1951. Yet it would still be a step-by-step process. On 15 February 1951, a month and a half after the Hoey Committee released its report, Hoover testified before the House Appropriations Committee. He assured the committee the FBI Identification Division had "proven its great value in the security field" by screening the fingerprint records of all people who applied for federal employment. In its efforts, Hoover said, it had weeded out "mental cases, murderers, thieves, sex deviates, and other criminally inclined misfits."[82]

Hoover then testified about the FBI focus on "sex deviates," which he described as "comparatively new" and "brought about because of the investigations of other congressional committees into *sex deviates in Government service*." (Actually, Hoover's FBI first focused on gays systematically in 1937, and it created the first version of the Sex Deviates Program in April 1950, before the Wherry Committee even met.) Significantly, though, Hoover also confirmed for the House Appropriations Committee that his FBI had "worked in conjunction with [the] committees" and arranged for the fingerprints of "all persons who are arrested for sex crimes" to be sent to the FBI. Hoover even offered a statistic. He noted, "Since April 1, 1950, to date [31 January 1951], we have made 406 identifications of individuals who were arrested as sex deviates who were employees of the Federal Government." Hence, we have both the meeting Flanagan had with FBI officials and Hoover's statement here to confirm the fact that his FBI maintained a direct connection to both the Wherry and Hoey Committees, even if we cannot know the full extent of its cooperation because of apparent record destruction.[83]

Two months after Hoover's appearance before the House Appropriations Committee, the committee released to the press the hearings transcript. Journalists immediately focused on Hoover's statement and his citation of 406 identified sex deviates in government. A journalist from the *Washington Times-Herald*, for example, although unsurprisingly conflating McCarthyism with the Lavender Scare, cited the 406 number as proof McCarthy was correct about subversives and inquired of the FBI whether any arrests had been made prior to April 1950 and after Senator McCarthy's 20 February speech singling out gays. This inquiry led FBI officials to discover their 406 number was incorrect and sparked an internal FBI crisis that would finally lead Hoover to revamp the Sex Deviates Program.[84]

When double checking their records following the press inquiry, FBI officials discovered conflicting numbers. They first noted a number of 363 identified sex deviates from the period 1947 to 1950. The 406 number, however, only dated *from* 1950. When recalculating even that number, FBI officials counted 234 sex deviate civilian federal employees, 133 identified individuals in the army and air force, and 41 in the navy and marines, for a total of 408. Worse yet, when agents counted individuals identified as sex deviates since Hoover's February 1951 testimony, the total number shot up to 508. Fortunately for Hoover and his carefully crafted public image, the *Times-Herald* reporter "was friendly" toward the bureau and did not report the incorrect explanation for the 406 number originally given him (it originated from Blick's list plus those arrested since 1950). As a heavy-handed taskmaster, Hoover demanded accuracy from all of his FBI agents and officials. If they failed him, even only by a count of two, they would be officially rebuked. In this instance, they were.[85]

Out of this internal bureau brouhaha, FBI officials began to recognize that the Sex Deviates Program as currently configured was flawed. They recognized that the Identification Division records and files used to identify individuals were in many instances out of date and, therefore, "there was no affirmative way of showing that [an] individual was still in Government service." They further realized FBI officials came to the 406 number "out of a series of confused speculations," including the use of two copies of the same records. FBI Assistant Director Nichols, head of the Crime Records

Division, advised Hoover's right-hand man, Tolson, that the Identification Division was already recalculating the number of sex deviates "by individual Government agencies," and he suggested revisiting each of the 406 cases as well as revisiting "this issue [the Sex Deviates Program] in greater detail later on." Indeed they would. It would take two more months, however, before Hoover would formulate a more formal program (and combined central file) to disseminate information about gays to various government agencies and departments to ensure their ouster.[86]

The work of these politicians and committees found resonance among some members of the US public. One concerned citizen wrote President Truman at the end of March 1950, "The best thing for our country and our foreign policy is for you to get rid of . . . 'the Reds' and 'Homos' in the State Department." Another, from Florida, agreed with this type of assessment. He wrote the president that if the "State Department can acquire and harbor 91 homosexuals who presumably had something to do with shaping our foreign policy or slanting the information on which it is based, the State Department is capable of anything." The correspondent found this fact "revolting." He warned Truman that Washington "seems intent on imitating the vices of Pagan Rome."[87]

To these citizens, and some self-serving politicians, there was little difference between "homos" and "reds." Given public attitudes toward homosexuality in the 1950s, the two groups seemed to have similar "subversive" traits. Gays and communists kept their true identities hidden, both seemed to move around in a secretive underworld, both had a common sense of loyalty, and both had their own publications and places to meet. Most obviously, though, gays and communists together did not conform to 1950s US society and culture. That was the *public perception*, and one commonly embraced—publicly at least—by politicians. FBI officials, in contrast, tasked with ferreting out gays and investigating those who might be gay, carefully distinguished gays from communists. Unlike some vocal politicians, to national security bureaucrats in the FBI, the two were not conflated.[88]

Nearly anyone was subject to FBI investigation when rumors about one's sexuality were raised. In July 1950 an informant of army intelligence learned from a Defense Department employee about a man who was a "self-admitted pervert." This man told the Defense Department employee about "matters of perversion," including the allegation that Senator Henry Cabot Lodge Jr. was a homosexual and "social contact" and frequent visitor of another man who was also "an alleged pervert and Communist Party member."[89]

FBI agents, of course, investigated the allegations, including a search of FBI files for any corroborating information. They found none. FBI Assistant Director Nichols, in fact, characterized the charges against Lodge as "unreliable" and "unfounded." Lodge, of course, was considered, also in Nichols's words, "friendly" toward the FBI. Intriguingly, Lodge had defeated the politically damaged Senator David I. Walsh—the senator who was gay baited during the Second World War era—in 1946 to return to the Senate after having resigned from the Senate to serve valiantly in the Second World War. Lodge was a moderate internationalist Republican who helped to convince Dwight Eisenhower to run for the presidency, even serving as the former general's political campaign manager. So he was not without the position and status, given the uncorroborated nature of his alleged associations, to insulate him; even still, the FBI investigated and forever filed the scurrilous information in Hoover's secret office file.[90]

In the political context of an intensified Lavender Scare, replete with committees forming to study the issue, hearings being held in public and in secret, and focused public interest, the Thayer case unfolded. On 16 February 1950, Hottel reported to Hoover that Thayer was rumored to be assuming a position at the CIA. FBI supervisor Gordon Nease, in Crime Records, also reported to Hoover information suggesting Thayer was to be transferred to the CIA to take a "top job." In response, FBI supervisor Cartha DeLoach contacted CIA officials who told him Thayer was not an employee of that agency. Nevertheless, in the effort to get to the bottom of whether Thayer would work at the CIA, FBI officials learned that Carmel Offie—a close friend of Thayer's employed by the CIA Office of Policy Coordination (the CIA covert operations branch)—"if contacted could furnish further derogatory information concerning Thayer."[91]

FBI officials then learned to their great interest that none other than Blick had arrested Offie in 1943 on a morals charge. Offie was apprehended cruising men in Lafayette Park, just across the street from the White House. Hoover found it "amazing" that the CIA had given Offie "such a high position." He ordered an FBI probe but, because Offie had a large number of friends in influential positions, Hoover demanded it be circumspect. Given the intimate ties between Thayer and Offie, moreover, the FBI probes of both would for a time parallel.[92]

In April 1950 FBI officials learned that Senator McCarthy intended to call upon the State Department to fire Thayer, whom he regarded as "one of the worst types of degenerates." McCarthy had learned about Thayer in late February when an anonymous letter writer provided the senator alleged details. The letter claimed, for example, that Thayer was a "high-class homosexual" and that he might have had a sexual relationship with Offie. Who provided this information to McCarthy is not clear, and with available evidence its veracity is not knowable. We do know, however, that shortly after McCarthy's inaugural Wheeling speech, FBI officials secretly began to provide him information about the communist issue culled from FBI files. To ensure the strict confidentiality of the supplied information, FBI officials gave it to McCarthy typed on blind memoranda—documents with no indication of sender or recipient so they could not be traced back to their source. The information McCarthy received concerning Thayer was typed in the form of a blind memorandum and contained specific suggestions for McCarthy, such as to look into why the FBI did not investigate Thayer before he joined the VOA and why the FBI only received Thayer's loyalty form at a late date. Given this bureau-related information, was it FBI officials who sent McCarthy the anonymous letter? Was it someone in the State Department? We cannot know for certain, but the phrase "high-class homosexual" originated in State Department records, information the FBI also had. We do know, in fact, that several years later they would share information about Thayer with the senator from Wisconsin.[93]

On 25 April 1950, just weeks after Hoover expressed amazement over the revelation that Offie was apparently gay, Senator McCarthy engaged Senator Millard Tydings in debate on the floor of the US Senate. Tydings challenged McCarthy to provide proof of his alleged 205 "card-carrying Communists" in the State Department. McCarthy defended himself with information not about a communist in government but about a confirmed homosexual in the CIA. Although he did not offer a name, McCarthy was referring to Offie. McCarthy said that this man had been arrested on a morals charge for "hanging around the men's room in Lafayette Park," and he then publicly questioned why the CIA had not, to date, fired him. Later that day,

Senator Wherry felt "privileged" to report that the "head of a Government agency" informed him only thirty minutes before that the man McCarthy had referenced had been finally, that day, fired. Wherry then vowed to "continue . . . to do everything I can to clean out moral perverts and subversives from Government," and he said he was "willing to be associated with any man [he meant McCarthy] who has the courage of his convictions in an endeavor to accomplish that objective." Because the two senators had for all intents and purposes publicly outed Offie, the White House demanded his immediate resignation—and got it. The pretext for the firing was the fact that, in 1948, when filling out his application to work at the CIA, Offie failed to disclose his 1943 arrest in Lafayette Park.[94]

Hoover, however, was not content with Offie simply being separated from the CIA. Because Offie had found employment in the CIA in part by concealing his past, and because he had intimate ties to another presumed "high-class homosexual" (Thayer), the FBI director ordered an investigation. Hoover justified the probe by contending that in failing to disclose his 1943 arrest, Offie had committed fraud. Justice Department officials disagreed with Hoover's opinion and refused to pursue a prosecution under that charge, but this in no way prevented Hoover from ordering an intensive investigation.[95]

After Offie was fired, Jay Lovestone offered him a job with the American Federation of Labor (AFL) Free Trade Union Committee. According to Hoover, Lovestone—although an opponent of Stalin, an avowed anticommunist at this point, and a man cooperating with the CIA through the Free Trade Union Committee—was suspect. He was a former socialist and former high-ranking Communist Party official who, Hoover claimed, was once an agent of Russian intelligence in 1935. Lovestone, moreover, supposedly advocated the establishment of socialism in the United States "through the organized labor movement." Because Lovestone now had under his employ the former CIA officer and "high-class homosexual" Offie, FBI officials on 10 July 1950 ordered "discreet" physical surveillance.[96]

FBI agents followed Offie everywhere to ascertain his "contacts and activities." Their surveillance began on 17 July with agents using a 1947 Pontiac sedan to follow him across Washington, DC. They observed Offie, for example, making a telephone call and drinking a soda at a drugstore on Connecticut Avenue. They also saw him at one point carrying a suspicious manila envelope that "appeared to contain three cylindrical objects about the size of Ediphone records." Agents further watched Offie's house from the vantage point of their car but some seventy-five yards away and shielded by "heavy shrubbery." Offie was observed in this manner while dining with an unidentified man on his front porch.[97]

FBI agents seemed to take an unusual interest in Offie's travels around metropolitan Washington, DC. They observed him on 16th Street engaging an enlisted soldier in conversation, after which he walked over to 17th Street and entered Mickey's Grille—which agents described as a "hangout for perverts." Offie was observed there drinking a beer and reading a newspaper. He then visited a second gay establishment, David's Bar, on 17th Street, where he consulted a phonebook before returning home. Although the details are not at all clear, the WFO apparently had conducted "very sloppy work" when watching Offie, which led bureau officials on 20 July to terminate (temporarily) their physical surveillance.[98]

FBI agents resumed their "discreet investigation of Offie" the following month when he returned to work in New York City. Part of this effort was to determine where Offie lived in the city and whether he still maintained a residence in Washington, DC.[99] (Offie lived and worked in Washington, DC, but commuted to New York when necessary for his job.) Meanwhile, on 27 July 1950 FBI officials authorized an illegal break-in of his Washington, DC, home either to search his personal papers and belongings or to surreptitiously install a microphone. Because of heavy redactions in FBI documents, there is no way to determine exactly what FBI officials had sought, but the memo concerning it was nevertheless captioned "JUNE"—the FBI code word used on documents to denote illegal break-ins.[100]

FBI agents eventually determined Offie had decided to maintain his Washington, DC, address, which prompted Hottel to submit regular reports on his activities. Hottel observed, moreover, in "view of the delicate nature" of the Offie investigation, a "great degree of discretion . . . must be exercised." FBI agents continued to follow Offie throughout Washington, DC, while investigating his financial affairs in search of any irregularities. FBI agents also continued to submit to headquarters—and vice versa—memoranda captioned "JUNE" over subsequent months.[101]

With the FBI documents regarding Offie heavily redacted, it is impossible to determine the precise nature of the FBI surveillance of him. Nevertheless, it seems clear FBI agents were looking for some avenue to exploit so as to neutralize this "known homosexual" who had worked in the CIA and now worked, as Westbrook Pegler wrote, for the "mysterious character" Lovestone.[102] (It is possible, though not proven, Hoover could have leaked nation about Offie to the arch-conservative Pegler.) One means FBI agents continually pursued was prosecuting Offie for not reporting to the CIA his 1943 arrest.[103] It is also clear FBI officials were convinced Offie must have been compromised or willingly engaged in some form of espionage precisely because he was a "deviant"; he was a former CIA and State Department officer, and he knew numerous influential people—none of which in any way was proof of being a traitor.

By December 1950, FBI agents investigated Offie and Lovestone together for suspected espionage. What specifically interested them was that Offie, while a State Department employee, might have "obtained considerable funds from dealing in illegal money transactions in Europe." This uncorroborated lead stemmed, in part, from Offie's relationship with Thayer, alleged to have engaged in the black market when stationed in Yugoslavia. This led SAC Hottel to recommend an examination of Offie's tax returns for the years 1946–1948.[104]

FBI agents continued their surveillance and investigation of Offie into 1951, by which time FBI officials decided to engineer his dismissal from the AFL. This was to be accomplished by leaking selected "information of a derogatory nature" to an unknown recipient—but probably to McCarthy or the SISS—"on a strictly confidential basis, which would enable" the recipient "to make an independent investigation looking toward the elimination of Offie from his present employment in the AF of L." The head of the FBI Identification Division, Assistant Director Tracy, advised Hoover, "It will be worthwhile to render every possible assistance in this situation for the reason that in his present position, Offie is dangerous to the security of the country." For unknown reasons, FBI officials decided, at that time, not to disseminate their information.[105]

Within days of FBI officials considering disseminating information to have Offie fired from his position, by 20 June 1951 Hoover had completely redesigned the Sex Deviates Program and created for it a dedicated and combined file. In so doing, he vastly expanded bureau efforts to disseminate information about gays in government to ensure their separation from federal employment. Indeed, Hoover effectively made the FBI *the* central player in the Lavender Scare. Over time, the program would expand to include even those working outside of government, and its concomitant file would grow to gargantuan proportions. On 20 June 1951 Hoover issued a memo to

FBI officials and supervisors establishing a "uniform policy for the handling of the increasing number of reports and allegations concerning present and past employees of the United States Government who assertedly [*sic*] are sex deviates." His new policy and procedures would go into effect "immediately in instances where the allegation comes to the Bureau's attention from sources other than fingerprints." The reference to fingerprints shows Hoover was moving the Sex Deviates Program well beyond that set up in April 1950 to include allegations and other FBI information.[106]

Hoover's new policy mandated that whenever the bureau learned "of *an allegation* that a present or former employee of any branch of the United States Government is a sex deviate," the information "in all cases" except "involving military personnel" was to "be disseminated by letter" to the chief of the Investigations Division of the CSC. In the letter, Hoover required FBI personnel to "identify the employing agency and whether it has been advised." He also required the information to be disseminated to the particular part of the government employing the subject.[107]

What is significant here, though, and in the policy's remaining particulars, is Hoover's mandated use of FBI letters when disseminating information to the CSC. Hoover's FBI used a variety of different types of documents, including letters, reports, memoranda, teletypes, and so forth; the type used always depended upon the unique situation presented. FBI letters left no doubt about the source of information: letters had on their heads the FBI seal, thus identifying their origin, and they were signed by an FBI agent or official. So for this aspect of the Sex Deviates Program policy—disseminating information to the CSC—the FBI clearly identified itself as the source of the information.

After the FBI forwarded information to the CSC, if the subject worked in the executive branch, Hoover's policy about further dissemination then varied depending upon the subject's exact status. If he or she was a current civilian employee, then FBI information was also forwarded to that person's "employing agency." If the subject was a former employee, then FBI information was only sent to the CSC. If the subject was a member of the "National Military Establishment," FBI personnel were required to forward it via blind memorandum through the bureau's liaison with a particular military branch's intelligence service.[108] Unlike letters, blind memos were FBI documents with no letterhead or signatures; they contained nothing, including watermarks, that would identify the FBI as the source of the document. This was the means by which FBI officials leaked information they did not want traced back to the FBI because a reader of a blind memo could never know its origins. As one FBI official himself put it, blind memos were "used in those instances where the Bureau's identity must not be revealed as the source."[109]

If the FBI information was about a suspected gay federal employee in the legislative branch, Hoover's FBI dissemination procedures were different. For the Sex Deviates Program policy, Hoover divided the legislative branch into four categories: the Senate, the House, the General Accounting Office (GAO), and the Government Printing Office (GPO). Hoover included along with the Senate the Botanical Gardens and the Library of Congress.[110]

If the FBI information dealt with an employee of the Senate, Botanical Gardens, or Library of Congress, Hoover required it to be disseminated by letter to the chair of the Senate Committee on Rules and Administration (Senator Carl Hayden of Arizona). If the bureau information concerned an employee of the House, it was disseminated by letter to the chair of the House Committee on Administration. If the information concerned an employee of the GAO or GPO, it was disseminated in blind memo format through FBI liaison with the GAO or GPO assistant director and director of personnel (V. J. Kirby and S. Preston Hipsley, respectively).[111]

If FBI information concerned a suspected gay employee of the judicial branch, Hoover required FBI personnel to disseminate it via blind memo, again through official FBI liaison, to the assistant director of the administrative office at the Supreme Court (Elmer Whitehurst).[112] To fully appreciate the significance of this, it is important to understand that "as a general practice" the FBI did "not disseminate information to the Judicial Branch of the Federal Government." Therefore, Hoover's inclusion of the judicial branch in the FBI Sex Deviates Program was a significant development.[113]

Hoover's procedures for dissemination of information via the Sex Deviates Program also mandated how the FBI information should be reported in either a letter or blind memo. FBI officials and supervisors were to include five items: first, the date and location of the "alleged act of sexual perversion"; second, where, exactly, the subject worked; third, "other pertinent facts, including the disposition [of the person's case], if known"; fourth, whether the FBI investigation had verified the sex allegations, meaning the details of them; and fifth, the statement that the FBI was disseminating facts "for information [purposes]."[114]

The FBI Sex Deviates Program also mandated that any information about gay employees originating from another government agency, in Hoover's words, "should be disseminated, and the memorandum should specifically state that the allegation came from another Government investigative agency." FBI personnel were told, however, never to disclose the name of that agency. Additionally, Hoover required that an FBI supervisor search for "additional derogatory information suitable for dissemination" in FBI files and "incorporate such information in the memorandum and letter." If the supervisor could locate no information, he was required to note that fact in either the cover memo or, if no cover memo was used, "on the yellow copy of the letter."[115]

Hoover further advised FBI personnel that if information was developed about a "sex deviate" who also happened to be under investigation by FBI agents, "the investigative reports may be disseminated" following standard dissemination procedures "to the Civil Service Commission and to the employing agency by cover memorandum when that agency is in the Executive Branch of Government." Yet if there was a question over whether an agency could be trusted to preserve the FBI's confidentiality, then "it should be resolved by furnishing the agency a blind memorandum instead of the reports."[116]

Hoover also advised that in cases dealing with employees of the legislative and judicial branches, "nothing more than a blind memorandum or letter" containing the "pertinent facts regarding the sex charge will be disseminated to them." Additional information, Hoover wrote, uncovered in FBI files about the employee was to be included only in the cover memo or yellow copy of the letter.[117]

If the FBI source of information about a suspected "sex deviate," furthermore, originated with a police department or an individual, bureau policy mandated that the source thenceforth should be identified when disseminating it in either a memo or letter unless the source wished to remain confidential. Anonymous source information, Hoover advised, was not to be disseminated unless the facts of the case could be verified by a government agency; "nonspecific" information was never to be disseminated.[118]

Finally, to ensure "proper indexing by the Records Section," every FBI supervisor was required, and "will be held personally responsible," to "underline in green pencil the names of individuals mentioned in any report, letter, memorandum, newspaper article, or other communication who are *alleged* to be sex deviates."[119]

It was a confluence of events that led Hoover to create his Sex Deviates

Program and, hence, create for the FBI a central role, by widely disseminating information about them, in the purge of gays from government. It is helpful to review the confluence of events that affected Hoover's decision. First, of course, was the evolution of the gays-in-government issue—not necessarily something new but an issue present since the Second World War and resurgent again after 1947—which now rose to the level of an intense national political scandal after McCarthy's 1950 speech, Republican efforts to leverage the issue for political purposes, and the subsequent State Department purge and backlash of the "ninety-one."

This prompted Hoover to forward to the White House on 10 April 1950 Blick's list of gays arrested since 1947 who claimed federal employment and create the first version of the Sex Deviates Program. Significantly, the executive director of the CSC subsequently pointed out to the White House serious flaws in Hoover's list; flaws he noted would cause "confusion and embarrassment." This was followed in the same month (May 1950) with the formation of the two-man Wherry Committee. Wherry focused public attention on Blick's fabricated number of gays in government and in the capital, suggesting the magnitude of the threat now facing the country. Significantly, his committee also recommended establishing intergovernmental liaison arrangements "for the exchange of information . . . and teamwork in ridding them [gays] from government." Hoover, having been embarrassed by the CSC while Wherry made the issue prominent, would have to respond.

Following the recommendations of the Wherry Committee came the more significant Hoey Committee and its former FBI-agent chief counsel seeking access to government "names and files"—which he was denied—in an effort to devise a master index for dissemination purposes. Hoover cooperated to some extent with Flanagan, with whom he shared similar views about the threat of gays in government, yet FBI officials explained to Flanagan that the "job of policing the federal service should not be placed with the FBI." Actually, it would be Hoover, perhaps getting the idea here, who later directed his supervisors to create a master index for dissemination purposes.

When testifying before the Hoey Committee, Assistant to the Director Ladd explained how the Federal Loyalty Program officially did not permit specific investigative focus on one's sexuality. He also explained how police departments shared with the FBI fingerprints of those arrested for sex crimes and admitted how it came about only after the gay issue had been popularized in the headlines. Even more significantly, while not divulging the FBI's early Sex Deviates Program, Ladd testified that regardless of these efforts, still, no agency existed with the "definite responsibility" of "seeking out perverts" in government. In the end, the Hoey Committee directly recommended the federal government "adopt and maintain a realistic and vigilant attitude" to the gays-in-government issue and not, employing loaded and gendered language, "pussyfoot" about it. Again, at this point the Lavender Scare as a public issue rose to its pinnacle, and it became "standard," as Johnson pointed out, to purge gays from federal employment. Additionally, it was also easier to locate and purge gays than communists, hence satisfying a desire to see bureaucratic and political success in the era of McCarthy.

So it is perhaps little surprise, given the connection between all of these events, and after FBI officials discovered serious flaws in their original Sex Deviates Program, that Hoover by June 1951 decided his FBI would, in fact, play the central role as the federal agency with "definite responsibility," at least in disseminating information about "sex deviates" to ensure their firing. Flanagan had tried and failed, thanks to the Truman administration denying him access to records, to create a central index of "perverts" for dissemination purposes. The police fingerprint liaison with the FBI and thence the CSC, moreover, was obviously insufficient and under criticism. There existed, moreover, by the summer of 1951 a political atmosphere—with two congressional committees calling for federal coordination on the issue and the public fully embracing the purge of gays from government—in which Hoover perhaps felt compelled to respond.

Yet the specific way in which Hoover responded was significant. He did so obsequiously and carefully. It appears, moreover, that he responded with the Sex Deviates Program on his own authority. There is no extant document in the Harry S. Truman Presidential Library to indicate the attorney general, or anyone else, authorized the more detailed program in the summer of 1951. We know the White House was aware the FBI was forwarding fingerprint records to the CSC after April 1950, but it apparently knew nothing about Hoover's revised efforts. Indeed, it was only in 1954 that FBI officials recommended to Hoover "that the Attorney General should be informed of the Bureau's policy of dissemination relating to information involving sex deviates who have been present or past employees of any branch of the United States Government."[120] The specific procedures FBI officials developed for disseminating information, either via identifiable FBI letter or blind memorandum, further illustrate Hoover's desire to keep the FBI role as a source of information confidential. Given the central congressional role in pushing the Lavender Scare and calling for liaisons between federal agencies and the FBI being, in part, responsive to such political pressure, FBI officials disseminated information to the Senate and House via FBI letters. Information going to the judicial branch, military departments, GAO, and GPO, however, Hoover mandated be in the form of a blind memo, thus concealing the FBI as the source of information.

The central role of the FBI in disseminating information to ensure the firing of gays from government is further highlighted by the fact that Hoover's FBI did not simply pass on information about "sex deviates" it happened to come across (from police departments, for example). It became Sex Deviates Program policy to include in its disseminated letters or blind memos information from FBI files or allegations it received about targets. It was also mandated that FBI supervisors carefully index names of not just known but suspected "sex deviates" in all manner of FBI records, newspapers, and other sources. It was in the end, to reiterate, Hoover's FBI that created the master index for dissemination purposes, making the bureau the preeminent federal agency targeting gays.

The FBI role in disseminating information about "sex deviates," however, did not remain restricted to federal employment. By October 1954, Hoover had decided "in appropriate instances where the best interests of the *Bureau* is [sic] served, information concerning sex deviates employed by institutions of higher learning or law enforcement agencies is disseminated to proper officials of such organizations."[121] Universities were included in the program because "on a few occasions" Hoover had ordered the "confidential" dissemination of information to George Washington University (GWU) and New York University (NYU) "concerning sex deviates or Communists employed as teachers" at GWU and the "sex deviate practices of an instructor who was involved in the Police Training Field" at NYU who also survived a "Security Investigation." Interestingly, Hoover gave the responsibility for disseminating this information specifically to the FBI Training and Inspection Division, which previously had never undertaken any FBI dissemination role. Two things should be noted about GWU, however. First, the university was Hoover's alma mater and one of his favored sources for FBI agent recruitment. Second, at some point an FBI official retired and assumed the position of director of alumni relations at GWU, a post from which he maintained contact with the FBI (see Chapter 6). As demonstrated above, he would have been an ideal liaison at GWU for Hoover.[122]

The FBI Sex Deviates program could only function with information. Along with the program, therefore, was a dedicated Sex Deviates File to facilitate dissemination of information. Despite the fact the entire content of this file was incinerated in 1977 and 1978, we nevertheless know something about it. In December 1977, in the post-Hoover era, with new legislation mandating National Archives approval prior to the destruction of federal records, FBI officials sought permission to "dispose immediately of two files, together with index cards, abstracts, [photographs,] and related documentation no longer needed for its current operation." This was the Sex Deviates File, and the National Archives record of the disposal request broadly described its contents.

FBI officials flagged two numbered files for destruction.[123] One was FBI File 105-34074, which FBI officials described as covering "the period 1937–1977 and relates to the subject of 'sex offenders.'" This file, of course, given its starting date and contents, contained information dating to the Charles Mattson kidnapping and the man presumed to be the perpetrator, a "degenerate." The file number, moreover, contained two parts. The 105 number designated the file, broadly, as "foreign counterintelligence," suggesting the given 1951 security rationale of spies blackmailing gay federal employees for collecting information on gays.[124] The second number identified the specific subject, in this case, "sex offenders."[125]

The second file number was 105-12189, described as covering the years 1942–1977, related to the "subject of 'sex perverts in Government service.'" An archivist inaccurately described this file as "part of the name-check loyalty program involving Federal employees." Sex deviates were security-risk targets, not Federal Loyalty Program ones. The archivist wrote, however, that he surveyed both files and found the "bulk of their contents [to] consist of copies of FBI investigative reports relating to individuals accused of or charged with sexual or morals offenses." He also described the files as containing a "small amount of correspondence, memoranda, and newspaper clippings on these same matters." The archivist, Henry J. Wolfinger, unilaterally deemed these files to have insufficient "research value to warrant permanent retention." They were, therefore, destroyed.[126]

Wolfinger's description of the two files also offers an indication of the size and general content of the Sex Deviates File. He described the records in the files as containing "massive amounts of material that relate to matters of individual sexual conduct and thus seem to infringe on personal privacy." He also described many of the records as containing "unsubstantiated accusations and allegations" (which was in line with what FBI officials were to report). He even calculated the size of the file as it was constituted in 1977. He described its volume as being 99 cubic feet—which he lamely claimed reduced its research value as a result of its size—which translated to approximately 330,000 pages of material.[127]

The Sex Deviates File though, in reality, was not exclusively composed of these two 105-numbered files. Through my own and others' extensive research on this and other topics, we know there were other related FBI files. One was headquarters FBI File 94-4-980, related to "Sex Degenerates and Sex Offenders."[128] A 94 FBI file classification referred to "research matters." My research has uncovered that this 94 file of "Sex Offender research material" was maintained in the "Special Projects Unit, Crime Research Section, Crime Records Division." It was used as part of Hoover's educational campaign involving published FBI articles and Hoover speeches to alter US public opinion in the fields of obscenity, pornography, and sex crimes. Significantly, the fact that the Crime Records Division—the Hoover-era FBI liaison with Congress and the media—maintained this particular file also shows that Crime Records after June 1951 maintained the Sex Deviates File. If the purpose of the Sex Deviates Program was to disseminate information about gays (significantly, to Congress), Crime Records would be the logical FBI division to carry out that main task. In addition, some FBI records copied *into* the Sex Deviates File remain extant in individual FBI files, and they include, handwritten in their margins, the FBI file numbers cited above. They were also sometimes stamped "crime research."[129]

Another file evidentially related to the Sex Deviates Program and File was FBI File 121-WF-14345, captioned "Sex Deviates in Government." FBI file designation 121, which FBI officials declared obsolete in 1953, referred to "Loyalty of Government Employees." The WF in the file number—the FBI Record/Information Dissemination Section added the WF to the file number in their response to me—indicates the file was maintained in the bureau's WFO. Yet this file, too, was "destroyed on March 7, 1977," months *before* the National Archives official assented to the destruction of the 105-numbered Sex Deviates Files, thus raising questions as to its disposition.[130]

Yet another FBI file number I have uncovered, evidentially related to the Sex Deviates Program and File, was 94-HQ-65 SUB P, related to "Sex Deviates in Washington, DC." The P refers to pervert, and the file comprised the solicitation arrest records the Washington, DC, Metropolitan Police Department routinely shared with the FBI. This was another "research matters" file as well as an FBI headquarters file. When I filed a FOIA request for this file, the FBI replied that its "central indices to our Central Records System reflect there were records potentially responsive to the FOIA"; however, they "were not in their expected location and could not be located." It would seem reasonable to assume that these records, like the previous ones, were destroyed.[131]

Another field office file dedicated to gays and lesbians was San Francisco File 94-843, under which information about the lesbian group Daughters of Bilitis (DoB; see Chapter 5) was filed in that field office. The earliest document from this file dates to November 1956 and is captioned "Homosexual Activity in San Francisco, Research Matter." Another is stamped "Research (Crime Records)," and a revealing third has written on it "Place in P*, Homo file" suggesting it was similar to the Sex Deviates in Washington, DC, headquarters file.[132]

Clearly, the FBI Sex Deviates File was a composite of more than just the two 105 files FBI officials carefully bothered seeking permission to incinerate in December 1977. It contained at least two "research matters" files, an (eventually) obsolete WFO loyalty file, and the FBI San Francisco Field Office research file. It is probably safe to assume other field offices in regions with large gay and lesbian populations (large coastal cities, usually) maintained similar files. The very fact that information about gays was included in "research" files makes clear that Hoover's Crime Records Division, in one manner, used the Sex Deviates File or related material to assist in the preparation of articles, under Hoover's byline, in an effort to educate the US public on the dangers of sex offenders. For example, in 1957 Hoover published an article nationwide, "Needed: A Quarantine to Prevent Crime." In general terms, he argued about the admittedly radical need to isolate those with mental illnesses (it was clear to the public who was included). He wrote (actually a ghostwriter in Crime Records wrote), "Law enforcement agencies and medical authorities must be given the opportunity to bring sex deviates—and other mentally and physically ill people—into treatment at the earliest possible moment." He continued, "Compulsory quarantine is the only way in which we can really protect ourselves and our children and still do our conscientious duty toward the pitiable men—and women—who are criminals in spite of themselves."[133] This article, in fact, caught the attention of members of the Los Angeles Mattachine Society Area Council (see Chapter 5), who, in an oblique effort to place themselves outside of the category of the sex deviate (i.e., the other) in which Hoover had squarely placed them, wrote in their April 1957 newsletter that they "applaud his stand and hope that it will lead to future consideration to do more for mental illness."[134] Finally, if we know that just the two 105 files constituted 330,000 pages of material, the inclusion of the remaining four files and other field office files obviously would increase that number, probably significantly if not exponentially, beyond 330,000 pages.

The transmission of derogatory personal information did not only flow from the FBI to special recipients. Certain individuals in government agencies or working for congressional committees regularly provided information to the FBI. Often, the person forwarding information to the bureau was a former FBI agent, such as Don Connors, who worked for the SISS. In November 1951, he offered FBI officials a copy of Finlator's 22 July 1948 report about Thayer, a report Finlator had already given to FBI officials. Connors inquired of FBI officials if they would ascertain the identities of the unnamed informants mentioned in the State Department report and furnish these names so his committee could interview them. Given the sensitive nature of the bureau's original source, Hoover denied the request. The loss of another opportunity to destroy Thayer prompted Tolson to observe it was a "shame that such a man can remain in Govt Service." The FBI director wrote, "I certainly concur."[135]

On 17 April 1952, the SAC of the FBI New York Field Office, Edward Scheidt, reported to Hoover allegations that Democratic governor of Illinois and prominent potential candidate for president, Adlai Stevenson, was gay. SAC Scheidt developed this information from a New York City detective tasked to transport, from Illinois to New York, Bradley University basketball players who faced prosecution for accepting bribes to fix games. The scandal was one of the biggest in US sporting history. The detective first told Scheidt members of the Peoria Police Department had told him two prominent persons in Illinois "were nothing but trouble to law enforcement officers." They were David Owen, the president of Bradley University, and Adlai Stevenson. Scheidt told Hoover, moreover, that one of the basketball players under indictment allegedly was arrested in Owen's house, "where he was being hidden," and when he was taken into custody "President Owen carried on like a hysterical woman." Even worse, the basketball players told their driver, Scheidt's source, "The two best known homosexuals in the state were President Owen and Governor Stevenson." Stevenson, they said, was known by his gay pseudonym "Adeline," and this would prevent him from running for president.[136]

This sexual allegation concerning a prominent national political figure was ultimately filed in Hoover's Official and Confidential File (one of his secret office files). Originally, however, SAC Scheidt's memo was stamped "CRIME REC," and a notation of "Sex Offenders" was penned in the margin, indicating it was initially filed in the FBI Sex Deviates File (94-4-980).[137]

With this information in hand, FBI Director Hoover ordered Assistant Director Ladd to prepare a "blind memorandum concerning Governor Stevenson, who, it has been alleged, is a known homosexual." The blind memo was a brief one and summarized the information SAC Scheidt had reported.[138] A month later, on 24 July 1952 and in the midst of the Democratic National Convention, Milton Jones, a unit chief in the Crime Records Division, wrote a synopsis of the "highlights of a detailed summary memorandum on Stevenson" for his boss, head of Crime Records, FBI Assistant Director Nichols. Jones wrote a notation on the memo, "Tickler in Crime Records doesn't contain VI." Section VI of the blind memo contained the information about Stevenson's "alleged sexual perversion," but the notation would seem to indicate that with Stevenson's nomination as the Democratic presidential candidate imminent, FBI officials removed the Stevenson information from the Sex Deviates File and placed it in Hoover's office file. Interestingly, even Stevenson's Sex Deviates File index card was placed in Hoover's office file, making it, by happenstance, the only Sex Deviates index card we know to have survived destruction. A notation on the card indicated that Stevenson's name had originally been listed on Owen's Sex Deviates index card, but FBI officials decided Stevenson warranted his own card. It was Stevenson's card, moreover, that identified the particular Sex Deviates File (94-4-980) in which his information was originally kept.[139]

This was not all. With the presidential campaign on, by the end of August 1952, Nichols informed Hoover that Milt Hill was recently given the responsibility to write the "official Republican biography of Governor Stevenson." Nichols described Hill as one of his friends, "close to Arthur Summerfield of the Republican National Committee," a friend of Republican presidential candidate Eisenhower, cautious, "intensely anti-Communist," and probably most important of all, "very loyal to the Bureau."[140]

Nichols further explained to Hoover that Hill was gleaning some information about Stevenson from former FBI agent Orval Yarger. In Nichols's opinion, Yarger "had a very good record in the Bureau" and had demanded that Hill and the Republicans never associate his name with the FBI because he would "under no circumstances participate in any activities which might embarrass the Bureau." Hill described Yarger's character to Nichols as a "man of high principle" and one with an "excellent attitude" but a man with strong "feelings towards the situation in Illinois which he blames to [*sic*] Governor Stevenson." Nichols elaborated that Yarger did not know about Hill's relationship with Nichols and that "Hill is furnishing me details which Yarger is furnishing him." Regarding this relationship, Nichols advised Hoover that the FBI should "maintain Hill's confidence at any cost."[141]

Yarger told Hill that Stevenson held personal animosity toward Hoover stemming from a perceived snub of Stevenson. Yarger, in fact, reported that Stevenson allegedly called Hoover that "bastard in the Bureau." Even worse, and obliquely linking Stevenson's supposed views to the Lavender Scare, Yarger reported that Stevenson's "feelings" likely originated "from his old associations in the State Department."[142]

A particular piece of information from Yarger, though, was of interest to Nichols. Hill told Nichols that Yarger, who refused to name his source, knew about some "scuttlebutt" concerning Stevenson's sexuality. According to Yarger, while in New York City at one point "Stevenson was arrested on a morals charge, put up bond, and elected to forfeit." He also claimed that recently syndicated articles, using Stevenson's divorced (1949) wife as a source, had "knocked down all of the whispers as to the reason for the divorce but never explained why she really divorced Stevenson."[143]

Yarger was referring to a mid-August 1952 article originally published in the *Chicago Daily News* by journalist Jay McMullen. With Stevenson running for the presidency, interest suddenly developed as to why he divorced his wife. In her interview with McMullen, according to scandal magazine *Confidential* in 1953, "she hinted that there was a deeper, sinister, never-revealed reason for her divorce." Supposedly, she told the reporter Stevenson was gay, which "reflected on the manhood of the father of her three sons." *Confidential* framed her supposed action as the "start of the nastiest, most widely circulated hearsay in the annals of rumor-mongering." It was plausible to the public, moreover, given the recent and popular gays-in-government issue with the State Department. Only at the end of its piece did *Confidential* proclaim the Stevenson story a "dastardly and deliberate lie" from a woman craving public attention who regretted divorcing her husband now that he was on the cusp of becoming president. Ironically, even though *Confidential* had proclaimed the rumor false, by so vividly discussing the tawdry tale it was nevertheless helping to keep a story alive in 1953 about a prominent and still viable politician. It did so, moreover, because in the 1950s stories about homosexuality sold countless issues of *Confidential.* Homosexuality, in fact, was a common theme, and source of revenue, for the lurid scandal magazine.[144]

What, precisely, was the nature of the relationship between Hill and FBI Assistant Director Nichols, who had nothing but effusive praise for Hill and whom he took pains to note "was very loyal to the Bureau"? Was the relationship strictly one-sided, whereby Hill was feeding information to the FBI, or did the relationship go both ways? It would seem strange that the man tasked with writing the official Republican biography of its presidential opponent, and who was linked to a former FBI agent and maintained a friendship with a senior FBI official, would not ask for bureau information. If he did not directly ask Nichols, were FBI officials thinking about indirectly leaking information to Hill through Yarger, the former FBI agent for whom Nichols also had nothing but effusive praise? We may never know, but as FBI historian Theoharis has observed, Nichols's memorandum recounting all of this was "delicately worded" and never directly documented any FBI assistance. Theoharis concluded, "Given the sensitivity of his meeting with a Republican operative seeking information helpful to a partisan adversary during a presidential campaign, it is not surprising that Nichols did not record in writing his actions or Hoover's response."[145]

During August 1952, FBI officials got wind of a rumor that "some high official" had been spreading rumors Stevenson was "queer" and the "FBI had a file on him." The "high official," it turns out, allegedly was the FBI SAC of the WFO, Hottel. The rumor made its way to the FBI from someone in the Washington, DC, Metropolitan Police Department. Apparently somebody having a drink at the Mayflower Hotel bar overheard a group of people, including Hottel, talking about Stevenson being gay and that Hottel claimed the FBI had a file on him. Even worse, the rumor had been passed on to the attorney general and White House press secretary through Stevenson campaign official Frank Barry.[146]

Because these rumors involved the allegation that the FBI had a file on Stevenson and that an FBI employee was spreading sexual rumors about him, Hoover sought to insulate the FBI from the rumor. To do this,

Hottel—who actually had a history of getting into trouble with Hoover, such as his being placed on probation in 1950 for "too many rumors circulating" about his activities—was directed to write a memo making clear that he had not visited the Mayflower Hotel in more than a year, certainly not during the month the alleged event transpired. He also wrote that he "could not have made any statement to the effect that the FBI has a file on Stevenson" because, as a matter of fact, given his position in the FBI, he did not know whether a file even existed. FBI agents also interviewed various people involved with the rumor spreading to document that they, in fact, had heard false information. Hoover was always careful to protect the image of his FBI from rumor and gossip—in this case even if the rumor, regardless of its precise details, happened to be true![147]

Then again, in November 1952, even more information about the Stevenson-Owen homosexual allegation was reported to the FBI. This time, Illinois Senator Everett Dirksen reported to FBI officials that Bradley University's board of trustees had discovered Owen was gay, and after more than a week's worth of meetings, decided to place him "on an extended leave of absence and then relieve him of his position in order to avoid as much publicity as possible." Senator Dirksen claimed Owen's sexual issues were not new but dated to his Second World War naval service in the Pacific. Dirksen then obliquely linked Stevenson to Owen because the latter "was a frequent visitor at the Governor's Mansion . . . and there were numerous rumors about that situation." He also claimed communists were afoot at Bradley University among the faculty, that they were blackmailing Owen about his homosexuality, that drug use was rampant at the university, and that students there had the ability to purchase good grades. All of the information beyond Owen's sexuality, though, FBI officials dismissed as "unfounded."[148]

Senator Dirksen also suggested FBI agents interview two individuals about these allegations. One was a vice president of Keystone Steel and Wire Company and the other the president of a bank. He also hoped FBI officials would "conduct an investigation within its jurisdiction." FBI agents followed up on all of this, but what most concerned FBI officials regarding Dirksen's allegations were his motivations for reporting this to the FBI. Dirksen's actions in this regard actually highlight the deep concern in the 1950s with allegations of homosexuality as well as the byzantine steps some took to avoid even remotely being associated with them during the Lavender Scare.[149]

FBI Assistant Director Alan Belmont thought Senator Dirksen might be "endeavoring to keep his 'political skirts' clean" regarding the gay allegations for three reasons. First, Dirksen held an honorary degree from Bradley University. Second, Dirksen had played a key role in helping Owen become a staff officer for Admiral Chester Nimitz during the war. Third, Senator Dirksen had a history of helping Owen to hire faculty members. Belmont thought Senator Dirksen, by arranging an FBI investigation "camouflaged with information of alleged activities at Bradley University which appear baseless," would be protected if the Owen gay allegations became public because he could say he reported it to the FBI, which then investigated them. Moreover, the Bradley Board of Trustees, Belmont speculated, could also fire Owen, claiming it was premised on the FBI's investigation.[150]

FBI agents interviewed the two sources suggested by Senator Dirksen. They offered FBI agents what they knew, or heard, about Owen's sexuality and that rumors about it originated in the basketball game-fixing scandal when one player, Gene Melchiorre, tried to pressure Owen by gay baiting him to intercede and stop legal proceedings against him. In the course of the FBI investigation, though, none of the related charges Dirksen claimed were associated with Bradley University rang true, and in any event, Owen had resigned his post by this point (January 1953). FBI officials learned, however, that the Bradley University Board of Trustees had hired the Pinkerton Detective Agency to conduct an investigation. The Pinkertons, they learned, allegedly had "linked Governor Adlai Stevenson with Owen as members of an exclusive group of sexually abnormal individuals in New York City." There was one problem with the Pinkerton's investigation and report, however; the Pinkertons could not prove their contentions, suggesting the evidence on which the allegation rested was little more than rumor.[151]

One of the two individuals Senator Dirksen suggested FBI agents interview, moreover, said the "Pinkerton report would be available to the FBI." He even offered FBI agents the names of four Bradley University Board of Trustee members who had "access to the same information."[152] FBI agents interviewed the four trustees, and none of them confirmed any of the allegations about nefarious activity on the campus of Bradley University. They did, however, comment on the sexual allegations surrounding Owen and Stevenson.

One stated that although Owen's "dismissal was justified," he felt the way the board carried it out was not. Another told FBI agents he personally knew the Pinkerton's source concerning Owen's sexuality, and he promised to make it "available to the Chicago Division." He commented, however, that the Pinkertons "admitted that absolute proof was lacking but a strong indication of perversion on the part of Owen existed." The sum of this "strong" evidence was guilt by association: Owen "was often in the company of other men known to frequent establishments which catered to individuals desiring indulgence in acts of perversion." As to the allegation linking Owen to Stevenson as part of a New York City gay sex ring, one of the trustees explained that "the rumor connecting Stevenson with immoral acts was common in the Illinois area." None of the trustees offered the FBI the Pinkerton report, and because the report failed to substantiate "subversive information," the FBI agent who interviewed the trustees did not ask for it.[153]

Eight years later, in 1961, FBI agents tried to confirm the allegations about Stevenson's and Owen's activities in New York City, that Stevenson used the pseudonym "Adelaide" (a version of Adeline), and that he had been arrested on morals charges. They also tried to gain access to the Pinkerton report. FBI officials at some unidentified time "made discreet inquiries at the Pinkerton Detective Agency" and elsewhere but learned that "all known copies of the Pinkerton report" had been destroyed. The deputy New York City police commissioner also dismissed the rumor of Stevenson's arrest by stating, "If persons of prominence were found under the circumstances mentioned . . . he would have been aware of the fact." FBI agents, in fact, failed to substantiate any of these allegations. This renewed effort, moreover, was part of an FBI background check on Stevenson made upon President John F. Kennedy's nomination of him for UN ambassador, and the unsubstantiated allegations were disseminated to the White House. That Hoover offered unproven allegations to the White House suggests he was trying to influence the success of the nomination. None of this information Hoover offered, however, prevented Stevenson's nomination from proceeding. Hoover subsequently and obliquely hinted at the gay rumors surrounding Stevenson to the Johnson administration—with whom Hoover shared a close and cooperative relationship—but exactly why we do not know. These examples nevertheless illustrate how serious and intense the gay issue was and how Hoover made use of allegations his FBI collected via its augmented 1951 Sex Deviates Program in efforts to influence events.[154]

Hoover may have failed using sexual innuendo to influence the appointment of Stevenson as UN ambassador, but he was successful in foiling the appointment of another individual slated for a position in the Eisenhower

White House. Arthur Vandenberg Jr., son of the prominent Republican senator from Michigan, joined the Eisenhower presidential campaign in 1952 as a political secretary.[155] Eisenhower, of course, won that election. Regarded by many as a valuable campaign asset and holding a prominent Republican political surname, Vandenberg was selected to serve in the White House. Before he could become a presidential aide, however, Vandenberg had to pass an FBI background check. Given the intensity of the communists- and gays-in-government issues prior to Eisenhower's election, the president-elect decided to have FBI background checks not only on cabinet officials but "all other high posts."[156]

By December 1952, Vandenberg's background check was well under way, including an interview with two senior FBI officials. In the course of the interview, Vandenberg asked the FBI officials how they handled rumors. He was told that unless a rumor was positively disproved, FBI agents included it in their report to demonstrate the thoroughness of their investigations; they left no stone unturned. Vandenberg expressed agreement with this statement, but several days after the interview he suddenly checked himself into a hospital.[157]

On 30 December 1952, Hoover met with Eisenhower to discuss the progress of the FBI background checks. At one point, Vandenberg's situation came up. Hoover told the president-elect that Vandenberg had requested the FBI delay interviewing his male roommate until Vandenberg had checked out of the hospital. Hoover, in fact, was making it explicitly clear to Eisenhower that FBI agents had uncovered the fact that Vandenberg was gay. (FBI agents had already investigated another gay man linked to Vandenberg.) Hoover, moreover, explained to Eisenhower that if Vandenberg withdrew himself from consideration for the White House position then no formal FBI report on him would go forward. Vandenberg, wishing to avoid the irreparable ramifications of being exposed by the FBI as gay in the 1950s, withdrew his name but used his recent health issues—stomach ulcers (possibly stress induced)—as his rationale.[158]

Beginning in late 1952, after an army intelligence officer alleged Carmel Offie had breached US security, FBI officials again focused on him. The officer, Colonel Willis Perry, claimed that on 3 October 1952 Offie had taken possession of a classified document concerning the Mutual Security Agency's offshore procurement program. (Created in October 1951, the Mutual

Security Agency replaced the Marshall Plan by offering both economic and military aid to foreign nations.) Given FBI officials' previous suspicion Offie had engaged in espionage—which in December 1951 they had dismissed after finding information that "logically refute[d]" the charge—and given his homosexuality, which to some made him an automatic security risk, Hoover ordered agents to interview Offie and learn how he acquired the documents.[159]

Twice FBI agents tried to interview Offie and twice he refused; he only relented after Lovestone authorized his cooperation. FBI agents then learned Offie was the liaison between the American Federation of Labor and the Mutual Security Agency, and his responsibility was to assist in stimulating foreign employment. Regarding the secret expenditure figures he had received, Offie denied knowing they were classified but expressed his faith that government officials would never have given him anything he should not have. Despite the agents having regarded Offie as uncooperative and "insolent" when they first contacted him, in their final interview they suddenly found him cooperative and "most affable." FBI officials then disseminated the contents of the Offie interview to the CIA, military intelligence, and the State Department.[160]

Hoover, however, was not satisfied with Offie's explanation and ordered FBI agents to interview the director of the Mutual Security Agency, Averell Harriman, to ascertain whether Offie "was a proper person" to have received the classified information and whether the official who had given it to him was authorized to do so. Upon interviewing Harriman's executive assistant, FBI agents learned Offie and his supplier of information were, in fact, "entitled to receive classified information concerning" the Offshore Procurement Program.[161]

Regardless of the fact Offie had not violated any law and had not engaged in any questionable activity whatsoever, Hoover was still not satisfied. After learning Offie was "seeking a position in the Federal Government," FBI officials disseminated to the CSC and another unidentified recipient (but it appears to be someone in Congress) details about Offie's 1943 arrest in Lafayette Park. A handwritten notation on a 3 January 1953 FBI document from Crime Records head Nichols to Tolson confirms that this information was leaked via the bureau's Sex Deviate Program on 11 December 1951.[162] FBI officials, moreover, seem to have been successful, though at a later date. On 4 February 1953, Hoover advised Tolson, Ladd, and Nichols "that Offie had been offered a $25,000 a year position" rescinded "at the last moment" when a "congressional committee" visited the White House and revealed Offie's 1943 arrest for soliciting sex from a man. Regarding Offie, Hoover was moved to write, "It seems to be an inherent part of a pervert's makeup to be also a pathological liar." The reformatted Sex Deviates Program worked.[163]

The following day, Hoover then disseminated derogatory information about Offie and his associates to Undersecretary of State Walter Bedell Smith and President Eisenhower's administrative assistant, General Robert Cutler. Hoover informed both men that a new report indicated "quite a number of people in the State Department" were linked to Offie. The list of presumed homosexuals included Douglas MacArthur II, Alexander Kirk, Lovestone, Air Force Major Don Reynolds, a Mr. Harper, Irving Brown, Lloyd W. Henderson, Robert P. Joyce, Thayer, and James C. Dunn. The revelations Hoover offered had "very much surprised" Cutler because he personally knew some of the people mentioned "and found it difficult to believe they would knowingly be associating with a person like Offie." Hoover assured Cutler, however, that "there was no question about Offie" being homosexual because the FBI had his arrest record in its files. Regarding this, Smith "was extremely pleased" Hoover had revealed the list to Cutler because Smith had been trying to convince Cutler "many of the appointees" needed security checks.[164] Hoover agreed with Smith's assessment, especially regarding Offie, Lovestone, and Brown—Brown worked with Lovestone as the Free Trade Union Committee's European representative—because he had "grave doubts re this trio."[165]

After doing all of this, because of Offie's supposed desire to assume yet another government post, on 11 February 1953, Hoover disseminated derogatory information about his sexuality and associations to Attorney General Herbert Brownell, Smith, Cutler, and White House Chief of Staff Sherman Adams. The document Hoover provided these men listed the "pervert allegations" against Offie, including his 1943 arrest and the details of how he was fired from the CIA. It also listed his "contacts in government," some of whom appeared on the list Hoover had previously shared with Smith and Cutler. Sixteen days later, Hoover sent Brownell, Adams, and Cutler a "supplementary memorandum" that added one more salacious detail about Offie. According to Hoover, on 15 October 1949, while being interviewed in his CIA office, Offie had made "improper [sexual] advances" toward an

official while this man was pointing out on a map where he had served during the Second World War. This information was then incorporated into the
FBI Sex Deviate File, as indicated on one of the internal FBI documents.[166]

On 26 January 1953, FBI Assistant Director Nichols received an "informal"
request from Roy Cohn, chief legal counsel to Senator McCarthy's Permanent Subcommittee on Investigations (aka, the McCarthy Committee).
Cohn had a list of VOA employees for whom he wanted FBI name checks.
Nichols subsequently learned from McCarthy's assistant legal counsel (and
former FBI agent) Don Surine that McCarthy and Senator Homer Ferguson
of the Foreign Relations Committee had planned to hold a joint investigation of the VOA in New York. Surine claimed that some members of the
VOA were engaging in influence peddling and that Thayer headed up its
"left-wing apparatus." Regarding Thayer, Surine said McCarthy hoped to
"get him before the Committee in the near future." Regarding this, Hoover
responded internally, "They certainly should expose him & his present tie-
in with State Dept."[167]

Nichols then took Cohn's name-check request to Deputy Attorney
General William Rogers. Rogers authorized the check and requested an
FBI summary memorandum on Thayer, who had appeared on Cohn's
list. Hoover provided this memorandum and then informed Rogers he intended to forward the Thayer memo to McCarthy's committee. Hoover was
careful to note, however, that the memo was only based on the FBI's *security*
investigation of Thayer because the president had excluded Federal Loyalty
Program files from dissemination. (The FBI conducted both a security and
loyalty investigation of Thayer, but officials only included in their loyalty
report information they could confirm on their own and without compromising Finlator. Otherwise, the two investigations were similar.) In the end,
Rogers directed Hoover not to give the McCarthy Committee the memo.[168]

Previously and repeatedly, FBI officials were stymied in their efforts to
end Thayer's career because their information about his alleged homosexuality originated from their confidential and sensitive State Department
source and not the gumshoe efforts of FBI agents. McCarthy's name-check
request, however, seemingly provided a solution to their sourcing dilemma.
According to Assistant FBI Director Belmont, "by merely giving [McCarthy]
the substance of the information obtained through [Finlator] . . . neither

his cooperation with the Bureau nor the confidential sources of his information will be uncovered."[169]

Belmont, therefore, recommended providing Cohn a copy of the FBI security report on Thayer. Before this could be done, however, because the McCarthy-Ferguson VOA hearings were to be public, Deputy Attorney General Rogers had to be consulted. Yet again, bureau officials were thwarted when Rogers asked them not to disseminate their memo to McCarthy because he did not want Secretary of State John Foster Dulles to think the Justice Department was "feeding material" to McCarthy's committee. On 9 March 1953, however, Rogers consulted with the State Department's new security chief, Robert W. Scott McLeod (a former FBI agent) and learned that the State Department had already decided Thayer had to go. Rogers, therefore, authorized the bureau's dissemination of the Thayer report to Senator McCarthy. It was handed over as a blind memo on 11 March 1953.[170]

McLeod was hired as administrator (head) of the State Department Bureau of Security and Consular Affairs in late February 1953. As a former FBI agent, his taking this position was a significant development for the FBI efforts to eliminate gays from government. Unlike Finlator's problematic relationship with the FBI, McLeod maintained a close, deferential, and intimate working relationship with FBI Director Hoover throughout his tenure at the State Department (and beyond), the details of which historians previously did not fully appreciate. Indeed, immediately after taking office, McLeod began summarily purging gays by firing "eight homosexuals from the State Department as security risks."[171] As was often the case, Hoover benefitted repeatedly when his former FBI agents or officials—provided they stayed on good terms with the taskmaster Hoover—took positions with congressional committees, other agencies of the federal government, or nongovernmental positions. These linkages gave Hoover significant leverage and access to information.

Hoover even played a significant role in having McLeod hired. The FBI director provided Undersecretary of State Smith a list of former FBI agents he might consider for the job. Eventually, it came down to former FBI agent J. Walter Yeagley and McLeod. After a phone call on 19 February 1953 from Smith, in which Hoover "favorably recommended" both and said the choice was a "toss-up," McLeod landed the job. On 26 February, Hoover wrote McLeod a congratulatory letter. He told McLeod his "many friends in the FBI join me in wishing you every possible success, and I hope you will never hesitate to call upon us when we may be of service to you." (McLeod, in fact, did just that—repeatedly.) In reply to Hoover's congratulations (and offer), McLeod expressed how "difficult" it was to "tell you how very much I appreciate your note of February 26." He explained his new job was "terribly complex," and "it would be impossible to do a really effective job if it were not for the fact that you have offered your cooperation."[172]

The same day McLeod wrote Hoover, an FBI inspector alerted the director that McLeod called to request a "copy of Elbert Hubbard's 'Loyalty'" for his office.[173] Always one to emphasize the importance of loyalty to the FBI—where a cult of personality existed that centered squarely on the domineering Hoover—every bureau office had on the wall a plaque of Hubbard's loyalty pledge. It read:

> If you work for a man, in heaven's name work for him; speak well of him and stand by the institution he represents.
>
> Remember—an ounce of loyalty is worth a pound of cleverness.
>
> If you must growl, condemn, and eternally find fault, why—resign your position and when you are on the outside, damn to your heart's content—but as long as you are part of the institution do not condemn it; if you do, the first high wind that comes along will blow you away, and probably you will never know why.
>
> —Elbert Hubbard[174]

Hoover happily offered McLeod the plaque—a symbol, indeed, of McLeod's steadfast loyalty and deference not to the State Department but to Hoover—adding, "If Mr. Hubbard's words were adhered to by everyone in government it would certainly be to the advantage of all."[175]

As he was "just digging in over at the State Department," McLeod quickly found himself, as FBI Assistant Director Nichols described it, "in water which might get over his head." Nichols advised Tolson that McLeod "hoped the Bureau would help him in every possible way and that he wanted to know what he could do for the Bureau." Nichols advised McLeod, at that point and before arranging one of many meetings for him with Hoover, FBI officials "would certainly call upon him as matters occur."[176]

McLeod's preliminary efforts in his new job seemed, in fact, to please FBI officials a great deal. At one point in mid-March 1953, while Nichols was eating lunch in the Justice Department cafeteria, he engaged Assistant

US Attorney Tom Donegan (who indicted Hiss) in a conversation about McLeod. Donegan was aghast that when meeting with State Department officials, McLeod asserted that Donegan's grand jury was not going to receive nor was entitled to any State Department files. Donegan told Nichols he "expected some such attitude from the whole crowd in the State Department" but "was amazed when Scott McLeod took this position," and he "could not understand it." Nichols replied that McLeod not only had a "good record" but was, in his view, "very much opposed to anybody with communist taints" and, moreover, was earnestly working to eliminate "undesirables" at the State Department.[177]

On the afternoon of 24 March, McLeod telephoned Nichols to tell him he felt "there is only one person he can turn to who can give him some guidance, namely, the Director." He then asked if Hoover would be willing to meet with him. FBI officials obliged the request. Although no extant record survives to indicate what they discussed, a sycophantic McLeod repeatedly met with, telephoned, and corresponded with Hoover.[178]

A couple of months later, after having irked the FBI director in the demonstratively public Dulles-McLeod controversy (detailed below), McLeod made certain to mollify Hoover. Apparently, personnel in his security bureau, in McLeod's view, were blaming the FBI for their own errors. This prompted McLeod to telephone Nichols to tell him he was notifying his people the "FBI cannot be blamed for the shortcomings of the State Department." He also told Nichols "he was feeling pretty low; that one of the reasons he took the job was he thought he might be of some service to the Bureau," and he did not feel like he was accomplishing this. Nichols told McLeod the "only way improvement will come will be through really bearing down and that we just were not going to put up any more with having the buck passed to us." McLeod asked to meet with Hoover personally, and the FBI director agreed.[179]

For a time, rumors about McLeod's bad "attitude" made their way to FBI headquarters. One such rumor, which Tolson heard, had it that McLeod "may well be under the complete domination of General Bedell Smith" at the State Department. Underlying the rumor was McLeod's newly "aggressive attitude" and new unwillingness to provide information to members of Congress (also a reaction to the Dulles-McLeod controversy). Hoover, however, after one of his many meetings with McLeod, assured Tolson that the "attitude of Mr. McLeod toward the Bureau, and his desire for cooperation, are very wholesome."[180]

We may not know the intimate details and precise advice and assistance Hoover offered McLeod in his repeated meetings with him either as chief of the State Department Security Division or later (1954), when he was promoted to deputy undersecretary of state for operations, but it is clear they maintained an intimate relationship. We do have examples, though, that illustrate how close their relationship was. When McLeod traveled abroad as part of his duties in administering the Refugee Relief Act, Hoover issued orders (replete with McLeod's travel itinerary) to his FBI legal attachés—FBI agents attached to US embassies to liaise with foreign police and intelligence agencies—to offer McLeod the "usual courtesies if their offices are contacted." In mid-November 1953, for example, McLeod traveled to European capitals and again in 1956 to East Asia and Australia. These courtesies included offering any kind of help, assistance, or travel and accommodation arrangements that amounted to first-class treatment. Hoover only ever extended such "courtesies" to prominent personalities or people close to him.[181]

By 1956 FBI officials and Hoover were quite pleased with McLeod's relationship with the bureau. In one summary of his recent activities, FBI Liaison Section Chief Ralph Roach wrote, "Mr. McLeod has been most cooperative with the Bureau and is considered an excellent liaison contact."[182] Then, within a year, McLeod found himself under consideration for the post of US ambassador to Ireland. As part of Senate confirmation hearings, Senator Styles Bridges, for whom McLeod had once worked as a staffer, included in the official record the text of a speech McLeod had given in Topeka, Kansas. In the speech McLeod asserted, "I have the greatest admiration and respect for J. Edgar Hoover, the Director of the Bureau. I am honored to be numbered among his friends, and I lean on him for counsel and guidance at all times." McLeod even noted in his speech that to keep the State Department Security Division functioning well, he hired "on a contract basis the services of Mr. James Egan," a former FBI supervisor famous for his work apprehending celebrity gangsters in the 1930s.[183] McLeod, in fact, had built his State Department Security Division team from former FBI agents and claimed to have purged 500 State Department employees in his first few weeks on the job.[184]

After Hoover wrote McLeod a note to congratulate him on his confirmation as ambassador, McLeod was moved to write an effusive thank you that exemplified his long relationship with the FBI director. McLeod told Hoover he found "it difficult to express fully my appreciation for the support which you and the Federal Bureau of Investigation have given me during the last four years." He admitted to Hoover, revealingly, that State Department insiders often criticized him "for being 'too much FBI.'" After McLeod left his position at the department, Hoover placed him, again revealingly, on the FBI's Special Correspondents' List and "on a first name basis," no less. This was Hoover's list of trusted individuals who would be leaked FBI information if necessary, for example, to influence public opinion. Perhaps most revealing of all about Hoover's close relationship with McLeod was Hoover's note to McLeod's wife after McLeod prematurely died of a massive heart attack in 1961 at age forty-seven. In the letter Hoover called McLeod by his nickname, and FBI officials even noted on the bureau's file copy of the letter McLeod "was known to the Director as 'Scottie.'"[185]

On 4 March 1953, at the same time Hoover was sharing FBI information about Thayer, Bohlen, and Offie with Senator McCarthy and others, he forwarded to White House Chief of Staff Adams a summary of information on Thayer. The thirty-eight-page summary focused on the allegations that Thayer, while in the OSS, was a "close associate of the Russians and other Communists." Although the allegations of homosexuality were seemingly downplayed in the report—inasmuch as they appear near the end of it—this information was the most important, hence the last read and most remembered. Hoover detailed Thayer's sexual life and associations, mostly using State Department files as his source. One of those associations was State Department employee Colonel Ira W. Porter, whom one State Department informant described as a "notorious homosexual." The informant—described in one internal FBI memo as a State Department "undercover operator . . . used in the investigations of homosexuals"—noted Thayer and Porter were "very good friends," and Porter was "a very large and masculine man, who had a great record in World War II as a full colonel, and that it is almost impossible for anyone to surmise Porter is a homosexual." The informant said Thayer ended his friendship with Porter after Porter "propositioned him to engage in homosexual acts," but before that happened the two believed they had caught Thayer at his New York City apartment in bed with another man. The informant claimed Porter "later told him that Thayer is 'as queer as a $3 bill,'" and despite being married, Thayer was a "high-class homosexual and is known only among high-class homosexuals."[186]

This same State Department informant/operative also reported that in 1948 he serendipitously ran into Porter in New York City and ended up having dinner and drinks with him and Thayer. Over dinner the informant said Porter and Thayer acknowledged their mutual friendship with Offie and noted he had resigned from the State Department. Also mentioned over dinner was Major Rankin Robert, whom the informant said Porter described as a "very famous homosexual." Another common friend's name that came up was Mike Petrovich, whom Thayer is supposed to have described as "'gay,' which [the] informant states is a homosexual term meaning an active or participating homosexual." The informant further claimed that while sharing a taxi, Thayer propositioned him to "engage in homosexual relations," and rounding out the trifecta, he even claimed Offie had once solicited sex from him.[187]

The FBI summary had even more to report about Porter and his association with Thayer. At one point, while still a friend of Porter's and while Porter worked at the State Department, Thayer "either stayed at Porter's home [in Washington, DC] or visited with him." Porter was subsequently "asked to resign from the State Department because he was found to be a notorious homosexual who . . . had brought in several other homosexuals into that division who subsequently had to be weeded out." The FBI Thayer summary even included the suggestive fact that "Porter often came in on Monday morning looking bleary-eyed and reported that he had had a 'terrific weekend' and that 'Charlie Thayer was by to see me and we had a wild time.'" The informant admitted, however, that the basis of his belief in Thayer's homosexuality was Thayer's "close personal association with Porter."[188]

Also listed as a questionable associate of Thayer's in the FBI summary was Nicholas Nabokoff. The summary noted Nabokoff worked with Thayer, was his roommate in New York, and "was obviously a homosexual." FBI evidence of his sexuality included his effeminate manner and speech and his common greeting of "Hello, darling." The FBI summary reported the "majority of the people" at the New York VOA office thought Thayer and Nabokoff were a "pair" as well as the "laughing stock of the office." Even worse, Thayer supposedly "often brought in young men friends to spend the night with him." This included a three-month period when Thayer and Nabokoff "had a young French boy named Jacques Brosse living with them," a twenty-five-year-old employee of the United Nations. Brosse was reportedly "very effeminate and obviously a 'queer.'"[189]

The FBI summary listed further examples from various informants suggesting Thayer was gay, he had communist sympathies or was friendly toward communists, he had engaged in the black market in Europe, and he had fathered an illegitimate child. But it was, in reality, the allusions to his presumed sexuality that effectively torpedoed Thayer's diplomatic career because Hoover also forwarded the Thayer memorandum to Undersecretary of State Smith. Smith, who learned about Thayer and Offie in February 1953, had asked Hoover for a copy of the FBI summary so that he could share it with Donald Lourie, the undersecretary of state in charge of personnel, who ultimately would ask for Thayer's resignation. Beyond Thayer, the memorandum (and other cases) also undoubtedly helped to influence President Eisenhower's issuance in April 1953 of Executive Order 10450, which expanded the Federal Loyalty Program beyond loyalty and subversion cases to security matters. Now, federal employees could be fired for "habitual drunkenness, narcotic addiction, sex perversion, deliberate misrepresentation," or any other perceived behavior that showed one "not reliable or trustworthy."[190]

Rumor and innuendo about Thayer's supposed homosexuality flowed freely around the nation's capital during 1953. Exacerbating it were his linkages to Bohlen and Offie (and others) along with the fact that even those two were targets of McCarthyites and internal security bureaucrats, all of which rose to a crescendo eventually leading to Thayer's downfall. It was Hoover, though, who forced the issue. Free-flowing rumors about a State Department employee were one thing, but when it became known that Hoover's FBI—the most revered investigative agency in the federal government, the one with the most gravitas, and the one officially responsible for both security and loyalty investigations—had a report apparently documenting Thayer's homosexuality, Thayer was (and in Hoover's view, finally) finished.

FBI Assistant Director Belmont even reiterated as much in February 1953. He wrote that none of the information FBI agents obtained from the State Department as part of the FBI security investigation of Thayer was included in its loyalty report, as the requirements of the loyalty program then excluded "information concerning a person's morals." (Really, they were protecting their source.) When FBI officials later initiated a formal loyalty probe of Thayer, however, "considerable information bearing on Thayer's homosexuality was volunteered by witnesses who were interviewed by Agents of this Bureau." FBI agents had reinterviewed some State Department witnesses. Because this information was then considered "volunteered, it was included in the loyalty reports which were subsequently disseminated." Therefore, on 6 March 1953, Undersecretary Lourie wrote Thayer—serving as the US counsel general in Munich—that proceedings were being initiated to dismiss him from the Foreign Service "on charges of misconduct pertaining to morality." As was so typical in cases of this kind, Thayer was advised that if he chose to waive these proceedings, and clearly the proceedings would have been an embarrassment for him, he would be permitted to resign. He chose the latter option, quitting on 23 March, with his resignation being made public on 26 May 1953. Officially, Thayer claimed that he wanted to devote his time to writing, which is, in fact, how he subsequently tried to make a living.[191]

Thayer was understandably embarrassed over the reasons for which he was fired. He referred to it sarcastically—perhaps with a mind toward Dreyfus—as "l'affaire." He told friends and acquaintances that he had not fought the firing because his enemies, particularly McCarthy, had been provided enough information to "smear me pretty badly, at least in the eyes of the puritanical public." He refused to tell people the reason he was terminated—allegations of homosexuality—and, instead, told them it had to do with "an old issue involving a young lady," which he "preferred not to have . . . made public" to save his family from "embarrassment." To one correspondent he admitted, incredibly, to this version of his story "only because I fear other more sordid charges might easily gain currency and naturally disturb editors and publishers." Clearly, he feared the stories of his supposed sexuality would undermine what he had hoped to be a successful writing career. In the 1950s, even if unfounded, this was a valid concern.[192]

Within days of Thayer's departure, another State Department official linked to Thayer was similarly forced to resign. Samuel Reber was deputy high commissioner for Germany and had devoted to his country more than a quarter of a century of service. When responding to my FOIA request for information about Reber, the FBI released little, and this precludes us from understanding the bureau's role in Reber's departure. What was released, a 27 May 1955 (file copy) memo from Hoover to a redacted recipient outside of the FBI, in fact, states plainly, "The FBI has conducted no investigation concerning Samuel Reber." An internal notation on the document also states, according to a State Department source, Reber had "admitted that he had participated in acts of homosexuality and asked for psychiatric aid. As a result Reber's resignation was requested." Significantly, because the document was the bureau's file copy, it also had an attached "note on yellow" summarizing information the FBI held on Reber. The note listed for each paragraph FBI file numbers indicating which FBI file was the source of information. Some cited numbers, immediately following Hoover's claim of no investigation, were 105-12189-1422, 1458, and 1514. The file number 105-12189 was one of those for the Sex Deviates File (sex perverts in government service) and cited three different individual documents (1422, 1458, 1514) that held information regarding Reber. Clearly, FBI officials did, in fact, collect and compile information about Reber, information placed in their Sex Deviates File, which existed for the express purpose of disseminating such information to purge gays from federal employment. Additionally, the fact that the serials were numbered in the thousands also suggests the intensity of FBI efforts regarding the Sex Deviates Program and File by the mid-1950s. The file was growing exponentially, and Reber was of interest to the FBI.[193]

The scrutiny Thayer, Offie, and company received at this juncture, and the intensity of the FBI efforts, must be understood within the context of acrimonious national political developments in 1953. The newly inaugurated President Eisenhower, although sympathetic to the anticommunists in his Republican Party, was nevertheless not a right-winger. He was a moderate. Given the McCarthyites' attacks on the Roosevelt and Truman administrations for "selling out" US interests to the communists at Yalta, when Eisenhower announced his nomination for US ambassador to the Soviet Union, Chip Bohlen, on 27 February 1953, partisan political tensions were only exacerbated. Eisenhower nominated the highly qualified Bohlen, a career diplomat present at the Yalta Conference as Roosevelt's interpreter, who had even publicly defended the conference from its conservative critics. Making matters even more concerning, at least for those with inside knowledge, was the fact that Bohlen was related to Thayer as his brother-in-law. Because of this relationship and Bohlen's other acquaintances, some of whom were gay, conservative Republicans (and the FBI director) attempted to forestall his nomination by gay baiting him.[194]

Just over two weeks before Eisenhower's Bohlen announcement, Secretary of State Dulles asked Hoover to investigate Bohlen's past. Hoover honored the request and ordered the preparation of a summary for the secretary of state, attorney general, and White House. Included in the twenty-one-page summary were the typical sundries, such as birth, education, and employment history, including the observation that Bohlen had "established himself as the leading diplomatic expert of the Department in all matters concerning the relationship between the United States and the Soviet Union." The real meat of the document, however, was in its second section.[195]

A curious inclusion in the FBI Bohlen summary was none other than Offie, who at this point was the Washington, DC, representative of the Free Trade Union Committee of the AFL. FBI agents interviewed Offie, who said he had first met Bohlen in July 1934 at the US Embassy in Moscow. Although they had never been stationed together, Offie said he was "well acquainted" with Bohlen, having met him repeatedly in various capital cities. He even said he had stayed at Bohlen's Washington, DC, home for three months during 1948. Offie then described Bohlen as "an extremely intelligent and attractive fellow" but one who had a history of drinking frequently.[196]

Regarding Bohlen's stance toward the Soviets, Offie had nothing good to report. He disagreed with Bohlen's positions, viewing his stance toward Russia as similar to the friendly tone of FDR advisor Harry Hopkins. He also castigated Bohlen for defending the Yalta Accords and said he was puzzled by Bohlen's "attitude of appeasement." Offie said although he believed Bohlen to be a loyal US citizen, he nevertheless could not recommend him as ambassador to the USSR because to "send a man who prospered and who helped along the appeasement period is wrong."[197]

The FBI summary on Bohlen then (perhaps unsurprisingly) went into detail about Offie's character, much of which information FBI officials had received from the State Department Bureau of Security and Consular Affairs. The information was clearly meant to cast aspersions on Bohlen through guilt by association and therefore should be reiterated in some detail. The summary, for example, described Offie as a former Foreign Service officer connected to Bohlen and single but "not effeminate." Once while visiting "an admitted homosexual" in Washington, DC (the State Department's undercover operator), Offie solicited this man, telling him "I'd like to sleep with you." The man said, "Offie is as queer as a $3 bill" and is "known among the Washington higher homosexuals as 'one of us.'" Another self-admitting gay source reported Offie "has the reputation of being homosexual and is well known." Yet another gay man known to this particular source reported, "Offie is certainly a homosexual" but said he never had "relations with Offie because 'We are not sexually attracted to each other.'"[198]

The Bohlen summary detailed Offie's arrest record. It included the fact that Offie had been arrested on 8 September 1943 by morals squad officers Pitts and Blick for trying to "induce him [Pitts] to engage in a homosexual act." Offie posted collateral and forfeited it, thereby accepting a charge of disorderly conduct. Getting to the point of the problem of association with Offie, the FBI summary reported that, according to the Bureau of Security and Consular Affairs, "Offie had listed Charles E. Bohlen as a character reference."[199]

Another self-admitting gay source used by the State Department Security Division also provided information besmirching Bohlen's moral character. This source claimed to have used Bohlen as a reference when he applied for a job with the War Assets Administration and subsequently was separated from the Foreign Service "for being a homosexual." This was not all. The source reportedly was also kicked out of the US Navy for being gay and was arrested by the Washington Park Police on 15 April 1948 "on a charge of perversion." The source further claimed to have served with Bohlen in Moscow during 1934. Given the source's history, he then went on to claim he could "separate the 'queer' from the men" to "spot" gays "very easily." He believed he had a "sixth sense" about it. Using what in the twenty-first-century we call "gaydar," this man concluded Bohlen was gay because he "walks, acts, and talks like a homosexual."[200]

The FBI Bohlen summary also cited the work of John Matson, a State Department security agent whose job was to read reports and index names of "State Department employees suspected of homosexuality." Matson reported that the department, indeed, had an index card on Bohlen, which indicated he "was associated with sexual perverts." FBI agents, especially given FBI Director Hoover's close relationship with the new head of the State Department Security Division, reviewed that department's records and reported their result in the Bohlen summary.[201]

One suspect culled, in part, from the State Department's index and making an appearance in Thayer's summary was Nabokoff. An interesting character, Nabokoff was a Russian refugee of the Bolshevik Revolution and grandson of Dimitri Nabokoff, Tsar Alexander II's minister of justice. Nabokoff attended the elite Imperial Lyceum in St. Petersburg, studied music in Germany, studied philosophy in Paris, and eventually settled in the United States to teach music. When the Second World War started, he took a job as a translator and cultural advisor. A twice-married bisexual man, Nabokoff in January 1947 joined the VOA in New York, where he worked with Thayer. Later, he was seen at Bohlen's Washington, DC, residence by none other than State Department Soviet expert and author of the Truman Doctrine, George Kennan. Like others, Nabokoff had listed Bohlen (along with Kennan) as a reference when he applied for his VOA job. Nabokoff had long been suspected of being gay (and a drug addict) as far back as when the FBI first investigated his background in the late 1940s but could not substantiate the charges.[202] State Department security officers interviewed Nabokoff on 25 June 1948, when he denied being gay and having sex with Thayer but did not deny associating with many different types of gays, with whom he said he had "no antipathy," such as a Russian ballet dancer and a French poet, among many others. In fact, the FBI reported in the Bohlen summary that Nabokoff "finds some of them to be the most charming people whose friendship he does not care to lose."[203]

FBI officials also included in their Bohlen summary, again originating from the State Department Security Division, information from a one-time, short-term house guest of Nabokoff's and Thayer's in New York City during the late 1940s, Brosse, also noted in the Thayer summary just weeks before. When interviewed by a State Department security officer, Brosse "admitted [to] homosexual activities of every type known and stated that he would engage in any type of homosexual activity." He told the security officer he had such sex in Nabokoff's and Thayer's apartment in New York, but not with them, though he had, in fact, heard Nabokoff was gay. Regarding Thayer, Brosse said his bedroom was opposite Thayer's, and he saw him "take men friends into the bedroom until two or three in the morning," yet he never heard anything nor did he know if Thayer was homosexual.[204]

Not only because Thayer's name came up in regard to Nabokoff and Brosse but because Thayer was Bohlen's brother-in-law and a questionable figure himself, he was unsurprisingly singled out in the FBI Bohlen summary. It reiterated that Thayer denied to State Department officials being homosexual but State Department files "contain an admission on the part of Thayer to engaging in one act of homosexuality while on foreign assignment" (the department official would not say with whom or where), and he had fathered an illegitimate child.[205]

Shocking and salacious stories of homosexuality such as these were not restricted to Bohlen's associates. A female FBI source reported her discomfort at being in proximity with Bohlen because "there is a definite shading in his conversation and in his manner of speech which indicates effeminacy." Even worse, she observed his "habit of running his tongue over his lip in the manner utilized by a woman." Also, she reported that when Bohlen spoke

with Thayer his "tone" was not "normal" and, instead, "was decidedly different, sounded effeminate, and was 'quite girlish.'" Yet when Bohlen spoke
French, she reported, he did not sound effeminate at all![206]

The remainder of the FBI summary listed the various, but nonsensa-
tional, views of Bohlen by former ambassador to Russia William Bullitt,
former communist leader Lovestone, Stalin and Lenin biographer Isaac
Don Levine, former ambassador to Poland Arthur Bliss Lane, and former
New York Times reporter Ray Benton Brock. Clearly, though, the detailed
allusions to Bohlen's purported homosexuality and, more significantly, his
associations with known or suspected gays were central to the FBI report.
Yet some derogatory, sexually themed information was not included in the
Bohlen summary because, in Hoover's view, it could not be "substantiated."
One example was provided by the columnist Drew Pearson, who claimed to
have heard a rumor that Bohlen, in his youth, had engaged in homosexual
activity, but when FBI agents asked Bohlen about it, he denied the story. Another originated from aide to Senator McCarthy and former FBI agent Surine, who claimed McLeod had confirmed the existence in his department
files of "several allegations" concerning Bohlen's homosexuality. (Clearly,
substantiality was not the real reason for excluding this particular tidbit.)
All the other unproven and unsubstantiated allegations of sex and associations with gays, however, Hoover somehow found substantiated enough
to include in the Bohlen summary report. In point of fact, Hoover—who
always claimed his FBI never made recommendations but just reported the
facts—was painting a picture of Bohlen he hoped would lead to a certain
conclusion.[207]

On 17 March 1953, at the urging of President Eisenhower, Secretary of
State Dulles requested Hoover's opinion on the Bohlen nomination. Normally, Hoover worked in indirect ways to undermine those who failed to
meet his standards—as he had done years before with Welles—but because the president directed Dulles to ask for Hoover's opinion, Hoover
(because he was insulated here) offered it. He told Dulles he "would not
be inclined . . . to give Bohlen a complete clearance." The basis of Hoover's
opinion was the "fact that several of his [Bohlen's] closest friends and intimate associates were known homosexuals."[208]

Then, on 18 March 1953, Dulles (along with Bohlen) testified in a three-
hour closed session before the Senate Foreign Relations Committee. Dulles
reported on the FBI investigation of Bohlen, about which homophobic
Senator Alexander Wiley of Wisconsin (see Chapter 5) later told reporters

it had "left no doubt of Mr. Bohlen's loyalty and security." The committee then voted unanimously to approve Bohlen's nomination. One wonders if Dulles offered an abridged reiteration of the FBI's report.[209]

The executive session vote enraged conservative senators opposed to the Bohlen nomination. Senator McCarthy charged Secretary Dulles with ramming the nomination through the Senate, calling it a "tremendous mistake." He then urged Dulles to have President Eisenhower examine the Bohlen "file" in hopes that he would withdraw the nomination. Senator Bridges joined McCarthy in his opposition, saying the Foreign Relations Committee should have the chance to read the FBI report itself rather than rely on "an evaluation of that report by the man who made the appointment." Bridges was referring to Dulles, not Eisenhower.[210]

That same day, 18 March, Hoover received a hurried telephone call from Senator McCarthy. McCarthy wanted Hoover to tell him "in complete confidence" whether Bohlen was a homosexual, as rumored. Hoover replied that because he was asked to investigate only after Eisenhower had made the nomination, determining whether Bohlen was gay "was very hard to evaluate." Hoover added that the "only way you could prove it was either by admission or by arrest and forfeiture of collateral." Nevertheless, Hoover told McCarthy "it is fact" that Bohlen associated with individuals such as Offie, whom Hoover described as his "very close buddy," who "is a well-known homosexual." Hoover also told McCarthy he had "no evidence to show any overt act" of homosexuality on the part of Bohlen, but, in his view, Bohlen "had certainly used very bad judgement in associating with homosexuals." McCarthy ended his conversation with Hoover by requesting access to any public-source materials the FBI might have on Bohlen for his use in continuing the fight on the Senate floor, but Hoover declined the request.[211]

The following day the issue exploded publicly after it was revealed that Secretary Dulles and State Department Security Chief McLeod had exchanged "heated words" over interpreting the FBI Bohlen summary. After the exchange McLeod reportedly threatened to resign. Senator McCarthy quickly asserted that he wanted to question McLeod in executive session, that day, about the matter. McLeod never showed up for questioning because he was summoned to the White House following the revelation. It was reported in the papers that Vice President Nixon was even enlisted to pressure McCarthy "not to summon the angry McLeod." The president, meanwhile, alluding to McCarthyite criticism of Bohlen's associations, publicly expressed his support for Bohlen, including stating he was once a guest in Bohlen's home and had even played golf with the man.[212]

With congressional criticism now focused on the secretary of state, Dulles hastily convened a press conference and tried to answer, and clarify, some of the charges made against him. Senator McCarran, for example, claimed Dulles had "summarily overridden" McLeod's objections. Dulles replied, according to the *New York Times*, that McLeod had never made "an attempt at evaluation" of the FBI summary. Dulles said that although McLeod had called the secretary's attention to "certain parts of the FBI report," in the end "there was no difference of opinion" between the two men. Dulles also denied the assertion McLeod was resigning. Senator McCarran "flatly" disagreed with Dulles, however, claiming McLeod "could not clear Bohlen." Senator McCarthy retorted that Dulles's words were "in complete conflict" with what legislators knew. The *Times* even reported that McLeod continued to hold "very close" relations with the "Senate right-wing Republicans and Democrats." Always one to crave the limelight, McCarthy even brazenly added, according to the *Chicago Tribune*, "I know what's in Bohlen's file, and to say that he is a security risk is putting it too weak."[213]

On 23 March 1953, the Dulles-McLeod brouhaha over the Bohlen nomination continued unabated. Senator McCarthy began to demand Bohlen take a lie-detector test, an assertion, as we will see, suggesting McLeod was his source of information. McCarthy asserted, "Let's find out the facts in the conflict of statements. There is no reason on God's earth why we shouldn't have McLeod's side of the story." He then suggested that the "nature of the evidence affecting Bohlen is such that we can't discuss it on the Senate floor without violating security." If the derogatory evidence against Bohlen were true, McCarthy warned, "Moscow is the last place on earth where Bohlen should be sent."[214]

McLeod in fact never testified before the Senate on this matter, as McCarthy wanted. Dulles strictly forbade it. Dulles made the FBI summary on Bohlen, though, available to Majority Leader Taft and Senator John Sparkman of Alabama. Taft replied that he found nothing in the FBI report to suggest Bohlen was even remotely soft on communism. He said there was nothing in it to "raise even a prima facie case or to supply any prime evidence that Mr. Bohlen had in any way ever done anything which could make him a bad security risk." Getting more to the heart of McCarthy and company's concerns, Taft continued, "The associations he had are those which anyone might have had with persons who were friends of many other people, who may have stayed overnight at his home, or for the weekend, with him and Mrs. Bohlen."[215]

Taft also told the Senate that McLeod had offered him written confirmation he had no information concerning Bohlen that Secretary Dulles had not seen. McCarthy's forces replied, again, Dulles had "overruled" McLeod. Taft stated flatly McLeod would not be asked to testify in opposition to the secretary of state. According to the *New York Times*, McCarthy offered no "specific charge" Bohlen "was either an associate of communism or a security risk," but he did link the nominee to Yalta and Hiss. Perhaps trying to shift the debate away from its salacious aspects, McCarthy said the nomination was "an inexcusable mistake" on the part of Dulles and Eisenhower.[216]

On 24 March, an anxious McLeod met with Hoover about the recent press blowup. Hoover observed McLeod "seemed to be quite depressed" about it, noting that "he had been on the point of resigning several times." McLeod told Hoover, in point of fact, that "he had made an evaluation of the FBI summary on Bohlen" and felt he "could not conscientiously" offer Bohlen a security clearance. Regarding the press coverage, McLeod said he was terribly embarrassed about it and pointed out he was being blamed for leaking the information to the press. Although he denied leaking anything to the press, McLeod did not deny leaking information to senators. McLeod even claimed Secretary Dulles opposed Bohlen's nomination "but had gone along with the appointment because of the President's personal desire and interest."[217]

The same day the McCarthy-Bridges-McCarran faction raised a fuss over Bohlen's loyalty and security clearance, Undersecretary of State Smith contacted FBI officials, telling them McLeod thought the FBI investigation of Bohlen "was a bad job and that several matters were not followed up." Smith could offer no specifics about McLeod's criticisms of the FBI, but he noted McLeod believed the bureau should give Bohlen a "lie-detector test." Significantly, Smith also alleged "on two different occasions" McLeod had "talked to either Senator McCarthy, or one of his investigators, prior to newspaper publicity re Dulles-McLeod controversy over issuance of security clearance for Bohlen." Smith believed the leak "was through McCarthy's office," and he said the "President wanted to fire McLeod for such a leak." Smith convinced the president, however, that firing McLeod was "bad tactics at that time." Hoover ordered his staff to follow this up "promptly."[218]

An official in the FBI Liaison Section named Quigley immediately

contacted Undersecretary Smith for further details. Smith said the day before the Dulles-McLeod issue appeared in the newspapers, he had spoken
with McLeod. According to Smith, "it was very evident" McLeod was upset, and when asked, McLeod told Smith after he had read the FBI Bohlen
summary "he could not in his own mind give Bohlen a security clearance."
Explaining his views to Smith, McLeod said his years working as an FBI
agent had given him a "sixth sense" about such matters. Smith replied that
"he and the Secretary and the White House were well satisfied" with the FBI
report, and they should not tell "the Director how an investigation should
be conducted." Smith also told Quigley he and McLeod did not go into
detail about what, exactly, McLeod found unsatisfactory in the summary,
but Smith did relate to McLeod that he saw "nothing of a derogatory nature which should prevent Bohlen being given a security clearance." Smith,
though, according to Quigley, "did admit that it [the summary] contained
the usual suspicions, which appear to be groundless."[219]

After the issue broke in the newspapers, because McCarthy had quoted
Dulles directly, Smith concluded the "only source who could have given
these quotes was McLeod inasmuch as McLeod and the Secretary were the
only ones present when these remarks were made." Smith also reported that
a member of the Senate Foreign Relations Committee told him "McLeod
contacted Senator Bridges when the Bohlen matter broke in the newspapers
and asked Bridges if he resigned . . . could he have his old job back." Smith
told Quigley he was offering "this information in the strictest confidence
for the Director and did not want it disseminated outside the Bureau under
any circumstances."[220]

On 26 March 1953, Hoover discussed the matter personally with Undersecretary Smith. Smith told Hoover he did not think much of McLeod's
criticism of the FBI because "McLeod had had a pretty bad day." Hoover
promised to have someone talk with McLeod "because if we missed anything
[in the FBI report] we would like to know it." Smith then asked whether
the FBI was conducting a "full field investigation on McLeod." Smith was
understandably concerned given McLeod's recent flap in the press and because McLeod had links to several senators. Referencing McLeod, Smith
said, "When a man gets in very close political liaison for a while his attitude
changes." Smith wondered if McLeod "had become very political minded."
Hoover agreed McLeod's actions "did not show loyalty."[221]

It was common for Hoover and other FBI officials to document their
opinions and recommendations by hand, right on FBI documents. Hoover

did just this with his memo recapitulating his conversation with Under-secretary Smith, but he never mentioned anything about McLeod leak-ing information. Instead, Hoover scrawled for his underlings, "I still want McLeod queried re defects in our Thayer investigation." Hoover, who had a long-established link to McCarthy dating from 1950 and probably did not mind McLeod's extra effort to undermine the Bohlen nomination, clearly had his own priorities.[222]

Undersecretary Smith allowed the FBI to interview McLeod about his views of the Bohlen summary. On 30 March, FBI Agent Quigley interviewed McLeod at the State Department, and McLeod said he wanted to tell "his side of the story."[223] McLeod said he had a conference with Undersecretary Smith the day after Dulles's Senate testimony. The two discussed whether the FBI summary was the result of a name-check or full-field investigation; Smith believed the former and McLeod the latter. McLeod advised Smith, however, not to raise the issue with Hoover because Dulles had already told the committee it was the summary of an in-depth investigation, and McLeod did not want to create "controversy with the Director" because he did not want to be so openly "critical of the FBI's investigation." Because the matter was now being raised, McLeod told Quigley his concerns.[224]

McLeod had three primary issues. First, he believed the FBI should have investigated other people who had referenced Bohlen for their jobs. Second, he thought the FBI should have interviewed people Bohlen had listed as ref-erences when he first joined the State Department in 1929. Finally, McLeod questioned whether Bohlen had actually graduated from St. Paul Prep School. The State Department Biographical Register indicated that Bohlen had graduated, whereas the State Department security file on Bohlen sug-gested "he had gotten into difficulty, had been investigated, and dismissed." This was an allusion to the Pearson allegation Hoover deleted from the FBI summary. Finally, McLeod emphasized to Quigley he "was considerably dis-turbed" that Undersecretary Smith had violated his confidence and talked to the FBI. McLeod thought Smith was "ratting" him out. He also wanted Quigley to tell Hoover he had "no intention of being critical" of the FBI and expressed his desire to talk with Hoover in person.[225]

When Hoover read Quigley's memo about the interview, he demanded to "know why we didn't pursue these 3 points." FBI Assistant Director Alex Rosen, head of the FBI Investigative and Accounting Division, subsequently studied and reported on the matter. Regarding the references issue—which brought up Nabokoff and his ex-wives, Brosse, Thayer, Offie, and others—Rosen concluded McLeod was "in error" regarding the reference issue on many counts. (Exactly which are not clear because of heavy redactions.) Regarding Bohlen's original 1920s job references, Rosen dismissed it as absurd to find and interview people from "a quarter of a century ago." Finally, about the prep school, Rosen wrote that ordinarily the FBI never looked into prep school records, but in this case FBI agents, in fact, had done so; they found Bohlen had graduated. In quick succession, Rosen shot down all of McLeod's criticisms.[226]

McLeod was also in hot water with his superiors at the State Department. On 16 March 1953, Secretary of State Dulles asked Hoover to update McLeod's background check dating from December 1949, when he joined Senator Styles Bridges's staff. FBI agents followed through with a "complete character and fitness" inquiry and loyalty investigation. They unearthed "nothing of a derogatory nature" regarding McLeod's "character or integrity." Hoover reported his findings to Dulles, the attorney general, and the White House. Thereafter, Hoover's good relationship with McLeod as head of State Department Security continued unabated—until McLeod left that position to become US ambassador to Ireland.[227]

Bohlen was confirmed by a vote of 74 to 13 as US ambassador to the Soviet Union on 27 March 1953.[228]

At times, Hoover did not hesitate to assist other government agencies when the issue was gays in government. Such was the case with the Federal Security Agency (FSA), a federal agency created in 1939 to help promote social and economic betterment by handling issues of education, health, youth, and social security—in 1953 it became part of the newly established Department of Health, Education, and Welfare (the forerunner of the Department of Health and Human Services). On 11 March 1953, SAC Hottel of the bureau's WFO reported that Blick told him FSA personnel officer Leo Miller ordered investigators within the Public Health Service to "stop taking statements regarding homosexuals or questioning them concerning their homosexual activities." Instead, according to Blick, Miller said he would handle these cases personally. Miller supposedly also directed, "In no case are the security men, even if they 'stumble onto a homo,' to take his or her resignation." Hoover's atypical reaction to this revelation was simply to comment that it "was a most unusual procedure." Hottel filed this information, moreover, in his field office Sex Deviates in Government File (121-14345).[229]

About a week later, Republican US Representative Fred Busbey of the House Appropriations Committee informed Hoover his committee learned the FSA had "run into a rather bad homosexual situation." Even more alarming, Busbey told Hoover a *Washington Post* reporter was investigating, and it was "urgent" that "they get this situation cleaned out as soon as possible." Busbey was so concerned he asked Hoover to assign FSA an FBI agent because, in his view, the matter was so delicate that FSA administrator Oveta Culp Hobby could not handle it. Busbey had spoken with Hobby and noted she "was very anxious to cooperate and would act quickly on any suggestion that would be worthwhile."[230]

Hoover asked Busbey whether Hobby had anybody in charge of FSA security, then relayed the story about Miller. Busbey said the FSA had no functioning security officer but pointed out its Public Health Service had one. To Busbey, though, nothing was working because Hobby "could not deal with anyone in her own office because of the setup [i.e., the multibranched nature of FSA] there." To that, Hoover said he would offer her names of ex-FBI agents he "could vouch for" to handle FSA security and, in particular, this situation. He also suggested sending an FBI agent to work with Public Health Service security to offer advice and help get FSA security procedures in order. Busbey then contacted Hobby about the matter, leading Hoover to dispatch FBI Inspector Leo Laughlin to interview Hobby.[231]

Officially classified as an FBI executive, Supervisor Laughlin headed the Liaison-Loyalty Branch of the FBI Domestic Intelligence Division. This division oversaw the Federal Loyalty Program and spearheaded liaisons with government agencies and senior officials. Laughlin interviewed Hobby, her administrative assistant, and insurance magnate Frank Walsh, who worked with the House Appropriations Committee. Laughlin reported Hobby "was almost frantic" because journalists were scrutinizing the FSA, and dealing with a situation of this kind "was something new to her." Hobby informed Laughlin that Walsh had "uncovered 35 to 40 homosexuals in FSA," but none of the security officers under the various FSA services were functioning properly. Laughlin, interestingly, advised Hobby the FBI did not investigate homosexuals "as such" but nevertheless told her "homosexuality can be the basis for removal from Federal Government Service." He outlined the "steps which could be taken to oust such people" and suggested she consult with the CSC for "compliance with existing required procedures." He suggested to Hobby, "If the allegations regarding homosexuality are well founded and, particularly, if they are backed up with a police or criminal record, one way of getting rid of an employee would be merely calling the employee in, confronting him with the evidence, and asking for his resignation." Recognizing her need to hire a qualified security officer, Hobby asked Laughlin whether the FBI could "detail" an FBI agent to FSA. He replied this was "impossible" but noted Hoover could suggest names of former FBI agents who might be interested in the job. Laughlin then told her about Miller and his views on the homosexual problem, to which she expressed amazement. She reiterated it only underscored the importance of hiring a "reliable security officer." The name of at least one allegedly gay employee was then raised at the meeting, that of Harold Dotterer, "in charge of the General Services Branch, FSA." FBI agents checked his name against FBI file indices, but nothing "derogatory" was found. FBI officials also promised to run a check of George Morse, the security officer at the Public Health Service, and William Mallard, the FSA security officer (they both passed).[232]

FBI Director Hoover was pleased with Laughlin's work in this matter as evidenced by his penning on a memo: "Well handled by Laughlin." (Indeed, Laughlin's success in handling the FSA matter contributed to his promotion as SAC of the WFO the following September.) Hoover then wrote to Hobby recommending four ex-FBI agents "you may wish to consider for the position of Security Officer in the Federal Security Agency." Hoover advised Hobby that all "had excellent records" and were "well qualified" for the job. He also said he would be pleased to continue helping her. The names he offered were J. Walter Yeagley, Robert Guerin, Burton Wiand, and Leonard Edwards.[233]

Within days Hobby's administrative assistant, Jack Beardwood, visited FBI headquarters to follow up. Aware that winning Hoover's cooperation meant not publicly embarrassing the FBI, Beardwood first apologized for a *Washington Post* story that suggested FSA had handed the bureau a case involving internal corruption at his agency—it involved somebody using government supplies to construct a summer home. The story, however, mentioned nothing about the so-called FSA homosexual problem. He then told FBI officials his agency had not yet contacted any of the ex-FBI agents Hoover suggested because the security position had yet to be finalized. Beardwood added, however, "that in view of the time element" and the need to hire a security officer "in a hurry," he was considering simply recommending to Hobby the security officer at the Public Health Service, Morse, or asking Yeagley, one of the ex-FBI agents from Hoover's list. Asked what the FBI thought of the Morse suggestion, FBI Inspector Laughlin, in line with standard FBI policy, refused to offer an official recommendation. FBI Director Hoover, however, in light of the *Post* story, ordered his staff "to be most careful in our dealings with FSA as they seem irresponsible and like to misuse [the] FBI name."[234]

On 31 March 1953, at the urging of White House Chief of Staff Adams, Hobby met with FBI Director Hoover and Philip Young, the newly installed head of the CSC. In the meeting, Hobby stressed how difficult it was to organize a security office because the FSA comprised six different branches. She also said certain members of Congress were pressuring her to elevate the security officer at the Public Health Service to head FSA security, but she was uncertain of that idea's efficacy. Given these problems, she said, Chief of Staff Adams recommended Hobby consult with Hoover.[235]

Hoover expressed sympathy for Hobby, saying her concerns with hiring a security officer internally were "well founded." He therefore recommended hiring an experienced outsider who, in his view, would be more effective and objective. Hoover, naturally, recommended hiring a former FBI agent.[236] Hobby agreed because the new security officer would be facing the "fact that FSA had several hundred or more sex deviates," which concerned her greatly. How the number escalated from forty homosexuals to several hundred is not clear. In any event, Hobby said she offered the job to ex-FBI agent Yeagley, but he was not interested. She then suggested to Hoover two new names. One was the deputy superintendent of the Washington, DC, police, due to retire, and the other a man who had connections to army intelligence. Hoover agreed to check their backgrounds, and he suggested yet another former FBI agent for the job, Daniel O'Connor.[237]

After his agents made their checks, Hoover passed the information on to Hobby. He also asked former FBI agent Yeagley why he turned down the job. He was not interested in the job, he told Hoover, because its salary was less than his current one at the Reconstruction Finance Corporation, and he feared being answerable to the FSA, which, in his opinion, "was in pretty bad shape." Yeagley told Hoover, though, he was embarrassed to reject the offer because the FBI director recommended him and because "Mrs. Hobby needs help very badly." Former FBI agent O'Connor also turned down the job because of its paltry salary ($10,800 annually). O'Connor believed, and relayed to Hoover, the FSA was "confused" and really did not understand the root of its problems.[238]

Hobby, her assistants, and FBI officials continued to go back and forth concerning name checks of potential candidates for the security position.[239]

Finally, in May 1953, now Secretary Hobby of the Department of Health, Education, and Welfare—into which the functions of the FSA were transferred—independently hired former FBI agent Frederick Schmidt, a man not on Hoover's list. Shortly afterward, Hobby began to hear rumors Hoover had fired Schmidt. She reached out to Hoover about it and told him Busbey was pressuring her department to "fire 600 people overnight [but] that it just cannot be done." Hoover advised Hobby, "for the purpose of window-dressing," against the mass firings because if anything emerged about an improper firing, legislators would only be encouraged to complain more. As Hobby's apparent confidant and advisor, Hoover promised to talk with Busbey. He straightened things out with the US representative, even making clear to him that although he had not recommended Schmidt, he was qualified for the FSA security job. Because Hobby failed to hire someone from Hoover's list, afterward he refused to offer any further personnel recommendations to Hobby even after she inquired about hiring an inspector in charge of her investigative staff. As with his relationships with ex-FBI agents, enjoying Hoover's cooperation came at a cost.[240]

FBI officials remained interested in Offie, both directly and indirectly, from the early 1950s through the early 1970s. The exact reason for their interest is difficult to ascertain given heavy redactions in his FBI file, but it is possible to glean a general idea of what piqued their curiosity. In March 1953, FBI agents tried to uncover details about Offie's sponsorship of an individual through the Displaced Persons Act.[241] This led Hoover, for unknown reasons, to order agents in late March and early April 1953 to interview a woman associated with Offie in both Germany and the United States. Hoover demanded "any information whatsoever" she might have "concerning Carmel Offie's homosexual activities." Hoover made explicitly clear, moreover, that the interviewing agent be aware that the "primary desire of the Bureau is to secure data concerning Offie and his homosexual activities." Exactly why Hoover was interested in compiling even more salacious details about Offie is not readily clear. The month before he had already reported such details about Offie in both the Thayer and Bohlen summaries. Two documents recording Hoover's interest in Offie's "homosexual activities" at that time, however, were copied to the FBI Sex Deviate Program File. It would seem, then, that Hoover had decided to individually target Offie now in an effort to torpedo his career.[242]

Hoover's curiosity over Offie's sponsorship of a displaced person then evolved into an interest in federal bureaucrats who admitted immigrants into the United States. This emerged after 5 July 1953, when journalist Pearson published in his column, the "Washington Merry-Go-Round," a piece about the raucous goings-on at a Senate immigration hearing considering President Eisenhower's immigration bill. Some senators wanted to "bottle up" the bill, which intended to admit some 240,000 Eastern European refugees and liberalize the 1950 Internal Security Act. What caught Hoover's fancy, however, was the statement by Air Force Major Don Reynolds—who only four months before had caught Hoover's attention as a possible homosexual—that the bureaucrats who processed immigrants were "loaded with Communists, sex deviates, and Jews." Reynolds even listed the names of these individuals for the committee. In response, FBI officials forwarded unspecified information from FBI files to the CSC via the Sex Deviates Program.[243]

In May 1953, FBI officials made an effort to win access to State Department records to gather even more data about Offie. McLeod responded by providing Hoover a summary of the information in his files rather than offering the files themselves. Upon receipt of the summary, however, FBI Assistant Director Belmont observed it contained nothing "concerning Offie's sex deviate activities not previously available in Bureau files." Nevertheless, the summary also was incorporated into the Sex Deviates File.[244]

Over time, the Eisenhower White House, for unknown reasons, became interested in the activities of Lovestone, linked to Offie. This interest, in part, led FBI officials to continue their surveillance and investigations into Offie's activities, but none of this information was reported to the White House. FBI agents tried continuously to develop derogatory information about Offie, including the allegation that he had violated the White Slave Traffic Act—the law pertaining to interstate prostitution rings. Some of the information FBI agents developed here, yet again, was added to the FBI Sex Deviates File.[245]

In the midst of this intensive monitoring of Offie—who by this point had moved to a farm in rural Virginia—he solicited the FBI for help. During the winter of 1954, Offie was the victim of repeated burglaries at his farm. The thieves stole his valuables but were mostly interested in the contents of his liquor cabinet. He changed the locks on his doors several times, but this failed to deter his frequent prowlers, who simply removed a door from its hinges. At this point he telephoned the FBI for advice and help. He asked if FBI officials could either refer him to a private detective agency or have an FBI agent lift footprints and fingerprints over a single weekend. Given Hoover's disdain for Offie and repeated attempts to undermine him, Hoover demanded that "this character" not be given "any advice or counsels." To Hoover, Offie did not deserve any help with his burglary problem because he "is a stinker in his own right."[246] It should be noted Hoover had a history of assisting those in his good standing: in 1943 he willingly helped Interior Secretary Harold Ickes discover who was stealing chicken eggs from the Ickes' farm.[247]

Vandenberg was not the only gay Eisenhower staffer isolated from any association with the president. On the night of 12 April 1957, Blick's morals squad arrested a White House staffer at GWU who had sexually solicited one of its undercover officers. While in jail, a fellow White House staffer who somehow heard of the arrest telephoned his arrested friend in jail. Because being a gay federal employee was considered a security breach, the police eventually turned the arrested man over to the Secret Service and revealed the telephone call he had received. The Secret Service subsequently investigated the matter, including polygraphing the man arrested. This led Secret Service agents to discover two other White House staffers "involved in homosexual activities." All three worked in the White House correspondence office, and all were promptly asked to resign. They did so immediately.[248]

This incident led Eisenhower staff secretary and defense liaison officer General Andrew Goodpaster to question whether there were any other gay White House staffers and, because all three had passed FBI background checks, whether the "broad field of security has been breached." The White House, therefore, asked the FBI to investigate a possible security breach and determine whether there were other gays in the administration. Hoover asked for access to Secret Service records and directed FBI Assistant Director Belmont to "take immediate action."[249]

A couple of days later, when talking with Goodpaster, Hoover took pains to point out to him various details in the "original [FBI] investigative reports of these three individuals" that cast aspersions on their characters. Hoover was defending the original FBI background checks and centering blame for the men being hired elsewhere. Hoover suggested Goodpaster might personally "look into the background of these three cases since they had gotten appointed, and this might be something to keep in mind for future cases."

Hoover then summarized for Goodpaster what the FBI had originally un-earthed about the men, including the fact that one man's mother had signed a Communist Party nominating petition in 1946. Hoover also described one of the men, using gay stereotypes and gendered language, as "shy, blush-ing, and bashful," a "muddleheaded type of idealist," and a "soft ideological thinker who could never be classified as a conservative" and hence work in the White House. Another of the three, Hoover pointed out, had been described as not suitable for work dealing with the public "due to [his] lack of maturity, responsibility and political judgement." Even worse, one of the three had previously "been hospitalized for ten months while in the army due to psychoneurosis" and had even "been characterized as egotistical." As icing on his defensive cake, again alluding to the origins of one of the men's homosexuality, Hoover took pains to point out that his "father and brothers have arrest records, which include arrests for nonsupport, reckless driving, drunk and disorderly, and assault and battery of a minor." Worse still, "his sister has two illegitimate children."[250]

The incident with the three gay White House staffers also led Hoover to reveal to White House officials another homosexual matter FBI agents were investigating involving journalist Joseph Alsop. Hoover had already informed the attorney general and his deputy about it, but because one of the three fired staffers admitted to seeing information related to Alsop, he believed it was time to bring White House Chief of Staff Adams into the loop.[251]

Joseph Alsop and his brother Stewart were well-connected journalists in Washington, DC. Sons of privilege related to the Roosevelts, the Alsops attended the Groton School, then went on to Ivy League universities; Joseph attended Harvard and Stewart went to Yale. Both brothers served in the Second World War, though Stewart had joined the British Army because the US Armed Forces rejected him given his blood pressure problems. After the war the brothers began working together as journalists, writing a col-umn called the "Capital Parade," then later "Matter of Fact." Stewart lived in Washington, DC, and covered domestic politics, and Joseph traveled the world covering foreign affairs.[252]

While Joseph Alsop was in Moscow to interview First Secretary of the Soviet Communist Party Nikita Khrushchev, he found himself in trouble. After having experienced several "homosexual invitations" during his trip, while dining in a Moscow restaurant on 17 February 1957, Alsop, who was gay, met a young man who told Alsop he was also gay—"an athletic blonde, pleasant-faced, pleasant-mannered fellow"—and became interested in him. Following dinner Alsop accompanied the man to his hotel room for an hour, after which the man invited him to return the next day. Alsop did just this, expecting a sexual encounter, when undercover KGB officers burst into the room and arrested him. The entire incident, in fact, was a KGB setup all along, designed to leverage the prominent US journalist into cooperating with Soviet intelligence. Interrogated for hours, Alsop was only permitted to leave after he told the KGB officers he was expected for dinner at the US Embassy. Not wanting to arouse official US suspicion, they let him go but arranged to meet Alsop, again, the next day.[253]

Meeting with him again, the KGB officers told Alsop they wanted his help in the name of peace. Continuing their pressure tactics, the KGB agents met him again in Leningrad, and at this point Alsop worried about what the KGB might do to him. He eventually contacted a friend at the US Embassy who then informed Ambassador Bohlen about the situation. To get Alsop away from the KGB officers, Bohlen summoned him to the embassy on false pretenses, then spirited the journalist out of the country. Alsop traveled to Paris, where a CIA officer met and debriefed the journalist. Alsop, moreover, refused to hide the fact that he was gay. He even willingly signed a detailed statement with full knowledge both the CIA and FBI directors would read it.[254]

Back in Washington, DC, CIA Director Allen Dulles notified his brother, Secretary of State John Foster Dulles, and FBI Director Hoover about the Alsop situation. In typical Hoover fashion, he ordered the compilation of a memorandum detailing FBI information about both Alsop brothers. As prominent journalists with connections among the Washington, DC, elite, the Alsops were long an interest of FBI officials.[255] At the time, incidentally, FBI officials were already suggesting possible prosecution of the brothers for allegedly publishing information about a classified National Security Council directive. FBI agents failed to interview Joseph Alsop about it because he was in Moscow at the time, where he found himself in altogether different trouble.[256]

To FBI officials, moreover, stories about the Alsops's sexual preferences were nothing new. Dating from May 1954, FBI agents began to hear rumors that both Alsop brothers were "queers" and even that "their homosexual activities" got them into trouble in South America.[257] Three months after this, FBI officials then learned from a source in the State Department, through their Liaison Section, that Joseph Alsop was gay. The FBI State Department contact (McLeod) decided to offer the information to the FBI because "Alsop has numerous highly placed contacts within the State Department and for this reason [name deleted but McLeod] has not disseminated this information within the State Department." The State Department's informant, however, was a gay former Foreign Service officer who had confessed his sexuality, then resigned his post. He continued to feed security officers at the State Department information "regarding other employees," leading to his designation as a "reliable" source.[258]

The confidential State Department source was James S. Waddington, an administrative/personnel officer in Frankfurt, Germany, who in July 1954 reported he had met Alsop while stationed in Germany either during 1951 or 1952. Alsop was visiting somebody there whose name is redacted in FBI documents. Alsop allegedly asked Waddington to "obtain for him the services of a 'warmer' (homosexual)." (The term Alsop is supposed to have used was an English derivation of a German term for a gay man: *warmer bruder* [hot brother].) Waddington failed to locate one, however.[259] So instead, "Waddington finally engaged in a homosexual experience with Joe Alsop to satisfy Alsop's desires."[260] But this was not all. Also in May 1954, a source in the Washington, DC, Metropolitan Police Department reported to FBI officials that one of its gay informants told them the "Alsop brothers were homosexuals." Even more, the source claimed to have seen one of the Alsops in bed with Vandenberg, and the two "were members of a group of homosexuals."[261]

FBI Director Hoover and CIA Director Dulles kept in close contact about Joseph Alsop. Both pledged to keep each other informed with developments on their respective sides of the Alsop case. Dulles promised to tell Hoover about any further contacts Alsop had with Soviet officials, and Hoover promised to keep Dulles informed if the FBI disseminated any information about Alsop while he was still in Europe. In one example, Dulles forwarded a report to Hoover on the CIA interview with Alsop, in which the journalist freely admitted to being an "incurable homosexual since boyhood" and having kept this fact secret. Sadly reflecting 1950s sexual self-loathing, Alsop described his sexuality thus, "If I do no harm to anyone, if I am no trouble to anyone, I should not be too much troubled myself." Alternatively, Hoover expressed concern to Dulles that Alsop refused to name other gays, especially in Washington, DC, and asked him to report any of this should Alsop name names, "particularly any which may be in Government circles." Hoover's official interest centered on whether Alsop, or those connected to him, could be blackmailed by Soviet agents; his real interest, though, was in rooting out undesirable gays from government. This was ironic, too, because by outing himself Alsop believed he had made the blackmail issue moot. Later, after the KGB issue had faded, and as Alsop began to critique the Eisenhower administration's handling of foreign affairs, internal discussions about Alsop's Moscow incident continued, including with the chair of the Joint Chiefs of Staff considering informing Alsop's publishers about it. Whether this happened, we do not know. The Alsop brothers' syndicated column did stop around this time in 1958, however. Clearly, though, in the heat of the Lavender Scare, even cooperating with the federal government in matters involving one's sexuality provided no assurances.[262]

The preceding constitutes how Hoover's FBI systematically investigated and sought to destroy the careers of individuals who were gay, or presumed to be gay, in the federal government at the height of the Lavender Scare. One or several FBI targets, unsurprisingly, led FBI agents to others who were then targeted for elimination. It must be kept in mind, however, that there were many other ordinary gays and lesbians who fell victim to internal security bureaucrats—whether at the State Department, FBI, or CSC—and who subsequently lost their careers and in some instances had their lives ruined. Documenting the nature and scope of these investigations is exceedingly difficult (if not impossible) given that historians must rely upon FOIA requests to win access to pertinent FBI files. Without knowing precisely who was targeted, and then establishing whether he or she is deceased, it is nearly impossible to reconstruct the complete history of FBI officials' efforts. This is especially problematic because the FBI Sex Deviates Program File was destroyed in the late 1970s.

We can get some vague idea as to how many gays and lesbians were dismissed from government employment during the Lavender Scare, but given the stigma of homosexuality in the 1950s and the reluctance of dismissed persons to admit why they were fired, we may never know an exact number. One historian has estimated that about 600 federal workers were fired for being gay.[263] During the year 1953—when Thayer was fired, Offie denied a job, and Bohlen's sexuality questioned—534 employees of the State Department were dismissed for "security" rather than "loyalty" reasons. The difference is significant because so-called security risks included alcoholics, people with financial difficulties, or homosexuals. It is probably safe to assume that many, if not most, of these were gay, simply given the times. During the following year, 1954, officials of the Commerce Department dismissed 132 "security risks." That year, President Eisenhower also cited the total number of "security risks" dismissed as 2,200. How many of these were gay is impossible to determine, and how many were subjects of FBI investigation is not knowable. Given how FBI officials pursued influential gays, where they were often circumspect in their efforts, it would seem their efforts against ordinary gays and lesbians would have been easy pickings.[264] There was one unexpected effect of all of this, however. Some brave gay men and women in light of the repression of the Lavender Scare began to organize themselves in search of equality. Unfortunately, they also became targets of FBI repression.

CHAPTER 5

"Take This Crowd On and Make Them 'Put Up or Shut Up'"

The FBI; the Mattachine Society; ONE, Inc.; and the Daughters of Bilitis

On 26 January 1956, Unit Chief Milton Jones of the Crime Records Division, the part of the Federal Bureau of Investigation (FBI) responsible for maintaining the Sex Deviates File, forwarded a memo to his superior, Assistant Director Louis Nichols, describing the content of a gay magazine in his possession. The magazine was the November 1955 issue of *ONE*, which contained a story by David Freeman—the pseudonym of Mattachine cofounder and radical homophile activist Chuck Rowland—that not only claimed gays worked in the FBI but suggested FBI Director J. Edgar Hoover, himself, was a closeted homosexual.[1]

Having intensively investigated both Mattachine and ONE, Inc., for the previous three years but unearthing nothing to indicate either group was an internal security threat, FBI agents had restricted themselves to monitoring the groups' publications. Now, with a controversial and derogatory public charge made concerning the bureau and its director, FBI officials, in the midst of the Lavender Scare, found themselves in a precarious position. Should they respond to the public charge, or should they leave it alone?

Jones did not think the matter worth pursuing. He suggested to Assistant Director Nichols that *ONE* "should not be dignified" with an FBI response. When Associate Director Clyde Tolson, according to popular rumor Hoover's secret lover, read Jones's suggestion, he pointedly disagreed. Taking an entirely different tactic, Tolson, always in the forefront in protecting Hoover's carefully crafted public image, argued instead that "we should take this crowd on and make them 'put up or shut up.'" (Tolson's use of "put up or shut up" is interesting because it was a common refrain of Hoover's he typically scribbled in the margins of FBI documents whenever upset.) When Hoover was made aware of Tolson's opinion, moreover, the

FBI director agreed with it. FBI agents thereafter targeted not only the offending *ONE* but the entire homophile movement in a concerted effort to silence its members.[2]

In many ways the Second World War gave rise to the homophile movement of the 1950s and 1960s. The mass mobilization of millions of young men and women from across the country who then found themselves in intimate, same-sex environments led those who were gay to realize they were not alone. Pursuing same-sex relationships while at war, many of these people refused to resume their previously isolated lives in morally repressive and distant areas of the country, so, instead, they relocated to large urban areas, especially those on the country's coasts. There, though still facing serious social restrictions, they could nevertheless experience some measure of a gay identity by socializing in gay bars, using pseudonyms to conceal and protect their identities and hence their jobs, reading emerging gay and lesbian literature, and joining nascent gay and lesbian social organizations such as the Veterans Benevolent Association in New York or the Knights of the Clock in Los Angeles.[3]

These developments, in conjunction with the rise of another in a series of sex-crime panics between 1947 and 1955, undoubtedly contributed to widespread and irrational fears among some segments of the population that perceived a threat from the gay and lesbian community. The resultant Lavender Scare brought increased raids on gay bars, military discharges of gays and lesbians, government and private-sector purges of gays and lesbians from jobs, and the enactment of state and municipal sexual psychopath laws, all of which made living an openly gay life seemingly impossible. Regardless of these fast-evolving impediments, and indeed because of them, some brave individuals nevertheless organized themselves in an attempt to effect positive change in the face of negative retribution.[4]

Amid these developments, the first significant US gay rights group formed in Los Angeles, California, in 1950. The effort, moreover, had a decidedly left-wing bent: the core founding members included former Communist Party members Harry Hay, Chuck Rowland, and Bob Hull. Given their shared experiences in radical politics and contemporary national developments, these highly motivated, politically minded men believed the time was right for a genuine effort at gay equality. As Rowland later reflected on the idealism of the moment, "We had just won the war. We had rid the world of fascism, except in Spain. We came back, and we were going to save the world."[5]

Most significant among the core founders was Hay. He was born on 7 April 1912 in Worthing, England, to upper-middle-class parents whose international work in mining made them wealthy. Traveling extensively, the Hays eventually settled in California, where as a child Harry thereafter grew up. Because his mother was born in Arizona, and his father was a naturalized citizen from New Zealand, even though born in England, Hay was a natural-born US citizen. (Questions over Hay's citizenship, however, would concern FBI officials at a later date.) Hay's childhood was one familiar to millions of gay people. Sometime during his teenage years he began to realize he had same-sex attraction. Concurrently, while he was working on a family farm, the hired hands there introduced him to socialism. In both respects, sexually and politically, Hay's life thereafter, significantly, would never be the same again.[6] After high school Hay attended Stanford University, where he was exposed to myriad new activities, including what would become a lifelong passion, drama. Hay's time at Stanford was short-lived, however. After a sudden illness, he was forced to drop out. He then moved to Los Angeles and pursued his acting interests while continuing to explore his sexuality, having affairs with various actors until one—Will Greer, who later famously played Grandpa Walton on television—introduced him to the Communist Party. It was not long before Hay became an active party member. The Communist Party, however, was intolerant of homosexuality, and Hay's communist friends encouraged him to distance himself from his sexual feelings and other gays.[7] Acceding to their advice but clearly still struggling with his own sexual identity, in 1938 he met a young party member named Anita Platky.[8] That same year Hay married her and formally joined the party. That Hay married was unsurprising. Many gay men of his era married women; they did so either because social and familial pressures demanded their betrothals or because it was a convenient way of masking one's true sexuality and fitting in. Years later, after Hay divorced his wife, she alluded to his disinterest in her but his love of leftist politics when she quipped, "You didn't marry me—you married the Communist Party."[9]

Although Hay was consumed with leftist politics during his marriage, he was also coming to terms with his homosexuality and considering that along political lines. No doubt because of his politics and organizing, in 1948 he began to ponder organizing gays. Hay was involved in presidential politics as a supporter of Henry Wallace's progressive campaign for the White House, and after drinking copious amounts of beer he resolved briefly with others to form an openly gay group called "Bachelors for Wallace." Enamored with the idea, Hay subsequently jotted down his ideas, but in subsequent days his now-sober compatriots unsurprisingly developed cold feet. His Bachelors for Wallace idea remained just that—a fleeting and fanciful idea.[10]

Beyond politics in 1948, Hay pursued other interests, including teaching a music history class at the People's Educational Center. Over subsequent years he continued to think about organizing a gay rights group until in 1950 he put those ideas to paper, again, and shared them with friend and fellow communist Hull, a student in his music class. When an excited Hull subsequently showed his former lover, now roommate, and fellow communist Rowland what Hay had written, it excited the activist and organizer in Rowland. "My God, I could have written this myself!" Rowland blurted out. In short order, in November of 1950 in the Silver Lake District of Los Angeles, where Hay resided, the men met to discuss the proposal. Also present were Hay's boyfriend, Rudi Gernreich, and Dale Jennings, a writer and longtime activist who had dared to champion interned Japanese Americans during the war. Over several meetings the men refined their ideas, significantly modeling their organization after the Communist Party, of which at least three of them had been members. Part of that involved devising a theoretical basis to underpin the organization because, as Rowland put it, "having been a Communist, you've got to work with a theory." Hay suggested basing it upon the idea that gays were an "oppressed cultural minority." The others agreed.[11]

They decided to call their group the Mattachine Foundation. Hay derived the name "Mattachine" from his interest in music and performance history. He learned that members of an obscure medieval French masque group had successfully, in public, satirized the French aristocracy by concealing their faces. This was a brave act, indeed, given the ruthless and repressive tendencies of the French aristocracy. Hay believed the name aptly fit gay men in the 1950s because they were forced to conceal themselves from society for fear of violent retribution and attack.[12] Additionally, Hay and company structured their group after the Freemasons, believing their (and the communists') secretive structure would sustain and protect members at a time of rabid homophobia. From the communists the men borrowed the party's secretive cell structure, and from the Freemasons they adopted the series of "orders," with the founding members serving as anonymous members of the so-called Fifth Order. Members of the four lower orders and various Mattachine informal discussion groups similarly remained anonymous, employing pseudonyms.[13] The Mattachine Foundation formalized and incorporated its mission by 1951, stating three purposes: to unite gays both among themselves and with heterosexual society, to educate the public about homosexuality, and to engage in activist politics.[14]

Regardless of these goals, the political context in which Mattachine appeared was crucial to its development. Paralleling Mattachine's evolution was the rise of McCarthyism and the intensification of the Lavender Scare. On 9 February 1950 Joseph McCarthy delivered his infamous Wheeling speech about "205 known Communists" allegedly inhabiting the State Department, a speech that propelled the junior senator from Wisconsin into the limelight and initiated the witch hunt that took on his name. Eleven days later on the floor of the Senate McCarthy furthered his claims but also singled out two cases in which he conflated communism with homosexuality. McCarthy had unwittingly focused public scrutiny on gays and, in the midst of a new sex-crime panic, unwittingly linked them to the exploding communists-in-government issue. This link quickly took on a life of its own, popularizing the Lavender Scare, which over subsequent years and decades only intensified and long outlived McCarthyism. It was no less than the advent of McCarthyism and the simultaneous Lavender Scare, then, that Mattachine faced as it organized.[15]

As a new organization, Mattachine's first challenge was not McCarthyism but a tangle in which Jennings found himself during March 1952. Jennings was arrested and jailed in a Los Angeles police entrapment scheme. According to Jennings's account, after visiting a public restroom, he was followed home by what he described as a "big, rough-looking character." Jennings tried but failed to dissuade the man from following him. When he finally arrived home, according to Jennings, the man forced his way into Jennings's house, where he then made repeated sexual advances. Jennings claimed to express disinterest, but the man grabbed Jennings's hand and forced it down the front of his trousers. Afterward he identified himself as a Los Angeles vice detective, handcuffed Jennings, and arrested him for violating section 647.5 of the state's penal code: lewd vagrancy.[16]

Jennings spent the night in jail, and the following day Hay bailed him out. Typically in these circumstances during the 1950s, most men never dared challenge this type of charge in open court for fear of public exposure, loss of employment, and social stigmatization. Most men either quickly admitted guilt and paid a fine, or more typically posted, then forfeited, collateral, anxious to move beyond the event (as Carmel Offie and others had done). Jennings, however, resisted this typical route. Instead, and audaciously for the time, he decided to "make a big thing out of this" by freely admitting to a judge he was gay and innocent of lewd conduct.[17] Because Jennings was a founding member, the leaders of Mattachine hastily called an emergency meeting. Taking Jennings's lead, they decided to use his arrest to publicize how gays were routinely subjected to police entrapment.[18]

Regardless of its activist desire to expose corrupt police practices, Mattachine's leadership was unwilling to expose members by publicly leading the campaign. To insulate themselves, they created an ancillary organization, the Citizens' Committee to Outlaw Entrapment, to spearhead the public relations effort. They printed leaflets that Mattachine members then distributed across Los Angeles in multiple venues, from public restrooms and beaches to various shops in different locations. The campaign was successful inasmuch as the committee received positive feedback in the form of mail from concerned citizens, some of whom offered money to defer the cost of Jennings's legal defense.[19]

Jennings then hired a lawyer, George Shibley—a heterosexual man not afraid to tackle such a controversial and stigmatizing case—and the two appeared before Judge Hunt in municipal court in July. Shibley refuted the charges, boldly claiming that "the only pervert in this courtroom is the arresting officer." Thanks to one member, the jury was unable to return a unanimous verdict of not guilty. The result was a hung jury, but because the district attorney was unwilling to retry the case, Jennings and Mattachine effectively had at hand their first victory for gay rights.[20]

Feeling jubilant and motivated, Mattachine members publicized their victory, this time explicitly asking for money to protect other victims of entrapment. Mattachine members also began to lobby those running for various political offices, such as those running for mayor, Los Angeles city council, and the board of supervisors, in an attempt to elicit their positions on police targeting of gays. The resulting publicity caused Mattachine's formal membership to grow from eighteen members to thirty, a significant number given the staunch homophobia of the era. Beyond an increase in formal membership, new Mattachine informal discussion groups also organized because established ones were reportedly flooded with attendees. The Jennings arrest and publicity, significantly, also brought into Mattachine's ranks certain individuals, some of whom in subsequent years assumed various leadership roles in the homophile movement.[21]

Among these new members were Jim Kepner, Kenneth Burns, and W. Dorr Legg. Kepner was a socialist, eventual Communist Party member, science fiction fan, and future editor of *ONE* magazine who disliked the secrecy of Mattachine yet sympathized with the idea of fighting for equality.[22] Kenneth Burns was an engineer who had once studied to be an Episcopal priest and who believed gays should slowly integrate into society to achieve acceptance. Eventually, he would rise to lead the Mattachine Society (the name change is discussed below).[23] W. Dorr Legg, a native of Michigan who had a penchant for African American lovers and advocated for racial equality, was formerly a professor of landscape architecture in Oregon before moving to Los Angeles in 1952, where he joined first the Knights of the Clock and then Mattachine.[24]

With these developments, Mattachine emerged into the public sphere, ultimately to become the subject of an intensive FBI investigation. Public scrutiny focused on the group in March 1953 after Paul Coates, a *Los Angeles Mirror* reporter and sometime TV personality renowned for his sensational exposé interviews, obtained copies of Mattachine's lobbying questionnaires, then published an article questioning the legitimacy of the group. Coates singled out Mattachine's lawyer, Fred Snider, whom he described as an "unfriendly witness at the Un-American Activities Committee [HUAC] hearings." More to the point, though, because the State Department had concluded gays were "bad security risks," Coates raised the specter of Mattachine being a potentially dangerous group. In Coates's view, because gays were a "scorned part of the community" he found it understandable that they would band together for "protection." Yet Coates suggested that by doing so, under the right conditions (such as the recent Lavender Scare), "they might swing tremendous political power." Feeding on popular cold war–era fears and biases about gays as somehow weak and liable to blackmail, Coates speculated that a "well-trained subversive could move in and forge that power into a dangerous political weapon."[25]

This sudden public focus energized by McCarthyite fears and the Lavender Scare, in conjunction with the sudden growth of the Mattachine's membership list, led some members to tremble over the potential of a punitive and public government reaction. Amplifying their fears, ironically enough, was the secretive architecture of their organization—a measure intended to protect them. Most members, for example, had no idea who had even founded or led the group. This led a number of bellicose and motivated Mattachine members, mainly from the San Francisco area, to lead an insurgency to change the nature of the organization. Mattachine member Hal Call, for example, a war veteran and journalist who joined a discussion group in Berkeley during 1953, was concerned with public charges conflating homosexuality and communism. "We wanted to see Mattachine grow and spread," he later commented, "and we didn't think that this could be done as long as Mattachine was a secret organization." Call knew, however, that going public would inevitably draw FBI attention, yet he was confident because "before we went public we wanted to make sure that we didn't have a person in our midst who could be revealed as a Communist and disgrace us all." Call had heard rumors that some of Mattachine's leaders were communists or had communist connections. "They had to go," he said. "Mattachine had to be free of Communists."[26]

Mattachine's founders worried about the future of the organization and similarly feared a public backlash, especially after some members demanded more openness and inquired about the founders' identities. This led the leadership to convene a general meeting in April to reconsider the nature of the organization and draft a constitution. The meeting was heated because of an ideological battle between two camps. On the one hand the founding members—Hay, Rowland, and Hull—advocated the view of gays as a repressed minority encompassing a unique culture and had set up Mattachine's secretive hierarchy for that very reason. On the other hand were the stalwart insurgents such as Burns, Call, Don Lucas, David Finn, and Gerard Brissette, who regarded gays as no different from average people except in their sexuality and who, given public charges, sought a more transparent organization. The latter group, moreover, was deeply concerned with the idea of gays as security risks especially because Mattachine, itself, was being labeled publicly a potentially subversive organization—as evidenced in the Coates article. Burns led the insurgents, but no real progress was made at the April meeting, requiring a second one the following month.[27]

During the May meeting, the debate between the two camps was heated and bitter. Call demanded the group write into its constitution a provision asserting its opposition to subversiveness. Finn, an irascible friend of Call's and fervent anticommunist, charged that Mattachine had been infiltrated by communists. Weary of the debate, Mattachine's founders decided quietly to relinquish their leadership positions, but the debate between the two factions continued nevertheless.[28] At a subsequent November general meeting, the insurgents having taken over and consolidated their leadership positions, one last fight revealed the polarity and bitterness of the times. The two camps argued over revising the Mattachine constitution preamble, leading Finn to cut off Rowland in his denunciation of the revision. Angered and anxious to silence continued opposition, Finn proclaimed to the group "that he had been closely associated with the FBI for many years and would consider it his duty to report the activities of the Convention" if it did not "reaffirm" Mattachine's newly adopted principles.[29] With this threat the insurgents silenced further opposition and finalized their reorganization of the group, including renaming it the Mattachine Society, with Burns as its new leader. The overall significance of the meetings was that Mattachine had largely dropped its veil of secrecy to become a more transparent organization, still advocating gay rights and acceptance but with a markedly different philosophical bent.

Deeply disenchanted with these developments, some members—such as Rowland, Kepner, Jennings, and Legg—left Mattachine to work with the recently founded ONE, Inc. Although little experienced with publishing, ONE, Inc. was, in fact, the first to publish a homophile magazine, also called *ONE*. Mattachine members disillusioned by that group's ceaseless squabbling formed the new organization in late 1952. The name of the organization and magazine derived from two sources. The first came from the Scottish essayist Thomas Carlyle's famous stanza, "a mystic bond of brotherhood makes all men one." The other was a more mundane but popular Second World War joke involving confused soldiers counting off in the ranks, asking, "Are you one?" The punchline was the effeminate reply, "Why yes, are you?" First led by Martin Block, Don Slater, and Jennings, the group maintained an activist, gay rights bent and focused boldly on controversial issues such as police entrapment, the conflation of communism and subversion with homosexuality, and even gay marriage. *ONE*, however, while having some ties to Mattachine, was nevertheless independent of it and, in its work—publishing on average 3,000 to 5,000 copies of the magazine per month—was less cautious and more firebrand than the reformatted Mattachine Society.[30]

The FBI surveillance of both Mattachine and *ONE* began at this moment. Shortly following publication of the Coates article in the *Los Angeles Mirror,*

FBI agents from the Los Angeles Field Office liaised with an informant who offered them elaboration on the newspaper article. The informant, however, merely reiterated the information in the article about Mattachine's questionnaire and its post office box, which Coates had identified. The Los Angeles special agent in charge (SAC), moreover, delayed reporting any of this to headquarters until May 1953, when another FBI informer—described as a "sex deviate"—provided the San Diego Field Office a copy of the April 1953 issue of *ONE* magazine. What interested FBI officials in this specific issue was the article "Are You Now or Have You Ever Been a Homosexual?" The article, which focused on the popular issue of loyalty, made the claim FBI agents had looked into the personal lives of a West Coast airline's employees and had found a large number of homosexuals among them. An FBI agent then supposedly questioned these individuals about their sexuality while confronting them with their signed loyalty oaths, leading to many being fired. To the SAC of the San Diego office, the content of the publication indicated "that the writer of the article at least is pro-communist." Reflecting the paucity of FBI information about the group, moreover, FBI agents considered *ONE*—which they described as "written for Sex Deviates"—a publication of the Mattachine Society, which, in reality, it was not.[31]

The bureau's interest resulted in an internal security investigation—under the FBI program code-named COMINFIL—of both ONE, Inc., and the Mattachine Society on the assumption that the two were linked and infiltrated by communists. Hoover ordered FBI field offices on the West Coast to investigate the two thoroughly and report to headquarters all information. To learn more about their targets, FBI agents scoured the records of the Los Angeles Post Office to determine who had rented a post office box for ONE, Inc. They also consulted the Los Angeles County clerk's office to examine the group's articles of incorporation, which detailed the magazine's claimed purpose; agents learned it was to "publish and disseminate a magazine dealing primarily with homosexuality from the scientific, historical, and critical point of view and to aid in the social integration and rehabilitation of the sexual variant." The agents also took note of the group's directors—Block, Jennings, and Tony Reyes—and they reported the notary of the articles of incorporation, Mattachine lawyer Snider. Beyond these sources, in their efforts to develop further intelligence, FBI agents also consulted the Retail Merchants Credit Association, the Los Angeles Police Department, and the Los Angeles County Sheriff's Office, all to develop further information on those associated with the magazine. The agents learned only that Jennings was mentioned in a "West Coast Communist newspaper" during the summer of 1948.[32]

A week later, on 14 July, the San Francisco Field Office reported to Hoover information originating from three informants regarding the origins and expansion on the West Coast of the Mattachine Society. More specifically, the SAC in San Francisco focused on the leader of Mattachine's San Francisco "region"—probably Brissette—whom he described as a professor at Berkeley but someone the university refused employment in 1950 for his refusal to sign a loyalty oath.[33] From information originating with an informant, the agent described the group as holding weekly meetings in which between thirty and thirty-six "homosexuals" participated. The informant reported, moreover, that "nothing subversive was discussed and very little was accomplished because the homosexuals became too involved in discussing their own problems of adjustment to the world about them."[34]

The SAC also informed Hoover that a female informant attended and reported on one specific meeting, on the night of 27 May 1953, at an apartment on Larkin Street involving thirty-two people, two of whom were members of the military. (The female informant pointedly noted that "she was the only person who was not a homosexual.") One attendee, she observed, "was a uniformed Coast Guardsman from Government Island, Alameda," and another was a marine but in civilian clothing. The SAC explained to Hoover he had not forwarded this information to military officials because the informant was unable to identify them. Irked by this decision, Hoover overruled the San Francisco SAC, ordering him to forward the information to both the Coast Guard and Marine Corps. The SAC at that field office immediately complied, adhering to the Sex Deviates Program procedure.[35]

The female and two other informants provided further information to FBI agents who then forwarded it to Hoover. The female informant warned that Mattachine members believed the "FBI would eventually investigate them," which led the group to make plans to publicize themselves in an effort to offset any negative backlash. This informant also gave FBI agents a list of Mattachine members in the San Francisco branch, a copy of the Mattachine Society's constitution, and a "schedule of the Oakland-Berkeley meetings and activities." Another male informant, described as "of unknown reliability but who was in a position to know," offered agents "substantially the same information" as the female informant but reported that Mattachine had existed "for a long while." He also reported that "there was a movement afoot in Los Angeles to break away from the Mattachine

Foundation and establish the Mattachine Society." The reason given for the desired break was that some members suspected two unnamed Mattachine leaders were procommunist. The informant further reported that Mattachine "was definitely not subversive" but was devoted to education and ending discrimination. The informant, significantly, told FBI agents "he would be glad to cooperate with the FBI in the future."[36]

This informant was Mattachine member and San Francisco insurgent Finn, who by his own account met with two FBI agents in San Francisco following Mattachine's 23–24 May 1953 convention. In an effort to convince FBI agents Mattachine was working to purge itself of communists, he gave them a copy of the group's constitution and described his and other members' anticommunist efforts. Although the FBI report detailing this incident does not use names of informants but instead (redacted) symbol numbers (an FBI code comprising a letter followed by a numeral, often used for informants) and lists three informants as sources, it is clear this specific information was from Finn. Finn himself wrote that he was approached by two FBI agents after Mattachine's May convention. In the FBI report only one coded informant of the three was listed as having met with two agents, and the meeting took place on 29 May 1953. The dates of the other two informants, one from the University of California at Berkeley and the other a woman, along with the content of their information, do not match up with what Finn publicly admitted to his colleagues. Interestingly, moreover, upon the death of Call in 2000, fellow Mattachine insurgent Lucas eulogized that the two had "built relationships with City Hall, the police, the FBI, and the establishment." As Lucas's comment indicates, FBI agents found multiple and prominent informants among Mattachine's San Francisco insurgents.[37]

Given what FBI officials subsequently did with the information provided by these proactive Mattachine informants, the insurgents' strategy to avoid FBI scrutiny by informing for the bureau can only be viewed as naive. After receiving the report detailing the informants' information, Hoover, not convinced the group was free of subversives, forwarded it to the Justice Department Criminal Division for possible prosecution, citing President Eisenhower's Executive Order 10450. Because of popular perception that Harry Truman's loyalty program was inadequate and failing in its purpose, Eisenhower sought to augment the loyalty program with a so-called security program designed to ensure nobody the federal government employed was a security risk. Eisenhower's program, significantly and especially, focused on gays among other so-called undesirables (such as drunks, adulterers, and parents of illegitimate children) as national security threats.[38]

By late 1953, FBI agents had investigated the backgrounds of various leading members of the Mattachine Society and *ONE*. FBI agents, for example, investigated and obtained a copy of Mattachine's questionnaire sent to candidates for elective office in Los Angeles, the same questionnaire that had drawn Coates's interest.[39] An FBI informant in the Los Angeles Post Office also provided agents information about Mattachine's new leader, Burns, including the information on his application for a new post office box for the Mattachine Society. This information included Burns's occupation and place of employment as well as his personal references. FBI agents then used this information to conduct a background check of Burns, consulting the Retail Merchants Credit Association, the Los Angeles Police Department, Los Angeles County Sheriff's Office, and the voting registrar. Yet another source gave FBI agents a detailed summary of all the places Burns had lived.[40] FBI agents also ascertained that Freeman (the pseudonym of Rowland, but FBI agents did not yet know this) was a member of the Communist Party between 1946 and 1948.[41]

In a letter "addressed to a person appearing on the mailing list of the Mattachine Foundation" that FBI agents had somehow obtained (probably from an informant), they learned that Mattachine Society members were meeting at the Red Cross Blood Center on South Vermont Street to donate blood as part of their Blood Bank Program, intended to demonstrate that the group "realizes its social obligations." Regarding this, on the administrative page of the FBI report, the Los Angeles SAC noted, "We will ascertain the subversive and criminal records of additional people who gave blood on August 7, 1953, and had such contribution credited to the Mattachine Society."[42] FBI agents, although indirectly, also attempted to look into Hay's background when they investigated names listed on a letter Mattachine had mailed in reply to somebody's correspondence. The letter was signed "Mrs. Henry Hay," which, in all likelihood, was actually Harry Hay.[43] In any event, FBI agents took the name "Mrs. Henry Hay" to the Los Angeles Police Department, Los Angeles County Sheriff's Office, and Retail Merchants Credit Association and unearthed no information on her, but seemingly did not link the surname to Harry Hay.[44]

* * *

FBI agents were aware of Hay long before he organized Mattachine, before a version of his name appeared on one of its letters, and well before he even conceived the idea of a gay rights group. He first became a subject of FBI investigation, in fact, because of his leftist politics. FBI agents first learned of Hay in mid-February 1943, when an informant referred to as "Source A" in FBI files provided the Los Angeles Field Office a letter Hay had written in 1938 to the chair of the Los Angeles Communist Party Membership Committee. Hay's letter was valuable to FBI agents—and to historians today because it offers previously unknown information about his past. The letter provides details about Hay's membership in the Communist Party. In the letter, Hay asked for readmission to the Communist Party, explaining he had first joined it using the pseudonym Karen Hunter shortly after his twenty-second birthday in the spring of 1934. He explained that his initial "allegiance" was a "purely emotional one." He also explained that, at the time, the "Sunday School instruction for new members," as he put it, "was purely perfunctory." Hay said the unit of which he had been a new member—in effect, his cell—had a policy of "shoving the new member into action out of which they hoped to God political development would eventually spring." None of this appealed to the young Hay, nor did the negative attitudes of party members at that time, leading him to drop out and pursue artistic interests among leftist theater groups around Los Angeles. By 1938, however, these groups had all gone defunct, so Hay reevaluated his relationship with the Communist Party and wanted to return to the fold. This time, as he told the chair of the Membership Committee, he wanted to use the pseudonym "Mac'h Eann" (Eann MacDonald), which, Hay explained, was "one of the gaidhlic [sic] appendages of my own name, Harry Hay." He also expressed a desire to be admitted into "one of the unexposed Studio units" of the Communist Party because he wanted to form a "Labor Front Theatre." He hoped this would attract what he regarded as true party members, and, he argued, in time, the inevitable result would be that the "jaded bourgeoise [sic] finds itself coming at least once for each play."[45]

An FBI agent in Los Angeles, after receiving this letter, investigated the lead to learn that Hay "was employed as a senior material planner by the Interstate Aircraft and Engineering Corporation" but had lost his job as a result of staffing issues. Upon further investigation, moreover, in which FBI agents obtained three photographs of Hay, an agent confirmed with "Source

B" the photos were a "true likeness" of the educational director of the Joe Hill Branch of the Communist Party in Los Angeles. The war-related work contracted to this company and Hay's apparent status as an important local Communist Party member—all despite the fact that the Soviet Union was an ally of the United States during the Second World War—explain FBI interest in Hay's activities.[46]

FBI interest in Hay was wide ranging. In August 1943, an FBI agent in New York City looked into Hay's background after learning he was once employed there before moving to Los Angeles. (After they married, Hay and his wife lived in New York until the 1941 Pearl Harbor attack.) The agent consulted with the metropolitan draft board, where he learned intimate details about Hay, including that he was being treated for secondary stage syphilis, information that seemingly confirmed to FBI agents his subversive nature because communists were popularly regarded as having innately weak moral characters. Some people at the time would consider having a venereal disease confirmation of this along with psychological problems, which some also believed to be behind one's adherence to communism (and, for that matter, homosexuality, though no FBI agent had yet established this link with Hay). The FBI agent also gleaned from his draft records information about Hay's educational background, his employment history, his marital status, and his return to Los Angeles. With all of this information collected, FBI officials deemed Hay a threat and ordered his name placed in the bureau's Custodial Detention Index. FBI policy mandated the Los Angeles Field Office monitor Hay as an individual listed in this index and continually update its information to reflect his current status and activities.[47]

The Custodial Detention Index was created in September 1939 following the outbreak of the Second World War in Europe. Through the index, FBI Director Hoover wanted his agents to identify, broadly, "persons of German, Italian, and Communist sympathies." The idea was that in the event of war, these already-identified individuals would be detained as potential threats. This index had no statutory backing, a significant problem because FBI officials had no legal authority to detain anybody, but by June of 1940, after the fact of its creation, Hoover sought approval to create this index from Attorney General Robert Jackson. Jackson offered his assent, basing detention authority on John Adams's infamous 1798 Alien Detention Act. When Francis Biddle, a civil-libertarian-minded man, replaced Jackson in 1941, he ordered Hoover to terminate the Custodial Detention Index. Although Biddle was, in fact, willing to accede to the detention of foreign nationals in the United States, he was not willing to authorize the detention of communists nor did he have any desire to prosecute US citizens on the list simply for their radical politics. Hoover did not comply with the attorney general's wishes, however. He retained the program, cleverly renaming it the Security Index. Technically, then, Hoover obeyed his superior's orders by ending the Custodial Detention Index but only inasmuch as he relabeled it. Hay's name would continue to be listed for decades.[48]

For the next eighteen years, FBI agents kept tabs on Hay as a subject in the Custodial Detention Index, particularly his activities within leftist and communist circles, reflecting the dominant concerns of the FBI at that time. FBI agents learned, for example, that Hay had been transferred from the Joe Hill Branch of the Communist Party to the Midtown Section and that he "was controlled though June 1943." "Controlled" was the Communist Party's term for Hay having paid his dues through the summer of 1943. Hay was also reported to have "participated" in a union rally led by labor leader William Z. Foster in Los Angeles on 18 July 1943. FBI agents also checked into Hay's background, noting his boyhood immigration to the United States as well as information about his parents, spouse, and various places of employment to that date; the facts of a National Labor Relations Board complaint he had filed; and his credit background (he had none). Finally, the SAC in Los Angeles noted in a report that a thirty-day mail cover—a surveillance method in which FBI agents recorded the addresses of incoming and outgoing mail—had been placed on Hay's place of residence. FBI agents noted several pieces of mail (the names and addresses have all been redacted in FBI files), including the "regularly received" *Daily People's World* and *In Fact* magazines.[49]

By November 1945, FBI agents developed even more information about Hay. One means of confirming Hay's current employment status and place of residence was having an FBI agent telephone him directly "through use of an appropriate pretext." A pretext interview was an FBI investigative tactic in which agents confirmed details about their targets without ever revealing, either to the target or his or her employer, that the caller worked for the FBI. The FBI agent who phoned Hay on 26 October learned directly from him that he worked as a machinist at the Salsburg Motor Company, the "successor corporation" to Hay's previous employer, and he confirmed Hay's home address.[50]

FBI agents also learned further details about Hay from their informants dubbed Source A and Source B. Source A said Hay regularly attended bimonthly meetings of the Echo Park Communist Political Association Club and that he was made a delegate to the Southern California District Communist Political Association Convention. In 1944, given the spirit of wartime unity, the Communist Party USA renamed itself the Communist Political Association and presented itself less as a political party and more as a political pressure group working to support leftist candidates in both the Democratic and Republican Parties. From Source B, FBI agents learned that Hay played no "active role" at the convention but attended all of its sessions.[51]

By October 1948, FBI officials in Washington, DC, grew worried the Los Angeles Field Office had not kept them up to date with information about Hay over the previous three years. FBI Director Hoover wrote the Los Angeles SAC noting the absence of regular reports on Hay and informed him that, normally, although regular reports were not required "on Security Index card subjects unless the subject is also a top functionary," he nevertheless wanted regular reports on Hay. Actually there was not an absence of reports so much as only the presence of one brief report reiterating Hay's status as a naturalized citizen dating from 1947. Hoover's thinking was premised on the "tense international situation at the present time." Hoover was referencing the increased tensions between the United States and the Soviet Union during the Truman presidency as reflected in the Berlin Airlift, which had begun only four months earlier. Given these international realities, Hoover believed Hay and his links to the "Communist Party and related groups" indicated he and they should be "considered a threat to the internal security" and therefore were worthy of more intense FBI scrutiny.[52]

The Los Angeles SAC responded with a new report in February 1949 that detailed FBI agents' increased monitoring of Hay's activities. FBI agents confirmed, through informants, that as of May 1947 Hay was a member not only of the Communist Party but of the United Automobile Workers Union. Agents also learned at this point, again from an informant, that "during the latter part of 1946" Hay taught Marxism classes for the Communist Party, and in 1947 he continued this activity but this time "in private homes." Finally, the Los Angeles SAC reported that, among others, Hay had written the US attorney to protest the fact that ten local Communist Party "functionaries" had received government subpoenas.[53]

FBI officials did not confine themselves to collecting information about Hay's Communist Party activities from FBI agents' fieldwork. In July 1949 a member of Hay's own family in Wisconsin wrote the FBI while apparently staying at the Brown Palace Hotel in Denver, Colorado (the letter was written on that hotel's stationery). This relative had learned Hay and his wife were communists and holding meetings at their home, yet despite the adage "blood is thicker than water," he or she believed the "security of the United States is more important to me than anything else." This person, although conceding the "Communist Party is a legal organization" nevertheless believed the "activities of its members are against the best interests of the United States" and therefore offered up Hay to the FBI.

FBI Director Hoover responded noting that he "appreciate[d] your writing to me as you have" and promising to give the letter "appropriate attention." Even more, Hoover offered Hay's relative the name of the FBI SAC in Milwaukee, instructing the letter writer to direct all future correspondence through that agent and office. Hoover subsequently informed the Milwaukee SAC that any future information he might receive should immediately be forwarded to the Los Angeles Field Office.[54]

Over subsequent years, FBI agents casually noted changes in Hay's life and periodically updated his Security Index card—the name of the index had changed by this point—with his latest address or place of employment. The internal document FBI agents used to update one's security information illustrates, in fact, the *political* focus of FBI officials when monitoring their targets. The form, which asked for work and home addresses, also asked for aliases, race, sex, and whether the individual was native born, naturalized, or an alien. It also singled out the target's political affiliation inasmuch as it specified categories of "Communist, Socialist Workers Party, Independent Socialist League," or "miscellaneous." The form also contained two notations specific to the FBI and in bureau jargon that, by 1950, would involve Hay. In November 1950, Hay's Security Index card was "tabbed" for "COMSAB" (communist sabotage), FBI parlance for a target employed by a company holding a government contract, who therefore fell under suspicion as a potential saboteur. Hay's political affiliation and job, then, not any clear evidence of a threat, served as the FBI basis for government detention. It should be noted as well that by 1950 Hay had actually left the Communist Party and formed Mattachine. Yet despite the aggressive FBI interest in his political affiliations and activism, there is nothing whatsoever mentioning this significant development in his FBI file that year (or the FBI Mattachine file later). One explanation for this was the FBI reliance on informers. Because Hay carefully kept his gay and straight (i.e., communist) worlds separate, the bureau's communist informers—the primary source of FBI information on Hay—knew nothing of his gay organizing.[55]

As with Hay, FBI agents and officials first learned of Mattachine cofounders Rowland and Hull as a result of the men's earlier Communist Party activity. Born on 24 August 1917 in Gary, South Dakota, where he would also be raised, Rowland graduated from high school and attended college for just one year (1935–1936) before dropping out to work in his father's drugstore between 1936 and 1941. Moving on with life away from his family, Rowland bounced around in various jobs, first in Ohio, then Arizona, before being drafted into the US Army in December 1942 for service during the Second World War. Because of his poor eyesight, however, Rowland was not shipped overseas; instead, he remained in the United States, ultimately rising to the rank of staff sergeant but only in "limited service" primarily as an "educational instructor." His military service afforded him the opportunity, however, to continue with higher education. For three months in 1943 he studied German, area studies, and military science at Michigan State College before receiving an honorable discharge in the spring of 1946. With the war over, Rowland returned to live with his parents and resumed working for his father until the latter's death. Afterward, in February 1947, he moved to Minneapolis, took a job with the Western Electric Company, joined the Communist Party, and perhaps (it is not clear) resumed his collegiate studies.[56]

Given extensive FBI infiltration of the Communist Party, it took only a few months before FBI agents knew of Rowland's existence and entrée into radical politics. In late March 1947, as the cold war was heating up and the federal government began to assume a permanent national security footing, Rowland felt compelled, along with eight others, to contact State Representative Leonard Dickenson beseeching him to drop a bill he sponsored seeking to exclude Communist Party candidates from the Minnesota ballot. Upon receiving the signed telegram, Dickenson contacted the FBI St. Paul Field Office, which in turn led FBI agents to open an investigation of Rowland and other local communists.[57]

It did not take long before FBI agents learned all about Rowland's various and extensive party activities between 1947 and 1949. They learned of his interests in forming youth clubs, including his working with American

Youth for Democracy, a group included on the attorney general's list of subversive organizations. In pursuing Rowland's involvement in this type of work, ultimately as educational director of the Youth Commission of the Communist Party, FBI agents took notice of his opinion that FBI Director Hoover was a red-baiter. They noted Rowland also worked to organize a veteran's conference and listed, in detail, his attendance at various Communist Party meetings, conferences, and conventions. In short, they were keyed in to the fact that he was a serious and active member.[58]

As a result, in May 1948 the FBI SAC in St. Paul recommended that Rowland not only be listed in the Security Index but "be made a key figure because of his potential dangerousness." The basis for this conclusion was that Rowland "devotes his full time to the Communist Party and is presently executive secretary of the Minnesota chapter of the American Youth for Democracy." Hoover approved both this designation and inclusion in the Security Index, after which the SAC in St. Paul forwarded a photograph of Rowland, acquired from his former employer, and a sample of his handwriting, provided by an informant in the Communist Party, to the FBI laboratory division for inclusion in the "National Security File."[59]

Hull was born on 31 May 1918 in Minneapolis, Minnesota. He was educated first as a musician at the St. Louis Institute of Music but then transferred to the University of Minnesota to take a degree in chemistry by 1940. Classified 4F, Hull was not drafted for service during the Second World War. By 1948 he joined the Communist Party in Minneapolis, undoubtedly where he met Rowland, with whom at one time he had a relationship. The relationship did not last, but the two nevertheless maintained a long-term friendship and remained roommates even when later relocating to the West Coast.[60]

By the late spring of 1949, for reasons of employment, Rowland decided to move to Los Angeles, and Hull accompanied him. Naturally, because Rowland was listed in the FBI Security Index, FBI agents kept close tabs on Rowland's (along with Hull's) movements and activities. In June 1949, the SAC in Los Angeles submitted a report to FBI headquarters on Rowland in which he noted his Communist Party activities in Minnesota and subsequent move to California, including his Los Angeles address, which a confidential informant, styled T-12 (possibly a wiretap), provided after Rowland relayed it to his mother. The SAC noted further that FBI agents were working to confirm the address as well as Rowland's place of employment.[61]

Within a month FBI agents confirmed Rowland's home address and employer by using a pretext telephone call. Without identifying themselves on the phone, an FBI agent called up his residence—which the bureau had already ascertained was a boarding house through a "discreet inquiry"—and with some concocted rationale asked if Rowland lived there. Agents did the same thing with his employer, a furniture manufacturer, to confirm his place of employment. All other investigative avenues, including liaison with the Los Angeles Police Department, Los Angeles County Sheriff's Office, and the local credit bureau, unearthed no information. With all of this new information about Rowland, his Security Index card was then updated.[62]

Only by November 1950—the same month incidentally in which Hay, Rowland, and Hull began discussing the formation of Mattachine—did FBI agents learn that Rowland and Hull were gay. In the course of maintaining regular contact with Communist Party informants, one of them, identified as informant T-3 in FBI records but actually a man named Frederick C. Price, revealed to FBI agents Rowland's and Hull's sexuality. According to an FBI report, Price was a "self-admitting member of the Communist Party" but had "disassociated himself" from it, the Civil Rights Congress, and the California Labor School. Further described as a "former and close associate" of Rowland and Hull dating from March 1950, Price, "acting in a totally unsolicited manner," volunteered to FBI agents not only that he, himself, was homosexual (and discharged from the army for it) but that Rowland and Hull lived together, and both were also gay. Price had reason to know this. Hull in June 1950 had recruited Price—whom FBI agents described as a "high school student at the Metropolitan High School under the G.I. Bill"—to join the Los Angeles County Communist Party. Ironically, and perhaps perceptively, some members of the party were wary of this new recruit because they felt "he might possibly be a stool pigeon or a plant." Hull retorted that if the party remained overcautious, it would never recruit new members. A couple of years later, yet another informant, apparently from his boarding house or neighborhood, also described both Rowland and Hull as "sexually queer." Interestingly, this final description of their sexuality was listed in an FBI document under a section titled "Health," alluding to the prejudices about the psychological well-being of gays during that era.[63]

The FBI had at hand dozens of informants in or associated with the Communist Party from whom they gleaned information about both Rowland and Hull, but Price offered the reason for Rowland's ouster from the party. Price, who in another document was designated informant T-18, told FBI agents that the Los Angeles County Communist Party had expelled

Rowland because he fled to Mexico in 1950 to "hide" and "escape possible arrest at the outbreak of the Korean War." Rowland went to Mexico with Hull because they feared with the outbreak of war that a cold war–inspired panic might ensue and spark a "Communist roundup." It is unclear, however, if this was the real reason Rowland was kicked out of the Communist Party. During the summer of 1950 Hull, himself, was also expelled from the party but expressly for the reason he was gay. (Communist Party members, like most everyone else in that era, were rabidly homophobic.) Given their close relationship and apparently known sexuality, it would logically follow that both men were likely dismissed for being gay. It makes little sense that the party would purge Rowland but not Hull for fleeing to Mexico; however, the charge of homosexuality for both their ousters makes more sense.[64]

Given the fact that both men had been expelled from the Communist Party with prejudice and were no longer active among any worrisome leftist groups, the SAC of the Los Angeles Field Office requested permission from Hoover to interview both men to learn further information about the Communist Party.[65] Hoover assented to the request, and on 20 August 1952 two FBI agents called on Rowland at his residence in Norwalk, California. After the agents identified themselves and asked if Rowland would talk with them, he perhaps unsurprisingly told them he was "too busy to talk with the Federal Bureau of Investigation." The agents assured Rowland that their interview would take little of his time, to which Rowland somewhat amusingly commented, "I have to mow my lawn. I have nothing to say to the FBI." To make his point clear, Rowland then proceeded to pull his lawnmower out of his garage, after which the agents departed. Hull, who was still living with Rowland at the time, was also interviewed at their common address eight days later. When asked to be interviewed, Hull replied, "It is not required for me to talk to the FBI, is it?" He was told it was not. In a more straightforward manner than his roommate, Hull then dismissed the agents by saying, "Well, let's leave it at that, then. I don't care to talk with you."[66]

When writing up their reports, the agents took Rowland's and Hull's behavior to indicate their "sympathies still reside with the Communist movement" and recommended their names "be retained on the Security Index." Hull was on the index for his connection to Rowland as well as his leftist sympathies. Interestingly, these agents, despite their and Hoover's knowledge about Rowland's and Hull's sexuality, never used that information as a reason either should remain on the Security Index. Even after FBI agents had established a clear connection between Rowland, Hull, and

Mattachine—after an informant in their boarding house reported seeing "quantities of literature and letterhead stationery of the Mattachine Society" and issues of *ONE* "advocating marriage among men"—they did *not*, in fact, consider this evidence in any significant way when deciding whether either should remain in the Security Index. In short, they did not conflate being gay with being a communist, and kept both men in the index.[67]

In 1953 when investigating ONE, Inc., FBI agents looked into the backgrounds of those listed as directors in the magazine: Block, Reyes, and Jennings; they also investigated Slater, who had helped found *ONE* and was listed as a contributing editor. FBI agents ascertained that Block operated a bookstore (the Studio Bookshop on Hollywood Boulevard), that he had been cited for a traffic violation in 1953, and that he was of "Jewish descent." Of more interest to FBI agents was Jennings. To learn as much as they could about Jennings, FBI agents liaised with the Los Angeles Police Department, and they interviewed informants. FBI agents discovered several things, including that in 1946 Jennings had filed for divorce from his wife, citing the common rationale "cruelty." They also learned, to their great interest, a rumor that in 1950 while Jennings was producing a play in Fillmore, California, a person saw him with a copy of the radical newspaper the *National Guardian* and asked him if he was a communist. Jennings reportedly replied, "Yes, I am a dirty Red. I have a right, however, to be a Communist same as other people have a right to their views." Additionally, FBI agents noted that a car registered to Jennings was spotted near the headquarters of the Morgan Hull section of the Los Angeles Communist Party. FBI agents also learned, of course, the details about his recent arrest and trial. Beyond Jennings, FBI agents investigated the background of his lawyer, Shibley. An FBI source contacted Shibley's secretary, who confirmed he was not a lawyer for *ONE* but only hired to defend Jennings. The secretary reported, moreover, that although Jennings had invited Shibley to attend Mattachine meetings, he declined. FBI agents thoroughly investigated Shibley's background, noting his ties to leftist lawyers. As for Reyes, FBI agents learned little. They ascertained he was employed as a ceramics worker and that in 1950 he was arrested for lewd vagrancy—for which he paid a $100 fine and was placed on one year's probation. FBI officials also took note of an advertisement Reyes had placed in the June 1953 issue of *ONE* listing apartments for rent in New Haven, Connecticut. FBI agents subsequently investigated Reyes's rental agency to "ascertain the criminal, credit, and subversive records" of those who managed it. They unearthed nothing despite their informant being a "self-confessed homosexual whose past information has proven reliable." Finally, regarding Slater, FBI agents noted his places of employment and that, like Reyes, he had been arrested on 25 September 1951 for lewd vagrancy and, therefore, was forced to register in California as a "sex offender." They also recognized something for which, among his friends, Slater was notorious: a long list of traffic violations.[68]

Some Mattachine members, or simply those attending Mattachine discussion groups, were also members of the military. When FBI agents acquired information about these particular people, adhering to Sex Deviates Program procedure, it was immediately forwarded to their respective military branches. The SAC in Los Angeles, for example, forwarded a copy of an FBI report detailing such information about Mattachine and ONE, Inc., members to the Air Force Office of Special Investigations at that time.[69]

Despite the fact that Mattachine was, indeed, founded by former members of the Communist Party and organized in ways similar to the Communist Party (and the Freemasons), and despite the fact that some of these individuals were affiliated with *ONE*, FBI officials determined about the two groups in December 1953—in large measure thanks to informants such as Finn and their own failure to realize *ONE* was actually separate from Mattachine—that "no Communist infiltration or control is indicated." As a result, they "closed" their active investigation but continued to collect issues of *ONE* and anything Mattachine published. FBI agents also maintained liaison with the Los Angeles vice squad and antisubversive detail, which continued surveillance of the groups and would, when necessary, inform FBI agents of any indication of "Communist infiltration."[70]

Both Mattachine's change of focus in 1953 away from its secretive nature and view of gays as a repressed minority and toward a more open and avowedly less communist organization, along with the intercession of Mattachine informers, convinced FBI officials the group was not under communist control. To FBI officials, because the group openly proclaimed its goals to educate the public about gays, to make homosexuality more acceptable, and to conduct itself "in a law-abiding manner" and was "opposed to indecent public behavior and acts contributing to the delinquency of minors," it received a clean bill of health from FBI officials.[71] By March 1954, moreover, because FBI officials had deemed Mattachine and *ONE* as "no internal security interest," they even rejected a request by the Air Force Office of Special Investigations to establish a mail cover on the Mattachine Society.[72] Finally, in May 1954, FBI officials even rejected, on the same basis as that request, a query of its Los Angeles Field Office to provide expenses for an informant to attend Mattachine's spring convention. For the following year and a half, FBI officials showed little interest in the Mattachine Society or *ONE* other than collecting issues of their magazines.[73]

By 1954, via their interest in Hay's communist background, FBI officials became interested, again, in Hay's citizenship because of "discrepancies in the information set forth in the files of the Los Angeles Office concerning the place of birth of subject's father." What concerned the Los Angeles Field Office was Hay's claim of "derivative United States citizenship as a result of his father's naturalization in 1892, [but the] place of naturalization [was] not stated." That FBI officials were so concerned reflected the xenophobic belief that subversives infiltrated from abroad. The "discrepancy" also reflected a possible remedy if Hay was deemed a threat: deportation. The Los Angeles SAC, therefore, requested that FBI headquarters inquire with the Immigration and Naturalization Service (INS) about Hay's father and his immigration status. Yet again, it should be noted, there was no reference as of 1954 to Hay's Mattachine connections in his FBI file despite the fact that since 1953 the FBI had begun its intensive, and in-depth, investigation of Mattachine.[74]

By April 1954, FBI officials had an answer about Hay's father. The INS reported it had no record of Hay's father's naturalization, but noted its archive dated only to 1906. FBI officials were advised, therefore, that Hay's father would have been naturalized in a court of law. The FBI Washington, DC, Field Office (WFO) also reported it was searching passport records for naturalization information because as a mining engineer Hay's father traveled extensively.[75]

By May FBI agents discovered Hay's father had, in fact, been naturalized in 1892 in Oakland, California. What is more, they observed that Hay's mother was born in Fort Bowie, Arizona, but then moved to England. FBI agents also noted Hay's parents' extensive travel habits.[76] By July, FBI agents further established that Hay was four years old when he entered the United States.[77] By August, FBI agents failed to find any information on Hay's immigration status in State Department records; they had also searched the FBI fingerprint file, but document redactions make it impossible to determine if it was Hay's fingerprints or his father's they sought.[78] Lastly, also

during 1954, in addition to COMSAB, Hay was "tabbed" for what FBI officials called "DETCOM," or detain as communist. To reiterate, in the event
of a national emergency, Hay and others like him would presumably be
detained by the government given their political affiliations.[79]

By 1955, FBI interest in Hay shifted, but again it never included information about Hay's founding or ouster from the Mattachine Society. The
context of this shift was FBI informant Stephen Wereb's testimony before
HUAC as it held hearings in San Diego investigating alleged communist
activities in California. FBI agents had recruited Wereb, who owned a typewriter service in Inglewood, California, to be an informant on the Communist Party, which he was between October 1943 and the end of 1947. Wereb
fell into this line of work after attending a social event at which he met an
FBI agent to whom he complained about constantly encountering communist literature during his various business travels. Once recruited, Wereb
infiltrated the Los Angeles County Communist Party, took a Marxist training course, then became a functionary of the party. He served variously as a
local press director, treasurer, and convention delegate.[80]

At one point in his testimony, Wereb was asked if the Communist Party
at any time during his infiltration openly advocated the use of violence or
advocated revolution. Wereb replied in the affirmative, stating that in his
Marxism classes his instructors taught that one day the Communist Party
would do just this. Then he singled out two teachers, one of whom was Hay.
According to Wereb, Hay argued that one goal of Marxism and Leninism
was to "overhaul" the election system in the United States to permit, for
example, one member of the entire National Maritime Union to vote for all
members—this idea was based on the fact that at any given time, one-third
of the union members were at sea. The problem, Wereb explained, was that
the Communist Party would make certain that this lone voter was *their*
"stooge." Because an FBI informant publicly testified before HUAC, the San
Diego SAC reported it to FBI Director Hoover along with quoting and citing the testimony from the printed HUAC hearings.[81]

Because Wereb had mentioned Hay's name publicly and in relation to
violence and revolution, which suggested the possibility of a Smith Act violation, the Los Angeles SAC next reported to Hoover that Hay's Security
Index card was current and up to date.[82] By mid-June 1955, after FBI agents
investigated to confirm Hay's current status—they learned that he still held
a manufacturing job; was primarily involved in the dramatic division of the
Hollywood Arts, Sciences, and Professions Council (HASP); and had been

subpoenaed to appear before HUAC in Los Angeles on 27 June 1955—the SAC recommended Hay be removed from the Security Index because he no longer met the index criteria.[83]

That criteria, outlined in SAC Letter 55-30 (Hoover issued SAC letters to update SACs on current bureau rules and procedures) involved whether Hay had been a member of the Communist Party within the past five years. He had not. The criteria also involved whether Hay had "acted in a leadership capacity in one or more front organizations which adhere to the policies and doctrines of a revolutionary group within the last three years." Again, Hay had not. Even though by 1955 Hay had, in fact, been tabbed for both DETCOM and COMSAB, he also no longer met the requirements for those designations as outlined in SAC Letter 55-12. For all of these reasons then, the Los Angeles SAC recommended Hay's removal from the Security Index. On 28 June 1955, FBI officials authorized the request; he was formally removed from the index on 26 July 1955.[84]

Just months later things changed quickly for Hay vis-à-vis the Security Index. On 2 July 1955 Hay, along with his lawyer, Frank Pestana, testified before HUAC in Los Angeles. He testified that although he was born in England in 1912, because his parents were both citizens of the United States at the time of his birth, he was, in fact, a US citizen. He also testified that, for employment, he was a production control engineer who made burners and boilers. Committee staffer Frank Tavenner then asked Hay whether he had worked as a teacher. Upon this seemingly innocuous question, Hay conferred with his lawyer and then declined to answer, citing his First and Fifth Amendment rights. Asked if he had any music training, he similarly declined to answer. Asked if he had taught classes at the California Labor School, information Tavenner claimed the committee had discovered in its investigations, Hay declined to answer. Asked if he knew whether the Communist Party selected people to teach at that school, Hay declined to answer. Asked if the Communist Party instructed him to teach classes there, Hay declined to answer. Tavenner then advised Hay that an undercover FBI informer named Wereb, who had infiltrated the party, testified that the Communist Party had ordered Hay to teach classes at the party's Hawthorne Club. Hay responded, "I wish to state that I have neither opinions nor recollections to give to stool pigeons and their buddies on this committee." After that remark, Tavenner asked Hay if anything Wereb had said was untrue, but Hay declined to answer. Tavenner also directly asked Hay if he taught a class on Marxism, if he was—or ever was—a member of the Communist

Party, and whether it was the Communist Party's "plan" to deny membership before HUAC. All of these questions Hay declined to answer.[85]

Hay's testimony was brief but fiery. In later years he concluded the committee did not press him further, nor seek a contempt charge for his stool-
pigeon remark, because he exuded what he described as a "gay consciousness"
with his impertinent and grandiloquent way of answering their questions. Hay
believed this encouraged the committee chair, uncomfortable with Hay's
demeanor, to dismiss him to maintain order—his answers had repeatedly
induced laughter from those in the gallery.[86]

By August of 1955 the Los Angeles SAC reported these details to Hoover.[87]
Six months later, the SAC again wrote Hoover, reiterating the details of his
previous report, advising the FBI director that Hay's case had been reevaluated, and recommending, again, that Hay be removed from the Security
Index because his activities were restricted to membership with HASP.
The SAC also advised Hoover, "No request for interview [of Hay] is being
submitted at this time, inasmuch as it is believed that an attempt to interview Hay would be unavailing in view of his refusal to testify before HCUA
[House Committee on Un-American Activities]."[88]

Upon receipt of this memorandum, however, an FBI official in Washington, DC, noted a discrepancy among dates in an FBI report from February
1954 in which an FBI informant reported Hay was a member of the Los
Angeles Communist Party "as of early 1950." Because this, apparently, fell
within the five-year time span of the Security Index criteria (dating from
when the Los Angeles Field Office had originally removed Hay from the
index), he asked that a form FD-122 be filed on Hay. This was the form used
to list a person in the Security Index. Hay remained on the index.[89]

Meanwhile, in April 1954 FBI agents and officials continued to collect information about Mattachine and ONE, Inc. For example, the senior senator
from Wisconsin, Alexander Wiley, having received a copy of *ONE* in the
mail, not only registered a complaint with the postmaster general because
he described the magazine as "devoted to the advancement of sexual perversion" but forwarded a copy of the complaint to FBI Assistant Director
Nichols, the bureau's liaison with Congress. Nichols subsequently reported
it to FBI Associate Director Tolson and filed a copy of the memorandum in
the FBI Sex Deviates File—the only bureau response at this point. (Nichols's

Crime Records Division, remember, maintained the sensitive Sex Deviates File.[90])

Around that same time, FBI agents also somehow acquired a verbatim transcript from a Los Angeles talk show called *Confidential File*, hosted by Coates, the same journalist whose 1953 article sparked initial FBI interest in Mattachine and *ONE*. The transcript was added to the FBI file on the Mattachine Society. For an April 1954 episode titled "Homosexuals and the Problem They Present," after having interviewed a psychiatrist who explained the "causes" of homosexuality somehow being rooted in an "overdominate [*sic*] mother and an extremely passive father," Coates interviewed the secretary of the Mattachine Society, who concealed his identity behind the pseudonym Curtis White. When asked, White explained he had no personality problems, had never been arrested, had no desire for treatment "to be transformed into a heterosexual," and believed homosexuality was not "abnormal." White then described the educational, research, and antidiscrimination goals of Mattachine and estimated its membership at about 160. Asked whether gay bars were used to recruit others to homosexuality, White said he did not know enough about the issue but thought it "merits looking into." On a personal note, White also said his appearance on the show would both out himself to his family and result in his being fired from his job (he was); White hoped, however, that his appearance would "be of some use" to others like himself. Coates then interviewed a city police captain who countered that gay bars were prime targets for blackmailers and gay recruiters. The captain then singled out other "danger spots," such as theaters, parks, and public restrooms.[91]

The post-1953 lackadaisical, collection-only FBI interest in Mattachine and *ONE* came to an abrupt end, however, by January 1956 after an anonymously delivered issue of *ONE*, published just two months before, arrived at FBI headquarters. In that issue FBI officials found what they regarded an intemperate article that pointedly mentioned the bureau.

"How Much Do We Know about the Homosexual Male?" was written by Rowland under his pseudonym David Freeman. In it, Rowland argued, "Homosexuals have existed in all parts of the world, among all peoples and all cultures, since man's emergence in the watered valleys of our young planet." In terms of the modern world, he segregated "homosexual society" into three disparate groups: the Revolutionaries, the Tories, and the Liberals. Revolutionaries, Rowland wrote, "can be found swishing down Hollywood

Boulevard or Constitution Avenue." Liberals, on the other hand, were those creative individuals who became actors, artists, doctors, and lawyers and who viewed "the world with an element of detachment." Rowland's third group, the Tories, sparked a renewed and, indeed, intensified FBI interest in both *ONE* and Mattachine, leading to an extensive FBI investigative and surveillance effort to silence the groups. About this particular segment of the gay population, Rowland wrote, "The Tories are the elegant ones who have decided to express their social hostility by being more correct than the foremost representatives of the dominant (and dominating) culture. They work for TIME magazine or the NEW YORKER. They are in the diplomatic service; they occupy key positions with oil companies or the FBI (it's true!)."[92]

FBI Director Hoover was always sensitive to any negative comments made about his FBI, but he was especially sensitive toward, and sought retribution against, anyone suggesting, as the Rowland articled did, gays worked in the FBI. Although Rowland never explicitly named Hoover in the article, Hoover was undoubtedly the FBI member he had in mind. Hoover, a man who lived with his mother until her death in 1938 (by which time he was forty-three years old) and who then remained a lifelong bachelor, was long subjected to rumors about his sexuality, especially from his political enemies. For years, because his private life did not fit the expected role 1950s society demanded of men, Hoover's opponents circulated rumors that questioned the FBI director's sexuality, and in light of the rise of McCarthyism and the Lavender Scare of the 1950s, Hoover had *any* such rumors quickly, quietly, and sometimes ruthlessly quashed. Yet because of this particular comment and the previous FBI investigations of both Mattachine and *ONE*, one FBI official recommended that the bureau should not dignify the magazine with an official reply. Associate FBI Director Tolson, always protective of his boss and sensitive to rumors about his own alleged relationship with Hoover, could not have disagreed more. In a national political context in which gays were viewed as moral and medical deviants, criminals, and as bad or actually worse than communists, there was no other possibility than a response from the most prominent agency responsible for rooting both out. Tolson insisted, "We should take this crowd on and make them put up or shut up." In response, Hoover wrote, "I concur."[93]

The two top FBI officials' comments triggered a renewed and intensive FBI investigation of both *ONE* and Mattachine. Hoover ordered his subordinates to check FBI files for any reference to Freeman, but, given the name was a pseudonym, they found none. Hoover then sent an airtel—an FBI message of highest priority posted via airmail—to the Los Angeles Field Office, ordering it to "have two mature and experienced Agents contact [deleted but Freeman] in the immediate future and tell him the Bureau will not countenance such baseless charges appearing in this magazine and for him either to 'put up or shut up.'" The Los Angeles Field Office was ordered to complete this within a week.[94]

At this point, agents in Los Angeles were unable to locate Freeman or to ascertain his true identity (Rowland). As a result, on 31 January 1956 two FBI agents made an impromptu visit to room 326 at 232 South Hill Street, the offices of ONE, Inc., where they found William Lambert—who had adopted the new appellation W. Dorr Legg and who was the business manager of *ONE*. When asked who he was, Legg refused to identify himself, leading FBI agents to ascertain his former name at a later date through an informer. When asked other questions about Freeman, Legg claimed to know nothing about him and, moreover, he was not authorized to release any information about *ONE*'s employees. The two agents left, but because they were still unable to develop information about Freeman, they returned to *ONE*'s office during the morning of 2 February to reinterview "Lambert," whom one scholar has described as "imperious and domineering." When the agents showed Legg their identifications, he reportedly grabbed one agent's credentials and wrote down his name. Asked if he might be William Lambert, Legg responded: "I might and I might not." Asked if he was an editor of *ONE*, Legg refused to confirm. When asked again about Freeman and the November 1955 issue of *ONE*, Legg responded each time by directing the agents to the magazine's attorney, Eric Julber. The agents then directly asked Legg whether he had any information about the FBI employing "a homosexual or a sexual deviant." According to the agents' report, he responded, "Do you have information that there are none?" The agents then "specifically" warned Legg that the "FBI would not tolerate any such baseless statement in this or any other publication." To that, Legg responded, "That's an interesting statement." Then, as the two agents were leaving the office, Legg reportedly asked them, "By the way, gentlemen, would you have any objection if this interview had been 'taped'?" The FBI agents responded they "had no objection." Lastly, in their report the two agents noted that the ramshackle nature of the office indicated to them the conversation likely was not recorded. Clearly, though, they were worried it was recorded.[95]

Five days later, FBI officials in Washington, DC, evaluated the results of the meeting and how to follow up. In their view, the agents' interview with Legg indicated he was "strictly no good"—usually nobody FBI agents confronted for claiming Hoover was gay argued back—and that he was either the author or editor of the offending article. Moreover, because Legg had invoked the name of *ONE*'s lawyer, FBI officials turned to focus on Julber's background. According to FBI agents, Julber was suspect because he had "appeared on platforms with Communist Party members"; defended the group American Youth for Democracy; worked in a Students for Wallace campaign; and shared an office with another lawyer who, according to the ex-communist and informer Louis Budenz, was a member of the Communist Party. Also, the car of a woman associated with him had been spotted parked near the location of a Communist Party meeting in 1948.[96]

In deciding what to do next, Chief Jones of the FBI Crime Records Division advised that because of the "unsavory nature of this entire crowd," the bureau should not attempt to interview anyone else, especially Julber, because he "would endeavor to embarrass the Bureau." Jones noted that in any interview FBI agents would "not have the element of surprise" and, as evidenced in the Legg interview, they would run the risk of the interview being recorded. Concluding his suggestions, Jones warned his superiors that further interviews would only lead the FBI "to lose more than could be gained." Tolson, however, again disagreed and overruled the cautious and sage advice of his subordinate. He wrote, "I think we should open an investigation on Julber and also get a line on Lambert."[97]

Hoover thereafter ordered the Los Angeles Field Office not to interview Julber until agents had conducted a thorough investigation of him. In this investigation, the FBI director ordered agents to contact "confidential sources, informants, the Los Angeles Police Department, and the Los Angeles County Sheriff's office." Agents were further directed to conduct neighborhood investigations and interviews with former employers. Beyond Julber, Hoover also ordered agents to investigate Lambert because "no derogatory information could be identified with him in Bufiles [bureau files]." (Interestingly, Legg's previous name of Lambert stymied FBI agents for some time in trying to ascertain his identity and activity.) They were further directed to develop information about *ONE* magazine and ONE, Inc., to ascertain "how they are financed" and whether they were "properly registered to do business in California." FBI agents were also ordered to interview post office officials to determine whether *ONE* had violated obscenity law when mailing its magazine to subscribers. This particular avenue would become the new FBI line of attack to silence the now rabble-rousing homophile movement. Paradoxically, however, the FBI's own Interstate Transportation of Obscene Matter Desk had advised FBI officials that the November 1955 issue of ONE was in no way consistent with previous and successful FBI obscenity cases, and it suggested the case be referred to the Justice Department for an opinion about prosecution. FBI agents were then directed to investigate the background of the management team of ONE, as listed in the magazine, and report to FBI headquarters not using normal procedures but via the Crime Records Division—the section of the bureau that maintained the FBI Sex Deviates File. In this way, whatever FBI agents developed, the information could easily be incorporated into this file or disseminated.[98]

Within days, responding to FBI officials' obscenity query, Chief Post Office Inspector D. H. Stevens reported that the post office solicitor had already reviewed the October 1954 issue of ONE, impounded it, and ordered the magazine to "show cause why the publication should not be declared nonmailable." The post office made a move before the FBI as a result of Senator Wiley's previous complaint about ONE. Post office inspectors in this particular situation were concerned with an aggregate of items: a seemingly lurid short story about a successful lesbian love affair (unsuccessful ones, according to historian Rodger Streitmatter, rarely caught the eye of censors), "obscene because [it was] lustfully stimulating to the average homosexual reader," a risqué poem containing "filthy words" describing a British homosexual scandal, and a Swiss advertisement that, itself, was not considered obscene but that nevertheless led people to obscene material; also included in the magazine was a suggestive advertisement with a picture for "Moon-Glow" see-through pajamas. Ironically enough, this issue of ONE also contained an article discussing "The Law of Mailable Material" that, although written anonymously, was in fact authored by Julber. ONE responded to the post office action by filing an injunction with the Federal District Court in Los Angeles. Stevens, moreover, advised FBI officials that he would also have the November 1955 issue of ONE reviewed to determine if a similar action with this issue could be taken with ONE overall.[99]

ONE thereupon began an effort to win its case, a legal fight that would ultimately take the poorly funded magazine all the way to the US Supreme Court in a decision that would have significant ramifications for all subsequent gay publications. The legal battle, however, was a hard-fought one. On 11 January 1956, Julber submitted ONE's argument to District Judge Thurmond Clarke, trying to persuade him that the post office claim the magazine was obscene lacked merit, therefore making *ONE* mailable. Probably to avoid undue publicity, both parties in the case asked for a summary judgment, handed down on 3 April against the magazine. Julber thereafter appealed the decision to the US Court of Appeals for the Ninth Circuit.[100]

Following Judge Clarke's ruling, senior FBI officials asked for a review of the bureau's case, which FBI official Jones compiled on 6 March 1956. In it, Jones informed his superiors that after the post office had impounded the October 1954 issue of *ONE,* the magazine had not applied for a new second-class mailing permit. Instead, FBI officials were informed, the postal inspector believed *ONE* was still being mailed in small numbers or *ONE* supporters were placing it in mailboxes across Los Angeles. Whether this was true, the postal inspector said, interestingly enough, he would not on his own review further issues of *ONE* because taking further action "would constitute a form of censorship." Instead, the post office would only act, FBI official Jones reported, if a particular issue was brought to "its attention as an unmailable item."[101]

FBI officials decided, therefore, in light of the fact that the federal district court had ruled the October 1954 issue "obscene," to forward the November and December 1955 issues of *ONE* to the Justice Department "for an opinion relative to its obscene nature." If the Justice Department deemed those two issues obscene, then FBI agents would interview Julber "concerning the slanderous statements about the FBI." Julber, thereupon, would be told of "the Bureau's extreme displeasure and told to 'put up or shut up.'"[102] Incidentally, because Julber was defending *ONE,* and given popular prejudices of what constituted a homosexual, FBI officials suspected he was gay. They learned from Assistant US Attorney Joseph Mullender Jr. that Julber was a "rather mild-mannered individual with somewhat effeminate characteristics." One FBI source even proactively "inquired as to whether [deleted but Julber] was 'gay' (homosexual)." The source reported to FBI agents, "No, he's all right." Julber, who worked for *ONE* on a pro bono basis, initially thought handling the case would enhance his legal reputation; he quickly learned, however, that it also led many to question his sexuality.[103]

ONE's involvement in a federal legal case concerning the mailability of its magazine had subsidiary ramifications for the FBI probe of both Mattachine and *ONE.* The legal case finally convinced FBI officials there was "no present organizational connection" between the two groups. This led bureau officials to open in Los Angeles a separate case file for ONE, Inc. FBI agents also finally ascertained, apparently from the informant discussed below, that Lambert was also Legg, *ONE*'s business manager and the irascible man they previously had questioned. The informant was at *ONE*'s printer, Abbey Lithographers, a company, in fact, owned and operated by Jennings's sister and her husband out of their basement. Although we cannot know with absolute certainty the identity of the informant, it is probably a safe assumption, given the small size of the business, that the FBI informant (a man) was Jennings's brother-in-law. Abbey Lithographers, apparently, was a two-person operation, and we know FBI agents first reached out to its informant (Jennings's brother-in-law) via a pretext interview during which they established that Abbey was, in fact, the printer of *ONE* and that the informant held "most of the back copies." The informant also told FBI agents that "on at least one occasion he questioned [deleted but Legg] whom he recalls under the name of William Lambert" about certain items in the magazine he believed "might be viewed as obscene and improper for him to print." The informant assured FBI agents, moreover, that *ONE*'s lawyer reviewed everything prior to publication to avoid any legal troubles. The informant also said he was "anxious to cooperate with the Bureau in any matter" and promised to keep his relationship with the agents confidential. He provided FBI agents the October, November, and December 1955 issues of *ONE* and told the agents that 5,000 copies of the January 1956 issue had been printed. Apparently having not received a copy of it from their informant, FBI agents subsequently purchased the January 1956 issue at a newsstand. The SAC of the Los Angeles Field Office then reported to Hoover that his agents had collected nearly every issue of the magazine for inspection. After examining the October 1954 issue of *ONE*, furthermore, agents believed that in addition to possible domestic interstate transportation of obscene materials charges, they might even be able to charge ONE with violating federal law relative to the international transportation of obscene materials because *ONE* reportedly had been distributed in Copenhagen, Denmark. The agents also reported that their "efforts to identify David L. Freeman have been unsuccessful to date."[104]

The eventual FBI discovery that the "sarcastic" Lambert was Legg triggered a renewed and focused effort to unearth information about him.[105] FBI agents went to great lengths in developing information about Lambert. They covertly tailed him, for example, and on 28 February 1956 "through confidential techniques" took photographs of him. They observed he had moved into a small house at 1717 South Mansfield Avenue in Los Angeles, which the agents described as a "colored section of town," where Legg was living with a "Negro." This led agents to record the license plate number of the car parked in front of the house.[106]

Because Legg had, in the view of FBI officials, engaged in "covert activities," they suspected he might have been "wanted" by other FBI field offices. They cited a couple of examples of "covert activities" that prompted this suspicion, included his taking a post office box without offering a home or work address, which led post office officials to demand the information; he also, apparently, gave a false address when registering to vote. FBI agents checked that address, only to learn it was a ceramics shop.[107]

In their widespread efforts to gather more data about Legg, FBI agents coordinated with field offices in Detroit, Michigan, and Portland, Oregon. FBI agents learned that while living in Detroit in 1949, Legg was arrested on a charge of "gross indecency" after being caught in a car "performing an act of oral perversion" with his African American boyfriend. As punishment for this crime, both men were sentenced to one year's probation. The FBI SAC in Detroit, moreover, citing Legg's arrest record, further described him as "uncooperative, suspicious with superior intelligence, and not psychotic. He was considered as 'very arrogant' by the examiners according to the file." Regarding his sexuality, the SAC further noted that "his deviated interests are of long standing and not amenable to treatment." FBI agents also learned he was arrested in May 1954 for "suspicion of burglary" in "skid row" but was subsequently released. Agents in Portland, Oregon, also ascertained that during the Second World War Legg was "suspected in 1943 of having Nazi Bund literature," a charge that, in the end, turned out to have no merit. Upon receiving Legg's mug shot from Detroit and confirming their information with the Los Angeles Police Department, FBI agents finally identified Legg as Lambert.[108]

In March 1956, again in light of the pending *ONE* appeal and the bureau's interest in using obscenity law[109] to silence the homophile movement, the New York Field Office forwarded to headquarters two copies of the *Mattachine Review* (March and April 1956; the Mattachine Society established its magazine in January 1955.) They noted the magazine was connected to the Mattachine Society in Los Angeles and it, like *ONE*, addressed "problems of homosexuality in the community." The New York SAC especially singled out the *Review*'s articles exploring "searches and seizures" and the "rights of citizens at the time of arrest."[110] This was followed by a complaint from Republican Senator Gordon Allott of Colorado, who in July 1956 received in the mail a pamphlet from the Mattachine Society that specifically advertised this magazine. After receiving the pamphlet, the senator "was very much upset and agitated," which led him to telephone FBI Assistant Director Nichols, after which he forwarded the pamphlet to him. The two developments prompted Nichols to advise Hoover to have the bureau's Loyalty Unit and Domestic Intelligence Division review the matter and offer an opinion about starting an investigation. Hoover, however, ordered the Los Angeles Field Office to provide headquarters "current information" about this, and he notified its superiors that "no active investigation need be conducted for this purpose." The Los Angeles Field Office responded by forwarding to Hoover, and other field offices, a summary memorandum of the Mattachine Society and *ONE* investigations.[111]

Seven days after FBI agents interviewed Jennings's brother-in-law, an interview in which they tried and failed to identify Freeman, FBI agents finally ascertained that Rowland was the true identity behind the pseudonym Freeman. What allowed FBI agents finally to identify him was an internal power struggle at ONE, Inc. By 1953 the magazine began to see marked success and even turned a profit, which in many ways spelled doom for its more radical, idealistic, and former Communist Party members, such as Jennings and Rowland. Between 1953 and 1956 Rowland served in various positions at *ONE*, whether on the editorial board, as a corporate member, or head of ONE, Inc.'s Social Services Division. Yet heated disagreements about *ONE*'s mission and future, compounded by Jennings's authoritarian editorship, led Rowland in October 1953 to resign from the editorial board and focus, instead, on running his Social Services Division. Jennings, too, inevitably butted heads with others at the magazine, leading to his resignation in March 1954. Rowland completely withdrew from ONE, Inc., on 1 March 1956, by which time Irma "Corky" Wolf (known as Ann Carll Reid on the magazine's masthead) had become *ONE*'s editor.[112]

By mid-March 1956, FBI agents interviewed somebody at *ONE*, whose name is redacted in FBI files, but who clearly was the editor, Wolf. In the interview, Wolf admitted to being listed as Reid in the magazine. She also advised FBI agents that both Julber and Legg had advised ONE's members not to talk with FBI agents. Legg had even shared with ONE's members his own raucous experience with FBI agents. Wolf, however, decided to talk with FBI agents, and she did so for an hour and a half. In their interview with Wolf, the FBI agents covered "one by one" the names of people they suspected were connected with *ONE*. Wolf "admitted that Chuck Rowland, who served as a staff member of the publication, is identical with David L. Freeman and wrote the article appearing in the November 1955 issue, which made reference to the FBI." Wolf further told the agents that Rowland had been expelled from the Communist Party but was still sympathetic to its thinking. Wolf continued that because of Rowland's political biases and disagreements with staff members—"particularly concerning his above-mentioned article"—he had recently resigned. Wolf apparently also offered the agents Rowland's home address and place of employment, the Morris Furniture Company. She then offered up the real names of others associated with *ONE* and in particular those listed on the masthead. With all of this information in hand, the Los Angeles SAC asked Hoover for instructions about interviewing Rowland, noting for the director that FBI agents had previously attempted to interview him in August 1952 but with no success. Hoover instructed the Los Angeles Field Office, in light of *ONE*'s pending legal appeal, not to interview Rowland.[113]

Soon thereafter, on 16 March 1956, FBI Director Hoover formally consented to FBI agents' request from some months before that Hay's name be placed back in the Security Index. The reason Hoover gave for Hay being relisted in the index was "in view of Hay's refusal to answer questions concerning Communist membership on the basis of the Fifth Amendment before the House Committee on Un-American Activities . . . plus his extensive subversive background." By 5 April 1956, Hay was back in the Security Index. Clearly, though, Hay was relisted not because of any evidence he was a genuine threat (or gay) but because of his dramatic refusal to cooperate with HUAC. In other words, he was relisted for political reasons.[114]

Hay's reappearance in the FBI Security Index in 1956 coincided, actually, with the bureau's second round of intense targeting of the Mattachine Society. Yet again, however, FBI agents never linked Hay to Mattachine, and no information exists about Hay's participation with Mattachine in either the FBI file on him or on Mattachine—except for the one notation of the name "Mrs. Henry Hay" on a Mattachine letter obtained from an informant. To reiterate, FBI agents checked into the name and learned nothing. That no information about Mattachine exists in Hay's individual FBI file is significant because FBI officials were interested in any and all information that even hinted at his "subversive" nature. Hay's being involved with, let alone having founded, a group seemingly responsible (to the FBI) for slandering Hoover and the FBI certainly would have qualified in that regard. Hay, however, remained a stubbornly secretive man and, in any event, had been out of Mattachine for more than three years at this point, so FBI sources inside Mattachine (mostly connected with the San Francisco insurgents) simply did not know who he was.[115]

Not realizing Hay's relationship to Mattachine, for the next five years FBI agents instead worked to ascertain Hay's activities in the Communist Party or sympathetic groups. In May and June 1956, for example, FBI agents again made "pretext inquiries" with Hay's employer to confirm Hay's current home address and employment status. They also questioned informants who reiterated Hay's membership with HASP, which, according to those agents, was the Southern California Chapter of the National Council of Arts, Sciences, and Professions and was, according to HUAC, a "Communist front." What's more, these informants also relayed to FBI agents that in November 1955 Hay had sent "greetings" to John Howard Lawson, the radical playwright, screenwriter, and Communist Party member, one of the Hollywood Ten who spent time in jail. This association concerned FBI agents because, from their perspective, Lawson was "an important figure in the CP's organization in the Hollywood film industry." At this same time, the Los Angeles SAC recommended on an administrative page keeping Hay in the Security Index "in view of his refusal to answer questions concerning CP membership" before HUAC.[116]

Over this five-year period FBI agents were unable to develop any new information about Hay's activities other than noting his place of employment, residence, and the fact that he had divorced his wife. The Los Angeles Field Office shared the information FBI officials maintained on Hay, however, with unspecified recipients in 1958 and 1959. The explanation for this paucity of information about Hay, over this period, was the fact that by this point he had quit the Communist Party.[117]

After FBI agents realized Hay was not associating with anyone from the Communist Party—incidentally, he had also walked away, for the time being, from his homophile activities—and because he no longer met the criteria for being listed in the Security Index, in June 1961 the SAC in Los Angeles asked Hoover for permission to recruit Hay as an FBI informant. The SAC noted for Hoover that if an initial interview with Hay went well, and if Hay was "cooperative," the Los Angeles Field Office would begin to "direct his activities" at a later date, but only after an extensive and up-to-date "background investigation." Hay seemed to be a good candidate for recruitment because the long FBI investigation revealed he had no relatives "connected with the CP" and because it seemed clear Hay had not been "expelled or rejected from the CP" but had left it on his own volition. For these reasons, the SAC "desired to ascertain subject's present attitude towards the CP and to also ascertain if he will cooperate with the FBI." An FBI official noted on the SAC's memo for Hoover that Hay had not been interviewed previously and that he had been an uncooperative witness before HUAC. Hoover approved the SAC's request.[118]

On 4 August 1961, two FBI agents arrived at Hay's home on Westwood Boulevard in Los Angeles to interview him. The agents began their interview by explaining to Hay their jurisdiction "in security matters." Incensed, Hay interrupted the agents before they could even ask for his cooperation. According to the agents' report, and perhaps reflecting Hay's own self-styled "gay consciousness," he "immediately stated that he had nothing to say and did not wish to talk to the FBI and terminated the interview." Hay's response was not surprising. As a long Communist Party member and gay man, he would have had an almost innate distrust of FBI agents. Hay knew about some of the past FBI interest in him beyond even the fact that an FBI informer had testified about him before HUAC. In 1948, when Hay worked at Leahy Manufacturing, a longtime friend warned Hay that FBI agents had inquired about him at his workplace and "knew all about you." The fact of the matter was, however, Hay knew almost nothing about the FBI *surveillance* of him, or of Mattachine, beyond suspicion; but those suspicions were enough to color his view of the FBI. Even though Hay refused to cooperate with FBI agents as an informer, and contrary to the FBI reaction when he refused to cooperate with HUAC, the Los Angeles SAC recommended because of Hay's "lack of activity" in the Communist Party since 1950, or "CP front activity" in the past five years, that he be removed from the Security Index. He was, in fact, finally removed from it. The FBI apparently never connected Hay to Mattachine.[119]

On 14 May 1956, Assistant Attorney General Warren Olney finally responded to Hoover concerning the bureau's inquiry as to whether the November and December 1955 issues of *ONE* were obscene and therefore prosecutable under federal law. Olney told Hoover the obscenity of the two issues was "not free from doubt," and he informed the FBI director, in any event, the department could not entertain further prosecutions until *ONE*'s pending appeal had been resolved. FBI officials remained optimistic, though, about a possible further prosecution of *ONE*, arguing, "We may well be able to make such a move should the pending appeal of the magazine against postal authorities be found in favor of the Government." Hoover, therefore, ordered the Los Angeles Field Office to follow "closely" the appeal and to submit to headquarters all issues of *ONE*. About one month later, as a result of all of this, the SAC of the Los Angeles Field Office suggested placing the bureau's investigation of *ONE* in a "pending inactive status" until the legal appeals of *ONE* were exhausted. FBI officials agreed, believing they could "proceed no further until we know the results of the appeal and receive the [final] departmental ruling." In the meantime, FBI agents continued to collect and compile information about gays, as exemplified in the San Francisco SAC's marginalia on a memo regarding gay-related information that office received in December 1956: "Place in P* Homo file."[120]

Five years after the formation of the male-dominated Mattachine Foundation (then Society), a uniquely lesbian homophile organization formed in San Francisco. Mattachine had a handful of lesbian members, but given the dominant patriarchal attitudes of the 1950s, they and their interests were subsumed by the men and theirs. So it is not surprising that a separate women's group would form on the West Coast. Originally conceived as a social group intended to facilitate meeting others like themselves, but to do so in a nonthreatening, risk-averse manner—meaning not in a bar that could be raided—the group first started meeting in members' homes. The founding members were a diverse bunch and included Rose Bamberger, a young Filipino woman credited with developing the idea of a "secret society of lesbians."[121] Also among the founders, and the two who would become most responsible for shaping and leading the group, were Phyllis Lyon and her partner, Del Martin. Both women grew up in the San Francisco region but only met later in life while employed by the same publishing company in Seattle. By 1953, together as a couple, they returned to San Francisco to live.[122]

During late September 1955, several couples came together to hold their first meeting, and among myriad issues discussed was, naturally, what to name their organization. Several suggestions were offered, but the women settled on the Daughters of Bilitis (DoB). The name not only fit their unique interests and the larger ideals of the homophile movement but the moniker itself provided a certain level of security because the name did not automatically reveal—at least to outsiders—what the group was about. The name "Bilitis" stemmed from the work of nineteenth-century poet Pierre Louys and his "Songs of Bilitis," which happened to have been republished at the time and were popular among certain circles. His poems included a fictional female character who became intimately involved with the ancient female Greek icon, Sappho, from the island of Lesbos. Educated lesbians of the 1950s would doubtless have recognized the Bilitis reference, especially because in the past the designation Sappho, or Sapphist, had already for a century or more been used as a popular term for a woman with same-sex attraction. To heterosexuals in the 1950s, on the other hand, the name would have raised few suspicions and only left the impression the group was yet another in a long list of sororal organizations.[123]

Before long the women began drafting a constitution and bylaws, with a conscious eye toward protecting themselves from public and police harassment. Given popular 1950s notions that gays and lesbians targeted youths in some insidious effort to turn these impressionable youngsters toward a life of deviancy, the women pointedly included in the document's language the requirement that all members be over the age of twenty-one and of "good moral character." Their intention was to insulate themselves from the oppressors' most common excuse for targeting gays, protecting youth. Time and again, moral leaders and law enforcement officials cited moral turpitude and impressionable youth as their *raison d'être*. Having finalized organizational documents, the women then elected their leadership, with Martin serving as president and Lyon as secretary.[124]

Almost immediately some members began to question the purpose and direction of the group. Some wanted the DoB to remain exclusively a lesbian social organization, and other more politically minded and motivated members wanted to involve the group in the burgeoning homophile movement and the nascent struggle for gay acceptance. DoB leadership had already, perhaps unsurprisingly, reached out to Mattachine and ONE, Inc., in Los Angeles—the only other formal gay groups in existence, really—as well as to Donald Webster Cory's book service in New York for literature on homosexuality. At the time, these were the few sources of positive information available to gays and lesbians as opposed to the standard negative sources, which painted those with same-sex attraction somehow as moral, legal, and medical deviants. Martin and Lyon even attended a conference hosted by ONE in 1956, where they learned more about homophile activities and organizing, prompting them to steer the DoB toward loftier goals.[125]

By the spring of 1956, unable to reconcile the divide between those who sought activism and those who only wanted to socialize, DoB leadership simply decided to embrace the former. This led the more socially inclined members to leave the organization, but now it had a reenergized purpose. Under the leadership of Martin and Lyon, the DoB maintained a working relationship with Mattachine and ONE, Inc., crafted and published its own newsletter (*The Ladder*), and fully embraced the broad common goals of the homophile movement: education of the public and of gays, participation in professional research about gays, and promoting the decriminalization of homosexuality.[126]

Because the FBI has released only thirty-four pages of records from its headquarters file and heavily redacted files from its San Francisco, Los Angeles, New York, and Boston Field Offices, having destroyed the rest, it remains notoriously difficult to reconstruct the bureau's interest in and investigation of the DoB. The first extant FBI notation of the DoB, however, dates to 1956, the year following the group's formation. As part of the bureau's renewed and intensified efforts that year to target and silence Mattachine and, more particularly ONE, Inc., the FBI San Francisco Field Office shared with the Los Angeles Field Office information it had collected in an effort to complete the Los Angeles Field Office's file. Specifically, the SAC in San Francisco photocopied and forwarded to Los Angeles forty-nine different issues of the *Mattachine Review*, but he tacked on at the end the October 1956 issue of *The Ladder*—the inaugural issue of the DoB newsletter. That newsletter detailed for readers the formation of DoB the previous year and explained exactly what its goals were, what its name meant, and the fact that it was joining *ONE* and the *Mattachine Review* in disseminating information, but from the "feminine viewpoint," about the homophile movement.[127] The San Francisco SAC also forwarded information to the New York Field Office informing it that, to date, the DoB had not opened a chapter in that area but had plans to do so.[128]

By late February 1957, an FBI agent in San Francisco learned more about the DoB but this time from a potential confidential informant (PCI) who had provided information about Mattachine relocating its headquarters to San Francisco and its efforts to "expand activities of the male and female queer sections, because of their sanctuary here in San Francisco as a bohemian city." The informant described the DoB to his FBI agent handler as a "companion organization of the Mattachine" Society that "will also operate on a more definite status." Such a description was the sort that usually irked members of the DoB. Although it, indeed, cooperated on many issues and in different ways with Mattachine and ONE, Inc., the DoB was an independent organization but nevertheless and typically was regarded by outsiders as little more than the women's auxiliary of Mattachine. The FBI informant, at that time, reportedly was also working to compile a "list of its members" as well as the membership lists of Mattachine.[129]

In the year 1957, the DoB attempted to expand its reach by opening a chapter in Los Angeles. In an effort to do this, in January 1957, while attending sessions of ONE, Inc.'s annual midwinter meeting in Los Angeles, Martin made reservations at the Clark Hotel in downtown Los Angeles for sixteen women to have a "get-acquainted brunch" to discuss forming the new DoB chapter. Because this transpired amid the renewed and intensified FBI effort to investigate and silence ONE, Inc., it did not take long before FBI agents learned about this breakfast. They probably learned about it, in fact, through their monitoring of homophile publications and, in this instance, from an advertisement by *ONE* announcing the $1.00 January brunch as one of various events surrounding the midwinter meeting. Only after the DoB held the breakfast, however, did FBI agents visit the Clark Hotel, where they asked to review hotel records. By doing this they learned Martin had made the reservations and when doing so had described her organization to hotel staff as a "tour group," a misleading designation that perhaps struck them somehow as subversive. This prompted FBI agents to search their files in Los Angeles for more detailed information about DoB, and they located it in a booklet agents had obtained while collecting information on *ONE*. The booklet, published by ONE, Inc., in fact, described the first meeting of the DoB as well as the group's "aims and purposes." This merely recounted information FBI agents had already developed.[130]

The next extant reference to the DoB in FBI files appears in August 1959. During that month, two San Francisco–based FBI agents conducted an investigation focusing on two Mattachine publications: the *Mattachine Review* and *Newsletter*. The agents were able to confirm Mattachine's San Francisco Area Council was responsible for producing these, and the Pan Graphic Press along with member Call were responsible for printing them. When writing up the investigative report, one agent listed the various

Mattachine area councils, including their addresses. Finally, and because of the established DoB links with Mattachine, the agent added the office address and telephone number of the DoB, yet again describing it as a "lesbian organization and closely associated with the Mattachine Society." The agent was also careful to note that the "Mattachine Society membership consists of males only, all alleged to be homosexuals."[131]

The agent then noted for his SAC that Lyon was listed, this time, as the DoB president and Martin its vice president (among others whose names are redacted). The agent also singled out the stated "purpose of [the] organization to educate the public to accept the Lesbian homosexual into society." Interestingly, though, the agent ended his report with an observation, probably reflecting the dominant view of FBI personnel and other law-enforcement figures about the evolving social structure of San Francisco and the efforts being undertaken to deal with it. He wrote:

> It will be noted there has been a large number of homosexuals and Lesbians drifting into San Francisco and most of the contact are gathering spots for these individuals which are so called "queer bars". Statements have been made by informants that there are approximately 40 queer bars in San Francisco at the present time. Investigation is being conducted to identify and list the owners of all of these bars.[132]

FBI agents, indeed, identified these bars. The day after the report noting the existence of the DoB, an FBI agent provided his SAC a list of San Francisco's "known hangouts of homosexuals." This list was confirmed, apparently, by two sources, one of whom was a "confidential source." This list was then shared with military authorities, who took what was described as "disciplinary action . . . against the first ten bars on the list."[133]

The next extant bureau notation—in its headquarters file—of the DoB dates to 1961. In March of that year the FBI Phoenix Field Office requested from headquarters information regarding the DoB. FBI records do not make clear the reason the Phoenix Field Office was interested in this information, but it most likely had to do with the formation of a DoB chapter in that city. Dating from 1957, as *The Ladder* reached increasing numbers of lesbians, Martin and company realized the need for local organizations, if only to help educate lesbians or offer them a sympathetic ear when they faced difficulties. They used *The Ladder*, then, to encourage the formation of DoB chapters nationwide. One such chapter, in fact, was formed in Phoenix during the late 1960s, with the assistance of Shirley Willer of the later New York chapter of the DoB. At this particular moment, though, it appears an early, if failed, DoB effort to organize in that city was under way.[134]

When collating information to send to Phoenix—ostensibly, the document subject line states, for "police training" reasons—the Los Angeles SAC forwarded information from the Los Angeles Police Department Intelligence Division. This information included the address and telephone number of the DoB chapter in San Francisco and its basic purpose of education and acceptance, described as "following the lines of its male counterpart, the Mattachine Society." This information further included the notion that both the Mattachine and DoB "appear to have been infiltrated by certain communists" but with no elaboration or details.[135]

The Phoenix Field Office was further told by the Los Angeles SAC about the leadership of the DoB in San Francisco, its "philosophy" of education of gays, its desire to reform the legal code, and the fact that different branches had opened "all over California." The SAC also listed the (redacted) names of three DoB members in Los Angeles the police surveilled. Offering further details, the SAC noted that one of them "was a female operative of DOB and held business meeting[s] at her home the first Wednesday of each month," and another was somehow connected to the University of California at Los Angeles and attended monthly DoB and Mattachine meetings. All of this information, though, suggests the extent of police surveillance efforts regarding gays and lesbians, let alone that of the FBI and the liaison between the two.[136]

The FBI decision to place the *ONE* investigation in "pending inactive status" until *ONE*'s appeals had been exhausted resulted, in effect, in an end to the active FBI effort to silence the groups, even though the Ninth Circuit Court of Appeals on 27 February 1957 upheld the ruling of the Los Angeles federal district court, observing that *ONE* "has a primary purpose of exciting lust, lewd, and lascivious thought and sensual desires in the minds of persons reading it."[137] Julber appealed the case to the US Supreme Court, filing his petition on 18 July 1957. The justices initially, and unprecedentedly, voted eight to one to delay a decision on whether to hear *ONE*'s appeal until a similar case involving two nudist magazines—*Sunshine and Health* and *Sun*—reached them, as was expected. This occurred three months later, when the justices voted five to four to hear the *ONE* and nudist cases together. (The Supreme Court required at least four votes to hear a case.) Moreover, a minority of justices—Felix Frankfurter, William O. Douglas, John Marshall Harlan, and Charles Whittaker—voted to reverse the lower court's ruling, but because their view was not the majority the case would, normally, have been argued before the Court. Yet it was not. Instead of Julber and US Solicitor General J. Lee Rankin submitting briefs and making oral arguments, the Court simply voted on the appeal at a later date. In a five to four decision in January 1958, the Supreme Court reversed the appeals court ruling, but the justices offered no explanation for their decision. Instead, they merely announced the reversal by applying the Court's new *Roth* standard for obscenity, which had only been established the previous year. The decision was a watershed, for it affirmed the right of gay publications to be mailed, ensuring a vital avenue of communication for gay rights groups and others.[138]

Despite the massive FBI surveillance of ONE, Inc., and Mattachine and the bureau's efforts to silence their gay advocacy by pursuing obscenity cases against them, both organizations survived. They not only survived but both were successful in their advocacy efforts—as they were constituted during the early homophile era—and even won a landmark legal battle despite FBI scrutiny. We know less about the FBI surveillance of the DoB because of the continued FBI records destruction, whether of DoB investigative files or the individual files of its leaders or members. It is clear, however, the FBI did maintain a significant interest in the group despite the fact that male-dominated groups seemed to elicit greater interest in midcentury US patriarchal, hypermasculine culture—they were perceived as the greater threat. FBI surveillance and investigative efforts did not stop. In fact, as the homophile movement spread eastward and evolved to become more militant by the late 1950s and early 1960s, FBI interest only intensified.

Charles Fletcher Mattson
Age 10
Height 4' 6"
Weight 65 to 70 lbs.
Spread pug nose few
freckles on nose, brown
eyes, dark hair cut short
in Front (needed hair
cut)
small hands & features.
Wearing blue knickers, b
blue sport short (shorts
& sleeves) brown Alaska
fur seal slippers, dark
blue zipper jacket.

Ten-year-old Charles Mattson, whose kidnapping in 1936 and murder in 1937 sparked the FBI's systematic monitoring of gays. (Image from Mattson FBI file)

FDR's Secretary of State Cordell Hull (left) and Undersecretary of State Sumner Welles (right) outside of the State Department. Hull used FBI information about Welles's sexuality to have him ousted. (National Archives)

Senator David I. Walsh of Massachusetts, who was gay baited during the Second World War. (Library of Congress)

FBI Assistant to the Director Edward A. Tamm, who handled FBI investigative and liaison activities, including coordinating the investigation of Philip Faymonville. (National Archives)

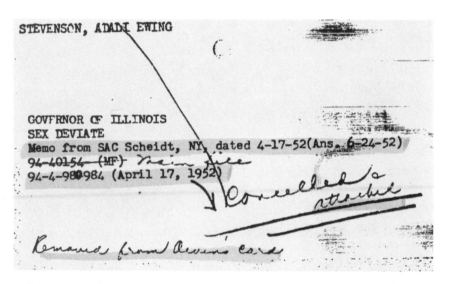

Adlai Stevenson's index card from the Sex Deviates File, the only known surviving such index card. (Image from Hoover Official & Confidential FBI file)

FBI Director Hoover (grey-striped suit, middle) and his assistant directors, including Clyde Tolson (third from right) and Louis Nichols (second from right), head of the Crime Records Division where the Sex Deviates File was housed. (National Archives)

Two-time Democratic presidential candidate Adlai Stevenson, who was gay baited and whose name was included in the FBI's Sex Deviates File. (Library of Congress)

Charles Thayer (left) and Nicolas Nabokoff (center) with unidentified man. Thayer and Nabokoff worked for the State Department's Voice of America, and both were victims of the Lavender Scare. (Harry S. Truman Library, copyright unknown)

Federal Security Agency Administrator Oveta Culp Hobby in 1953, who asked
J. Edgar Hoover for advice on how to handle gays. (Library of Congress)

UNITED STATES DEPARTMENT OF JUSTICE

FEDERAL BUREAU OF INVESTIGATION

June 20, 1951

In Reply, Please Refer to File No.

WASHINGTON 25, D. C.

MEMO FOR MR.	HOOVER	BELMONT	HOLLOMAN	NAUGHTEN
	TOLSON	BOWLES	JONES, M. A.	NEASE
	CLEGG	BROWN, B. C.	KEAY	PARSONS
	CONNELLEY	CALLAHAN	LAUGHLIN	PENNINGTON
	CLAVIN	CALLAN	LEONARD	PONTZ
	HARBO	CONRAD	LONG	PRICE
	LADD	DOWNING	MASON, E. D.	RENNEBERGER
	NICHOLS	EDWARDS, H. L.	McGUIRE	ROGERS
	ROSEN	EGAN	McINTIRE, K. R.	SIZOO
	TRACY	FEENEY	MOBLEY	TAMM, Q.
	ALDEN	GEARTY, G.	MOHR	WAIKART
	BAUMGARDNER	HENNRICH	NANNA	AND SUPERVISORS

RE: SEX DEVIATES IN GOVERNMENT SERVICE

For the purpose of establishing a uniform policy for the handling of the increasing number of reports and allegations concerning present and past employees of the United States Government who assertedly are sex deviates, the following procedure will become effective immediately in instances where the allegation comes to the Bureau's attention from sources other than fingerprints.

Upon the receipt of an allegation that a present or former employee of any branch of the United States Government is a sex deviate such information in all cases, except those involving military personnel, should be disseminated by letter to Mr. James E. Hatcher, Chief, Investigations Division, U. S. Civil Service Commission, Attention: Mr. Emery J. Adams. This letter should identify the employing agency and whether it has been advised. In addition, this information should be disseminated as follows:

A. EXECUTIVE.

    1. Civilian Employees.

        (a) If a present employee - to the employing agency.

        (b) If a former employee - to the Civil Service Commission only.

    2. Military Personnel

        Information concerning members of the National Military Establishment should be furnished by blind memorandum, via Liaison, to the Service Intelligence Agency.

J. Edgar Hoover's 20 June 1951 memo detailing the revised Sex Deviates Program, which began in April 1950 as a limited fingerprint check and arrest record program. (Document provided via FOIA; special thanks to Charles Francis and Matt Apuzzo for sharing it)

Frank Kameny, co-founder of the Mattachine Society of Washington. (Penn State University Archives, Jack Nichols Collection)

FBI Agent Richard Nichols Sr. and his first wife. Father of Mattachine Society of Washington co-founder Jack Nichols. Nichols Sr. failed to report his son's homosexuality to the FBI and was censured and transferred for it. (Penn State University Archives, Jack Nichols Collection)

Jack Nichols, Frank Kameny, and others of the Mattachine Society of Washington (MSW) were the first to picket the White House for gay rights in April 1965. (Penn State University Archives, Jack Nichols Collection)

Jack Nichols (center) and Frank Kameny (second from right) in 1965 with East Coast Homophile Organization (ECHO) leaders. (Penn State University Archives, Jack Nichols Collection)

White House Aide Walter Jenkins, longtime assistant to LBJ, who was arrested for soliciting gay sex in October 1964. (LBJ Presidential Library)

Presidential advisor and future Supreme Court Justice Abe Fortas, who was gay baited, receiving the "Johnson treatment" in July 1965. (LBJ Presidential Library, photo by Yoichi Okamoto)

FBI Assistant Director William Sullivan and Hoover. After leaving the FBI on bad terms, Sullivan would write about Hoover's focus on Jenkins and Fortas. (National Archives)

Jackie Hormona, participant in the Stonewall uprising, a Gay Liberation Front protest in New York. (Photo by and used with permission of John Lauritsen of the GLF)

CHAPTER 6

"Something Uniquely Nasty"

The FBI; the Mattachine Societies of New York and Washington, DC; Donald Webster Cory; and ECHO

Following *ONE*'s victory in the US Supreme Court, Federal Bureau of Investigation (FBI) officials' efforts to silence gay magazines using federal obscenity law effectively ended. ONE, Inc., continued its publishing, and the Mattachine Society, which had reformatted its image away from its more radical past and secretive, Communist Party–like structure, was also safe. Although FBI agents continued to passively monitor both ONE, Inc., and Mattachine in California, mainly by reading their respective magazines, they never resumed any investigation with the aim of silencing either group. Instead, FBI interest was drawn to the East Coast of the United States, where Mattachine Society chapters began to appear and where they began to act in more militant ways as a result of facing homophobic discrimination.

In California, meanwhile, ONE, Inc., continued its radical and provocative homophile activism, but Mattachine existed with the more limited aims of helping gays adjust in society and educating the public about homosexuality. By discarding the more activist approach of its founders, which had previously served to draw in highly motivated members, the Mattachine Society began to shrink. Membership dwindled, the San Diego branch closed, and discussion groups vanished one after another.[1] Nevertheless, Mattachine survived. It attempted to expand its reach beyond California, and affiliate branches appeared in some locations across the country. The San Francisco branch became the organization's national headquarters. Mattachine Society chapters appeared in New York; Boston; Denver; Philadelphia; Detroit; Chicago; and Washington, DC. Many of these chapters remained small and some barely operational, such as in Chicago, Boston, and Detroit. FBI officials showed little to no interest in these smaller outfits, and, instead, they directed FBI agents to monitor the larger ones, especially in New York City and Washington, DC. By 1961, as a result of internal conflict, the Mattachine Society's national organization collapsed. The New York, San Francisco, and Chicago chapters became independent. The Boston and Denver chapters closed, and the Philadelphia chapter evolved into the Janus Society, which drew limited FBI interest.[2]

The Mattachine Society of New York was organized in 1955 primarily by two individuals, Tony Segura and Sam Morford, but the group did have organizational forebears. After the Second World War, several gay men in New York City formed the Veterans Benevolent Association. The war had significant social effects on the lives of gay men and women, leading them to discover one another and develop close bonds, ultimately contributing to a robust gay identity. These developments led these New Yorkers to form a social club for those with same-sex attraction. Over time, by 1954, a secretive offshoot calling itself the League evolved out of the Veterans Benevolent Association. Although there were 100 official members, they were terrified of police raids and unable to accomplish anything, and within just one year the League went defunct.[3]

There was another, short-lived attempt at forming a gay rights group prior to the rise of the Mattachine Society of New York. Called Homosexuals Anonymous, this group was organized in large measure by controversial homophile activist Edward Sagarin, more popularly known among gays as Donald Webster Cory, the pseudonym he used among them and under which he published. Cory became something of a hero to many gays and lesbians in the 1950s after he published the book *The Homosexual in America* (1951), which offered gay men and women one of the first arguments that ran counter to the dominant and negative view of them as moral, criminal, and medical deviants. Instead, Cory argued gays were a genuine, if repressed, segment of society who were not criminals but victims of an unjust system. He argued, remarkably well ahead of his time, that if there was something wrong with gays, it was caused by their mistreatment at the hands of the dominant culture. He wrote that "homosexuals are a minority group, consisting of large numbers of people who belong, participate, and are constantly aware of something that binds them to others and separates them from the larger stream of life; yet a group without a spokesman, without a leader, without a publication, without an organization, without a philosophy of life, without an accepted justification for its own existence."[4] He also stood firm on the nature of homosexuality: "It is entirely involuntary and beyond control, because *one did not choose to want to be homosexual.*"[5]

A gay man and something of a contradiction (he was also married to a woman), Sagarin, as a middle-aged man, evolved to become controversial after he returned to university, earning a BA, MA, and PhD in sociology. Shortly before these developments, he had resigned from Mattachine New York after failing to be elected its leader. This disappointment led Sagarin to become disenchanted with the homophile movement, which, in any event, was evolving in ways beyond "Cory." Instead, pursuing his education, Sagarin came under the influence of Albert Ellis, a professor who advocated that homosexuality was a pathology and could be cured, and others in the field of sociology who held similar views. He even chose as his dissertation topic the Mattachine Society of New York. A major problem with his dissertation, however, was that Sagarin never revealed in his writing, or to his doctoral committee, that he was personally and heavily involved in the group under his pseudonym Cory. He even went so far as to write about "Cory" in his dissertation, employing the third person. He later became a professor of sociology and reputed expert on deviancy dating from the late 1960s onward, arguing in a proliferation of publications that homosexuality was, in fact, psychopathy.

This intellectual shift has led at least one scholar to describe him as a Jekyll and Hyde personality, between the pseudonym he used as a sympathetic gay advocate when writing *The Homosexual in America* and the legal name he used when writing as a sociologist that gays were "deviants"—albeit curable deviants. In stark contrast to this, in 1951 the Cory persona called for "an ordinary, everyday, matter-of-fact word" for homosexuals "without glorification or condemnation." He had expressed contempt for the word "deviate" as nothing but a "repulsive [word,] grouping . . . homosexuals with all sexual nonconformists: the sadist, the child-molester, and others." Perhaps the most illuminating example, however, was Sagarin's view expressed in his 1966 PhD dissertation utterly contradicting Cory's previous opinion expressed in his 1951 book: "Despite its [Mattachine Society's] denials, and in spite of its intentions, Mattachine thus becomes an agency proselytizing for the spread of homosexuality. When confronted with such evidence, the leaders reply, 'No one was ever converted to homosexuality.' There are many assumptions in such an unproved statement." Sagarin then cited contemporary studies of sex offenders "seduced into homosexuality." Even more, in one of the books he published as a sociologist, *Odd Man In: Societies of Deviants in America* (1969), Sagarin argued that the best gays could ever hope for was to form self-help groups akin to Alcoholics Anonymous. He regarded civil liberties groups such as Mattachine as leading gays to ultimate failure with their rejection of the pathological sources of homosexuality.[6]

After he received his PhD, Sagarin wrote his friend and homophile activist, Franklin Edward "Frank" Kameny, founder of the Mattachine Society of Washington, DC (MSW) that he would "be most distressed with my thesis, but I can do nothing about this." After subsequently reading some of Sagarin's related writings, the often blunt Kameny replied, "I say, for the moment, merely that it is an open question, at the very least, as to just who it is who has the ideology—the homosexual or the psychiatrists—and which is trying to shape reality. You have forged a two-edged sword which can be potentially deadly and totally destructive of any kind of dissent, nonconformity, change, or social progress, and can be used to perpetuate error permanently."[7]

Sagarin could be just as blunt with Kameny, particularly with his new frame of mind about gay individuals and homosexuality in general. He wrote Kameny, in 1968, after the latter coined the popular locution "Gay is good":

> Alas, I do not think gay is good, and I do not think the slogan is good, and I do not think it is good for gay people to have such a slogan, and I do not think it is good for a society for people to say that gay is good, although it is bad for a society to say that gay is bad, and it is good for a society that people have the courage and fight to say that gay is good even though gay is not good. Whew! Don't quote that—I may want to refine it a bit!"[8]

Yet it was Sagarin who helped form one of the earliest gay rights groups. He and several others formed Homosexuals Anonymous in February 1952 in New York City and, according to Roy Blick of the Washington, DC, Metropolitan Police Morals Division, it was closely associated with the Civil Rights Congress, a leftist civil liberties group that engaged in political action and, itself, a target of McCarthyites. One of the main efforts of Homosexuals Anonymous, according to Blick, was to assist those discharged from the military with the now infamous blue discharge—a dishonorable conduct discharge—and help them have their separations amended to honorable discharges.[9]

FBI agents and officials learned of the group through an unexpected and bizarre channel of information. In December 1951 an FBI informant named Phillip Louis Ellison was asked by his handler, Special Agent Francis Cotter, "to obtain copies of photographs of Soviet Embassy Receptions." The embassy had hired Ellison, a professional photographer, to snap pictures of its functions, which serendipitously placed him in a good position not only to provide the bureau the photographs but to glean for his FBI agent handler information about those attending the receptions. This he did, leading his handler to judge Ellison's informant work "reliable."[10]

Shortly afterward Ellison felt compelled to out himself to Special Agent Cotter. In addition to telling him he was gay, he admitted to being arrested in both Los Angeles and Washington, DC, "for soliciting acts of perversion." A highly motivated, bigoted, and apparently self-loathing individual who was also a Second World War veteran and member of the American Legion, Ellison embraced a widely popular, if unfounded, assumption of the time about the relationship of gays to communists. He "told SA Cotter that Communists have 'used' homosexuals throughout the world, and added that he would like to 'use' his homosexuality 'against them.'" By early March 1952, Ellison wrote Cotter that he had attended a meeting of people "who are starting a Homos Anonymous [in Washington, DC], patterned after an established HA in New York." Ellison also reported that a man who used the pen name Donald Webster Cory was "one of the organizers."[11]

Ellison further reported to Cotter that he had spoken with Cory. Given his interest in the New York chapter of Homosexuals Anonymous, Cory invited Ellison to a meeting there and told him, in the words of Ellison, that he "could invite another homo as a guest." Even more, Ellison reported that he had also learned of the existence of "an established Homo Veterans Association [probably the Veterans Benevolent Association], throughout the country" but that most of its members were "Jews." Ellison told his FBI handler that he would try to attend the meeting in New York out of "curiosity [*sic*]." Ellison concluded his letter by reporting to Cotter that a "well-known, normal, lawyer will address the New York group on the homo and the law."[12]

FBI officials forwarded all of this information to the bureau's New York Field Office for further investigation. FBI agents in New York indeed learned further details, and they did so by using another informant, a man "who has been very cooperative and of great assistance in the past in investigations involving homosexuals" and who had been invited to speak before Homosexuals Anonymous. This informant was Dr. Alfred Gross, a psychologist working for an organization called the George W. Henry Foundation.[13] (The FBI intended to conceal his identity in FBI documents, but forgot to redact his surname just once.) The foundation was a splinter group from something called the Quaker Emergency Committee, an organization formed in 1945 by the Society of Friends to offer assistance and support to young gay men arrested on morals charges. Internal differences, however, led to a split and the creation of the George W. Henry Foundation, which continued to offer, in the words of Sagarin, "aid, advice, and encouragement to youths who were troubled, particularly (although not exclusively) with the problems of homosexuality." This group worked with gays in trouble with the police out of a sense of charity, but in reality it chose to see them as people afflicted with some sort of abnormal social defect. Founder George Henry even testified before the Hoey Committee in 1950 as an expert witness on homosexuality.[14]

It was Gross, significantly, who revealed to FBI agents that the renowned Cory, popular author of *The Homosexual in America*, was, in fact, the pseudonym of Sagarin. Gross also revealed to FBI agents that Sagarin was the "proprietor of the Cory Book Service" in New York City, which "specializes in books by and about homosexuals, and [he] sponsors a book-of-the-month type of club for the distribution of these books among homosexuals." With this knowledge, it was then easy for FBI agents to fill in the details of Sagarin's particulars, such as his address. Gross even offered a physical description. In Gross's view—ironic given his surname—Sagarin was short and thin, had "dark, prominent eyeballs," and had an overall build Gross characterized as "cadaverous looking." Gross's description, actually, seems to have reflected the biased opinion he developed regarding Sagarin, as will be illustrated below.[15]

It should be noted at this point that FBI records repeatedly referred to Sagarin's group as Homosexuals Anonymous. When writing his 1966 sociology dissertation on the Mattachine Society of New York, however, Sagarin described in the third person one "Donald Webster Cory and several of his friends and correspondents" as having created an informal discussion group in 1952, to which he referred in his thesis as the "group."[16] Why, exactly, Sagarin did not call it Homosexuals Anonymous is not altogether clear. Sometimes gays described their organizations to straights using Alcoholics Anonymous as a rough analogy. This was an easy way to justify and offset suspicions about their organizations to heterosexuals in an era when homosexuality was not only roundly condemned but targeted by the police, moralists, and medical professionals as something dangerous. An early version of Mattachine did exactly this in the nation's capital (discussed below) when trying to arrange a meeting space. What is more, even in his dissertation Sagarin compared Mattachine's anonymous nature with Alcoholics Anonymous.[17] Perhaps Sagarin had explained his group to Ellison in this manner when meeting him in Washington, DC; or, perhaps, calling it the "group" was a way Sagarin masked the fact that he was, in fact, Cory, and the organization was his. There is no way to know for certain.

The invitation Sagarin had extended to Gross to speak before Homosexuals Anonymous convinced Gross in his opinion. When Gross was asked to give that talk in April 1952, he emphasized to Sagarin that the "Foundation specifically discouraged groups of this sort." He agreed to "speak as an individual," however, because he thought his experience in assisting "troubled" gays might be worthwhile to a group he probably thought included some. Having had some difficulty finding the home of its host, Gross arrived late to the meeting. When he did arrive, he was oddly "surprised to learn that it was composed entirely of homosexuals." There were about twenty men at the meeting "in various social attitudes" who were drinking alcohol and "having a good time gossiping among themselves." Gross, an apparent teetotaler, which undoubtedly reflected the original Quaker background of his foundation, found the drinking objectionable and questioned in his own mind "whether a serious address could be made to the accompaniment of clinking glasses." He was further put off by Sagarin's failures as a host because he "made no effort to provide the speaker with more acceptable refreshment."[18]

Gross spoke briefly, and in his remarks he equated the meeting with first-century Christians "living under the Caesars" and "in fear of the police seizing the assembly." He then offered what he believed a "coldly factual" assessment of what gays faced in the United States during the 1950s. He said the "homosexual had no rights as such that the community was bound to respect," and they should be aware the group would be judged "by the conduct of its worst members." He then described gays with the "now familiar theme of the homosexual as a minority group, subject to the disabilities of minority groups." Gross offered those present this advice: "to conduct themselves so as to command the respect of men by their public conduct, etc."[19]

It was not long before Sagarin had upset Gross because, in the doctor's view, the host had "set me up as a straw man to demolish my positions." Sagarin, apparently rebutting Gross's talk, began to argue about the accomplishments of "so-called Great Men of History who happened to be homosexual," which Gross took to be a rebuke. Making matters worse, and to the consternation of Gross, attendees continually arrived late to the meeting. After six rambunctious but tardy men arrived, according to Gross, they announced he "had talked enough" and wanted questions answered. This upset Gross. One of them, an "especially annoying individual," questioned Gross's comparison of gays to ancient Christians. He did this, according to Gross, because the man had recently seen the 1951 Roman epic film *Quo Vadis.* Even worse, in Gross's view, this rabble rouser was a doctoral student at Columbia University, was drunk, and "was an effeminate individual of the sort described among the cognoscenti as 'piss-elegant'" but more commonly known as a "pretentious fool."[20]

The final straw in this meeting for Gross was his realization that among the twenty-plus men there was none other than George Sylvester Viereck, the notorious German agent in the United States during the Second World War.[21] Given Gross's perception of the rude manner in which he was treated, then upon seeing a noted subversive, Gross concluded that members of Sagarin's group were only "digging their own grave." In particular, and perfectly in line with contemporary assumptions about gays in the 1950s, Gross worried about "Mr. Viereck having access to a group of individuals who are . . . easily influenced by circumstances," especially "if any are in Government employment." It was at this point Gross felt compelled to leave. He told those assembled it was late, and he needed to return home. Later, Gross concluded that his time spent at the meeting "was simply a wasted evening" and only "furnished ample confirmation of Dr. [George W.] Henry's theory of the unwisdom [*sic*] of homosexual group meetings."[22]

One week after attending the Homosexuals Anonymous meeting, Gross decided to report all of this to the FBI. He contacted Special Agent Thomas Minogue at the New York Field Office, told him about the meeting, in whose home it was held, how often they met, and that "these homosexuals have formed their organization to fight for their 'civil liberties.'" Gross told Minogue the members "were not too pleased" with his talk "since he is strongly against such organizations." Explaining himself, Gross told the FBI agent he was reporting this information "because one of the ringleaders of this group was George Sylvester Viereck, the man who was sent to prison during WWII for violation of the registration act." In his report, Minogue alluded to Gross's bona fides by citing his employment with the George W. Henry Foundation and the fact that "homosexuals [are] referred to him for psychiatric purposes by churches, other doctors, hospitals, and magistrates in the New York area." Minogue also observed that Gross "has been extremely helpful to this office in the past."[23]

At the end of May 1952, the special agent in charge (SAC) of the New York Field Office forwarded this information to FBI Director J. Edgar Hoover but to the attention of Assistant Director Louis B. Nichols. Nichols, it must be remembered, was head of the Crime Records Division, the part of the FBI that maintained the Sex Deviates File and that also disseminated its contents to ensure the termination of gay employees in the federal government and beyond. In the memo to Hoover, the SAC wrote that Gross "feels that Sagarin is [a] bad influence among the homosexuals in New York City and the vincinity [*sic*] in that his activity among the homosexuals tends to encourage homosexuality rather than reduce it." Moreover, the SAC reported, Gross reiterated "that Sagarin is a homosexual and a despicable person."[24]

As mentioned previously, the League, where Segura and Morford first found themselves, was the organization out of which, indirectly, the Mattachine Society of New York would emerge. Segura was a Cuban immigrant and research chemist with a degree from Emory University. In 1954, he read Cory's *The Homosexual in America* (1951), which offered "encouragement to those who, being homosexual like myself, are seeking the answers to the many questions they face in life."[25] The book inspired Segura and led him to find and join the League, where he met Morford. A disaffected League member, Morford was a clinical psychologist who for decades had been living an openly gay life. In late 1955, while at a psychological conference in San Francisco, he heard a talk given by Dr. Evelyn Hooker, one of the few psychologists who conducted research into noninstitutionalized gay men and therefore reached different conclusions than those psychologists who commonly regarded homosexuals as ill while studying only clinical cases. After talking with Hooker, Morford learned about the Mattachine Society (with whom Hooker worked), eventually visited it, and obtained its imprimatur to start a New York chapter. Armed with a mailing list of gay New Yorkers he obtained in San Francisco, Morford and Segura began their organizing.[26]

The New York Mattachine Society was an active group. As in California, the New York members organized gay discussion groups, published a local newsletter, distributed the national *Mattachine Review* in the city, organized social activities, sponsored lectures, and participated in gay-related research projects.[27] Almost immediately, because *ONE*'s legal case was meandering through the federal court system, FBI agents took notice of the New York group. In April 1956, the FBI SAC in New York forwarded to FBI Director Hoover two copies of the *Mattachine Review* (the March and April 1956 issues) and a single copy of *ONE* (the January 1956 issue) he had "received anonymously through the mails." This FBI agent was interested in these magazines because they were "published ostensibly for homosexuals" and particularly because they discussed the rights of individuals when arrested.[28]

Several months later, acceding to orders from headquarters, the New York Field Office received a summary memorandum from the Los Angeles Field Office detailing the organization and activities of the Mattachine Society "because chapters of the Society exist within their territories." This memorandum summarized all the FBI information about Mattachine dating from 1953. By the time the New York Field Office received the memo, Hoover had already ordered FBI agents to escalate their investigations of *ONE* and Mattachine after publication of *ONE*'s article mentioning gays in the FBI. Included in the memo was a list, obtained from an FBI informant within Mattachine, of the various Mattachine area councils and chapters in California and across the country, including those in Chicago, New York, Virginia, Florida, and New Orleans. The memo also noted, according to another FBI informant, that Mattachine's membership "had dropped from 300 to less than 100 inasmuch as they were getting rid of all the dead weight who did not pay dues."[29]

By November 1956, the FBI New York Field Office had also acquired from a redacted source (via the FBI San Francisco Field Office) a letter from the New York Mattachine addressed to a "Mr. Goodie." The letter told Goodie the group would be "delighted" to meet him and provided him copies of the group's newsletter. The newsletter interested FBI agents inasmuch as it noted the New York chapter's activities and that no chapter of the Daughters of Bilitis (DoB) existed there, but that the group hoped one would be established soon. (Interestingly, in the opinion of the New York Mattachine, "the ladies are rather shy and not too anxious to join organizations."[30])

For several years thereafter, FBI interest in the activities of the New York Mattachine seemed to fade. That changed, however, on 8 June 1959, when someone from FBI headquarters telephoned Assistant Special Agent in Charge (ASAC) E. H. Winterrowd, ordering the New York Field Office to monitor a talk to be given at a 10 June New York Mattachine Society meeting.[31] FBI officials' interest was the fact that *New York Post* journalist William

Dufty, a man noted for his exposés, including stories about the FBI and Hoover, was slated to speak before the group at Freedom House on West 40th Street. FBI officials learned of his lecture through an advertisement for it in the 30 May issue of the *Nation*, noting that Dufty was going to speak on "The Vice-Squad." Yet because Mattachine "is an organization of homosexuals," ASAC Winterrowd thought an FBI agent should not monitor the talk. Instead, he suggested employing an informant. Moreover, the New York Field Office shared this information with the New York City Police Department and Transit Police on 8 June, both of whom said they would send undercover officers, but only the Transit Police did.[32]

Two separate FBI informants, in fact, attended this Mattachine meeting, one of whom was determined "reliable," and the other's reliability was uncertain. The "reliable" informant noted about eighty people were in attendance, and he seemed impressed that "three or four women" were included. He observed that Dufty was "critical" of both the New York City vice squad and the Federal Narcotics Bureau, noting that both "engaged in entrapment as far as addicts and homosexuals were concerned." Dufty also pointed out that immigrants arrested on morals charges would not have been arrested for the same activity in their home countries. The only mention of the FBI, the informant reported, was when Dufty (ironically) made a joke about undercover agents being easy to spot because the FBI refused to hire anyone under 5'10"; thus anyone under that height could never be an undercover agent.[33]

Interestingly, when reporting all of this to Hoover the New York SAC recapitulated the information about the advertisement in the *Nation* and the background of Dufty. He then reported to the director what must have seemed subversive: "According to the informant, Dufty defended the rights of the homosexual and stated his own opinion was that there was no reason for these people to be taken into Court for their activities. He added that sex is a normal thing and the activities of the homosexual are legitimate."[34]

The New York SAC then included four separate examples of Dufty's "references to the FBI," most of which originated from the second informant. These included the observation that the word of FBI agents was not questioned in court, unlike that of vice-squad cops; that FBI agents ignored drug cases because they were not newsworthy; that the FBI was interested in communist influence among unions; and, of course, the FBI joke, which the second informer failed to report as a joke. The New York Field Office did not include the Transit Police report in its memo to Hoover, having only received that information on 2 July 1959. The Transit Police report, though, was more extensive and mentioned use of a recording device, but it ended up "not working too well."[35]

While FBI agents were developing information on the New York chapter of the Mattachine Society, an early chapter—a predecessor group, really—of what would become the MSW began to form in Washington, DC. This occurred about a year after other chapters had formed in Chicago, New York, and elsewhere and was stimulated, in large measure, by the federal government effort to purge gay employees from its ranks. The man responsible for forming this early Washington, DC, chapter was a thirty-year-old, probably unemployed, gay man named Buell Dwight Huggins. Born and raised in Illinois, Huggins began studying at the University of Illinois, Urbana, in September 1940. While exploring his sexuality at that young age, in March 1941 Huggins solicited a fellow student in a campus restroom and was promptly reported to the university police. University officials who confronted Huggins told him he would not be expelled provided he attended weekly "psychotherapeutic treatment" sessions with the university's assistant director of personnel and assistant professor of psychology, William M. Gilbert.[36]

To help him overcome his apparent deviancy, Gilbert advised Huggins to "smoke a pipe, never carry an umbrella, assume a more masculine gait of walk, [and] have many dates with girls." Unsurprisingly, according to Huggins, these sessions with Gilbert were a failure and did nothing to stem his same-sex urges, including the doctor's attempt at hypnosis.[37] As a result, according to Huggins, after only eighteen months of higher education, he was expelled in February 1942.[38]

After his expulsion, Huggins moved to Washington, DC, to find work. This was not a surprising development. In the years before attending the University of Illinois and over subsequent summer breaks, Huggins took temporary clerking jobs with the federal government in Illinois and Washington, DC, to earn tuition money. He worked variously as a clerk-typist for the US attorney's office in Chicago; junior clerk–stenographer at the Savannah Ordnance Depot in Illinois; assistant clerk with the Civil Service Commission (CSC) in Washington, DC; and junior clerk–stenographer with the US Public Health Service in the capital city. Having been forced out of the University of Illinois, Huggins looked to the only work experience he had in hopes of finding some sort of gainful employment. This led him back to Washington, DC, a city that also happened to have a significant gay population and gay subculture, which must have also figured into Huggins's decision.[39]

Huggins was successful in finding work, but never anything that really satisfied him. As a result, he took one menial job after another. In July 1942, for example, he began work, again, as a clerk-stenographer with the Public Health Service in Bethesda, Maryland, only to resign two months later to take a seemingly better job with the Office for Emergency Management. He then quit this job within a year because he was "not satisfied" and took another with the War Food Administration in the Department of Agriculture, but he would eventually come to detest even this. After only four months in the Agriculture Department, in 1947 he took a job in the US Post Office solicitor's bureau, where he remained through December 1954, his longest-lasting job in the capital. He quit this job after seven years, departed Washington, DC, for several months, then returned to take another job in the spring of 1955 with the Internal Revenue Service (IRS) that lasted only one month. He quit, reportedly, "due to an illness in [his] family."[40]

Sometime during early to mid-1954, Huggins formed his Mattachine chapter in Washington, DC. The August–September 1954 newsletter of the New York Mattachine noted that "word has been received from Washington that a member of the Society who is currently living there has had a preliminary meeting with a group of people interested in forming a chapter there." The newsletter informed New York members if anyone was interested, and "New York members are especially welcome," that meetings were held in the capital on Sundays.[41] The national Mattachine Society normally assigned its chapters numbers, under a larger "area council" such as Los Angeles or San Francisco, and the chapters often gave themselves individualized names. Little documentary evidence has survived about this early chapter in Washington, DC, but Huggins named it the Council for Repeal of Unjust Laws. No doubt reflecting his own background, and fears stemming from the Lavender Scare, Huggins's group focused on reforming US law and its unequal and unfair targeting of gays. The national Mattachine organization, however, worried that Huggins had set a lofty and controversial goal and, under pressure, persuaded him to conform to the more mundane educational and research mission of the national organization.[42] He rented a post office box for the group (P.O. Box 8815 at the city's southeast station), published a newsletter starting in July 1956, and invited speakers to

Mattachine meetings. Over time the group grew to forty members, a membership roughly equivalent to the other major Mattachine chapters.[43]

Huggins's Washington, DC, chapter fell under FBI scrutiny in February 1957—a full year before the FBI terminated its investigations of ONE, Inc., and Mattachine—when retired FBI assistant director D. Milton Ladd forwarded to the FBI two copies of the Mattachine Washington, DC, newsletter. At the time Ladd was serving as administrative director of the Commission on Government Security, a body established in 1955 to evaluate the laws, regulations, and procedures of the federal government to determine if they were adequate to ensure national security. In some unknown manner this commission had acquired the December 1956 and January 1957 newsletters. The December newsletter detailed a legal case in Idaho in which sixteen men were arrested on morals charges; the January letter discussed a local morals case, the murder of a gay man by a marine, and the possibility of gays in Congress.[44]

After detailing for the SAC of the Washington, DC, Field Office (WFO) Mattachine's overarching educational-research-ethical mission—a mission, ironically, the organization's leaders hoped would keep government harassment at bay—Hoover ordered the SAC to "conduct an inquiry" to determine who was leading the Washington, DC, chapter and who constituted its membership. In Hoover's opinion, because "it is possible" the leadership and members of this chapter might be federal employees, "their activities in this regard may have some bearing on the Security of Government Employees Program [i.e., the Federal Loyalty-Security Program]." He wanted a list of Mattachine members reconstructed and FBI indices consulted to determine if any of these people had been investigated as part of the Federal Loyalty-Security Program. Hoover ended his memo with a curt "Expedite."[45]

Because the Washington, DC, Mattachine Society listed its post office box on its newsletter, FBI agents quickly and easily ascertained that Huggins was the one who rented it. Name in hand, the Washington, DC, SAC initiated a request, noting Hoover's expedited order, with the St. Louis Field Office requesting a "review of [deleted but Huggins's] personnel file [at the National Personnel Records Center] for background information and any indication he is a homosexual." Afterward, the SAC learned from the Office of Naval Intelligence (ONI) that navy investigators had placed the California Mattachine Society under a mail cover, which, on the California

...d at least, the ONI extended to Huggins's Mattachine post office box. FBI agents also checked into Huggins's credit rating records, inquired about his previous employment at the post office, and liaised with the Washington, DC, Metropolitan Police Department and US Park Police to determine if he had an arrest record. The assumption was that a "sex deviant" would have been picked up at some point on a morals charge, and if so, to FBI officials, this was proof of homosexuality. Huggins, however, had no arrest record.[46]

FBI agents also contacted the CSC (from which they learned of Huggins's temporary employment there) and the State Department to determine if he was employed or had contacts there. The State Department, of course, was a particular and popular focus during the Lavender Scare. When Huggins wrote to the American Civil Liberties Union (ACLU) in 1964 to reiterate his story, he wrote that he knew an employee of the State Department who lost his job "on the ground that he was a friend of mine." Huggins's friend, moreover, confided to him that State Department Security Division personnel got their information from the FBI. In addition to this, FBI agents also contacted the Morals Division of the Washington, DC, Metropolitan Police Department, led by Blick, for further information on Huggins, but that division had none to share.[47]

The FBI investigation of Huggins was extensive and looked far into his past. FBI agents learned, for example, that in 1942, after he was expelled from college, which resulted in forfeiture of his draft deferment, Huggins applied with the Selective Service for conscientious objector status. He was promptly denied and then appealed the decision. Sometime in mid-April 1942, Huggins apparently decided his best chances of avoiding the potential horrors of war or the consequences of being an objector—conscientious objectors were forced to serve in civilian public service often at very low or no pay and in questionable conditions—was to be up front about his homosexuality. Huggins wrote a letter to his local draft board withdrawing his appeal on the grounds that, according to FBI records, "he was convinced that his being in a group of virile, heterosexual males at any camp would be disastrous to all concerned." Huggins's strategy apparently worked. The US attorney's office ended its investigation of Huggins's objector appeal, and he was never drafted.[48]

This was not all FBI agents investigated. In his 1964 letter to the ACLU, albeit with a time-induced foggy memory, Huggins related his multiple efforts over many years to contact the University of Illinois about his dismissal, including his contacting the university "security officer." He came to believe that not only was the FBI preventing him from winning promotion or gainful employment but that the university, too, must have been leaking information to sully his reputation. Huggins's reasoning was that he had had therapy sessions regarding his homosexuality at the university prior to his expulsion. He claimed his therapist at the university, Gilbert, told him after his final session that FBI agents had asked about him.[49] Huggins's fears were not unfounded, but, in fact, no FBI agent asked about him during 1942. Instead, on 8 June 1955, the day after Huggins had called someone at the university demanding to be shown his university records, somebody there "confidentially" reported to an FBI agent Huggins had claimed "information contained in the file concerning homosexual activities on his part had been instrumental in making it difficult for him to obtain promotion in the position he held with the U.S. Government in Washington, D.C." Also according to the FBI information, Huggins "indicated he was at that time a homosexual and he intended to continue as one." When asked by the university official about the "nature" of his government job, a perceptive Huggins refused to answer, and he "was somewhat ambiguous in statements concerning such employment in Washington, D.C." According to a later FBI document, Huggins was apparently unemployed at this juncture, having quit his job with the IRS, as he claimed, because of an illness in his family. Clearly, FBI officials learned of Huggins even before they learned about his organization.[50]

The same or another FBI "Confidential Source of Information" at the University of Illinois, probably Gilbert, then provided further information (redacted in FBI files) from some university records. Some of this information, indeed, included that from the University of Illinois Counseling Bureau, and it reported the lack of progress in Huggins's therapy sessions and the recommendation "that he be separated from the University." The FBI investigation also revealed that in 1952 Huggins had applied to law school in California, where he revealed openly his dismissal from the University of Illinois because of his homosexuality. The California Committee of Bar Examiners thereupon requested further elaboration from Huggins, but it appears he then dropped the matter. FBI agents also got hold of records from the university recorder's office about Huggins, but the entire page's worth of information was redacted.[51]

Given FBI agents' failure to develop a list of Washington, DC, Mattachine members, on 16 April 1957 Hoover reiterated his order to the WFO to reconstruct the list, and he ordered agents to "ascertain the present employment of" Huggins. Hoover was particularly interested in this information because of Huggins's law school application. Hoover warned the SAC that the "possibility exists he may be engaged in the practice of law."[52]

To step up efforts to develop the membership list, the Washington, DC, SAC established a mail cover, this time on Huggins's 8815 post office box, rented for Mattachine. The SAC believed this surveillance technique "both necessary and desirable" given the "lack of other established sources which could assist in identifying the organization's members." The SAC was hopeful this effort would be "productive" because, he observed, this post office box was the "only known means by which society members communicate with the local officer, B. D. Huggins."[53] FBI agents' mail cover lasted for thirty days and focused upon return addresses with the express goal of identifying Washington, DC, Mattachine members. The effort proved fleeting, however, because FBI agents were unable to compile a list as a result of the paltry correspondence sent to Huggins's post office box.[54]

Within a year, FBI agents were able to develop information, however general in content, that the Washington, DC, Mattachine Society was growing. On 19 June 1958, a canon at the Episcopal Church on Rhode Island Avenue phoned the FBI WFO to report the Mattachine Society was holding meetings, free of charge, in the church facilities. The canon reported that in these meetings, which he equated with Alcoholics Anonymous because it was his understanding that they sought a cure, "about 40 people" were in attendance. Seemingly uncomfortable with the parish priest allowing the meetings, the canon asked if the FBI could provide him any information on Mattachine. He was told FBI information could not be released to unauthorized persons. With this, the reporting FBI agent suggested providing the Metropolitan Police Department this information.[55]

Having done so, the Washington SAC subsequently reported to Hoover that a police officer had covertly attended the 18 June meeting of Mattachine, after which he shared his report with the bureau (a copy is not extant in FBI records). He then asked Hoover for permission to approach the episcopal canon and priest to glean further information about the names of Mattachine members who met in the church. Hoover assented because the canon had previously provided information, and he gave permission to contact the priest provided he proved trustworthy.[56]

By 14 August 1958, the SAC reported to Hoover. The agents only interviewed the canon, however, who said the church had ended the Mattachine meetings because the group could not prove its members were working to "correct the affliction of its members." In the canon's view, Mattachine was "merely an organization for 'boys to meet boys.'" He further advised FBI agents not to approach the priest because, in his view, he would regard anything Mattachine members told him as confidential information, tantamount to the bonds of the Catholic confessional. The Washington, DC, SAC advised Hoover that, in his opinion, contacting the priest would only be "unproductive" and probably "lead to embarrassment for the Bureau." Instead, he believed the best course of action was to get information about Mattachine from Blick of the Washington, DC, Metropolitan Police Department Morals Division.[57]

Huggins, who seemed to have a propensity for stirring up trouble, would have further run-ins with the FBI even after his Mattachine years. In 1962 he attempted to resume his collegiate studies and wrote Southern Illinois University. In his letter of interest, because he figured the admissions office would find out anyway, he revealed not only that he was gay but that he knew gay students and instructors at that institution. According to Huggins, this led the university to send its "security officer" to interview him. This officer told Huggins he was a former FBI agent, whereupon Huggins brashly said he "used to have a friend in Washington who had homosexual relations with an agent of the FBI." Huggins later told the ACLU this officer contacted the FBI, "and two of their agents came to see me to get my friend's name, so they could give him a hounding." This, more or less, but in fact, happened. According to FBI records, in 1962 two FBI agents visited Huggins and "admonished" him "for having made an unfounded allegation of homosexual activities by a special agent."[58]

This is not all. In October 1972, some five months after Hoover's death, a motivated Huggins decided to call the Springfield, Illinois, Field Office to ascertain the name of the FBI agent, "a fat, pot-bellied man who did not clearly present his identification" to him but who had confronted him in 1962. The other agent who confronted Huggins he identified as working out of the Carbondale, Illinois, Field Office, and Huggins claimed to have previously tried to contact him. When talking to the agent at Springfield, a man named James Colby, Huggins relayed his story, which the agent claimed could not be true. According to Huggins, Colby "was extremely rude and hateful and shouted," apparently having looked at Huggins's file, "that I had been removed from every college campus in the United States." Huggins admitted that he was forced out of the University of Illinois for being gay and "because a stupid, crackpot psychologist could not turn me into a heterosexual with his silly hypnosis and psychotherapeutic treatment." He then told the agent that ever since he had "been denied all opportunity and have been adversely affected job-wise."[59]

Four months after this visit, thirty-one years to the month he was dismissed from the University of Illinois, Huggins wrote Acting FBI Director L. Patrick Gray demanding that Agent Colby and the two agents who visited him in 1962 be fired and barred from any government employment. He asked to be provided after-the-fact proof of this action. Huggins admonished Gray not simply to transfer the agents "to the cold of Point Barrow, Alaska, or the heat of Biloxi, Mississippi" or to dispatch FBI agents to harass him. "The stunt-pulling days of government agents and security officers," Huggins wrote, "are over."[60]

Upon receipt of Huggins's letter, FBI officials noted he "appears mental," leading them to create a "mental card" with his name on it. The incident and letter led FBI officials to search their files for information about Huggins, and they referenced a variety of FBI files in which his name appeared.[61] Then, in July 1974, employing the stronger, amended, Freedom of Information Act (FOIA), Huggins again wrote the FBI director attempting to access his FBI file. He was still convinced the FBI and the University of Illinois had colluded to ruin his life. At first denied access to anything, the following year he appealed, whereupon the FBI released his own letters to the bureau and an FBI memorandum dated 22 April 1957 (cited in this chapter) that innocuously listed his places of employment and residence. Huggins was denied all other information because it was "contained in investigatory records compiled for law-enforcement purposes" and was therefore exempt from the FOIA.[62]

Revealingly, the FBI internal notes about Huggins's 1970s correspondence released to this author—in addition to noting his statement to the draft board in 1942 that he was an active Mattachine member and pointing out he was "an admitted homosexual," was admonished by FBI agents in 1962, and was denied reentry into the University of Illinois—significantly reference the fact that information about him was filed in the FBI Sex Deviates File. The number 105-12189-2841 is listed at the bottom of the FBI internal note.[63] The Sex Deviates File was composed of several FBI files, one being file 105-12189 (Sex Perverts in Government Service). As an on-again, off-again federal employee and leader of a gay rights group, Huggins clearly would have fallen under FBI interest via its Sex Deviates Program, and did.

In both his letter to the ACLU and his various calls and letters to the FBI after Hoover's death, Huggins made clear he believed the University of Illinois and the FBI had disseminated information about his homosexuality to prevent him from finding employment. Though time led him to confuse dates, and despite being denied access to government records, Huggins in fact was not far off the mark. Although officials at the University of Illinois did not proactively disseminate information to Huggins's potential employers, one or more persons there did freely share with FBI agents information about Huggins from university records, including supposedly confidential medical information about his psychotherapeutic sessions. FBI agents also aggressively compiled information about Huggins from a wide variety of sources. With little doubt, especially given the fact that Huggins had a Sex Deviates File number, this contributed to his inability to hold onto a government job after 1955, after he had founded his Washington, DC, Mattachine chapter. The FBI memo of 22 April 1957 released to Huggins in the 1970s lists his various government jobs, and that list stopped in 1955. Even in his appeal for FBI records in the 1970s, Huggins pointedly told FBI Director Clarence Kelley he was unemployed, indigent, and unable to pay FOIA fees. It seems clear Huggins, a gay rights activist, was effectively purged from a government job during the Lavender Scare, then unable to find a new one (the point of the Sex Deviates Program) after he "quit" his IRS job in 1955. Furthermore, given the fact that his employment record listed reasons for his quitting some jobs (family health reasons, etc.), it would follow that he was probably pressured into resigning or did so out of fear and intimidation. Huggins certainly voiced his fears about this, and he clearly felt the long-term effects of being a victim of the Lavender Scare.

The Washington, DC, Mattachine Society only lasted a few years, and by the end of the 1950s it more or less faded into nonexistence. It also seemed to fade from people's memories because, after its successor formed, few seemed to even remember it. Perhaps the most significant event leading to the group's demise was Huggins's departure by December 1957 (eleven months after the FBI began investigating it). He returned to Illinois, yet again citing personal and family reasons, but the real reason probably was his inability to find work. It would seem that thanks to FBI harassment, and without his drive and leadership, the group just could not survive.[64]

The national Mattachine Society also did not survive. After years of internecine conflict and petty disputes between the various Mattachine chapters, particularly between the San Francisco and New York branches, in the spring of 1961 the national organization collapsed. Afterward, Mattachine chapters across the country were left to their own devices, resulting in some surviving and others going defunct. Out of these various failures, a new Mattachine organization rose in the nation's capital, and, like its progenitors, it also fell under FBI scrutiny.[65]

FBI awareness and surveillance of the soon-to-be dubbed MSW began immediately. On the very day, 1 August 1961, cofounders Frank Kameny and John Richard "Jack" Nichols Jr. among others, met in the Hay-Adams Hotel, one block away from the White House, to organize the MSW, Blick, deputy chief of police and head of the Morals Division, contacted the FBI WFO to notify FBI agents of the scheduled 8:00 p.m. meeting to be held in Room 120. Even more, when looking into the tip, an FBI agent learned from a hotel employee the name and address of the person from New York City who reserved the room, and while the meeting was in progress, this person also made a point of walking past the open meeting-room door several times and "observed about 16 well-dressed men in discussion." According to the employee, they were discussing drawing up "bylaws" and "resolutions," were "well behaved," and ordered sixteen cups of coffee.[66]

The driving force behind the MSW, and the man most responsible for its establishment, was the thirty-six-year-old Kameny. A native New Yorker of Jewish descent, with a Polish immigrant father and New Yorker mother, Kameny, like many gays and lesbians at the time, served his country in the Second World War. In fact, his college education was interrupted after only two years (he was a student from 1941 to 1943) to serve in the US Army. In November 1944 Kameny was shipped to the European theater as a crewmember on an 81 mm mortar squad and saw frontline combat duty in Holland, the Rhineland, and Germany. During the Allied occupation of Europe, Kameny served as a German interpreter, then a clerk, before returning home with an honorable discharge. Following the war, Kameny returned to Queens College in New York to finish his undergraduate degree in physics, with a minor in mathematics, while conducting some undergraduate research studying optics. After graduation in 1948, Kameny then won a scholarship at Harvard University to study astronomy, a subject about which he had been passionate since childhood. He took both his master's degree and doctorate there, graduating in 1956 and having written a dissertation in which he measured the brightness of particular types of stars using the new photoelectric detectors of the time, which converted light into a measurable electrical signal.[67]

Kameny's acceptance of his homosexuality and experiences in gay subculture, and hence his future trouble with authorities, actually began before he completed his PhD. His experience, moreover, was not at all unlike the experiences of other gay men in the 1950s. While a graduate student, Kameny completed his astronomical research at the University of Arizona Steward Observatory between 1953 and 1954. Being so far from home, he unsurprisingly felt comfortable experimenting with his sexuality. Kameny then took a one-year job at the Armagh Observatory in Northern Ireland, where he combined dissertation research with employment as the chief assistant to the director of the observatory, Eric Lindsay. He also continued to explore his sexual feelings while in Europe, so far from home. Afterward Kameny returned to Harvard to write his thesis, "dividing my time 50–50 between my thesis and cruising the gay bar scene in Boston and Cambridge," and in the midst of this he decided to travel the country.[68]

"I enjoy travel," Kameny later wrote, "and find much pleasure and intellectual stimulation in meeting new people of all kinds."[69] Being a poor graduate student, he headed westward by bus. During a visit to San Francisco, an unsurprising destination for any newly out gay man, Kameny found himself in trouble with the San Francisco Police Department. While at the East Bay Bus Terminal after midnight on 29 August 1956, Kameny, according to the police report, was in the lavatory "for half an hour." While he was standing at a urinal, another man "reached over and touched the private parts of Kameny." Kameny later said he was "approached and, for less than 5 seconds, was sexually molested by another man." He also said later he had not solicited or invited the man's action. Moments afterward, however, two inspectors of the San Francisco Police Sex Detail arrested both men for violating the municipal ordinance against lewd and indecent acts. When the police questioned both men about the incident, according to the arrest report, they admitted guilt.[70] Most gay men in the 1950s would never dare contest such charges leveled against them by the police, and neither did Kameny. Instead, he accepted willingly a sentence of six months' probation and a fine of $50, hoping to put the incident behind him. He later described the arrest and court appearance as "painful" and ones "of extreme tension." After six months, and in accordance with the law's provisions, Kameny's charge was expunged on 12 March 1957. Yet it was this arrest record, which Kameny was told and thereby believed would be expunged once it expired, that would come back to haunt him and forever alter the course of his life.[71]

After graduating with his PhD, Kameny took a job as a research associate with the astronomy department at Georgetown University. He helped to plan observations of solar eclipses there, lectured, guided graduate students, and built for the college observatory an astronomical photoelectric photometer. Working for a Jesuit institution as a gay man unsurprisingly did not fit Kameny's character or interests, so by the summer of 1957 he sought new employment with the federal government and cited "dissatisfaction" as the reason he wanted to leave Georgetown.[72] Kameny would now work as a civilian employee of the Research and Analysis Branch of the Army Map Service Geodetic Division using his astronomical expertise to increase the accuracy of military maps. When he filled out his job application, however, Kameny listed his San Francisco arrest as "Disorderly Conduct; San Francisco; Not Guilty; Charge Dismissed" rather than the more technically accurate charge of "lewd and indecent acts." Because of the nature of his federal employment, even though he had no security clearance, Kameny would be subject to a background check, and it would be this personal oversight in his record the CSC investigators and his boss would cite—"falsification of official government documents in connection with your employment at the Army Map Service"—when later firing him. In reality, he would lose his job for being gay.[73]

In early September 1957, the Army Map Service sent Kameny to Hawaii for a one-month temporary assignment as part of his map-surveying duties to inspect "occultation field survey parties." While Kameny was working in the territory of Hawaii, the CSC sent him a vague letter notifying him that "it is necessary that you return at once to the Army Map Service in connection with certain administrative requirements." The CSC also told Kameny it "hoped that the interruption of your work will be only temporary." Not knowing what the letter was about, and indeed it seemed innocuous enough, Kameny did not really give it a second thought; he decided to finish up his work and return to the capital at the conclusion of the week. When he did return to Washington, DC, he was confronted by what he described later as "some two-bit Civil Service Commission investigator" who said, "We have information that leads us to believe you are homosexual. Do you have any comment?"[74]

Kameny's only response was to inquire about the information the CSC claimed to have. The official refused to tell him. Instead, the investigator continued to press Kameny about his sexual encounters and other homosexual activities. He refused to answer. The investigation continued for the remainder of 1957, and by 10 December 1957, basing its decision on the claim Kameny had falsified his job application, the CSC terminated his employment effective 20 December. Kameny assumed, unsurprisingly, although no extant evidence exists to prove it (it is probable given police sharing of arrestees' fingerprint records with the FBI), his San Francisco arrest record had been forwarded to the FBI, which then shared it with the CSC.[75]

Shocked and frustrated by this action, Kameny initiated administrative appeals with the CSC and the Army Map Service, but they were fruitless. On 11 December 1957, one day after receiving official notification of his termination, Kameny filed his first administrative appeal and was promptly denied. About two weeks later and in person, he then met with the Army Map Service commanding officer, Colonel F. O. Diercks, and its civilian personnel officer, B. D. Hull, in a vain effort to explain "his failure to list more complete information" on his application. After Kameny made his plea, Colonel Diercks asked him to submit a written version of his appeal, and after reviewing it the colonel "would then present to Doctor Kameny his final decision."[76]

Kameny wrote a long and detailed memorandum, including with it three character statements and a brief autobiography "to assist you in evaluating the trustworthiness of my sworn statement in denial of the charge brought against me." Kameny wrote further that he lived an "honorable life," had nothing of which to be ashamed, and "much of which I am proud." He argued that he never had in his possession a physical record of the exact charge leveled against him in San Francisco, and when he wrote on his job application "Disorderly Conduct," he was writing what he "assumed, honestly, to be the title of the charge." He had previously, and fruitlessly, made this argument in an addendum to his original 11 December appeal, explaining that when he originally listed disorderly conduct on his job application, although confused, he honestly meant the lewd and indecent acts charge. In other words, as he later wrote to Mattachine New York and ONE magazine, "I did not, until much later, know the official name of the offense with which I was charged." He also argued that California law allowed him to write that he was "not guilty" and "case dismissed" after having served his probationary period.[77]

Incredibly, Kameny managed to have noted psychiatrist Dr. Benjamin Karpman write one of his character references. Long a specialist in human sexuality, Karpman was the author of the first medical text on "sex offenders," a significant contributor to the development of the Washington, DC, sexual psychopath law, and a believer that homosexuality could be cured. Yet Karpman was also a staunch opponent of gay harassment. Probably because Kameny needed the letter quickly, in reality he and his lawyer, Joseph Fanelli, wrote the letter and then sent it to Karpman for his approval. Karpman asked for several changes to the letter, and Kameny promptly complied.[78] When Karpman submitted the document, he noted that after four sessions with Kameny, he believed Kameny had "entered the lavatory for entirely legitimate purposes." Karpman elaborated, with the version of events Kameny provided:

> Almost as soon as he entered, he noticed the man loitering who was later to become involved in the act in question. This person, when first observed, was peering over the top of the partition between the two stalls. At the time it did not occur to Dr. Kameny that anything of a sexual nature was in the man's mind. When the man emerged from the stall, went to the urinal several places down from where Dr. Kameny was standing, and then moved to the urinal adjoining his and reached out and placed his hand on Dr. Kameny's genitals, Dr. Kameny says " . . . this was unexpected. I was immobile for a moment, and then when in a flash I realized what it meant, I promptly removed his hand from my body, straightened out my clothes and went out." Near the exit of the lavatory, as he was leaving, he was arrested.

Karpman also argued he believed Kameny "was brought up in a quite normal environment" and had exhibited no "odd, peculiar behaviors either in childhood or adolescence which sometimes are signs and symptoms of the deviation yet to come." He also noted Kameny's adult sex life "has been quite withing [*sic*] the limits of the normal." Karpman admitted, however, Kameny had engaged in a "certain amount of experimentation" but characterized it as "common and usual among young people." Karpman also wrote that Kameny was "at present courting a young woman with serious intentions" and believed "he will marry and assume a normal life as so many others do." "I believe," Karpman wrote, "he is entirely marriageable." Concluding his statement, Karpman wrote, "These lavatories are used so often by sexual deviates that any normal person cannot enter them without running the risk of being involved in something or other."[79]

Kameny's inclusion of his dating a woman in the Karpman letter, actually, was something he described in a letter to Karpman as an "afterthought" to a conversation he had with him about relationships and marriage. This sudden, heterosexual relationship was to Kameny, moreover, a "possible item which you may care to work into any letter you write, or use as background for any comments or verdicts you make." Kameny wrote further he was not certain why he failed to mention any of this in his original conversation with Karpman, except "your question about marriage left me, for some reason, feeling on the defensive." This aspect of Karpman's character statement, in other words, was a late, and considered, addition. As Kameny put it in his letter to Karpman, after describing this woman and the types of dates they enjoyed, "I would be pleased to marry her, altho [sic] I'm not sure of her feelings—if she is. We're not by any means engaged, but she has no objection to my telling people, as I've told a number, in recent months, that we're considering the possibility of becoming engaged. Whether anything will come of this, of course, is difficult to say."[80]

It seems unlikely Kameny was serious about dating a woman. Instead, albeit unsurprisingly and understandably, it would appear he was prepared to do whatever was necessary to salvage his career. Kameny's dating a woman and, perhaps, marrying her to mask his true sexuality and protect his job was, in fact, no different from the recourse of untold numbers of gay men of that era. It is also significant to note that Kameny's views on gay rights, and how gays should regard themselves—with his famous future line, "Gay is good"—had yet to evolve and reach fruition. That could only come after Kameny experienced all of the various and traumatic life events he was to experience.

Despite his oral and written appeals and letter from his prominent psychiatrist, Kameny was denied reinstatement. Ignoring the argument in Kameny's appeal, Colonel Diercks wrote that his "answer has failed to show that you were unaware of the charge" of lewd and indecent acts in San Francisco. "That you did know of this charge," the Colonel elaborated, "is proved by the fact that you appealed to the Municipal Court . . . to set aside the plea or verdict of guilty." To the colonel, "this proves that you were found guilty of the charge," and "even though the court set aside the conviction verdict after completion of your six (6) months' probation, you were convicted of the charge as entered." In concluding his decision, Colonel Diercks wrote, coldly, that Kameny's severance "was considered justifiable to better promote the efficiency of the Federal service." Kameny was also informed that "no action will be taken to reinstate you to your former position." In a tragically ironic sense, it seems accurate to speculate that if Kameny had simply not listed his incident from San Francisco on his application, because technically the charge had been dismissed, the CSC might never have looked into the charge, and he might never have found himself in the position he did (and might never have become a prominent activist). It would seem, in the end, his scrupulous honesty did him in.[81]

Even worse, afterward, Kameny could not find work. He was effectively blackballed. As an astronomer his skill set was uniquely specialized, job opportunities were limited, and given the small pool of professional astronomers, everyone knew about his situation. He applied for jobs and was granted interviews but was never hired because of background checks and security clearances. (Certainly the FBI was involved at this point.) Kameny's position was all but hopeless because this all transpired in the midst of the Lavender Scare. Moreover, because he was jobless and his appeals had failed, Kameny spent a good deal of time writing letters, hoping in vain his situation would be rectified. He wrote the chair of the CSC, the chairs of both the House and Senate Civil Service Committees, and even President Dwight Eisenhower, all with no success.[82]

After a flurry of correspondence with CSC officials, a frustrated Kameny wrote one, "You go right on throwing competent, highly trained scientists and others out of the government, and make them completely unavailable for work elsewhere, on inane, trivial, irrelevant, irrational, outmoded grounds of so-called suitability, and through the application of meaningless, erroneous, logically baseless 'security' criteria. You drive them to starvation, into other fields, or out of the country." Kameny then described for CSC officials the effects their antigay policies had on those fired, using himself as an example: "As a case in point, as a qualified scientist in a field in which there is a severe shortage of manpower, jobless, I am existing on less than 25 cents' worth of food per day and will be able to do that only until the less-than-$2 which I have to my name, as my total financial resources, is gone. This is hardly the proper utilization of available trained manpower."[83]

It was a no-win situation for Kameny. A revealing internal memo from the CSC dated November 1964 made clear the typical stance of the CSC, and hence the entire federal government (including the FBI), when it came to allegations of homosexuality among federal employees. After outlining CSC policy about security and suitability issues surrounding homosexuality, O. Glenn Stahl, director of policy and standards, argued that "it is evident that we set homosexuality apart from other forms of immoral conduct and take a much more severe attitude toward it." He concluded, in a remarkably honest manner, "the result is that our evaluations are quite subjective, depending on the strength of the reviewing official's personal aversion to homosexuality in general and his reaction to the circumstances of the particular case at hand." He continued, "Some feel that 'once a homo, always a homo,' and tend to find against anyone who has ever engaged in such activity." Stahl concluded with continued honesty, presciently getting to the true heart of the purge of gay employees:

> In summary it seems clear that this is an area in which there is little objectivity. Although it is Commission Policy to rule in favor of the individual if there is evidence of rehabilitation, in actual practice we rarely find evidence of rehabilitation. Really, we do not apply Commission policy at all; we apply our own individual emotional reactions and moral standards. Our tendency to "lean over backwards" to rule against a homosexual is simply a manifestation of the revulsion which homosexuality inspires in the normal person. What it boils down to is that most men look upon homosexuality as something uniquely nasty, not just as a form of immorality. It is problematical whether any study of the subject could result in overcoming an attitude this ingrained.[84]

Kameny next decided to take his case before the courts. He hired a sympathetic attorney and filed his first case with the US district court, asking for an injunction against the Army Map Service and his job reinstated. The US attorneys, however, asked the court for a summary judgment in the case, which the court granted in favor of Kameny's dismissal. Kameny and his attorney then appealed this decision, arguing that the commanding officer of the Army Map Service had not granted a full and proper hearing during Kameny's administrative appeal. The appeals court, however, disagreed. The judges cited the code of federal regulations, which stated an employee could be fired at any time with written notice, and Kameny was not necessarily entitled to a hearing, which was entirely at the discretion of the commanding officer. Kameny, in other words, lost his case for a second time.[85]

Kameny wanted to take his appeal to the next level, the US Supreme Court, but his attorney advised against it. He thought the effort would be futile and refused to take Kameny's case any further. Undaunted, Kameny decided to write and file the appeal himself. As he later commented on writing a legal appeal to the Supreme Court, "My petition simply set out my case." Kameny argued that the basis of the federal government's firing of gays was "immoral conduct," which he said "is a matter of personal opinion and individual belief." Kameny reasoned because the federal government was not an individual citizen but a representative body of the collective whole, it had "no power or authority to have any view at all." Kameny, furthermore, argued homosexuality was "affirmatively moral," a position he later concluded was probably a first in any legal proceeding. In March 1961, the Supreme Court denied Kameny certiorari, refusing to review his case.[86]

His legal options now exhausted and gainful employment eluding him, Kameny began to move in new directions. "Preparing the petition was extremely useful," he later noted, "because it forced me to sit down and think through and formulate my entire ideology on this whole issue."[87] While fighting his legal case, Kameny had learned about the homophile movement, and he learned of the existence of the Mattachine Society and ONE, Inc. He even made some preliminary contacts with them, seeking any help he could find fighting his legal battles, but during the same month the Supreme Court turned him away, the national Mattachine Society had folded. Nevertheless Kameny decided he had "gone as far as I could go acting as an individual and that the time had come to act through an organization." Because the national Mattachine Society was now gone, Kameny would have to create his own.[88]

In forming the MSW, however, Kameny did not act alone. Kameny's youthful cofounder was twenty-three-year-old Nichols. (In the 1990s, Nichols described his relationship with Kameny in terms of himself being Tonto to Kameny's Lone Ranger.[89]) Nichols met Kameny amid the latter's legal battles in 1960, when the two became friends. Nichols was an ironic and interesting young man for Kameny to befriend. From Washington, DC, Nichols was also the son of an FBI agent of the same name. Nichols came out of the closet in high school, and, like many others, had read Cory's *The Homosexual in America*. It inspired the young man, ultimately, to become an activist for gay rights.[90]

Kameny also had the assistance of the New York Mattachine Society. He had already reached out during his legal fight to both the San Francisco and New York chapters, and when he and Nichols finally brought forward the idea of forming a chapter in Washington, DC, Curtis Dewees and Al de Dion of the New York chapter jumped at the opportunity. According to Kameny, however, Dewees and de Dion's interests really were rooted in gaining leverage in their internal power struggle within the dying national

Mattachine Society rather than actually helping found a new chapter. As Kameny later put it, "They figured they would have no trouble in controlling us and looked forward to having a flunky, which I had no intention whatsoever of being." Their help was significant nevertheless. They had an extensive mailing list of people on the East Coast interested in the Mattachine Society, and they sent out invitations asking people to attend the organizational meeting of the MSW in the Hay-Adams Hotel. Dewees and de Dion also attended that meeting, lending their Mattachine and organizing experience to the MSW.[91]

According to Kameny, an undercover officer from the Morals Division of the Metropolitan Police Department also attended the meeting. Kameny later keenly concluded that the Morals Division must have gotten itself on the New York Mattachine's mailing list and, hence, knew about the meeting (the police may also have had an informant on the list). Given the intensity with which Blick's Morals Division targeted gays, another meeting attendee actually recognized the man, Officer Louis Fouchette, whereupon he pointed him out to Kameny. Never one to back down, Kameny stood up and said to the gathering, "I understand there's a representative of the Metropolitan Police Department here. Could he please identify himself and tell us why he's here?" Kameny knew that, if asked, the police were required to identify themselves, which Fouchette did and then, apparently embarrassed, departed.[92]

After the preliminary organizational meeting, on 15 November 1961 the MSW was formally created. At this first official meeting, the members finalized their constitution and bylaws, elected officers (with Kameny as leader), planned to obtain a post office box, and did all the other sundry things new organizations do when formed. Missing, however, was Nichols. The young Nichols decided to visit his grandparents in Florida, where he met and became infatuated with a man. His interests now diverted, Nichols began pursuing personal interests, living on and off in Washington, DC, and traveling to different parts of the country, all to win over his love interest. The result was Nichols being largely absent during most of the initial formative year of the MSW. By January 1963, with Nichols's youthful infatuation exhausted, he returned to work with Kameny and the MSW. Kameny, somewhat of a taskmaster, let Nichols know he did not appreciate the younger man's behavior and elicited a promise from him to remain and to work hard.[93]

Interestingly, at this point in his activism, Nichols decided to let his FBI agent father know about his activities. Unsurprisingly, Nichols's membership in and work with the MSW greatly concerned his father. As an FBI agent he knew full well the extent to which Hoover targeted gays and their organizations, but when he expressed his worry to his son, he framed it in rather selfish terms. Nichols Sr. said his son's participation in Mattachine had the likely potential to threaten his father's retirement from the FBI, only a few years off. Nichols's father was vulnerable inasmuch as Hoover could fire him on the grounds that he was a security risk. Over the years, Hoover unhesitatingly quashed any allusions, no matter how small, to linkages between his FBI and homosexuals. He also had no qualms about firing agents he did not like, even if those agents were close to retirement, and their separation would ruin their financial futures. So Nichols Sr.'s worries, if selfish, were well founded nevertheless. To remedy the problem, his son promised to conceal his true identity and linkage to Mattachine behind a pseudonym—not an unusual thing for gay men at the time or for most Mattachine members in any event—at least until his father had retired. He chose the name Warren D. Adkins.

Meanwhile, FBI officials and agents were working to develop information about this new Mattachine organization in Washington, DC. FBI agents investigated Mattachine from multiple angles, including and significantly by developing confidential informants. On 27 May 1962, one such potential informant telephoned a clerk at the FBI WFO, saying he "wished to furnish information concerning a newly formed organization in WDC known as THE MANAGING SOCIETY [*sic*], which he stated was supposed to be a homosexual society but instead has proven communist infiltrated." The clerk misheard the caller when he named the Mattachine Society and wrote "managing." The FBI clerk instructed this person to follow up by visiting the WFO the following day, where he would be interviewed.[94]

We know the identity of the informant—Warren Scarberry of Suitland, Maryland—because an FBI redactor failed, just once, to black it out in the middle of a sentence. Scarberry appeared at the WFO on 29 May 1962 and was interviewed by an FBI agent and the clerk who took the telephone call. He claimed to be a member of the Mattachine Society, and "he wished to furnish the FBI a couple of names of members who are government employees." He offered them Kameny's name—"the president of this organization"—and another whose name is redacted and unrecoverable. When asked why he was offering the FBI information, Scarberry answered, "he was angry with the homosexual element in this town and that this is his way of getting even with them."[95]

Scarberry also told the FBI agent and clerk a member of the organization had a "homosexual affair" with somebody who applied and was interviewed for a job with the Central Intelligence Agency (CIA), but the names are redacted in the FBI memo. He further warned FBI agents, correctly, that most members of the MSW employed pseudonyms both in their meetings and "when they receive mail from the society." Scarberry also informed the FBI agents and clerk that the secretary of the MSW, whose name he did not know (Bruce Schuyler was secretary), had a master list of "all members, their addresses, and their assigned code names." He said he might be able to get hold of this list for the FBI because the "secretary has taken a like [*sic*] to him."[96]

On 31 May, Scarberry again telephoned the FBI agent who had interviewed him and reported he was unable to secure the list of Mattachine members. He did claim to have, however, a "list of homosexuals who reside in the Metropolitan area" that included some addresses and phone numbers, but Scarberry was uncertain whether anyone on the list was an employee of the federal government. Ultimately, Scarberry handed over a list of eighty-five names, telling an FBI agent he still hoped to get hold of Mattachine's membership list.[97]

Scarberry's full identity is confirmed by an extant document in the organizations series Mattachine Society of Washington section of the Frank Kameny Papers at the Library of Congress. Scarberry, apparently, was a man who for unknown reasons repeatedly claimed to be a member of, and spokesperson for, the MSW. He even seemed to have gone so far as to make "reservations and other arrangements and commitments in the name of our Society." Concerned by his activity, members of the executive board of the MSW wrote him on 26 May 1965 warning that if he persisted in his "fraudulent misrepresentation, however slight," they would press charges. What, exactly, Scarberry's relationship (if any) was with the MSW remains unknown. He suggested to the FBI he was an MSW member. Was he a disaffected former member? Was he an angry and resentful gay man in the region? Was he mentally unstable? Was he even gay? Genealogical records show he was married (and is now deceased), but in reality that reveals little. To date there are no answers to these questions.[98]

Seemingly infiltrated by the FBI, Kameny and his MSW nevertheless moved forward with their advocacy efforts. As historian John D'Emilio has pointed out, Kameny took a much more militant tack than the earlier, national, homophile movement, which limited itself to an educational, social support, and research mission. As D'Emilio quoted Kameny, "It is absolutely necessary to be prepared to take definite, unequivocal positions upon supposedly controversial matters. We should have a clear, explicit, consistent viewpoint, and we should not be timid in presenting it." Kameny's approach, then, would be modeled after part of the African American civil rights movement and include direct action and aggressive advocacy.[99]

In late August 1962, the MSW issued a news release announcing its formation. Characterizing its mission as "dedicated to improving the status of the homosexual in our society," the MSW described gays in the 1960s as "where the Negro was in the 1920s, except that the Negro has had, at worst, the mere indifference of his government, and, at best, its active assistance, whereas the homosexual has always had to contend with the active hostility of his government." The MSW then outlined its four-pronged "primary effort" against the discriminatory policies of the CSC, the exclusionary policies of the military, the "illogical" security clearance system, and the iniquities of local laws.[100]

These goals reflected Kameny's personal experience and, indeed, he would be the driving force behind the organization during its formative years. He began his aggressive, direct-action efforts with a letter-writing campaign to virtually every senior government official from the president and his cabinet down to every US representative and senator. They each received a letter, a copy of the Mattachine news release, and the organizational statement of purpose. Inevitably, some of this information—particularly that sent to the military cabinet posts, Secretary of the Navy Fred Korth and Defense Secretary Robert McNamara—made its way into the hands of FBI officials. FBI officials also received a copy of the MSW constitution from its informant, Scarberry, who also grossly overestimated the total membership of the MSW for FBI agents at 200 to 300 members. FBI officials then shared this information with Blick of the Metropolitan Police Department Morals Division because they "considered it valuable in connection with the activities of his Division." In return, Blick provided FBI agents a photo of Kameny.[101]

FBI Director Hoover was also a recipient of a MSW letter, and in true Hoover fashion he did not acknowledge it. Ever the militant organization, however, Mattachine wrote Hoover, again, precisely because of his silence. On 16 February 1963, five months after sending the first letter, Schuyler, the secretary of the MSW, wrote the FBI director noting that MSW "had neither the pleasure of a response, nor even the common courtesy of an acknowledgment." He said MSW expected the same "prompt, proper, full, constructive attention" and letter of reply he believed other, more mainstream minority groups would have received from Hoover. (Hoover, actually, would not necessarily have replied to those groups any more than Mattachine.) He told Hoover the concerns of gays were "valid ones," and "our problems are real ones." He continued, "They will not vanish if you look the other way long enough." Hoover, quite to the contrary, was not looking the other way; he was looking for information he could use to identify Mattachine members to ensure they were purged from any federal jobs and perhaps even beyond. In any event, FBI agents turned to their files and conducted a name check of Schuyler but found only that he had written previous letters to the FBI.[102]

Interestingly, extant FBI records on the MSW include a memo written by an agent in the WFO captioned "Mattachine Society of Washington." (The FBI, today, denies having a file on MSW.) The memo, of which five copies were made for Hoover, warned that a "source" had advised that the MSW, led by Kameny, "plans to submit a letter, probably sometime in September, 1962, to all Members of the United States House of Representatives and of the United States Senate." The memo noted this letter "will decry alleged mistreatment of homosexuals and will ask for equality for homosexuals in our society." The end of the memo included a notation that the Washington, DC, Metropolitan Police Department had raided a "homosexual club," and, worse yet, Kameny had dared to complain about it. It would seem that because five copies were made for Hoover, he planned to forward them to the leadership of both the House and Senate as well as his superiors to warn them in advance of Kameny's plans and strategy.[103]

Over the years, Kameny's MSW not only sent multiple letters to FBI Director Hoover at various points, it also placed him on the mailing list of the group's monthly newsletter, called the *Gazette*. Perhaps unsurprisingly, this action raised the ire of FBI officials. In late July 1964, Unit Chief Milton Jones of the Crime Records Division discovered this fact and informed his superior, FBI Assistant Director Cartha DeLoach, head of the Crime Records Division—the part of the FBI in which the Sex Deviates file was maintained—suggesting a response. Jones described MSW for DeLoach as a group that sought to "legalize the activities of homosexuals" while mounting an "active campaign" to permit them to hold federal employment. Revealing FBI homophobia, he described the *Gazette* as "disgusting and offensive" and advised DeLoach that the FBI respond to MSW's placing Hoover on its mailing list with a "vigorous objection." More specifically, Jones advised having "two Agents from the Crime Records Division contact the president of this group to advise him in strong terms that Mr. Hoover objects to receiving this material, and his name should immediately be removed from their mailing list." Hoover wrote on the memo, "Right."[104]

FBI officials repeatedly tried, and failed, to confront Kameny. Finally, according to Kameny himself, FBI official John W. O'Beirne contacted Kameny by telephone on 6 August and requested a meeting in his FBI office. Assenting to the meeting, Kameny, along with the editor of the *Gazette*, Robert King, met O'Beirne at 12:30 p.m. the following day. O'Beirne and another Crime Records Division official then proceeded to interview the two men.[105]

O'Beirne told Kameny and King "that the presence of Mr. Hoover's name on their mailing list is considered offensive" and asked them "to delete" it. Undoubtedly Hoover and FBI officials wondered if the inclusion was yet another allusion to rumors about the director's sexuality; rumors FBI officials always worked quickly and unhesitatingly to silence. Kameny, however, told him MSW had placed numerous government officials on its mailing list, and Hoover, as an important government bureaucrat, was simply one of those individuals. From O'Beirne's perspective, Kameny's placing Hoover's and other prominent government officials' names on the list "was to attempt to influence these officials to become more understanding of the aims of their group." Undeterred, O'Beirne explained that because Congress made laws and the attorney general set legal policy, "there would appear no need to forward such material to the FBI." From Kameny's perspective, O'Beirne was suggesting that the director did not want to be associated with any suspicious groups. Kameny then decided to reframe the discussion in terms of civil rights and how MSW not only deserved the backing of the FBI but had a legal right to mail its newsletter to whomever it wished. King, according to FBI officials, then assured them "they did not wish to antagonize officials by sending material which was strongly resented." King also invited Hoover to the forthcoming October MSW convention. Regarding removing Hoover from the list, Kameny told O'Beirne he would have to discuss the issue with Mattachine board members, and the meeting ended.[106]

Jones later informed DeLoach the meeting lasted a mere eight minutes, and "there was no discussion or argument concerning the legal, moral, or social merits" of the Mattachine Society. He also noted the interview was "calm and dispassionate." Finally, whatever response Kameny and

King offered, in Jones's view, "it has been clearly made a matter of record that the receipt of such items is considered offensive and are [sic] not desired."[107]

Kameny later noted that at this point he came to suspect the FBI was monitoring him and the MSW. Everyone in Mattachine except Kameny used pseudonyms. Even more, nobody in MSW placed a byline on any of the articles in the newsletter. Instead, those associated with the newsletter were simply listed on its masthead, and Kameny's name was never listed in the newsletter. The fact that O'Beirne phoned Kameny, himself, struck him as odd and led him to conclude FBI agents were collecting information about MSW because upon receiving the newsletter they went directly to him. A Mattachine officer, Gail Johnson, subsequently wrote O'Beirne promising to remove Hoover's name from the mailing list provided the FBI destroy all files on Mattachine. She also asked for the name of an alternate FBI official to receive the newsletter and said MSW reserved the right to mail Hoover particular items its members felt were important. Johnson made sure to explain Kameny's rationalization as to why he believed the FBI had a file. Kameny and MSW, unsurprisingly, never received a response.[108]

Although MSW received no FBI response, Johnson's letter and response to the bureau nevertheless stirred irritation among FBI officials. Jones characterized the MSW letter as nothing but a "blatant attempt to open a controversy with the Bureau." He suggested that any "further contact with them will be exploited to the Bureau's disadvantage." Jones believed it "apparent" that MSW was attempting to draw government officials into their efforts for "recognition," so any future FBI communications would simply "serve their ulterior motives." Jones, therefore, suggested not responding to the letter and ignoring all future MSW correspondence. Hoover agreed.[109]

Even before the 1964 FBI demand that Hoover's name be removed from a Mattachine mailing list, leading to Kameny's deduction about FBI surveillance, in June 1962 Kameny and other members of the MSW, perhaps unsurprisingly, suspected FBI agents were monitoring the group. In line with their extensive letter-writing campaign, they decided to appeal to Hoover's superior. Kameny fired off a letter to Attorney General Robert Kennedy demanding an end to FBI harassment. Perceptively, Kameny told Kennedy that "in the course of FBI interrogations, recently," people were asked about the MSW, asked for membership lists, asked whether "particular people belonged to the group," and asked about the location of meetings. "One was even asked," Kameny stunningly wrote Kennedy, "to act as an informer for the FBI, to gain and to pass on to them the names of members and other information about the Society and its activities." Whether Kameny and company were clued in to the exact work of Scarberry remains unknowable but possible.[110]

In typical verbose Kameny style, he referred to FBI actions against MSW "as being equivalent, de facto, even if, perhaps, not de jure (although possibly that too) to improper harassment and intimidation." He told Kennedy that because his group engaged only in legal activities, "however unpopular," it had a right to do so without being the "objects of official interrogation, harassment, and intimidation, and without making themselves the objects of official inquiry, infiltration, and informants."[111]

Kennedy referred the letter to Hoover, who ordered DeLoach to provide him background information on Kameny's charges. Information about Kameny is redacted in the memo DeLoach's subordinate, D. C. Morrell, prepared for him, but regarding Kameny's charges the FBI official said he did not "know what Dr. Kameny is referring to specifically." (He probably would not have known about the WFO use of informers, or he wrote the memo intentionally leaving out any sensitive information because it was a response to Kennedy.) He speculated, however, it may have had something to do with two FBI cases (redacted in the document) that both "involved crimes perpetrated by sex deviates." He thought this might be the case because "criminal informants having known homosexual tendencies" had provided leads in these cases. Morrell then wrote, disingenuously, "Certainly, the Bureau has not engaged in harassment or intimidation of this or any other group, and inquiries that have been necessitated as a result of matters coming within our jurisdiction have been from the standpoint of criminal intelligence." He advised Attorney General Kennedy not to respond to Kameny's letter.[112]

Hoover responded to the attorney general on 9 July 1962. In his memo, Hoover recapitulated for Kennedy what bureau files contained about Kameny and the Mattachine Society. (The Kameny portion, however, has also been redacted completely, but undoubtedly it noted his firing from the Army Map Service.) Hoover, in an attempt at deflection, added a small paragraph at the end about the FBI investigating "crimes perpetrated by sex deviates" and that some members of Mattachine "are considered as possible suspects" in sex crimes. Ever the master bureaucrat, Hoover thus provided his superior a law-enforcement rationale as to why Kameny believed the FBI was investigating him and why he was upset enough to write Kennedy.

Hoover advised the attorney general that Kameny's "malicious and un-founded charges" should not be acknowledged.[113]

Clearly, though, FBI agents were engaged in investigative behavior that a target would, rationally, find harassing and intimidating. FBI agents, more-over, did employ the use of informants vis-à-vis Mattachine. They did so not for criminal investigations but to ascertain further information about a civil rights group out of favor with most of US society, especially Hoover's FBI. It should also be noted that Hoover did not like the Kennedys. Un-like previous presidents (except Harry Truman), with whom Hoover culti-vated a close working relationship, President John F. Kennedy presented a unique problem inasmuch as he appointed his brother as attorney general. Normally, Hoover bypassed his nominal boss, the attorney general, when cultivating his unique relationships with the chief executives, but given the familial relationship between the two, Hoover could not do this during the early 1960s. Instead, he kept information in his files about the president's peccadilloes, information he could use for leverage if needed while keeping the president and attorney general in the dark about FBI operations—such as using informants within Mattachine to collect noncriminal information.

FBI agents remained on alert for any information regarding the activi-ties, real or proposed, of the MSW. In June 1963, such information fell right into their laps when the MSW secretary, Schuyler, again wrote Hoover personally inviting him to a lecture MSW was hosting by none other than Cory. The topic of Cory's talk was "The Homosexual: Minority Rights, Civil Rights, Human Rights," and it was to be held in the Gramercy Inn on Rhode Island Avenue.[114]

FBI officials were so interested in this lecture given their focus on MSW, and concerned Hoover was invited, that they made certain one of their informants attended. The informant (Scarberry?) attended the invitation-only lecture with a "homosexual who belongs to the society and who had re-ceived an invitation." The informant told his FBI handler that at the talk, he had recognized two "homosexuals about whom he has furnished informa-tion previously" and one other. Attending the lecture were about seventy-five individuals of whom, the informant reported, about 25 percent were homosexuals "with whom he had previously come in contact in the past." He did not know the others but given "their appearance and mannerism appeared to be homosexuals." Cory's talk, in the informant's view, offered "nothing new" and merely reiterated the "'party line' of the Mattachine

Society" about gays experiencing discrimination, not being security threats, and receiving unfair dishonorable discharges from the military. The informant made sure to buy two copies of Cory's book, one of which the author signed, and five pieces of Mattachine literature.[115]

The FBI agent handling this informant noted in his report that the informer had also participated in the "March on Washington Now" of 14 June 1963. The march, which started in Lafayette Park and ended at the Justice Department, was part of the black civil rights movement and focused on fair housing and employment laws in the capital. Several thousand marchers, both African American and Caucasian, took part in the protest. The informant told his FBI handler he participated "because he was sympathetic with the plight of the Negro in Washington." Moreover, the informant said he had asked a "Negro male to let him carry" a sign that read "Equality for All," which he, in fact, carried along Pennsylvania Avenue. It was not unusual for MSW members to participate in other civil rights activities. Much better known was their participation, albeit subdued, in the much larger August 1963 March on Washington organized by Martin Luther King Jr.[116]

By 1965 Kameny and the MSW would borrow from the black civil rights movement and initiate their own picketing of federal buildings, including the White House. FBI records indicate, however, that the MSW had planned this sort of protest two years before their now-famous 1965 efforts. The same informant who passed along information about the Cory lecture also told his FBI handler that a "leader" from the New York Mattachine Society had contacted him and said that "he was bringing approximately fifty homosexuals to Washington, D.C., in August, 1963, to picket the White House." Reportedly, the picketers had planned to carry "placards enscribed [*sic*] with slogans criticizing the government for discriminating against homosexuals in government employment." The New York Mattachine leader said he was trying to recruit gays in Washington, DC, for the protest, and the informant promised he would help, putting him in a position to provide information to his FBI handler.[117]

In August 1963, an FBI agent at the WFO received an anonymous phone call from a man, "apparently a Caucasian," who said "homosexuals may picket the Department of Justice [on] Friday, September 6, 1963, inferring they would protest that the FBI discriminates against homosexuals." In furtherance of this lead, the WFO SAC told Hoover that FBI agents "will contact informants in the homosexual field" to confirm the information.[118]

FBI agents in New York also reached out to informants and developed further information about the planned picketing. They learned the demonstration targeting the White House had been rescheduled for October, and it would be a joint effort between the New York Mattachine and MSW involving, according to one informant, "approximately 100 members." Regardless of their plans, the demonstration never materialized. According to one New York informant, the plan "never got out of the idea stage, and was merely brought up at a meeting by one of the members because of the publicity being given to the Negro march on Washington at that time." Hoover had his subordinates draw up memos on 5 September and 22 October outlining this information, apparently, for administration officials.[119]

To celebrate the second anniversary of Kameny's MSW, in November 1963 the group spearheaded a two-month fund-raising campaign. Citing the need to pay legal fees and raise funds to host the 1964 East Coast Homophile Organizations (ECHO) Convention, MSW mailed letters asking "friends" of the group to help it raise $1,499.99. One of these fund-raising letters found its way to an education counseling office at George Washington University (GWU). An employee of that office, not knowing where to direct the letter, gave it to the university's director of alumni relations. That director, Stanley Tracy, happened to be a former FBI assistant director who once headed the bureau's Identification Division (the original home of the 1950 Sex Deviates Program). According to Tracy, because MSW had requested use of a university classroom one year earlier, which it was denied, and was now soliciting money from the university, he handed the document over to Inspector Edward Kemper in the Crime Records Division "for completion of the Bureau's records."[120]

What is more, when Unit Chief Jones of the Crime Records Division explained all of this to his boss, Assistant Director DeLoach, almost as an aside and with imprecise language he described MSW as having "exerted pressure on the Civil Service Commission to discontinue its policy of excluding homosexuals from government." Upon reading this sentence, an exasperated FBI Director Hoover underlined it and scribbled on the memo: "Has Civil Service done this?" Hoover read the sentence as suggesting MSW might actually have been successful in persuading the CSC to stop discriminating against gays.[121]

Hoover's inquiry led Jones to research the question. He located in FBI files a 1962 letter the chair of the CSC had sent MSW explaining that gays were not considered suitable employees. Jones also inquired with the bureau's administrative division and its liaison section about whether the CSC, in fact, had changed its policy. They reported to Jones it had not. Hoover was not satisfied, however, and ordered the liaison section to verify the assertion with the CSC. Because the FBI was a central player in the intricate and extensive efforts to exclude gays from federal employment, and disseminated information widely across the government, especially to the CSC, Hoover was unsurprisingly, if a bit irrationally, concerned the CSC might have changed its antigay policy. His inquiry also suggests Hoover believed gay groups might be successful in the 1960s. The documents outlining all of this, moreover, were copied to the FBI Sex Deviates File.[122]

In April 1964, FBI officials' interest in the activities of MSW members took a bizarre turn, and, because of FBI file redactions, their interest remains unclear. On 9 April the SAC of the WFO advised Hoover that a member of the Mattachine Society planned to host a social function at the Syriana Club on Connecticut Avenue. The event was called the "Academy Awards of Washington, DC." The SAC told Hoover about 200 people were expected to attend, and most attendees "will be dressed as females," where they were expected to compete for different awards. Among the awards were "'bitch' of the year, hostess of the year, Miss Washington, best-dressed homosexual, and others." The winners, according to the SAC, "will be presented with engraved trophies." The SAC said Blick, of the Metropolitan Police Department, "has been advised." In many locations, men dressing as women was illegal, and those who did it were commonly arrested.[123]

The following month, this party resurfaced in another FBI memo—a form FD-209, used to summarize information from an informant. In an incident that remains unclear, an FBI agent approached his "homosexual" informant to inquire about a "victim" who had disappeared, and he showed him an artist's rendering of the suspect. The informant, however, failed to make an identification. The informant also could not identify other suspects in a group photograph. The informant did note, however, he had attended the Academy Awards of Washington, DC, event, where he had won the "gayest guy in 1963" award. He also noted for his FBI agent handler that there were "now three 'Hollywood Houses' housing homosexuals in the capital," and "the homosexual activities at 'Utopia' located at Connecticut Avenue and Q Streets area are still numerous." How any of this fits together and relates to the MSW, beyond it being a group composed of gays, remains unknown. Perhaps FBI officials were interested in (or just biased about) tying a civil rights group to criminal activity involving gays.[124]

In 1962 Kameny decided it would be in everyone's greater interest if the various and disparate gay groups fighting for equality on the East Coast worked in harmony. To effect this arrangement, four groups met in Philadelphia during January 1963, including the MSW, the New York Mattachine Society, the DoB of New York, and the Janus Society of Philadelphia. Not developing a new homophile group per se, what they organized can best be described as a confederation of homophile organizations seeking innovative avenues of cooperation to advance their common agendas. They called their loose affiliation ECHO, and, according to historian John D'Emilio, "ECHO played a critical role in solidifying a militant wing of the movement."[125]

One of their ideas, apparently spearheaded by Kameny, was to create informative pamphlets, distributed starting in the fall of 1964 by ECHO, for gays who might find themselves interrogated or arrested. As common targets of police harassment—at the hands of morals squads, park police, and transit police, especially in Washington, DC—gays were often susceptible to legal difficulties simply by being ignorant of their legal rights when questioned or arrested. Kameny and ECHO, therefore, wrote and distributed two pamphlets, "How to Handle a Federal Interrogation" and "If You Are Arrested." FBI officials got hold of these pamphlets from an "undercover investigator" of the US Army who had infiltrated a meeting of the MSW at which the pamphlets were distributed. In addition to being filed in the FBI Mattachine and DoB files, the pamphlets and memo were also placed in three FBI files concerning gays: File 121-14345, the WFO file for Sex Deviates in Government; File 94-65 Sub P, the FBI headquarters file for Sex Deviates in Washington, DC; and File 105-34074, the Sex Deviates File.[126]

In "How to Handle a Federal Interrogation," ECHO offered gays eleven points of advice: (1) no one was required to submit to interrogation; (2) citizens have the right not to speak and on matters of homosexuality should not speak; (3) for every question on homosexuality offer the same answer about it being an issue "of no proper concern to the Government"; (4) sign nothing, take no lie detector test, offer no names; (5) do not submit to "unannounced visitation by investigators at your home or" workplace; (6) do not fall for persuasive interrogation tactics; (7) "say NOTHING whatever" about homosexuality; (8) confirm no information interrogators might claim to have; (9) insist upon being treated with respect; (10) speaking to a lawyer about the interrogation is permissible and advisable; (11) do not resign your job out of fear or intimidation.[127]

In the pamphlet "If You Are Arrested," readers were informed about their rights under the law. Among these were particular details about sexual acts deemed illegal, the vague nature of disorderly conduct laws, that the police must inform those arrested as to the charges if asked, and that the police could not enter a home or hotel room without a warrant. Readers of the pamphlet were also given advice on what to do if arrested. Included in this advice was to remember the right to a telephone call, that one had to submit to fingerprinting and photographing, to offer no information beyond one's name, never reveal where one is employed, make and sign no statements, plead not guilty, do not forfeit collateral, get a lawyer, and "behave with dignity."[128] By 1965 the US Army was investigating who published and distributed these pamphlets. In their efforts, army investigators kept FBI officials informed of their progress. Army investigators learned that the pamphlets were printed by the Gay Publishing Company in Toronto, Ontario, Canada, but they were limited in what they could accomplish because of limited jurisdiction and resources. They therefore asked if FBI agents could discover who contracted for the pamphlets, how many were printed, whether any Canadian laws had been violated, and whether any information existed on the associate editors of the Gay Publishing Company. The FBI was in a position to ascertain this information because the bureau maintained foreign LEGATs—FBI agents stationed in US embassies and consulates abroad—who liaised with foreign police and intelligence agencies. Given redactions in FBI files, however, it is not clear what, if anything, FBI agents learned. However, this information (perhaps inevitably) was filed in the FBI Sex Deviates File.[129]

With the East Coast homophile groups cooperating with one another by the mid-1960s, the New York branch of the DoB drew FBI attention, especially when that chapter hosted in 1964 the third biennial DoB conference. The DoB chapters attending included San Francisco, Chicago, and New York but not the Los Angeles chapter because it had recently gone defunct.[130] In mid-April 1964, a member of the Cleveland, Ohio, chapter of the Citizens for Decent Literature contacted the FBI Cleveland Field Office to report information she had learned about the pending DoB convention in New York. This unidentified woman (her name is redacted in FBI documents) informed FBI agents she had learned DoB was planning to hold its national convention in New York City at the Hotel New Yorker on 20 June 1964.[131]

After being made aware of these developments, FBI Director Hoover forwarded this information to his bureau's New York Field Office and ordered the SAC there to "furnish this information to local authorities and follow this matter for possible Bureau interest." The FBI documents detailing this information, interestingly enough, were labeled and filed under a white-slave-trafficking classification. The White Slave Trafficking Act was passed in 1910 and hence was one of the oldest FBI filing classifications. The vaguely worded law, although intended to target prostitution rings, in the end only helped to expand bureau investigations beyond prostitution and crime fighting to the realm of morality policing. Federal law enforcers, in fact, often times used the law to investigate matters well beyond the scope of criminal prostitution, and in this case because a New York hotel was slated as the proposed site for the DoB convention, it would seem FBI officials, officially or bureaucratically at least, regarded a group of lesbians meeting there to constitute a possible white-slave-trafficking case. FBI agents, in point of fact, often and in particular investigated white-slave-trafficking cases when they involved hotels, clubs, truck stops, or massage parlors.[132]

What, exactly, FBI officials did with this information remains unclear. On 8 June 1964 FBI agents interviewed a (redacted) source from the Hotel New Yorker, undoubtedly management, who told them Shirley Willer, the president of New York chapter of DoB, on 7 February had attempted to make reservations with the hotel to host its conference. The manager asked Willer for a $400 deposit but never received it. He also attempted to ascertain "any credit rating on the organization," and when that failed he canceled the tentative reservation. According to DoB leaders Del Martin and Phillis Lyon, however, the hotel management continually delayed finalization of the reservation by repeatedly demanding of DoB constantly changing requirements. Extant FBI records confirm this. They indicate that hotel management not only demanded the $400 deposit but also demanded more detailed information about the DoB before finalizing the reservation. In response, Ev Howe, national treasurer of the DoB, sent the hotel a letter explaining that the group was headquartered in San Francisco and that the State of California had even incorporated the group. Howe also explained that the overarching mission of the DoB was to advocate for the integration of homosexuals into US society, and, moreover, the group successfully, and with no trouble, had held conventions at different hotels in California. Howe also forwarded with her letter two copies of *The Ladder*. In the end this failed to satisfy the hotel managers. The group ended up holding its biennial convention, instead, at the Barbizon-Plaza Hotel on 20–21 June 1964.[133]

After the failure of the DoB to make reservations with the Hotel New Yorker, FBI agents repeatedly tried to ascertain where, in fact, the group afterward held its convention. FBI agents asked the management of the Hotel New Yorker this very question, in fact, and they queried the Convention Bureau of New York City. Neither knew the new location. It seems clear given the date of Willer's initial contact with the hotel (February 1964), the date of the FBI first learning of the DoB plans and then advising the New York Field Office about them (late April 1964), and the time FBI agents interviewed the hotel manager (early June 1964), the FBI could not, in fact, have actively sabotaged the DoB Convention reservations, as has been proposed elsewhere. What FBI officials did do, however, was to take the FBI memorandum outlining this hotel brouhaha and file it in the Sex Deviates File, for on the margin of one DoB document was written, "Unrecorded copy filed in 105-34074-47162." This was one of the file numbers associated with the Sex Deviates File, and as reflected in the serial (document number 47162), by the mid-1960s the file had grown staggeringly large.[134]

Reflecting the web of connections and liaisons FBI officials maintained, which enabled them to collect vast amounts of information about gays and lesbians, in January 1965 the US Post Office forwarded to the FBI information it knew bureau officials would find interesting. An official in the US Post Office Division of Personnel Security noticed that the December 1964 issue of *Drum* magazine—a gay magazine published by the Philadelphia-based Janus Society, a group that evolved after the national Mattachine organization had dissolved—indicated the January 1965 issue was to include an article titled "I Was a Homosexual for the FBI." When FBI officials received the magazine, it was routed to the Crime Research Section of the Crime Records Division, those responsible for maintaining the Sex Deviates File and the bureau's experts on gays.[135]

When the January issue was finally published, FBI officials found nothing in the magazine. Two months later, however, because of publishing delays, the article appeared. When Unit Chief Jones of the Crime Records Division read this piece, he found it "strictly trash" and nothing but a "parody" written by one P. Arody. The piece was obviously a take on the "I Was a Communist for the FBI" stories (published as a book and made into a radio series and a film) of Pittsburgh native and FBI informer Matt Cvetic. The article, in part, read:

> As an *agent provacature* [sic] for the FBI, I have seen how homosexuals operate—how they disguise themselves as heterosexuals and infiltrate industry and Government in order to gain employment; how they lull their families and friends into thinking they are what they call "straight" to escape the ostracism that is their just due; and how they issue deceitful propaganda claiming that they are really no different from our normal world.

Probably incensed at the gall of the magazine, Jones consulted with the Impersonation Desk of the FBI General Investigative Division for an opinion about possible criminal investigation. Those officials were not interested, however. Jones advised his superior, therefore, "Past experience has shown that there is nothing to be gained by contacting the individuals connected with this type of publication." He further suggested taking "no action with reference to the article," probably reflecting the FBI experience with Kameny and the MSW newsletter, yet advised that the FBI Liaison Section of the Domestic Intelligence Division stay in touch with the US Post Office to see if it took action.[136]

By the spring of 1965, after news reports indicated the Cuban government was sending gays to forced labor camps as an "alarming political and social matter" because "no homosexual represents the revolution, which is a movement of he-men," ECHO decided the time was right for picketing. Previous efforts to organize a picket, spearheaded by the New York Mattachine Society in conjunction with the MSW, had failed to materialize. Now, with a militant confederation of gay activist groups in the forefront of homophile activity (ECHO) and several years of militant activism under their belts, Nichols and others led the effort for a series of pickets.[137]

Nichols, enraged by the Cuban action, had to push for the effort because in the past Kameny wanted to reserve picketing only for issues that had the potential to win public sympathy for gays. Nichols argued that Cuba—not only a cold war opponent but gay oppressor using Nazi-like tactics—was just that kind of issue, and he convinced Kameny. They decided to picket the White House on 17 April 1965 because the United States maintained no diplomatic relations with the Castro regime and, hence, there was no Cuban embassy in the capital; the United Nations was picketed separately and independently by the New York Mattachine the following day. At Kameny's insistence, moreover, and perhaps reflecting ideas put forward in his pamphlets, the men wore suits and the women dresses and conducted themselves in a stoic, orderly manner. Mattachine would also notify the targets in advance of the picketing. Kameny did not want to leave anything open to critics.[138] Subsequent pickets were planned between May and October: on 29 May a second White House protest, on 26 June at the CSC, on 4 July at Independence Hall in Philadelphia, on 31 July at the Pentagon, on 28 August at the State Department, and on 23 October 1965 yet again at the White House.[139]

After one of the White House pickets, according to Nichols, his FBI-agent father again became distraught over his son's public activities. According to Nichols Jr., "He was worried that J. Edgar Hoover would connect me with him (because of our names) and that he might have trouble on his job." At some point following the protest, Nichols Sr. visited his son to discuss the picketing. Before doing so, however, his father searched Nichols Jr.'s house for FBI microphones, fearing Hoover might already know about his son and that he had marched in front of the White House. He then "began an angry lecture, accusing Jack of putting his career in jeopardy." Nichols Jr. thought his father was paranoid, self-centered, and only concerned with his career, especially after Nichols Sr. created a family tree for Jack to illustrate how easily the FBI could trace him back to his father. Nichols Sr. even threatened his son's life, he was so upset. A now-angry son admonished his father for demeaning him, and, in fact, after this confrontation, he never saw or spoke with his father again.[140]

Within a few months of this confrontation (if not actually before), during early 1966, FBI officials came to learn exactly who Nichols Jr. was, including his use of a pseudonym. On 6 February 1966 his stepfather in Florida (his mother divorced his father after the Second World War) called the FBI and relayed that his stepson was a member of the MSW and asked for information about the group. Nichols Jr.'s stepfather was told FBI information was confidential, but his call had the effect, whether intentional, of outing his stepson and the fact that his father was an FBI agent. This triggered an internal FBI inquiry concerning Special Agent John Richard Nichols Sr. and his failure to report his son's status to FBI officials.[141]

Officials in the FBI Administrative Division confronted Special Agent

Nichols about the telephone call and his son, after which he offered FBI officials details. He revealed his son was, in fact, a "homosexual." He told them his son was the product of his first marriage, lived in Washington, DC, and worked as a counselor at the Capital Radio Engineering Institute (today Capital Technology University). Special Agent Nichols also told them his son was "Executive Director of the Mattachine Society of Washington under the name of Warren Adkins."[142]

In attempting to explain himself, Nichols Sr. told his superiors he divorced his wife in July 1946, after which his wife took legal custody of their son. Nichols Sr. then remarried in March 1948 and was transferred to Philadelphia in 1949, where his ex-wife soon also relocated. He then said when he visited his son he "determined that he was a disciplinary problem," whereupon Nichols Jr.'s stepfather asked him to take custody of his son. Nichols Jr.'s mother objected, but during one visit with his father and stepmother, she apparently ascertained that her fourteen-year-old stepson was gay. Special Agent Nichols told his superiors he was "completely shocked at this and did not confront his son with this information at that time." He also noted his son had tried running away at this time and associated with an Iranian family.[143]

Special Agent Nichols then advised his FBI superiors that in September 1954, shortly after he had been transferred to Washington, DC, Nichols Jr. outed himself to his father. When asked why he had not revealed this fact to the FBI, Special Agent Nichols answered that it was because he had not raised his son. He also said, until the present time, he had asked his son to keep his sexuality private to "protect his father and the Bureau from embarrassment." Nichols Sr. then claimed the "situation has caused him considerable emotional concern," prompting him to seek advice from clergy members. They offered no answers, so Nichols Sr. said he tried to direct his son toward the "Christian faith," but only learned his son "was a confirmed atheist." Nichols Sr. also claimed his son ran away with a girl at one point, then asked him for money; he said he gave his son the money, thinking "he was beginning to act in a normal manner."[144]

Special Agent Nichols then explained he had been restrained and only "maintained occasional contact with his son" since being transferred to Washington, DC, "so as not to jeopardize his family or embarrass the Bureau." He then relayed details about his latest meeting with his son, two or three months previous, when he learned his son was a leading member of MSW and wrote "articles for homosexual magazines." This revelation prompted FBI officials to search FBI files, where they found Nichols Jr.'s pseudonym (Warren Adkins) listed in a May 1965 issue of *Eastern Mattachine Magazine* and listed as a staffer for the MSW newsletter, the *Gazette*. Nichols Sr. also noted that recently his son had shown him copies of letters MSW had planned to mail to clergy and government officials, including Hoover.[145]

Special Agent Nichols then advised his superiors that six or eight months ago, his son told him his stepfather, an alcoholic, "had called the Capital Radio Engineering Institute and threatened [him] with bodily harm." This prompted Nichols Jr. to move to a new address in Arlington, Virginia. Meanwhile, his stepfather made repeated attempts to contact Special Agent Nichols, but he ignored the calls. At this point, now pointedly concerned about his job, Special Agent Nichols said he now only maintained "occasional contact" with his son out of a desire to "influence his son to think someday as a normal male." He also told FBI officials although he would like to continue seeing his son on occasion, he also did "not want to jeopardize his job or family and if asked to do so by the Bureau, he will stop seeing his son."[146]

After interviewing Special Agent Nichols, FBI officials searched FBI files for the MSW letter Nichols noted that his son had a hand in sending to top government officials. Although they could not locate it, they nevertheless noted that one copy was forwarded to the president following picketing of the White House. FBI officials then ran a name check of both Jack Nichols and his pseudonym, Warren Adkins, but turned up nothing other than the Adkins references in the MSW publications. FBI agents further consulted with the Washington, DC, Metropolitan Police Department but unearthed nothing except a 1964 traffic citation.[147]

FBI officials in the Administrative Division found Special Agent Nichols's "failure to advise the Bureau of this problem involving his son" to be "inexcusable." They did not find the fact that Nichols Jr. was using a pseudonym adequate in light of the fact that he and his father shared identical names, which, in FBI officials' view, "could develop into a source of great embarrassment to the Bureau; particularly in view of his son's more active role in the Mattachine Society." Therefore, the FBI Administrative Division suggested censuring Special Agent Nichols, placing him on probation, and transferring him out of Washington, DC, "for his flagrant disregard of regulations which require that employees immediately advise the Bureau of any situation which could possibly be a source of embarrassment to the

Bureau." In the Hoover FBI, being transferred to an undesirable FBI field office was common punishment for those who upset the FBI director. To date, because the FBI has not yet released Special Agent Nichols's personnel file, there is no way of knowing if he was punished in this manner, but there is no reason to believe he would not have been; Hoover even initialed the memo regarding all of this. It is clear Nichols Sr. never spoke with his son again after this point.[148]

FBI officials seemingly only caught on to the pickets after the CSC received Kameny's notice of the pending demonstration. After receiving the notice, someone at the CSC notified an FBI supervisor, who, in turn, notified the FBI WFO. An FBI agent there then shared the information with a captain in the Metropolitan Police Department investigations squad. The reason the FBI seems to have been interested only after the CSC learned of the protest can be understood in a couple of ways. First, the White House picket was overshadowed by a larger antiwar demonstration at the Washington Monument. Only a handful of protestors appeared at the White House—twelve according to the *New York Times*—whereas 20,000 participated in the other protest. Also, Mattachine's demonstration was the first of its kind and hence not anticipated, if given any thought whatsoever. During the Lavender Scare the CSC and FBI cooperated intimately in ascertaining who in government was homosexual and then worked together to ensure their firing. So a sudden gay protest before the CSC building would certainly have caught their attention.[149]

The Pentagon was Mattachine's next target for picketing, on 31 July 1965. For this demonstration the Joint Chiefs of Staff (JCS) ordered a chief warrant officer of the US Army Criminal Investigation Division to photograph the picketers using a telephoto lens. He photographed all of the pickets, of whom the army could only identify one, probably Kameny because his redacted name is at the top of the FBI memo with "(PHD)" bizarrely not blacked out. The army investigator also photographed all of the cars and most of their license plates, then shared this information with an FBI agent, because one of the picketers, described as a "white male, age 34, 5'9" with a crew-cut, weighing approximately 155 pounds," was believed to be a government employee. The FBI WFO was tasked with the job of identifying him, and on the FBI memo about this is a cryptic handwritten notation by "J.E.K.": "Handled. Not good."[150]

Who this was is not presently known, or exactly why members of the JCS were so interested in the protest beyond it happening at the Pentagon.

Interestingly, however, there is evidence Elijah Hadn "Lige" Clarke—Nichols Jr.'s partner and fellow Mattachine member—drove and dropped off several picketers, then went directly to his job in the Pentagon! Clarke was serving in the army at the time and, perhaps revealingly, worked in the offices of the JCS. It is difficult to conclude definitively Clarke was the individual of interest to the army and FBI because, at the time, Clarke was only twenty-three years old and therefore did not fit the description of the older man given. The description, of course, could have been in error, so it still could have been him (especially given his connection to Nichols Jr. and hence the FBI no less), and he well could have been the trigger for the photographing; in which case, "Not good," indeed.[151]

The next picket took place on 28 August 1965 at the State Department in the Foggy Bottom section of Washington, DC. Alerted to the protest apparently by Mattachine's own advance notice, FBI officials informed the State Department, the Metropolitan Police Department, the Secret Service, and the military intelligence agencies, including the army investigator who had photographed the picketers at the Pentagon. Interestingly, FBI agents do not appear to have surveilled the Mattachine protestors. Instead, a detective of the Washington, DC, Metropolitan Police Department Special Investigations squad watched and reported on them. He noted for the FBI that ten men and two women began picketing at 2:00 p.m. and stopped at 4:00 p.m. He took note of what was written on their placards, such as "Sexual Conduct Is Irrelevant to State Department Employees" and reported that they behaved in an "orderly" manner, with "no unusual incidents."[152]

The only other extant document in the FBI MSW file about the picket of the State Department is a newspaper clipping from the *Washington Post*. According to the *Post*, Secretary of State Dean Rusk said the "demonstration would have no effect on the department's personnel policies." Rusk said the State Department would never knowingly hire a homosexual but would fire one if discovered because of his or her blackmail potential and unstable nature. Rusk said the State Department had to "exact standards of conduct which are far higher than the conduct of the general society in which we operate."[153]

Finally, on 23 October 1965, ECHO picketed the White House for a final time. This time a New York City police detective learned of the planned demonstration and alerted the FBI New York Field Office, especially to the fact that the New York Mattachine had organized buses to transport protestors to Washington, DC. The SAC of that office then wrote a memo on the planned demonstration and forwarded it to Hoover. FBI officials in Washington, DC, then forwarded this information to their Justice Department superiors, the various military branches, and the Secret Service and ordered the WFO to provide the Metropolitan Police Department the information. The police, however, already knew about the planned demonstration because, as with all other pickets, Kameny informed them in advance to avoid spontaneous trouble. The deputy chief of police, Howard Covell, then advised his deputy chiefs, detectives, and precinct captains of the planned demonstration and instructed them to be prepared for any possible developments with this protest.[154]

Unlike with all previous Mattachine-ECHO pickets, FBI agents were assigned to surveil this one. They noted that more than thirty protestors, including "at various times" several women, paraded before the White House. The agents also listed all thirteen of the statements on the protestors' various placards, such as, "Government Policy toward Homosexuals Creates Security Risks," "Legality," "Demonstration Sponsored by Mattachine Society of Washington, D.C., Post Office Box 11032," etc. Not only this, the FBI agents noted the protest inspired an "anti-picket line" of two teenagers with signs reading: "Are You Kidding?," and "Get Serious," whom the police kept at a distance. At the end of the demonstration, "Mr. Kameny presented a letter addressed to the president of the United States," which was accepted by agents of the Secret Service. Finally, the FBI agents noted that no arrests or other incidents transpired. The agents' report was then distributed to various FBI field offices and to the military branches.[155]

Following MSW's 1965 series of pickets protesting federal discrimination and treatment of gays, FBI interest in the group began to wane. MSW shifted its advocacy efforts over the next few years toward offering legal assistance to fired gay federal employees. The case of Bruce Scott was one of them. Scott was arrested in 1947 for loitering in Lafayette Park, a known gay cruising area, but only lost his job with the Labor Department in 1957 when cold war priorities, McCarthyism, and the Lavender Scare all coalesced with new security clearance requirements for federal employees. Now jobless and destitute, Scott appealed to Kameny and the MSW for help, and Kameny, as an active member of the ACLU, directed him to his local chapter. Scott's case was a significant one, which by 1965 he won. The ruling required the CSC thereafter to have hard evidence supporting its claims of homosexual or immoral misconduct. This was a watershed moment for the CSC because its ability simply to dismiss employees with little more than rumor or suspicious associations (such as loitering in a gay cruising area) was at an end.[156]

The CSC resisted change, however. It not only regarded living a secret gay life as a threat but started viewing engagement in what it called "notoriously disgraceful conduct"—in other words being a member of a gay civil rights group—as a basis for job termination. Kameny and the MSW, however, kept fighting and advocating for gay federal employees until, finally, by 1968 the CSC relented and ended its routine firing of gay employees. Even more, during the following year, MSW saw victory in the case of Clifford Norton, another man who lost his job after being arrested in Lafayette Park. However, in his case, unlike Scott's, the CSC had evidence, a witness, and a confession. The court then ruled that immoral conduct alone, and on one's personal time, was not sufficient to warrant termination of federal employment. In other words, the CSC could no longer fire anyone simply for being gay, a huge victory for the MSW and gay rights. For agencies outside CSC coverage, political appointees, or those engaged in national security work, however—such as at the FBI, CIA, National Security Agency (NSA), and military—antigay employment discrimination continued unabated.[157]

With the near demise of the gays-in-government issue, FBI interest specifically in the MSW and ECHO eventually ran its course. Yet FBI interest in, obsession with, and responses to gay issues during the 1960s were not restricted to militant activists and groups such as Kameny's MSW. Just as gay issues permeated national politics and government during the Truman and Eisenhower administrations, they would continue as issues for the subsequent Lyndon B. Johnson and Richard Nixon administrations.

CHAPTER 7

"It's a Thing That You Just Can't Tell"

The FBI and the Johnson and Nixon Administrations

Walter Jenkins, a forty-seven-year-old senior Lyndon B. Johnson (LBJ) aide, worked until 7 p.m. on Wednesday, 7 October 1964. This was nothing new. For more than a quarter of a century, Jenkins worked tirelessly for LBJ, devoting to him exceptionally long hours, usually well past the standard 5:00 quitting time and including weekends. Jenkins was not simply an employee of the domineering Texas politician. He was also his friend. Jenkins first started working for LBJ when the future president was elected to the US House of Representatives in the 1930s, and he continued working for him after LBJ became a senator, vice president, and then president of the United States. On this particular night in 1964, Jenkins had been invited to an office-warming party for *Newsweek* magazine. So at 7:00, with plans to meet his wife there, he departed the White House for the party.[1]

Jenkins and his wife mingled at the party for about an hour. Sometime after 8:00 they said their good-byes, going their separate ways for the evening. Marjorie Jenkins headed to a dinner party, and her husband said that after another drink he was returning to work at the White House. To his wife, this was not out of the ordinary. He, however, lied to her. Instead of returning to work, feeling exhausted and drunk, he headed for a nearby Young Men's Christian Association (YMCA) looking for sex. A man soliciting anonymous sex with another man at a YMCA was not unique. It was quite common, in fact, for gay men to cruise YMCAs, especially in an era when society shunned those with same-sex desires and forced them underground. Jenkins's problem when visiting the YMCA that night, though, was the fact undercover vice officers were also there. At 8:35 p.m., they arrested Jenkins in the YMCA basement men's room for engaging in a sex act with a sixty-year-old retired army veteran, Andy Choka, who was missing from the Old Soldier's Home.[2]

In custody, Jenkins cooperated fully with the police. He never denied what he had done or tried to conceal his identity. He even admitted to having been arrested in the very same men's room in January 1959 and to having posted and forfeited $25 collateral. As was standard practice in 1959, the police had forwarded Jenkins's fingerprint arrest information to the FBI. Significantly, it noted only that he was arrested as a "suspicious person" and failed completely to mention his sexual liaison. Only later did the police update Jenkins's 1959 arrest record to reflect "pervert," but they failed to forward the updated record to the FBI. This explains why Jenkins had no difficulty with his background check upon becoming a White House aide. In Jenkins's current police dilemma, he also posted and forfeited collateral (at the suggestion of the police), but this time it was $50, and this time he could not avoid the FBI.[3]

FBI Assistant Director Cartha DeLoach, head of the Crime Records Division, the FBI liaison to LBJ, and a personal friend of Jenkins, learned of the arrest the following day. As a man close to both LBJ and Jenkins—indeed the assistant FBI director golfed with Jenkins, attended church with Jenkins, and their families even spent Easter together at Camp David with LBJ's permission—DeLoach was stunned. Previously, he had viewed Jenkins as "one of the better people I'd met in government." FBI Assistant Director Les Trotter, who headed the Identification Division, was the one who told DeLoach about Jenkins's arrest. Trotter only learned about it himself after the police forwarded to the FBI Jenkins's fingerprints and arrest record, long standard procedure in morals cases involving homosexuality.[4]

Because he served as the direct FBI liaison to LBJ, and indeed because he expected the president to phone him as soon as he learned about Jenkins, DeLoach tried to learn all the details he could beforehand. He quietly dispatched two FBI agents to talk with the Metropolitan Police Department to obtain more details about the arrest. According to DeLoach, after the agents reported in, he then "knew the story was true. It was no mistake, and certainly no frame." DeLoach claimed in his memoir to have waited impatiently that day for LBJ to call, and he wrote that the president indeed called him. But LBJ could not have done so about the arrest, because the president only learned about Jenkins a week later.[5]

LBJ only found out about Jenkins on the afternoon of 14 October, after his political ally (and future Supreme Court justice) Abe Fortas called and told him about a "very serious problem that came up today." Jenkins had visited Fortas that morning to tell him he had "got himself involved in quite a serious situation," and when Fortas told LBJ about it, Fortas said he hoped some "very unpleasant publicity, which might otherwise have developed, has been averted." Revealing nothing initially, Fortas advised LBJ, if asked, not to say anything publicly except that he heard about it and hoped to learn more. Fortas then told the president he was handling the situation by having Jenkins check into George Washington Hospital for "hypertension and acute nervous exhaustion." Fortas called it a "weird situation," and before revealing the details he asked the president if it was "alright to talk on this phone." LBJ said it was. Fortas then said Jenkins had visited him after learning from Liz Carpenter, the First Lady's press secretary, that a reporter at the *Washington Star* learned of Jenkins's arrest "on a morals charge" a week ago and planned to write about it. Fortas then told LBJ he and Clark Clifford subsequently visited the *Star,* the *Washington Daily News,* and the *Washington Post* to try to convince them not to publish the story.[6]

LBJ asked, "Could this be true?" Fortas replied, "Mr. President, I'm afraid so." LBJ then inquired about who was involved, and Fortas said: "Just some bum. It happened at the YMCA." Fortas tried to explain Jenkins's situation, his voice growing ever softer, almost inaudible really, and seemingly out of embarrassment, "It's just a case of a fella going off his rocker for long enough to get involved in that kind of thing." He told the president that they had explained to the newspapers that Jenkins was drunk, tired, and had a "complete blackout about the period." Yet Fortas admitted to the president the truth, "He does remember." Fortas advised, moreover, that Jenkins "shouldn't be around the White House," and this was why he checked into the hospital for several days. Fortas added that he refused even to reveal the truth to Jenkins's wife, "except that he [Jenkins] was exhausted."[7]

Aghast hearing this about his longtime friend and aide, LBJ replied, "I just can't believe this." He then asked if Jenkins had ever done this before. Fortas said Jenkins told him he had not, but that the *Star* had a record of a previous arrest in 1959. Fortas said he "didn't have the heart to ask him about that 1959 thing, which we'll have to do one of these days."[8]

Fortas and Johnson knew they could not keep the story quiet for long. Fortas warned that the Republican National Committee would have it, if they did not already, and would use it in the presidential campaign. Fortas told LBJ he had talked with "Deke [DeLoach] and put to him the question of the police blotter and what, if anything, could be done. He offered to do that." Yet Fortas believed it was too late. He, despite having already let slip the truth, reiterated for LBJ, "My impression of it is he blanked out and he doesn't know anything." Fortas believed that the situation, politically, was "in as good shape as it can be right now."[9]

Concluding their conversation, Fortas exclaimed, "This of all things. It's just incredible." LBJ asked if Jenkins had been framed, and Fortas said he had not been. He also added, "There must be something latent there, a psychiatric problem he managed to handle all these years, but it's there." When LBJ asked how this might play out, Fortas said with the Republicans it "will add fuel to the general attack on moral standards." At the present, however, Fortas said it was important, first, to keep it out of the news and, second, to "set the stage for the future," which involved getting Jenkins out of the White House and explaining it. LBJ then suggested telling Jenkins's wife the truth, but Fortas said he did not think it was a good idea because she had problems. "It might knock her off her rocker," he explained to a surprised LBJ. Jenkins's family doctor did not think she should be told either, he said, but he thought they could tell Lady Bird Johnson, her close friend.[10]

Lady Bird, indeed, was told about it. She talked with Jenkins's wife and informed LBJ on 15 October that a devastated Marjorie blamed the president and White House for overworking Jenkins, leading him to do what he did. Lady Bird, moreover, wanted the president to offer Jenkins some kind of public support, including finding him a job. LBJ was worried, however, about the political ramifications of such a move. He was also concerned with Marjorie's being angry with him in that it might lead her to talk to the press. He wanted someone to set her straight on the details about Jenkins, hoping to defuse her blame.[11]

Republicans, indeed, immediately learned about the Jenkins incident and with no hesitation used it. The same day LBJ talked with Fortas about trying to keep the issue quiet, Republican National Committee (RNC) Chair Dean Burch, who had learned about both of Jenkins's arrests, issued a statement to the United Press accusing the White House of suppressing the story; the following day he erroneously accused LBJ of a five-year cover-up of Jenkins's first arrest. Barry Goldwater, the Republican presidential nominee in 1964, however, said he would not comment on Jenkins unless it became a national security issue. Regardless of his promise, Goldwater repeatedly referenced Jenkins in subsequent political speeches. The RNC move forced LBJ's hand. He asked Jenkins to resign the same day he talked with Fortas and ordered FBI Director J. Edgar Hoover to investigate the matter thoroughly.[12]

Having already spoken with Fortas in the afternoon, LBJ then spoke on the phone with DeLoach at 9:00 p.m. that evening. DeLoach wrote in his

memoir that LBJ asked him if the story was true—he told him it was—
and that LBJ believed Jenkins must have been framed by the Republicans
"because we're kicking their butts." DeLoach also wrote that he told Johnson the Republicans were not behind it, and "Walter did what they said he
did." Consciously or not, surprisingly or not, DeLoach had simplified his
response to LBJ for his memoir. LBJ's telephone conversation with DeLoach
was recorded, and it shows that the president actually asked DeLoach if
he thought Jenkins could have been framed. DeLoach answered: "Yes, sir,
he could have been framed. It's entirely possible. . . . It's entirely possible
they [the police] could have been bribed, or entirely possible they're lying
about it." Regarding the RNC using the Jenkins story to its benefit, DeLoach
told Johnson he thought the Republicans would undoubtedly "push it," and
"this guy Burch, who is a first-class bastard . . . is the one who issued the
statement to the United Press" about LBJ trying to cover up the Jenkins
incident. DeLoach also told LBJ he "had this thing taken out of three newspapers today [14 October]."[13]

A shocked and curious LBJ then asked DeLoach, "Who was supposed
to have been workin' on who?" DeLoach answered somewhat confusingly,
"Walter was supposed to be the active one, Mr. President. In other words
this 62-year-old man was letting Walter have it and Walter was taking it."
In his memoir, DeLoach claimed LBJ then ordered him to visit Jenkins at
the hospital, with the First Lady, to get Jenkins's side of the story. The taped
conversation confirms LBJ did ask DeLoach to visit Jenkins, but he never
mentioned the First Lady. Whatever the manner of events, DeLoach immediately took a taxicab to the White House, where he met with Lady Bird
Johnson, Clifford, and Fortas. DeLoach told them the president wanted him
to visit Jenkins, but Fortas and Clifford warned that the press was camped
out at the hospital. DeLoach then phoned Jenkins's doctor, who advised
him he would have to come another time because Jenkins was sedated.[14]

LBJ did not limit the FBI investigation to Jenkins. In light of the Jenkins scandal, he demanded the FBI check everyone. On 17 October one of
the president's special assistants called FBI Assistant Director DeLoach asking him how many people LBJ "had brought to the White House had been
given full field investigations." He advised DeLoach, moreover, that of the
John F. Kennedy (JFK) staff holdovers, seventeen were LBJ people, and he
named them. DeLoach later learned that only eight of the seventeen had full
FBI field investigations, and so he directed the section chief of the Special

Investigations Division, W. V. Cleveland, to complete the remainder immediately. (The only names not redacted on the FBI-released list were Jenkins and Jack Valenti.)[15]

On 18 October, DeLoach finally visited Jenkins at the hospital. Instead of taking Lady Bird Johnson, he was accompanied by two FBI agents who interviewed Jenkins. Beyond Jenkins, Hoover later claimed his agents interviewed, in total, some 500 people. Jenkins admitted to FBI agents he was arrested in both 1959 and 1964 but claimed to have been "enticed" into the first arrest and that he was drunk, tired, and sick during the second. He also said he did not recall any other incidents but also did not deny any by saying if he had been arrested he would have been drunk. Jenkins also assured FBI agents he was not being blackmailed.[16]

A former FBI assistant director, William Sullivan, wrote about Jenkins in his memoir, a book he wrote after Hoover fired him and published following the FBI director's death. He wrote that LBJ wanted the FBI to "prove that the object of Jenkins's attention [Choka] was being paid by the Republican National Committee and that the whole incident was a frame-up, a Republican plot." Sullivan pointed to FBI Assistant Director DeLoach as the man assigned to establish these facts for LBJ.[17]

Sullivan wrote his memoir with an eye toward settling some scores, but his assertions nevertheless have some air of truth. When LBJ first spoke with Fortas at 3:00 p.m. on 14 October, for example, Fortas commented extensively on his efforts to protect Jenkins and the president. These efforts included convincing Jenkins to check into the hospital, advising LBJ what to say publicly, trying to keep the story from being published, and telling the president that "if there is any break [in the news] about the blotter entry on the police record, Walter won't be available, and we'll just have to work out some way of saying it's just a frame up."[18] According to Sullivan, moreover, LBJ wanted the FBI to "bear down" on Choka about his possible connections to the RNC and a frame-up. Sullivan claimed FBI agents indeed confronted Choka, but it led nowhere. Sullivan also claimed LBJ wanted DeLoach to extract from Jenkins's doctor a public statement about Jenkins's "diseased brain" being the cause of his trouble. The doctor refused. Sullivan even claimed LBJ wanted FBI pressure placed on the police officer who had arrested Jenkins in 1959 and that DeLoach asked Johnson aide Bill Moyers to have the secretary of the interior pressure that police officer. Again, according to Sullivan, this failed. Sullivan disingenuously wrote in his memoir,

"The courage shown by both Jenkins's doctor and the policeman restored some faith I used to have in human beings."[19]

This was not all. In a recorded phone call with DeLoach on 27 October, DeLoach told LBJ he did not think Choka "was part of any frame up," and he cited his previous arrests and homosexual reputation in the army as proof. "I don't think he was a plant, Mr. President," DeLoach said (the conversation DeLoach recalled incorrectly for his memoir). Unconvinced, LBJ pressed DeLoach about "pursuing him [Choka] further" as well as the police officer to learn all the details. This is when DeLoach, in point of fact, suggested using Moyers to pressure the interior secretary to act, just as Sullivan claimed. What Sullivan wrote is striking, in fact, because it so closely adhered to the taped conversation between LBJ and DeLoach. It seems unlikely Sullivan would have had access to the tape when writing his memoir, but he would have had access to any memos DeLoach wrote about the phone conversation. One wonders how he got them, though, when writing his book after having been fired.[20]

Sullivan also claimed in his memoir that DeLoach, who aspired to be Hoover's successor as FBI director, used the Jenkins incident to try to embarrass the now-elderly Hoover into retiring. Sullivan claimed DeLoach encouraged Hoover to send Jenkins a get-well card and flowers, which he, in fact, did. Hoover's action was then reported in the newspapers, suggesting the FBI director had shown favoritism in his investigation of Jenkins. That Hoover had offered flowers to a gay man, particularly when rumors about Hoover's own sexuality floated around Washington, DC, must also have figured into the picture. According to Sullivan, DeLoach "managed to convince Hoover he had done the right thing after all" because the flowers were sent prior to the FBI investigation of Jenkins. We do not know if Sullivan was being truthful here, but Hoover did, in fact, send the flowers, and it was reported in the newspapers. FBI officials of the Hoover era were renowned for their byzantine machinations, but whether DeLoach—both a friend of Jenkins and a man who defended Hoover long after the FBI director's death—in fact did what Sullivan claimed is questionable.[21]

In his report on Jenkins for the White House, Hoover wrote that his agents had uncovered no national security breach. FBI agents unsurprisingly found, however, that Jenkins maintained contact with known or suspected "sex deviates," but they could not prove he had sex with them. The chair of psychiatry at George Washington University (GWU), moreover, also assured FBI officials that Jenkins was suffering from severe depression and that "his general adjustment is within the normal range and that his present condition was the culmination of extreme tensions."[22]

On 23 October LBJ spoke with Hoover on the phone, thanking him for a thorough investigation and the compassionate way he handled it. LBJ told Hoover that Jenkins "knew that these people were sex deviates," and although he did not deny what he did, he was apprehensive about admitting to it. Hoover told the president he thought Jenkins was a "desperately ill man" who should be institutionalized, perhaps at Walter Reed (because of his Second World War military service). He also offered his explanation for sending Jenkins flowers. LBJ shrugged it off, though, telling Hoover it proved nothing except that he was a "compassionate man, an understanding man" and that he was proud of him and DeLoach. LBJ also assured Hoover his job was secure, assuming Hoover was worried. (By this point Hoover had passed the mandatory federal retirement age of seventy and only retained his job because LBJ, through executive order, exempted him.) LBJ later commented to DeLoach that he thought "history will record he's a bigger man for having done it." No matter how LBJ phrased it, this was a terribly ironic and embarrassing position in which Hoover found himself. Given his decades-long history of tirelessly targeting "sex deviates," publishing articles about them as a threat to children, and ensuring they lost their jobs (thereby ruining their lives) through wide dissemination of intimate details about them, he sent flowers to a gay man because he was close to the president.[23]

On Halloween, Hoover again telephoned LBJ with a follow-up on Jenkins. Hoover said he talked to "Abe Fortas about it" and told the president US Navy intelligence was investigating a man with "some deviation" who was apparently linked to Jenkins and worked for an assistant secretary in the Pentagon. Hoover explained that the FBI took over that investigation on 30 October. LBJ said he had heard about the navy investigation, in fact, and especially that questions arose over the suspect's effeminate "way he combed his hair, the way he did something else, but they had no act of his or [evidence] he had done nothing [sic]."[24] Hoover explained that the investigation was based on suspicions about "his mannerisms, and so forth." LBJ interrupted Hoover, saying the navy suspect "worked for me for 4 or 5 years, but he wasn't even suspicious to me. I guess you gonna have to teach me something about this stuff!"[25]

LBJ's comment seemed to befuddle Hoover, but in a hesitant and half-laughing voice he replied, "You know I often wonder what the next crisis is going to be." LBJ jumped in, "I swear I can't recognize 'em, I don't know anything about it." Hoover then calmly explained, in his typically enunciating voice: "It's a thing that you just can't tell, sometimes just like in this Jenkins matter there was no indication in any way. I knew him pretty well and DeLoach did also. There was no suspicion, no indication. There are some people who walk kind of funny, and so forth, that you might kind of think are a little bit off, and maybe queer. But there was no indication of that in the Jenkins case." Hoover then advised the president that with the election pending, different public charges were apt to be made about the Jenkins affair. "One of these dirty columnists," he warned, "is very apt to carry something in a column" soon.

LBJ then ended the conversation with a directive for Hoover: "You might give some thought to what we ought to do with all secretaries and undersecretaries and assistant secretaries, and you and Deke [DeLoach] give a little thought to this from my standpoint, kind of representing me. I don't want to run you crazy over there, but I rather think you ought to take everybody [and investigate them] from me right on down."

Hoover said Dwight Eisenhower, in fact, had done just this. He said Eisenhower had instructed every cabinet officer to personally call Hoover to request the FBI "investigate them, John Foster Dulles all the way down the line, including this fellow Vandenberg." Hoover said this was standard policy until JFK became president. He then quickly added, seemingly contradicting himself, that with the LBJ administration everyone in the cabinet had been investigated five years ago (when JFK was president) except the postmaster general and secretary of health, education, and welfare. LBJ replied, "You give some thought to that because I have implicit confidence in what you say, [and] we'll do [it]."[26]

The Jenkins story made for good copy in the nation's capital just before a presidential election. As historian David Johnson has pointed out, however, it was not an issue for Frank Kameny's Mattachine Society of Washington, DC (MSW). Its members were not much interested in defending closeted, heterosexually married gays with political power who ended up arrested while cruising notorious areas most careful gay men knew to avoid. Even worse, the bad press coverage over Jenkins created a political climate in which the Johnson administration could not respond in any positive way to Kameny's and MSW's demands to end gay discrimination even if it wanted to.[27]

FBI Director Hoover, meanwhile, proceeded with background investigations of all White House staffers—that is, beyond investigating merely the seventeen carryover staffers and the cabinet—and he did so along the lines of his conversation with LBJ on Halloween. About a month after that conversation, on 27 November, LBJ telephoned DeLoach about the investigations. He asked whether FBI agents had finished their investigations of the cabinet, to which DeLoach said they had not. LBJ then directed DeLoach, in line with Hoover's advice, to have presidential assistant Moyers inform each cabinet member he needed to "personally request" that Hoover's FBI "conduct full field investigations" of him or bring older investigations up to date. LBJ also told DeLoach "no further appointments would be announced unless full field investigations were first conducted."[28]

This was not all. LBJ also requested full FBI field investigations of "all individuals who entertain in the White House in the future . . . prior to the time they entertain." DeLoach advised the president, however, that making such extensive investigations of entertainers "would create a considerable burden upon the FBI." So DeLoach instead suggested an alternative. He said it would be easy for the FBI to "conduct name checks and possibly knock some of these people out by merely a review of the files." LBJ agreed and advised him to coordinate with the White House social secretary, but the real contact person was White House Aide Mildred Stegall, who coordinated background checks with the FBI.[29]

LBJ did not limit his interest in background checks to his own staff. In late October 1964, Johnson had Moyers ask DeLoach for name checks on fifteen members of Goldwater's staff. FBI agents, indeed, went forward with the name checks, and DeLoach subsequently advised Moyers nothing "derogatory" was found for thirteen names on the list. No extant document survives telling us anything more than this, however, but it seems logical it likely had to do with LBJ's personal interest in discovering if the Republicans had somehow set up Jenkins.[30]

The shock of the Jenkins revelation, and the fact that Republicans had so quickly used it against LBJ in the election, further led him to have Hoover's FBI investigate even beyond his political staff to root out other "employees of the White House who are suspected of homosexual tendencies." In light of the Jenkins incident and highlighting the perseverance of homophobic politics, LBJ regarded them as "possible sources of embarrassment at the White House at the present time." In this regard, Moyers forwarded to the FBI at least two names of suspected homosexuals on the White House staff.

Redactions make a full understanding impossible, but one appeared to be a White House butler or usher, and the other was employed in another part of the executive mansion.[31]

With concerns only escalating over potential gays in the White House, FBI officials came to focus their attention on one particular LBJ aide, Jack Valenti. On 12 November 1964, the FBI special agent in charge (SAC) of the Los Angeles Field Office told Hoover an informant claimed the RNC had hired an ex-FBI agent who, after the Jenkins incident became public, was investigating a similar matter concerning Valenti. The ex-FBI agent supposedly learned that Valenti, renowned for his parties in Houston, had invited to one a photographer with the "reputation of being a homosexual." Even worse, Valenti and this man were supposed to be "having an affair for a number of years," and Valenti had supposedly "gone to great lengths to impress the President" with this photographer's work.[32]

This was not all. On the morning of 19 October 1964, Section Chief Cleveland reported that an unsolicited bureau informant in New York claimed Valenti should be investigated "as a sex pervert." Explaining himself before hanging up the phone, the informant said he had read that Valenti often swam nude in the White House pool! Even though this was likely from a crank, it lent weight to the rumors already surrounding Valenti and, in a larger sense, the gay panic at the White House.[33]

By 18 November, an impatient LBJ asked DeLoach whether the FBI had unearthed "any derogatory information concerning people around him." DeLoach informed the president that Hoover was in the process of forwarding him a memo about "Valenti's association with a homosexual in California and Texas." LBJ said he already knew about this, and he "felt that Valenti was all right." On the other hand, LBJ admitted, he also once believed "Jenkins had been alright." DeLoach suggested Valenti read the FBI memo and then "submit an affidavit" offering his side of the story "concerning his association with this homosexual." LBJ disagreed. He believed the move improper because, unlike Jenkins, Valenti had done nothing wrong, and he should not have to defend himself that way. LBJ then asserted, referencing Valenti's reputation as a heterosexual philanderer, "that Valenti was attracted to the women and not to the men." LBJ also told DeLoach the FBI should not interview the photographer.[34]

When speaking with the president on the phone on 25 November, however, DeLoach told him he "felt very strongly that the bare record should not stand without some interview of the photographer in question." After "reconsidering this matter," LBJ relented. He then gave his permission for FBI agents to interview the photographer, reflecting how intimately LBJ worked with the FBI. The president was making calls on FBI investigative procedure.[35]

FBI agents located the photographer in New York City and arranged an interview for 1 December 1964. When questioned, the man admitted to having "homosexual tendencies" and admitted to having been arrested on a morals charge in California while drunk. FBI agents even noted intimate details about this man's sex life, including the fact that "due to a prostrate [*sic*] condition he has not been able to engage in any homosexual activities for a period of over five years." It was not out of the ordinary for FBI agents to note such intimate details of gay men's activities. Their interest did not reflect voyeurism as much as manipulation. Such embarrassing detail was valuable to FBI officials when confronting someone with it, especially when trying to pressure them, or someone connected to them, to resign from a job. Regarding Valenti, though, the man said he had known him for twelve or fifteen years but only "on a limited basis," and he had twice been Valenti's house guest. When asked about Valenti's sexuality, the man said, "Valenti has never engaged in homosexual activities and does not have these tendencies." He added, "He could never under any circumstances consider Valenti as 'sexually attractive,' but merely thought of him as a very charming 'and intelligent individual.'" To him, Valenti was a "woman's man." The man refused, however, to provide a signed statement to any of this because of "mental and physical exhaustion." The FBI report on the man's interview, moreover, was filed in the FBI Sex Deviates File (sex offenders). The Valenti matter was thereafter closed.[36]

Given the Jenkins and Valenti issues, it is perhaps not surprising FBI officials were interested in any sex rumors concerning members of the Johnson administration. On 28 May 1965, FBI officials learned from an informant who regularly exposed "security risks" in an anticommunist newsletter that National Security Advisor McGeorge Bundy "had a 'sex relationship'" with a "convicted homosexual." Upon further investigation, FBI officials learned this was not, in fact, true. They learned, instead, Bundy had supposedly had a heterosexual affair with someone who worked for him. Even worse, according to this informant, LBJ allegedly impregnated a woman, and Valenti "arranged for an abortion." Regardless of its fantastic nature, FBI agents checked all of this information and, of course, found no substantiation for it. FBI officials even noted, "Our Special Inquiry investigation," which LBJ had demanded they conduct on all staff, "of McGeorge Bundy did not indicate he had homosexual tendencies." Hoover, clearly interested in any and all sex scandal allegations, had all this information forwarded to the White House.[37]

By late April 1966, Valenti resigned his post at the LBJ White House to become president of the Motion Picture Producers Association. It was from this position in 1968, significantly, that he helped to devise the US movie rating system. His change in careers did not end FBI interest in his activities, however. Several times during the remainder of his life, Valenti was considered for different presidential appointments and thus had FBI background checks made on him, though at no time did the issue of his alleged gay associations ever come up. When it came to Hollywood, though, especially where Hollywood intersected with the carefully crafted FBI public image, Hoover and FBI officials were always acutely interested in gay issues.

One Hollywood personality who took center stage for the FBI officials was actor Rock Hudson. It was not, in fact, only when Hudson contracted HIV and developed AIDS in 1984, followed by his tragic death in 1985, that the public learned about his sexuality. In and around Hollywood, at least, whether as rumor or firsthand knowledge, the notion that Hudson was gay was common knowledge. FBI officials knew about it, at latest, dating from 1965. Exactly what their interest in the actor's sexuality was in 1965 remains somewhat clouded because of extensive redactions in his FBI file, but one can make an educated guess.

In mid-May 1965, after the FBI learned the Los Angeles Field Office files "contain[ed] no derogatory subversive references to Hudson," the Washington, DC, Field Office (WFO) requested permission from headquarters to interview Hudson. FBI Director Hoover replied that only after a thorough search of FBI files would he consent to an interview. FBI officials conducted their search, and even though the document about it is now mostly redacted, some facts can be ascertained. On a 21 May 1965 reference slip listing the FBI files consulted in the search, two file numbers remain unredacted. They were FBI files 105-34074-34-57 and 105-34074-2613. As discussed in Chapter 4, these are files from the FBI Sex Deviates File. The content of these particular files remains unknown; however, an FBI official characterized the results of the file search of Hudson as finding "no derogatory security-type information concerning Hudson." This suggests FBI officials found nothing linking Hudson to any government employees, which also suggests this may have been the root of their original interest. With the request coming so soon after the Jenkins and Valenti affairs, it possibly had something to do with name checks of possible White House entertainment (or celebrity visitors/presidential associations). In any event, FBI officials recommended FBI agents interview the actor.[38]

Hoover consented to the interview, but "in view of the information that Hudson had homosexual tendencies," he ordered the Los Angeles Field Office to use "two mature, experienced Special Agents." Although the information about Hudson's sexuality originated from the Los Angeles Field Office, it did not come from its files. Instead, that office reported it was "common knowledge in the motion picture industry that Hudson is suspected of having homosexual tendencies."[39]

The FBI agents' report on their interview with Hudson was merely one page long. It primarily focused on Hudson's ex-wife, Phyllis Gates, the fact that she was living in Europe, and the fact that Hudson paid her alimony checks through an advertising agency. The Los Angeles Field Office prepared five copies of the memo for headquarters, two for the WFO, and one for the San Francisco Field Office. Hoover intended to disseminate the information; he had to admonish the Los Angeles Field Office to update the memo "in a form suitable for dissemination" to reflect the "basis for your interview with Hudson."[40]

Following these events, there appeared a curious FBI document in Hudson's file dated 22 December 1965. The document was written by an FBI SAC—his location is unknown because of redactions—who detailed the recruitment of an informant who was willing and enthusiastic about assisting the bureau, had "great respect for the Bureau," and agreed to provide any information "of value" to the FBI on a confidential and discreet basis. Again, details are lacking because of redactions, but in the margin of the document is a notation that it was also filed in the Sex Deviates File (105-12189, Sex Perverts in Government).[41]

Ten months later, in October 1966, Stegall, special assistant to LBJ and as of 1964 one of his assistants who handled FBI issues, asked the bureau to conduct name-check requests on a list of individuals, including Hudson. DeLoach reported to LBJ aides Marvin Watson and Stegall that the bureau's fingerprint and central files contained "no pertinent derogatory information" about any of the names submitted and forwarded information from "FBI Identification Records" for each. Hudson's memo started with the typical FBI claim he "has not been the subject of an FBI investigation," but then noted the 1965 claim of a male informant to having had an affair with

Hudson replete with having "indulged in homosexual acts with Hudson." The memo further noted it was Hollywood "common knowledge" Hudson was gay, and in May 1961 a New York informant "stated that Hudson definitely was a homosexual." (The FBI copy of the memo cited the Sex Deviates File as the source for the New York informant.[42])

Most concerning to FBI officials regarding Hudson was information that came to them in September 1967 suggesting the actor was going to play an FBI agent who has an affair with a jewel thief in the forthcoming film *The Quiet Couple*. Hoover and FBI officials relentlessly guarded their carefully crafted FBI image. They would never allow an FBI agent to be portrayed on film as consorting with a criminal or, worse yet, allow a commonly known gay actor to play an FBI agent. This particular information, though, came from the 5 September 1967 issue of the Hollywood periodical *Daily Variety* and another source that also noted Hudson was to costar with Claudia Cardinale, and filming was scheduled to begin in November. The FBI Los Angeles Field Office advised that it planned to inquire with Columbia Pictures and with the Creative Management Agency for further information.[43]

A source at the Creative Management Agency advised FBI agents that Hudson, indeed, was slated to star in the film. The source noted, however, that the film was merely in the planning stages and would be produced by an Italian company. The source further advised that the *Daily Variety* piece had erred, and Hudson's character was supposed to be associated with the US Embassy in Italy, not specifically with any government agency. The source told FBI agents to contact her in mid-October, by which time she would have the script in hand. FBI agents did exactly this and learned from the source that she "feels certain that Hudson's role is not that of an FBI agent." Finally, by late November, another source told FBI agents Hudson's character was, in fact, to be a New York police officer visiting Italy.[44]

Hoover's and FBI officials' interest in homosexuality in Hollywood was not restricted to actors such as Hudson during the 1960s. They were also interested in filmmaker Andy Warhol. As an avant-garde artist and flamboyant gay man famous for pushing artistic boundaries in the 1960s—his most prolific era as an artist—who earned significant public interest, it is perhaps unsurprising that Warhol drew FBI scrutiny. Extant FBI files about Warhol center on the production of his 1968 film *Lonesome Cowboys*. One of Hoover's interests was in defending and protecting orthodox US values—at least as he understood them from his puritanical perspective—and he tried to do this, particularly in the 1960s, with respect to Warhol by seeking a legal case against him about *Lonesome Cowboys* violating federal obscenity law.

Warhol filmed *Lonesome Cowboys* in January 1968 at the Linda Vista Ranch in Oracle, Arizona, which was in the process of becoming an artists' commune as it is today. On 27 January somebody from Oracle filed a complaint with the FBI that Warhol and company had "made an obscene film." The FBI Phoenix SAC informed headquarters he would investigate, including ascertaining the identities of everyone who participated in the making of the film and how the film was transported (the key to a federal antiobscenity law prosecution), searching at the ranch, surveying local newspapers, and interviewing witnesses.[45]

FBI agents proceeded with their investigation and reported that among the actors was the wife of a University of Arizona art professor, a couple from California, multiple actors from New York, and a "girl by the name of Viva [the actor Janet Hoffman], last name unknown." The Phoenix SAC noted, moreover, "All of the male individuals had long hair." One informant said he saw no "obscene sex acts" but did see Viva filmed "in the nude." An informant at the ranch told FBI agents, additionally, Warhol had paid them $333.72 for a week's stay, and arrangements for the stay were made through the Art Department of the University of Arizona.[46]

FBI agents also interviewed a witness to the filmmaking, probably their original informant, who told them somebody at the ranch called him and said that "he should come over and watch it because he could not believe what they were doing." The witness described the actors, including the comment by one that "he enjoyed sexual relations with a horse more than he did with a man or girl." He also described the actors taking the clothing off Viva, then "performing a sexual act of cunnilingus" on her while a "second man was licking her breasts." The whole scene, the witness reported, lasted about ten minutes, and some of the actors "had reached a sexual climax." Viva was reported as yelling out, after it was all over: "I have fucked half of you here, and none of you are a good fuck." The witness also described a scene in which "unnatural sex acts took place," including men playing "with each other's rear ends," and "one fellow was hanging by his knees, face down, out of a tree and kissing on the lips one of the other men on a horse." The informant described them as all looking like hippies and using "very vulgar" language. This and other titillating descriptions of the filming were included in the FBI agent's report, but these particular pages of the report (pages seven through thirteen) were sent specially to FBI headquarters under obscene cover—the FBI method of mailing obscene items, sealed in a manila envelope with the word "OBSCENE" written on it in capital letters.[47]

FBI agents interviewed many witnesses about the film, including the couple in the process of selling the ranch to those who intended to convert it into an art community. They described, for example, where some individuals stayed on the ranch. Warhol stayed in Cabin 33 with another man, and the ranch owners believed the two "to be lovers" in that "they both slept in the same bed." The man staying with Warhol, moreover, was described as acting "like a big sissy and did not take part in the movie." Further alluding to his sexuality, this man supposedly "wore ankle-strap thongs."[48]

Another witness, an eighteen-year-old man who lived at the ranch, reported that one Saturday while he was with his fifteen-year-old sister, he saw some of the male actors filmed naked. There were six or seven men who paired up, naked, in sleeping bags. They then filmed inside one of the cabins, but the witness was not permitted to watch. The filming lasted for an hour, and the young witness concluded "that these naked men were doing acts of sexual perversion" and "used very foul language." The witness even reported finding an abandoned pair of shorts in the area of the nude filming after they all had left the ranch, leading him to deduce one of the naked men forgot them. This and other descriptions of sex acts in the film were forwarded to FBI headquarters under obscene cover.[49]

By May 1968, FBI agents learned that the film would be titled *Lonesome Cowboys* and that it was transported from Arizona to New York on 30 January 1968. Thereafter, FBI officials directed agents to try to develop an interstate-transportation-of-obscene-items (ITOM) case against Warhol between the Phoenix, New York, and San Francisco offices, covering where it was made, edited, and screened. Part of FBI agents' investigation included collecting evidence of the airline tickets Warhol and company had purchased. When the film was eventually shown at the San Francisco International Film Festival in November 1968, moreover, two FBI agents attended the midnight screening and wrote detailed reports about the film, scene by scene. Again, not voyeurs, they were documenting as evidence for prosecution the obscene nature of the film at a public screening.[50]

In September 1969 the US attorney in Phoenix, Arizona, reviewed the FBI reports about the film. He also attended an August screening of *Lonesome Cowboys* in Scottsdale. He concluded, "The movie had no redeeming value whatsoever," but it was not "obscene within the definition of that word as defined by the Supreme Court of the United States." Part of his conclusion was the fact that some scenes reported by FBI informants had not been included in the final product. By 1969, after several Supreme Court opinions, the legal standard for what was and was not obscene, and therefore prosecutable under the law, had dramatically changed. This foreclosed Hoover's ability to target risqué films such as the kind controversial gay artist Warhol made during the 1960s. It did nothing, however, to stem his interest in gay celebrities.[51]

The FBI undoubtedly monitored the sexuality of many Hollywood celebrities and other notable people, but, to reiterate, because no central FBI index of gays or suspected gays exists, many of their identities are unknown. One must rely on extant FBI files that have, for whatever reason, come to light. One example is African American author James Baldwin. In a brief episode in July 1964, Hoover penned on an FBI memo about Baldwin: "Isn't Baldwin a well-known pervert?" Unit Chief Milton Jones of the Crime Records Division replied, "It is not a matter of official record that he is a pervert; however the theme of homosexuality has figured prominently in two of his three published novels."[52] One final example of a Hollywood celebrity, however, sheds some light on another avenue of investigation FBI agents took when it came to gays. This FBI subject was Władziu Valentino Liberace.

The details are somewhat murky, but in May 1966 Liberace and four other individuals were named as victims in connection with a federal investigation for extortion in an interstate-transportation-in-aid-of-racketeering case out of New York. As a result of extensive redactions it is impossible to ascertain the details of Liberace's case—other than the fact that Hoover denied a request to interview him—but, in the least, the FBI investigated the matter, opening a file on him through an FBI program called Compromise and Extortion of Homosexuals. FBI officials assigned this program a code name, HOMEX, and it comprised a headquarters file (166-1778) and three field office files (Washington, DC; New York; and Chicago).[53]

To date, the FBI has released very little about this program, precluding full understanding of its nature, but there was a similar program that might shed some light on its basic nature. The FBI code-named program PORNEX, short for pornography extortion, targeted organized crime attempts to blackmail those in the pornography industry in Los Angeles during the late 1970s and early 1980s. It employed undercover FBI agents using a false pornography distribution company in an effort to dismantle the Mafia on the West Coast. This program, however, was a uniquely post-Hoover FBI operation. During the Hoover years, FBI agents did not engage in true and extensive undercover work. Quite the contrary, in fact. Hoover's FBI agents were forced to adhere to a rigid dress code, strict physical appearance, and code of conduct. FBI officials, in any event, prioritized radical politics and noncriminal intelligence gathering over criminal law enforcement, especially undercover work and targeting the Mafia. So the exact nature of HOMEX remains murky until the FBI releases further information.[54]

There exists general information about the extortion ring itself, however. By February 1966, nine members of the national ring were arrested in New York City. Dating from 1961, it engaged in various forms of extortion, from small-scale robberies of men seeking gay sex—they used young decoys (members of the ring) who took them to hotel rooms and promptly robbed them—to large-scale extortion scams involving tens of thousands of dollars and targeting the affluent. The extortionists typically posed as police officers threatening to arrest their victims if they refused to pay. According to the *New York Times*, "writers, teachers, lawyers, and businessmen" all were targeted. One arrested ring member, who later in life came out as gay, Edward Murphy, was thought to be an FBI informant, but whether he played a role in HOMEX remains unknown. Suffice it to say, clearly, the FBI code-named HOMEX Program focused on gays as susceptible to blackmail—significantly, criminal and not foreign intelligence blackmail—through which FBI agents easily could have collected sensitive information about the private lives of a wide variety of gay US citizens. One extortion victim FBI agents interviewed became so distraught he committed suicide shortly afterward. Clearly, it would have taken minimal effort for FBI officials to use or copy to the bureau's Sex Deviates File anything they learned. In fact, it seems probable they would have done so.[55]

Allegations of homosexuality in the 1950s and 1960s, whether even true, had tremendous power, and their employment was sometimes terribly ironic. Such was the case with Supreme Court Justice Fortas. An informal but trusted advisor to LBJ and a man who played a central role in dealing with the Jenkins scandal, Fortas himself was eventually gay baited. He was not caught in a compromising homosexual liaison, but rumors about his sexuality surfaced in 1967 and were later leaked to journalists who then decided not to use the information. The hope was, however, that the embarrassing information could help influence Fortas to resign his seat on the Supreme Court.

Fortas was a longtime friend of LBJ. When LBJ first ran for the US Senate in 1948, he faced a tough three-way primary election—the primary was where the real race occurred in solidly Democratic Texas. The primary resulted in former governor of Texas Coke Stevenson having a plurality of the vote, and LBJ came in second. Because nobody won a majority, a runoff election was scheduled. LBJ won, but whispers of fraud permeated the election, leading Stevenson to seek judicial intervention. In court, Fortas represented LBJ, and he triumphed; LBJ became a senator, and Fortas thereafter served him as an invaluable advisor all the way to the White House.

By the spring of 1965, LBJ decided to elevate Fortas to the Supreme Court. Before doing so, however, he spoke with DeLoach and asked him to update the FBI investigation of Fortas because he "was seriously thinking of appointing Abe Fortas to a major departmental position." LBJ's allusion to an executive department was his way of masking his real interest in appointing Fortas to the Court. A master of working and leveraging legislators, LBJ wanted FBI agents to interview specific liberal senators, including Howard Cannon (Nevada), Eugene McCarthy (Minnesota), Paul Douglas (Illinois), Robert Kennedy (New York), Ted Kennedy (Massachusetts), Thomas Kuchel (California), and Everett Dirksen (Illinois) to get them on record about Fortas to prevent them from later saying anything negative about him in public. LBJ also wanted conservative senators Roman Hruska (Nebraska), Bourke Hickenlooper (Iowa), Norris Cotton (New Hampshire), and George Murphy (California) interviewed, though he did not think they would cause any trouble. Hoover's FBI agents did exactly as the president wished, and the senators offered no objection to Fortas; thus, interestingly enough, FBI agents helped to pave the way for Fortas's nomination.[56]

LBJ then turned his now-famous methods of bending people to his will to convince Justice Arthur Goldberg—who had only been on the Court for three years—to retire and thereby vacate a seat for Fortas. He agreed. On 28 July 1965, LBJ nominated Fortas to the High Court. During the confirmation hearings, FBI Assistant Director DeLoach, LBJ's FBI liaison and confidant, continued to assist the president with the Fortas vote count. The Senate confirmed Fortas by voice vote on 11 August 1965, and afterward he and DeLoach continued to maintain a friendship and close working relationship.[57]

Shortly after taking the bench, Fortas then began to engage in a pattern of troubling and unethical activity that, ultimately, would lead to his downfall. On 3 January 1966, Fortas accepted a $20,000 check from the Wolfson Family Foundation—the charitable organization set up by industrialist Louis Wolfson. The check, actually, was merely the first offering of an arrangement whereby Fortas was to receive annual payments of $20,000 for "continuing services" to the foundation. Fortas, moreover, had a previous relationship with Wolfson. Encountering trouble with the Securities and Exchange Commission (SEC) in 1964, before Fortas was elevated to the Court, Wolfson hired as legal representation Fortas's law firm. After Wolfson was indicted for SEC violations in September 1966, it still took three months before Fortas decided to return the $20,000 given to him.[58]

Accepting money from Wolfson was not an isolated incident for Fortas. During the summer of 1967, Fortas gave a series of lectures in a seminar at American University Law School and received as remuneration $15,000. When both incidents later became public, critics rightfully charged the justice with ethical violations. They said he had engaged in conduct that gave, in the least, the appearance of impropriety, and his acceptance of money similarly raised eyebrows.[59]

The year 1967 would bring further allegations of irregularities on the part of Fortas, but this time they evolved from financial ones to sexual. In July 1967, an informant for the FBI WFO, whom an FBI agent described as an "active and aggressive homosexual . . . [who] over the years has provided a great deal of reliable information," reported to the FBI that someone he knew "had 'balled' with Abe Fortas on several occasions prior to Mr. Fortas' becoming a Justice of the United States Supreme Court." The informant explained to the FBI agent "that to 'ball' is to have a homosexual relationship with another male." After learning about this, FBI officials Clyde Tolson and DeLoach both advised Hoover to forward the information to Attorney General Ramsey Clark. The byzantine Hoover disagreed and, instead, wrote on the memo, "DeLoach should see Fortas."[60]

DeLoach visited Fortas at his home on the afternoon of 24 July 1967. He told the justice about the allegation and allowed him to inspect the FBI memo about it, while adding that Hoover "wanted this matter discreetly and informally brought to his attention so that he would be aware of such an allegation." DeLoach advised Fortas that the "FBI was taking no further action" regarding the claim. Fortas responded that the allegations were "ridiculous and absolutely false" and that he "had never committed homosexual acts at any time." Fortas, moreover, apparently knew the man who had leveled the charge, as he told DeLoach he "always felt a little suspicious toward" him because he seemed "somewhat effeminate and that he never tried to date the girls [deleted but a location]." Fortas then thanked DeLoach and asked him to express his appreciation to Hoover "for having handled the matter in this manner."[61]

Hearing this must have been terribly ironic for Fortas because both he and DeLoach three years before had worked together on the Jenkins matter. Fortas, in fact, was stunned by Jenkins's activities and arrest, and he, with DeLoach, worked tirelessly to handle the matter for the president. Now he found himself the target of homosexual allegations and was told about it by the one agency he knew took special interest in such matters. Did Hoover handle the matter in the way he did to let Fortas know, regardless of whether the rumor was true (it likely was not true given Fortas's history of heterosexual peccadilloes), he had damning information about the man now in an influential judicial position? Or was Hoover letting him know about the allegation because Fortas was close to LBJ, and Hoover relied upon the good graces of the president to retain his position as FBI director? Both speculations are possible, and both could be true, but Hoover's exact motivation cannot be known with any certainty.

In June 1968, Chief Justice Earl Warren then announced his retirement. LBJ decided, as one of his final presidential acts, to elevate his man, Fortas, to the top chair on the Supreme Court. The Warren Court had become famous by this point for issuing one ruling after another that dramatically altered US jurisprudence. Whether it was ending racial segregation or the liberalization of federal obscenity law, many conservatives were upset by what they perceived as an activist court. So when the liberal LBJ decided to nominate his close friend and former advisor as chief justice, the decision created a wellspring of opposition not only because the liberal Fortas was LBJ's choice but because the presidential election was nearing, and conservatives, sensing a victory, wanted the next president to fill the seat. Nineteen Republicans vowed to oppose the nomination, and they threatened, for the first time in history, to filibuster a Supreme Court nomination.[62]

This, of course, is exactly what happened. In their calls for LBJ to withdraw the Fortas nomination, opponents raised the issue of his having accepted the $15,000 from American University and cited violations of judicial ethics (they did not yet know about the Wolfson money). Meanwhile, Republicans proceeded with their filibuster on 25 September, which continued through 1 October, all the while gaining momentum until a vote to end the filibuster failed. Fortas then asked the president to withdraw his name from candidacy, and the president did so.[63]

This was not the end of controversy surrounding Fortas. With Richard Nixon squeaking out a victory over Hubert Humphrey in the 1968 presidential election, FBI Director Hoover now had an ideological ally in the White House. Almost immediately, Hoover began to help Nixon—who campaigned not only on invoking the "great silent majority" of upstanding citizens who paid their taxes and wanted the Vietnam War ended with honor but on the dangerous permissiveness of both the Johnson administration and Supreme Court—to change the political makeup of the Court. On 23 April 1969, President Nixon phoned Hoover to discuss a few matters, one of them being Justice Fortas. Nixon told Hoover he had heard *Life* magazine was about to publish "an exposé of Abe Fortas." Hoover confirmed this for Nixon, saying journalist William Lambert had a "very strong story," and Lambert even offered it to Fortas for comment prior to publication. Lambert's story was the first public revelation of Fortas's $20,000 check from Wolfson. Nixon asked Hoover why Fortas would do such a thing, and Hoover replied, revealingly, "He has not only done that, but I showed Assistant Attorney General Will Wilson the other day an article which was in the paper about three months ago" about Fortas and some other men buying a building in Arlington, Virginia, and renting it to the General Services Administration (GSA). Hoover characterized the purchase as a "tax dodge" and told Nixon he was investigating Fortas to "find out what pressure, if any, has been brought to bear on GSA by Fortas or anybody in his behalf to get these buildings rented to the Government." Hoover added that if there was pressure, then this "is a conflict of interest and I am hoping to dig something up." Nixon replied, according to Hoover, that Fortas "ought to be off" the Supreme Court.[64]

When Lambert's article, "Fortas of the Supreme Court: A Question of Ethics," was published in *Life* on 9 May 1969 (but given to the press on 4 May), given previous questions about Fortas's dealings, it created a firestorm. Public opinion was squarely against Fortas. Republicans called for his resignation, and Democratic legislators chose to remain silent and not defend the embattled justice, though some did express their belief that the Nixon administration had helped Lambert. Attorney General John Mitchell, moreover, compiled documents supportive of prosecution of Fortas and had them sent to the justice to pressure him into resigning. In the end it was just too much, and Fortas tendered his resignation from the Supreme Court, giving Nixon an opportunity (one of four, actually) to appoint a justice.[65]

Journalist Lambert, politically a Republican, got some of his information for the Fortas article from the Justice Department and the Internal Revenue Service (IRS). Lambert told historian Alexander Charns, however, he got nothing from the Nixon administration, and he "stayed the hell away from the bureau" even though he had contacts there. The fact of the matter was Lambert got some of his information from Justice Department sources, including Assistant Attorney General Wilson and Wolfson attorney Bill Bittman, a former Justice Department prosecutor who obviously would still have had contacts at the department and possibly even the FBI. Historian Athan Theoharis has pointed out that Hoover wrote Attorney General Mitchell on 2 June 1969 to tell him a "reliable source" confided that someone in the Justice "Department furnished considerable information to William Lambert" for his Fortas exposé. Theoharis also noted that in 1971, White House Aide E. Howard Hunt had attempted, but failed, to pass falsified information to Lambert for another exposé on JFK's role in the Diem assassination in Vietnam. Lambert, however, refused to use a document he could not authenticate.[66]

Although Lambert "stayed the hell away" from his FBI sources when *writing* his story, he clearly learned information about Fortas from the FBI or somebody with access to FBI information. On 29 August 1969, *New York Times* reporter Fred Graham—who himself had extensively covered the Fortas story, including writing a piece on Lambert's exposé in *Life* magazine—talked with Lambert. Graham made notes of his conversation, and he observed that Lambert, in addition to himself,

> also knows about the report that the FBI had a morals file on Fortas. One of his contacts telephoned him shortly after the *Life* story broke, informing him that the Washington field office of the FBI had a file that showed that Fortas had been identified as a man who had been accused of homosexual relations with a 16-year-old boy. Lambert said he didn't want to see the file, although his friend said he could bootleg it out of the FBI's office for him if he were interested.

Lambert's wording here is significant. He did not merely say the FBI had information about Fortas, which any unknowing person could claim. Instead, he specifically said the WFO had the file. As we have seen, this was exactly the case, and only someone in the FBI or Justice Department would know such details. Use of the word "bootleg," moreover, might suggest it was somebody in the Justice Department, not the FBI. It cannot be proven for certain.[67]

Equally revealing is the fact that at another time Hoover disseminated information to alter the makeup of the Supreme Court. After Republican House Minority Leader Gerald Ford, without any conclusive evidence, in the spring of 1970 called for an investigation and impeachment of Justice William O. Douglas for alleged improprieties, Nixon decided to lend his support. When speaking on the phone with Hoover in early June, Nixon asked Hoover if he could provide Ford any information he had on Douglas to assist the US representative in his efforts. Hoover told Nixon he would give the information to Ford. Nothing came of the matter because Hoover had no proof of any wrongdoing on Douglas's part, but it illustrates that Hoover had no compunction about disseminating information to others who could effect a change on the Supreme Court bench and, hence, its political philosophy. Like other conservatives, Hoover did not like what he perceived as increasingly liberal rulings from the Court, especially those related to federal obscenity law.[68]

Just like the Johnson administration before it and the Eisenhower administration before that, even the morality-crusading Nixon White House was not exempt from gay baiting. Late in the afternoon on Wednesday, 11 June 1969, pugnacious columnist Jack Anderson, without an appointment, stopped by FBI Assistant to the Director for Investigations DeLoach's office (DeLoach was promoted to this position in 1965). Long considered by Hoover a troublemaking journalist—for decades FBI officials investigated Anderson for illegal access to classified government documents—Anderson worked for noted columnist Drew Pearson, helping him with his widely popular column the "Washington Merry-Go Round," which Anderson would inherit after Pearson's death. Anderson also published articles on his own in different venues. He dropped in on DeLoach because Hoover had issued standing orders not to cooperate with Pearson, so this was the only way he would be able to speak with an FBI official. That Wednesday, Anderson told DeLoach "he picked up some very damaging information regarding three White House aides." His source, he told DeLoach, was another White House aide he described as "absolutely reliable."[69]

Anderson proceeded to explain to DeLoach that Nixon White House Chief of Staff Robert Haldeman, domestic affairs advisor John Ehrlichman, and Special Assistant to the President Dwight Chapin were all homosexuals. The journalist said the three men would meet early in the morning before work to "engage in homosexual and perverted activities" and sometimes did the same thing at Haldeman's Watergate apartment. Anderson told De-Loach the story was a "bombshell," and he wanted to publish it in Pearson's column, but he needed "further evidence."[70]

DeLoach stopped Anderson after he made that comment and pointed out to him that the FBI was under obligation to "report this matter to the White House." Anderson said he understood but asked DeLoach not to reveal his name if he did. "I made no reply in this regard," DeLoach later told FBI Associate Director Tolson. DeLoach also reported to Tolson his belief that Anderson "dumped" the story on the FBI so he would "be in the position to indicate, publicly or otherwise" the FBI knew about it. DeLoach also observed that Anderson had been close to Humphrey, the Democratic presidential candidate in 1968, and so probably had it out for Nixon. After Anderson departed, DeLoach consulted the FBI Special Inquiry Files but found nothing to corroborate the allegations against any of Nixon's aides. DeLoach advised Tolson the FBI had no choice but to inform the White House, but he wondered if Hoover wanted to handle it himself and inform the president, the attorney general, or Ehrlichman. Tolson suggested adding Henry Kissinger to the list.[71]

Afterward, DeLoach forwarded to Tolson and Hoover the FBI summary reports on Haldeman, Ehrlichman, and Chapin, and on 24 June the FBI director spoke with Attorney General Mitchell and forwarded to him a report on the Anderson allegations. Hoover then visited Ehrlichman, who had already spoken with the attorney general and who asked Hoover for a written account of Anderson's sudden visit. The FBI director complied, after which Ehrlichman assured Hoover that Anderson's claims were a "complete fabrication."[72]

Hoover then met with Chief of Staff Haldeman on 1 July. Worried about how the homosexual allegations might play out, Haldeman suggested Hoover arrange for sworn statements to be taken from himself, Ehrlichman, and Chapin and for Hoover to retain custody of the statements. Hoover commented he thought Anderson and Pearson were "rat[s] of the worst type," and he tried to assure Haldeman by telling him "they tackle me about once a month." He also told him his initial "reaction was of such outrage and disgust" he "did not want to dignify it" with a response to Anderson. Haldeman then told Hoover he believed Anderson intentionally gave De-Loach the story to put himself "in a position where he could say this information was supplied to the Bureau," and if the FBI did not investigate, then Anderson could claim "it was hushed up by the White House or the Attorney General."[73]

Hoover, who already suspected this, agreed with Haldeman's assertion and added that Anderson probably said he got the information from a White House aide to "divert us," but he also believed it was entirely possible that Anderson, indeed, had a White House source because Pearson and Anderson "have contacts in almost every department." Haldeman then told Hoover there were two possible responses they could make: either do nothing or have an FBI official take down the sworn statements. With this, Hoover changed his mind about not responding and agreed to take the sworn statements. That way, Haldeman argued, if Pearson and Anderson made hay of the story, the White House could "say the FBI was investigating the charges."[74]

Hoover added that Pearson and Anderson often played good cop and bad cop. Pearson, Hoover said, was the "bad boy" and Anderson the "good boy" in that if the situation became too controversial Anderson would claim to have prevented Pearson from publishing it. Hoover thought, in any event, that "they dare not publish it because there would be a libel suit." Haldeman, however, disagreed with the FBI director, saying he believed Pearson would have no qualms about publishing the story. Hoover agreed inasmuch as he thought Pearson and Anderson were "pretty shrewd in the way they phrase things." He thought that if they were going to use the story, they would "do it in such a way that it is not libel, but near it." The FBI director added, "Anderson is no friend of this Bureau" but remarked that Anderson was at least a "rather nice-looking fellow," whereas Pearson "looks like a rat" and "looks like a skunk and is one."[75]

That same day, Hoover dispatched FBI Assistant Director Joseph Casper of the Training Division and FBI Supervisory Agent George Quinn, along with Hoover's personal secretary, Erma Metcalf, to the White House to take the sworn statements from Haldeman, Ehrlichman, and Chapin. They completed the task over two days (1–2 July). Assistant Director Casper reported that all present "cooperated fully" and were told that FBI agents would not investigate the matter further. According to Hoover, "all three under oath emphatically denied" Anderson's claims. Hoover maintained custody of the statements and filed them in his secret office file.[76]

Pearson and Anderson never published their story, and the matter seems to have ended there, but Hoover had a long and storied history with Anderson—whom he viscerally detested since the 1950s. In November 1950 Jean Kerr, Senator Joseph McCarthy's administrative assistant and future wife, broke her hip. McCarthy and Kerr decided to take some time off in Hawaii, during which time Kerr could recuperate. As he often did with prominent personalities, Hoover ordered local FBI agents to assist McCarthy and Kerr while there in any way. By April 1951, after Anderson learned about this, he telephoned the FBI asking about the assistance. He even admitted he was trying to prove that the FBI and McCarthy were linked. There was, of course, a quietly established link, but an FBI official told Anderson the FBI always strove to remain a neutral body. Anderson's bravado angered Hoover, who commented, "This fellow Anderson and his ilk have minds that are lower than the regurgitated filth of vultures."[77]

In 1971, Anderson again wrote about Hoover in his column. By this point public attitudes had changed with the strife of Vietnam and tumult of the 1960s, eroding former deference to, and respect for, among others, the FBI director. This only prompted Anderson to single out Hoover, repeatedly, for attack. He wrote about Hoover's embarrassment for having never arrested anyone in the 1930s and his subsequent hastily arranged personal arrest of Alvin "Kreepy" Karpis in New Orleans but only after FBI agents had done the dangerous work. Anderson also wrote about Hoover's refusal to leave his bulletproof Cadillac when a long-haired young man was loitering near Hoover's home, and how a seemingly frightened Hoover sometimes had the police stationed outside his home. When he learned about the column, an angry Hoover referred to Anderson as a "jackal." Likewise, when Anderson soon thereafter wrote about President Nixon using US Air Force jets to shuttle his dog, King Timahoe, cross country, Hoover similarly remarked, "Nothing is too low for this 'jackal' to cover."[78]

In February 1971, Anderson continued targeting the FBI director by boldly using FBI surveillance tactics against Hoover, then writing about them. He had Hoover physically surveilled and even rummaged through his trash to learn details about the FBI director's life. In a column titled "The Real Hoover Is No Superman" and in another titled "Hoover Neither Hero nor Ogre," Anderson documented Hoover's comings and goings, his picking up the now-enfeebled Tolson every morning, their daily lunch excursions, and even that Hoover's trash indicated that the FBI director suffered from gastrointestinal distress. Anderson even claimed Hoover refused to eat food thoughtful citizens sent him for fear it might be poisoned. So, Anderson claimed, Hoover donated the food to orphanages. Anderson even answered questions about Hoover's presumed homosexuality on a Boston radio show, though he answered them obliquely (calling Hoover and Tolson odd "bachelors" who "grew up together at the FBI"). Hoover, in his typical style, commented at FBI headquarters Anderson was the "jackal of the news media. No one but a scavenger would rummage thru garbage and trash such as Anderson states was done." Regarding the food comment, he called Anderson a "malicious liar." One FBI official was worried Hoover might wish to publicly express his anger at Anderson's columns, and he warned that Hoover's trash comment should not be made public because "in the past" FBI agents had, indeed, used "trash covers" in their investigations, and if this was learned "it would be inimical to the Bureau's best interests."[79]

With Hoover's death in May 1972, Anderson continued unabated his FBI-centered columns, which raised further questions about the FBI interest in homosexuality, among other issues. Just days after Hoover's death, Anderson wrote a column taking Hoover's replacement, L. Patrick Gray, to task for claiming publicly that the FBI had no secret files. Anderson cited, by file number even, specific files Hoover's FBI had kept on prominent personalities. One of them, he said, was Hudson, in whose file Anderson claimed the new FBI director would find "titillating tidbits."[80]

Anderson's revelation triggered an FBI investigation to discover who leaked Hudson's file (and several others) to the journalist. In the end, FBI officials decided somebody in the Secret Service had leaked the materials to Anderson, and in their reports they asserted the typical FBI finesse by claiming FBI agents had never investigated Hudson. What they meant was FBI agents never conducted an official field investigation of Hudson, but FBI agents did, in fact, conduct a name-check search of FBI files in reference to him and collect information about him from FBI informants and an interview. Technically speaking, this was not an official FBI investigation per se, but obviously FBI officials were interested in Hudson and collected and compiled information about him, including using the FBI Sex Deviates File.[81]

Anderson's various published attacks on the FBI, particularly his revelations after Hoover's death of FBI files and investigations, greatly concerned

FBI officials. Significantly, except for FBI Director Gray, who was Nixon's man, all of the FBI top officials were still Hoover men—trained and indoctrinated with his methods—who carried on the old way of doing things. By the end of 1972, after learning that Anderson planned to argue that FBI agent morale was down, FBI supervisors decided to survey agent attitudes in the field offices. Not a scientific survey, FBI officials merely asked SACs across the country to report on their offices' morale situation. Perhaps not surprisingly, and maybe even a little humorously in retrospect, they all naturally reported that FBI agent morale was "so overwhelming, enthusiastic and immediate that they completely belie any contention to the contrary and, accordingly, are being made a matter of record"![82]

FBI officials in the immediate post-Hoover era were not finished with Anderson, however. In March 1973, they compiled in a blind memo of "public source data" on Anderson, civil liberties lawyer Joseph Rauh, and one other individual whose name is redacted in FBI documents. For Anderson, this meant a compilation of his various articles criticizing the bureau. FBI officials then disseminated this document to conservative Republican Senator Hruska, who had a reputation for being outspoken and was a repeated target of Anderson—the journalist claimed Hruska was a part owner of pornography theaters. What Hruska did with the information, if anything, remains unknown, but clearly FBI officials even after Hoover's death were disseminating information that could be used against the rabble-rousing Anderson.[83]

The Nixon White House, concerned with leaks to the press and always looking for any angle to use against its enemies, was deeply interested in the gay issue and what information the FBI might have. On 25 November 1970 White House Chief of Staff Haldeman called Hoover seeking such information. Haldeman told Hoover that Nixon wanted, assuming Hoover already had the information at hand rather than having to investigate, a "rundown on the homosexuals known and suspected in the Washington press corps." Hoover told Haldeman he "thought we have some of that material." Haldeman mentioned some names (redacted in the FBI record) of journalists rumored to be gay and reiterated to Hoover that "the President has an interest in what, if anything else," the FBI knew. Hoover replied that he "would get after that right away." Handwritten notations on the FBI memo documenting the request indicate that FBI officials indeed compiled and sent the requested information in letter format, dated 27 November 1970, to Haldeman.[84]

To date this letter has not surfaced, and it remains to be seen if or how the Nixon White House used the information Hoover provided. Even the details of what, exactly, Hoover provided, remain mysterious. Several examples, however, documenting Nixon's willingness to gay bait his perceived enemies and his general views on homosexuality exist. Shortly after being elected, for example, Nixon chose William Rogers to be his secretary of state (1969–1973). Nixon had a problem with Rogers, however, in that he was part of that eastern establishment a paranoid Nixon perceived as somehow against him. Even though Rogers was long a Nixon confidant, Nixon never passed on an opportunity to humiliate Rogers. This included his starting a rumor that Rogers was gay—Nixon called him a "fag"—and that he supported a young lover in Georgetown.[85]

In late April 1971, following the traditional annual White House conference on children and youth—a meeting presidents had sponsored for more than seventy years—because issues of gay rights had been raised, Nixon, Kissinger, and Haldeman were moved to discuss homosexuality shortly afterward in the Oval Office. In the recorded conversation, a disingenuous Nixon said he did not want his "views misunderstood" about the "gay thing." He then claimed, incredibly, to be the "most tolerant person on that of anybody in this shop" and expressed his opinion that gays were "born that way, the tendency is there." As a man with apparent cognitive dissonance, Nixon then said, "My point is, that Boy Scout leaders, YMCA leaders, and others, bring them in that direction, and teachers." He then compared current homosexuality with that of ancient Rome, arguing that "once a society moves in that direction, the vitality goes out of that society."[86]

Kissinger agreed with the president, noting incorrectly, "That's certainly been the case in antiquity. The Romans were notorious homosexuals."

With that prompt, Nixon cut off Kissinger, then cited, again inaccurately, the ancient Greeks as another example of a society plagued by homosexuality. "By God," he exclaimed, "I am not going to have a situation where we pass along a law indicating, 'Well, now, kids, just go out and be gay.' They can do it. Just leave them alone. That's a lifestyle I don't want to touch." To that, Chief of Staff Haldeman commented to Nixon, "I'm afraid that's what they're doing now." Nixon admonished him, however, "Just leave them alone." Kissinger then warned of the dangers of the federal government embracing gay rights: "It's one thing for people, to, you know, like some people we know, who would do it discreetly, but to make that a national policy."[87]

The following month, while Nixon stood in a White House receiving line shaking hands with guests, he could not help but comment to his chief of staff afterward about one man from California who told Nixon he, like the president, was a Quaker: "He was an obvious, roaring fag." Later, while Nixon was watching TV, he came across the soon-to-be popular show *All in the Family*, which he mistook for a movie. The particular episode Nixon saw had one of Archie Bunker's old friends come out as gay.[88] To Nixon it was "glorifying homosexuality. I mean, the guys were admitting they were homosexuals and so forth." Nixon then described the gay character entering Bunker's house inasmuch as he was "obviously queer—he wears an ascot and so forth and he uses the language—but he's not offensively so." After some discussion of the episode, Nixon claimed to "not mind the homosexuality." He said, in fact, he understood it. "But, nevertheless," the president continued, the "point that I make is that Goddamn it, I do not think that you glorify on public television homosexuality . . . any more than you glorify whores." Nixon then wondered what effect such programming had on young boys. The president cited the Boys Clubs because "we constantly had to clean up the staffs to keep the Goddamned fags out of it." Nixon claimed it "outraged" him because he feared for the future of the country. He again cited the ancient Greeks, claiming "homosexuality destroyed them." "Sure, Aristotle was a homo," he said. "We all know that, so was Socrates." As for Rome, in Nixon's humble opinion, "The last six Roman emperors were fags." He then cited gays as undermining Britain and France, but indirectly praised Russia, of all countries, for "root[ing] them out." He claimed drugs and homosexuality were the "enemies of strong societies," and "communists and the left wingers are pushing" both. "They're trying to destroy us," Nixon claimed. He then added, "Goddamn it, we have got to stand up to these people," whom Nixon cited as not only those "in the ratty part" of San Francisco but also among the "upper class." Nixon continued: "It is the most faggot goddamned thing you could ever imagine. . . . It's just terrible. I mean I don't even want to shake hands with anybody from San Francisco." Nixon even claimed women in the early 1970s dressed terribly because the clothing "designers hate women."[89]

On 22 December 1971, Nixon discussed with Ehrlichman the leak of classified National Security Council information to journalist Anderson. He directed his aide to find out if the navy yeoman who provided Anderson the information was gay because, in Nixon's mind, that could be an indicator of his motivation. Nixon, moreover, wanted the yeoman taped in an interview. "I want a direct question about homosexuality asked," Nixon said. "You never know what you're going to find," said Nixon, who once claimed he wanted to leave gays alone.[90]

Nixon's men—those who engaged in political dirty tricks—also used homosexuality against his enemies. One of them planned to donate $200 in the name of the Gay Liberation Front (for the GLF, see Chapter 8) to Pete McCloskey, a Republican who challenged Nixon in the Republican presidential primaries on an antiwar platform, then quit the party to become a Democrat. In the end, the Nixon operative, in the words of journalist Rick Perlstein, "chickened out" and configured the donation as originating from a socialist group. Another Nixon man spread rumors that Democratic Senator Henry "Scoop" Jackson, who was running for the Democratic presidential nomination in 1972, had been arrested by the Washington, DC, police for gay solicitation. Nixon and his men seemed to know few bounds.[91]

Gay baiting and the political use of homosexuality was nothing new, but Nixon, in his bitter and vindictive ways, took it to extremes. LBJ and Nixon, and the people who worked for them, were people of their times. Yet times were changing. By the end of the 1960s the reserved homophile movement had given way to the militant homophile movement, reflected so well in Kameny and ECHO, and even this would give way to a far more radical alternative. Inspired by the black power and women's liberation movements and other radicalized forces by the end of that decade, even the gay rights movement would become radicalized after a riot in New York City. The FBI would, of course, continue to be interested but, as always, within the context of that particular era.

CHAPTER 8

"I'm Ready to Die for the Cause!"

The FBI Confronts Gay Liberation

On one Sunday evening in Chicago, 19 April 1970, a member of that city's Mattachine Society attended the group's regular meeting at the Second Unitarian Church on West Barry Avenue. About midway through, several "hippie types" crashed the gathering of otherwise reserved homophile advocates and proceeded to disrupt it. Homophile activists were typically demure and concealed their identities behind pseudonyms even among kindred spirits. The interlopers shouted out "radical statements" such as "I'm ready to die for the cause!" Not content with departing after the sudden disruption, they proceeded to do what they intended all along: recruit new members to their radical, militant cause. They passed out fliers for those interested in moving beyond reserved, low-key activism and those who expressed interest in joining the recently formed Gay Liberation Front (GLF) of Chicago. The particular Mattachine member noted above, however, was so "very much disturbed" by these radicals' intrusion, he was moved late that night to contact the Chicago Field Office and report the incident.[1]

The Chicago GLF disruption and recruiting tactics perfectly capture the change in attitudes, strategies, and, in fact, the rift among gay rights activists during the late 1960s and early 1970s. The gay liberation movement was rooted not only in gay men's and lesbian women's experiences since the Second World War but also stemmed from gays witnessing and participating in the struggles of other minorities and women and their quest for equality. They sought to emulate and replicate these various movements and their philosophical and tactical successes.

Gays and lesbians read about, witnessed in person, and saw on television the nonviolent and assimilationist principles of Martin Luther King Jr. and his Southern Christian Leadership Conference (SCLC), the Student Nonviolent Coordinating Committee (SNCC), and the Freedom Rides led by the Congress for Racial Equality (CORE) in which participants braved brutal violence and humiliation, all for a higher purpose. The homophile movement, in fact, had been significantly influenced by King, seeking to copy what gay liberationists later described as a passive and acceptable approach to gay civil rights and liberties. For those predisposed to the radicalism of the 1960s, however, the results achieved by homophile activists prior to 1969 were limited and unsatisfying.

By the late 1960s, gays and lesbians watched, and some participated in, the African American civil rights movement as it was morphing and evolving. These activists expanded their work from integration and equality to targeting related issues of poverty and housing. Regardless of winning lawsuits and gaining some encoded legal rights, African Americans continued to face stringent racial discrimination, ferocious oppression, and race-based economic inequity. Out of this seemingly hopeless situation, riots erupted across the country between 1964 and 1968, whether in Los Angeles; Newark; Detroit; Washington, DC; or any number of smaller locations. Achieving wins on paper, yet experiencing unending social stagnation nationally, some decided a more radical movement was needed. All of this gave rise to the militant black power movement.

Gays and lesbians also witnessed the rise of new figures in the African American civil rights movement. They learned about Robert Williams, who decided the legal system had failed African Americans, leading him to drift away from King's nonviolent principles and begin advocating for self-defense. They saw Gloria Richardson, who decided African Americans were only making limited progress and had little protection, so she began to carry a gun while embracing the concept of self-protection.[2] Most notably, gays and lesbians witnessed the militancy of Malcolm X and Stokely Carmichael. These and other militants came to question racial integration and assimilation and emphasized black pride and black autonomy. Some formed radical groups, such as the Black Panther Party (BPP) in 1966. The BPP members embraced along with their political agenda African American self-defense as a priority. Although only a minority in the African American civil rights movement, black power advocates received considerable press attention and public scrutiny.

The women's liberation movement also influenced the gay liberation movement. For more than a century women, including many lesbians working quietly among their groups, had fought for equal political rights, and in the 1950s and 1960s many worked as civil rights activists and antiwar organizers. In *The Feminine Mystique,* Betty Friedan questioned the dominant 1950s notion of women's expected domestic roles, their stunted career paths, and unhappy existence based on what US culture and social values demanded. By 1966 Friedan, Pauli Murray (a black civil rights activist), and others created the National Organization for Women (NOW), calling for women to be liberated—a term dating from at least 1898 but used more contextually in the mid-1960s[3]—from the social and sexual status society had imposed upon them.

Those who would take up the banner of gay liberation were perhaps most influenced by the rise of the New Left, known by its advocates as the Movement. Students were the heart and soul of the New Left—whether protesting the Vietnam War, advocating for social progress, or fighting for greater democracy—and some of them would go on to form gay liberation groups on college and university campuses, often without official recognition. Yet the core of what would become the wider gay liberation movement would be an eclectic and diverse bunch heavily influenced by the New Left Movement. The New Left began after SNCC and Students for a Democratic Society (SDS) had rejected traditional leftist politics and embarked on community organizing. They decided it was best to organize black communities directly for action rather than trying to convince white communities to support equality. By 1966, in fact, SNCC devoted itself completely to the idea of minority self-organizing.

A radical offshoot of the civil rights movement, the New Left emerged from multifaceted forces, including the free speech movement in Berkeley, California, to offer an alternative to traditional leftist politics. Its activists would further embrace the counterculture movement and advocate for social revolution, rejecting the strictures of traditional society, the Democratic Party, and even the Communist Party.[4] Emulating this, gay liberationists would reject out of hand the philosophy, strategies, and goals of their predecessor—the homophile movement—including even its militant East Coast wing.

Standard histories of the GLF, about which scholarship is thin, have it that the group formed immediately following the two-day Stonewall riots that began on 28 June 1969 in the Greenwich Village section of New York City. According to the Red Butterfly—a Marxist cell of the GLF formed by John Lauritsen and others as "radical intelligentsia within GLF, concerned with developing a theory of gay liberation and linking it to other movements for social change"[5]—radical and militant gay groups, as early as the spring of 1969, had formed in California and Minnesota.[6]

More broadly, gay men and lesbian women during the 1960s watched and participated as other struggling minority groups turned to radicalization. The GLF, itself, wrote in a pamphlet about its history that gays "could sympathize most readily with other oppressed peoples, having been oppressed themselves for many centuries."[7] As radical activist and GLF member Martha Shelley put it:

> The civil rights movement gave me a deep underpinning. The women's movement questioned sexual roles. The yippies [the radical Youth International Party] and the left-wing movements of the sixties questioned the politics I grew up with, questioned the economic and social underpinnings of the whole society. Then the drugs, LSD, and writers and philosophers caused me to really question everything, and to say, "The whole perception of reality I was raised with is fucked up, totally crazy, certifiably insane."[8]

Another group that significantly helped to radicalize gays was the BPP. According to the Red Butterfly cell, it influenced gays to "start to think of no longer sitting around and hiding the fact that they too were oppressed." "The time had come," the Red Butterfly announced, "to stand up and confront the old ways and moral standards, in and out of the movement, and wherever Gays were openly being ridiculed."[9]

The gay liberation movement, however, only "fully came to light"[10] following the June 1969 Stonewall riots. New York City of the late 1960s was not the gay-tolerant place it would later become. The New York Police Department routinely arrested gay men for solicitation—one historian estimated the numbers during the mid-1960s to be as high as 400 men a month—and the New York Liquor Authority liberally interpreted its regulatory function to regard any bar that served gays as engaging in disorderly conduct and therefore subject to closure. Members of organized crime saw the potential in an assured, if illegal, gay drinking and socializing population. The situation perfectly fit the Mafia's typical modus operandi. Like other Mafia operations—such as the extortion of pornographers during the 1970s and 1980s—their targets could not report exploitive tactics because of police targeting of gays. They also would not dare resist the Mafia for fear of violent retribution. So Mafia-connected bars and clubs ironically (given organized crime's homophobia) began to cater to the gay community—a group with expendable income—with watered-down drinks and inflated prices. Strangely enough, these establishments were relatively safe meeting places because the Mafia paid off corrupt police precincts to leave them alone. One such bar was the Stonewall Inn in Greenwich Village.[11]

Rampant targeting, exploitation, and harassment of gays eventually came to a head on Friday, 27 June 1969, at the Stonewall Inn. Just before midnight, two detectives and some regular police officers planned to raid the popular gay bar. The raid was a function of that year's mayoral political campaign, in which the incumbent, Mayor John Lindsay, backed police raids of so-called problem bars because they left the impression the mayor was cracking down on crime (both organized crime and gays) to improve conditions in the city, always popular with voters. This was not unique to this period. Later, in 1972, Lindsay would similarly target the popular and iconic porn film *Deep Throat* in Times Square because that would assure votes. Lindsay also had the benefit of a cooperative local precinct commander willing to carry out the raids.[12]

The Stonewall Inn, moreover, was a tempting target. Not only was it a popular hangout among young, gay men but its patrons were diverse. There were white men, people of color, and a fair number of drag queens. Making it even more tempting for the police was the fact that the bar had no liquor license. There were, of course, popular rumors of mob ties—rumors that happened to be true. The establishment also provided as entertainment scantily clad go-go boys, which only contributed to the perception of a vice problem. Overall, the bar had a reputation for unruliness in a busy, if bohemian, section of the city.[13]

Gay bar raids were routine, of course, but what made this one unique was the backlash. Normally gays were deferential to the police and rarely resisted arrest, seemingly accepting their fates while loaded en masse into paddy wagons. Not this time. Given the intensified targeting of gays, exploitation of gays, given the times, given developing militancy in various civil rights movements, the bar's patrons resisted. As bar-goers filed out of Stonewall one by one, a crowd began to form outside. Not content with observation, it began to jeer the police as they loaded bar employees and several drag queens into a paddy wagon.[14]

Then, as a police officer was escorting a lesbian outside, she began to resist. Some in the growing crowd began throwing beer cans and bottles at the police vans and cars. Some people even threw coins. The ruckus then rapidly escalated from bottles and coins sailing through the air to dislodged cobblestones. The police took refuge in the bar awaiting backup, leading several angry men to tear up a parking meter and use it as a battering ram to smash down the bar door.[15]

The bar then somehow caught fire and was engulfed. Rioting continued throughout the night, including the spectacle of Puerto Rican transvestites attacking police riot lines. Protests continued into the following day, and particularly the next night. The situation did not diminish. Angry, young, gay men taunted the police and threw just about anything at them, including garbage and bricks. Someone even spray painted the phrase "gay power" on walls, a derivative of Carmichael's black power. Famously, a group of men conducted a chorus line, replete with full leg kicks, until the police dispersed them. One estimate has it that some 400 police officers confronted a crowd of about 2,000. It was a full-fledged gay uprising. The gay New York beat poet Allen Ginsberg said of it: "They've lost that wounded look that fags all had ten years ago."[16]

Following the Stonewall riots, some newly radicalized gays—those who by this point had been influenced by the New Left and counterculture ideas—sought out the Mattachine Society and the Daughters of Bilitis (DoB). These meetings were significant inasmuch as younger gays immediately recognized in the homophile movement a reserved and cautious attitude that clashed with their more avant-garde thinking. Yet the very presence of homophile groups did have an impact. As historian Toby Marotta has put it, the homophile movement influenced the rise of gay liberation "less by promoting liberationist activity than by letting homosexuals partial to New Left political perspectives know that they would have to pursue liberationist aims on their own."[17]

They decided they needed to join others in the New Left Movement. To end oppression, broadly conceived, they needed to work with black power advocates, anti–Vietnam War protestors, and others to radically transform US society and values as the only solution to their problems. Ironically, though, and perhaps unexpectedly, it began with Mattachine New York. Michael Brown, a New Left activist who happened to be gay, contacted Mattachine emphasizing the need for a response to Stonewall. The president of Mattachine New York, Dick Leitsch, agreed, and together they formed something called the Action Committee of Mattachine. After a few meetings Brown quickly found his ideology more in line with theirs than Mattachine's, an organization long concerned with not antagonizing authorities. Among the members he recruited to the new group were Bill Weaver, whom Brown knew from the Fifth Avenue Vietnam Peace Parade Committee, and Shelley, who had resigned as president of DoB New York to participate in radical politics.[18]

They saw an opportunity for protest after they learned about a planned demonstration outside of a women's prison near Greenwich Village. Its purpose was to support BPP members who had been arrested. Being in sympathy with the views and goals of the BPP, and seeking an opportunity to unite with other radical groups, members of the Action Committee decided to participate in the demonstration. Respecting Mattachine's concerns about angering authorities, members of the group decided not to identify themselves with Mattachine and, instead, someone suggested using the name Gay Liberation Front, after which Shelley pounded on the meeting table and exclaimed, "THAT'S IT. THAT'S IT. We're the Gay Liberation Front!" The name stuck from that point onward.[19]

After the offshoot group participated in the prison march using their new moniker, Leitsch learned about it and became upset. He asked about the GLF, "What's this? Another new gay organization?" He then inquired of Shelley if she and others were forming a new group. To this Shelley replied, "No, that's just the name of our march committee." She and the others quickly realized they could never continue as part of Mattachine. She later commented about her reply to Leitsch, "I think in my heart I knew I was lying."[20]

With views and tactics clearly out of sync with Mattachine's, and experiencing recurring friction with Mattachine's cautious leadership, the members of the Action Committee soon afterward met other leftists who wanted to organize gays differently. These included Bill Katzenberg and Charles Pitts. Katzenberg was a member of SDS and thought gays could be organized like the student group; Pitts worked in radio—for New York's WBAI—and was well known for outing himself on air and publicly discussing homosexuality. They held a meeting in late July at Alternate University, a radical education center located in a Manhattan industrial loft, that the members of the Action Committee and others attended. (Alternate U., as they called it, would be the location of future GLF meetings and dances because they wanted to avoid mob-run gay bars.) The meeting was a success and led to another at which fifty or sixty attendees discussed their concerns and decided to organize a larger GLF. They announced its formation in the underground newspaper the *Rat.*[21]

Unlike the homophile movement, the GLF members proudly used the word "gay" in their group's name. According to Jerry Hoose, a young man long immersed in the local gay scene who attended the meeting, they decided on using "gay-something or homosexual-something" in their name but settled on the former.[22] At the time, the word "gay" was considered a slur by many, and, in fact, some in the media even considered it obscene. The word homosexual, a clinical term invented by heterosexuals, would not be used because it represented the social values gay liberationists wanted to overturn. The remainder of the group's name, in addition to representing their goal of liberation from imposed social values, was borrowed from the South Vietnamese National Liberation Front—the alliance of those seeking to overthrow their repressive government and oust US forces. As Shelley put it, members of the South Vietnamese National Liberation Front "were heroic in the eyes of the left, all of these little Vietnamese peasants running around in their conical hats and black pajamas, daring to stand up to the most powerful army in the world, with all its tanks and helicopters and napalm. It was David against Goliath, fighting for their nation and for the liberation of their people."[23] In the view of the GLF, this reflected their broader domestic interest in liberation from oppressors, and they hoped the radical name might attract young supporters with similar viewpoints.

The membership of the GLF was varied and diverse. One reason for this was its decentralized, anarchist nature. Its members did not want to create a formalized structure with strict membership requirements, dues, elected officers, formal voting, or formal committees—like that of the homophile movement. Essentially, anyone who attended a meeting was considered a member and was encouraged to join any one of several project groups, or cells. As they put it themselves, "GLF is you. Everyone is welcome at meetings."[24] Although most GLF members were Caucasian, about a third to a quarter consisted of people of color. Many of these members organized themselves in a cell called Third World Gay Revolutionaries.[25] Beyond its racial diversity, the GLF also included members from a wide variety of different socioeconomic backgrounds, "from the criminal underclass to the upper class," but mainly those from the middle and working classes. Only a few, however, came from the upper classes—graduate students, artisans, and those with elite educational backgrounds.[26]

The GLF was also diverse in terms of the political views of its members. It included radicals, revolutionaries, and cultural and political reformers. The most active GLF members were radicals, which reflected the influence of both the New Left and the 1960s counterculture movements. A significant part of this involved the idea that people needed to embrace new ways of thinking, a new "consciousness" that would permit them to recognize inherent problems in society and implement a revolution in social mores and values. They would transform the political system for the better. These radicals saw living an avowedly open gay life, in a group with no formal structure, as directly challenging existing social values and therefore making a significant political statement.[27]

GLF revolutionaries (a minority faction) were those who embraced more traditional leftist views, such as Marxism or socialism, and hoped to effect political and economic change in society. Focused on the effects of capitalism as the cause of US social inequality, they did not believe the consciousness focus of the radicals should be the group's primary effort. In constant conflict with the majority radicals, the revolutionaries, such as Lauritsen, organized their own cell, the Red Butterfly, and remained largely upset that the GLF refused to have an organized structure in favor of decentralized cells. The Red Butterfly dedicated itself to forming an intellectual theory for gay liberation and reached out to the other movements.[28]

The third minority political component of the GLF was made up of the reformers, whether cultural or political. They were unique from the other factions given the means by which they hoped to effect change. Cultural reformers wanted gays to come out of the closet and live open lives because, they believed, if heterosexuals were more exposed to gay subculture, they would have little choice but to accept gays for who they were. GLF member Leo Martello exemplified this view by demanding his compatriots call themselves "gay" rather than accept negative, socially imposed descriptions. Political reformers, on the other hand, wanted to use influence—focusing on those in power—to win acceptance as a legitimate minority and thereby end various forms of repression. Reformers, of whatever stripe, looked to political demonstrations and confronting politicians as their priority.[29]

To best understand the FBI monitoring of the GLF and its various chapters across the country, we first need to understand the context in which the FBI and J. Edgar Hoover operated from the mid-1960s through the early 1970s. Beginning in 1965, FBI Director Hoover significantly reduced the number of wiretaps and bugs FBI agents employed in their investigations after Attorney General Katzenbach suddenly required his prior approval of them upon the discovery of illegal electronic surveillance during the Fred Black case. (Black was convicted in 1964 of income-tax evasion, and his deeds were uncovered through an illegal FBI bug in his home and office, installed on Hoover's authority in 1962; in 1966 his case and knowledge of the listening devices were before the Supreme Court.) Hoover also reduced the use of wiretaps, bugs, and other sensitive FBI activity because the Senate, at the time, was scrutinizing their use in organized crime cases, and he was concerned further revelations of FBI use of illegal surveillance techniques would irreparably harm the FBI.[30]

Hoover was also worried about additional exposure of illegal FBI activity, particularly given increased public criticism during the turbulent 1960s. On 8 March 1971 a social protest group led by Haverford College physics professor William Davidon broke into the FBI resident agency in Media, Pennsylvania (near Philadelphia) and pilfered FBI files. The files documented FBI improprieties, including its illegal COINTELPRO disruption program. COINTELPRO began in 1956 and targeted the Communist Party, Socialist Workers Party, Ku Klux Klan, black nationalist groups, and the New Left not for prosecution but for disruption because, at the time, prosecutions had become too difficult. The public also learned of FBI targeting of student and war activists, leading Hoover to terminate COINTELPRO.[31]

The Hoover FBI at this point, during both the Lyndon B. Johnson (LBJ) and Richard Nixon administrations, had also vastly increased its role as a political intelligence arm of the White House. In 1965, moreover, Hoover had reached the mandatory federal retirement age of seventy and only retained his job and powerful position because LBJ issued an executive order exempting Hoover from retirement. As a result, Hoover felt compelled to ingratiate himself with LBJ by providing him a steady flow of information about his political opponents, including war protestors. Hoover used FBI agents to monitor the 1964 Democratic National Convention and the activities of civil rights activists there. When Nixon became president in 1969, Hoover had an ideological ally in the White House and still only retained his position because of LBJ's standing executive order. The order, technically, could have been revoked at any time, so Hoover continued providing the Nixon White House political intelligence. Hoover created a special program, code-named INLET (intelligence letters), through which he provided the administration sensitive information. FBI agents, moreover, wiretapped members of the Nixon administration and journalists, all to discover the source of leaks. Yet Nixon ultimately became displeased with Hoover's efforts, partly for failing to uncover leakers and partly because he hesitated to employ more intrusive surveillance techniques given the increase in criticism of the government along with the FBI and Hoover's liability for revelations of illegal activity.

The FBI investigation of the GLF, therefore, occurred in the midst of these developments. On the one hand, extant documents seem to indicate FBI agents were somewhat restrained in how they monitored the GLF, mainly using informants rather than more intrusive techniques. On the other hand Hoover seemed more than willing to develop information about these radical activists, equating them with the New Left, especially when their activities intersected with the political interests of the White House. In an overarching sense, the disjointed and anarchist style of the GLF seemed to confound FBI agents, who had difficulty describing GLF structure (or lack thereof). When the Gay Activists Alliance (GAA) formed later, because it was more traditional in its organizational methods, FBI agents had an easier time investigating it.

The FBI first focused on the GLF in early August 1969, just weeks after the group's formation. FBI Director Hoover ordered the New York Field Office (in New York City) to "identify officers, aims, and objectives pursuant to Sec. 87E, M of I [Manual of Instructions]."[32] Section 87 of the FBI Manual of Instructions dealt with the use of so-called subversive informants, those used to investigate "subversive activities," which the bureau defined as "activities aimed at overthrowing, destroying, or undermining the Government of the United States or any of its political subdivisions." FBI agents typically used subversive informants when monitoring the Communist Party or any other group that, in their view, held revolutionary goals. When investigating the GLF, then, FBI agents' primary investigative tool was informants. Given that the GLF had formed in New York City, that was, unsurprisingly, the locus of FBI investigative efforts.[33]

Within a year, Hoover ordered FBI agents to determine whether the GLF "is connected with any New Left organizations or if it is a New Left–type organization." He was particularly interested in those GLF groups on college and university campuses. Hoover's later interest was to determine via the FBI's COMINFIL Program whether the GLF was under the influence of communists, similar to his worries in the 1950s that Mattachine might have been infiltrated. Hoover's concern with subversive infiltration can best be seen in an open letter he wrote, and President Nixon issued, to college and university students in September 1970. Hoover and Nixon were concerned with unrest on college campuses, leading Hoover to warn of the influence of extremists—he identified the SDS, among others, as the extremists—on students nationwide:

> The extremists are a small minority of students and faculty members who have lost faith in America. They ridicule the flag, poke fun at American institutions, seek to destroy our society. They are not interested in genuine reform. They

take advantage of the tensions, strife, and often legitimate frustrations of students to promote campus chaos. They have no rational, intelligent plan of the future either for the university or the Nation.[34]

It appears FBI officials first learned of the GLF—which they initially described, but then crossed out, as the "Fag Liberation Movement"—in connection with its support of imprisoned Vietnam War resisters and absent-without-leave (AWOL) soldiers who rose up and rioted at the Fort Dix stockades because of deplorable conditions there.[35] Thereafter, FBI agents mobilized their network of informants, or developed new ones, and began collecting varied information on the GLF.

From the summer of 1969 through 1970, FBI agents collected from informants copies of various New York area GLF newsletters, including a publication called the *GLF News*, the Red Butterfly cell newsletter and pamphlets, *Come Out!* (a GLF bimonthly publication), a flier called *Third World Gay Revolution Preamble*, the *Gay Journal*, and a host of other items the FBI has redacted in its files.[36] The FBI special agent in charge (SAC) in Buffalo also forwarded to the New York Field Office, under obscene cover— meaning using the special FBI procedure for handling and mailing items deemed obscene—copies of the radical GLF publication *Gay Flames*, which advocated joining with the BPP. The link to the BPP must have greatly interested and concerned FBI agents because the bureau long targeted the BPP under its illegal COINTELPRO disruption program. The Buffalo Field Office acquired its *Gay Flames* issues from US Customs officials who seized them from a Volkswagen bus entering the United States at the Peace Bridge. The magazines were sent under FBI obscene cover because they contained a gay cartoon strip called "The Lavender Kid and Butch" that depicted men with full frontal nudity. Using the obscene cover procedure when investigating gay groups was nothing new. FBI agents previously used it when forwarding to headquarters information about a gay bar in Texas and information about Andy Warhol.[37]

The literature these informants provided, indeed, offered FBI agents details about the aims and objectives of the GLF that FBI officials compiled but seemingly did not study in any singular analysis of the group. The *Gay Liberation Front Newsletter*, which FBI agents collected in August of 1969 shortly after the group formed, revealed that GLF was a "group of radical homosexuals dedicated to the elimination of the oppression of the homosexual community, and the creation of a society where all men and women can participate freely and to the fullness of their ability." It also educated FBI agents about some GLF activities, including a demonstration to "demand the freedom of prostitutes, [Black] panthers, and all other political prisoners," a "free beer party" to prepare for the Nagasaki Day antiwar rally, and a dance to raise funds. The bottom of the newsletter, which must have caught agents' attention, read: "All Power to the People; Gay Power to the Gay People."[38]

A second *Gay Liberation Front Newsletter* reiterated the ever-present danger of police raids on gay bars and the harassment of gays on New York City streets. "These actions," the GLF wrote, "seem to give credence to the rumor that chief pig Mitchell and super-pig Trickie-Dickie have launched a national crackdown on gay 'ghettos.'" As the GLF saw it, the New York City Police Department and Nixon "want to isolate and divide the people: gay and straight, black and white, workers and youth," and it was "up to gay people to not atagonize [*sic*] potential friends; i.e., we don't harass those who don't harass us."[39]

An issue of the *GLF News* that fell into FBI agents' hands during 1970 quoted abolitionist John Brown: "If it is deemed necessary that I should forfeit my life for the furtherance of the ends of justice, and mingle blood further with the blood of my children and with the blood of millions . . . whose rights are disregarded by wicked, cruel and unjust enactments, I say, let it be done." Given FBI concerns that the GLF sympathized with the BPP and wanted to reach out to its members, this statement must have greatly concerned FBI officials. The remainder of the *GLF News* listed various GLF meetings and the times and meeting dates of study groups. It also announced the formation of different radical gay and lesbian groups, such as the Radical Study Group, Lesbian Consciousness-Raising Group, Gay Male Consciousness-Raising Group, and a Co-ed Consciousness-Raising Group. Finally, the publication alerted readers about where one could hear "news of the gay community" on the radio in New York, WBAI-FM. All of these constituted potential investigative leads for FBI agents.[40]

The revolutionary Red Butterfly cell's *National Newsletter* of 10 March 1970 recounted the story, and resultant public gay protest, of a young gay man who panicked during a gay bar raid in Greenwich Village. He had run upstairs and apparently leapt from a second-story window only to impale himself below on an iron fence. At the time he was in critical condition in the hospital and still under police arrest. The newsletter then noted the growth across the country of the gay liberation movement. Reflecting the change in the gay rights movement, the newsletter observed, "What was once a quiet plea for 'tolerance' and 'acceptance'—the homophile era—has become a militant demand." The newsletter also noted gay liberation was growing alongside women's liberation, and the "oppression of our own people is part of the general oppression of minorities in America." The newsletter then invoked the phrase coined by militant homophile activist Frank Kameny: "Gay is good!"[41]

The issue of *Gay Flames* collected by FBI agents and sent to the New York Field Office under bureau obscene cover revealed to FBI officials the preferred connections of the radical GLF. *Gay Flames* explained its sympathies with the BPP under an article titled "Gay People Help Plan New World." During 1970 about thirty New York GLF members and members of Radical Lesbians were invited and traveled to Philadelphia to attend the BPP-sponsored plenary session of the Revolutionary Peoples' Constitutional Convention, an ultimately failed attempt to create a broad-based revolutionary movement. After attending various talks and meetings, these gay liberation advocates decided to recognize the "BPP as being presently the vanguard of the peoples' revolution." They regarded the BPP as the "clearest of all US radical groups in its understanding of the nature of the fight of the peoples of the whole world."[42]

The November 1970 issue of *Gay Flames*, in addition to recounting the experience of a black male transvestite in Bellevue Hospital, took up the issue of the GLF experience with the Communist Party and its discriminatory bias. The newsletter noted "Revolutionary Gays" had from time to time "confronted the Communist Party, U.S.A., about their anti-gay beliefs." Moreover, despite the GLF being fully in support of Angela Davis—the radical and communist whose firearm was used to murder a judge—the Communist Party was not interested in GLF support. "We can march beside them," *Gay Flames* observed, "as long as we do not carry our own banners or camp it up too much." The newsletter also noted that three times in the past the Communist Party had evicted gays from its picket lines and, in the future, the GLF hoped to have sufficient "numbers to physically resist" this.[43]

Perhaps most revealing for FBI agents was the GLF announcement of its formation in the underground newspaper, the *Rat*. Three GLF members—Michael Brown, Lois Hart, and Ron Ballard[44]—prepared the statement in the form of a series of questions put to fictional and anonymous GLF members. The first question asked, "What is the Gay Liberation Front?" In perusing the *Rat*, FBI agents learned about its radical goal of "complete sexual liberation for all people [, which] cannot come about unless existing social institutions are abolished." They learned that the GLF rejected "society's attempt to impose sexual roles and definitions of our nature," and "Babylon has forced us to commit ourselves to one thing . . . revolution."[45]

Secondly, the article in the *Rat* asked fictional members, "What makes you revolutionaries?" The answer was that after the Stonewall riots "we've come to realize that all our frustrations and feelings of oppression are real." In the blunt way so characteristic of radical gay liberationists, the article continued: "The society has fucked with us . . . within our families, on our jobs, in our education, in the streets, in our bedrooms; in short, it has shit all over us." Moreover, and undoubtedly of great interest to FBI agents, was the subsequent comment: "We identify ourselves with all the oppressed: the Vietnamese struggle, the third world, the blacks, the workers . . . all those oppressed by this rotten, dirty, vile, fucked-up, capitalist conspiracy."[46]

When asked specifically to identify oppression of gays, a fictional interviewee in the *Rat* depicted the existence of a gay man during the homophile era as someone having to "live two separate existences, which precludes his being able to live fully in either." Then, reflecting the radical liberationist background of the article's authors, the mock interviewee then criticized society's dominant value system and "socialization process," which, in his view, were "nothing but a phony morality impressed upon us by church, media, psychiatry, and education, which tells us that if we're not married heterosexual producers and pacified workers and soldiers that we are sick degenerate outcasts."[47]

Of particular interest to FBI agents (as one underlined the response) was the answer to the question, "What does the GLF intend to do?" The pretend interviewee answered:

> We are relating the militancy generated by the bar bust and by increasing
> pig harassment to a program that allows homosexuals and sexually liberated
> persons to confront themselves and society through encounter groups,
> demonstrations, dances, a newspaper, and by just being ourselves on the street.
> The program will create revolution of the mind and body as we all confron[t]
> the opposition. At this time we have specific plans to open a coffeehouse, a
> working commune, and experimental living communes. We hope to extend
> the coffeehouse idea as an alternative to the exploitive overpriced syndicate
> [Mafia-] run gay bar."[48]

With this varied and detailed information provided to FBI agents through their so-called subversive informants, the agents then had enough information with which to conduct physical surveillance of GLF activities and activists. During the first full week of August 1969 FBI agents observed, and reported in detail, a series of political demonstrations in New York City. Organized by the Fifth Avenue Vietnam Peace Parade Committee, the demonstrations were to culminate at week's end with a Nagasaki Day demonstration. The agents noted that participating in the demonstrations, among other groups, were members of the GLF.[49] An FBI agent reported, however, that the "GLF appeared to be a group more interested in obtaining more freedom for homosexuals rather than a group motivated by strictly political ideologies." The SAC of the New York Field Office, moreover, prepared a memo for Hoover outlining all of this information and the various groups that participated in the weeklong demonstration, and he distributed it, locally, to the various military branches and the Secret Service.[50]

FBI agents in New York City also began accumulating information about the GLF and its members from interviews with informants, some of which proved illuminating and others less so. On 6 December 1969 one informant visited the New York Field Office to report information on GLF members (the names are redacted in FBI files), where they held their meetings, and their connections with the BPP. The informant, who said he knew an FBI agent for nine years, then asked that an agent go with him to a GLF meeting the following day. He was told that this could not happen. This particular informant, however, was deemed by FBI agents an "unstable individual" who "appeared to be emotionally unstable during his visit to the office this date."[51]

Three days later another FBI informant was interviewed in the New York Field Office. He provided information about another individual (whose name is redacted) and about Noel (Joel) Fabricant, who published the tabloid-style *Gay Scenes*, the *East Village Other*, and *Gay Power*. The primary GLF newspaper, *ComeOut!*, for which Shelley was the typesetter, criticized Fabricant, who championed the Mafia-run gay bars and who publicly identified gays in print and attacked them, as interested only in profit. In the simplistic view of the FBI agent who interviewed the informant, "The purpose, activities, and objectives of the GLF are quite similar to those of the Mattachine Society. Both organizations are composed of homosexuals who organized in order to gain recognition of their problems and to gain social acceptance." More to the point of their differences, the agent wrote simplistically, "The main difference between the Mattachine Society and the GLF is that the members of the GLF are younger and more liberal."[52]

When asked, the informant told his FBI agent handler he was unaware of "actual contact between the GLF and the Black Panthers." He also told him about a heated political discussion during a GLF meeting of about forty or fifty members held at an Episcopal church on Sunday, 7 December 1969. The informant identified five individuals, including John Sirgal, GLF founding member John O'Brien, and reformist GLF member Martello (the FBI has redacted the other names). The informant told the FBI agent that after Sirgal and O'Brien talked, "other members of the GLF spoke out against their political views, and these members received applause from the remaining members of the GLF." In the view of the informant, O'Brien "appeared to be very knowledgeable in regard to visits of various dignitaries [e.g., Nixon] to NYC," and the GLF planned to picket Mayor Lindsay's second inauguration. A longtime activist with experience working with the SNCC, National Association for the Advancement of Colored People (NAACP), CORE, and multiple antiwar groups, O'Brien was a Stonewall participant before helping to found the GLF in New York City. Yet, after the informant offered all these details to the FBI, the agent who interviewed him wrote about him, "It is to be noted . . . [he] appeared to be in a highly emotional state, was quite tense, and appears to be disturbed." The FBI agent also wrote that the informant's file "should be reviewed" because he was repeatedly "on the verge of crying," was "on record as a homosexual," and in the future should he always be interviewed by two agents.[53]

This particular FBI informant seems to have been something of a problem for the New York Field Office, but he probably reflected the nature of some troubled gay men of the 1960s and 1970s (and before) who felt compelled to inform on other gays. What is more, over December 1969 and January 1970 this informant repeatedly telephoned a particular FBI special agent in the New York Field Office to provide "non-specific information concerning the GLF." The problem for the FBI agent was that this information was simply a "re-hash of information [he] previously provided." Worse yet, the informant often "provides information in a highly emotional and disjointed fashion" and mostly discussed personal issues with the FBI agent. According to an FBI memo, "His emotional moods range from high elevation to severe depression," and he apparently called the FBI office "at a moment's whim." At one point, concerned with this informant's intense interest in the FBI, an agent was forced to tell him that "he was not being directed by the FBI, that he was not being asked to do anything on behalf of the FBI, and that any decision of his to attend any meeting of the GLF or involvement with any group or organization was strictly on his own."[54]

FBI agents continued to collect information about the GLF, and it primarily came from GLF publications offered by informants. FBI agents especially were interested in any GLF activities that intersected with the New Left or antiwar demonstrations. Among some of the publications collected during 1970 were the *Gay Liberation Front Bulletin*, which advertised the group's various events, such as general meetings, study group meetings, workshops, a newspaper contributors' meeting, and classes at Alternate University.[55] Another was the *Rat*, the underground New Left newspaper, which described the GLF for FBI agents as a "radical and revolutionary organization based on anarchist guidelines, similar to the Black Panthers and Weathermen." This, alone, would have been enough to catch the interest of FBI officials, but the *Rat* also noted, oddly, that the GLF, although "worth watching," seems to contain "only one or two radical individuals present at any given time." The *Rat* also saw in the GLF "no immediate threat" because members of the group "represent[ed] themselves as a homophile organization but are unlike such respectable and dedicated organizations as the Daughters of Bilitis and Mattachine." Finally, the *Rat* also retold the story of the panicked man who fell and impaled himself on a fence during a gay bar raid.[56]

Another issue of the *Rat* vividly described the GLF as "springing up like warts all over the bland face of Amerika, causing shudders of indigestion in the delicately-balanced bowels of the Movement." It noted that the GLF had branches across the country and planned to "make our own revolution because we're sick of revolutionary posters which depict straight he-man types and earth mothers with guns and babies." This particular issue also suggested disgust with liberals and BPP members who referred to gays with "their term of universal contempt—'faggot.'" The author, Shelley, former president of the New York DoB, explained that she did not seek tolerance but understanding of gays. "You will never be rid of us," she wrote, "because we reproduce ourselves out of your bodies—and out of your minds. We are one with you."[57]

At one point, somebody from the New Left underground Liberation News Service even suggested arranging a meeting between "some friends and comrades from the Gay Liberation Front" and the BPP. The purpose, according to the FBI "highly placed, sensitive source," was "to talk over what they are doing and how they can work together and things like that." According to Shelley, the "Black Panthers later came around" to working with the GLF, "but at first they were very homophobic." Ultimately, Huey Newton, cofounder of the BPP, had to appeal to his members to unite with the GLF, "whatever your personal opinions and your insecurities about homosexuality and the various liberation movements among homosexuals and women." Despite the desire of members of the GLF to work with other leftist and radical groups for a common purpose, they never did significantly breach the divide between them over sexual bigotry. In addition to the BPP, the GLF even became alienated from various New Left groups.[58]

During July 1970 the GLF again caught the attention of FBI agents for participating in a demonstration before the international group World Assembly of Youth. The assembly was formed in London during 1948 after noncommunist groups withdrew from the leftist World Federation of Democratic Youth. With the onset of the cold war, some US officials came to suspect the federation was a communist front. The new group proclaimed its goal was to seek to "promote better understanding among the youth of different nations, strengthen and extend youth movements, give youth a chance to gain needed experience for adult responsibility, and to express its voice to the United Nations." Given the FBI director's longtime interest in protecting and insulating the moral integrity of US youth from subversive influence, FBI agents kept Hoover informed of these developments.[59]

The bureau's information, of course, originated from one of its many informants. On 15 July 1970, protestors passed out a flier to World Assembly of Youth delegates visiting the United Nations in New York City to celebrate the twenty-fifth anniversary of that body's founding. The flier told the delegates "American Revolutionaries Want to Meet You" to discuss how the delegates "are being sheltered from the realities of the American political scene," imploring them to "hear representatives of the American Revolutionary Movement." Moreover, the flier invited them to a meeting at the Hotel Diplomat that would include speakers from the Youth International Party, the BPP, the women's liberation movement, the Puerto Rican Liberation Front (aka, the Young Lords Party), the Committee of Returned Volunteers, and the GLF. Handing out these fliers was part of a larger leftist heckling effort directed at delegates from South Vietnam, South Korea, and Taiwan.[60]

It appears the FBI distributed a letterhead memo about this incident to unknown recipients (but probably military agencies), because the SAC of the New York Field Office sent Hoover twelve copies of it with the typical FBI notation at the bottom indicating the bureau was loaning the document to "your agency." However, the FBI has withheld in their entirety multiple pages of documents related to this incident, which prevents full understanding of what and who held FBI officials' interest in it.

In a second letterhead memo—fifteen copies of which were forwarded from the New York Field Office to Hoover—the SAC reported on the scheduled meeting at the Hotel Diplomat. FBI agents preferred, it appears, to use an informant to monitor the event, which seems in line with their investigative tactic with the GLF. Reverend James Bevel, a leader in the SCLC, spoke at the meeting about the US government being the "greatest menace" to humanity at the time and accused it of engaging in genocide. He then singled out Hoover as a "threat to the sanity and well-being of human beings." Attorney William Kunstler, who defended the political activists charged with causing a riot at the 1968 Democratic National Convention, accused Hoover of using the FBI for political purposes when the FBI director publicly called the BPP the greatest threat to US security.

The GLF came into the picture here because of friction between the various groups, which, according to the *New York Times*, had met for the first time, "cooperating in a deliberative session." The *Times* reported, moreover, that GLF member Tom Finley commented about this being the first time his group was invited to such a meeting. Whatever the intentions of the groups, the parley of radicals soured, the New York SAC told Hoover, after Willie Amarfio—a delegate from Ghana and follower of African independence leader Kwame Nkrumah—"castigated the American movement people for aligning themselves with a frivolous organization such as the homosexual Gay Liberation Front." This comment led Finley and six other GLF members to storm out of the meeting at the Hotel Diplomat and some advocates of women's liberation to heckle Amarfio. Finley later returned and told those assembled he could not "continue to participate in a meeting when what I stand for is subject to assault." A Canadian woman then told the crowd "male chauvinism permeates the World Youth Assembly."[61]

For the remainder of 1970 and 1971, FBI agents monitored rallies and protests, noting the participation of the GLF. It is difficult, however, to know precisely who and what FBI agents investigated because the FBI has withheld many pages of documents in their entirety. In one example, in late September 1970 FBI agents watched "an anti-war picket line demonstration" in front of the Hotel Americana. The National Guard Association of the United States—a lobbying organization for the National Guard—was holding its annual convention in the hotel and, outside on the street, the Vietnam Veterans against the War protested the guard's recent participation in the Kent State shooting. Over subsequent days protests at the convention continued and expanded to include many different groups, including, by the third day, the GLF. The SAC of the New York Field Office forwarded to Hoover eleven copies of a memo about these demonstrations and "disseminated [it] locally" to the various military branches.[62]

The following month, October 1970, FBI agents again reported to Hoover about a demonstration at the UN Plaza in which the GLF participated. This particular demonstration was directed against President Nixon and was sponsored by the New York Peace Action Coalition. Hoover would have been keenly interested in this anti-Nixon demonstration as part of his bureau's INLET program. Between 1969 and 1972 FBI officials shared with the Nixon White House wide-ranging political intelligence via INLET, particularly anything Hoover thought might interest the president. This program, in its systematic and formalized nature, surpassed the previous FBI efforts to provide the White House political intelligence, dating back to Herbert Hoover and Franklin D. Roosevelt.[63]

Four days later an FBI agent in the New York Field Office wrote a memo for his superior about one of the activists who participated in the anti-Nixon demonstration. Unfortunately, the FBI has redacted most of the document, but it did leave unredacted a parenthetical notation under the memo's subject line that reads, "SM - C (Key Activist)." This referred to the FBI code-named Key Activist Program, a part of its larger, secret, and illegal COINTELPRO disruption program, which targeted New Left activists. The Key Activist Program focused on "individuals in the Students for a Democratic Society and the anti–Vietnam war groups [who] are extremely active and most vocal in their statements denouncing the United States and calling for civil disobedience and other forms of unlawful and disruptive acts." Each activist target was the subject of an "intensive investigation" that typically included the use of informants, physical surveillance, or technical surveillance (wiretaps or bugs). The Key Activist Program, moreover, was not designed as a means to ensure prosecution of activists but to see that they were, in the words of FBI officials, "neutralize[d]." Whether the individual in this heavily redacted document was a member of the GLF (as well as the SDS) or just associated with it is not known, but the document does illustrate the close connections between the New Left and GLF, the context in which FBI officials viewed the GLF, and perhaps its disruption efforts against the movements.[64]

The only other example of gays crossing paths with the FBI COINTEL-PRO program dates to 1960. That year in New York City, FBI officials planned to target a "key figure" in the Communist Party who happened to be gay. Knowing the Communist Party was just as homophobic as US political parties at that time, FBI officials hoped the arrest of this particular party official and subsequent publicity about his sexuality would "embarrass the Party" and contribute to its destabilization. The plan ultimately failed, however, because this person suddenly quit the party, but the example nevertheless illustrates the lengths to which FBI officials went in their illegal disruption tactics and interest in surveilling gays and lesbians.[65]

FBI agents noted the seemingly inexhaustible GLF links to different groups or participation in further demonstrations through 1970 and 1971. These included GLF attendance at the SDS conference at Columbia University; its "student agitation" there; its participation in the workshop-style conference Alternatives for a New Society at Carnegie-Mellon University in Pittsburgh; its demonstration in Detroit; its linkages with the Venceremos Brigade, an SDS-formed group that maintained a relationship with Cuba, and with the Young Lords Party demonstration at the United Nations; its relationship to the Student Mobilization Committee to End the War in Vietnam; its demonstration on the steps of the New York Capitol in Albany (a copy of this memo was filed in the FBI Sex Deviates File); the GLF march in Atlanta; its demonstration in Los Angeles in front of a bar that displayed a "Faggots stay out" sign (a copy of this memo was filed in the FBI Sex Deviates File); its 1971 plans to celebrate Gay Pride Week in New York City; its demonstration at the University of Missouri; its disruptive demonstration at the University of Michigan; and any number of seemingly endless incidents. FBI agents kept close tabs on GLF activities nationwide. Although often not the primary subject of investigation, GLF members or their links to New Left groups inevitably warranted, in FBI agents' view, a "full search" of FBI file indices.[66]

One of the best examples illustrating FBI officials' perceptions of the GLF involved one agent in Detroit who reported his informant's opinion about a heterosexual man and his girlfriend, members of the SDS, who "use the GLM [Gay Liberation Movement] as a device to further 'new left' agitation." (An unrecorded copy of this particular memo was filed in the FBI Sex Deviates File.) Ultimately, the SAC of the Detroit Field Office (as in other locations) reported to Hoover that his office concluded the GLF was not a "viable New Left–oriented group" because it merely supported New Left activity and did not take "any independent aggressive action on a New Left project or activity." The GLF in Detroit, according to the SAC there, did not seem to fall under the parameters of FBI investigative guidelines for "security interest" investigations.[67]

GLF members naturally suspected that FBI agents were interested in their activities and were monitoring them. When first joining the DoB in New York, Shelley was warned to use a pseudonym when writing her name on the membership list. She really did not see the point of doing this but decided on a compromise. She listed her surname as Shelley even though her actual name was Altman (Shelley was a nickname her first girlfriend had given her because Martha wrote poetry, which reminded her girlfriend of the poet Percy Shelley). Yet because she wanted to receive mail from the DoB, she then wrote down her address as "in care of Martha Altman." After doing this, she said to the DoB leaders, "This is totally stupid. If the FBI wants to find me, they will find me." Not until she participated in the GLF, however, did Shelley become convinced the FBI was interested her.[68]

Lauritsen, a member of the Marxist Red Butterfly cell of the GLF, also believed the FBI was monitoring GLF activity. When the GLF Radical Study Group, headed by Arthur Evans, convened its first meeting in the fall of 1969, Lauritsen "noticed a car parked down the street with men who appeared to be surveilling us as we entered the apartment building." Although FBI agents primarily relied upon informants, they also engaged in this type of physical surveillance. Furthermore, given Hoover's code of conduct for FBI agents, which included a strict dress code, it was something of a running joke among radicals because they could easily spot FBI agents tailing them. They stuck out, with their dark suits and ties. It was not until the 1970s, after Hoover's death, that FBI agents began concealing their identities through undercover operations.[69]

As a more or less united national movement, the GLF lasted only about two years. It was unable to sustain itself given its decentralized, anarchist structure, lack of a stable and active membership base, and involvement in varied issues beyond gay rights. In short, it simply could not maintain cohesive momentum organizationally or politically to remain a viable and united group. The fact that members of the GLF regularly departed to join other groups—such as the GAA—and the fact that the GLF had become alienated from other leftist organizations that just could not overcome their antigay bias also contributed to the group's demise. However, some motivated GLF members lingered on one way or another, and FBI officials remained interested in their activities as they related to the upcoming 1972 Democratic and Republican National Conventions, both held in Miami Beach, Florida.

FBI concern with potential GLF demonstrating and protesting at both political conventions began on 2 November 1971, after FBI Director Hoover learned about the seemingly coordinated plans among leftists to protest the Republican National Convention. At the time the Republicans had planned to hold their convention in San Diego, but they later relocated it to Miami Beach, where the Democrats also organized their convention. Hoover advised all FBI field offices that activists John Froines and Rennie Davis of the People's Coalition for Peace and Justice—an antiwar and antipoverty group—and Jerry Rubin of the Youth International Party (the "yippies") had "recently made statements" about organized "massive demonstrations" planned for the Republican National Convention. He further advised the SACs that the Peace Action Council in Los Angeles planned to protest a dinner to honor Nixon and that the People's Coalition for Peace and Justice regarded these protests as merely "phase I of a program to 'evict Nixon' from the White House."[70]

Because all of this activity indicated an effort to bring "all possible pressure and embarrassment . . . on the President and other public officials during the forthcoming election campaign," Hoover advised the SACs to monitor sources and report to headquarters. Hoover ordered his agents to forward information promptly by teletype—an instant electronic communication method—"in a form suitable for dissemination." He further ordered his agents to evaluate their coverage of dissident groups and, where that "coverage is considered weak," undertake "special efforts" to rectify that.[71]

Hoover admonished his agents, furthermore, that he would "not tolerate incomplete or delayed reporting." He emphasized to them that he wanted complete, clear, and detailed reports from agents and advised them to follow closely the FBI Manual of Rules and Regulations. "It must be born in mind," he told the SACs, "that the President and his Administration will rely, to a large degree, on information that we furnish." Hoover finally ordered his agents to adhere "rigidly" to one more set of instructions. Any memos FBI agents sent related to demonstrations targeting the president were to be captioned TROPUS. When FBI agents obtained information about "demonstrations at the Republican National Convention, teletypes and intra-bureau communication should carry the code word 'CALREP.'" This code word referred to the Republican National Convention in California, later changed to code name MIREP (Miami Republican), and the Democratic National Convention was MIDEM.[72]

FBI officials first became interested in possible GLF convention protests on 1 April 1972 after the Miami Field Office alerted Hoover that an informant "claimed there are at least two thousand representatives of the GLF who will be coming down for the convention, for the purpose of demonstrating." The Miami SAC took note of the assumed leader of the GLF demonstration, Bob Johnson of the Washington, DC, GLF, and noted the names of others from Washington, DC; Chicago; and New York (whose names are redacted in FBI files). FBI concern with GLF convention protests reflected the worries of the Nixon administration over antiwar demonstrations disrupting the Republican National Convention and can be viewed in light of FBI Director Hoover responding to the political interests of his superiors. Hoover subsequently ordered all FBI field offices, because he "anticipated that these two events will draw extremists and other violence-prone activists to Miami Beach," to report all related information to headquarters, including what the underground press printed because it might "reveal the nature of the plans being made by these groups." Hoover hoped to be able to use federal antiriot laws against these groups.[73]

In response, the Chicago Field Office found nothing in its indices regarding the subjects noted in the teletype from Miami. The Washington, DC, Field Office (WFO) consulted with informants "familiar with the WDC [Washington, DC] Gay Community" and "advised that [deleted but presumably members of the GLF of Washington, DC] are unknown to them personally," and they knew "[deleted but presumably Johnson] . . . in name only." Reflecting the collapse of the GLF network by 1972, the SAC of the New York Field Office reported nothing about the individuals in the Miami teletype and, moreover, said that the "GLF is no longer functioning in the NYC area, having disintegrated during May 1971." He added that no gay organization in New York City had plans to attend the Democratic National Convention.[74]

Other FBI field offices also responded to the warning from the Miami

SAC. On 25 April 1972, the SAC of the San Diego Field Office reported on the activities of the local GLF. He noted that GLF members had placed posters on the campus of San Diego State College, held a "Gay-In" at Presidio Park, and a member wrote a letter to the campus newspaper complaining that those same posters had been torn down. The SAC further noted that the GLF protested police harassment in the city and was not an approved campus student organization.[75]

Of particular interest to FBI agents in San Diego was a letter in the 31 December 1971 edition of the *Berkeley Tribe*, which the SAC described as a "New Left underground type newspaper." The letter was written by Steve Bell, whom the San Diego SAC described as the president of the local GLF chapter. In his letter, Bell asked that all gay groups planning to protest at the Republican National Convention coordinate with the GLF to achieve a more effective demonstration. The SAC described Bell as a man who had engaged in a previous protest in Chicago, worked with the Committee to Investigate Right Wing Terrorism, and attended a convention of radical groups in San Diego, seemingly to demonstrate his history of political agitation. Regardless of all of this, however, the San Diego Field Office reported that none of its informants were "familiar with New Left and related extremist activities," nor could local law-enforcement agencies provide any "information concerning the GLF or its members." The San Diego SAC did report, however, that one informant "familiar with New Left subversive activities in the San Diego area . . . has advised that the GLF is not active in plans, programs, or other preparations for the Republican National Convention." Hoover provided the memo describing all of this to officials of the US Army because of "their interest in the 1972 Republican Convention" and members of the Secret Service "in view of their protective responsibilities."[76]

On 2 May 1972, FBI Director Hoover was found dead, lying on the floor of his bedroom in his pajamas. He had expired from a massive heart attack. Hoover was the one FBI official most responsible for pushing the monitoring of gays, but in the months immediately following his death in no way did FBI agents stop monitoring the GLF or other gay groups. FBI efforts for the time being continued seamlessly. On 1 June 1972, the acting FBI director, Nixon ally L. Patrick Gray, issued updated orders to FBI agents regarding demonstrations at the national political conventions. First, he ordered agents to begin using the code name MIREP for the Republican National Convention because the location had been changed from California. Second, he ordered that information on protest groups be forwarded "promptly and on a continuing basis" to both headquarters and the Miami Field Office. Informants, Gray noted, should be employed to learn about the activities of groups with a history of violence, that engaged in civil disobedience, that planned convention protests, or that were "known to be under the control or influence of the Communist Party or other revolutionary groups." Moreover, he said these informants should be willing to travel with their groups to Miami, and agents should forward travel details about them to headquarters and the Miami Field Office. Finally, through the SAC of the WFO, Gray ordered that "homosexual matters in connection with demonstrations at the National Conventions" be "handled in WFO under the GLF title." [77]

Accordingly, the New York Field Office reported that "by means of a discreet telephonic inquiry to the reservation office of the Greyhound Bus Company," it had determined that nobody from the GLF had chartered a bus to Miami for the Democratic National Convention. Similarly, the Los Angeles SAC reported that a Greyhound bus had departed that city on 7 July but had "no passengers aboard ticketed for Miami." The SAC of the WFO reported to Gray in a teletype captioned "Communist Infiltration" that multiple informants had indicated that the GLF, SCLC, National Welfare Rights Organization, and the National Tenants Organization had not chartered a bus to Miami. The Savannah, Georgia, Field Office also reported that no one from the GLF had chartered a bus, nor did its informant have knowledge of the group intending to travel to Miami. The Chicago Field Office also reported that the GLF did not charter a bus or arrange a "gay caravan" by car to Miami. The Cincinnati Field Office advised that Greyhound and Continental Trailway reported "no unusual traffic congregated in or left their respective terminals destined for Miami." Likewise, no chartered buses left for Miami from Philadelphia. [78]

Extant documents indicate that FBI agents only established that three GLF members (or former members by this point) had traveled to Miami to engage in protest. Yet it does not seem the agents even realized these three were former GLF members. FBI agents were able to establish, via an informant, that a group of gays through something called the National Coalition of Gay Organizations of Washington, DC, had organized a trip to Miami. Most of these men were not GLF members, however, whether current or former. Instead, they included Kameny of the Mattachine Society of Washington, DC (MSW); W. Randolph Dowling, who headed a gay commune in the capital; Ty Jameson, Bill Bricker, Steve Hoglund, and Dave Livingston of the GAA (although Bricker and Livingston were ultimately unable to travel to Florida); Chuck Avery of the Poor People's Party; and finally Jim Fouratt, Michael Bumblebee, and Steve Mann of the GLF. The teletype referencing all of these attendees was filed in the FBI Sex Deviates File.[79]

Highlighting FBI agents' ignorance of group member identities, just four days later, on 10 July 1972, the SAC of the WFO reported to Gray new and apparently final information about the GLF and the Democratic National Convention. According to an FBI informant the GLF did not charter a bus to Miami; the "GLF had given up their plans to travel to Miami because of the cost involved." About two months later, the SAC then learned and reported to Gray that a "branch of the GLF has not been reported to exist at WDC since approximately January 1972." Finally, with "no outstanding leads in this matter," the WFO "placed in a closed status" its inquiry into the GLF.[80]

FBI field offices nationwide continued to submit detailed information to headquarters and the Miami Field Office regarding New Left and antiwar groups that planned to protest at the two national political conventions in Miami. Never, however, did FBI agents develop any information about GLF activities except regarding the few individuals previously noted, whom FBI officials did not seem to link to the GLF. This all makes sense because as an organization the GLF had ceased to exist by this point. Yet there was one final, if odd, incident in FBI files in which the GLF name appeared.

During the afternoon of Sunday, 3 October 1977, an explosion occurred at the Atherton, California, home of Edward Derry, the general manager of the Coors Beer Distributorship in San Francisco. Derry was at home when the explosion took place, and after firefighters extinguished the blaze, they found remnants of a glass jar that contained a flammable liquid—in other words, a Molotov cocktail. The damage to Derry's house was minimal, and shortly after the incident the Atherton Police Department received two anonymous telephone calls from a single individual who ridiculed Derry and said, fumbling, "The New World . . . make that Gay Liberation Front" claimed responsibility for the firebombing.[81]

The telephone call and confused claim of responsibility did not convince FBI agents, however. The nature of the bombing, making use of a simple Molotov cocktail, and the hesitation of the caller, who began by invoking the name of the New World Liberation Front—a violent leftist group in San Francisco—but then switched to name the defunct GLF, led FBI agents to conclude that the incident "does not fit into the pattern of prior terrorist activity in the San Francisco Bay Area." Underpinning their conclusion was the fact that at the time Coors was being criticized for donating money to "anti-homosexual organizations," was experiencing labor trouble, and "has been the target of New World Liberation Front attacks." Since July 1977, the New World Liberation Front had targeted Coors distributors in a variety of bombings, some successful and some not, leading the company to offer a $25,000 reward for information on the perpetrators. The nature of the telephone call seemed to convince FBI agents that "one or two disgruntled former employees" were behind the attack, apparently because they fumbled and confused the name of the terrorist group while using a bomb inconsistent with those used by the New World Liberation Front. Ultimately, FBI officials dropped the investigation because it did not fall under the purview of the bureau. Thereafter, the GLF would no longer interest FBI officials.[82]

On 15 April 1972, a group called the Inner Circle held a dinner at the New York Hilton Hotel. It was the organization's fiftieth such dinner, a gala event dating to 1922. Composed of current and former reporters who covered New York City Hall, the Inner Circle also continued its twenty-five-year tradition of satirizing politics and politicians, what they innovated and dubbed during the 1920s "stunt dinners."[83] The event, today, is comparable to the more popular and annual Gridiron Dinner in Washington, DC. Dignitaries of all sorts attended these dinners, and such an assemblage of press, power, service, and influence inevitably drew significant attention. For the semicentennial dinner, the Inner Circle reporters performed a parody they called the "Golden Touch." One act portrayed a mayoral fund-raising campaign party with a fictitious mayor continually interrupted with telephone calls. Another mocked two contemporary events of that year: the upcoming Democratic National Convention and President Nixon's trip to China. The reporters portrayed a Democratic National Convention that welcomed the Republican Nixon and two Chinese reporters—named Ping and Pong. When asked by Ping and Pong why the Republican president was at the Democratic National Convention, the reporter playing Nixon replied, "My visit to China worked. I'm here to offer the Democrats equal time on my visit to Russia. It's the democratic way."[84]

This was not the only drama at the Inner Circle dinner that night. With Mayor Lindsay and others in attendance, including FBI Assistant Director John Malone—head of the New York Field Office, the only field office run by a high-ranking FBI official—during an intermission members of the GAA suddenly appeared to disrupt the dinner. Born as an offshoot of the GLF, the GAA became renowned for something called "zapping," a publicity-generating protest tactic involving boldly and publicly confronting public officials to focus popular attention on gay issues. The GAA decided to crash the dinner after a homosexual civil rights bill was defeated at City Hall and after its opponents derisively claimed the "flamboyance" of the GAA was responsible for the failure of the bill. The GAA was further motivated by its members' belief that Mayor Lindsay was dishonest in claiming to back the measure.[85]

According to the account Malone wrote for FBI Director Hoover, "approximately twenty-five young, crudely dressed" GAA members "invaded the ballroom" and started passing out leaflets noting the unfair treatment gays received in the press and at the hands of government. As the activists were distributing the leaflets, "one tried to talk into the microphone on the stage." Yet because the curtain was drawn for intermission, Malone reported that this person could not be seen from the center part of the ballroom. Finally, "men in dinner jackets" confronted the GAA members and asked them to leave, then escorted them out. As they exited, two GAA members were assaulted, including the one trying to speak over the microphone, a development that would only create further publicity for the group. Back in Washington, DC, Hoover had Malone's memo filed in the FBI Sex Deviates File.[86]

The GAA was formed by twelve disenchanted members of the GLF on 23 December 1969. The men at the core of this dozen were the reformist-minded Marty Robinson, Jim Owles, and Arthur Evans. These particular members had difficulty agreeing ideologically or organizationally with the radicals and revolutionaries who dominated the GLF. In just weeks (Robinson and Owles had only joined GLF in September) they came to realize that the decentralized, anarchist nature of the GLF had permitted nearly anyone or any GLF group/cell to hamstring the organization's efforts, draw attention away from uniquely gay issues, and sow dissension. These disenchanted GLF members also disagreed with involving the GLF in myriad issues beyond gay rights, such as the antiwar movement and supporting the BPP. Although they avidly agreed with confrontational protest techniques themselves, they eventually decided GLF radicals and revolutionaries were more interested in employing these techniques to promote a goal of social revolution rather than focusing on achievable equal rights for gays. They feared the goal of uniting and politicizing gays was being undermined in favor of unrealistic causes. Over a brief period, these disagreements led to personal resentments, then alienation.[87]

The only solution these members saw was to leave the GLF and form a new group that was still militant and liberationist but dedicated exclusively to gay rights. Thus they formed the GAA. The GAA sought to politicize gays, going beyond what its members viewed as the reserved failures of the Mattachine Society, but considering themselves not as radical as the GLF. Whereas the GLF had rejected gay subculture—gay bars in New York run by the Mafia, cruising, and promiscuity—the GAA defended it. They believed it was vital to be liberated from the mores of the dominant, repressive, heterosexual culture. They would employ "zaps," moreover, to achieve these ends, particularly to politicize gays by drawing the attention of mainstream media.

To achieve all of this regardless of its nontraditional politics, the GAA would be carefully organized with elected officers, rules of membership, standing committees, and Robert's Rules of Order—all quite the opposite of the GLF. Its formation also reflected the late 1960s, as Marotta has observed: "Underlying GAA's limited but liberationist goals, its nonviolent but militant strategy, and its structured but participatory framework was an attempt to reconcile political convictions and organizational considerations so as to appeal to homosexuals ready to become political but wary of extremes."[88]

Zapping would be the primary GAA political tool. As Marotta has written, "Robinson and Owles had learned [while with the GLF] that homosexuals could infiltrate political gatherings and make themselves heard through sheer brashness."[89] These zaps, in particular the effort at the Inner Circle dinner—some two years after the formation of GAA—brought FBI officials' scrutiny of GAA activities, but the affair also brought significant media attention to GAA, even if the case, legally speaking, was not a success. After the GAA members disrupted the Inner Circle dinner, they were attacked by several individuals, including the president of the Uniformed Firefighters Association and former Golden Gloves boxer Michael Maye. As the activists were being escorted from the hotel, twenty-one-year-old GAA member and Columbia University student Morty Manford engaged Maye in an altercation.[90] According to Maye's account, Manford grabbed his crotch and tore his pants, leading Maye to punch him in the head and then shove him, which caused Manford to fall down an escalator in a "semiconscious" state. A witness testified that the 6 foot 2 inch, 210-pound Maye then pushed through the crowd and down the escalator, where he ground his foot into Manford's groin repeatedly. After it was over, Maye stood up, straightened his dinner jacket, and allegedly said, "Well, we won't have any more trouble from him tonight."[91]

Manford and six other GAA members then filed charges against Maye and several others who assaulted them, but the only person they could positively identify was Maye. The district attorney and grand jury subsequently charged him not with assault but simple harassment, an action the GAA publicly characterized as "prejudice against homosexuals" because "if an ordinary person committed this act," he would have automatically faced more serious charges.[92] Maye defended himself from this criticism by saying publicly that the Inner Circle "was invaded by aggressive individuals seeking to disrupt the affair and provoke and incite the guests by obscene language and action." He added, "The invaders attempted to tear clothing off guests and pulled hair, scratched and bit before they were ejected." He admitted, however, only to punching Manford.[93]

In the end, however, the harassment charge against Maye was dismissed but not by a jury. The case was heard only in front of a judge, without a jury. The judge, Shirley Levittan, claimed the witnesses statements were too inconsistent to proceed. She added that although it was apparent "several melees" between GAA members and Inner Circle guests broke out (and despite Maye's admission in the press about his punch), it was "far from clear who did what and to whom." Maye later referred to the court proceedings as "pretty sad" and a "waste of time." He added his thought that it was a "damn shame" money was spent on the case when robberies and rapes were occurring throughout the city. GAA victim Manford called the result "obscene" and an "affront to the American principle of equal application under the law." He also accused the district attorney of bias both in reducing the charge against Maye and in not investigating "without bias and favoritism." Manford then tried filing a new complaint against a second assailant, but it failed at the grand jury level.[94]

The incident—which interested FBI officials enough that they filed a memo about it in the Sex Deviates File—reflected the political strategy of the GAA. Its members, including Manford, might not have won their legal battles, but the case did elicit extensive press coverage. That coverage included intimate details of the case, such as Maye admitting, at least, to punching Manford and then being cleared of harassment. Readers of the fifteen stories about the incident in the mainstream press, not just the underground or gay press, were then exposed to the unequal treatment of gays both in public and before the courts—the exact goal of the GAA zapping strategy. GAA members hoped to use mainstream media to better educate the public about such events and politicize usually diffident gays. The strategy also had the unintended consequence of drawing the ire and interest of FBI agents and officials.

FBI interest in the GAA had first appeared during mid-December 1971, when an FBI agent on Long Island reported witnessing one of its demonstrations in the hamlet of Hauppauge. Fourteen members of the GAA were demonstrating at the Suffolk County Police Department after two GAA members were arrested on charges of sodomy. During the course of the demonstration, the FBI agent learned from a police department source, a scuffle ensued, leading three of the activists, two men and a woman, to be arrested for assault.[95]

A couple of days later, the New York Field Office learned further details about the demonstration and arrests and forwarded them to Hoover. The New York SAC reported that the three arrested GAA members were Charles Burch, Sylvia (Tony) Rivera—a transvestite—and Corona Perrotta. Each were charged with disorderly conduct and harassment, then released on $100 bond. The New York Field Office searched its file indices and found nothing on Rivera or Perrotta, but did learn that Burch had been arrested four months earlier during another demonstration. Nothing more was reported to Hoover after this, but FBI attention turned nevertheless to the GAA political demonstrations.[96]

Of far more significance and interest to FBI officials were the GAA planned activities at the national political conventions the next year in Miami Beach. In this regard, FBI agents investigated the GAA actions in a similar vein as they did suspected GLF protests in Florida. This is reflected in the first report Hoover received about possible GAA activity in March 1972. The Miami SAC reported rumors, from a questionable source, that the GAA "discussed the possibility of committing violence at the Democratic National Convention" using "handguns." The SAC also reported contradictory intelligence about the GAA "that any form of violence would be in direct conflict with the very nature of most homosexuals, who are peaceful by nature and avoid violence." Although this view was based on stereotypes, it nevertheless accurately reflected the way in which the GAA conducted its demonstrations. Although always blunt and militant in protests, and despite its members occasionally becoming involved in fisticuffs, the GAA was a decidedly nonviolent organization.[97]

It did not take long, however, for FBI agents to gather more accurate information about the GAA and its planned work in Miami. On 21 April 1972, the Miami SAC reported to Hoover that the GAA met every Tuesday in a local Lutheran church, where its members planned a "series of 'zaps' in the Miami area during the Democratic National Convention, designed to draw attention to, and sympathy for, the GAA cause." The GAA zaps included a demonstration portraying a gay wedding and another a gay dance. The SAC wrote Hoover, perhaps suggesting a possibility for an arrest charge, that "both of these actions are believed to be illegal" but that "these 'zaps' are still in the formative stage."[98]

By June 1972, the Miami SAC reported that a source indicated the GAA, along with the American Civil Liberties Union (ACLU), would demonstrate at the federal courthouse in Miami. When FBI agents arrived at the courthouse, however, they found no demonstration. Undaunted, the FBI agents made further inquiries only to learn that GAA members were actually inside the courthouse pursuing a complaint they filed against the Miami Beach Police Department. The complaint was over a local ordinance that made it illegal for men to impersonate women, a significant part of gay subculture and part of their planned zaps. When observing the hearing, the FBI agents overheard one GAA member remark that "there would be 500 sisters in for the conventions." The judge then determined the ordinance "vague," and he issued an injunction because it created a "chilling effect on the First Amendment rights." He said the GAA members had a right to dress as they wished and should not be subject to arrest. FBI officials deemed all of this important enough to copy to the FBI Sex Deviates File.[99]

At about the same time and shortly after Hoover's death, the Miami SAC distributed an airtel to the acting FBI director and fourteen bureau field offices concerning the GAA. In it, the SAC reported that a source had given him a "list of gay organizations, along with their leaders, who will be attending the upcoming Miami" national political conventions. The five-page list covered various organizations, including the GLF, but mostly listed the GAA chapters. The Miami SAC asked FBI agents to "conduct indices, credit, and arrest checks and furnish photographs of individuals who are marked . . . as being in their division and any information concerning any violence which they may have been involved in." This memo would be the basis of subsequent FBI inquiries into the GAA and political demonstrations in Florida.[100]

Just before this airtel was distributed, FBI agents finally learned, conclusively, that the GLF was largely defunct and therefore would not be a presence at the Miami conventions. Instead, "logical sources of information" informed FBI agents that "activity among Gay Demonstrators will be through the Gay Activists Alliance." FBI agents nevertheless kept their GLF file "open in the event that there is a change in the organization's plans."[101]

In short order, various FBI field offices nationwide began reporting on the individuals listed in the Miami airtel. On 30 June the Philadelphia Field Office reported, "Indices are negative regarding all individuals listed." Those listed in the Miami memo were Jeffrey Escoffier, Henry Langhorne, Mathew Grande, Richard Kiniry, Richard Marcucci, and James Guthrie—a graduate student and member of Homophiles of Penn State.[102] The Alexandria, Virginia, Field Office reported on Allan Vick of the Gay People's Alliance of Washington, DC. The agents learned that Vick and his roommate were George Washington University (GWU) students; they listed the address of their apartment, source of income, the identity of Vick's mother, and the fact that a search of local police records produced "negative results."[103] The Chicago Field Office reported that its searches unearthed nothing about John Abney and Paul Miline of the Chicago GAA and Advocates of Gay Action, respectively. Similarly, that office found nothing negative about William Kelley of Homosexuals Organized for Political Education except that he was also the vice president of a Mattachine group. The Chicago SAC did report, however, information about Chuck Lamont of the GAA Chicago chapter. The SAC reported that Lamont was also a spokesperson for the National Coalition of Gay Organizations and had been in Miami to organize protests at the Democratic National Convention. The SAC concluded, however, "Individuals and possibly even groups from Chicago will be present during the national political conventions, but to date, no plans or organization has been undertaken at Chicago for mass appearance or activity by any Chicago elements at the conventions."[104]

The SAC of the New York Field Office advised Acting FBI Director Gray that his agents had inquired with the New York Police Department Intelligence Division and Security and Investigations Section but failed to unearth any information on Mark Wald, Deni Covello, Renee Cafiero, Brian Campbell, John Howard, Bob McMorray, Joseph Christie, Edward Eisenberg, Hal

Offen, Michael Murphy, Claude Wynne, Paul Stack, Jerry Hoppe, Jim Fou-ratt, or Roy Birchard. The SAC advised that during August 1971 FBI agents had identified Owles as the president of the GAA in New York, but they had "no information indicating Owles has been involved in any violent activities in the past."[105]

The SAC of the Richmond, Virginia, Field Office looked into the back-ground of University of Virginia (UVA) students Peter Andren and Ken Roberts. He reported that his office's files contained no information on ei-ther Andren or Roberts. The FBI resident agency in Charlottesville also had no information about these two in relation to "its overall coverage of New Left activities at the University of Virginia" or "in connection with any dem-onstrations or other activities." In ascertaining this information, FBI agents coordinated with someone at UVA who checked the student directory for the two men's names. Similarly the Charlottesville Police, county sheriff, and UVA Security Department reported no information on Andren or Rob-erts. Also, the Baltimore Field Office reported that its "informants who are familiar with New Left activities in the Baltimore, Maryland area . . . know of no activities or members of the GAA."[106]

The SAC of the Charlotte, North Carolina, Field Office forwarded to Gray a report on Brad Keistler of that city's GLF chapter. Yet the only thing the office could find was that Keistler "is the owner and operator of a 1965 Ford Mustang, blue, bearing 1972 [redacted but license plates]."[107] Two indi-viduals on the Miami Field Office's list, Ronald Alheim and Ernie Reaugh, were from Albany, New York, and associated with the GLF. The SAC of the Albany Field Office sent Gray an airtel on the two, in which one (the names are redacted and it is unclear who) was described as having "appeared in public demonstrations in Albany sponsored by the Gay Liberation Front, is very intelligent, [and] is [a] completely peaceful minded individual who is interested in gaining legislation to help homosexuals." This person had no plans to travel to Miami. The other individual the SAC described as having "participated in various demonstrations in Albany; [and] Washing-ton, D.C.," and in both locations the police arrested him. What is more, the SAC also described him as "known locally as a radical, and is friendly with several nationally known radicals." Finally, the Albany SAC reported that a "police official from [deleted]" who had access to "intelligence information during MIDEM [Democratic National Convention], concerning the Gay Alliance, is a closeted homosexual." Even worse, this police official report-edly shared this information with a member of the GAA. Nobody knew, however, who this official was or in which department he worked. The SAC, therefore, warned Gray, "Miami should be very circumspect in disseminating information concerning source as it is expected he will travel to MIREP [the Republican National Convention]." Several days later, the SAC further reported that the GAA of Albany had no plans for Miami.[108]

The Boston Field Office reported information on the background of Paul MacPhail Jr. FBI agents there "conducted [an] investigation of [deleted but MacPhail] under BSfile" and ascertained basic data about him, including his place of employment. The only negative thing the Boston SAC reported was that MacPhail "was [minimally] involved with New University Conference activities," and these were the "only known New Left or radical activities on the part of the subject." The New University Conference was organized in March 1968 by faculty and graduate students to promote leftist activity on college campuses, oppose Department of Defense research programs, and advocate for radical causes.[109]

Given the prevalence of student involvement in New Left activities and protests, FBI agents paid particular attention to the activities of the GAA on or near university campuses. One location that, in particular, concerned FBI agents was the Ohio State University (OSU) in Columbus, where student protestors had torched the ROTC building. FBI interest in the OSU GAA chapter began in October 1971, when gay students forced the university-recognized GLF chapter to be renamed the GAA. Former OSU GLF member Jeff Arnold commented to the *Ohio State Lantern* that the GLF had alienated many gays "because it was involved in anti-war and civil rights movements that were not gay related," and "many people just couldn't relate to other issues."[110]

After taking notice of this article in the student newspaper, FBI agents began to investigate the GLF changing its name and being an officially recognized student organization. An FBI agent out of the Cincinnati Field Office recruited a university source who allowed him to review the "record folder" that contained the GLF petition for official recognition and change of status. Of interest to the FBI agent was the stated purpose of the new group. GAA described its purpose as "educational, political, social, service, and cultural." The FBI agents also noted the date, in March 1971, when the university Student Assembly approved the petition as well as the name of the student who prepared the petition, Marti Bergstein, and the group's faculty advisor, philosophy professor Richard Garner. Finally, the agent obtained and listed the names of all of the officers of both the GLF and GAA groups.[111]

This surveillance was intensified after FBI agents, who routinely monitored the student newspaper at OSU, read a story headlined "Gays Want Representation at Democratic Convention." Coming just three months after FBI officials first became aware of and interested in potential GLF protests at the national political conventions, it is not surprising that upon reading this article FBI agents investigated deeper. The article reported that if the Democrats did not include gays as delegates to their convention, the GAA would "take legal action against the Ohio Democratic Party." The article also identified two members of the GAA—junior Jeff Orth and sophomore Sue Vasbinder, coordinator of the campus GAA—and an FBI agent underlined their names in the article, indicating that their names were indexed.[112]

FBI agents' interest in OSU GAA activities was not restricted to official university sanction of the organization or proposed conflict with the Ohio Democratic Party. In March 1972, an FBI agent clipped a story from the *Ohio State Lantern* about three GAA nonstudent members being prosecuted for cross-dressing, a story that seemingly confirmed the radical nature and outside influence of the group. The judge sentenced the three men to ninety days in jail but promised to suspend eighty days of the sentence if the men promised no longer to wear women's clothing. In reaction, one of the defendants claimed the police and courts were biased and discriminated against gays, citing as evidence the judge referring to homosexuality as "unnatural" along with his view that cross-dressing was intended to "aggravate others."[113]

Contributing to the intensive Cincinnati Field Office interest in the activities of the OSU and Columbus GAA chapters was an FBI communication from the San Francisco Field Office to Cincinnati—and ten other field offices plus three military branches—about the potential "revolutionary activities" of an organization called Vocations for Social Change. A nonprofit group founded in 1967, Vocations for Social Change promoted educational efforts to effect social betterment and advertised leftist groups nationwide in its bimonthly newsletter. What drew the concern of FBI agents monitoring the OSU GAA was an advertisement in the newsletter for the 1972 Columbus Gay Pride event, which included an "All-Ohio Gay Conference." According to the communication from San Francisco, FBI officials believed this was an "excellent opportunity to place informants" in the organizations listed in the communication. As such, the Cincinnati Field Office and others were directed to "take appropriate action regarding such organizations . . . which may be in their respective territories."[114]

The intense focus the Columbus GAA received from FBI agents included their monitoring some GAA meetings. Extant FBI documents indicate that informants told an FBI agent the GAA held monthly meetings on 5 April, 31 May, and during late June 1972. An FBI agent learned that the group even met during the summer quarter of 1972. He also reported that the GAA had a meeting scheduled for the end of September, when the autumn quarter had resumed. After the September meeting was held, an FBI agent wrote a report for his SAC listing the newly elected officers, that forty people attended the meeting, and that they discussed "running a male for Homecoming Queen at OSU" as well as Gay Pride Week festivities. An FBI memo was also created for the GAA October meeting (at which they decided in the affirmative to run for homecoming queen).[115]

Into 1973, FBI agents continued to monitor the OSU GAA. They received information about its January meeting, including not only a list of its officers but the fact that member Patrick Miller was running for city council. By April, no longer monitoring the GAA on a monthly basis, an FBI agent noted that the "Gay Activists Alliance (GAA) continued to operate as a recognized student organization at OSU." Significantly, however, by this point the agent had observed that "there was no indication [deleted] that GAA had been formed for the purpose of engaging in revolutionary-type activities or had participated in any such activities." What is more, an informant told the FBI agents the group was "relatively inactive" and had not hosted any event, such as a "gay dance," since January 1973. By July the FBI agent further reported that the GAA continued to exist as a student organization but had not been very active.[116]

By October 1973, FBI agents continued to monitor the GAA, still listing its officers and recognizing its association with OSU, but at this point they merely noted its civil rights mission and counseling and service work. This sort of monitoring continued into 1974, including an informant saying that the GAA did not participate in any demonstrations or cause the university any trouble. FBI agents also observed that the GAA was not "dedicated to the overthrow of the U.S. Government" and had not engaged in "seditious conspiracy." Afterward, FBI agents continued to monitor its publication, *Columbus Gay Activists*, but otherwise closed their inquiries on the OSU GAA.[117]

When the national political conventions concluded, FBI officials found nothing about the GAA to confirm their worst fears. For example, in March 1973 the SAC of the New York Field Office advised Acting FBI Director Gray that the GAA "exerted almost no influence during the Republican National Convention." Instead, he reported that GAA members "advocated non-violence and were concerned primarily in demonstrating in favor of equal rights for homosexuals" and "although opposed to the 'establishment,' ha[ve] not been active in the current revolutionary movement in NYC."[118] This realization marked the end of the intensive FBI interest in the GAA. Although FBI agents and officials did not completely stop their inquiries, those inquiries thereafter became ad hoc and limited. An example of this can be seen in the FBI response to a 1976 letter the GAA of Houston sent to Gray. The letter asked the FBI director about the bureau's policy regarding the employment of gays, and what the FBI did if one was discovered. Gray responded with a simple, curt, and unelaborated: "In answer to your inquiry, this is to advise that it is contrary to the policy of the FBI to employ homosexuals."[119]

The FBI surveillance of both the GLF and the GAA was characterized by Hoover's curtailment of FBI investigative activity dating from the mid- to late 1960s onward. With public scrutiny and questioning of government activity at a peak and Hoover having passed the mandatory retirement age of seventy, a politically vulnerable FBI director was unwilling to go too far in possibly compromising his or the bureau's stature. This was reflected in his reluctance to use wiretaps and bugs after 1966 and his worries about revelations of sensitive FBI operations following the Media, Pennsylvania, burglary in early 1971. The evolving Civil Service Commission (CSC) policy regarding gays and federal employment was also changing in 1968 and 1969. No longer could non-security-related gay civil servants so easily be manipulated into resigning or be fired with only circumstantial evidence at hand. Hoover, therefore, did not have the easy and automatic rationale he once had, during the 1950s and early 1960s, to widely disseminate information about gays to ensure their firing without question. Again, he would be more circumspect and focused on gay group's links to New Left politics.

Hoover's FBI remained content to collect most of its information about both the GLF and GAA through extensive use of informants. Meanwhile FBI agents monitored both groups in the context of their larger concerns with the New Left rather than their links to federal employees. Although the agents initially perceived both groups to be part and parcel of the New

Left—usually in an effort to confirm whether they had engaged in radical or violent activity, including protests—as they investigated they eventually determined the groups' goals were, albeit in radical ways, the mere acceptance of gays and equal rights. FBI officials then seemed to lose interest by 1972, especially after Hoover's death, in favor of the greater perceived threat of New Left activity. Within a few years, as gay rights activism became more mainstream and focused more on employment discrimination and attainable civil rights, as reflected in the 1976 GAA letter to FBI Director Gray about gay employees, FBI surveillance interests shifted to these areas.

Epilogue

With J. Edgar Hoover's death in May 1972 and the ultrapartisan and vindictive Richard Nixon—a president always seeking any angle, any information, to "screw over" an enemy—relegated to history, FBI abuses were becoming public, and ever so slowly the FBI began to change. Because he was FBI director for nearly fifty years, the bureau *was* Hoover. The FBI culture was a function of his unique personality, and it operated under his keen sense of politics, making it in many ways a cult of personality. In Hoover's absence, senior FBI officials—indoctrinated in the Hoover FBI culture—continued managing the bureau but without the presence of the domineering bulldog himself, and with public scrutiny at new heights, some level of change was, perhaps, inevitable.

The FBI was and always had been, in fact, a federal bureau responsive not only to Hoover's whims but to particular influences in US culture and whichever president happened to occupy the White House. In many ways the Gerald Ford administration was a natural corrective to the cancer growing on the Nixon presidency. With antiwar and antigovernment protest at a peak and a shift from cold war deference to reflexive distrust of the chief executive, Ford served as the antithesis to the byzantine and manipulative Nixon. His attorney general, Edward Levi, for example, issued guidelines intended to rein in FBI investigative abuses until a more permanent solution was implemented (it never was).[1] Ford seemed affable and trustworthy, and he offered a much-needed restorative to the presidential image even if it, perhaps unfairly, included the former star athlete being perceived as a clumsy oaf. Ford undermined his own presidency, however, with his pardon of Nixon. Although he may have had good, if naive, intentions, his action resulted in the only unelected president in US history remaining unelected.

With the election of Jimmy Carter in 1976, a moral man but not a moralizer like Nixon, the image of the presidency significantly changed, both for the better and worse. The FBI also changed in response to the political and policy interests of the Carter White House. When assuming the presidency, in a conscious effort to reduce the imperial vestiges the presidency had assumed, Carter invoked a new presidential style modeled after another southerner. Thomas Jefferson, who saw excess regality in the presidency following George Washington and John Adams, strove for something simpler and more democratic. At his inauguration, Carter intentionally wore a common business suit rather than more traditional formal menswear, a modern reflection of when Jefferson met dignitaries at the White House wearing his tattered robe and slippers. Just as Jefferson had famously walked to and from his inauguration rather than using the imperious presidential carriage pulled by multiple white horses, Carter walked from the Capitol to the White House. He also dispensed with the marine guard at the White House, sold the presidential yacht, and refused to use *Hail to the Chief* prior to his appearances.[2]

President Carter also extended the Levi guidelines restricting FBI investigations and signed into law the 1978 Foreign Intelligence Surveillance Act (FISA) requiring court-issued warrants for wiretaps in domestic national security cases. This was, again, the antithesis of Nixon, who famously said in his 1977 interview with David Frost, "Well, if the president does it, that means it is not illegal." With Carter, presidential accountability and decency was resurrected. Carter even made one of his priorities respecting human rights abroad and equality at home, yet when it came to gays—being the sometimes astute politician he was—Carter could only offer lip service. It was no small matter, though, that Carter was the first president to meet with and speak favorably of gays, yet the country was not yet ready for federally legislated equality.

In June 1977, for example, Carter's vice president, Walter Mondale, was dispatched to San Francisco to give a speech about Israel and the Middle East. During the speech, vocal gay rights protestors interrupted the vice president, demanding that the Carter administration respond to the various local and state efforts to undermine recently enacted ordinances outlawing discrimination against gays and lesbians. The most prominent of these efforts was the one spearheaded in Florida by singer and fundamentalist, born-again Christian Anita Bryant. After the ruckus, some were motivated to write Mondale. One woman pointed out that he and the president had "been speaking out on behalf of human rights, not only for elsewhere but here too, I hope." She hoped he would "speak to us about the issue of gay rights but you never came out." A man wrote apologizing for the interruption, but called Mondale and Carter out on the carpet for advocating human rights abroad while ignoring gay rights at home. He compared Mondale's public criticism of South African apartheid to his silence on "gay aparteid [*sic*] in Florida." Some writers were not quite as civil-liberty minded, however. One asked Mondale, "I have always understood homosexuality was unlawful; if so why can't they be stopped from demonstrating and public appearance of any kind?" She pondered, "Why are they allowed to call themselves 'gays' when the dictionary definition" meant happy? "What is wrong with queers?," she asked the vice president, while arguing that their goal was to teach and legalize homosexuality.[3]

One of Mondale's aides responded to these and other writers with a form letter exemplifying the Carter administration's political finesse of gay rights. The form letter read:

> The Vice President was invited to speak to a specific group in San Francisco and had remarks prepared for that occasion. The issue of gay rights is a complex topic which should be addressed in a deliberate manner, not as part of a shouting match with protestors disinterested in meaningful dialogue. The incident was unfortunate, but we hope that there will be ample opportunity for all sides to have their views heard on this question.

The San Francisco incident even prompted Mondale to ask his aides for a draft statement on "homosexual rights." Mondale's domestic policy advisor, Gail Harrison, replied that the issue involved "two difficult questions." "The first," she said, "is really a judgement about lifestyle." She used herself as an example, explaining how she had grown up in a rural part of the United States, where "strong family values" were predominant, which suggested to her that many citizens "could never regard homosexuality as consistent with those values." She advised him that the "federal government should not be in the position of condoning that way of life." The second question involved whether Mondale and the administration should support a federal law prohibiting discrimination against gays and lesbians. She advised him, "What is really at issue, and we have seen controversies in Florida and elsewhere, are a variety of state and local ordinances affecting the rights of homosexuals. These are problems that in my view should be resolved at the state and local level."[4]

Mondale's subsequent letters to concerned citizens were thereafter written with this advice adopted and in mind. After one letter writer warned about the "horrible witch hunt" taking place in Florida, an aide responded that the situation in Florida was strictly a state affair and "outside the jurisdiction of the Federal government." Then came the finesse, "This issue, however, will be closely watched by the appropriate Federal officials to assure that no one is subject to any discriminatory infringement of his or her federal rights." That was easily said because no significant federal protections for gays existed during the 1970s.[5] By 1978 Mondale's—and by extension the Carter administration's—standard response to letter writers on gay rights was thus:

> This administration is firmly committed to full civil rights for all citizens. Our stand on this issue is a matter of public record, and we continue to be deeply troubled by violations of the human and civil rights of any American. Be assured that the administration shares your concern and will continue to support equal *federal* treatment for all Americans. We should note, however, that many of the recent controversies surrounding homosexual rights have involved decisions and ordinances by local governments; thus, we suggest that your views be shared also with your local officials.[6]

Although the Carter administration was willing to speak out in generally supportive terms about gay rights, like no previous administration before it, for political reasons it was unwilling and unable to tackle the issue on the federal level.

This is evident in how the Carter administration handled the issue of Civil Service Commission (CSC) reform. A centerpiece of Carter's domestic political agenda, he planned a complete overhaul of the system, something not accomplished in ninety-four years. It would include new negotiating and bargaining rights, better definition of prohibited practices, merit rewards, and so forth. One thing it failed to do, however, was address antigay employment discrimination, but the Carter administration did consider its inclusion. Margaret Constanza, assistant to the president for public liaison, listed for President Carter the pros and cons of the issue. Pros included consistency with Carter's human rights stand and public support for gays, support for the estimated 20-million-strong gay community, and avoiding a possible negative confrontation with the gay community. Cons included "criticism and abuse for defending the constitutional rights of gay people" and jeopardizing the reform bill by supporting gays. Constanza further noted that gays already had some protections from the CSC and had never exerted any significant political pressure on Carter's reform issue. Constanza was referencing the fact that in 1975 the CSC, as a result of a lawsuit in which Frank Kameny involved himself, had eliminated "homosexuality as a factor for consideration in hiring, firing, and promotion." Richard Pettigrew, special assistant to the president for reorganization, who had worked in Florida and knew well the effects of the Bryant antigay campaign, supported Constanza's view and advised the president not to include gays in

CSC reform. He argued, "If a battle erupts in Congress this year, 'gay rights,' to the extent currently recognized, will sustain serious setbacks." Instead, Pettigrew suggested "quiet consultation" with gay groups to "urge them to leave well enough alone." The cons unsurprisingly triumphed. Carter agreed with them, and the administration pointedly excluded gay rights from federal legislation overhauling the CSC. The most the administration could offer gays and lesbians was continued supportive rhetoric, and even that caused them difficulty. In the 1980 presidential election, Carter was pointedly and unfairly attacked by both the Moral Majority and Ronald Reagan campaign for allegedly proactively seeking legal recognition for an "alternative lifestyle."[7]

Regardless of the Carter administration's political reluctance when it came to gay rights, its overall human rights platform and supportive rhetoric nevertheless had a discernible internal governmental impact. It was at this precise time (1977–1978), without coincidence, that FBI officials decided to incinerate the FBI Sex Deviates File. Effectively, this was a recognition that its purpose—ensuring the termination of gay employees through the dissemination of sensitive information about them—was over. As already noted, just two years before the FBI decision, the CSC had stopped its own overt, antigay discrimination, and Hoover, who rabidly pursued and drove the issue for decades, was dead. Significant to this evolution was the fact that none of his inculcated bureau protégées succeeded in replacing him as FBI director, and President Carter rhetorically voiced his support for gays in particular and human rights more generally.

Having always been acutely sensitive to changing political winds and shifting sands in Washington, DC, FBI officials followed suit, anxious to restore the ruptured FBI image in the wake of shocking revelations of extensive FBI abuses. Significantly, however, FBI officials did not do this by falling in line with Carter's views and embracing human rights. Not in the least. Instead, they reacted by promptly disposing of the evidence. With deferential National Archives approval, the FBI incinerated the Sex Deviates File and related files, including indices, which together well exceeded 330,000 pages of damning evidence. With minimal effort, FBI officials eradicated forty years' worth of detailed, voluminous, historical records. This was the FBI way of dealing with a newly emerging minority slowly gaining acceptance and now seeking legal equality and federal recognition. If FBI officials could avoid any further embarrassing revelations from their sordid past, they would do so, and they did.

This did not mean, however, that FBI interest in gays became extinct. It did not, but it did shift in different directions. This is evident in how FBI officials dealt with two markedly different gay groups: the National Gay Task Force (NGTF) and AIDS Coalition to Unleash Power (ACT-UP).[8] In 1973, unable to see eye to eye with the Gay Activist Alliance (GAA) leadership, member Bruce Voeller resigned to form his own gay rights group. He called it the NGTF, and it was headquartered in New York City. Voeller envisioned a gay version of the National Association for the Advancement of Colored People (NAACP), using legal means to advance gay rights while bringing together disparate (reformist and radical) gay factions. The NGTF was remarkably successful. In March 1977 it became the first gay rights group invited to the (Carter) White House—arranged by Constanza—where it discussed gay and lesbian issues. Because the group formed after Hoover's death, FBI interest in the NGTF focused mostly on a criminal harassment matter and the issue of employment equity.[9]

In April 1978, the NGTF received a threatening letter in response to one of its direct-mail fund-raising efforts aiming to educate the public after Bryant's Save Our Children campaign. Originating from Red Top, South Carolina, a man using the name Stem Wilson wrote on an NGTF donation flier: "We don't want you cock sucking queers down here—I personally have killed three of your kinds myself. Stay up north and suck all them nigger Yankee dicks you want." NGTF directors Jean O'Leary and Voeller forwarded the bigoted threat to the Department of Justice (DOJ), seeking action.[10]

Assistant Attorney General Patricia Wald, in the Office of Legislative Affairs, forwarded the threat to the FBI. Reflecting a new attitude at the White House, Wald had been designated by the Carter administration as the DOJ liaison for the NGTF. She asked FBI officials whether the bureau had jurisdiction in the matter and, if so, if they could look into the threat. If the FBI could not do anything, Wald asked that FBI officials forward the threatening note to the appropriate local or state authorities.[11]

FBI agents in South Carolina investigated Wilson, but unearthed no references to anyone with that identity living in the Charleston region. They also checked with postal authorities, who told FBI agents that the post office box listed on the note was a fabricated one. Because FBI agents were unable to develop any leads, the assistant US attorney in Charleston refused to authorize further investigation. The matter was also referred to the assistant US attorney in New York, but he refused to do anything, citing the lack of a "specific threat to injure the addressee or any other person." Wald reported these developments to O'Leary and Voeller, noting that in her view the FBI's "cooperation . . . responding to your concerns has been superb."[12]

The second matter in which the FBI and NGTF crossed paths involved federal employment discrimination. In January 1980 Attorney General Benjamin Civiletti initiated a new civil liberties focus and created new policy for the DOJ, including creating a position of civil-liberties coordinator to help DOJ personnel in reporting civil-liberties issues and dealing effectively with civil-liberties groups. Upon learning that Sana Shtasel had been appointed civil-liberties coordinator, NGTF officials C. F. Brydon and Lucia Valeska wrote her to express their concern over several issues, including the FBI antigay hiring policy. They urged Shtasel to help them convince FBI Director William Webster to overturn that policy. Brydon and Valeska noted that Webster had already "expressed a willingness to review policy in this area but said he didn't expect to see any changes for several years." They called Webster's reticence "government-sanctioned prejudice" and "intolerable and unsupportable by any objective fact." Their efforts, of course, were ignored, and the FBI continued its homophobic discrimination policy. Webster continued to cite the baseless and age-old refrain that gays constituted a national security threat inasmuch as they could be blackmailed into betraying state secrets.[13]

The NGTF did not give up, however. Twice in September 1982, Mel Boozer, the NGTF director of civil rights advocacy, wrote the FBI with concerns over the bureau's treatment of gays. On 16 September, he accused the FBI of wantonly mistreating the gay and lesbian community. The FBI responded that it was "in no way involved in any arbitrary and capricious treatment of the gay community." Boozer then wrote the FBI on 29 September asking why it "continues to bar homosexual Americans from employment as FBI agents." He called its discrimination unfair and unwise—because it robbed the FBI of talented agents—and compared it with the Secret Service, which did not have a similarly discriminatory policy.[14]

FBI Assistant Director Roger Young, head of the office of congressional and public affairs, responded to Boozer simply by reiterating FBI Director Webster's "official stand on the hiring and retention of homosexuals." It read, "A number of factors are considered in employment decisions. During a background investigation, it must be emphasized, the FBI does not inquire into an individual's sexual preferences. However, where information is developed that an individual has engaged in homosexual conduct, it is considered a significant factor in FBI decisionmaking, both with respect to decisions on hiring and the retention of employees." In other words, Webster's FBI practiced what in the 1990s would be called a don't ask, don't tell (DADT) policy. Much as the Clinton-Bush era DADT policy failed miserably, the FBI version also failed to live up to its wording.[15]

ACT-UP was a product of the 1980s and the Reagan administration's failures to stem the AIDS crisis. When medical doctors first noticed AIDS in January 1981, they were baffled. They did not know what it was and did not even know what to call it. After recognizing that it was hitting the gay and bisexual community almost exclusively, and because the resultant skin lesions resembled a form of skin cancer, doctors first referred to it as the "gay cancer." After thousands of deaths, by 1983–1984 French and US doctors finally determined AIDS resulted from a virus that attacked the immune system. By March 1985 the Food and Drug Administration (FDA) approved a test to detect the virus. Negative public attitudes about the epidemic only began to shift in 1985, after noted Hollywood actor Rock Hudson died of AIDS and when Elizabeth Taylor became an advocate for people suffering from AIDS, demanding that something be done. Over the next two years exponential numbers of gay men contracted the illness and died, which decimated much of the gay community, while the Reagan administration sat idle, reluctant even to reference the crisis. In reaction to the epidemic and Reagan's intransigence, but especially his FDA's refusal to approve drugs to treat the illness, in March 1987 hundreds of gay activists came together to form the AIDS Coalition to Unleash Power.[16]

ACT-UP was a single-issue advocacy group. It devoted all its energies to pressuring the government to do something about the lack of drugs to treat AIDS. Employing the zapping strategy of the GAA, ACT-UP worked to create as much trouble as it could, and generate as much publicity as possible, to focus public attention where its members wanted it. They were loud, rude, disruptive, and heavily engaged in civil disobedience. Their disorderly, raucous meetings, in fact, were in many ways reminiscent of the Gay Liberation Front (GLF), but ACT-UP, in reality, was a new development in gay rights organizing.[17]

To date, the FBI has released only fifteen pages of documents regarding ACT-UP, making it terribly difficult to understand the FBI interest. Given the fact that ACT-UP remains a part of contemporary US history, moreover, and because many of its members are still very much alive, the FBI will not release any information about those individuals and the possible FBI interest in their relationship to ACT-UP. In the fifteen pages released to me via the Freedom of Information Act (FOIA), however, are three FBI "Numerous Reference Search Slips." These are slips of paper on which FBI personnel list, from the bureau's central indices, the FBI file numbers of documents related to a subject (in this case ACT-UP) for either an FOIA request or an internal bureau file search. The three slips, together, list thirty-five separate files related to ACT-UP, with many of them constituting but one serial (one page) in a file. Most of the files listed (twenty-four of them) were classified as Freedom of Information Act, meaning that they were documents related to public requests for files (one extant example is from a journalist). Eleven of the files listed were classified as relating to "civil unrest."

The civil-unrest-related FBI files on ACT-UP mostly described planned demonstrations or marches at federal buildings or public parks in different US cities, or local law-enforcement information about ACT-UP forwarded to the FBI. One document was a request from the FBI legal attaché in Bern, Switzerland, for an FBI file check on ACT-UP because the group had caused trouble at a Swiss pharmaceutical company. Another document summarized information from the Secret Service about an ACT-UP plan to protest at former President George H. W. Bush's summer home in Kennebunkport, Maine. This constitutes all the information, right now, about the FBI and ACT-UP. Was the FBI interest more extensive? Was its interest limited only to summarizing and disseminating information about raucous demonstrations on federal property in the 1980s and 1990s because the Sex Deviates Program and File were finished? Did FBI officials take any action to disrupt or prosecute ACT-UP or to disseminate information about its members? To date these questions remain unanswered.[18]

There exists one final example of post–Sex Deviates Program FBI interest in gays. Between June 1989 and May 1990, FBI officials maintained a cooperative relationship with the US Customs Service whereby each agency shared with the other material from their respective collections of obscene materials. The purpose was to increase the volume of their collections in the belief that with more obscene samples, identifications of the sources of the interstate transportation of obscene materials would be revealed. It did no such thing. This was a watershed, if fleeting, moment for the FBI when it came to collecting information to add to its long-lived (dating to 1942) and gargantuan Obscene File, because forty-four years earlier FBI officials tried to win access to the Customs Bureau's obscenity collection but failed. (The head of the Customs Bureau at the time believed it was legally bound not to share its collection.) In this instance the FBI gained access, but the FBI Obscene File would remain in existence for only three more years.[19]

In 1989 and 1990, however, some of the material the Customs Service shared with the FBI included an assortment of eighty-five gay magazines. What, exactly, the FBI interest in these magazine was remains unknown. Exactly what kind of magazines these were, whether pornographic or advocacy periodicals, is not known either. If one assumes—and that is all it would be, an assumption—the magazines were pornographic in nature, that might explain the FBI interest, but even here federal prosecutions of smut had all but vanished by the 1990s. Between 1978 and 1986 only 100 people nationwide, out of a population of 240 million, had been charged with violations of federal antiobscenity law, and of these only 71 were convicted. By the 1990s, moreover, federal efforts in the area of obscenity law focused almost exclusively on child pornography. So why collect eighty-five gay magazines? We simply do not know, but it is difficult to imagine the FBI would have attempted to undertake another effort, as it had tried in the 1950s, to silence the gay movement by targeting its magazines. Legally, it would have been difficult, and more likely impossible, by the 1990s.[20]

In the 1990s there were some significant developments for the post–cold war FBI. The fifty-year-old FBI Obscene File was terminated, the rumors over Hoover's sexuality gained renewed vigor with Anthony Summers's sensational biography, and in 1993 the FBI antigay discriminatory hiring policy ended. The FBI finally ending its homophobic hiring policy was, ironically enough, the harbinger of a larger wave ending one aspect of federal gay discrimination in that decade. Joining the FBI were the Central Intelligence Agency (CIA) and National Security Agency (NSA), both of which eventually organized gay support groups within their respective agencies: the Agency Network of Gay and Lesbian Employees (ANGLE) at the CIA, and the Gay, Lesbian, and Bisexual Employees (GLOBE) at the NSA. By 1995, President Clinton even issued an executive order ending gay discrimination for openly gay individuals seeking security clearances needed for national security and intelligence work. Yet the final FBI step in ending its decades-long animus toward those with same-sex attraction did not come easily. It was the result of a lawsuit initiated by a fired gay FBI agent.[21]

Frank Buttino grew up in a prototypical small town in upstate New York. He was a third-generation Italian American playing out the dream sought by many of the so-called New Immigrants, who arrived in this country after 1880. He was masculine, played high school football, and dated girls.

Although he recognized the presence of same-sex attraction as a young man, given the pressures of heterosexual US culture at midcentury, he dismissed these feelings like so many others like him. Studious and a hard worker, Buttino attended Colgate University in 1963, continued to date women, and was even sexually intimate with them. After college he returned home to become a high school teacher and football coach, which he found unsatisfying. The 1960s and the civil rights movement had a significant effect on the young college grad, motivating him to contribute. Inspired by President John F. Kennedy's 1961 call to service, Buttino decided to join the FBI.[22]

Buttino became a special agent in 1969 and over the next two decades grew into a model investigator. In a somewhat ironic sense given how he would dramatically change the bureau, Buttino even had the chance to meet the vaunted FBI director in 1972, shortly before Hoover died. As an agent, Buttino worked a wide variety of cases. He investigated criminal cases, served as an undercover agent, and even worked in the areas of foreign counterintelligence and terrorism. All the while the FBI decorated him repeatedly for his excellence. Being an undercover FBI agent necessarily meant he had limited contact with other bureau personnel. Ironically, this afforded Buttino the opportunity to explore his sexual identity, and he began a gay relationship with another man, which, of course, he kept confidential. He continued to date women, however, until fully embracing his true sexual identity, something that happened only after he had become an FBI agent.[23]

When exploring his sexuality, Buttino was cautious and circumspect. He refused to visit any gay bars or other such open venues. He met and dated men by answering personal ads in gay magazines, and he never revealed his occupation to anyone until he felt he knew and could trust him or her. He found that people were typically standoffish, especially gay men, after learning he was an FBI agent. In 1988, one of his personal ad correspondents mailed one of his letters to his parents. It was an apparent effort to out him. Later that year, the same person sent another of Buttino's letters and a postcard to his FBI field office in San Diego. (The identity of this mysterious mailer would never be established.) When his superiors asked him about the items, he lied and said they were not his. It was this incident that triggered an FBI inquiry into Buttino's personal life and sexuality that would last months.[24]

Worried about what the FBI might do, Buttino promptly removed anything from his home the FBI might find questionable. He had no pornography but did have copies of the gay periodical the *Advocate* as well as some gay newspapers. When gathering these items, he could not locate the materials that were sent to his parents. He came to realize that someone had broken into his house and taken them, a mystery that would never be solved. Buttino was also given advice on how to handle the FBI inquiry. He was told to explain that he was a closeted gay man, he did not frequent gay bars, and he did not belong to any gay rights groups.[25]

By December 1988, Buttino was recalled to FBI headquarters to speak with the Office of Professional Responsibility (OPR), the section of the FBI handling the inquiry. Before his interview commenced, Buttino immediately admitted he had lied about the letter sent to his field office and even confessed the letter was, indeed, his. He also outed himself as gay, not only a first for Buttino but probably a first for the FBI. He decided, naively as it turned out, his only chance to save his job was to be cooperative. One of the two agents interviewing him said he had never seen a case like his before: an FBI agent with an excellent record discovered to be gay. The agent told him, "You could be a test case in the bureau, Frank. Bureau policy may be established on the basis of this case." Those words would prove prophetic.[26]

In their interview—interrogation is perhaps more apt—with Buttino, the two FBI agents asked him intimate questions about the sort of sex he engaged in, including whether he had sex with other FBI agents. They also insisted he name names. Buttino thought to himself, "What were they thinking? What was on the bureau's mind? Did they think there was a gay sex ring in the FBI?" To the sex-with-agents question, Buttino nodded yes because, as he told them, he had once had sex with a female FBI agent six years before. He refused to offer any names, however. The agents pressed on, forcing Buttino to question the relevance of the sex questions. The agents said the FBI demanded a full accounting, then disingenuously claimed heterosexual agents in a similar situation would be asked the same questions. So they continued asking about oral sex, anal sex, masturbation, and whether he played the active or passive role.[27]

The FBI was not, as some presume, interested in these tawdry details out of some quirky sense of voyeurism. There was an all-too-real method to the bureau's madness. For decades FBI agents collected and recorded intimate sexual details of their subject's lives because they could be useful, and they were particularly useful when it came to gays. It was a simple matter in homophobic culture to pressure gay employees to resign, but especially by documenting for the record all the sordid and embarrassing details of their personal lives. It was understood these details could be made public in any number of ways. Sexual details, whether or not true, were also useful in a more general sense to pressure people into doing what FBI officials wanted. As Hoover had once told Senator Joseph McCarthy in 1953, during the Charles Bohlen nomination fight, homosexuality "was a very hard thing to prove and the only way you could prove it was either by admission or by arrest and forfeiture of collateral."[28] If a suspected gay employee did not admit to homosexuality, he or she (or anyone) could easily be pressured to resign through an implied threat of exposure of sordid sex details, regardless of their veracity. This was the reason the FBI Sex Deviates Program required all sexual detail to be included in reports disseminated to recipients. A slightly different example also sheds light on the FBI interest in sexual details. Civil rights activist Martin Luther King Jr., whom FBI agents tape recorded engaging in sex with a woman who was not his wife, anonymously sent King the tape prior to his acceptance of the Nobel Peace Prize in 1964. They hoped to pressure him into not accepting the prestigious award. They failed.

Upon returning to San Diego, Buttino consulted a lawyer from the gay community. The lawyer suggested Buttino make use of media publicity as a means of applying pressure on the FBI, which, without public exposure, would simply do as it pleased. At that point, Buttino resisted the idea because he still hoped, naively as it turned out, to save his job. He knew going to the media would not advance that goal. In the long run, however, he would be forced to go public.[29]

In a subsequent interview at FBI headquarters, one of the same two FBI agents who interviewed Buttino informally admitted that with his spotless record, "You're our worst nightmare." Yet they continued to press him with questions such as asking him to name names and asking why he kept his sexuality from his family. Buttino even consented to a polygraph, not fully appreciating how a polygraph examiner could interpret the results to fit preconceived notions. As it turned out, the FBI agent administering the test freely admitted to being a homophobe, even commenting that homosexuality was a "distraction from our [FBI] strength." Like the others, he also asked Buttino intimate and personal, sex-related questions during the polygraph interview; afterward he claimed Buttino's answers indicated dishonesty.[30]

In September 1989 Buttino was placed on a twenty-day administrative leave, with pay, for his "past and present conduct and association with unknown individuals in the homosexual community." To the bureau these things suggested the possibility of his being coerced and indicated Buttino was somehow untrustworthy. The FBI also cited Buttino's refusal to cooperate fully in the investigation (by not naming names). The administrative leave was extended for months, until the FBI finally decided to fire Buttino.[31]

In early 1990, FBI officials revoked Buttino's security clearance (technically not for being gay but for being untruthful), which meant it was only a matter of time before he was fired. The stark reality was that no FBI agent could conduct his or her job without a security clearance. At this point Buttino fully appreciated the fact that, from the start, the FBI had no other goal in mind than forcing him out. The fact that it had dragged the inquiry out for so long had given him hope, but, ironically, the extended effort also reflected changing times. In the past, during the Hoover era, Buttino would have been fired on the spot. Now, in changing political waters, with gay rights advancing more quickly than any previous time, the bureau proceeded carefully and methodically toward its intended goal.[32]

Buttino nevertheless pursued administrative appeals and wrote his US representative seeking assistance. Representative Don Edwards, a Democrat from California, wrote FBI Director William Sessions on Buttino's behalf, but the letter went unanswered until it was too late. By 29 May 1990, Buttino's administrative appeal over revocation of his security clearance was denied, and on 20 June he was formally fired. Now he went forward with his lawsuit, which inevitably drew press interest, and he began answering reporters' questions. Buttino explained that "there is a difference between FBI employees in the field and the bureaucrats at headquarters." Later, a veteran FBI agent told him he thought Buttino had been caught between the old Hoover people still in charge at FBI headquarters and a new FBI slowly emerging.[33]

In the subsequent legal battle, the DOJ lawyers sought a summary judgment in the case whereas Buttino and his lawyers tried to turn it into a class-action lawsuit. Buttino wanted to expand the case beyond himself, but the government wanted to end it and, if possible, avoid further publicity. In court, the judge ordered the FBI to turn over all documents since 1985 related to the "hiring, firing, and disciplinary practices of all FBI agents," a huge victory for Buttino. This led the Buttino legal team to acquire as a coplaintiff a woman, Dana Tillson, denied an FBI job because she was a lesbian.[34]

Buttino and his lawyers also learned that the FBI never seriously investigated the break-in at his home nor the anonymous letters mailed concerning him, and instead was more interested in Buttino's own actions. They also learned that the FBI had taped his polygraph session in Washington, DC, and in investigations of suspected gay employees mere suspicion rather than proof was enough to warrant separation. Significantly, they learned that FBI pressure tactics included the threat of outing gay employees through an updated background investigation—a background check would necessitate interviewing family, friends, and neighbors and asking them intimate and detailed questions about the FBI employee, effectively outing him or her as homosexual. Ironically, Buttino had unknowingly negated this tactic by initially demanding an updated background investigation! This may well have contributed to the lengthy FBI administrative inquiry.[35]

Surveying the records released by the FBI, Buttino's lawyers learned, to their astonishment, that over the short two-year period of his lawsuit FBI headquarters had initiated more than 1,000 administrative inquiries of FBI employees who engaged in sexual improprieties, generically. Yet those who engaged in heterosexual irregularities were never fired and always mildly punished, but anyone even suspected of homosexuality was forced out, often in ways not even requiring a formal firing. Realizing the scope and insidiousness of the FBI discrimination, Buttino now recognized his case was larger than himself. "I'm afraid if I lose," he told another concerned FBI employee on the phone, "the witch hunt for gays and lesbians in the bureau will begin." Buttino at this point decided to write a book about his experiences to document the FBI treatment of gays in the event he lost his case.[36]

As it turned out, Buttino's fears were unfounded. On 13 February 1992 the court denied the government's motion for a summary judgment. A few months later, after more legal wrangling, the court then elevated Buttino's case to class-action status. His case was no longer that of a single gay man suing to win back his job but, now, a lawsuit on behalf of all gays and lesbians the FBI fired or rejected for employment. With the mass of evidence Buttino and his lawyers extracted from the FBI, and the class-action suit granted, the writing was now on the wall for the bureau. Negotiations commenced to settle Buttino's legal action, including pressure exerted on the DOJ and FBI from the recently inaugurated Bill Clinton administration. Buttino and the FBI settled out of court for an undisclosed sum, but Buttino was forced to agree not to return to the FBI. Significantly, the FBI implemented a new policy regarding gay employees. No longer would the FBI discriminate against gays for what they did in private, nor would the FBI ask job applicants about their sexuality or sexual conduct. On 10 December

1993, FBI Director Louis Freeh, only three months on the job and supportive of a change, sent all FBI field offices instructions for the bureau's new policy regarding gay and lesbian employees, effectively ending a half-century of bureau homophobia.[37]

Given the fifty-plus-year FBI history of antigay animus, Buttino's legal victory was, to put it mildly, a watershed moment. It was truly earthshattering and hugely significant because the one federal agency that, more than any other, viciously targeted gays and had created a deep-seated and well-earned reputation for its intense homophobia would now—albeit thanks to a lawsuit and pressure from President Clinton and Attorney General Janet Reno—be the reluctant trailblazer in ending federal gay discrimination. As already noted, within two years Clinton would end gay discrimination in awarding security clearances and intelligence work, while the two most significant US foreign intelligence agencies would organize gay support groups for their employees. Only after the election of Barack Obama did the FBI fully embrace its LGBT employees. In 2012 the FBI posted to its bureau careers website information about its Lesbian, Gay, Bisexual, Transgender Program, aimed at addressing diversity issues and better educating FBI employees about them. Perhaps predictably, and illustrating the resiliency of visceral homophobia among some segments in the United States, at least one "family values" group warned in its usual siege-mentality way that under the Obama administration the FBI was "embracing the gay agenda, having a gay advisory committee, welcoming homosexuals as FBI agents, getting involved with pride events, but more than that going to gay pride events and encouraging homosexual activists to report hate crimes and working with them against profamily groups."[38]

The FBI was interested, obsessed really, with gays and lesbians for fifty-six years. There is no simple or single explanation for this interest, however. It involved myriad influences, coalescing at opportune times, including things as obvious as Hoover's puritanical moralism and homophobia. It is important to recognize, though, that among FBI officials and others, when it came to gays, given the country's dominant patriarchal and heterosexual culture, which perceived men's supposed violations of gender expectations as the greater threat, gay men were more of a preoccupation. This explains the disproportionate paper trail FBI agents left behind, so much more focused on gay men's activities and organizing than women's. In a significant way, moreover, it was society's particular construction of homophobia and shifting cultural perceptions of gays over time that largely defined FBI interests. Always present at the FBI since 1937 was animus toward gays.

Although not the definitive or single explanation, this reality nevertheless helps us to understand why the FBI played no role whatsoever in either the 1920s Newport US Navy scandal or the Leopold and Loeb murder investigation. Newport constituted the first major and controversial federal effort targeting gays, and Leopold and Loeb were two vicious sociopaths who targeted a helpless child simply to see if they could get away with murder. Yet the FBI neither lent investigative assistance (Hoover was not yet director) to the navy nor investigated the matter of Leopold and Loeb. It also never initiated systematic targeting of gays as a clear and present threat to youth during the mid-1920s (by which time Hoover *was* FBI director). At the time, US society and culture did not yet perceive gays as an overarching threat that warranted such an effort or FBI interest. Instead, immigrants and radicals were the overarching perceived threat, and the excesses of wealth were perceived to be the cause of moral decay leading to the murder of a well-to-do child in the New Era. The times were not right for systematic targeting of gays.

That all changed with the Great Depression, however. The greatest economic calamity in human history dramatically altered social and cultural perceptions of sexuality. In the decidedly masculine and heterosexual culture of the United States, as fathers and husbands from all social classes failed as wage earners and supporters of their families, as jobless and homeless men congregated together as vagrants and transients, as culturally defined gender roles utterly failed, citizens reassessed their views of those with same-sex attraction. After three years of this, the federal government stepped in with the New Deal in an attempt to alleviate massive social dislocation. Its intimate involvement, like never before, in the lives of ordinary people, concurrent with social reconsideration of one particular segment of society, led to the widespread federal discovery of homosexuals. When another youngster was viciously murdered, a crime in some ways eerily reminiscent of both the Lindbergh kidnapping and the Leopold and Loeb case, the public had a profoundly different reaction. A "degenerate" was to blame as in the 1920s, but now his kind had become a demonstrable and widespread (not a function of wealth) threat to US youth amid economic disaster.

The politics of bureaucracy also played a significant role in FBI Director Hoover's initiation of systematic collection of information about "sex offenders." As a holdover, conservative bureaucrat amid liberal New Deal-ers, Hoover never passed up an opportunity to ingratiate himself with Pres-ident Franklin D. Roosevelt (FDR), both to preserve his job and expand his bureau. So when FDR decided to speak out publicly about the Charles Mattson murder, undoubtedly outraged but equally sensing an opportunity to push his federal crime-control program, the head of the FBI had little choice but to respond. Hoover had two bureaucratic motivations: catering to FDR's wishes and compensating for his previous claim that child kidnap-ping/murder cases had been extinguished and were a thing of the past. All of this coalesced into a massive and systematic FBI investigative effort vis-à-vis "sex offenders." Unable to solve the Mattson murder, FBI officials compiled their newly acquired information and used it, instead, to educate the public over decades about this particular "criminal menace."

As the United States shifted from Great Depression to the Second World War, federal perceptions of gays evolved. If gays were a dangerous criminal threat to children and society in the 1930s, during the 1940s their stigma-tized position in society meant they would be security threats in wartime. Although FBI targeting of gays—or those perceived to be gay—in federal positions was not nearly as extensive during the Second World War as it would become afterward, it was nevertheless a significant evolutionary step. The president's most valued foreign policy advisor, Sumner Welles, was dis-covered soliciting gay sex, which the president was willing to overlook. Out-wardly, Hoover had to respect FDR's wishes, suggesting that the president assign Welles a traveling companion, but behind the scenes Hoover directed interested parties to information that would undermine Welles. Hoover also never hesitated to investigate Senator David Walsh and Philip Faymonville when they were gay baited. Although neither was found guilty of any sexual misconduct, the fact that their presumed sexuality was used against them says something about how US society perceived gays. The FBI investiga-tions, moreover, although exonerating both men, nevertheless contributed to the ends of their respective careers. The tinge of homosexual rumor and FBI inquiry was simply too much for either to overcome. On the part of the FBI, its agents' collection of information about "sex perverts" then ex-panded from a criminal and educational effort to a noncriminal intelligence gathering and national security concern.

Then came the cold war, by which point the FBI role had dramatically changed from top law-enforcement arm to domestic intelligence agency and guardian of national security. Hoover's bureau also enjoyed deferential treatment because the public and politicians believed investigative secrecy was a vital element to ensuring national security in the face of subversive threats. As the threat of communists in government was then complemented by a perceived threat of gays in government, the FBI interest in gays evolved—skyrocketed—yet again. For a second time, gays in the midst of crisis (economic and social collapse in 1937; fears of social and political subversion after 1947) were singled out as a unique threat, as bad as or worse than the communists. Unlike the Second World War examples, this time the targeting was intensified and systematic.

Yet again, national and bureaucratic politics played a hand. In light of the intense national political phenomenon that was McCarthyism, it was difficult to single out, identify, and purge communist subversives in government. It was far easier, given popular stereotypes about identifying gays and intensified homophobia since the 1937 sex-crime panic complemented by the 1947 one, to root out *this* particular subversive element as a companion to the communists-in-government issue. Hoover recognized the efficacy of the effort when he implemented an early version of the Sex Deviates Program and forwarded to the White House in April 1950 his list of gay men arrested in Washington, DC, who claimed federal employment. The result, however, was only embarrassment for Hoover inasmuch as the executive director of the CSC pointed out the flaws in Hoover's list and possible embarrassment if it were acted upon.

Then came not one but two congressional inquiries into the threat posed by gays in government. Hoover's FBI cooperated with both committees. They concluded, without critical evaluation of the so-called evidence and no contrary argument, that more needed to be done to divest the federal bureaucracy of "sex deviates," who, in a national security state, could be blackmailed into betraying secrets. As head of a federal bureau responsive to the demands of society and politics, Hoover, in light of his embarrassing list of arrested gays, had to respond. Yet he responded in what is perhaps classic Hoover fashion, with an obsequious, bureau-authorized program and file to disseminate—widely but shrewdly—information about gays across government (and then beyond) to ensure their segregation from employment. Not the lone actor in these efforts, Hoover's FBI instead made itself the central player with at hand a gargantuan and indexed master file.

In FBI officials' efforts, it did not matter if information about a subject's sexuality was true. Rumor and innuendo were sufficient and, by FBI policy, were intentionally but quietly collected, included in, and disseminated from the Sex Deviates File. This afforded Hoover significant leverage behind the scenes to influence events and appointments as he saw fit, and in typical, obsequious, Hoover fashion. Not always successful (the Charles Bohlen nomination for instance), Hoover nevertheless insisted his FBI never made conclusions or policy recommendations, but as a master bureaucrat with an astute sense of politics, he knew how to paint a damning portrait by including in FBI background reports all the sordid details and rumors about a person's life and associations; hence, the reason FBI agents were required to collect all the sordid details and include them in the Sex Deviates File.

The FBI efforts vis-à-vis gays, moreover, were not restricted to the federal government or high-level appointments. Not at all. An unknown number of lower-level civil servants, national security bureaucrats, military personnel, and political appointees also had information collected and disseminated about them. The Sex Deviates Program, in fact, mandated how information about people in each of these categories was to be disseminated. With the Sex Deviates File destroyed, however, there is no way of knowing exactly how many of these people Hoover's FBI was ultimately responsible for ousting from government. Given the sheer breadth of FBI efforts in this area, the massive size (330,000-plus pages) of the Sex Deviates and related files, and the size of government at the time, it is probably a safe assumption the number is easily (or conservatively) in the thousands.

Concurrent with the rise of the public Lavender Scare after 1947–1950 was the development after the Second World War of the first true gay rights advocacy groups: the Mattachine Society; ONE, Inc.; and the Daughters of Bilitis (DoB). FBI officials targeted them in the belief subversive forces could take advantage of scorned members of society and manipulate them. Hence, both Mattachine and ONE, Inc., were initially surveilled via the FBI's COMINFIL program. FBI agents cleared them both, but several years later when *ONE* (Chuck Rowland) dared to accuse the FBI of employing gays, and even inferred it was led by one, the FBI responded with vigor to silence both groups and terminate their publishing efforts using federal obscenity law. The lesbian group DoB, which formed immediately before the second FBI targeting effort, hence fell under FBI scrutiny as part of this intensified effort. Although the FBI failed to silence or even stop the early homophile movement, its efforts nevertheless had a definite chilling effect, making it a federal agency all gays feared. As a worried and anonymous gay correspondent wrote to *ONE* in 1953, "I do not wish to have any traceable link with your publication. A hint of such activity in my FBI records would be sufficient to put me on the outside looking in, because of our supposed proneness to blackmail."[39]

FBI officials continued their gay targeting with the later, more militant, East Coast–centered homophile movement of the 1960s. FBI agents monitored the New York Mattachine and New York DoB, documented the work and organizing of early gay rights pioneer Donald Webster Cory, and worked tirelessly to reconstruct the membership list of Frank Kameny's Mattachine Society of Washington (MSW) and its predecessor. They intensively investigated Buell Dwight Huggins, blacklisting him from federal employment, and identified and compiled information about Kameny. In time FBI officials even identified Kameny's MSW cofounder, Jack Nichols, whose father was an FBI agent, which must have caused, in the least, considerable consternation at FBI headquarters. Nichols's father, in fact, apparently provided the bureau all of the details about his son. FBI agents even monitored the Kameny-inspired picketing of federal buildings in and around Washington, DC, sponsored by the East Coast Homophile Organizations (ECHO). FBI agents seemingly left no stone unturned.

Meanwhile, as a political issue, homosexuality continued to hold considerable sway during both the Johnson and Nixon administrations. The revelation that LBJ's longtime aide Walter Jenkins was homosexual can be compared with the case of FDR's valued advisor Welles. Whereas Hoover, who had a close relationship with FDR, had to guide Welles's enemies to information that would lead to his career termination, this was not necessary in the Jenkins case. As with FDR, Hoover was equally close to LBJ and equally dependent upon him for his job, if not more so. Yet unlike FDR, LBJ feared the presence of gays in or associated with his administration and, given the different times, wanted them isolated. Present throughout the Jenkins case was Hoover deliberately funneling to LBJ information about gays in government, or those associated with the administration, phone calls to the president with the latest information in the Jenkins matter, and a perceptive LBJ even telling Hoover not to worry about his job because the president supported him. LBJ's concerns connected to wider FBI interests in gays in Hollywood as potential White House guests, entertainment, or associates and even an actor slated to portray an FBI agent on the silver screen. Hoover was even interested in stopping the avant-garde gay filmmaker Andy Warhol by using antiobscenity law, and he collected information about other prominent gay men, such as Liberace, via the FBI HOMEX Program in the 1960s. FBI efforts to collect damaging information on gays and lesbians by the 1960s were widespread and varied.

With Nixon in the White House in 1969, the politics of homosexuality took a nastier turn. Nixon and Hoover were ideological allies, with a cooperative history dating to the 1950s and Alger Hiss, and the FBI director did what he could to satisfy the Nixon administration's desire for sensitive information. Whether it was helping in whatever way to undermine embattled Supreme Court Justice Abe Fortas, collecting and maintaining information attesting to Nixon's aides not being homosexual, or feeding the Nixon White House information it could use to gay bait enemies in the press corps, Hoover cooperated unhesitatingly. Although Nixon might have claimed in an Oval Office conversation he was not interested in singling out gays, he was a decidedly rabid homophobe and never hesitated, in fact, to gay bait those he perceived as his opponents. Hoover's FBI was a useful tool in this regard, and it is striking that this sort of nefarious activity—both gay baiting and disseminating information about alleged gays—ended shortly after Hoover's death and Nixon's political demise. Thereafter, though incrementally and quite slowly (over two decades), the FBI started to move in the direction of sexual equity.

FBI agents' ability to collect information about gays was not single-handed and did not happen in a vacuum. FBI officials from the start had at hand the means to collect massive amounts of data on people's private lives. The FBI maintained connections and liaison arrangements with a seemingly inexhaustible number of state and local police departments, morals squads, sheriff's offices, park police, university police departments and security offices, US attorney's offices and local prosecutors, branches of the military and especially their intelligence units, and virtually every branch and department of government on all levels, including the US Post Office. The bureau had long-established contacts with private, charitable, moral advocacy, and fraternal organizations, friendly elements in the media, and politicians whose sympathies were in line with FBI goals.

One of the most striking features of FBI agents' ability to collect massive amounts of information on gays was the techniques they employed. In certain instances, especially in which gays were presumed somehow to be a counterintelligence threat, FBI agents used clandestine personas, pretext interviews, mail covers, illegal break-ins, bugs, possibly even wiretaps, and physical surveillance that included photographing their targets. Yet the most extensive, and indeed striking, source of FBI information was informants. FBI agents had a seemingly inexhaustible supply of informants quite willing to share information they held about gays or those suspected of being gay. These informants came from all segments of society, most notably from gay men and women themselves. There were multiple reasons gays and lesbians so willingly informed on their own. These included resentment of others in their community, a strong sense of anticommunism and desire to purge subversives, a kind of self-legitimacy from cooperating with FBI agents (these informants were often described by agents as having emotional difficulties), an internal sense of self-loathing, or fear. Fearing police and federal targeting, David Finn and others at Mattachine, Dale Jennings's brother-in-law/printer, and the editor of *ONE* magazine, for example, naively believed that by cooperating with the FBI they were somehow protecting themselves or their groups from harassment, arrest, and probable ruination of their lives or political efforts. That, of course, came at the cost of providing information that could ruin other gay people's lives or even contribute to the undermining of their own efforts.

Some informants included those in the medical or therapeutic community who willingly proffered information revealed to them in confidence. Although there might not have been strict privacy laws at the time protecting such information, clearly the cooperation of psychologists, therapists, and university officials crossed ethical boundaries. Alfred Gross, a therapist who worked with gay men in the 1950s, not only went directly to the FBI with information about an early gay rights group but had a history of cooperating with FBI agents in matters of this kind. University of Illinois professor and psychologist William Gilbert, or another university official, seemingly had no problem sharing with FBI agents information from university counseling office records about his patient B. D. Huggins. FBI agents were successful in obtaining this sort of information given the deference afforded them during the early cold war. As protectors of the home front from subversive forces, willing and confidential cooperation was almost automatic and, indeed, expected. Secrecy was perceived as necessary to ensure US national security, so confidential medically related information was turned over probably in the belief that no one would be any the wiser and if, by chance, the patient was indeed a subversive, then so much the better.

Other FBI informants included those in other segments of society who, for whatever reason, had contact with gay people or their organizations. Those included informants in New Left groups, in or connected with the Black Panther Party (BPP), and associated with the World Youth Assembly, among others. Informants in the state vice society Citizens for Decent Literature provided FBI agents information about the DoB biennial convention, leading to FBI monitoring of lesbian activity in New York City through a white-slave-trafficking investigative classification. The reach of these informants was wide, including those in boardinghouses and among employers, but given the redacted nature of FBI records the preceding merely constitutes a broad sampling of the different types of informants FBI agents used to collect information about gays and lesbians. Most of the names, identities, and associations of FBI informants remain blacked out in FBI files. Suffice it to say, it is clear their numbers were legion.

Finally, and essential to FBI success in disseminating the mountain of information it collected about gays, was the FBI means of filing it. Although the formal Sex Deviates Program dates to 1950 and was augmented in 1951, in reality FBI agents had been collecting information in a systematic fashion about gays since 1937 and the Mattson kidnapping and murder. Previous to this, FBI agents collected general sexual and obscenity-related information, including some about homosexuality, in the course of other investigations (e.g., in enforcing the White Slave Trafficking Act).

Over time, since 1937, FBI filing of information evolved from research files referenced number 94, used initially to educate the public about the threat of "sex offenders" to the creation of counterintelligence files when gays were perceived to be liable to blackmail. Beyond these, there were related files, such as the headquarters 94 file dedicated to "Sex Deviates in Washington, D.C.," the FBI repository of records of those arrested on morals charges in the nation's capital and elsewhere. There was, for a time, the FBI Washington, DC, Field Office (WFO) file dedicated to "Sex Deviates in Government," until it was made obsolete (redundant, really) by 1953 with implementation of Dwight Eisenhower's security augmentation of the Federal Loyalty Program. Finally, in addition to various other field office 94 files, the FBI code-named HOMEX Program compiled information on prominent gay men supposedly vulnerable to criminal extortion.

For a half century FBI officials and agents were obsessed with gays, lesbians, and their respective organizations. That interest was a function of US social construction of homophobia, changing cultural perceptions of gays and lesbians; the moralism of government bureaucrats and politicians;

the effects of politics and bureaucracy in different eras; and notably, as with other groups, the rise of a concerted civil rights effort after the Second World War. Not a unique phenomenon, FBI surveillance and targeting of gays and lesbians and their respective groups should be placed squarely alongside its companion efforts against myriad other civil rights targets in the twentieth century.

Notes

Prologue

1. Athan Theoharis, *Chasing Spies: How the FBI Failed in Counterintelligence but Promoted the Politics of McCarthyism in the Cold War Years* (Chicago: Ivan R. Dee, 2002), 170–197. Theoharis has repeatedly analyzed these topics in his other works, including *The FBI and American Democracy: A Brief Critical History* (Lawrence: University Press of Kansas, 2004), *J. Edgar Hoover, Sex, and Crime* (Chicago: Ivan R. Dee, 1995), and *Abuse of Power: How Cold War Surveillance and Secrecy Policy Shaped the Response to 9/11* (Philadelphia, PA: Temple University Press, 2011).

2. Richard Gid Powers, *Broken: The Troubled Past and Uncertain Future of the FBI* (New York: Free Press, 2004); Rhodri Jeffreys-Jones, *The FBI: A History* (New Haven, CT: Yale University Press, 2007); Tim Weiner, *Enemies: A History of the FBI* (New York: Random House, 2012).

3. John D'Emilio, *Sexual Politics, Sexual Communities: The Making of a Homosexual Minority in the United States, 1940–1970,* 2nd ed. (Chicago: University of Chicago Press, 1998), 43–44, 46–47, 84, 124; Robert Dean, *Imperial Brotherhood: Gender and the Making of Cold War Foreign Policy* (Amherst: University of Massachusetts Press, 2001), chps. 4, 5, 6. See also Dean, "Charles W. Thayer: Purged from the State Department," in David L. Anderson, ed., *The Human Tradition in America since 1945* (Wilmington, DE: Scholarly Resources, 2003), 227–245.

4. Marcia M. Gallo, *Different Daughters: A History of the Daughters of Bilitis and the Rise of the Lesbian Rights Movement* (New York: Carrol and Graf, 2006), xvii–xx; David K. Johnson, *The Lavender Scare: The Cold War Persecution of Gays and Lesbians in the Federal Government* (Chicago: University of Chicago Press, 2004), 11–12, 56, 121, 127, 144–145.

5. Alexander Stephan, *"Communazis": FBI Surveillance of German Émigré Writers* (New Haven, CT: Yale University Press, 2000), 86–108; Adrea Weiss, "Communism, Perversion, and Other Crimes against the State: The FBI Files of Klaus and Erika Mann," *GLQ: A Journal of Lesbian and Gay Studies* 7, no. 3 (2001): 459–481; Lawrence R. Murphy, "The House on Pacific Street: Homosexuality, Intrigue, and Politics during World War II," *Journal of Homosexuality* 12, no. 1 (Fall 1985): 27–49; Irwin F. Gellman, *Secret Affairs: Franklin Roosevelt, Cordell Hull, and Sumner Welles* (Baltimore, MD: Johns Hopkins University Press, 1995); Mary Glantz, "An Officer and a Diplomat? The Ambiguous Position of Philip R. Faymonville and United States–Soviet Relations, 1941–1943," *Journal of Military History* 72 (January 2008): 141–177. The first, though still limited, examination of the FBI and Faymonville was by one of my students in her undergraduate thesis: Sabina Medilovic, "'Moral Degeneracy': FBI Investigation of Philip R. Faymonville of the Lend-Lease Mission to the Soviet Union" (history honors thesis, The Pennsylvania State University, 2008).

1. Was J. Edgar Hoover Gay? Does It Matter?

1. Athan Theoharis, *J. Edgar Hoover, Sex, and Crime* (Chicago: Ivan R. Dee, 1995), 33–34.

2. Ibid., 36–37. These are not the only examples.

3. Ibid., 11–14; Anthony Summers, *Official and Confidential: The Secret Life of J. Edgar Hoover* (New York: Putnam, 1993); Christopher Drew, "Gays Accuse US Agencies of Bias," *Chicago Tribune*, 2 May 1993.

4. Theoharis, *Hoover, Sex, and Crime*, 11, 14–15; Murray Weiss, "J. Edgar's Slip: Damning Pic Mysteriously Disappeared," *New York Post*, 11 February 1993.

5. *Naked Gun 33 1/3: The Final Insult*, directed by Peter Segal (Los Angeles: Paramount Pictures, 1994).

6. Theoharis, *Hoover, Sex, and Crime*, 44–45.

7. Ibid., 39–42. On Summers paying Rosenstiel, see Ronald Kessler, *Bureau: The Secret History of the FBI* (New York: St. Martin's, 2002), 108.

8. Summers, *Official and Confidential*, 254.

9. Theoharis, *Hoover, Sex, and Crime*, 42.

10. Ibid., 44–46.

11. Ibid., 46–48; Douglas M. Charles, "'Before the Colonel Arrived': Hoover, Donovan, Roosevelt, and the Origins of American Central Intelligence," *Intelligence and National Security* 20 (Summer 2005): 225–237.

12. Ray Wannall, *The Real J. Edgar Hoover, for the Record* (Paducah, KY: Turner, 2000), 159.

13. Cartha DeLoach, *Hoover's FBI: The Inside Story by Hoover's Trusted Lieutenant* (Washington, DC: Regnery, 1995), 62.

14. Ibid., 63.

15. Ibid., 65.

16. Cartha D. DeLoach, response to Ronald Kessler, "Did J. Edgar Hoover Really Wear Dresses?," History News Network, http://hnn.us/articles/814.html.

17. William W. Turner, *Hoover's FBI* (New York: Thunder's Mouth Press, 1993), xvi, 80–81.

18. Charles Kaiser, *The Gay Metropolis: The Landmark History of Gay Life in America since World War II* (New York: Harcourt Brace, 1997), 69–70.

19. Richard Gid Powers, *Secrecy and Power: The Life of J. Edgar Hoover* (New York: Free Press, 1987), 171–173; Powers, *Broken: The Troubled Past and Uncertain Future of the FBI* (New York: Free Press, 2004), 241–242.

20. Craig M. Loftin, *Masked Voices: Gay Men and Lesbians in Cold War America* (Albany: State University of New York Press, 2012), 177–179.

21. Claire Bond Potter, "Queer Hoover: Sex, Lies, and Political History," *Journal of the History of Sexuality* 15, no. 3 (September 2006): 355, 358.

22. Ibid., 361, 370.

23. Ibid., 365.

24. Ibid., 380.

25. Jay Hatheway, *The Gilded Age Construction of Modern American Homophobia* (New York: Palgrave Macmillan, 2003), 101–124; *Oxford English Dictionary*.

26. Hatheway, *Gilded Age Construction,* 49–55.

27. See George Chauncey, *Gay New York* (New York: BasicBooks, 1994), chp. 1; Hatheway, *Gilded Age Construction,* 55–60.

28. Chauncey, *Gay New York,* 13.

29. Ibid., 13–15. For *deviate* see the *Oxford English Dictionary.*

30. Chauncey, *Gay New York,* 15–16.

31. Hatheway, *Gilded Age Construction,* 11–21.

32. Ibid., 23–30.

33. John Loughery, *The Other Side of Silence: Men's Lives and Gay Identities—A Twentieth-Century History* (New York: Holt, 1998), 5–6.

34. Lawrence R. Murphy, *Perverts by Official Order: The Campaign against Homosexuals by the United States Navy* (New York: Harrington Park Press, 1988), 10–11; Loughery, *Other Side of Silence,* 6–7.

35. Murphy, *Perverts by Official Order,* 11–17; Ted Morgan, *FDR: A Biography* (New York: Simon and Schuster, 1985), 236–237.

36. Morgan, *FDR: A Biography,* 235–236; Loughery, *Other Side of Silence,* 8; Murphy, *Perverts by Official Order,* 16–17.

37. Loughery, *Other Side of Silence,* 8.

38. Murphy, *Perverts by Official Order,* 21–26, 60–64.

39. Ibid.

40. Ibid., 12, 26, 100–101; Loughery, *Other Side of Silence,* 10.

41. Loughery, *Other Side of Silence,* 10–11.

42. Letter, Josephus Daniels to Franklin Delano Roosevelt, 4 March 1921, in Newport Investigation 1921 folder, box 30, FDR Family, Business, and Personal Papers, FDR Presidential Library, Hyde Park, NY (hereafter FDRL).

43. Loughery, *Other Side of Silence,* 11.

44. "Lay Navy Scandal to F.D. Roosevelt," *New York Times,* 20 July 1921, 4.

45. Senator William H. King, Statement and Preliminary Minority Report, 18 July 1921, in Newport Investigation 1921 folder, box 30, FDR Family, Business, and Personal Papers, FDLR. See also "Minority Report Dissents; Senator King Holds Innuendoes against Officials Unjustified," *New York Times,* 20 July 1921, 4.

46. Franklin D. Roosevelt, Statement for the Press, 18 July 1921, in Newport Investigation 1921 folder, box 30, FDR Family, Business, and Personal Papers, FDLR.

47. See George Chauncey, "Christian Brotherhood or Sexual Perversion?: Homosexual Identities and the Construction of Sexual Boundaries in the World War I Era," in *Hidden from History: Reclaiming the Gay and Lesbian Past,* ed. Martin Duberman, Martha Vicinus, and George Chauncey Jr. (New York: Meridian, 1990), 294–317.

48. Leopold and Loeb trial transcript 1, 23 July 1924 and 25 July 1924, 20–24, Clarence Darrow Digital Collection, University of Minnesota Law Library, http://darrow.law .umn.edu/trials.php?tid'1.

49. Ibid., 25–32.

50. Ibid., 33–36.

51. Ibid., 36–38.

52. Ibid., 38–44.

53. Ibid., 46–56; John A. Farrell, *Clarence Darrow: Attorney for the Damned* (New York: Vintage, 2011), 334–335.

54. Farrell, *Clarence Darrow*, 335–338.

55. Clarence Darrow, *Attorney Clarence Darrow's Plea for Mercy and Prosecutor Robert E. Crowe's Demand for the Death Penalty in the Leopold-Loeb Case: The Crime of a Century* (Chicago: Wilson Publishing, 1924), 97, in Clarence Darrow Digital Collection, University of Minnesota Law Library, http://darrow.law.umn.edu/trials.php?tid'1.

56. "Franks Slayers Get Life Imprisonment; Youth Averts Noose," *New York Times*, 11 September 1924; "Assails Alienists of Franks Slayers," *New York Times*, 27 August 1924, 19.

57. Frederick Lewis Allen, *Only Yesterday: An Informal History of the 1920s* (New York: Harper and Row, 1931), 160, 161; Michael E. Parrish, *Anxious Decades: America in Prosperity and Depression, 1920–1941* (New York: Norton, 1992), 128.

2. "The Victim of a Degenerate"

1. "Tacoma Boy of 10 Is Kidnapped from Home by a Masked Man," *New York Times*, 28 December 1936; "Demented Man Is Hunted as Mattson Kidnapper," *New York Times*, 29 December 1936; Edward Tamm to J. Edgar Hoover, memo, 28 December 1936, FBI 7-1820-4; Tamm to Hoover, memo, 30 December 1936, FBI 7-1820-20; C. C. Spears, report, 2 January 1937, FBI 7-1820-147.

2. "Tacoma Snatch," *Time* (11 January 1937); "Wide Kidnap Hunt for Waley Aides," *New York Times*, 11 June 1935; Tamm to Hoover, memo, 28 December 1936; E. P. Coffey to Mr. Nathan, memo, 28 December 1936, FBI 7-1820-8; R. C. Suran to Edward Tamm, memo, 28 December 1936, FBI 7-1820-13.

3. J. Edgar Hoover to E. J. Connelley, letter, 1 January 1937, FBI 7-1820-62; "Ransom Payment for Mattson Boy Is Declared Near," *New York Times*, 30 December 1936; "Tacoma Kidnapper Keeps Boy Captive," *New York Times*, 31 December 1936; "Mattson Boy Safe, Kidnapper Tells Father of Victim," *New York Times*, 1 January 1937; "Mattsons Renew Plea to Abductor," *New York Times*, 3 January 1937; "US Agents 'Take' the Mattson Case," *New York Times*, January 4, 1937; Tamm to Hoover, memo, 28 December 1936; Edward Tamm to J. Edgar Hoover, memo, 28 December 1936, FBI 7-1820-5; single fingerprint report, 13 January 1937, FBI 7-1820-Not Recorded; J. Edgar Hoover to C. C. Spears, letter, 28 December 1936, FBI 7-1820-2.

4. E. J. Connelley to J. Edgar Hoover, letter, 5 January 1937, FBI 7-1820-146; Connelley to Hoover, letter, 8 January 1937, FBI 7-1820-179.

5. Edward A. Tamm, memo for the file, 30 December 1936, FBI 7-1820-14; "Halt Kidnap Hunt on Mattson's Plea for Safety of Son," *New York Times*, 5 January 1937; "Mattsons Clear Way for Abductor," *New York Times*, 6 January 1937; "Mattson Appeal Stirs New Hopes," *New York Times*, 7 January 1932; "New Mattson Ad Assures Abductor," *New York Times*, 8 January 1937; "Mattson Waiting Word for Ransom," *New York Times*, 9 January 1937; "Demand New Proof Mattson Boy Lives," *New York Times*, 10 January 1937; "Hunt Mattson Boy on Lonely Island," *New York Times*, 11 January 1937.

6. Edward Tamm to J. Edgar Hoover, memo, 11 January 1937, FBI 7-1820-215; "Mattson Boy Found Slain; Body Left in Lonely Brush; Killer's Footprints in Snow," *New York*

Times, 12 January 1937; Tamm to Hoover, memo, 11 January 1937, FBI 7-1820-232; Tamm to Hoover, memo, 12 January 1937, FBI 7-1820-259; H. W. G., note, 16 January 1937, FBI 7-1820-421; Hoover to All Field Divisions, teletype, 11 January 1937, FBI 7-1820-197; Tamm to Hoover, memo, 12 January 1937, FBI 7-1820-272.

7. "Mattson Boy Found Slain"; "Footprint Casts Aid Mattson Hunt," *New York Times,* 13 January 1937.

8. President's Statement on Mattson case, 12 January 1937, Official File 2523, Charles Mattson, FDR Library, Hyde Park, NY (hereafter FDRL); "President Spurs Kidnapper Hunt; Hoover Directs Search," *New York Times,* 13 January 1937, 4; Edward Tamm to J. Edgar Hoover, memo, 28 December 1936, FBI 7-1820-3.

9. As quoted in Margot Canaday, *The Straight State: Sexuality and Citizenship in Twentieth-Century America* (Princeton, NJ: Princeton University Press, 2009), 120.

10. "Ex-Convict Named in Mattson Hunt," *New York Times,* 14 January 1937.

11. "Police Find 'Lair' of Mattson Killer," *New York Times,* 15 January 1937; "Mattson Suspect Surrenders Self; a Degenerate Is Sought," *New York Times,* 16 January 1937. On the FBI interviewing hobos, see Special Agent in Charge (SAC) Omaha, report, 14 January 1937, FBI 7-1820-408. Interestingly, according to an FBI report describing Charles Mattson in detail the day he was abducted, he was not wearing underwear. See SAC Tacoma, report, 7 January 1937, FBI 7-1820-216, 15. One rumor reported in the press, alluding to the suspect, had it that investigators found a cave with a bloodstained mattress. FBI agents inquired into the story and found it false. See Edward Tamm to J. Edgar Hoover, memo, 17 January 1937, FBI 7-1820-471. On hobos and homosexuality, see also Frank Tobias Higbie, *Indispensable Outcasts: Hobo Workers and Community in the American Midwest, 1880–1930* (Urbana-Champaign: University of Illinois Press, 2003), 123–127; Todd DePastino, *Citizen Hobo: How a Century of Homelessness Shaped America* (Chicago: University of Chicago Press, 2003), 85–94.

12. Canaday, *Straight State,* 91–117.

13. Edward Tamm to J. Edgar Hoover, memo, 13 January 1937, FBI 7-1820-348; Tamm to Hoover, memo, 14 January 1937, FBI 7-1820-470; R. W. King to Hoover, letter, 12 January 1936 [*sic;* 1937], FBI 7-1820-453.

14. Edward Tamm to J. Edgar Hoover, memo, 5 January 1937, FBI 7-1820-121; SAC New York, report, 5 January 1937, FBI 7-1820-135; "Ransom Note Text Is Published; Previous Kidnap Threats Cited," *Sunday Star,* 3 January 1937, in FBI 7-1820-124X; "Slaughter of 2 Boys Admitted by Sex Slayer," *Washington Times,* 17 September 1937, in FBI 7-1820-11747; Guy Hottel to J. Edgar Hoover, letter, 12 January 1937, FBI 7-1820-330.

15. "Society Is Blamed for Case Murder," *New York Times,* 18 January 1937.

16. "112 Kidnappings Solved," *New York Times,* 23 January 1938; "Still Seeking Mattson Abductor," *New York Times,* 28 December 1942; "Confesses Killing of Mattson Child," *New York Times,* 13 July 1938; Ralph H. Major Jr., "New Moral Menace to Our Youth," *Coronet* (September 1950): 11. For the sex-crime panic and the *New York Times,* see Estelle B. Freedman, "'Uncontrolled Desires': The Response to the Sexual Psychopath, 1920–1960," *Journal of American History* 74 (June 1987): 83; (Deleted) to J. Edgar Hoover, letter, 11 January 1937, FBI 7-1820-252.

17. J. Edgar Hoover, "War on the Sex Criminal," *New York Herald Tribune*, 26 September 1937, 2.

18. Ibid.

19. Jack Frosch and Walter Bromberg, "Sex Offender: A Psychiatric Study," *American Journal of Orthopsychiatry* 9 (October 1939): 761–762; Freedman, "'Uncontrolled Desires,'" 88. A second sex-crime panic emerged between 1949 and 1955—see Neil Miller, *Sex-Crime Panic: A Journey to the Paranoid Heart of the 1950s* (New York: Alyson, 2002).

20. "Spurred by President, Hoover Flies Here to Push Hunt," *Washington Herald*, 13 January 1937, in Mattson FBI file. The Mattson kidnapping and murder file comprised 1,112 volumes of documents, or approximately 222,000 pages—David M. Hardy, FBI Records/ Information Dissemination Section, to Douglas M. Charles, letter, 5 September 2006.

21. See George Chauncey, *Gay New York: Gender, Urban Culture, and the Making of the Gay Male World, 1890–1940* (New York: BasicBooks, 1994), 353–354.

22. Canaday, *Straight State*, 4.

23. FBI Director J. Edgar Hoover, confidential memoranda, 24 August 1936, 25 August 1936, folder 136, Official and Confidential Files of J. Edgar Hoover (hereafter Hoover O&C); William Donovan and Edgar Ansel Mowrer, "Germans Said to Spend Vast Sums Abroad to Pave Way for Conquest," *New York Times*, 23 August 1940.

24. Henry Wolfinger, Records Disposition Division, to Directors of NCD and NNF, memo re: Disposition Job No. No1-65-78-5, 28 December 1977; James W. Awe, request for Records Disposition authority, 15 January 1978. I would like to thank Athan Theoharis for copies of these documents.

25. SAC Edward Scheidt, New York Field Office, to J. Edgar Hoover, memo, 17 April 1952, FBI 94-4-80-984, and Sex Deviate Index Card, both in Adlai Ewing Stevenson, folder 143, Adlai Stevenson, Hoover O&C. See also Athan Theoharis, "Secrecy and Power: Unanticipated Problems in Researching FBI Files," *Political Science Quarterly* 119, no. 2 (2004): 284. This document and index card of the Sex Offender File focused on Adlai Stevenson, Democratic presidential nominee. For FBI interest in his presumed sexuality, see Theoharis, "How the FBI Gaybaited Stevenson," *Nation* (7 May 1990): 1.

26. (Deleted) to Cartha DeLoach, memo, 7 July 1959, FBI 80-662-Not Recorded.

27. Wolfinger to Directors of NCD and NNF, memo re: Disposition Job No. No1-65-78-5.

28. For a description of these classifications and general data about them, see Gerald K. Haines and David A. Langbart, *Unlocking the Files of the FBI: A Guide to Its Records and Classification System* (Wilmington, DE: Scholarly Resources, 1993), 92–93, 105–107. Extant documents found in the survey of the 105 classification date to 1938. The Sex Deviates File, though (one of the 105 files), has documents dating to 1937, but this reflects the Mattson case. The Haines and Langbart book is the result of a court-ordered US National Archives survey of the general scope and content of FBI files.

29. Douglas M. Charles, *J. Edgar Hoover and the Anti-interventionists: FBI Political Surveillance and the Rise of the Domestic Security State, 1939–1945* (Columbus: Ohio State University Press, 2007), 33–38; FBI Director J. Edgar Hoover, confidential memo, 7 November 1938, in Athan Theoharis, ed., *From the Secret Files of J. Edgar Hoover* (Chicago: Ivan R. Dee, 1991), 183.

3. "Sex Perverts in Government Service"

1. The only other gay-related FBI targets I found for this period were German émigré writers Klaus and Erika Mann but it appears incidents of same-sex activity were simply noted in their files. Moreover, it is impossible for me to evaluate their FBI files in the sense of seeing things other historians would not recognize because the FBI response to my FOIA request was that the bureau had lost the files. For a limited and unsatisfactory understanding of the FBI interest, see Adrea Weiss, "Communism, Perversion, and Other Crimes against the State: The FBI Files of Klaus and Erika Mann," *GLQ: A Journal of Lesbian and Gay Studies* 7, no. 3 (2001): 459–481; Alexander Stephan, *"Communazis": FBI Surveillance of German Émigré Writers* (New Haven, CT: Yale University Press, 2000), 86–108.

2. J. Edgar Hoover, do-not-file memo, 30 January 1941, folder 157, Sumner Welles, Official and Confidential File of J. Edgar Hoover (hereafter Hoover O&C); Irwin F. Gellman, *Secret Affairs: Franklin Roosevelt, Cordell Hull, and Sumner Welles* (Baltimore: Johns Hopkins University Press, 1995), 395, 397–398.

3. Ibid.; memo for the director, 23 January 1941, folder 157, Sumner Welles, Hoover O&C.

4. Hoover, do-not-file memo, 30 January 1941; memo for the director, 23 January 1941.

5. Hoover, do-not-file memo, 30 January 1941; blind memo, 27 January 1941, folder 157, Sumner Welles, Hoover O&C.

6. Hoover, do-not-file memo, 30 January 1941.

7. Hoover, do-not-file memo, 3 January 1941, folder 157, Sumner Welles, Hoover O&C.

8. Ibid.

9. On Hoover's relationship with FDR and his catering to the president's interests, see Douglas M. Charles, *J. Edgar Hoover and the Anti-interventionists: FBI Political Surveillance and the Rise of the Domestic Security State, 1939–1945* (Columbus: Ohio State University Press, 2007).

10. Hoover, do-not-file memo, 30 January 1941.

11. Ibid.

12. Ibid.

13. Ibid.

14. The Welles story was first documented by Irwin F. Gellman, who also deftly details the political machinations with Welles's enemies. For the Bullitt incident, see Gellman's excellent book *Secret Affairs*, 240–241.

15. Louis Nichols to Clyde Tolson, do-not-file memo, 22 June 1942, folder 157, Sumner Welles, Hoover O&C.

16. Louis Nichols to Clyde Tolson, do-not-file memo, 17 July 1942, folder 157, Sumner Welles, Hoover O&C.

17. D. Milton Ladd to J. Edgar Hoover, memo, 4 September 1942, FBI 100-134410-NR, folder 157, Sumner Welles, Hoover O&C.

18. J. Edgar Hoover to Clyde Tolson and Edward Tamm, memo, 29 October 1942, folder 88, Cordell Hull, Hoover O&C.

19. J. Edgar Hoover, memo, 29 October 1942, folder 88, Cordell Hull, Hoover O&C.

20. Kimball to D. Milton Ladd, memo, 13 November 1942, folder 157, Sumner Welles, Hoover O&C.

21. See Douglas M. Charles, "Informing FDR: FBI Political Surveillance and the Isolationist-Interventionist Foreign Policy Debate, 1939–1945," *Diplomatic History* 24 (Spring 2000): 211–232.

22. Francis Biddle, *In Brief Authority* (Garden City, NY: Doubleday, 1962), 202.

23. P. E. Foxworth to J. Edgar Hoover, memo, 4 May 1942, FBI 62-68060-1.

24. J. Edgar Hoover to Attorney General Francis Biddle, personal and confidential memo, 13 May 1942, FBI 62-68060-1; Hoover to Biddle, personal and confidential memo, 13 May 1942, FBI 62-68060-2; memo re: Senator David I. Walsh—Alleged Fraud, 7 December 1942, FBI 62-68060-32. On Walsh and the Victory Program leak, see Charles, *J. Edgar Hoover and the Anti-interventionists*, chp. 5.

25. Morris Ernst to Franklin D. Roosevelt, letter, 24 April 1942, President's Secretary's File (hereafter PSF), Morris Ernst folder, Franklin D. Roosevelt Presidential Library, Hyde Park, NY (hereafter FDRL); Roosevelt to Ernst, memo, 27 April 1942, PSF, Ernst, FDRL; blind memo, re: William Elberfeld, with aliases, Espionage—G, Alien Enemy Control, 27 June 1942, folder 153, David. I. Walsh, Hoover O&C. On Walsh's nonconformist personal life, see Lawrence R. Murphy, "The House on Pacific Street: Homosexuality, Intrigue, and Politics during World War II," *Journal of Homosexuality* 12, no. 1 (Fall 1985): 23.

26. Memo on Walsh Case, 1 June 1942, HWG, folder 153, David I. Walsh, Hoover O&C; Blind memo, re: William Elberfeld, with aliases, Espionage—G, Alien Enemy Control, 27 June 1942, folder 153, David I. Walsh, Hoover O&C; "Scandal Scotched," *Newsweek* (1 June 1942): 30; "The Case of 'Senator X,'" *Time* (12 June 1942): 50.

27. The limerick can be found, naturally, on the Internet: http://www.jokes2go.com /poems/9669.html?22 .

28. Blind memo, re: William Elberfeld; minutes of cabinet meeting, 22 May 1942, Cabinet Meetings folder, box 1, Francis Biddle Papers, FDRL.

29. Blind memo, re: William Elberfeld, 6–7.

30. Ibid.

31. Ibid.

32. Ibid.

33. Ibid.

34. Ibid.

35. Ibid.; "FBI Clears Walsh, Barkley Asserts," *New York Times*, 21 May 1942, 6; "Tobey Asks Inquiry on Walsh Charge," *New York Times*, 22 May 1942, 10; "The Case of 'Senator X'" ; Walsh to Hoover, letter, 20 May 1942, Walsh folder, Hoover O&C; J. Edgar Hoover to David I. Walsh, letter, 21 May 1942, Walsh folder, Hoover O&C. For the foreign policy debate, see Wayne S. Cole's magnum opus, *Roosevelt and the Isolationists, 1932–1945* (Lincoln: University of Nebraska Press, 1983), or more recently Justus Doenecke, *Storm on the Horizon: The Challenge to American Intervention, 1939–1941* (Lanham, MD: Rowman and Littlefield, 2000). See also Charles, *J. Edgar Hoover and the Anti-interventionists*.

36. Affidavit executed by Gustave Herman Beekman, 18 May 1942, folder 153, David I. Walsh, Hoover O&C.

37. *New York Post* quoted in blind memo, re: William Elberfeld, 2–2b. On the FBI's relationship with the *Post,* see Matthew Cecil, *Hoover's FBI and the Fourth Estate: The Campaign to Control the Press and the Bureau's Image* (Lawrence: University Press of Kansas, 2014), 145, 155, 239.

38. Blind memo, re: William Elberfeld.

39. Ibid.

40. J. Edgar Hoover to Clyde Tolson and Edward Tamm, strictly confidential memo, 3 May 1943, folder 157, Sumner Welles, Hoover O&C; Gellman, *Secret Affairs,* 313.

41. Hoover to Tolson and Tamm, strictly confidential memo, 3 May 1943; Gellman, *Secret Affairs,* 314.

42. Gellman, *Secret Affairs,* 316–317.

43. J. Edgar Hoover to Edwin Watson, personal and confidential letter, 14 September 1943, folder 157, Sumner Welles, Hoover O&C; memo for the attorney general, 14 September 1943, folder 157, Sumner Welles, Hoover O&C.

44. SAC Los Angeles to J. Edgar Hoover and Louis Nichols, two telegrams, 2 September 1943, folder 157, Sumner Welles, Hoover O&C.

45. SAC Los Angeles to Hoover and Nichols, telegram, 2 September 1943; routing slip, ca. 2 September 1943, folder 157, Sumner Welles, Hoover O&C.

46. Hoover to Watson, personal and confidential letter, 14 September 1943; memo for the attorney general, 14 September 1943.

47. J. Edgar Hoover to Edwin Watson, personal and confidential letter and attachment, 3 September 1943, Official File 10-B, Sumner Welles, FDRL.

48. D. Milton Ladd to Edward Tamm, memo, 19 September 1942, FBI 64-4568-2.

49. Edward Tamm to J. Edgar Hoover, memo, 21 September 1942, FBI 64-4568-2.

50. See Athan Theoharis, *The FBI and American Democracy: A Brief Critical History* (Lawrence: University Press of Kansas, 2004), 49. For the delimitation proposal, see Proposal for Coordination of FBI, ONI, and MID, 5 June 1940, in RG 169, Records of the Military Intelligence Division, National Archives and Records Administration, Washington, DC (hereafter NARA).

51. Marshall to Hoover, letter, 25 September 1942, FBI 64-4568-1; Tamm to Hoover, memo, 21 September 1942. We know Beck's identity because FBI redactors overlooked his signature on an FBI report. The signature was stamped over, but the name was discernible upon closer inspection.

52. Raymond J. Batvinis, *The Origins of FBI Counterintelligence* (Lawrence: University Press of Kansas, 2007), 177–178. See also Douglas M. Charles, "'Before the Colonel Arrived': Hoover, Donovan, Roosevelt, and the Origins of American Central Intelligence," *Intelligence and National Security* 20 (Summer 2005): 225–237.

53. Batvinis, *Origins of FBI Counterintelligence,* 178–182.

54. For Beck's biographical and job details, see Raymond J. Batvinis, "The Strange Wartime Odyssey of Louis C. Beck," *World War II Quarterly* 5, no. 2 (Spring 2008): 16. Batvinis apparently did not have access to Faymonville's FBI file. For a description of the FBI SIS, see Sherman Miles to J. Edgar Hoover, memo, 23 July 1940, War Department files, Records of the Special and General Staffs, RG 165, 9794-186B/3, NARA.

55. Louis C. Beck to J. Edgar Hoover and Edward Tamm, memo, 26 September 1942,

FBI 64-4568-3. Michela's name is redacted in this document, but a later memo clearly states that "most of the information regarding Faymonville was furnished by General Joseph A. Michela." See (Deleted) to A. H. Belmont, memo, 29 April 1953, FBI 64-4568-40.

56. Beck to Hoover and Tamm, memo, 26 September 1942.

57. Ibid.

58. Ibid.

59. Ibid.

60. Ibid.

61. Ibid.

62. Ibid.

63. Louis C. Beck to Edward Tamm, memo, 3 October 1942, FBI 64-4568-4; Beck to Tamm, memo, 11 October 1942, FBI 64-4568-5.

64. Mary Glantz, "An Officer and a Diplomat? The Ambiguous Position of Philip R. Faymonville and United States–Soviet Relations, 1941–1943," *Journal of Military History* 72 (January 2008): 144, 145.

65. Glantz, "An Officer and a Diplomat?," 146–149. Questions about Faymonville's alleged Soviet sympathies have been explored for quite some time. See also John Daniel Langer, "The 'Red General': Philip R. Faymonville and the Soviet Union, 1917–1952," *Prologue* 8, no. 4 (1976): 209–221.

66. Glantz, "An Officer and a Diplomat?," 149–151.

67. Ibid., 157–161, 164–165, 167.

68. Beck to Tamm, memo, 11 October 1942.

69. Glantz, "An Officer and a Diplomat?," 162–163.

70. Ibid., 161–162.

71. Ibid., 168.

72. Memo, Special Investigation Conducted by Louis Beck, 20 May 1943, FBI 64-4568-19.

73. D. Milton Ladd to J. Edgar Hoover, memo, 20 March 1945, FBI 64-4568-31.

74. Edward Tamm to J. Edgar Hoover, memo, 22 January 1943, FBI 64-4568-9; (Deleted) to D. Milton Ladd, memo, 25 January 1943, FBI 64-4568-10; Edward Tamm to D. Milton Ladd, memo, 8 February 1943, FBI 64-4568-11; decoded message from Louis C. Beck, 25 February 1943, FBI 64-4568-13.

75. Decoded message from Louis C. Beck, 15 February 1943, FBI 64-4568-12.

76. Decoded message from Louis C. Beck, 8 May 1943, FBI 64-4568-17; decoded message from Beck, 24 May 1943, FBI 64-458-20.

77. (Deleted) to D. Milton Ladd, memo, 24 June 1943, FBI 64-4568-24; blind memo, Brigadier General Philip R. Faymonville Morals Charges, 25 August 1943, FBI 64-4568-6.

78. Ibid.

79. Ibid.

80. Ibid.

81. Ibid; Ladd to Hoover, memo, 20 March 1945.

82. D. Milton Ladd to J. Edgar Hoover, memo, 2 June 1943, FBI 64-4568-22.

83. J. Edgar Hoover to George Strong, personal and confidential letter and attached memoranda, 6 July 1943, FBI 64-4568-27.

84. D. Milton Ladd to J. Edgar Hoover, memo, 17 July 1943, FBI 64-4568-28.

85. Blind memo (by Louis C. Beck), Mr. Joseph E. Davies in Moscow 1943, 12 July 1943, FBI 64-4568-28; Mary Glantz, *FDR and the Soviet Union: The President's Battles over Foreign Policy* (Lawrence: University Press of Kansas, 2005), 125.

86. Blind memo (by Louis C. Beck), Mr. Joseph E. Davies in Moscow 1943, 12 July 1943, FBI 64-4568-28; Mary Glantz, *FDR and the Soviet Union: The President's Battles over Foreign Policy* (Lawrence: University Press of Kansas, 2005), 125.

87. Ibid.

88. Louis C. Beck to D. Milton Ladd, confidential memo, 23 July 1943, FBI 64-4568-29.

89. Regarding Spalding, see Glantz, "An Officer and a Diplomat?," 174, n. 143. For Burns's response, see James Burns to Harry Hopkins, memo, 16 August 1943, Faymonville folder, box 140, Harry Hopkins Papers, FDRL.

90. William Standley to Franklin D. Roosevelt, letter, 3 May 1943, Russia 1942–1943 folder, box 49, PSF, FDRL.

91. "Two Generals Demoted after Moscow Fiasco," *Chicago Tribune*, 18 November 1943, 8; "General Is Reduced after Duty in Soviet," *New York Times*, 18 November 1943, 3; Adam Lapin, "What They're Saying in Washington about Col. Faymonville," *Daily Worker*, 23 November 1943, 6, FBI 64–4568-A; Ladd to Hoover, memo, 20 March 1945, FBI 64-4568-31.

92. SAC Boston to J. Edgar Hoover, memo, 5 December 1945, FBI 64-4568-32; Philip Faymonville to Ella Winter, letter, 14 November 1945, FBI 64-4568-32; SAC Boston to J. Edgar Hoover, memo, 6 December 1945, FBI 64–4568–33.

93. Blind memo re: Joseph Davies and Philip Faymonville, 5 May 1949, FBI 64-4568-Not Recorded.

94. (Deleted) to Belmont, memo, 29 April 1953; Westbrook Pegler, "Fair Enough," *Washington Times-Herald*, 29 April 1953, FBI 65-4568-40. On Hoover's relationship with Pegler see Cecil, *Hoover's FBI and the Fourth Estate*, 219.

95. Louis Nichols to Clyde Tolson, memo, 5 May 1953, FBI 65-4568-39.

96. D. Milton Ladd to J. Edgar Hoover, memo, 8 May 1953, FBI 65-4568-42; Ladd to Hoover, memo, 30 April 1953, FBI 65-4568-41.

97. Minutes of cabinet meeting, 22 May 1942, Cabinet Meetings folder, box 1, Francis Biddle Papers, FDRL. For the claim that the FBI had whitewashed the Walsh incident, see C. A. Tripp, *The Homosexual Matrix* (New York: McGraw Hill, 1975), 212–13. On Roosevelt and sedition, see Athan Theoharis, "The FBI, the Roosevelt Administration, and the 'Subversive' Press," *Journalism History* 19 (Spring 1993): 3–10; Patrick S. Washburn, "FDR Versus His Own Attorney General: The Struggle over Sedition, 1941–1942," *Journalism Quarterly* 62 (Winter 1985): 717–724; Richard W. Steele, "The Great Debate: Roosevelt, the Media, and the Coming of the War, 1940–1941," *Journal of American History* 71 (June 1984): 69–92.

4. "Sex Deviates in Government Service"

1. James Patterson, *Grand Expectations: The United States, 1945–1974* (New York: Oxford University Press, 1996), 105–106.

2. On the contrast between Franklin D. Roosevelt and Harry Truman and the way in which cold war policy therefore evolved, see the thoughtful article by Athan Theoharis, "Roosevelt and Truman on Yalta: The Origins of the Cold War," *Political Science Quarterly* 87 (June 1972): 210–241.

3. Richard Polenberg, "Franklin Roosevelt and Civil Liberties: The Case of the Dies Committee," *Historian* 30 (1968): 165–178.

4. David Johnson, *The Lavender Scare: The Cold War Persecution of Gays and Lesbians in the Federal Government* (Chicago: University of Chicago Press, 2004), 21, 83–84.

5. Ibid., 21.

6. SAC San Antonio to J. Edgar Hoover, memo, 1 September 1947, FBI 80-662-(unreadable); Lieutenant (Deleted) to FBI Crime Lab, letter, 5 March 1964, FBI 80-662-308; FBI Lab Worksheet, 13 March 1964, FBI Lab Report, FBI 80-662-308; Hoover to Oak Park Police, 26 March 1964, FBI 80-662-308. On the FBI Obscene File, see Douglas M. Charles, *The FBI's Obscene File: J. Edgar Hoover and the Bureau's Crusade against Smut* (Lawrence: University Press of Kansas, 2012).

7. George Chauncey, "The Postwar Sex Crime Panic," in *True Stories from the American Past,* ed. William Graebner (New York: McGraw-Hill, 1993), 161–165; Estelle B. Freedman, "'Uncontrolled Desires': The Response to the Sexual Psychopath, 1920–1960," *Journal of American History* 74 (June 1987): 97; Johnson, *Lavender Scare,* 55–64.

8. J. Edgar Hoover, "How Safe Is Your Daughter?," *American Magazine* 144 (July 1947): 32–33, 102–104. Emphasis in original. "Hoover Asks Press to Help Crime War; Finds Menace in Parole," *New York Times,* 23 April 1937, 16.

9. The best account of the Lavender Scare, its origins, and its longevity, is Johnson's *Lavender Scare.*

10. Ralph H. Major Jr., "New Moral Menace to Our Youth," *Coronet* (September 1950): 101.

11. Ibid., 101–102.

12. Ibid., 102. Emphasis in original.

13. Ibid., 103, 104, 107, 108.

14. J. Paul De River, *The Sex Criminal: Documented Case Histories That Rip the Mask from Society's Most Fearsome Enemy* (Los Angeles: Associate Professional Services, 1965), 87–88.

15. Jack Lait and Lee Mortimer, *Washington Confidential* (New York: Crown, 1951), 90–98; Lait and Mortimer, *Chicago Confidential* (New York: Crown, 1950), 289, 291; Lait and Mortimer, *New York Confidential* (New York: Crown, 1948), 72–77. See in particular K. A. Cuordileone, "'Politics in an Age of Anxiety': Cold War Political Culture and the Crisis in American Masculinity, 1949–1960," *Journal of American History* 87 (September 2000): 515–545; Cuordileone, *Manhood and American Political Culture in the Cold War* (New York: Routledge, 2005); Allan Berube, *Coming Out under Fire: The History of Gay Men and Women in World War Two* (New York: Free Press, 1990), 255–279.

16. Glavin to Clyde Tolson, memo, 26 January 1949, FBI 100-360035-1.

17. Alex Rosen to D. Milton Ladd, memo, 28 January 1949, FBI 100-360035-2.

18. Ibid.

19. Ibid.; Alex Rosen to D. Milton Ladd, memo, 2 February 1949, FBI 100-360035-3. On Hoover's morality, see Charles, *FBI's Obscene File*, 17–18.

20. Keay to D. Milton Ladd, memo, 9 February 1949, FBI 100-360035-4.

21. Ibid.; J. Edgar Hoover to SAC Washington, DC, Field Office (hereafter WFO), memo, 22 March 1949, FBI 100-360035-7.

22. J. Edgar Hoover to SAC New York, memo, 10 February 1949, FBI 100-360035-4; SAC New York to Hoover, memo, 25 March 1949, FBI 100-360035-6.

23. Guy Hottel to J. Edgar Hoover, memo, 8 April 1949, FBI 100-360035-9; FBI Report, Subject: Charles Wheeler Thayer, 22 July 1948, Senate Internal Security Subcommittee (SISS) Name File, Charles Thayer, box 259, record group 46, National Archives and Records Administration, Washington, DC (hereafter NARA); Hoover to SAC WFO, memo, 22 March 1949, FBI 100-360035-7. See also Robert D. Dean, *Imperial Brotherhood: Gender and the Making of Cold War Foreign Policy* (Amherst: University of Massachusetts Press, 2001), 102.

24. D. Milton Ladd to J. Edgar Hoover, memo, 28 April 1949, FBI 100-360035-11; Ladd to Hoover, memo, 27 April 1949, FBI 100-360045-12.

25. Ladd to Hoover, memo, 28 April 1949.

26. Guy Hottel to J. Edgar Hoover, strictly confidential memo, 4 April 1949, FBI 100-360035-14; Dean, *Imperial Brotherhood*, 107–108.

27. FBI Report re: Charles Wheeler Thayer, 1 April 1949, FBI 100-360035-15.

28. Alex Rosen to D. Milton Ladd, memo, 22 April 1949, FBI 100-360035-16X.

29. J. Edgar Hoover to SAC WFO, memo, 29 April 1949, FBI 121-17249-1. On the FBI loyalty and security investigations, see J. Edgar Hoover, "Role of the FBI in the Federal Employee Security Program," *Northwestern University Law Review* 49 (1954): 333–347.

30. SAC Los Angeles to J. Edgar Hoover, memo, 9 May 1949, FBI 100-360035-17; Summary memo re: Charles Wheeler Thayer, March 1953, FBI 100-360035-23, 30–31.

31. *Congressional Record* (20 February 1950): 1961, 1978–1979.

32. Johnson, *Lavender Scare*, 15–16.

33. Robert Emmet Lee, *In the Public Interest: The Life of Robert Emmet Lee from the FBI to the FCC* (Lanham, MD: University Press of America, 1996), 118–119; Johnson, *Lavender Scare*, 23–24; John Earl Haynes, "Senator Joseph McCarthy's Lists and Venona," April 2007, http://www.johnearlhaynes.org/page62.html.

34. Special Agent (Deleted) to SAC WFO, memo, 5 August 1969, FBI 105-94852-3; David M. Hardy, FBI Section Chief, R/ID Section, to Douglas M. Charles, letter, 12 September 2013.

35. David M. Hardy, FBI Section Chief, R/ID Section, to Douglas M. Charles, letter and 1940 FBI background check reports re: Isham W. Perkins, 27 June 2013.

36. Johnson, *Lavender Scare*, 16–20.

37. "Perverts Called Government Peril," *New York Times*, 19 April 1950, 25.

38. J. Edgar Hoover to Sidney Souers, personal and confidential letter and list, 10 April 1950, box 147, Subject File FBI, President's Secretary's File, Harry S. Truman Presidential Library, Independence, MO (hereafter HSTL). I'd like to thank Steve Rosswurm for sharing his copy of this document I neglected to copy at the Truman Library.

39. Louis Nichols to Clyde Tolson, memo, 27 April 1951, FBI 67-37651-Not Recorded (but in section 3 of Quinn Tamm's FBI personnel file).

40. Lawson A. Moyer to Donald S. Dawson, memo, 8 May 1950, Sex Perversion File, box 32, Confidential File, White House Central Files, HSTL.

41. Ibid.

42. Ibid.

43. US Congress, Senate, *Report of the Investigations of the Junior Senator of Nebraska, a Member of the Subcommittee Appointed by the Subcommittee on Appropriations for the District of Columbia, on the Infiltration of Subversives and Moral Perverts in the Executive Branch of the United States Government*, S. doc. 4179, 81st Congress, 2nd sess., 1950 (hereafter Wherry Report), 2–3, 5, 13; Athan Theoharis, *Chasing Spies: How the FBI Failed in Counterintelligence but Promoted the Politics of McCarthyism in the Cold War Years* (Chicago: Ivan R. Dee, 2002), 174.

44. John Finlator, Traband, and Roy Blick, 29 March 1950, memorandum of conversation, Sex Perversion File, White House Confidential Files, HSTL.

45. Wherry Report, 8.

46. Ibid., 8, 6, 10.

47. Ibid., 10, 11–12.

48. Ibid., 14–15; Johnson, *Lavender Scare*, 84–89.

49. Johnson, *Lavender Scare*, 101–103.

50. Ibid., 104–105.

51. On FBI cooperation with Richard Nixon, Joseph McCarthy, HUAC, and SISS, see Athan Theoharis, *The FBI and American Democracy: A Brief Critical History* (Lawrence: University Press of Kansas, 2004), 77, 92–94, 94–95. On the FBI Responsibilities Program, see Cathleen Thom and Patrick Jung, "The Responsibilities Program of the FBI, 1951–1955," *Historian* 59, no. 2 (Winter 1997): 347–370. For the FBI relationship with the House Appropriations Committee, see Aaron J. Stockham, "'I Have Never Cut His Budget and I Never Expect To': The House Appropriations Committee Role in Increasing the Federal Bureau of Investigation's Cold War Power," *Historian* 75, no. 3 (Fall 2013): 499–516.

52. Stephen J. Spingarm, memo for the Hoey Subcommittee Sex Pervert Investigation File, 10 July 1950, Sex Perversion File, White House Confidential Files, box 32, HSTL; memo, Files Desired by Investigations Subcommittee in Conduct of Investigation, 27 June 1950, Sex Perversion File, White House Confidential Files, box 32, HSTL. See also Johnson, *Lavender Scare*, 105.

53. D. Milton Ladd to J. Edgar Hoover, memo, 18 July 1950, FBI 67-110597-127. One of the file numbers (105-12189-136) of the Sex Deviates File is written on the margin of this document, showing a copy of this memo was filed in it.

54. Ibid.

55. D. Milton Ladd to J. Edgar Hoover, memo, 20 July 1950, FBI 67-110597-128.

56. Ibid.

57. Ibid.

58. Ibid.

59. J. Edgar Hoover to SAC WFO, memo, 11 September 1950, FBI 67-110597-130.

60. Blind memo re: Mr. Francis D. Flanagan, 3 July 1952, FBI 67-110597-Not Recorded.

61. L. A. Hince to J. Edgar Hoover, memo, In-Service Training Course #15, 12 February 1940, FBI 67-110597-60.

62. Milton Jones to Louis Nichols, do-not-file memo, 9 April 1948, FBI 67-110597-124.

63. Spingarm, memo for the Hoey Subcommittee Sex Pervert Investigation File.

64. US Congress, Senate, Committee on Expenditures in Executive Departments, Investigations Subcommittee, *Hearings* Pursuant to S. Res. 280, Executive Session, 81st Congress, 2nd sess., 8 September 1950 (hereafter Hoey Committee Hearing), 2769.

65. J. Edgar Hoover to SAC Cleveland, memo, 24 July 1953, FBI 67-110597-136.

66. J. Edgar Hoover to SAC WFO, memo, 27 February 1956, FBI 67-110597-138.

67. Theoharis, *Chasing Spies*, 207–209.

68. Louis Nichols to Clyde Tolson, memo, 25 February 1954, FBI 62-97564-Not Recorded. There are only two references in extant FBI files regarding Roy Cohn's sexuality, and they are not at all clear because of redactions. Someone contacted Nichols on 21 May 1954 concerning rumors Cohn and David Schine, a McCarthy consultant, were gay, but Nichols said he knew nothing. The second reference was an anonymous letter signed "Revolted Republican" to the FBI making the same allegation but including McCarthy. See Nichols to Tolson, memo, 21 May 1954, FBI 62-97564-Not Recorded; anonymous communication, 29 May 1954, FBI 62-97564-Not Recorded.

69. Hoey Committee Hearing, 14 July 1950, 2130–2131.

70. Ibid., 2131.

71. Ibid., 2131–2132.

72. Ibid., 2132–2134, 2142.

73. Ibid., 2134.

74. Ibid., 2135–2138.

75. Ibid., 2139.

76. Ibid., 2140.

77. Ibid., 2142–2144.

78. Ibid., 2144.

79. US Congress, Senate, *Employment of Homosexuals and Other Sex Perverts in Government: Interim Report Submitted to the Committee on Expenditures in the Executive Department,* 81st Congress, 2nd sess., S. doc. 241 (Washington, DC: US Government Printing Office, 1950; hereafter Hoey Report), 19.

80. Ibid., 10–21.

81. Johnson, *Lavender Scare,* 117.

82. US Congress, House of Representatives, Committee on Appropriations, Subcommittee on the Department of Justice, *Hearings* for Department of Justice Appropriations for 1952, 82nd Congress, 1st sess., 15 February 1951 (Washington, DC: US Government Printing Office, 1951), 311.

83. Ibid., 319. Emphasis added.

84. Louis Nichols to Clyde Tolson, memo, 27 April 1951, FBI 67-37651-Not Recorded; J. Edgar Hoover to Supervisor Quinn Tamm, letter of reprimand, 2 May 1951, FBI 67-37651-258.

85. Nichols to Tolson, memo, 27 April 1951; Hoover to Tamm, letter of reprimand, 2 May 1951.

86. Nichols to Tolson, memo, 27 April 1951.

87. William Hogan to Harry S. Truman, letter, 31 March 1950, Official File 419K, box 1268, HSTL; Delmar Hill to Truman, letter, 28 March 1950, Official File 419K, box 1268, HSTL.

88. Johnson, *Lavender Scare*, 30–38; Lait and Mortimer, *Washington Confidential*, 90–98. For an examination of the difference between public conflation of gays and communists and the reality, see Douglas M. Charles, "Communist and Homosexual: The FBI, Harry Hay, and the Secret Side of the Lavender Scare, 1943–1961," *American Communist History* 11, no. 1 (2012): 101–124.

89. Milton Jones to Louis Nichols, 10 November 1952, addendum to memo, 14 November 1946, FBI 62-47774-13, folder 5, Henry Cabot Lodge Jr., Hoover O&C; Jones to Nichols, memo, 10 November 1952, folder 5, Henry Cabot Lodge Jr., Hoover O&C.

90. Jones to Nichols, 10 November 1952, addendum to memo, 14 November 1946.

91. Guy Hottel to J. Edgar Hoover, memo, 16 February 1950, FBI 100-360035-18; Gordon Nease to Hoover, memo, 4 March 1950, FBI 100-360035-Not Recorded (Charles Thayer file) and FBI 65-32871-3 (Carmel Offie file).

92. Gordon Nease to J. Edgar Hoover, memo, 4 March 1950, FBI 65-32871-3; Keay to Alan Belmont, memo, 8 March 1950, FBI 65-32871-4; D. Milton Ladd to Hoover, memo, 9 September 1943, FBI 65-32971-2; District of Columbia arrest record, Carmel Offie, 8 September 1943, in SISS Name File, Charles Thayer, NARA.

93. J. Edgar Hoover to attorney general, personal and confidential letter, 31 March 1950, FBI 121-17249-48; Alan Belmont to D. Milton Ladd, memo, 4 April 1950, FBI 100-360035-Not Recorded; (Signed An American who H.O.P.E.S.!) to McCarthy, anonymous letter and report, 26 February 1950, SISS Name File, Charles Thayer, NARA. On the FBI leaking information to McCarthy, see Athan Theoharis, "Secrecy and Power: Unanticipated Problems in Researching FBI Files," *Political Science Quarterly* 119 (2004): 275–278. For an alternate theory as to who provided Senator McCarthy this information, see Dean, *Imperial Brotherhood*, 271n3.

94. J. Edgar Hoover to Sherman Adams, personal and confidential letter, 11 February 1953, Carmel Offie folder, box 54, Henry R. McPhee files, Dwight D. Eisenhower Presidential Library (hereafter DDEL), Abilene, KS (acquired via Mandatory Review Request); summary memo re: Carmel Offie, 11 February 1953, Carmel Offie folder, box 54, Henry R. McPhee files, DDEL (acquired via Mandatory Review Request); *New York Times*, 26 April 1950, 3; *Congressional Record* (25 April 1950): 5703–5704, 5712.

95. Summary memo re: Carmel Offie, 11 February 1953.

96. Ibid.; Guy Hottel to J. Edgar Hoover, memo, 21 July 1950, FBI 65-32871-14. On Lovestone working with the Central Intelligence Agency, see Anthony Carew, "The American Labor Movement in Fizzland: The Free Trade Union Committee and the CIA," *Labor History* 39, no. 1 (1988): 25–42.

97. Ibid.; SAC New York, report, 18 October 1950, FBI 65-32871-45.

98. Keay to Alan Belmont, memo, 20 July 1950, FBI 65-32871-Not Recorded; D. Milton Ladd to J. Edgar Hoover, memo, 25 July 1950, FBI 65-32871-13; Hottel to Hoover, memo, 21 July 1950; Ray Wannall, memo, 31 August 1950, FBI 65-32871-21.

99. J. Edgar Hoover to Guy Hottel, personal and confidential memo, 31 August 1950, FBI 65-32871-Not Recorded.

100. Guy Hottel to J. Edgar Hoover, confidential JUNE memo, 27 July 1950, FBI 65-32871-19.

101. Guy Hottel to J. Edgar Hoover, memo, 19 September 1950, FBI 65-32871-23; Hottel to Hoover, memo, 11 September 1950, FBI 65-32871-27; Hoover to Hottel, memo, 11 December 1950, FBI 65-32871-53; Hoover to Hottel, JUNE memo, 28 August 1950, FBI 65-32871-19; Hennrich to Alan Belmont, JUNE memo, 21 September 1950, FBI 65-32871-26; Hoover to Hottel, JUNE memo, 21 September 1950, FBI 65-32871-26.

102. See Westbrook Pegler's column in the *Washington Times-Herald*, 30 December 1952.

103. Hennrich to Alan Belmont, memo, 6 October 1950, FBI 65-32871-39; Hennrich to Belmont, memo, 16 December 1950, FBI 32871-54.

104. J. Edgar Hoover to Guy Hottel, memo re Offie and Lovestone espionage, 4 December 1950, FBI 65-32871-48; Hottel to Hoover, memo, 20 November 1950, FBI 65-32871-51; Hottel to Hoover, memo, 22 November 1950, FBI 65-32871-52.

105. Hennrich to Alan Belmont, memo, 14 June 1951, FBI 65-32871-81; Stanley Tracy to J. Edgar Hoover, memo, 13 June 1951, FBI 65-32871-96.

106. Hoover to senior FBI officials and supervisors, memo, 20 June 1951, Freedom of Information Act (FOIA) request document. Thanks to *New York Times* reporter Matt Apuzzo and Charles Francis for sharing this document, which the FBI had not previously released. Francis obtained it in his efforts to compile FBI records concerning gays. See Matt Apuzzo, "Uncovered Papers Show Past Government Efforts to Drive Gays from Jobs," *New York Times*, 20 May 2014.

107. Hoover to senior FBI officials and supervisors, memo, 20 June 1951. Italics emphasis added; underlined emphasis in original.

108. Ibid.

109. As quoted in Athan Theoharis, *Abuse of Power: How Cold War Surveillance and Secrecy Policy Shaped the Response to 9/11* (Philadelphia, PA: Temple University Press, 2011), 78.

110. Hoover to senior FBI officials and supervisors, memo, 20 June 1951.

111. Ibid.

112. Ibid.

113. L. V. Boardman to J. Edgar Hoover, memo, 28 October 1954, FBI 62-93875-2503 (FBI Responsibilities Program File).

114. Hoover to senior FBI officials and supervisors, memo, 20 June 1951.

115. Ibid.

116. Ibid.

117. Ibid.

118. Ibid.

119. Ibid. Emphasis added.

120. L. V. Boardman to J. Edgar Hoover, memo, 28 October 1954, FBI 62-93875-2502.

121. Ibid. Emphasis added.

122. (Deleted) to Alex Rosen, memo, 22 October 1954, FBI 62-93875-Not Recorded.

123. Henry J. Wolfinger, Records Disposition Division, to Directors of NCD and NNF, memo re: Disposition Job No. No1-65-78-5, 28 December 1977; James W. Awe, Request for Records Disposition Authority, 15 January 1978. All in author's possession. I would like to thank Athan Theoharis for sharing with me these documents.

124. For the complete list of FBI file designations, see Gerald K. Haines and David A. Langbart, *Unlocking the Files of the FBI: A Guide to Its Records and Classification System* (Wilmington, DE: Scholarly Resources, 1993).

125. Wolfinger to Directors of NCD and NNF, memo, 28 December 1977.

126. Ibid. We can understand the National Archives rolling over to this FBI request in two ways. First, the Hoover era had just ended five years before, but that did not mean the automatic deference to the vaunted FBI ended. Indeed it had not. Second, the field of gay and lesbian history was just starting to develop and was still viewed by the larger historical discipline as an aberrant subfield. Thus, records relating to the field were regarded by archivists as not worthy of retention because they were salacious. In fact, Wolfinger conceded that "on the one hand, the records have some evidential value for documenting the FBI's interest and activities in gathering information on sexual offenders and homosexuals. On the other hand, however, the records contain massive amounts of material that relate to matters of individual sexual conduct and thus seem to infringe on personal privacy." He thought they could not be made available for research "without threatening damage to the reputations of numerous private citizens."

127. Ibid.

128. See Theoharis, *Abuse of Power*, 82.

129. (Deleted) to Cartha DeLoach, memo, 7 July 1959, FBI 80-662-Not Recorded (the administrative file of the FBI Obscene File). See also Charles, *FBI's Obscene File*, 43–44, 60–61.

130. David M. Hardy, FBI Section Chief, R/IDS, to Douglas M. Charles, letter, 8 August 2013. For the "121" being obsolete, see Haines and Langbart, *Unlocking the Files of the FBI*, 119.

131. David M. Hardy, FBI Section Chief, R/IDS, to Douglas M. Charles, letter, 19 July 2013.

132. Special Agent (Deleted) to SAC San Francisco, memo, 8 November 1956, FBI 94-843-1; Special Agent (Deleted) to SAC San Francisco, memo, 23 November 1956, FBI 94-843-5; Special Agent (Deleted) to SAC San Francisco, memo, 21 November 1956, FBI 94-843-6; Special Agent (Deleted) to SAC San Francisco, memo, 2 December 1956, FBI 94-843-7.

133. J. Edgar Hoover, "Needed: A Quarantine to Prevent Crime," *This Week* magazine, *Milwaukee Journal*, 10 March 1957, 8–10.

134. *Mattachine* (Los Angeles) *Newsletter* (April 1957) in FBI 100-45888-1A59.

135. Leo Laughlin to Alan Belmont, memo, 3 December 1951, FBI 100-360035-21.

136. New York SAC Edward Scheidt to J. Edgar Hoover, memo, 17 April 1952, folder 143, Adlai Stevenson, Hoover O&C; "8 Bradley Players Involved in Fixing Games," *New York Times*, 25 July 1951.

137. Ibid.

138. D. Milton Ladd to J. Edgar Hoover, memo and attached blind memo, 24 June 1952, folder 143, Adlai Stevenson, Hoover O&C.

139. Milton Jones to Louis Nichols, memo, 24 July 1952, folder 143, Adlai Stevenson, Hoover O&C; Jones to Nichols, memo, Summary of Information from FBI files, 24 July 1952, folder 143, Adlai Stevenson, Hoover O&C; Stevenson, Adlai Ewing, Sex Deviates index card, folder 143, Adlai Stevenson, Hoover O&C; "Stevenson Gaining," *New York Times*, 24 July 1952. One day later the nomination was sealed, and the next day Stevenson accepted the nomination.

140. Nichols to Hoover, memo, 29 August 1952, folder 143, Adlai Stevenson, Hoover O&C.

141. Ibid.

142. Ibid.

143. Ibid.

144. Joseph M. Porter, "How That Stevenson Rumor Started," *Confidential* 1, no. 4 (August 1953): 41–43, 59–60; Henry E. Scott, *Shocking True Story: The Rise and Fall of Confidential, "America's Most Scandalous Scandal Magazine"* (New York: Pantheon Books, 2010), 80.

145. Theoharis, *Chasing Spies*, 183.

146. J. Edgar Hoover to Clyde Tolson and Glavin, memo, 24 February 1950, no file number but in Leo Laughlin personnel file, section 2; D. Milton Ladd to J. Edgar Hoover, 15 August 1952, FBI 94-40154-10X1, folder 17, Adlai Stevenson, Hoover O&C; Theoharis, *Chasing Spies*, 183.

147. Guy Hottel to D. Milton Ladd, memo, 13 August 1953, FBI 94-40154-10X, folder 17, Adlai Stevenson, Hoover O&C; Theoharis, *Chasing Spies*, 183–184.

148. Alan Belmont to D. Milton Ladd, memo, 2 December 1952, folder 143, Adlai Stevenson, Hoover O&C.

149. Ibid.

150. Ibid.

151. Alan Belmont to D. Milton Ladd, memo, 6 January 1953, folder 143, Adlai Stevenson, Hoover O&C.

152. Ibid.

153. Alan Belmont to D. Milton Ladd, memo, 3 March 1953, folder 143, Adlai Stevenson, Hoover O&C. In April 1960 Owen was murdered by strangulation while staying in a Washington, DC, hotel. He was found lying naked beside his bed with his face badly beaten. He was only identified later via fingerprints. See A. K. Bowles to Les Trotter, memo, 8 April 1960, folder 19, David Blair Owen folder, Hoover O&C.

154. Cleveland to Evans, memo, 31 October 1964, folder 143, Adlai Stevenson, Hoover O&C; Theoharis, *Chasing Spies*, 185–186.

155. "Vandenberg Slated as Eisenhower Aide," *New York Times*, 31 May 1952, 18.

156. "Loyalty Checks 'Routine,'" *New York Times*, 26 November 1952, 9; "Check by FBI Denies Jobs to Two in Eisenhower Office," *New York Times*, 17 January 1953, 1; Theoharis, *Chasing Spies*, 186–187.

157. Theoharis, *Chasing Spies*, 188.

158. Ibid., 188–189; "Vandenberg Forgoes U.S. Post," *New York Times*, 14 April 1952, 31.

159. J. Edgar Hoover to SAC WFO, memo, 21 November 1952, FBI 65-32871-124; Branigan to Alan Belmont, memo, 19 December 1951, FBI 65-32871-117.

160. SAC WFO, report, 10 December 1952, FBI 65-32871-125 (marked "To be dissem., when invest. completed."); SAC WFO to J. Edgar Hoover, memo, 5 December 1952, FBI 65-32871-126; Branigan to Alan Belmont, memo, 10 December 1952, FBI 65-32871-131.

161. J. Edgar Hoover to SAC WFO, memo, 11 December 1952, FBI 65-32871-129; SAC WFO, report, 23 December 1952, FBI 65-32871-134.

162. J. Edgar Hoover to Sherman Adams, personal and confidential letter, 11 February 1953; Louis Nichols to Clyde Tolson, memo, 3 January 1953, FBI 65-32871-141.

163. J. Edgar Hoover to Clyde Tolson, D. Milton Ladd, and Louis Nichols, memo, 4 February 1953, FBI 65-32871-159; Branigan to Alan Belmont, memo, 27 February 1953, FBI 65-32871-165.

164. J. Edgar Hoover to Clyde Tolson, D. Milton Ladd, and Louis Nichols, memo, 5 February 1953, FBI 65-32871-154.

165. Hennrich to Alan Belmont, memo, 16 January 1952, FBI 65-32871-Not Recorded.

166. J. Edgar Hoover to Herbert Brownell, letter and report, 11 February 1953, FBI 65-32871-155; Hoover to Walter Bedell Smith, letter and report, 11 February 1953, FBI 65-32871-161; Hoover to Robert Cutler, letter and report, 11 February 1953, FBI 65-32871-163; Hoover to Sherman Adams, letter and report, 11 February 1953; Hoover to Herbert Brownell, letter and memo, 27 February 1953, FBI 65-32871-164; Hoover to Cutler, letter and memo, 27 February 1953, FBI 65-32871-168; Hoover to Adams, letter and memo, 27 February 1953, Carmel Offie Folder, McPhee files, DDEL; Alan Belmont to D. Milton Ladd, memo, 3 April 1953, FBI 65-32871-173 (this memo has on it a reference to it being filed in the Sex Deviates File).

167. Louis Nichols to Clyde Tolson, memo, 4 February 1953, FBI 100-360035-25; Alan Belmont to D. Milton Ladd, memo, 17 February 1953, FBI 100-360035-26.

168. Belmont to Ladd, memo, 17 February 1953.

169. Ibid.

170. Louis Nichols to Clyde Tolson, memo, 24 February 1953, FBI 121-17249-64; Alan Belmont to D. Milton Ladd, memo, 25 February 1953, FBI 100-360035-26; Belmont to Ladd, memo, 17 February 1953; Nichols to Tolson, memo, 9 March 1953, FBI 121-17249-66.

171. "Bohlen Report Builds Up Feud in State Dept.," *Chicago Daily Tribune*, 20 March 1953, 3.

172. J. Edgar Hoover to Clyde Tolson, D. Milton Ladd, and Louis Nichols, memo, 19 February 1953, FBI 77-57561-g; Milton Jones to Cartha DeLoach, memo, 16 January 1961, FBI 67-308303-153; J. Edgar Hoover to Scott McLeod, letter, 26 February 1953, FBI 62-99272-1X; McLeod to Hoover, letter, 9 March 1953, FBI 62-99272-1X1.

173. J. Edgar Hoover to Scott McLeod, letter, 9 March 1953, FBI 62-99272-1X1.

174. Richard Gid Powers, *Secrecy and Power: The Life of J. Edgar Hoover* (New York: Free Press, 1987), 356.

175. Hoover to McLeod, letter, 9 March 1953.

176. Louis Nichols to Clyde Tolson, memo, 3 March 1953, FBI 67-308303-105.

177. Louis Nichols to Clyde Tolson, memo, 14 March 1953, FBI 67-308303-106.

178. Louis Nichols to Clyde Tolson, memo, 24 March 1953, FBI 62-99272-1.

179. Louis Nichols to Clyde Tolson, memo, 25 May 1953, FBI 62-99272-3.

180. Clyde Tolson, memo re: Scott McLeod, no date, FBI 62-99272-5; J. Edgar Hoover to Clyde Tolson, memo, 17 July 1953, FBI 62-99272-5.

181. Keay to Alan Belmont, memo, 19 November 1953, FBI 62-99272-Not Recorded; Ralph Roach to Alan Belmont, memo, 13 February 1956, FBI 62-99272-18; Louis Nichols to Clyde Tolson, memo, 20 April 1954, FBI 62-99272-8.

182. Roach to Belmont, memo, 13 February 1956.

183. Ralph Roach to Alan Belmont, memo, 9 May 1957, FBI 62-99272-23; Mohr to J. Edgar Hoover, memo, 9 May 1957, FBI 62-99272-Not Recorded.

184. Richard Gid Powers, *Broken: The Troubled Past and Uncertain Future of the FBI* (New York: Free Press, 2004), 223.

185. Scott McLeod to J. Edgar Hoover, letter, 14 May 1957, FBI 62-99272-26; D. C. Morrell to Cartha DeLoach, memo, 14 September 1960, FBI 62-99272-29; Hoover to Edna McLeod, letter, 8 November 1961, FBI 62-99272-31.

186. J. Edgar Hoover to Sherman Adams, personal and confidential letter and attached summary memo re: Charles Thayer, 4 March 1953, Charles Thayer folder, box 70, McPhee files, DDEL (obtained via Mandatory Review Request). Many of the names are redacted but can be found extant in report by John Finlator, Subject Charles Wheeler Thayer, 22 July 1948, in SISS Name File, Charles Thayer, NARA. See also Belmont to Ladd, memo, 17 February 1953.

187. Ibid.

188. Ibid.

189. Ibid.

190. J. Edgar Hoover to Walter Bedell Smith, personal and confidential letter and memo, 4 March 1953, FBI 100-360035-23; Alan Belmont to D. Milton Ladd, memo, 4 March 1953, FBI 100-360035-23; J. Edgar Hoover to Clyde Tolson, D. Milton Ladd, and Louis Nichols, memo, 4 March 1953, FBI 100-360035-24; Democratic Senatorial Campaign Committee, memo, 9 February 1954, Security Risks folder, Charles S. Murphy Papers, box 37, HSTL.

191. Belmont to Ladd, memo, 17 February 1953; Donald Lourie to Charles Thayer, secret letter, 6 March 1953, FBI 121-17249-65; Alan Belmont to D. Milton Ladd, memo, 13 March 1953, FBI 121-17249-67; Sizoo to J. Edgar Hoover, memo, 9 June 1953, FBI 100-360035-29; "Bohlen's Relative Quits," *New York Times*, 27 March 1953, 8; entry for 23 March 1953, Charles Thayer diary, box 7, Charles Thayer Papers, HSTL.

192. Charles Thayer to Jacob Beam, US Embassy in Moscow, letter, 21 May 1953, Charles Thayer Papers, box 1, HSTL; Thayer to Joseph Alsop, letter, 20 June 1953, Charles Thayer Papers, box 1, HSTL; Thayer to Katherine Bunnell, letter, 30 March 1953, Charles Thayer Papers, box 1, HSTL; Thayer to Lurton Blassingame, letter, 31 March 1953, Charles Thayer Papers, box 1, HSTL; "Battle Joined," *Newsweek* (23 March 1953): 28.

193. J. Edgar Hoover to (Deleted), memo, 27 May 1955, FBI 100-418839-1; "Samuel Reber to Retire," *New York Times*, 30 May 1953, 13.

194. On the McCarthyites' view of the Bohlen nomination, see "Chip on Old Block," *Newsweek* (23 March 1953): 23–24. For a thorough discussion of the Bohlen nomination fight, see Dean, *Imperial Brotherhood*, 119–140.

195. Summary memo re: Charles Eustis Bohlen, 16 March 1953, folder 38, Charles Bohlen, Hoover O&C. I managed to obtain via Mandatory Review Request the White House copy of the Bohlen summary memo. It is significantly less redacted than the one in the Hoover Official and Confidential file. J. Edgar Hoover to White House Chief of Staff Sherman Adams, letter and summary memo, 16 March 1953, Charles Bohlen folder, box 8, Henry R. McPhee Records (hereafter Bohlen summary, W.H.), DDEL.

196. Bohlen summary, W.H.

197. Ibid.

198. Ibid.

199. Ibid.

200. Ibid.

201. Ibid.

202. FBI Report, Nicholas Nabokoff, 28 June 1948, FBI 123-1231-21; J. Edgar Hoover to SAC New York, memo, 14 June 1948, FBI 123-1231-1; FBI Report, Nicholas Nabokoff, 22 April 1943, FBI 123-1231-X3; FBI Report, Nicholas Nabokoff, 22 July 1948, FBI 123-1231-22. FBI file designation 123 was especially for Voice of America (VOA) investigations.

203. Bohlen summary, W.H. Nabokoff's name is redacted in the Bohlen summary, but the same information about him in the summary can also be found without his name redacted in memo, Subject Charles Wheeler Thayer, 22 July 1948, 5–6, in SISS Name File, Charles Thayer, NARA.

204. Bohlen summary, W. H. Brosse's name is similarly redacted, like Nabokoff's, but also can be found extant in a memo by John Finlator, Subject Charles Wheeler Thayer, 22 July 1948, 4–5, in SISS Name File, Charles Thayer, NARA.

205. Bohlen summary, W.H.

206. Ibid.

207. Alex Rosen to D. Milton Ladd, 16 March 1953, FBI 77-56416-99, folder 38, Charles Bohlen, Hoover O&C.

208. Louis Nichols to J. Edgar Hoover, memo, 16 March 1954, folder 38, Charles Bohlen, Hoover O&C.

209. "Senate Unit Backs Bohlen as Envoy by Vote of 15 to 0," *New York Times*, 19 March 1953.

210. Ibid.

211. J. Edgar Hoover to Clyde Tolson, D. Milton Ladd, and Louis Nichols, memo, 18 March 1953, folder 105, Joseph McCarthy, Hoover O&C.

212. "Bohlen Report Builds Up Feud in State Dept.," *Chicago Daily Tribune*, 20 March 1953, 3; Edward Folliard, "McCarthy Reiterates That He Can't Agree, Calls It His Duty to Fight Choice," *Washington Post*, 27 March 1953.

213. "Rips Dulles' 'Cover Up' on Bohlen Case," *Chicago Daily Tribune*, 21 March 1953; "Dulles Holds Firm in Senate Attacks on Bohlen Security," *New York Times*, 21 March 1953.

214. "McCarthy Demands Lie Test for Bohlen on Security Data," *Chicago Daily Tribune*, 24 March 1953.

215. "Taft, Sparkman Pore over FBI Data on Bohlen," *Chicago Daily Tribune*, 25 March 1953, 10; "2 Senators Study FBI Bohlen Data, Affirm Clearance," *New York Times*,

25 March 1953; William S. White, "Bitterness Marks Debate on Bohlen; Taft Defers Vote," *New York Times*, 26 March 1953, 1.

216. Ibid.

217. Memo for the Director's Personal Files, 16 April 1953, folder 38, Charles Bohlen, Hoover O&C.

218. Alan Belmont to D. Milton Ladd, memo, 25 March 1953, FBI 77-57561-7.

219. Ibid.

220. Ibid.

221. J. Edgar Hoover to Clyde Tolson, D. Milton Ladd, and Louis Nichols, memo, 26 March 1953, FBI 62-99272-Not Recorded.

222. Ibid.

223. Alan Belmont to D. Milton Ladd, memo, 30 March 1953, FBI 77-57561-8.

224. Ibid.

225. Ibid.

226. Ibid.; Clegg to Clyde Tolson, memo, 4 April 1953, FBI 77-57561-Not Recorded.

227. J. Edgar Hoover to John Foster Dulles, letter, 18 March 1953, FBI 77-57561-1; Dulles to Hoover, letter, 16 March 1953, FBI 77-57561-1; Hoover to Sherman Adams, personal and confidential letter and memo re McLeod, 1 April 1953, FBI 77-57561-2; Hoover to attorney general, personal and confidential letter, 1 April 1953, FBI 77-57561-3; Hoover to Dulles, personal and confidential letter and memo re McLeod, FBI 77-57561-4.

228. Robert C. Albright, "Bohlen Wins by 74-to-13 Senate Vote," *Washington Post*, 28 March 1953.

229. SAC WFO to J. Edgar Hoover, memo, 11 March 1953, FBI 62-69402-Not Recorded; Hoover to Tolson, Ladd, and Nichols, memo, 18 March 1953.

230. Hoover to Tolson, Ladd, and Nichols, memo, 18 March 1953.

231. Ibid.

232. Leo L. Laughlin, report of performance rating, 31 March 1953, FBI 67-58420-263; D. Milton Ladd to J. Edgar Hoover, memo, 19 March 1953, FBI 62-69402-75 and FBI 62-40772-Not Recorded (this copy of the same document does not have names redacted); Ladd to Hoover, (second) memo, 19 March 1953, 62-69402-75; Alan Belmont to D. Milton Ladd, memo, 24 March 1953, FBI 62-69402-74.

233. J. Edgar Hoover to Clyde Tolson and Glavin, memo, 9 September 1953, FBI 67-58420-268; Hoover to Oveta Culp Hobby, personal and confidential letter, 20 March 1953, FBI 62-40772-74.

234. Leo Laughlin to Alan Belmont, memo, 26 March 1953, FBI 62-69402-Not Recorded; Simeon Booker, "FBI Investigates Shortage in Two Supply Units of FSA," *Washington Post*, 26 March 1953.

235. J. Edgar Hoover to Clyde Tolson, D. Milton Ladd, and Louis Nichols, memo, 31 March 1953, FBI 62-69402-73.

236. Ibid.

237. Ibid.

238. Holloman to J. Edgar Hoover, memo, 31 March 1953, FBI 62-69402-78; memo, Mohr to Clyde Tolson, 14 April 1953, FBI 62-69402-82.

239. D. Milton Ladd to J. Edgar Hoover, memo, 25 April 1953, 62-69402-83; Leo Laughlin to Alan Belmont, memo, 4 May 1953, FBI 62-69402-84; Laughlin to Belmont, memo, 15 April 1953, FBI 62-69402-85.

240. J. Edgar Hoover to Clyde Tolson, D. Milton Ladd, and Louis Nichols, memo, 23 June 1953, FBI 62-69402-87; Hoover to Tolson, Glavin, Alex Rosen, and Nichols, memo, 25 June 1953, FBI 62-69402-88; Sizoo to Clyde Tolson, memo, 1 September 1954, FBI 62-69402-119.

241. (Deleted) to Foley, memo, 31 March 1953, FBI 65-32871-174; Alan Belmont to D. Milton Ladd, memo, 28 April 1953, FBI 65-32871-175.

242. J. Edgar Hoover to SAC WFO, memo, 29 April 1953, FBI 65-32871-175; SAC WFO to Hoover, memo, 17 June 1953, FBI 65-32871-182 (also in the Sex Deviates File).

243. Drew Pearson, "Senatorial Fireworks Rock Immigration Hearings," 5 July 1953, typescript copy of the "Washington Merry-Go-Round" column, Special and Digital Collections, American University Library, Washington, DC; Alan Belmont to D. Milton Ladd, memo, 8 July 1953, FBI 65-32871-183. The Carmel Offie FBI file is heavily redacted.

244. Alan Belmont to D. Milton Ladd, memo, 19 May 1953, FBI 65-32871-176; Belmont to Ladd, memo, 2 June 1953, FBI 65-32871-178; Belmont to Ladd, memo, 22 July 1953, FBI 65-32871-184.

245. Branigan to Alan Belmont, memo, 23 March 1954, FBI 65-32871-Not Recorded; Hennrich to Alan Belmont, memo, 15 March 1954, FBI 65-32871-(?); Branigan to Belmont, memo, 16 March 1954, FBI 65-32871-(?); Belmont to Ladd, memo, 19 February 1954, FBI 65-32871-194; SAC Richmond, report, 15 March 1954, FBI 65-32871-220; SAC Richmond to Hoover, memo, 3 April 1954, FBI 65-32871-229; SAC Richmond, report, 17 May 1954, FBI 65-32871-233; SAC WFO to J. Edgar Hoover, memo, 2 July 1954, FBI 65-32871-238 (copied to the Sex Deviate File as 105-12189-2183).

246. Les Trotter to Stanley Tracy, memo, 16 February 1954, FBI 65-32871-200; Cartha DeLoach to Clyde Tolson, memo, 2 March 1954, FBI 65-32871-199.

247. Douglas M. Charles, *J. Edgar Hoover and the Anti-interventionists: FBI Political Surveillance and the Rise of the Domestic Security State, 1939–1945* (Columbus: Ohio State University Press, 2007), 146.

248. J. Edgar Hoover to Clyde Tolson, L.V. Boardman, and Alan Belmont, memo, 17 April 1957; Hoover to Tolson, Boardman, Belmont, and Louis Nichols, memo, 17 April 1957, folder 159, White House Employees Homosexuals, Hoover O&C.

249. Ibid.

250. J. Edgar Hoover to Clyde Tolson, L.V. Boardman, Alan Belmont, and Louis Nichols, memo, 19 April 1957, folder 159, White House Employees Homosexuals, Hoover O&C.

251. Hoover to Tolson, Boardman, Belmont, and Nichols, memo, 17 April 1957.

252. "Joseph Alsop Dies," *New York Times*, 29 August 1989; Ann W. Engar, "Alsop, Stewart," American National Biography Online (February 2000), http://www.anb.org/articles/16/1603017.html.

253. Allen Dulles to J. Edgar Hoover, letter and memo prepared by Alsop, 1 April 1957, folder 26, Joseph Alsop, Hoover O&C; Theoharis, *Chasing Spies*, 191–192.

254. Theoharis, *Chasing Spies*, 192.

255. Ibid., 192–193.

256. (Deleted) to Alan Belmont, memo, 7 April 1957, FBI 100-354477-124.

257. Alan Belmont to L. V. Boardman, memo, 19 May 1954, FBI 100-354477-179.

258. L. V. Boardman to J. Edgar Hoover, memo and attached document, 3 August 1955, FBI 100-354477-189.

259. Ibid.

260. L. N. Conroy to Alex Rosen, memo and attached blind memo dated 16 July 1957, 15 July 1957, FBI 100-354477-(255?). The FBI redactors failed to delete Waddington's surname in this document, thus revealing it for us.

261. Alan Belmont to L. V. Boardman, memo and attached memo re: the Alsops, 29 March 1957, FBI 100-354477-218 (Alsop file). The copy of the 29 March 1957 memo in folder 26, Joseph Alsop, Hoover O&C (Hoover O&C version at Marquette University Library) contains Vandenberg's unredacted name. See also Theoharis, *Chasing Spies*, 193. For Waddington's position see *Foreign Service List, January 1, 1952* (Washington, DC: US Government Printing Office, 1952), 39.

262. Allen Dulles to Hoover, letter and memo prepared by Alsop, 1 April 1957, in folder 26, Joseph Alsop, Hoover O&C; letter, Hoover to Dulles, 19 April 1957; Theoharis, *Chasing Spies*, 193–197.

263. Johnson, *Lavender Scare*, 2.

264. Democratic Senatorial Campaign Committee, memo, 9 February 1954, 25–26, box 37, Charles S. Murphy Papers, HSTL; "Only 11 Fired in '53 on Loyalty Grounds, McLeod Report Says," *Washington Star*, 10 February 1954, box 37, Charles S. Murphy Papers, HSTL; James Donovan, "Commerce Dept. Aide Reports 132 Fired as Security Risks," *Washington Post*, 19 February 1954, box 37, Charles S. Murphy Papers, HSTL.

5. "Take This Crowd On and Make Them 'Put Up or Shut Up'"

1. Milton Jones to Louis Nichols, memo, 26 January 1956, FBI 100-403320-14.

2. Ibid.

3. Allan Berube, *Coming Out under Fire: The History of Gay Men and Women in World War Two* (New York: Free Press, 1990), 271–272; John D'Emilio, *Sexual Politics, Sexual Communities: The Making of a Homosexual Minority in the United States, 1940–1970*, 2nd ed. (Chicago: University of Chicago Press, 1998), 31–32. On gay and lesbian literature and communications networks and how this affected the development of gay and lesbian culture, see Martin Meeker, *Contacts Desired: Gay and Lesbian Communications and Community, 1940s–1970s* (Chicago: University of Chicago Press, 2006).

4. For the post–Second World War sex-crime panic, see George Chauncey, "The Postwar Sex Crime Panic," in *True Stories from the American Past*, ed. William Graebner (New York: McGraw-Hill, 1993), 160–178.

5. Chuck Rowland, quoted in Eric Marcus, *Making Gay History: The Half-Century Fight for Lesbian and Gay Equal Rights* (New York: Perennial, 2002), 10.

6. Stuart Timmons, *The Trouble with Harry Hay: Founder of the Modern Gay Movement* (Boston: Alyson, 1990), 32–36.

7. Hay believed in certain cases the party would make exceptions for gay members. See ibid., 108–109. On Communist Party homophobia and antigay policies, about which

the literature is thin, see Simon Karlinsky, "Russia's Gay Literature and Culture: The Impact of the October Revolution," in *Hidden from History: Reclaiming the Gay and Lesbian Past,* ed. Martin Duberman, Martha Vicinus, and George Chauncey Jr. (New York: Meridian, 1990), 347–364.

8. Timmons, *Trouble with Harry Hay,* 104.

9. Quoted in Timmons, *Trouble with Harry Hay,* 97.

10. Jonathan Katz, "The Founding of the Mattachine Society: An Interview with Henry Hay," *Radical America* 11, no. 4 (1977): 28–29.

11. Marcus, *Making Gay History,* 24; Dudley Clendinen, "William Dale Jennings, 82, Writer and Gay Rights Pioneer," *New York Times,* 22 May 2000, B7.

12. See D'Emilio, *Sexual Politics, Sexual Communities,* 63–64; Warren Johansson, "Mattachine Society," in *Encyclopedia of Homosexuality,* ed. Wayne R. Dynes (New York: Garland, 1990), 779.

13. On the founding of Mattachine, see D'Emilio, *Sexual Politics, Sexual Communities,* 63–64; Timmons, *Trouble with Harry Hay,* 96–101, 158–159; Dudley Clendinen, "Harry Hay, Early Proponent of Gay Rights, Dies at 90," *New York Times,* 25 October 2002, 33; Timmons, "Harry Hay," in *Gay Histories and Cultures: An Encyclopedia,* ed. George Haggerty (New York: Garland, 2000), 432; Clendinen, "William Dale Jennings."

14. For their goals, see Meeker, "Behind the Mask of Respectability," in Meeker, *Contacts Desired: Gay and Lesbian Communications and Community, 1940s–1970s* (Chicago: University of Chicago Press, 2006), 83.

15. Athan Theoharis, *The FBI and American Democracy: A Brief Critical History* (Lawrence: University Press of Kansas, 2004), 92; David K. Johnson, *The Lavender Scare: The Cold War Persecution of Gays and Lesbians in the Federal Government* (Chicago: University of Chicago Press, 2004), 15–16.

16. SAC Los Angeles, report, 9 September 1953, FBI 100-403320-4, 21; Dale Jennings, "To Be Accused Is to Be Guilty," *ONE: The Homosexual Magazine* (January 1953): 10–13. Jennings has the dates of his arrest and trial wrong in his article. FBI agents consulted Los Angeles Police files and recorded the dates I have used.

17. Jennings, quoted in James T. Sears, *Behind the Mask of the Mattachine: The Hal Call Chronicles and the Early Movement for Homosexual Emancipation* (New York: Harrington Park, 2006), 163. For Carmel Offie, see Gordon Nease to J. Edgar Hoover, memo, 4 March 1950, FBI 65-32871-3.

18. D'Emilio, *Sexual Politics, Sexual Communities,* 70.

19. Ibid., 70–71.

20. SAC Los Angeles, report, 9 September 1953, 21; George Shibley, quoted in Sears, *Behind the Mask of the Mattachine,* 163.

21. Sears, *Behind the Mask of the Mattachine,* 164; SAC Los Angeles, report, 9 September 1953.

22. Sears, *Behind the Mask of the Mattachine,* 164; Marcus, *Making Gay History,* 30–31; C. Todd White, *Pre-Gay L.A.: A Social History of the Movement for Homosexual Rights* (Urbana: University of Illinois Press, 2009), 65–69.

23. Sears, *Behind the Mask of the Mattachine,* 164, 230–231.

24. D'Emilio, *Sexual Politics, Sexual Communities,* 87–88.

25. Paul V. Coates, "Well, Medium, and Rare," *Los Angeles Mirror*, 12 March 1953, 8; "Paul Coates, 47, Coast Columnist" *New York Times*, 18 November 1968, 47.

26. Hal Call, quoted in Marcus, *Making Gay History*, 43–44.

27. D'Emilio, *Sexual Politics, Sexual Communities*, 76–81.

28. Ibid., 79–81.

29. Using his pseudonym, Chuck Rowland reported David Finn's accusation in his article. David Freeman, "Who Is This Man?," *ONE: The Homosexual Magazine* (March 1954): 16. See also D'Emilio, *Sexual Politics, Sexual Communities*, 84–85. Although this account is drawn from Rowland's article, as will be seen, Finn *was* an FBI informer.

30. Sears, *Behind the Mask of the Mattachine*, 167; Craig M. Loftin, *Masked Voices: Gay Men and Lesbians in Cold War America* (Albany: State University of New York Press, 2012), 20–21; White, *Pre-Gay L.A.*, 28–34. On *ONE*'s provocative nature, see the following issues and their cover stories, which the FBI specifically collected: "Are 'Normals' Abnormally Interested in Sex?," *ONE: The Homosexual Magazine* (November 1953); "Are Homosexuals Reds?," *ONE: The Homosexual Magazine* (September 1953); "Homosexual Marriage?," *ONE: The Homosexual Magazine* (August 1953). The content of these specific issues was also discussed in SAC Los Angeles to Federal Bureau of Investigation Headquarters, report, 31 December 1953, FBI 100-403320-7.

31. SAC San Diego to J. Edgar Hoover, memo, 21 May 1953, FBI 100-403320-1X. In an internal memo, FBI officials refuted the claim FBI agents had conducted investigations for a West Coast airline. See SAC Los Angeles to J. Edgar Hoover, memo, 9 September 1953, FBI 100-403329-4. Although redactions in the FBI files make it impossible to confirm, it would seem the 16 March 1953 informant was Paul Coates. With such an article published in Los Angeles, it is difficult to believe FBI agents would not have interviewed him. I submitted an FOIA request for FBI records on Coates, but the bureau claimed to have none; they could very likely have been destroyed.

32. On the FBI COMINFIL Program, see the final report, *Intelligence Activities and the Rights of Americans*, Book 2, Senate Select Committee to Study Governmental Operations with Respect to Intelligence Activities, 94th Congress, 2nd sess. (Washington, DC: US Government Printing Office, 1976), 48–49; SAC Los Angeles to J. Edgar Hoover, 6 July 1953, memo, FBI 100-403320-X2.

33. Sears describes Gerard Brissette as a chemistry lab technician at UC Berkeley in *Behind the Mask of the Mattachine*, 170.

34. SAC San Francisco, report, 14 July 1953, FBI 100-403320-1.

35. Ibid. and FBI 100-45888-10; J. Edgar Hoover to SAC San Francisco, memo, 6 August 1953, FBI 100-403320-1; Special Agent (Deleted) to SAC San Francisco, memo, 29 May 1953, FBI 100-45888-8; SAC San Francisco to Navy District Intelligence Officer, letter, 8 October 1953, FBI 100-37394-8; SAC San Francisco to Commander, 12th US Coast Guard District, letter, 8 October 1953, FBI 100-37394-9.

36. Special Agent (Deleted), notes taken at time of (female) interview, 6 June 1953, FBI 100-37394-1A(1); SAC San Francisco to SAC Los Angeles, memo, 4 November 1953, FBI 100-45888-29; SAC San Francisco, report, 14 July 1953, FBI 100-403320-1 and FBI 100-45888-10; Special Agent (Deleted) to SAC San Francisco, memo, 1 June 1953, FBI 100-45888-7.

37. For David Finn's own account of meeting with FBI agents, see D'Emilio, *Sexual Politics, Sexual Communities*, 84; Sears, *Behind the Mask of the Mattachine*, 246. Don Lucas paraphrased in Hal Call's obituary. Carol Ness, "Pioneering S.F. Gay Rights Advocate Hal Call," *San Francisco Chronicle*, 22 December 2000. Given the redacted nature of FBI files, it is difficult to determine definitively all who served as FBI informers. It is clear Finn was one, and given Lucas's comments about Call it would seem they were also working with the FBI. I tried to ascertain who the female informant was, but because there were several female members of Mattachine and because there are not enough specific details in the FBI files to get around the redacted name, it is impossible at this juncture to say. Suffice it to say, the informants seem to have come from the San Francisco insurgents.

38. J. Edgar Hoover to Warren Olney III, memo, 19 August 1953, FBI 100-403320-(unreadable). See also Ellen Schrecker, *Many Are the Crimes: McCarthyism in America* (New York: Little, Brown, 1998), 291.

39. SAC Los Angeles, report, 9 September 1953, 6–12.

40. Ibid., 11–13.

41. Ibid., 13, 49. In 1954 FBI agents interviewed Chuck Rowland (David Freeman), and he admitted his former Communist Party membership. See Milton Jones to Louis Nichols, memo, 10 February 1956, FBI 100-403320-16. It appears FBI agents also stumbled upon Bob Hull when searching through the records of the Retail Merchants Credit Association, but because they were uncertain about his identity they listed information about his chemistry degree and job as a chemist on an administrative page.

42. Mattachine Society to (Deleted), letter (date deleted but ca. August 1953), reprinted in SAC Los Angeles, report, 9 September 1953, 15–16; see also 50. Administrative pages were reserved for sensitive, embarrassing, or unverified information. On the FBI use of administrative pages, see Theoharis, *FBI and American Democracy*, 110–111. Mattachine's Blood Bank Program is discussed in Jeff Winters, "Can Homosexuals Organize?," *ONE: The Homosexual Magazine* (January 1954): 4–8.

43. On the identity of Mrs. Henry Hay, see Meeker, "Behind the Mask of Respectability," 86.

44. SAC Los Angeles, report, 9 September 1953, and FBI 100-45888-24, 14–15.

45. SAC Los Angeles, report, 12 June 1943, FBI 100-211619-1.

46. Ibid.

47. SAC New York, report, 20 August 1943, FBI 100-211619-2; J. Edgar Hoover to SAC Los Angeles, confidential memo, 10 August 1943, FBI 100-211619-Not Recorded. On the view of communists (and gays) having weak characters and psychological problems, see Johnson, *Lavender Scare*, 35–36.

48. Theoharis, *FBI and American Democracy*, 53–55.

49. SAC Los Angeles, report, 25 September 1943, FBI 100-211619-4.

50. SAC Los Angeles, report, 6 November 1945, FBI 100-211619-5.

51. Ibid.; Michael J. Heale, *American Anticommunism: Combating the Enemy Within, 1830–1970* (Baltimore, MD: Johns Hopkins University Press, 1990), 130.

52. J. Edgar Hoover to SAC Los Angeles, memo, 25 October 1948, no file number but seemingly attached to FBI 100-211619-7.

53. SAC Los Angeles, report, 16 February 1949, FBI 100-211619-7.

54. J. Edgar Hoover to (Deleted), letter, 26 July 1949, FBI 100-211619-8.

55. SAC Los Angeles to J. Edgar Hoover, memo, 13 November 1950, FBI 100-211619-10.

56. FBI Report, Charles Dennison Rowland, 14 May 1948, FBI 100-355009-2; FBI Report, Charles Dennison Rowland, 9 April 1948, FBI 100-355009-3.

57. FBI Report, Rowland, 14 May 1948.

58. FBI Report, Charles Dennison Rowland, 19 February 1954, FBI 100-355009-22.

59. SAC St. Paul to J. Edgar Hoover, letter, 14 May 1948, FBI 100-355009-6; SAC St. Paul to Hoover, memo, 14 May 1948, FBI 100-355009-7; SAC St. Paul to Hoover, memo, Atten: FBI Laboratory, 14 May 1948, FBI 100-355009-8.

60. FBI Report, Robert Booth Hull, 16 July 1952, FBI 100-392963-1.

61. FBI Report, Charles Dennison Rowland, 10 June 1049, FBI 100-355009-9.

62. FBI Report, Charles Dennison Rowland, 19 July 1949, FBI 100-355009-10; SAC St. Paul to J. Edgar Hoover, letter, 1 August 1949, FBI 100-355009-11.

63. FBI Report, Charles Dennison Rowland, 10 May 1950, FBI 100-355009-15; SAC Los Angeles to J. Edgar Hoover, memo, 17 July 1952, FBI 100-355009-19 and FBI 100-392963-1; FBI Report, Hull, 16 July 1952.

64. FBI Summary Report, Charles Dennison Rowland, 19 February 1954, FBI 100-355009-15; SAC Los Angeles to J. Edgar Hoover, memo, 17 July 1952; FBI Report, Hull, 16 July 1952. It should be noted that in interviews later in life, Rowland claimed to have quit the Communist Party before moving to Los Angeles with Hull, who remained in the party. The FBI information seems credible, and it is possible Rowland might have been sensitive for having been ousted from the party and avoided talking about it in interviews. Hull committed suicide in 1962. See D'Emilio, *Sexual Politics, Sexual Communities*, 61.

65. SAC Los Angeles to Hoover, memo, 17 July 1952.

66. FBI Report, Charles Dennison Rowland, 3 September 1952, FBI 100-355009-20; J. Edgar Hoover to SAC Los Angeles, memo, 12 August 1952, FBI 100-355009-20; FBI Report, Robert Booth Hull, 29 August 1952, FBI 100-392963-3.

67. FBI Summary Report, Charles Dennison Rowland, 19 February 1954, FBI 100-355009-22; SAC Los Angeles to J. Edgar Hoover, memo, 16 June 1955, FBI 100-392963-5.

68. SAC Los Angeles, report, 9 September 1953, FBI 100-4588-24, and FBI 100-37394-4, 21–25, 48, 50; SAC New Haven, report, 6 October 1953, FBI 100-403320-5. Block's bookstore is named in White, *Pre-Gay L.A.*, 34. For Jennings's biography, see also White, *Pre-Gay L.A.*, 20–23. The Slater "sex offender" comments come from Mattachine Society, memo, 10 June 1966, FBI-33796-110. On Slater's traffic ticket problems, see also Joseph Hansen, *A Few Doors West of Hope: The Life and Times of Dauntless Don Slater* (Universal City, CA: Homosexual Information Center, 1998), 12. C. Todd White also extensively discusses Slater's background.

69. SAC Los Angeles, report, 9 September 1953; SAC Los Angeles to Colonel (Deleted) of OSI, letter, 6 October 1953, FBI 100-45888-26.

70. SAC San Francisco to J. Edgar Hoover, memo, 7 October 1953, FBI 100-403320-6; SAC Los Angeles to Hoover, memo, 31 December 1953, FBI 100-403320-7 and FBI 100-45888-34.

71. SAC Los Angeles, report, 31 December 1953, FBI 100-403320-7.

72. (Deleted) to Alan Belmont, memo, 18 March 1954, FBI 100-403320-8.

73. J. Edgar Hoover to SAC Los Angeles, memo, 7 May 1954, FBI 100-403320-11; SAC Los Angeles to Hoover, airtel, 29 April 1954, FBI 100-403320-11.

74. SAC Los Angeles to J. Edgar Hoover, memo, 23 February 1954, FBI 100-211619-12.

75. SAC Washington, DC, Field Office (hereafter WFO) to J. Edgar Hoover, memo, 13 April 1954, FBI 100-211619-14.

76. SAC WFO, report, 21 May 1954, FBI, no number.

77. SAC Los Angeles to J. Edgar Hoover, memo, 6 July 1954, FBI 100-211619-17.

78. SAC WFO to J. Edgar Hoover, memo, 9 August 1954, FBI 100-211619-18.

79. SAC Los Angeles, report, 23 February 1954, FBI 100-211619-13. See especially this document's administrative page.

80. US House of Representatives, *Hearings before the Committee on Un-American Activities, Investigation of Communist Activities in the State of California*, Part 6, 83rd Congress, 2nd sess., 20 April 1954 (Washington, DC: US Government Printing Office, 1954), 4779–4782. For more on California and anticommunism, see Michael J. Heale, "Red Scare Politics: California's Campaign against Un-American Activities, 1940–1970," *Journal of American Studies* 20 (1986): 5–32.

81. US House of Representatives, *Hearings before the Committee on Un-American Activities*, 4791; SAC San Diego to J. Edgar Hoover, memo, 26 January 1955, FBI 100-211619-(deleted, but 21). Interestingly, the FBI has redacted the San Diego SAC's reiteration of what appears, publicly, in the published HUAC committee hearings.

82. SAC Los Angeles to J. Edgar Hoover, memo, 13 April 1955, FBI 100-211619-22. The Smith Act of 28 June 1940 prohibited any individual or organization from advocating the violent overthrow of the US government or membership in an organization advocating such a goal.

83. SAC Los Angeles, report, 16 June 1955, FBI 100-211619-23.

84. SAC Los Angeles to J. Edgar Hoover, memo, 16 June 1955, FBI 100-211619-24; SAC Los Angeles to Hoover, 7 July 1955, FBI 100-211619-25.

85. US House of Representatives, *Hearings before the Committee on Un-American Activities*, 84th Congress, 1st sess., 1–2 July 1955 (Washington, DC: US Government Printing Office, 1955), 1872–1875. In later years Harry Hay refuted the accuracy of the HUAC transcripts because, he claimed, he was asked if he was a member of the Communist Party in 1954 and 1955, to which he answered "no"—because he had quit in 1950—rather than the transcript's claim that he had refused to answer. See Timmons, *Trouble with Harry Hay*, 189–190.

86. Timmons, *Trouble with Harry Hay*, 189.

87. SAC Los Angeles to J. Edgar Hoover, memo, 11 August 1955, FBI 100-211619-26.

88. SAC Los Angeles to J. Edgar Hoover, memo, 28 February 1956, FBI 100-211619-27.

89. Ibid.; SAC Los Angeles, report, 23 February 1954, FBI 100-211619-13.

90. J. Edgar Hoover to SAC Los Angeles, memo, 7 May 1954, FBI 100-403320-11; SAC Los Angeles to J. Edgar Hoover, airtel, 29 April 1954, FBI 100-403320-11.

91. Federal Bureau of Investigation, memo, Confidential File, Mattachine Society, 8 May 1954, FBI 100-45888-61; Stephen Tropiano, *The Prime-Time Closet: A History of Gays and Lesbians on TV* (New York: Applause Theater and Cinema Books, 2002), 3–4. Tropiano notes that as late as the 1990s, White still did not want to reveal his true identity, but he does describe him as having had a successful career in public relations (318n13). James Sears describes Mattachine member Dale Olsen in 1954 as being responsible "for the mounting Mattachine correspondence" and as the later "public relations agent in Los Angeles" of actor Rock Hudson. Sears, *Behind the Mask of Mattachine*, 312, 314. An FBI document describing the 1954 Mattachine convention notes Olsen was elected "secretary for the Board of Directors, for recording and correspondence." Federal Bureau of Investigation, memo, Mattachine Society, 27 May 1954, FBI 100-45888-62. Another memo of 1956 describes Olsen as "secretary" of Mattachine. Special Agent (Deleted) to SAC Los Angeles, memo, 29 June 1956, FBI 100-45888-101. Olsen would seem to be the prime candidate for Curtis White.

92. David L. Freeman, "How Much Do We Know about the Homosexual Male?," *ONE: The Homosexual Magazine* (November 1955): 4–6. Issues of *ONE* can be found at the ONE Institute and Archives in Los Angeles, California.

93. Milton Jones to Louis Nichols, memo, 26 January 1956, FBI 100-403320-14.

94. J. Edgar Hoover to SAC Los Angeles, airtel, 27 January 1956, FBI 100-403320-15.

95. SAC Los Angeles to J. Edgar Hoover, teletype, 2 February 1956, FBI 100-403320-Not Recorded; SAC Los Angeles to Hoover, airtel, 2 February 1956, FBI 100-403320-18. On William Lambert/W. Dorr Legg's personality, see White, *Pre-Gay L.A.*, 30.

96. Milton Jones to Louis Nichols, memo, 7 February 1956, FBI 100-403320-15; Jones to Nichols, memo, 6 March 1956, FBI 100-403320-20.

97. Jones to Nichols, memo, 7 February 1956.

98. J. Edgar Hoover to SAC Los Angeles, memo, 15 February 1956, FBI 100-403320-14; Milton Jones to Louis Nichols, memo, 10 February 1956.

99. Ralph Roach to Alan Belmont, memo, 17 February 1956, FBI 100-403320-13; SAC Los Angeles to J. Edgar Hoover, memo, 2 March 1956, FBI 100-403320-21; Sears, *Behind the Mask of the Mattachine*, 454–455; *ONE: The Homosexual Magazine* (October 1954); Joyce Murdoch and Deb Price, *Courting Justice: Gay Men and Lesbians v. the Supreme Court* (New York: BasicBooks, 2001), 32–33; Rodger Streitmatter, *Unspeakable: The Rise of the Gay and Lesbian Press in America* (Boston: Faber and Faber, 1995), 33.

100. Eric Julber, Petition for Writ of Certiorari, US Supreme Court, *ONE, Inc. v. Olesen*, 355 US 371.

101. Milton Jones to Louis Nichols, memo, 6 March 1956, FBI 100-403320-20.

102. J. Edgar Hoover to Warren Olney III, memo, 12 March 1956, FBI 100-403320-21. They planned to go to Eric Julber because W. Dorr Legg had directed the FBI agents to *ONE*'s lawyer when he was interviewed.

103. SAC Los Angeles to Hoover, memo, 2 March 1956; Los Angeles Field Office, report, Eric Julber, 2 March 1956, FBI 100-40332-Not Recorded; for Julber's view on others questioning his own sexuality, see Murdoch and Price, *Courting Justice*, 29–30.

104. SAC Los Angeles to J. Edgar Hoover, memo, 9 March 1956, FBI 100-403320-22. See also the less redacted duplicate of this memo in file FBI 100-45888-95. The Los

Angeles Field Office had obtained all issues of *ONE* by March 1956. See SAC Los Angeles to Hoover, memo, 14 March 1956, FBI 100-403320-23. On the ownership of Abbey Lithographers, see White, *Pre-Gay L.A.*, 33, 37, 38. For further details about the FBI and antiobscenity work, see Douglas M. Charles, *The FBI's Obscene File: J. Edgar Hoover and the Bureau's Crusade against Smut* (Lawrence: University Press of Kansas, 2012). Jennings's brother-in-law, whose name we do not presently know, if indeed the informant, did not necessarily inform on the activities of a family member out of spite. It is possible he believed he was assuring FBI agents the magazine with which his brother-in-law was involved, and that he printed, was not illegal.

105. For the "sarcastic" reference, see Jones to Nichols, memo, 10 February 1956.

106. SAC Los Angeles to J. Edgar Hoover, memo, 2 March 1956; SAC Los Angeles to Hoover, memo, 9 March 1956, FBI 100-403320-22.

107. SAC Los Angeles to Hoover, memo, 9 March 1956. It is not clear if this was Reyes's ceramics shop or not.

108. SAC Los Angeles to Hoover, memo, 9 March 1956; SAC Detroit to SAC Los Angeles, airtel, 26 March 1956, FBI 100-403320-25; J. Edgar Hoover to SAC Los Angeles, memo, 22 March 1956, FBI 100-403320-24; SAC Detroit to Hoover, 28 March 1956, memo, FBI 100-403320-25; SAC Los Angeles to Hoover, memo, 30 March 1956, FBI 100-403320-26; SAC Portland to Hoover, memo, 2 April 1956, FBI 100-403320-27; SAC Detroit to Hoover, memo, 3 April 1956, FBI 100-403320-28.

109. On the use of obscenity in targeting gays within the context of defined gender roles on the West Coast, see also Whitney Strub, "The Clearly Obscene and the Queerly Obscene: Heteronormativity and Obscenity in Cold War Los Angeles," *American Quarterly* 60, no. 2 (June 2008): 373–398.

110. SAC New York to J. Edgar Hoover, memo, 11 April 1956, FBI 100-403320-30.

111. J. Edgar Hoover to SAC Los Angeles, memo, 31 July 1956, FBI 100-403320-36; Senator Gordon Allott to Louis Nichols, letter, 20 July 1956, FBI 100-403320-36; SAC Los Angeles to Hoover, memo, 23 August 1956, FBI 100-403320-37. On the start of the *Mattachine Review*, see Nan Alamilla Boyd, *Wide Open Town: A History of Queer San Francisco* (Berkeley: University of California Press, 2003), 167–168, 171–172.

112. For an accounting of the internal leadership troubles at *ONE*, see White, *Pre-Gay L.A.*, 41–73.

113. SAC Los Angeles to J. Edgar Hoover, airtel, 15 March 1956, FBI 100-403320-24; Hoover to SAC Los Angeles, memo, 22 March 1956, FBI 100-403320-31.

114. SAC Los Angeles to J. Edgar Hoover, memo, 5 April 1956, FBI 100-211619-28; Hoover to SAC Los Angeles, memo, 16 March 1956, FBI 100-211619-no serial.

115. See Charles, *FBI's Obscene File*.

116. SAC Los Angeles, report, 25 June 1956, FBI 100-211619-29.

117. SAC Los Angeles, report, 19 June 1957, FBI 100-211619-30; SAC Los Angeles, report, 9 July 1958, FBI 100-211619-31; SAC Los Angeles to J. Edgar Hoover, memo, 9 July 1958, FBI 100-211619-32; cover letter with attached memo on Hay, 9 July 1958, FBI 100-211619-32; SAC Los Angeles, report, 26 June 1959, FBI 100-211619-33; SAC Los Angeles, report, 27 June 1960, FBI 100-211619-34; SAC Los Angeles, report, 15 June 1961, FBI 100-211619-35.

118. SAC Los Angeles to J. Edgar Hoover, memo, 15 June 1961, FBI 100-211619-36.

119. SAC Los Angeles to J. Edgar Hoover, memo, 22 August 1961, FBI 100-211619-38. On Harry Hay's knowledge of the FBI's interest, see Timmons, *Trouble with Harry Hay*, 131.

120. Warren Olney III to J. Edgar Hoover, memo, 14 May 1956, FBI 100-403320-32; Hoover to SAC Los Angeles, memo, 22 May 1956, FBI 100-403320-32; Hoover to SAC Los Angeles, memo, 15 June 1956, FBI 100-403320-Not Recorded; Special Agent (Deleted) to SAC San Francisco, memo, 2 December 1956, FBI 94-843-7.

121. Quoted in Marcia Gallo, *Different Daughters: A History of the Daughters of Bilitis and the Rise of the Lesbian Rights Movement* (New York: Carroll and Graf, 2006), 1.

122. D'Emilio, *Sexual Politics, Sexual Communities*, 101–102.

123. Ibid., 102; Gallo, *Different Daughters*, 2–3.

124. Gallo, *Different Daughters*, 3–5.

125. Ibid., 5–8.

126. Ibid., 8–13; D'Emilio, *Sexual Politics, Sexual Communities*, 103. For an analysis of the Daughters of Bilitis in the context of women's rights, see Lyn Diane Franks, "Torchbearers and Front Runners: The Daughters of Bilitis and Women's Rights" (MA thesis, Murray State University, 2011).

127. SAC San Francisco to SAC Los Angeles, memo, 22 August 1956, FBI 100-45888-104; SAC San Francisco to SAC Los Angeles, memo, 8 November 1956, FBI 100-37394-34; *The Ladder* 1, no. 1 (October 1956).

128. SAC San Francisco to SAC New York, memo, 8 November 1956, FBI 100-37394-35; SAC Los Angeles to J. Edgar Hoover, memo, 23 August 1956, FBI (number illegible)-93.

129. Special Agent (Deleted) to SAC San Francisco, memo, 26 February 1957, FBI 100-373394-37. On the differences between Mattachine and Daughters of Bilitis see Boyd, *Wide Open Town*, 177–179.

130. SAC Los Angeles to J. Edgar Hoover, memo, 18 April 1957, FBI 100-37394-38 (see also duplicate copy in GLBT Historical Society); Harry W. Beckett, general manager Hotel Clark, to Dorothy Martin, letter, 21 January 1957, in Daughters of Bilitis (National Organization), 1956–1984, Subseries: *The Ladder* Files, 1956–1984, Correspondence, 1956–1958, CD, 1956–1958, Phyllis Lyon and Del Martin Papers, Gay, Lesbian, Bisexual, and Transgender Historical Society; "Daughters Hold Brunch in LA, Plans for Chapter Underway," *The Ladder* 1, no. 5 (February 1957): 11; Program of ONE Institute, *Los Angeles Mattachine Newsletter* (February 1957), FBI 100-45888-108; Gallo, *Different Daughters*, xix.

131. Special Agent (Deleted) to SAC San Francisco, memo, 6 August 1959, FBI 94-843-25.

132. Ibid.

133. Special Agent (Deleted) to SAC San Francisco, memo, 7 August 1959, FBI 94-843-26. Only five bars—the Paper Doll, 57 Club, Black Cat, Handlebar, and Spur Club—were listed on this document; the rest of the document had been withheld by the FBI.

134. Gallo, *Different Daughters*, 34–35, 129–130.

135. SAC Los Angeles to J. Edgar Hoover, memo, 19 April 1961, FBI 100-403320-86.

136. Ibid.

137. Appeals court, quoted in Murdoch and Price, *Courting Justice*, 33.

138. Supreme Court information comes from Murdoch and Price, *Courting Justice*, 41–47; "Homosexual Mag Not Obscene," *Los Angeles Daily News*, 20 January 1958. On *Roth*, see Whitney Strub, *Obscenity Rules: Roth v. United States and the Long Struggle over Sexual Expression* (Lawrence: University Press of Kansas, 2013).

6. "Something Uniquely Nasty"

1. John D'Emilio, *Sexual Politics, Sexual Communities: The Making of a Homosexual Minority in the United States, 1940–1970*, 2nd ed. (Chicago: University of Chicago Press, 1998), 82.

2. Ibid., 115. On Chicago, see John D. Poling, "Standing Up for Gay Rights," *Chicago History* 33 (Spring 2005): 4–17.

3. D'Emilio, *Sexual Politics, Sexual Communities*, 32, 89–90; James T. Sears, *Behind the Mask of the Mattachine: The Hal Call Chronicles and the Early Movement for Homosexual Emancipation* (Binghampton, NY: Harrington Park, 2006), 356, 373n8.

4. Donald Webster Cory, *The Homosexual in America: A Subjective Approach* (New York: Greenberg, 1951), 6.

5. Ibid., 183. Emphasis in original. For a recent assessment of *The Homosexual in America*, see Rick Valelly, "The Conflicted Gay Pioneer," *American Prospect* online, 8 October 2013.

6. See Martin Duberman, "Dr. Sagarin and Mr. Cory: The 'Father' of the Homophile Movement," *Harvard Gay and Lesbian Review* (Fall 1997): 7–14; Cory, *The Homosexual in America*, 106–107; Edward Sagarin, "Structure and Ideology in an Association of Deviants," (PhD diss., New York University, 1966), 370; Edward Sagarin, *Odd Man In: Societies of Deviants in America* (Chicago: Quadrangle, 1969), 31, 54–55, 108–109, 244–245.

7. Edward Sagarin to Frank Kameny, letter, 13 June 1967, box 9, folder 2, Frank Kameny Papers, Library of Congress; Kameny to Sagarin, letter, 3 February 1967, box 9, folder 2, Frank Kameny Papers, Library of Congress.

8. Edward Sagarin to Frank Kameny, page two of letter (as first page is missing), no date but ca. 1968, box 9, folder 2, Frank Kameny Papers, Library of Congress.

9. FBI memo, 14 March 1952, FBI 100-109371-2; SAC Washington, DC, Field Office (WFO) to J. Edgar Hoover, secret memo, 19 March 1952, FBI 100-109371-1.

10. SAC WFO to Hoover, secret memo, 19 March 1952.

11. Ibid.

12. Ibid.

13. Ibid.

14. Sagarin, "Structure and Ideology in an Association of Deviants," 59–61.

15. SAC WFO to Hoover, secret memo, 19 March 1952.

16. Sagarin, "Structure and Ideology in an Association of Deviants," 73–74.

17. Ibid., 79.

18. Alfred Gross to Executive Committee of the Foundation, Report on Meeting of Homosexual Group, 14 April 1952, FBI 100-109371-1a; Special Agent Thomas Minoque, letter and report, June 1952, FBI 100-109371-3.

19. Gross to Executive Committee, Report on Meeting of Homosexual Group, 14 April 1952.

20. Ibid.

21. On Viereck, see Douglas M. Charles, *J. Edgar Hoover and the Anti-interventionists: FBI Political Surveillance and the Rise of the Domestic Security State, 1929–1945* (Columbus: Ohio State University Press, 2007), 92–94.

22. Gross to Executive Committee, Report on Meeting of Homosexual Group, 14 April 1952.

23. Minoque, letter and report, June 1952.

24. SAC New York to J. Edgar Hoover, memo, ATTN: Asst. Dir. L. B. Nichols, 27 May 1953, FBI 100-109371-5.

25. Cory, *The Homosexual in America*, xvi–xvii.

26. D'Emilio, *Sexual Politics, Sexual Communities*, 89–90; Sears, *Behind the Mask of the Mattachine*, 356–357.

27. On the New York Mattachine's activities, see Sears, *Behind the Mask of the Mattachine*, 393–394.

28. SAC New York to J. Edgar Hoover, letter, 11 April 1956, FBI 100-132065-1.

29. SAC Los Angeles to J. Edgar Hoover, memo, 23 August 1956, FBI 100-132065-2.

30. SAC San Francisco to SAC New York, memo, 8 November 1956, FBI 100-132065-5; (Deleted but from New York Mattachine) to Mr. Goodie, letter, 12 September 1956, FBI 100-132065-5.

31. The name is redacted in FBI files, but it was possibly FBI Associate Director Clyde Tolson given that his initials appear on the side of the document.

32. ASAC E. H. Winterrowd to SAC New York, memo, 8 June 1959, FBI 100-132065-11; *Nation* (30 May 1959): 68; Supervisor (Deleted) to SAC New York, memo, 11 June 1959, FBI 100-132065-16.

33. Special Agent (Deleted) to SAC New York, memo and informant report, dated 11 June 1959 (but 22 June 1959), FBI 100-132065-12.

34. SAC New York to J. Edgar Hoover, airtel, 11 June 1959, FBI 100-132065-13.

35. Ibid.; Special Agent (Deleted) to SAC New York, memo, 19 June 1959, FBI 100-132065-14; Supervisor (Deleted) to SAC New York, memo, 2 July 1959, FBI 100-132065-15; Chief, Transit Police Department, Special Report Regarding June 10 Meeting of the Mattachine Society at Freedom Hall, 11 June 1959, FBI 100-132065-15.

36. B. D. Huggins to Mr. Reitman, letter and "personal and confidential" history of B. D. Huggins, 18 September 1964, folder 16, box 1063, American Civil Liberties Union (ACLU) Archives, Seeley G. Mudd Manuscript Library, Princeton University, Princeton, NJ. Used by permission of the Princeton University Library.

37. William Gilbert was something of an aficionado when it came to hypnosis. He wrote a foreword to Myron Teitelbaum, *Hypnosis Induction Technics*, 5th ed. (Springfield, IL: Charles C. Thomas, 1980).

38. Huggins to Reitman, letter and "personal and confidential" history.

39. SAC St. Louis to J. Edgar Hoover, memo, 22 April 1957, FBI 100-403320-49.

40. Ibid.

41. SAC San Francisco to SAC New York, Mattachine New York Area Council *Newsletter*, Issue 4 (August–September 1954) attached to memo, 8 November 1956, FBI 100-132065-5.

42. David K. Johnson, *The Lavender Scare: The Cold War Persecution of Gays and Lesbians in the Federal Government* (Chicago: University of Chicago Press, 2004), 172–173.

43. Ibid., 173; Special Agent (Deleted) to SAC WFO, memo, 19 June 1958, FBI 100-33796-17; FBI, "The Mattachine Society, Inc., Information Concerning (Internal Security)," memo, 12 April 1957, FBI 100-132065-6. Few documents from Huggins's group have survived, and from the two listed in endnote 44, counting backward, indicates the start of the newsletter occurred in July. On the lack of documents, see Johnson, *Lavender Scare*, 254n48.

44. J. Edgar Hoover to SAC WFO, memo, 4 March 1957, FBI 100-45888-109; Mattachine, Washington, DC, Area Council, *Newsletter* 2, no. 1 (January 1957); Mattachine, Washington, DC, Area Council, *Newsletter* 1, no. 6 (December 1956).

45. Hoover to SAC WFO, memo, 4 March 1957.

46. SAC WFO to SAC St. Louis, memo, 1 April 1957, FBI 100-33796-3; SAC WFO to J. Edgar Hoover, memo, 2 April 1957, FBI 100-33796-4.

47. FBI, "Mattachine Society, Inc., Information," 12 April 1957; Huggins to Reitman, letter and "personal and confidential" history; SAC WFO to J. Edgar Hoover, memo, 1 May 1957, FBI 100-33796-8.

48. FBI, "Mattachine Society, Inc., Information," 12 April 1957. On conscientious objectors to the Second World War, see Richard Polenberg, *War and Society: The United States, 1941–1945* (Westport, CT: Greenwood, 1972), 54–58.

49. Huggins to Reitman, letter and "personal and confidential" history, 3–4.

50. FBI, "Mattachine Society, Inc., Information," 12 April 1957; SAC St. Louis to Hoover, memo, 22 April 1957.

51. FBI, "Mattachine Society, Inc., Information," 12 April 1957.

52. J. Edgar Hoover to SAC WFO, memo, 16 April 1957, FBI 100-132065-6.

53. SAC WFO to Hoover, memo, 22 May 1957, FBI 100-33796-10; SAC Laughlin to Postmaster Roy M. North, letter, 4 June 1957, FBI 100-33796-11.

54. SAC WFO to J. Edgar Hoover, memo, 27 June 1957, FBI 100-33796-12; SAC WFO to Hoover, memo, 16 July 1957, FBI 100-33796-13.

55. Special Agent (Deleted) to SAC WFO, memo, 19 June 1958, FBI 100-33796-17.

56. SAC WFO to J. Edgar Hoover, memo, 24 July 1958, FBI 100-33796-18; Hoover to SAC WFO, memo, 1 August 1958, FBI 100-33796-19.

57. SAC WFO to Hoover, memo, 14 August 1958, FBI 100-33796-20.

58. Huggins to Reitman, letter and "personal and confidential" history, 6; Clarence Kelley to B. D. Huggins, FBI note on letter, 17 March 1975, FBI 62-115525-5.

59. B. D. Huggins to Patrick Gray, letter, 24 February 1973, FBI 62-115525-1.

60. Ibid.

61. FBI, reference slip, 27 February 1973, in FBI 62-115525.

62. B. D. Huggins to Clarence Kelley, letters, 29 July 1974, 13 March 1975, 19 February 1975, FBI 62-115525; Kelley to Huggins, letters, 7 August 1974, 11 March 1975, 17 March 1975, FBI 62-115525.

63. Kelley to Huggins, FBI note on letter, 17 March 1975.

64. Johnson, *Lavender Scare*, 173–174.

65. D'Emilio, *Sexual Politics, Sexual Communities*, 123.

66. SAC WFO to J. Edgar Hoover, memo, 8 August 1961, FBI 100-45888-131.

67. Franklin Edward Kameny, An Informal, Condensed Autobiography, attached to letter, Kameny to Commanding Officer, Army Map Service, 14 January 1958, Civil Service Personnel Folder, National Personnel Records Center, Valmeyer, Illinois (hereafter Kameny Civil Service Records). I would like to thank my friend Dr. Marek Kukula, the public astronomer at the Royal Observatory in Greenwich, for explaining to me Kameny's thesis.

68. Kay Tobin and Randy Wicker, *The Gay Crusaders: In-Depth Interviews with 15 Homosexuals—Men and Women Who Are Shaping America's Newest Sexual Revolution* (New York: Paperback Library, 1972), 91–92; Franklin Edward Kameny, Application for Federal Employment, US Civil Service Commission, 23 June 1957, in Kameny Civil Service Records.

69. Kameny, Informal, Condensed Autobiography.

70. San Francisco Police Department, Bureau of Identification, Criminal Record of Franklin E. Kameny, Kameny Civil Service Records; Kameny, Statement Regarding Arrest, 2 November 1958, box 44, folder 7, Frank Kameny Papers, Library of Congress; Kameny, Summary of Relevant Facts Regarding My Case against the Government, no date, box 44, folder 7, Frank Kameny Papers, Library of Congress.

71. Kameny to Commanding Officer, Army Map Service, 14 January 1958, letter and attachments (appeal, character statements, autobiography), Kameny Civil Service Records; Probation Officer's Report Recommending Dismissal Pursuant to Sec. 1203.4, 1 March 1957, Kameny Civil Service Records; David Carter, *Stonewall: The Riots That Sparked the Gay Revolution* (New York: St. Martin's, 2004), 21; Tobin and Wicker, *Gay Crusaders*, 91–92.

72. Kameny, Application for Federal Employment.

73. D. L. Mills, Request for Personnel Action, 20 December 1957, Kameny Civil Service Records; Johnson, *Lavender Scare*, 180, 181.

74. Robert F. Jacobs to Frank Kameny, memo, travel orders, 6 September 1957, Kameny Civil Service Records; B. D. Hull to Frank Kameny, letter, 15 October 1957, Kameny Civil Service Records. Hull letter also in box 43, folder 12, Frank Kameny Papers, Library of Congress. Kameny interview in Eric Marcus, *Making Gay History: The Half-Century Fight for Lesbian and Gay Equal Rights* (New York: HarperCollins, 2002), 80.

75. Hull to Kameny, letter, 10 December 1957; Johnson, *Lavender Scare*, 179–180. Johnson writes in a definitive manner that the FBI had forwarded the information, yet his endnote for this does not document a definitive source other than Kameny, who could only have been speculating. There is no indication of FBI involvement in Civil Service Commission records, and the FBI claims to have no file on Kameny. The Sex Deviates Program left it to the military or agency with jurisdiction to investigate its employees. It remains unclear where the US Army civilian personnel fell under this policy. The FBI may or may not have played a role in Kameny's firing.

76. B. D. Hull, memorandum for the record, 23 December 1957, Kameny Civil Service Records.

77. Kameny to Commanding Officer, Army Map Service, letter and attachments, 14 January 1958; Frank Kameny to Commanding Officer, Army Map Service, 20 December 1957, box 43, folder 12, Frank Kameny Papers, Library of Congress; Kameny to Mattachine New York, 5 May 1960, box 43, folder 12, Frank Kameny Papers, Library of Congress; Frank Kameny to *ONE* magazine, 27 August 1960, box 43, folder 12, Frank Kameny Papers, Library of Congress.

78. Frank Kameny to Benjamin Karpman, note and draft statement, no date, box 44, folder 4, Frank Kameny Papers, Library of Congress; Kameny to Karpman, second note and revised draft statement, no date, box 44, folder 4, Frank Kameny Papers, Library of Congress. On Karpman, see Genny Beemyn, *A Queer Capital: A History of Gay Life in Washington, D.C.* (New York: Routledge, 2014), 136–137.

79. Benjamin Karpman to Joseph Fanelli, letter, 27 January 1958, Kameny Civil Service Records.

80. Frank Kameny to Benjamin Karpman, letter, no date, box 44, folder 4, Frank Kameny Papers, Library of Congress.

81. Colonel F. O. Diercks to Frank Kameny, letter, 12 March 1958, Kameny Civil Service Records. See also *Kameny v. Brucker et al.*, 282f.2d 823 (1960). If, in fact, it was the FBI all along that had forwarded Kameny's arrest record to the Civil Service Commission, then it would not have mattered if he did not list his arrest. It is difficult to reconstruct the FBI role here.

82. Johnson, *Lavender Scare*, 180.

83. Frank Kameny to Harris Ellsworth, US Civil Service Commission, letter, 3 January 1959, box 44, folder 3, Frank Kameny Papers, Library of Congress.

84. O. Glenn Stahl to John W. Steele, memo re: Homosexuality and Government Employment, 17 November 1964, Freedom of Information Act (FOIA) request document. Thanks to *New York Times* reporter Matt Apuzzo and Charles Francis for sharing this document

85. *Kameny v. Brucker et al.*, 282f.2d 823 (1960).

86. Kameny, quoted in Marcus, *Making Gay History*, 80; *Kameny v. Brucker et al.*, 365 US 843. Kameny's petition for certiorari can be found in box 44, folder 8, Frank Kameny Papers, Library of Congress.

87. Kameny, quoted in Marcus, *Making Gay History*, 80.

88. Kameny, quoted in D'Emilio, *Sexual Politics, Sexual Communities*, 151.

89. J. Louis Campbell, *Jack Nichols, Gay Pioneer* (New York: Harrington Park, 2007), xvi.

90. D'Emilio, *Sexual Politics, Sexual Communities*, 152; Campbell, *Jack Nichols*, 44.

91. Albert J. de Dion to Frank Kameny, letter, 25 July 1961, box 78, folder 6, Frank Kameny Papers, Library of Congress; de Dion to friend, (mass) letter, 25 July 1961, box 78, folder 6, Frank Kameny Papers, Library of Congress; de Dion to Kameny, letter, 4 October 1961, box 78, folder 6, Frank Kameny Papers, Library of Congress; Marcus, *Making Gay History*, 81–82.

92. Ibid., 82; Johnson, *Lavender Scare*, 183.

93. Campbell, *Jack Nichols*, 70–72.

94. Clerk (name deleted) to SAC WFO, memo, 27 May 1962, FBI 100-33796-24.

95. Special Agent (Deleted) to SAC WFO, memo, 5 June 1962, FBI 100-33796-25.

96. Ibid.

97. Ibid.

98. Warren D. Adkins (pseudonym of Jack Nichols) to Warren Scarberry, letter, 26 May 1965, box 83, folder 2, Frank Kameny Papers, Library of Congress.

99. D'Emilio, *Sexual Politics, Sexual Communities*, 152–153.

100. Mattachine Society of Washington, DC, news release, 28 August 1962, FBI 100-33796-1A.

101. Form FD-340a, list of items filed in Mattachine Society of Washington, DC, File over 1962–1963, FBI 100-33796-1A; FBI memo, Mattachine Society of Washington, DC, 20 August 1962, FBI 100-33796-30; SAC WFO to J. Edgar Hoover, airtel, 20 August 962, FBI 100-33796-31; Special Agent (Deleted) to SAC WFO, memo, 21 August 1962, FBI 100-33796-32.

102. Bruce Schuyler to J. Edgar Hoover, letter, 16 February 1963, FBI 100-403320-93X, Dan Siminoski Collection, ONE Institute and Archive, Los Angeles; D. C. Morrell to Cartha DeLoach, memo, 14 March 1963, FBI 100-403320-93-X3, Dan Siminoski Collection, ONE Institute and Archive, Los Angeles.

103. FBI, "Mattachine Society of Washington [DC]," memo, 20 August 1962, FBI 100-33796-30; SAC WFO to J. Edgar Hoover, airtel, 20 August 1962, FBI 100-33796-31.

104. Milton Jones to Cartha DeLoach, memo, 20 July 1964, FBI 100-403320-109. This and the following particular FBI document about this episode were not released to me in my FOIA request. In fact, the FBI claims to have no file on Kameny at all, but these documents can be found in a different FOIA release in box 47, folder 3, Frank Kameny Papers, Library of Congress.

105. Marcus, *Making Gay History*, 91; Milton Jones to Cartha DeLoach, memo, 7 August 1964, FBI 100-403320-110. In Marcus's interview with him, Kameny identified this person as an agent; he was a headquarters official, and he said his name was John A. O'Beirne, but it was actually John W. O'Beirne. See O'Beirne's obituary in the *New York Times*, 9 September 1990.

106. Marcus, *Making Gay History*, 91–92; memo, Jones to DeLoach, 7 August 1964.

107. Jones to DeLoach, memo, 7 August 1964.

108. Marcus, *Making Gay History*, 92; Gail Johnson to John O'Beirne, letter, 1 October 1964, FBI 100-403320-111.

109. Milton Jones to Cartha DeLoach, memo, 9 October 1964, FBI 100-403320-111.

110. Frank Kameny to Robert F. Kennedy, letter, 28 June 1962, attached to memo, J. Edgar Hoover to Robert F. Kennedy, 9 July 1962, FBI 100-33796-29.

111. Ibid.

112. D. C. Morrell to Cartha DeLoach, memo, 9 July 1962, FBI 100-403320-88X2, Dan Siminoski Collection, ONE Institute and Archive, Los Angeles. This particular memo was not released to me in my FOIA request.

113. Hoover to Kennedy, memo, 9 July 1962, and FBI 100-403320-88X2.

114. SAC WFO to J. Edgar Hoover, airtel, 10 June 1963, FBI 100-33796-38; Bruce Schuyler to J. Edgar Hoover, letter, 4 June 1963, FBI 100-403320-Not Recorded.

115. Special Agent (Deleted) to SAC WFO, memo, 11 July 1963, FBI 100-33796-51; "Homosexual's Civil Rights Discussed in Lecture Here," *Washington Afro American*, 15 June 1963, 27, FBI 100-33796-42.

116. Ibid.; "Marchers in Capital Hear Washington Will Get Fair Housing Law," *New York Times*, 15 June 1963. On Mattachine Society of Washington (MSW) members marching in other events, see Campbell, *Jack Nichols*, 74.

117. SAC WFO to Hoover, airtel, 10 June 1963; Special Agent (Deleted) to SAC WFO, memo, 7 June 1963, FBI 100-33796-41.

118. Special Agent (Deleted) to SAC WFO, memo, 30 August 1963, FBI-100-33796-52; SAC WFO to J. Edgar Hoover, airtel, 3 September 1963, FBI 100-33796-54.

119. SAC WFO to J. Edgar Hoover, airtel, 5 September 1963, FBI 100-33796-56; FBI, memo, Proposed Demonstration at White House by Homosexuals in October 1963, 5 September 1963, FBI 100-33796-55 and FBI 100-132065-18; FBI, memo, Proposed Demonstration at White House by Homosexuals on October 25, 1963, 22 October 1963, FBI 100-33796-60; SAC New York to J. Edgar Hoover, memo, 22 October 1963, FBI 100-33796-64; Special Agent (Deleted) to SAC New York, memo, 30 October 1963, FBI 100-132065-22.

120. Stanley Tracy to Edward Kemper, letter and enclosure, 15 December 1963, FBI 100-403320-108; Milton Jones to Cartha DeLoach, memo, 19 December 1963, FBI 100-403320-110.

121. Jones to DeLoach, memo, 19 December 1963.

122. Milton Jones to Cartha DeLoach, memo, 23 December 1963, FBI 100-403320-106.

123. SAC WFO to J. Edgar Hoover, memo, 9 April 1964, FBI 100-33796-68.

124. Special Agent (Deleted) to SAC WFO, memo, 15 May 1964, FBI 100-33796-69.

125. D'Emilio, *Sexual Politics, Sexual Communities*, 161; Marc Stein, *City of Sisterly and Brotherly Loves: Lesbian and Gay Philadelphia, 1945–1972* (Chicago: University of Chicago Press, 2000), 200–201.

126. SAC WFO to J. Edgar Hoover, memo and attached pamphlets, 29 October 1964, FBI 100-33796-70 and FBI 100-403320-86.

127. Ibid., "How to Handle a Federal Interrogation" (pamphlet).

128. Ibid., "If You Are Arrested" (pamphlet).

129. J. Edgar Hoover to LEGAT Ottawa, memo, 16 September 1965, FBI 163-12514-1, Dan Siminoski Collection, ONE Institute and Archive, Los Angeles (this document was also filed in the FBI Sex Deviates File); Lt. Col. Donald Synnott to Special Agent (Deleted), letter, 7 September 1965, FBI 163-12514-163, Dan Siminoski Collection, ONE Institute and Archive, Los Angeles.

130. Marcia Gallo, *Different Daughters: The History of the Daughters of Bilitis and the Rise of the Lesbian Rights Movement* (New York: Carroll and Graf, 2006), 98.

131. SAC Cleveland to J. Edgar Hoover, memo, 22 April 1964, FBI 31-90277-1.

132. J. Edgar Hoover to SAC New York, memo, 30 April 1964, FBI 31-90277-2. On the FBI White Slave Trafficking Act file classification and the types of investigations it involved, see Gerald K. Haines and David A. Langbart, *Unlocking the Files of the FBI: A*

Guide to Its Records and Classification System (Wilmington, DE: Scholarly Resources, 1993), 29.

133. SAC New York to J. Edgar Hoover, memo, 19 June 1964, FBI 31-90277-4; "Homosexual Women Hear Psychologists," *New York Times*, 21 June 1964, 54. There are two differently redacted copies of this FBI memo. The copy at the ONE Institute and Archive in Los Angeles does not reveal Willer's name or the date of her contacting the Hotel New Yorker. The copy held by the GLBT Historical Society, however, reveals Willer's name and the date of her initial contact with the hotel. The ONE Institute copy, alternatively, reveals Ev Howe's name, and the GLBT Historical Society one does not. Such is FBI research.

134. SAC New York to Hoover, memo, 19 June 1964. For the interpretation that FBI agents "visited the Hotel New Yorker to urge them not to rent space to DOB," see Gallo, *Different Daughters*, xx.

135. J. J. Dunn to D. J. Brennan, memo, 22 January 1965, FBI 100-403320-119. This and the following FBI documents about this article were not released to me through my FOIA request but can be found in the FOIA release in Frank Kameny Papers, box 47, folder 3. Stein, *City of Sisterly and Brotherly Loves*, 231–240.

136. Milton Jones to Cartha DeLoach, memo, 10 February 1965, FBI 100-403320-120. On Matt Cvetic, see Daniel J. Leab, *I Was a Communist for the FBI: The Unhappy Life and Times of Matt Cvetic* (University Park: Pennsylvania State University Press, 2000).

137. D'Emilio, *Sexual Politics, Sexual Communities*, 164–165; "Cuban Government Is Alarmed by Increase in Homosexuality," *New York Times*, 16 April 1965, 2.

138. Campbell, *Jack Nichols*, 94–95.

139. D'Emilio, *Sexual Politics, Sexual Communities*, 165.

140. Jack Nichols to Dan Siminoski, letter, 7 January 1985, Dan Siminoski Collection, ONE Institute and Archive, Los Angeles, CA; Campbell, *Jack Nichols*, 94–95.

141. J. B. Adam to Assistant Director Callahan, memo, 14 February 1966, FBI 100-403320-138. A heavily redacted copy of this FOIA document can be found in folder 17, box 1, Jack Nichols Collection, Special Collections Library, Pennsylvania State University, University Park, PA. The copy I obtained via the FOIA is significantly less redacted.

142. Ibid.

143. Ibid.

144. Ibid.

145. Ibid.

146. Ibid.

147. Ibid.

148. Ibid.

149. "Homosexuals Stage Protest in Capital," *New York Times*, 30 May 1965, 42; D'Emilio, *Sexual Politics, Sexual Communities*, 165.

150. Special Agent (Deleted) to SAC WFO, memo, 24 August 1965, FBI 100-33796-76.

151. Campbell, *Jack Nichols*, 91, 97.

152. FBI, memo, "Picketing of the State Department," 26 August 1965, FBI 100-33796-78; SAC WFO to J. Edgar Hoover, airtel, 26 August 1965, FBI 100-33796-79; FBI, memo, "Picketing of the State Department Building," 3 September 1965, FBI 100-33796-80.

153. "Pickets Assail State Dept. Ban on Homosexuals," *Washington Post,* 29 August 1965, 27, FBI 100-33796-75.

154. FBI, memo, "East Coast Homophile Organization Planned Demonstration in Front of White House," 7 October 1965, FBI 100-33796-83; SAC New York to J. Edgar Hoover, airtel, 7 October 1965, FBI 100-33796-84; FBI, routing slip, 12 October 1965, FBI 100-33796-85; Howard Covell to Deputy Chiefs, District Inspectors, and Precinct Commanders, confidential letter, 19 October 1965, FBI 100-33796-86; SAC WFO to J. Edgar Hoover, airtel, 22 October 1965, FBI 100-33796-88.

155. FBI, memo, "East Coast Homophile Organization Demonstration in Front of White House," 25 October 1965, FBI 100-33796-91; SAC WFO to J. Edgar Hoover, airtel, 25 October 1965, FBI 100-33796-92.

156. Johnson, *Lavender Scare,* 156, 202–203.

157. Ibid., 204–208.

7. "It's a Thing That You Just Can't Tell"

1. "Text of the Summary of Report by FBI on the Security Aspects of the Jenkins Case," *New York Times,* 23 October 1964, 31.

2. Ibid.; "Choka Is Reported in Hands of CBS," *New York Times,* 16 October 1964, 20. On gays and the YMCA, and this particular YMCA, see Genny Beemyn, *A Queer Capital: A History of Gay Life in Washington, D.C.* (New York: Routledge, 2014), 35–39.

3. "Text of the Summary of Report by FBI on the Security Aspects of the Jenkins Case," 31.

4. Cartha D. DeLoach, *Hoover's FBI: The Inside Story by Hoover's Trusted Lieutenant* (Washington, DC: Regnery, 1995), 384; oral history interview with Cartha D. "Deke" DeLoach, 11 January 1992, Oral History Collection: Electronic Copy of Cartha D. "Deke" DeLoach OH, AC 96-12, Lyndon B. Johnson Presidential Library (hereafter LBJL), Austin, TX.

5. DeLoach, *Hoover's FBI,* 384–385.

6. Lyndon B. Johnson (LBJ), conversation with Abe Fortas, 14 October 1964, tape WH6410.08, program no. 6, citation number 5876, LBJL via the Miller Center, University of Virginia, millercenter.org; John Morris, "Johnson Friends Called on Press," *New York Times,* 16 October 1964, 20.

7. LBJ, conversation with Fortas, 14 October 1964, program no 6.

8. Ibid.

9. Ibid.; LBJ, conversation with Fortas, 14 October 1964, tape WH6410.08, program no. 7, citation number 5877.

10. Ibid.

11. LBJ, conversation with Lady Bird Johnson, 15 October 1964, tape WH6410.11, program no. 5, citation number 5895, LBJL via the Miller Center, University of Virginia, millercenter.org.

12. "Johnson Issues Reply on Jenkins," *Harvard Crimson* (16 October 1964); Max Frankel, "President's Aide Quits on Report of Morals Case," *New York Times,* 15 October 1964; Lyndon B. Johnson, "Statement by the President on Walter Jenkins," 15 October

1964, online by Gerhard Peters and John T. Woolley, American Presidency Project, http://www.presidency.ucsb.edu/ws/?pid'26611.

13. LBJ, conversation with Cartha DeLoach, 14 October 1964, tape WH6410.09, citation number 5884, LBJL via the Miller Center, University of Virginia, millercenter.org; DeLoach, *Hoover's FBI*, 385–387.

14. LBJ, conversation with DeLoach, 14 October 1964.

15. LBJ, conversation with Fortas, 14 October 1964, tape WH6410.09, citation number 5880, LBJL via the Miller Center, University of Virginia, millercenter.org; Cartha De-Loach to John Mohr, 17 October 1964, FBI 161-2624-Not Recorded.

16. DeLoach, *Hoover's FBI*, 386–387; Tom Wicker, "Jenkins Cleared of Security Slip in FBI Report," *New York Times*, 23 October 1964; "Text of the Summary of Report by FBI on the Security Aspects of the Jenkins Case," 31.

17. William C. Sullivan, *The Bureau: My Thirty Years in Hoover's FBI* (New York: Norton, 1979), 68.

18. LBJ, conversation with Fortas, 14 October 1964, program no. 7.

19. Sullivan, *Bureau*, 68–69.

20. LBJ, conversation with Fortas, 14 October 1964, tape WH6410.09, citation number 5881; LBJ, conversation with Clark Clifford, 14 October 1964, tape WH6410.10, citation number 5886; LBJ, conversation with DeLoach, 27 October 1964, tape WH6410.15, citation number 5971, LBJL via the Miller Center, University of Virginia, millercenter.org.

21. Sullivan, *Bureau*, 69; "Hoover Assailed on Jenkins Case," *New York Times*, 28 October 1964, 34.

22. Wicker, "Jenkins Cleared of Security Slip in FBI Report"; "Text of the Summary of Report by FBI on the Security Aspects of the Jenkins Case," 31.

23. LBJ, conversation with J. Edgar Hoover, 23 October 1964, tape WH6410.14, citation number 5948, LBJL via the Miller Center, University of Virginia, millercenter.org; LBJ, conversation with DeLoach, 27 October 1964. LBJ's executive order can be found in box 38, Hoover Retirement folder, White House Special Files: Staff Member and Office Files (SMOF), John Dean III files, Richard Nixon Presidential Library, Yorba Linda, CA.

24. LBJ, conversation with J. Edgar Hoover, 31 October 1964, tape WH6410.16, program no. 7, citation number 5989, LBJL via the Miller Center, University of Virginia, millercenter.org.

25. Ibid.

26. Ibid.

27. David Johnson, *The Lavender Scare: The Cold War Persecution of Gays and Lesbians in the Federal Government* (Chicago: University of Chicago Press, 2004), 198–199.

28. Cartha DeLoach to J. Edgar Hoover, memo, 27 November 1964, FBI 161-2624-41.

29. Ibid.; oral history interview with DeLoach, 11 January 1992.

30. William Sullivan to John Dean, memo, 31 January 1975, in US Senate, Select Committee to Study Governmental Operations with Respect to Intelligence Activities, *Hearings*, 94th Congress, 1st sess., vol. 6 (Washington, DC: US Government Printing Office, 1976), 539, exhibit 52.

31. DeLoach to Hoover, memo, 27 November 1964.

32. SAC Los Angeles to J. Edgar Hoover, airtel and letterhead memo, 12 November

1964, FBI 121-2624-39; W. V. Cleveland to Evans, memo, 16 November 1964, FBI 121-2624-40.

33. W. V. Cleveland to Evans, memo, 19 October 1964, FBI 161-2624-34.

34. Cartha DeLoach, memo, 18 November 1964, FBI 161-2624-37.

35. DeLoach to Hoover, memo, 27 November 1964.

36. W. V. Cleveland to Evans, memo, 2 December 1964, FBI 161-2624-44; Cartha De-Loach to Bill Moyers, letter, 2 December 1964, FBI 121-2624-45; SAC New York, report, Jack Joseph Valenti, 2 December 1964, FBI 161-2624-46 (unrecorded copy filed in 105-34074-26).

37. Ray Wannall to William Sullivan, memo, 28 May 1965, FBI 161-2624-51.

38. SAC WFO to J. Edgar Hoover, memo, 14 May 1965, FBI (file number redacted)-66; Hoover to SAC Los Angeles, memo, 28 May 1965, FBI (file number redacted, but Hudson FOIA release); FBI, reference slip, 21 May 1965, Hudson file; (Deleted) to William Sullivan, memo, 2 June 1965, FBI (file number redacted)-73.

39. (Deleted) to Sullivan, memo, 2 June 1965.

40. SAC Los Angeles to J. Edgar Hoover, memo, 9 July 1965, FBI (file number redacted)-75; Hoover to SAC Los Angeles, memo, 22 July 1965, FBI (file number redacted); SAC Los Angeles to Hoover, airtel and letterhead memo, 29 July 1965, FBI (file number redacted but Hudson FOIA release).

41. SAC (Deleted) to J. Edgar Hoover, attn: DeLoach, airtel, 22 December 1965, FBI 62-110654-4.

42. Cartha DeLoach to Marvin Watson and Mildred Stegall, letter and blind memo, 28 October 1966, FBI 62-5-26880.

43. SAC Los Angeles to J. Edgar Hoover, airtel, 8 September 1967, FBI 94-63352-1; "Rock Hudson and Claudia Cardinale 'The Quiet Couple,'" *Daily Variety*, 5 September 1967, FBI 94-63352-1.

44. SAC Los Angeles to J. Edgar Hoover, airtel, 5 October 1967, FBI 94-63352-2; SAC Los Angeles to Hoover, airtel, 30 October 1967, FBI 94-63352-3; SAC Los Angeles to Hoover, airtel, 28 November 1967, FBI 94-63352-4.

45. SAC Phoenix, report, 23 February 1968, FBI 145-4011-1.

46. Special Agent (Deleted), report, 23 February 1968, FBI 145-PX-230.

47. Special Agent (Deleted), report, under obscene cover, 23 February 1968, FBI 145-PX-230, 7–13. For the FBI interest in obscenity and pornography and its special procedures for the same, see Douglas M. Charles, *The FBI's Obscene File: J. Edgar Hoover and the Bureau's Crusade against Smut* (Lawrence: University Press of Kansas, 2012).

48. SAC Phoenix, report, 28 March 1968, FBI 145-4011-2.

49. SAC Phoenix, report, under obscene cover, 28 March 1968, FBI 145-4011-2, 13–17.

50. Special Agent (Deleted), report, 21 May 1968, FBI 145-PX-230; SAC Phoenix, report, 3 September 1968, FBI 145-4011-4; Special Agent (Deleted), report, 3 September 1968, FBI 145-PX-230; SAC New York to J. Edgar Hoover, memo, 30 September 1968, FBI 145-4011-5; SAC Phoenix, report, 16 January 1969, FBI 145-4011-6. For the film festival, see Charles, *FBI's Obscene File*, 65–67.

51. SAC Phoenix, report, 17 December 1969, FBI 145-4011-8.

52. M. A. Jones to DeLoach, memo, 17 July 1964, FBI 62-108763-29; William J.

Maxwell, *F. B. Eyes: How J. Edgar Hoover's Ghostreaders Framed African American Literature* (Princeton, NJ: Princeton University Press, 2015), 127. There is no indication on these extant documents of a Sex Deviates File number.

53. SAC New York to J. Edgar Hoover, airtel, subject: HOMEX, ITAR Extortion, 20 May 1966, FBI 166-1838-1; SAC Los Angeles to Hoover, airtel, 10 June 1966, FBI 166-1838-2; Gale to Cartha DeLoach, memo, 28 June 1966, FBI 166-1838-Not Recorded; Hoover to SACs in Los Angeles, New York, Chicago, and Las Vegas, airtel, 28 June 1966, FBI 166-1838-(?); SAC Los Angeles to Hoover, airtel, 22 June 1966, FBI 166-1838-4; SAC Washington, DC, Field Office (WFO) to Hoover, airtel, 4 August 1966, FBI 166-1838-4.

54. On PORNEX, see Charles, *FBI's Obscene File*, 106–118.

55. Jack Roth, "Nine Seized Here in Extortion Ring," *New York Times*, 18 February 1966, 19; "Blackmailer Gets Five-Year Sentence in Homosexual Case," *New York Times*, 17 August 1966, 23; David Carter, *Stonewall: The Riots That Sparked the Gay Revolution* (New York: St. Martin's, 2004), 90–94, 100, 252, 287–288.

56. Cartha DeLoach to Clyde Tolson, memo, 19 July 1965, FBI 161-2860-37; J. Edgar Hoover to Marvin Watson, letter and blind memo, 21 July 1965, FBI 121-2860-49. See also Alexander Charns, *Cloak and Gavel: FBI Wiretaps, Bugs, Informers, and the Supreme Court* (Urbana: University of Illinois Press, 1992), 53–54.

57. On DeLoach helping with the Fortas nomination, see Charns, *Cloak and Gavel*, 94, 176n39; "Senate Confirms Fortas for Court," *New York Times*, 12 August 1965, 13.

58. Fred Graham, "*Life* Says Fortas Received and Repaid a Wolfson Fee," *New York Times*, 5 May 1969; Fred Graham, "Fortas Quits the Supreme Court, Defends Dealings with Wolfson," *New York Times*, 16 May 1969.

59. Graham, "*Life* Says Fortas Received and Repaid a Wolfson Fee"; Charns, *Cloak and Gavel*, 95.

60. FBI, note attached to memo re: Abe Fortas, 20 July 1967, in folder 71, Abe Fortas, Official and Confidential File of J. Edgar Hoover, Marquette University Archives, Milwaukee, Wisconsin (hereafter Hoover O&C).

61. Cartha DeLoach to Clyde Tolson, memo, 24 July 1967, in folder 71, Abe Fortas, Hoover O&C.

62. "Object to LBJ Naming New Chief Justice," *Chicago Tribune*, 23 June 1968, A11; "Johnson Appoints Fortas to Head Supreme Court; Thornberry to Be Justice; Opposition Voiced," *New York Times*, 27 June 1968, 1; Marjorie Hunter, "19 in the Senate Study Filibuster," *New York Times*, 27 June 1968, 30.

63. "Critics of Fortas Begin Filibuster, Citing 'Propriety,'" *New York Times*, 26 September 1968, 1; "Senate Rejects Ending Fortas Filibuster; Next Move Appears to Be up to President," *Wall Street Journal*, 2 October 1968, 3; "Fortas Requests Name Be Axed; LBJ Complies," *Chicago Tribune*, 3 October 1968, 2.

64. J. Edgar Hoover to Clyde Tolson, Cartha DeLoach, Gale, Alex Rosen, William Sullivan, and Bishop, 23 April 1969, "Tolson File," in Athan Theoharis, ed., *From the Secret Files of J. Edgar Hoover* (Chicago: Ivan R. Dee, 1991), 245–246.

65. William Lambert, "Fortas of the Supreme Court: A Question of Ethics," *Life* (9 May 1969): 32–38; Fred Graham, "Some in G.O.P. Ask Fortas to Resign," *New York Times*, 6 May 1969, 1; Fred Graham, "Fortas's Old Form Faces U.S. Inquiry," *New York*

Times, 7 May 1969, 1; Graham, "Fortas Quits the Supreme Court"; Charns, *Cloak and Gavel,* 105.

66. Athan Theoharis and John Stuart Cox, *The Boss: J. Edgar Hoover and the Great American Inquisition* (Philadelphia, PA: Temple University Press, 1988), 404–405; Charns, *Cloak and Gavel,* 101.

67. Fred Graham, conversation with William Lambert, 29 August 1969, box 8, folder 5, Fred Graham Papers, Library of Congress, Washington, DC.

68. Theoharis and Cox, *Boss,* 405–407; Charles, *FBI's Obscene File,* 76.

69. Cartha DeLoach to Clyde Tolson, memo, 11 June 1969, folder 119, Richard Nixon—Homosexuals in Government, Hoover O&C.

70. Ibid.

71. Ibid.

72. Cartha DeLoach to Clyde Tolson, memo, 13 June 1969, folder 119, Richard Nixon—Homosexuals in Government, Hoover O&C; J. Edgar Hoover to John Ehrlichman, letter, 25 June 1969, folder 119, Richard Nixon—Homosexuals in Government, Hoover O&C; J. Edgar Hoover, memo for official and confidential files, 3 July 1969, folder 119, Richard Nixon—Homosexuals in Government, Hoover O&C.

73. J. Edgar Hoover, memo for personal files, 1 July 1969, folder 119, Richard Nixon—Homosexuals in Government, Hoover O&C.

74. Ibid.

75. Ibid.

76. Hoover, memo for official and confidential files, 3 July 1969; Joseph Casper to J. Edgar Hoover, memo, 2 July 1969, folder 119, Richard Nixon—Homosexuals in Government, Hoover O&C.

77. FBI, summary memo re: Jack Anderson, 30 August 1957, FBI 94-50053-2. See also Theoharis and Cox, *Boss,* 281.

78. FBI, memo re: Jack Anderson column, 11 January 1971, FBI 94-50053-38; Jack Anderson, "'First Dog' Given Royal Treatment," *Washington Post,* 20 January 1971, FBI 94-50053-39.

79. G. E. Malmfeldt to Bishop, memo, 11 February 1971, FBI 94-50053-51; Hoover comment on news clipping, FBI 94-50053-Not Recorded; FBI, memo, comments of Jack Anderson in radio telephone interview, 4 February 1971, FBI 94-50053-Not Recorded.

80. Jack Anderson, "Secret File Copies Offered FBI Head," *Washington Post,* 11 May 1972, "Washington Merry-Go Round," K13.

81. (Deleted) to E. S. Miller, memo, 22 May 1972, FBI 65-74630-3; (Deleted) to E. S. Miller, memo, 2? May 1972, FBI 65-74630-1; H. N. Bassett to Callahan, memo, 5 February 1975, FBI 94-50053-214X.

82. Walters to Felt, memo, 20 December 1972, FBI 94-50053-182.

83. Walter Jenkins to Baker, memo, 1 March 1973, FBI 94-50053-Not Recorded; Jack Anderson, "Hruska Helps a Contributor," *Free Lance-Star,* 22 April 1970, 3; Jack Anderson, "Sen. Hruska Vulnerable as 'Fixer,'" *Toledo Blade,* 21 April 1970, 26; Jack Anderson, "Hruska, Poff Fight Gun Curbs," *Free Lance-Star,* 7 March 1970, 3; Francis M. Gibbons, *Jack Anderson: Mormon Crusader in Gomorrah* (Lincoln, NE: Writers Club, 2003), 140.

84. J. Edgar Hoover to Clyde Tolson, William Sullivan, Bishop, Brennan, and Alex Rosen, memo, 25 November 1970, Clyde Tolson FBI File.

85. Rick Perlstein, *Nixonland: The Rise of a President and the Fracturing of America* (New York: Scribner, 2008), 369.

86. Douglas Brinkley and Luke A. Nichter, eds., *The Nixon Tapes* (New York: Houghton Mifflin Harcourt, 2014), 111–112.

87. Ibid., 112.

88. Perlstein, *Nixonland*, 589.

89. "Richard Nixon's Anti-Gay Rant," *Huffington Post*, 2 August 2013, http://www.huffingtonpost.com/2013/08/02/richardnixonantigayrant_n_3695785.html.

90. Brinkley and Nichter, *Nixon Tapes*, 335–336.

91. Perlstein, *Nixonland*, 631–633.

8. "I'm Ready to Die for the Cause!"

1. Special Agent (Deleted) to Special Agent in Charge (SAC) Chicago, memo, 19 April 1970, FBI 100-49116-3.

2. Jeanne Theoharis and Athan Theoharis, *These Yet to Be United States: Civil Rights and Civil Liberties in America since 1945* (Toronto, ON: Wadsworth, 2003), 78–80.

3. See the *Oxford English Dictionary* for the term's usage over time.

4. For an assessment of the contribution of the New Left, including to the gay rights movement, see Rhodri Jeffreys-Jones, *The American Left: Its Impact on Politics and Society since 1900* (Edinburgh: Edinburgh University Press, 2013), 119–146.

5. John Lauritsen, Red Butterfly, http://paganpressbooks.com/jpl/TRB.HTM.

6. "History of the Gay Liberation Movement," *Gay Liberation* (pamphlet, ca. 20 November 1970), 3, FBI 100-167120-1B2(3).

7. Ibid.

8. Martha Shelley, quoted in Eric Marcus, *Making Gay History: The Half-Century Fight for Lesbian and Gay Equal Rights* (New York: Perennial, 2002), 124.

9. "History of the Gay Liberation Movement," 3.

10. Ibid.

11. David Carter, *Stonewall: The Riots That Sparked the Gay Revolution* (New York: St. Martin's, 2004), 18–19.

12. John D'Emilio, *Sexual Politics, Sexual Communities: The Making of a Homosexual Minority in the United States, 1940–1970* (Chicago: University of Chicago Press, 1983), 231; Douglas M. Charles, *The FBI's Obscene File: J. Edgar Hoover and the Bureau's Crusade against Smut* (Lawrence: University Press of Kansas, 2012), 98.

13. D'Emilio, *Sexual Politics, Sexual Communities*, 231; Carter, *Stonewall*, 79–83, 113–114.

14. D'Emilio, *Sexual Politics, Sexual Communities*, 231.

15. Ibid., 232.

16. Ibid.

17. Toby Marotta, *The Politics of Homosexuality* (Boston: Houghton Mifflin, 1981), 76–77.

18. Ibid., 77–78.

19. Ibid., 78; Martha Shelley interview, *Voices of Feminism Oral History Project*, Sophia Smith Collection, Smith College, Northampton, MA, 35.

20. Shelley interview, 35; Marcus, *Making Gay History*, 133.

21. Marcus, *Making Gay History*, 79–82.

22. Public Broadcasting Service (PBS), "Biography: Stonewall Participants," *American Experience*, http://www.pbs.org/wgbh/americanexperience/features/biography/stonewallparticipants/.

23. Marcus, *Making Gay History*, 133.

24. *Gay Liberation Front Bulletin* 1, no. 3 (6 January 1970), FBI 100-167120-28; Marotta, *Politics of Homosexuality*, 92.

25. Shelley interview, 38.

26. Ibid.; John Lauritsen to Douglas M. Charles, email, 13 June 2013.

27. Marotta, *Politics of Homosexuality*, 83–89.

28. Lauritsen, Red Butterfly; Marotta, *Politics of Homosexuality*, 89–91.

29. Marotta, *Politics of Homosexuality*, 95, 103–104, 108–110, 111–115.

30. Tony Poveta et al., eds., *The FBI: A Comprehensive Reference Guide* (Phoenix, AZ: Oryx, 1999), 124–125.

31. Ibid., 125–127. On the Media, Pennsylvania, burglary and who was behind it, see Betty Medsger, *The Burglary: The Discovery of J. Edgar Hoover's Secret FBI* (New York: Knopf, 2014).

32. J. Edgar Hoover to SAC New York, memo, 7 August 1969, FBI 100-167120-1.

33. Senate Select Committee to Study Governmental Operations with Respect to Intelligence Activities, final report, *Supplementary Details Staff Reports on Intelligence Activities and the Rights of Americans*, book 3, 94th Congress, 2nd sess. (Washington, DC: US Government Printing Office, 1976), 234.

34. J. Edgar Hoover to SAC Kansas City, memo, 17 March 1971, FBI 100-464462-2; Hoover, "An Open Letter to College Students," 21 September 1970, Richard Nixon Presidential Library, http://www.nixonlibrary.gov/virtuallibrary/releases/jul10/58.pdf. Five days before releasing Hoover's letter, Nixon distributed an article from a college professor concerned with the effects of campus unrest. See "President Calls Peace on Campus Educators' Task," *New York Times*, 21 September 1970.

35. Hoover to SAC New York, memo, 7 August 1969; "150 Riot at Ft. Dix Stockade; Fires Set and Windows Broken," *New York Times*, 6 June 1969, 33.

36. All of these publications can be found in FBI 100-167120-1A, dated between 8 August 1969 and 31 December 1970. For more on these and other gay publications of the time, see Rodger Streitmatter, *Unspeakable: The Rise of the Gay and Lesbian Press in America* (Boston: Faber and Faber, 1995).

37. SAC Buffalo to SAC New York, memo, 13 November 1970, FBI 100-14970-3; Form FD-192, Gay Liberation Front, 10 December 1970, FBI 100-167120-1B1. On FBI use of its obscene materials filing procedure and interest in the collection of obscenity, see Charles, *FBI's Obscene File*.

38. *Gay Liberation Front Newsletter* (no date but ca. 8 August 1969), FBI 100-167120-1A1.

39. *Gay Liberation Front Newsletter* (no date but ca. 14 August 1969), FBI 100-167120-1A1.

40. *GLF News* 1, no. 2 (10 February 1970), FBI 100-167120-1A4.

41. *National Newsletter* 1, no. 1 (10 March 1970), FBI 100-167120-1A5.

42. *Gay Flames* 2 (11 September 1970), FBI 100-167120-1B1 (1 and 2).

43. *Gay Flames* 7 (14 November 1970), FBI 100-167120-1B2.

44. Marotta, *Politics of Homosexuality*, 82, 88.

45. *Rat* (12–20 August 1969): 7, FBI 100-167120-2.

46. Ibid.

47. Ibid.

48. Ibid.

49. Among the other groups FBI agents reported as present, given "signs and buttons worn by the demonstrators," were the Communist Party USA, W. E. B. Du Bois Clubs of America, GIs against the War, Veterans for Peace in Vietnam, American Servicemen's Union, Youth against War and Fascism, US Committee to Aid the National Liberation Front, Fifth Avenue Vietnam Peace Parade Committee, New York Student Mobilization Committee, Socialist Committee of Correspondents, WSP, LEMPA, CRV, and the Committee for Peace.

50. Special Agent (Deleted) to SAC New York, memo and report, 20 August 1969, FBI 100-167120-5; SAC New York to SAC Chicago, memo and report, 22 August 1969, FBI 100-167120-6; FBI, memo, "Fifth Avenue Vietnam Peace Parade Committee," 8 September 1969, FBI 100-167120-10; "8 Are Arrested in War Protests Here," *New York Times*, 7 August 1969, 10; "More Than 2,500 Mark Anniversary of the Bombing of Nagasaki with Peace Rally in Central Park," *New York Times*, 10 August 1969, 12; SAC New York to J. Edgar Hoover, confidential memo, 8 September 1969, FBI 100-167120-11.

51. Special Agent (Deleted) to SAC New York, memo, 6 December 1969, FBI 100-167120-18.

52. Special Agent (Deleted) to SAC New York, memo, 10 December 1969, FBI 100-167120-19; Shelley interview, 36. On Joel Fabricant, see "Joel Fabricant Perverts Gay Power," *ComeOut!* 1, no. 1 (14 November 1969): 3.

53. Special Agent (Deleted) to SAC New York, memo, 10 December 1969; Special Agent (Deleted) to SAC New York, memo, 16 December 1969, FBI 100-167120-20. On John O'Brien, see PBS, "Biography: Stonewall Participants."

54. Special Agent (Deleted) (331) to SAC New York, memo, 9 January 1970, FBI 100-167120-21; Special Agent (Deleted) (331) to SAC New York, memo, 13 January 1970, FBI 100-167120-22.

55. *Gay Liberation Front Bulletin* 1, no. 3 (6 January 1970), FBI 100-167120-28.

56. "Out of the Closets and into the Streets," *Rat* (20 March–4 April 1970): 10, FBI 100-167120-31.

57. Martha Shelley, "Gay Is Good," *Rat* (24 February–9 March 1970): 11, FBI 100-167120-32.

58. Special Agent (Deleted) (43) to SAC New York, memo, 22 May 1970, FBI 100-167120-39; Shelley interview, 36; Huey Newton, "A Letter from Huey to the Revolutionary Brothers and Sisters about the Women's Liberation and Gay Liberation Movements," *Black Panther* (21 August 1970), FBI 100-65673-9. On the problems of the Gay Liberation

Front with the homophobia of other radical groups, see Marotta, *Politics of Homosexuality*, 126–128.

59. "World Youth Parley Convenes in Turkey," *New York Times*, 14 August 1950, 11; "Youth Council Meets," *New York Times*, 2 August 1949, 10; "World Youth Parley Is Discussed Here," *New York Times*, 10 April 1951, 29.

60. FBI, memo, "World Youth Assembly," 16 July 1970, FBI 100-167120-52; SAC New York to J. Edgar Hoover, airtel, 16 July 1970, FBI 100-167120-53; "Saigon's Delegation Quits U.N. Meeting and Assails Leftists," *New York Times*, 16 July 1970, 5.

61. SAC New York to J. Edgar Hoover, memo, 13 August 1970, FBI 100-167120-60; FBI, memo, "[Title Deleted]," 13 August 1970, FBI 100-167120-59; "New Left Groups in Session Here," *New York Times*, 19 July 1970, 33.

62. FBI, memo, "Demonstrations against Convention of National Guard Association of the United States," 28 September 1970, FBI 100-167120-66; SAC New York to J. Edgar Hoover, airtel, 28 September 1970, FBI 100-167120-67.

63. SAC New York to J. Edgar Hoover, teletype, 15 October 1970, FBI 100-167120-72. For a discussion of the FBI role as the political intelligence arm of the White House, see Douglas M. Charles, *J. Edgar Hoover and the Anti-interventionists: FBI Political Surveillance and the Rise of the Domestic Security State* (Columbus: Ohio State University Press, 2007).

64. Special Agent (Deleted) to SAC New York, memo, 19 October 1970, FBI 100-167120-73; Senate Select Committee to Study Governmental Operations with Respect to Intelligence Activities, *Intelligence Activities and the Rights of Americans*, book 2, 90.

65. Ibid., book 3, 58.

66. SAC New York to J. Edgar Hoover, airtel, 4 November 1970, FBI 100-167120-76; SAC New York to Hoover, airtel, 18 November 1970, FBI 100-167120-82; Special Agent (Deleted) to SAC New York, memo, 15 June 1971, FBI 100-167120-123; SAC Pittsburgh to Hoover, airtel, 30 November 1970, FBI 100-52208-3; SAC Los Angeles to Hoover, airtel, 17 November 1970, FBI 100-167120-85; Special Agent (Deleted) to SAC New York, memo, 9 December 1970, FBI 100-167120-98; SAC New York to Hoover, airtel, 11 March 1971, FBI 100-167120-108; SAC New York to SAC Chicago, memo, 20 April 1971, FBI 100-167120-118; SAC Detroit to Hoover, memo, 17 June 1970, FBI 100-453225-1; FBI, memo, "Gay Liberation Movement," 17 June 1970, FBI 100-453225-1; SAC Albany to Hoover, airtel, 15 March 1971, FBI 100-464380-2 (a notation of 105-34074 on the memo's margin shows it was filed in the Sex Deviates File); SAC Los Angeles to Hoover, memo, 9 March 1970, FBI 100-449004-8; SAC Atlanta to Hoover, teletype, 27 June 1971, FBI 100-464380-3; Hoover to SAC Kansas City, memo, 17 March 1971, FBI 100-464462-2.

67. SAC New York to Hoover, airtel, 30 June 1971, FBI 100-464380-4; SAC Detroit to Hoover, memo, 28 October 1970, FBI 100-459225-5.

68. Shelley interview, 24–25.

69. Lauritsen to Charles, email, 13 June 2013.

70. J. Edgar Hoover to all SACs, personal attention airtel, 2 November 1971, FBI 100-32191-1.

71. Ibid.

72. Ibid.; J. Edgar Hoover to all SACs, airtel, 19 January 1972, FBI 100-32191-5.

73. SAC Miami to J. Edgar Hoover, New York, Chicago, Washington, DC (WFO),

teletype, 1 April 1972, FBI 100-470952-1; Hoover to all SACs, memo, 4 April 1972, FBI 100-32540-4; Hoover to all SACS, memo, 6 April 1972, FBI 100-32540-5; Special Agent (Deleted) to SAC Cleveland, memo, 14 April 1972, FBI 100-32540-9; SAC John W. Burns to all agents, memo, 17 April 1972, FBI 100-32540-12.

74. SAC Chicago to J. Edgar Hoover, teletype, 7 April 1972, FBI 100-470952-2; SAC WFO to Hoover, memo, 20 April 1972, FBI 100-470952-3; SAC New York to Hoover, airtel, 25 April 1972, FBI 100-470952-4.

75. SAC San Diego to J. Edgar Hoover, memo, 25 April 1972, FBI 100-470952-6 (this memo was also filed in the FBI Sex Deviates File); FBI, confidential memo, "Gay Liberation Front," 25 April 1972, FBI 100-470952-6.

76. Ibid.

77. Acting Director to all SACs, airtel, 1 June 1972, FBI 100-32540-39; SAC WFO to Acting Director, airtel, 30 June 1972, FBI 100-470952-12.

78. SAC New York to Acting Director, teletype, 5 July 1972, FBI 100-470952-1; SAC Los Angeles to Acting Director, teletype, 7 July 1972, FBI 100-47092-8; SAC WFO to Acting Director, teletype, 12 July 1972, FBI 100-470952-5; SAC Chicago to Acting Director, teletype, 8 July 1972, FBI 10047092-11; SAC Cincinnati to Acting Director, teletype, 8 July 1972, FBI 100-47092-(?); teletype, 18 July 1972, FBI 100-472348-2.

79. SAC WFO to Acting Director, airtel, 30 June 1972, FBI 100 470952-12; FBI, memo, "National Coalition of Gay Organizations Washington, D.C.," 30 June 1972, FBI 100-470952-12; SAC WFO to Acting Director, teletype, 6 July 1972, FBI 100-470952-14.

80. SAC WFO to Acting Director, teletype, 10 July 1972, FBI 100-472348-3; SAC WFO to Acting Director, memo, 25 September 1972, FBI 100-47234-6; Special Agent (Deleted) to SAC WFO, memo, 31 July 1972, FBI 100-52896-35.

81. SAC San Francisco to Clarence Kelley, teletype, 3 October 1977, FBI 174-7829-2.

82. Clarence Kelley to Deputy Attorney General, Assistant Attorney General, Secret Service, and ATF, teletype, 4 October 1977, FBI 174-7829-3; "Coors Offers Reward in Terrorist Bombing," *Pittsburgh Press*, 2 September 1977.

83. "Politics Reporters in New Stunt Club," *New York Times*, 25 February 1923.

84. "Politicians Spoofed in Songs and Story at Writer's Gambol," *New York Times*, 16 April 1972.

85. "Homosexual Bill Protecting Rights Is Killed by Council," *New York Times*, 28 January 1972; "Death of a Bill," letter to the editor, *New York Times*, 16 February 1972, 38.

86. "Homosexuals File Assault Charges against Maye and 6 Others," *New York Times*, 19 April 1972, 23; John Malone to J. Edgar Hoover, memo, 20 April 1972, FBI 100-469170-4.

87. Marotta, *Politics of Homosexuality*, 134, 136, 143.

88. Ibid., 144–145.

89. Ibid., 137.

90. "Maye Is Held as Harasser in Gay Alliance Outbreak," *New York Times*, 23 May 1972, 30; "Homosexuals File Assault Charges against Maye and 6 Others," 23.

91. "Maye Kicked Man, Witness Testifies," *New York Times*, 24 June 1972, 36; "Official Accuses Maye of Assault," *New York Times*, 25 April 1972, 11; "Court Told Maye Beat Homosexual," *New York Times*, 27 June 1972, 42; "Attack Charges Denied by Maye," *New York Times*, 28 June 1972, 46.

92. "Maye Is Held as Harasser in Gay Alliance Outbreak," 30.

93. "Gay Activist Charge Is Disputed by Maye," *New York Times*, 20 April 1972, 38.

94. "Maye Cleared of Harming Homosexual," *New York Times*, 6 July 1972, 38; "Frand Jury Clears 2d Fire Union Aide," *New York Times*, 8 July 1972, 30.

95. SAC New York to J. Edgar Hoover, teletype, 14 December 1971, FBI 100-469170-1.

96. SAC New York to J. Edgar Hoover, airtel, 16 December 1971, FBI 100-469170-2.

97. SAC Miami to J. Edgar Hoover, memo, 22 March 1972, FBI 100-469170-3.

98. SAC Miami to J. Edgar Hoover, memo, 21 April 1972, FBI 100-469170-5.

99. SAC Miami to Patrick Gray, airtel and memo, 23 June 1972, FBI 100-469170-9.

100. SAC Miami to Acting Director, airtel, 19 June 1972, FBI 100-469170-21.

101. Special Agent (Deleted) to SAC Miami, memo, 31 May 1972, FBI 100-16589-23.

102. SAC Philadelphia to Patrick Gray, airtel, 30 June 1972, FBI 100-469170-15.

103. SAC Alexandria to Patrick Gray, memo, 19 July 1972, FBI 100-469170-16. Bizarrely the FBI has redacted most of the names in the FBI reports, but the original memo from Miami listing all of these individuals is not at all redacted, so actual names can be matched to the corresponding FBI reports.

104. SAC Chicago to Patrick Gray, airtel, 5 July 1972, FBI 100-469170-17.

105. SAC New York to Patrick Gray, airtel, 6 July 1972, FBI 100-469170-18.

106. SAC Richmond to Patrick Gray, airtel, 6 July 1972, FBI 100-469170-19; Special Agent (Deleted) to SAC Baltimore, memo, 7 September 1972, FBI 100-30225-4.

107. SAC Charlotte to Patrick Gray, airtel, 6 July 1972, FBI 100-469170-20.

108. SAC Albany to Patrick Gray, teletype, 3 August 1972, FBI 100-469170-22; SAC Albany to Gray, teletype, 10 August 1972, FBI 100-469170-23.

109. SAC Boston to Patrick Gray, memo, 1 August 1972, FBI 100-469170-24. On the New University Conference, see Fred L. Pincus and Howard J. Ehrlich, "The New University Conference: A Study of Former Members," *Critical Sociology* 15 (1988): 145–147.

110. "Gay Lib: New Name and Policies," *Ohio State Lantern*, 28 October 1971, FBI 100-20096-3.

111. Special Agent (Deleted) to SAC Cincinnati, memo, 9 February 1972, FBI 100-20096-5.

112. "Gays Want Representation at Democratic Convention," *Ohio State Lantern*, 16 February 1972, FBI 100-20096-9.

113. "Three GAA Members Found Guilty of Violating Ordinance," *Ohio State Lantern*, 3 March 1972, FBI 100-20096-17.

114. SAC San Francisco to Cincinnati, "Vocations for Social Change," report, 9 June 1972, FBI 100-20096-44.

115. Special Agent (Deleted) to SAC Cincinnati, memo, 12 April 1972, FBI 100-20096-22; Special Agent (Deleted) to SAC Cincinnati, memo, 6 June 1972, FBI 100-20096-39; Special Agent (Deleted) to SAC Cincinnati, memo, 25 July 1972, FBI 100-20096-50; Special Agent (Deleted) to SAC Cincinnati, memo, 28 September 1972, FBI 100-20096-59; Special Agent (Deleted) to SAC Cincinnati, memo, 17 October 1972, FBI 100-20096-67.

116. Special Agent (Deleted) to SAC Cincinnati, memo, 30 January 1973, FBI 100-20096-76; Special Agent (Deleted) to SAC Cincinnati, memo, 30 April 1973, FBI

100-20096-82; Special Agent (Deleted) to SAC Cincinnati, memo, 20 July 1973, FBI 100-20096-86.

117. Special Agent (Deleted) to SAC Cincinnati, memo, 24 October 1973, FBI 100-20096-37; Special Agent (Deleted) to SAC Cincinnati, memo, 31 January 1974, FBI 100-20096-91; Special Agent (Deleted) to SAC Cincinnati, memo, 29 March 1974, FBI 100-20096-93; Special Agent (Deleted) to SAC Cincinnati, memo, 2 May 1975, FBI 100-20096-100.

118. SAC New York to Patrick Gray, memo, 6 March 1973, FBI 100-469170-25.

119. Sheri Cohen, Gay Activists Alliance of Houston, to Personnel Director, FBI Houston, letter, 23 June 1976, FBI 100-469170-28; SAC Houston to Patrick Gray, memo, 25 June 1976, FBI 100-469170-28; Patrick Gray to Sheri Cohen, letter, 15 July 1976, FBI 100-469170-28.

Epilogue

1. Athan Theoharis, *Abuse of Power: How Cold War Surveillance and Secrecy Policy Shaped the Response to 9/11* (Philadelphia, PA: Temple University Press, 2011), 146–147.

2. Melvyn Dubofsky and Athan Theoharis, *Imperial Democracy: The United States since 1945* (Englewood Cliffs, NJ: Prentice Hall, 1988), 250.

3. Cynthia Fressola to Walter Mondale, letter, 17 June 1977, Homosexual or "Gay" Rights folder, Central Files: Human Rights, Walter Mondale Vice Presidential Papers, Minnesota Historical Society Library, St. Paul, MN (hereafter Mondale VP Papers); William Palmatier to Mondale, letter, 23 June 1977, Homosexual or "Gay" Rights folder, Central Files: Human Rights, Mondale VP Papers; Mrs. E. George to Mondale, letter, 25 June 1977, Homosexual or "Gay" Rights folder, Central Files: Human Rights, Mondale VP Papers.

4. Gail Harrison to Walter Mondale, memo, 27 June 1977, in Homosexual or "Gay" Rights folder, Mondale VP papers.

5. Paul R. Gell to Mondale, letter, 25 June 1977; Jame Dyke to Gell, letter, 28 June 1977, in Homosexual or "Gay" Rights folder, Central Files: Human Rights, Mondale VP Papers.

6. James W. Dyke Jr. to Jane Purse, letter, 25 August 1978, in Homosexual or "Gay" Rights folder, Central Files: Human Rights, Mondale VP Papers. Emphasis added.

7. Jimmy Carter, "Civil Service Reform Act of 1978 Statement on Signing S. 2640 into Law," 13 October 1978, in Gerhard Peters and John T. Woolley, American Presidency Project, http://www.presidency.ucsb.edu/ws/?pid'29975; Margaret Constanza to Jimmy Carter, memo, 21 February 1978; Richard Pettigrew to Carter, memo, 22 February 1978; Stu Eizenstat and Steve Simmons to Carter, memo, 25 February 1978, in folder 2/27/78, Presidential Files, Office of Staff Secretary, Jimmy Carter Papers, Carter Presidential Library, Atlanta, GA; Jeanne Theoharis and Athan Theoharis, *These Yet to Be United States: Civil Rights and Civil Liberties since 1945* (Toronto, ON: Wadsworth, 2003), 235.

8. Both the extant NGTF and ACT-UP FBI files are small, perhaps indicating the bureau's post–Sex Deviates Program interest in gays and gay groups. It is also possible

the FBI has not released some files or has destroyed them. It makes sense, though, that after 1977 their previous focused interest in gays would be muted.

9. Neil Miller, *Out of the Past: Gay and Lesbian History from 1869 to the Present* (New York: Alyson, 2006), 352–353, 372; Task Force History, http://www.thetaskforce.org /about_us/history.

10. Jean O'Leary and Bruce Voeller to Patricia Wald, Office of Congressional Liaison, US Department of Justice, letter, 18 April 1978, FBI 9-6359-X.

11. Patricia Wald to John A. Mintz, letter, 27 April 1978, FBI 9-63959-X.

12. FBI, "Unknown Subject: Stem Wilson," memo, 7 June 1978, FBI 9-63959-2; FBI Director to Patricia Wald, memo, 15 June 1978, FBI 9-63959-3; Wald to Jean O'Leary and Bruce Voeller, letter, n.d. (1978), FBI 9-63959-4.

13. John Shenefield to all heads of offices, boards, bureaus, and divisions, memo, 19 March 1980, FBI 62-118584-1; C. F. Brydon and Lucia Valeska to Sana Shtasel, letter, 26 March 1980, FBI 62-118584-1.

14. Mel Boozer to William Webster, letter, 29 September 1982, FBI 62-118584-2; Roger Young to Mel Boozer, letter, 19 October 1982, FBI 62-118584-3.

15. Young to Boozer, letter, 19 October 1982.

16. Miller, *Out of the Past*, 409–426.

17. Ibid., 426–427.

18. SAC Los Angeles to FBI Director, teletype, 6 October 1989, FBI 157-35228-1 (157 refers to civil unrest); LEGAT (legal attaché) Bern to FBI Director, teletype, 11 February 1993, FBI 163A-BR-5070-1; FBI Director to LEGAT Bern, teletype, 23 February 1993, FBI 163A-BR-5070-2; LEGAT Bern to FBI Director, memo, 5 March 1993, FBI 163A-BR-5070-3; SAC Newark to FBI Director, teletype, 4 February 1993, FBI 163A-BR-5070-4.

19. Douglas M. Charles, *The FBI's Obscene File: J. Edgar Hoover and the Bureau's Crusade against Smut* (Lawrence: University Press of Kansas, 2012), 126–127.

20. Ibid., 122, 127.

21. On the Central Intelligence Agency, National Security Agency, and Bill Clinton, see Rhodri Jeffreys-Jones, *Cloak and Dollar: A History of American Secret Intelligence* (New Haven, CT: Yale University Press, 2002), 279–280.

22. Frank Buttino with Lou Buttino, *A Special Agent: Gay and inside the FBI* (New York: William Morrow, 1993), 18–21.

23. *Buttino v. Federal Bureau of Investigation*, No. C-90-1639-5BA (N.D. Cal. Feb. 12, 1992); Buttino, *Special Agent*, 28–29.

24. Buttino, *Special Agent*, 26–31, 83–85, 94–104.

25. Ibid., 101–103.

26. Ibid., 108–111.

27. Ibid., 115–116.

28. J. Edgar Hoover to Clyde Tolson, D. Milton Ladd, and Louis Nichols, memo, 18 March 1953, folder 105, Joseph McCarthy, Hoover O&C.

29. Buttino, *Special Agent*, 130.

30. Ibid., 141–143, 150–151.

31. Ibid., 174–175.

32. Ibid., 207–211.

33. Ibid., 212–238.

34. Ibid., 240–286.

35. Ibid.

36. Ibid., 289–314.

37. Ibid., 316–330; "FBI Settlement Bans Bias against Homosexuals," *New York Times*, 12 December 1993; "Gay Ex-Agent Settles Lawsuit out of Court," *Desert News*, 11 December 1993; FBI director to all FBI field offices, teletype, 10 December 1993, box 15, Frank Buttino case file, Frank Kameny Papers, Library of Congress, Washington, DC; Louis J. Freeh, *My FBI* (New York: St. Martin's, 2005), 177.

38. Neal Broverman, "Gays Control FBI, CIA, Trying to Subvert Christians, Right-winger Claims," *Advocate*, 3 October 2012, http://www.advocate.com/politics/washing tondc/2012/10/03/gayscontrolfbiandciaaccordingrightwingerbriancamenker.

39. S. A. to ONE, Inc., letter, 20 March 1953, in Craig M. Loftin, ed., *Letters to ONE: Gay and Lesbian Voices from the 1950s and 1960s* (Albany: State University of New York Press, 2012), 213.

Bibliography

Presidential Libraries: Manuscript Sources

Dwight D. Eisenhower Library, Abilene, KS
  Bohlen, Charles (FBI report on)
  McPhee, Henry R., Papers (via mandatory review request)
  Offie, Carmel (FBI reports on)
  Thayer, Charles (FBI report on)

Franklin D. Roosevelt Library, Hyde Park, NY
  Biddle, Francis, Papers
  Gellman, Irwin F., Papers
  Hopkins, Harry, Papers
  Official File
  President's Secretary's File
  Roosevelt, Franklin D., Family, Business, and Personal Papers

Harry S. Truman Library, Independence, MO
  Clifford, Clark, Papers
  Murphy, Charles, Papers
  Official File (419K)
  President's Secretary's File
  Thayer, Charles W., Papers
  White House Central Files (confidential files, sex perversion)

James Earl Carter Presidential Library, Atlanta, GA
  Presidential Files

Lyndon Baines Johnson Presidential Library, Austin, TX
  Johnson, Lyndon Baines, telephone audio recordings (most via the Miller Center,
      University of Virginia)
  Oral History Interviews

Richard Nixon Presidential Library, Yorba Linda, CA
  White House Special Files

Additional Manuscript Sources

American University, Washington, DC
  Pearson, Drew, Special and Digital Collections

Federal Bureau of Investigation
  AIDS Coalition to Unleash Power
  Alsop, Joseph and Stewart

Anderson, Jack

Arndt, Ernest (most destroyed October 1961 and 30 August 1982)

Baldwin, James

Boardman, Leland

Coates, Paul (FBI says it has no file)

Cohn, Roy

Compromise and Extortion of Homosexuals (HOMEX, FBI 166-1778)

Daughters of Bilitis (only thirty-four pages released; larger than what was released
     to me; rest destroyed by FBI)

Davies, John Paton

DeLoach, Cartha

Dowdy, John (only dates after 1970; some destroyed)

East Coast Homophile Organization

Faymonville, Philip

Federal Security Agency

Flanagan, Francis

Gay Activists Alliance

Gay Liberation Front

Gittings, Barbara (FBI says it has no file)

Hay, Harry

Hoey, Clyde (FBI says it has no file)

Hoey Committee (FBI says it has no file)

Homosexual Activity in San Francisco, Research Matter (FBI 94-SF-843)

Hoover, J. Edgar, Official and Confidential File

    Alsop, Joseph (folder 26)

    Bradley University (folder 18)

    Fortas, Abe (folder 71)

    Hoover, sexual allegation (folder X)

    Hull, Cordell (folder 88)

    Lodge Jr., Henry Cabot (folder 5)

    McCarthy, Joseph (folder 105)

    Nixon, Richard, homosexuals in government (folder 119)

    Owen, David Blair (folder 19)

    Stevenson, Adlai (folders 17 and 143)

    Walsh, David (folder 153)

    Welles, Sumner (folder 157)

    White House Employees—homosexuals (folder 159)

Hudson, Rock

Huggins, Buell Dwight

Hull, Bob

INLET

Jenkins, Walter

Jones, Milton

Kameny, Frank (FBI says it has no file, but mentioned in Mattachine Society of
     Washington, DC, file)

Kinsey, Alfred

Laughlin, Leo

Legg, W. Dorr (also in Mattachine file but redacted)

Liberace, Władziu Valentino

Los Angeles Daily Journal

Mann, Erika and Klaus (FBI cannot locate file)

Martin, Del (FBI says destroyed 3 March 1994)

Mattachine Society (Los Angeles; New York; San Francisco; Washington, DC)

Mattachine Society of Washington, DC

Mattachine Society/ONE, Incorporated (headquarters file)

Mattson, Charles (murder file; 1937–1980s)

McCarthy, Joseph

McLeod, Scott

Nabokoff, Nicholas

National Gay Task Force

New York University

Nichols Jr., John Richard (FBI says destroyed 14 August 2008, but have one memo)

Nichols Sr., John Richard (not yet released)

Nichols, Louis (Official and Confidential file)

Obscene File (administrative file)

Offie, Carmel

ONE, Incorporated

ONE: The Homosexual Magazine

Perkins, Isham

Pratt, Harden de Valson (FBI says it has no file)

Radical Lesbians

Reber, Samuel

Responsibilities Program File

Rowland, Chuck

Sagarin, Edward/aka Donald Webster Cory (at National Archives and Records Administration, Record Group 65, FBI)

Sex Degenerates and Sex Offenders (FBI 94-4-980)

Sex Deviates File (destroyed December 1977–January 1978; some case file documents extant)

Sex Deviates in Government (FBI 121-WF-14345; made obsolete in 1953; destroyed 7 March 1977)

Sex Deviates in Washington, DC (FBI 94-HQ-65 Sub. P; FBI lost it)

Sex Offenders Foreign Intelligence (FBI 105-34074)

Sex Perverts in Government Service (FBI 105-12189)

Society for Individual Rights

Spellman, Cardinal Francis

Tamm, Quinn

Thayer, Charles W.

Tolson, Clyde

US Army (records regarding gays and lesbians)

Valenti, Jack
Walsh, David I.
Warhol, Andy

Gay, Lesbian, Bisexual, and Transgender Historical Society, San Francisco, CA
Daughters of Bilitis (FBI documents by Freedom of Information Act request
[redactions different in hard copy versus online version])
Lyon, Phyllis, and Del Martin Papers (available online from Gale Cengage Learning)

Library of Congress, Washington, DC
Graham, Fred, Papers
Kameny, Frank, Papers

Marquette University, Special Collections and Archives, Milwaukee, WI
Federal Bureau of Investigation, Bulletins
Federal Bureau of Investigation, Destruction of Records
Federal Bureau of Investigation, Dissemination of Information
Federal Bureau of Investigation, Executive Conference
Federal Bureau of Investigation, Hoover, J. Edgar, Official and Confidential (most
extensive, least redacted copy)
Federal Bureau of Investigation, McCarthy, Joseph
Federal Bureau of Investigation, Responsibilities Program
Federal Bureau of Investigation, Special Agent in Charge (SAC) Letters

Michigan State University, Archives and Special Collections
Confidential Collection

Minnesota Historical Society Library St. Paul, MN
Mondale, Walter, Vice Presidential Papers

National Archives and Records Administration, College Park, MD
Records of the Federal Bureau of Investigation, RG 65
Records of the Military Intelligence Division, RG 169
National Personnel Records Center Annex
Kameny, Frank, Civil Service Records
Senate Internal Security Subcommittee (name file), RG 46

ONE Institute and Archives, Los Angeles, CA
Siminoski, Dan, Collection

Pennsylvania State University, University Park, PA
Nichols, Jack, Collection

Princeton University, Seeley G. Mudd Library
Huggins, Buell Dwight, Correspondence, American Civil Liberties Union Archives

University of Minnesota Law Library
Darrow, Clarence, Digital Collection

Government Reports and Publications

Congressional Record (1950)

US House of Representatives, Committee on Appropriations, Subcommittee on the Department of Justice. *Hearings* for Department of Justice Appropriations for 1952. 82nd Congress, 1st session, 15 February 1951. Washington, DC: US Government Printing Office, 1951.

US House of Representatives. *Hearings before the Committee on Un-American Activities, Investigation of Communist Activities in the State of California*, Part 6. 83rd Congress, 2nd session, 20 April 1954. Washington, DC: US Government Printing Office, 1954.

US Senate, Committee on Expenditures in the Executive Departments, Investigations Subcommittee. *Hearings* Pursuant to S. Res. 280, Executive Session Transcripts. 81st Congress, 2nd session, July 14–September 8, 1950. Washington, DC: US Government Printing Office, 1950 (Hoey hearings).

US Senate, Committee on Expenditures in the Executive Departments. Report No. 1747, *Employment of Moral Perverts by Government Agencies*. 81st Congress, 2nd session, 1950. Washington, DC: US Government Printing Office, 1950 (McClellan Report).

US Senate. *Employment of Homosexuals and Other Sex Perverts in Government: Interim Report Submitted to the Committee on Expenditures in the Executive Department*. 81st Congress, 2nd session, S. Doc. 241. Washington, DC: US Government Printing Office, 1950 (Hoey Report).

US Senate, Select Committee to Study Governmental Operations with Respect to Intelligence Activities. *Final Report: Intelligence Activities and the Rights of Americans*, Books 2 and 3. 94th Congress, 2nd session, 1976. Washington, DC: US Government Printing Office, 1976 (Church Committee Report).

US Senate, Select Committee to Study Governmental Operations with Respect to Intelligence Activities. *Hearings*. 94th Congress, 1st session, vol. 6. Washington, DC: US Government Printing Office, 1976 (Church Committee FBI hearings).

US Senate, Subcommittee Appointed by the Subcommittee on Appropriations for the District of Columbia, on the Infiltration of Subversives and Moral Perverts in the Executive Branch of the United States Government. *Report of the Investigations on the Junior Senator of Nebraska*, S. Doc. 4179. 81st Congress, 2nd session, 1950. Washington, DC: US Government Printing Office, 1950 (Wherry Report).

US Senate, Subcommittee of Subcommittee on Appropriations for the District of Columbia. *Report Made by the Chairman, the Senator from the State of Alabama, Mr. Hill, with Reference to Testimony on Subversive Activity and Homosexuals in the Government Service*, S. Doc. 4178. 81st Congress, 2nd session, May 1950 (Hill Report).

Oral History Interviews, Published Documents, and Correspondence

Brinkley, Douglas, and Luke A. Nichter, eds. *The Nixon Tapes*. New York: Houghton Mifflin Harcourt, 2014.

Katz, Jonathan Ned. *Gay American History: Lesbians and Gay Men in the USA*. Rev. ed. New York: Meridian, 1992.

Lauritsen, John, and John O'Brien. "Biography: Stonewall Participants," *American Experience*, Public Broadcasting Service.

Marcus, Eric. *Making Gay History: The Half-Century Fight for Lesbian and Gay Equal Rights*. New York: Perennial, 2002.

———. *Making History: The Struggle for Gay and Lesbian Equal Rights, 1945–1990—an Oral History*. New York: Harper Collins, 1992.

Shelley, Martha. Interview. *Voices of Feminism Oral History Project*. Sophia Smith Collection, Smith College, Northampton, MA.

Theoharis, Athan, ed. *From the Secret Files of J. Edgar Hoover*. Chicago: Ivan R. Dee, 1991.

Tobin, Kay, and Randy Wicker. *The Gay Crusaders: In depth Interviews with 15 Homosexuals—Men and Women Who Are Shaping America's Newest Sexual Revolution*. New York: Paperback Library, 1972.

Woolley, John T., and Gerhard Peters. American Presidency Project, online archive. University of California–Santa Barbara.

Newspapers and Periodicals

Advocate
American Magazine
Chicago Tribune
Confidential
Coronet
Daily Variety
Free Lance-Star
Harvard Crimson
Huffington Post
Los Angeles Daily News
Los Angeles Mirror
Los Angeles Times
Milwaukee Journal
Newsweek
New York Herald Tribune
New York Post
New York Times
Ohio State Lantern
Pittsburgh Press
San Francisco Chronicle
Sunday Star
Time
Toledo Blade
Wall Street Journal
Washington Afro American
Washington Herald
Washington Post

Washington Times
Washington Times-Herald

Memoirs and Other Primary Sources

Allen, Frederick Lewis. *Only Yesterday: An Informal History of the 1920s.* New York: Harper and Row, 1931.

Biddle, Francis. *In Brief Authority.* Garden City, NY: Doubleday, 1962.

Buttino, Frank. *A Special Agent: Gay and Inside the FBI.* New York: Morrow, 1993.

Cory, Donald Webster (pseudonym for Edward Sagarin). *The Homosexual in America: A Subjective Approach.* New York: Greenberg, 1951.

———. *The Lesbian in America.* New York: Citadel Press, 1964.

———, and John P. LeRoy. *The Homosexual and His Society.* New York: Citadel, 1963.

DeLoach, Cartha D. *Hoover's FBI: The Inside Story by Hoover's Trusted Lieutenant.* Washington, DC: Regnery, 1995.

———. Response to Ronald Kessler. "Did J. Edgar Hoover Really Wear Dresses?" History News Network. http://hnn.us/articles/814.html.

De River, J. Paul. *The Sex Criminal: Documented Case Histories That Rip the Mask from Society's Most Fearsome Enemy.* Los Angeles: Associate Professional Services, 1965.

Freeh, Louis J. *My FBI.* New York: St. Martin's, 2005.

Frosch, Jack, and Walter Bromberg. "Sex Offender: A Psychiatric Study." *American Journal of Orthopsychiatry* 9 (October 1939): 761–762.

Haines, Gerald K., and David A. Langbart. *Unlocking the Files of the FBI: A Guide to Its Records and Classification System.* Wilmington, DE: Scholarly Resources, 1993.

Haynes, John Earl. "Senator Joseph McCarthy's Lists and Venona." April 2007. http://www.johnearlhaynes.org/page62.html.

Hoover, J. Edgar. "How Safe Is Your Daughter?" *American Magazine* 144 (July 1947): 32–33, 102–104.

———. "Needed: A Quarantine to Prevent Crime." *This Week* (magazine), *Milwaukee Journal,* 10 March 1957, 8–10.

———. "Role of the FBI in the Federal Employee Security Program." *Northwestern University Law Review* 49 (1954): 333–347.

Lait, Jack, and Lee Mortimer. *Chicago Confidential.* New York: Crown, 1950.

———. *New York Confidential.* New York: Crown, 1948.

———. *U.S.A. Confidential.* New York: Crown, 1952.

———. *Washington Confidential.* New York: Crown, 1951.

Lee, Robert Emmet. *In the Public Interest: The Life of Robert Emmet Lee from the FBI to the FCC.* Lanham, MD: University Press of America, 1996.

Naked Gun 33 1/3: The Final Insult, film directed by Peter Sega. Los Angeles: Paramount Pictures, 1994.

Sagarin, Edward. *Odd Man In: Societies of Deviants in America.* Chicago: Quadrangle, 1969.

———. "Structure and Ideology in an Association of Deviants." PhD dissertation, New York University, 1966.

Sullivan, William C. *The Bureau: My Thirty Years in Hoover's FBI.* New York: Norton, 1979.

Turner, William W. *Hoover's FBI.* New York: Thunder's Mouth, 1993.

US Department of State. *Foreign Service List, January 1, 1952.* Washington, DC: US Government Printing Office, 1952.

Wannall, Ray. *The Real J. Edgar Hoover, for the Record.* Paducah, KY: Turner, 2000.

Secondary Sources

Altman, Dennis. *Homosexual Oppression and Liberation.* 2nd ed. New York: New York University Press, 1993.

Batvinis, Raymond J. *Hoover's Secret War against Axis Spies: FBI Counterintelligence during World War II.* Lawrence: University Press of Kansas, 2014.

———. *The Origins of FBI Counter-intelligence.* Lawrence: University Press of Kansas, 2007.

———. "The Strange Wartime Odyssey of Louis C. Beck." *World War II Quarterly* 5, no. 2 (Spring 2008).

Beemyn, Genny. *A Queer Capital: A History of Gay Life in Washington, D.C.* New York: Routledge, 2014.

Berube, Allan. *Coming Out under Fire: The History of Gay Men and Women in World War II.* New York: Free Press, 1990.

Boyd, Nan Alamilla. *Wide Open Town: A History of Queer San Francisco.* Berkeley: University of California Press, 2003.

Bullough, Vern L. *Before Stonewall: Activists for Gay and Lesbian Rights in Historical Context.* New York: Harrington Park, 2002.

Campbell III, J. Louis. *Jack Nichols, Gay Pioneer.* New York: Harrington Park, 2007.

Canaday, Margot. *The Straight State: Sexuality and Citizenship in Twentieth-Century America.* Princeton, NJ: Princeton University Press, 2009.

Carew, Anthony. "The American Labor Movement in Fizzland: The Free Trade Union Committee and the CIA." *Labor History* 39, no. 1 (1998): 25–42.

Carter, David. *Stonewall: The Riots That Sparked the Gay Revolution.* New York: St. Martin's Griffin, 2004.

Cecil, Matthew. *Hoover's FBI and the Fourth Estate: The Campaign to Control the Press and the Bureau's Image.* Lawrence: University Press of Kansas, 2014.

Charles, Douglas M. "'Before the Colonel Arrived': Hoover, Donovan, Roosevelt, and the Origins of American Central Intelligence." *Intelligence and National Security* 20 (Summer 2005): 225–237.

———. "Communist and Homosexual: The FBI, Harry Hay, and the Secret Side of the Lavender Scare, 1943–1961." *American Communist History* 11, no. 1 (2012): 101–124.

———. *The FBI's Obscene File: J. Edgar Hoover and the Bureau's Crusade against Smut.* Lawrence: University Press of Kansas, 2012.

———. "Informing FDR: FBI Political Surveillance and the Isolationist-Interventionist Foreign Policy Debate, 1939–1945." *Diplomatic History* 24 (Spring 2000): 211–232.

———. *J. Edgar Hoover and the Anti-interventionists: FBI Political Surveillance and the Rise of the Domestic Security State, 1939–1945.* Columbus: Ohio State University Press, 2007.

Charns, Alexander. *Cloak and Gavel: FBI Wiretaps, Bugs, Informers, and the Supreme Court.* Urbana: University of Illinois Press, 1992.

Chauncey, George. *Gay New York.* New York: BasicBooks, 1994.

———. "The Postwar Sex Crime Panic," in *True Stories from the American Past,* edited by William Graebner. New York: McGraw-Hill, 1993, 161–165.

Cole, Wayne S. *Roosevelt and the Isolationists, 1932–1945.* Lincoln: University of Nebraska Press, 1983.

Cuordileone, K. A. *Manhood and American Political Culture in the Cold War.* New York: Routledge, 2005.

———. "'Politics in an Age of Anxiety': Cold War Political Culture and the Crisis in American Masculinity, 1949–1960." *Journal of American History* 87 (September 2000): 515–545.

Dean, John. *The Rehnquist Choice: The Untold Story of the Nixon Appointment That Redefined the Supreme Court.* New York: Touchstone, 2001.

Dean, Robert. "Charles W. Thayer: Purged from the State Department," in *The Human Tradition in America since 1945,* edited by David L. Anderson. Wilmington: Scholarly Resources, 2003.

———. *Imperial Brotherhood: Gender and the Making of Cold War Foreign Policy.* Amherst: University of Massachusetts Press, 2001.

D'Emilio, John. *Sexual Politics, Sexual Communities: The Making of a Homosexual Minority in the United States, 1940–1970.* 2nd ed. Chicago: University of Chicago Press, 1998.

———, and Estelle B. Freedman. *Intimate Matters: A History of Sexuality in America.* 2nd ed. Chicago: University of Chicago Press, 1997.

DePastino, Todd. *Citizen Hobo: How a Century of Homelessness Shaped America.* Chicago: University of Chicago Press, 2003.

Doenecke, Justus. *Storm on the Horizon: The Challenge to American Intervention, 1939–1941.* Lanham, MD: Rowman and Littlefield, 2000.

Duberman, Martin. "Dr. Sagarin and Mr. Cory: The 'Father' of the Homophile Movement." *Harvard Gay and Lesbian Review* (Fall 1997): 7–14.

———, Martha Vicinus, and George Chauncey Jr., eds. *Hidden from History: Reclaiming the Gay and Lesbian Past.* New York: Meridian, 1990.

Dubofsky, Melvyn, and Athan Theoharis. *Imperial Democracy: The United States since 1945.* Englewood Cliffs, NJ: Prentice Hall, 1988.

Dynes, Wayne R., ed. *Encyclopedia of Homosexuality.* New York: Garland, 1990.

Farrell, John A. *Clarence Darrow: Attorney for the Damned.* New York: Vintage, 2011.

Feldstein, Mark. *Poisoning the Press: Richard Nixon, Jack Anderson, and the Rise of Washington's Scandal Culture.* New York: Farrar, Straus, and Giroux, 2010.

Franks, Lyn Diane. "Torchbearers and Front Runners: The Daughters of Bilitis and Women's Rights." MA thesis, Murray State University, 2011.

Freedman, Estelle B. "'Uncontrolled Desires': The Response to the Sexual Psychopath, 1920–1960." *Journal of American History* 74 (June 1987).

Gallo, Marcia M. *Different Daughters: A History of the Daughters of Bilitis and the Rise of the Lesbian Rights Movement.* New York: Carrol and Graf, 2006.

Gathorne-Hardy, Jonathan. *Sex, the Measure of All Things: A Life of Alfred C. Kinsey.* Bloomington: Indiana University Press, 1998.

Gellman, Irwin F. *Secret Affairs: Franklin Roosevelt, Cordell Hull, and Sumner Welles.* Baltimore, MD: Johns Hopkins University Press, 1995.

Gerstmann, Evan. *The Constitutional Underclass: Gays, Lesbians, and the Failure of Class-based Equal Protection.* Chicago: University of Chicago Press, 1999.

Gibbons, Francis M. *Jack Anderson: Mormon Crusader in Gomorrah.* Lincoln, NE: Writers Club Press, 2003.

Glantz, Mary. *FDR and the Soviet Union: The President's Battles over Foreign Policy.* Lawrence: University Press of Kansas, 2005.

———. "An Officer and a Diplomat? The Ambiguous Position of Philip R. Faymonville and United States–Soviet Relations, 1941–1943." *Journal of Military History* 72 (January 2008): 141–177.

Haggerty, George, ed. *Gay Histories and Cultures: An Encyclopedia.* New York: Garland, 2000.

Hansen, Joseph. *A Few Doors West of Hope: The Life and Times of Dauntless Don Slater.* Universal City, CA: Homosexual Information Center, 1998.

Hatheway, Jay. *The Gilded Age Construction of Modern American Homophobia.* New York: Palgrave Macmillan, 2003.

Heale, Michael J. *American Anticommunism: Combating the Enemy Within, 1830–1970.* Baltimore, MD: Johns Hopkins University Press, 1990.

———. "Red Scare Politics: California's Campaign against Un-American Activities, 1940–1970." *Journal of American Studies* 20 (1986): 5–32.

Higbie, Frank Tobias. *Indispensable Outcasts: Hobo Workers and Community in the American Midwest, 1880–1930.* Urbana: University of Illinois Press, 2003.

Howard, John. *Men Like That: A Southern Queer History.* Chicago: University of Chicago Press, 1999.

Hurewitz, Daniel. *Bohemian Los Angeles and the Making of Modern Politics.* Berkeley: University of California Press, 2007.

Jeffreys-Jones, Rhodri. *The American Left: Its Impact on Politics and Society since 1900.* Edinburgh: Edinburgh University Press, 2013.

———. *Cloak and Dollar: A History of American Secret Intelligence.* New Haven, CT: Yale University Press, 2002.

———. *The FBI: A History.* New Haven, CT: Yale University Press, 2007.

Johnson, David K. *The Lavender Scare: The Cold War Persecution of Gays and Lesbians in the Federal Government.* Chicago: University of Chicago Press, 2004.

Kaiser, Charles. *The Gay Metropolis: The Landmark History of Gay Life in America since World War II.* New York: Harcourt, Brace, 1997.

Kalman, Laura. *Abe Fortas: A Biography.* New Haven, CT: Yale University Press, 1990.

Katz, Jonathan. "The Founding of the Mattachine Society: An Interview with Henry Hay." *Radical America* 11, no. 4 (1977): 28–29.

Kessler, Ronald. *Bureau: The Secret History of the FBI.* New York: St. Martin's, 2002.

Langer, John Daniel. "The 'Red General': Philip R. Faymonville and the Soviet Union, 1917–1952." *Prologue* 8, no. 4 (1976): 209–221.

Leab, Daniel J. *I Was a Communist for the FBI: The Unhappy Life and Times of Matt Cvetic*. University Park: Pennsylvania State University Press, 2000.

Loftin, Craig M. *Masked Voices: Gay Men and Lesbians in Cold War America*. Albany: State University of New York Press, 2012.

———. ed. *Letters to ONE: Gay and Lesbian Voices from the 1950s and 1960s*. Albany: State University of New York Press, 2012.

Loughery, John. *The Other Side of Silence: Men's Lives and Gay Identities—a Twentieth-Century History*. New York: Holt, 1998.

Marotta, Toby. *The Politics of Homosexuality*. Boston: Houghton-Mifflin, 1981.

Maxwell, William. *F. B. Eyes: How J. Edgar Hoover's Ghostwriters Framed African American Literature*. Princeton, NJ: Princeton University Press, 2015.

Medilovic, Sabina. "'Moral Degeneracy': FBI Investigation of Philip R. Faymonville of the Lend-Lease Mission to the Soviet Union." History honors thesis, Pennsylvania State University, 2008.

Medsger, Betty. *The Burglary: The Discovery of J. Edgar Hoover's Secret FBI*. New York: Knopf, 2014.

Meeker, Martin. *Contacts Desired: Gay and Lesbian Communications and Community, 1940s–1970s*. Chicago: University of Chicago Press, 2006.

Miller, Neil. *Out of the Past: Gay and Lesbian History from 1869 to the Present*. New York: Alyson, 2006.

———. *Sex-Crime Panic: A Journey to the Paranoid Heart of the 1950s*. New York: Alyson, 2002.

Morgan, Ted. *FDR: A Biography*. New York: Simon and Schuster, 1985.

Murdoch, Joyce, and Deb Price. *Courting Justice: Gay Men and Lesbians v. the Supreme Court*. New York: BasicBooks, 2001.

Murphy, Lawrence R. "The House on Pacific Street: Homosexuality, Intrigue, and Politics during World War II." *Journal of Homosexuality* 12, no. 1 (Fall 1985): 27–49.

———. *Perverts by Official Order: The Campaign against Homosexuals by the United States Navy*. New York: Harrington Park, 1988.

O'Reilly, Kenneth. "Adlai Stevenson, McCarthyism, and the FBI." *Illinois Historical Journal* 81, no. 1 (Spring 1988): 45–60.

O'Toole, David. *Sex, Spies, and Videotape: Outing the Senator*. Worcester, MA: James Street, 2005.

Parrish, Michael E. *Anxious Decades: America in Prosperity and Depression, 1920–1941*. New York: Norton, 1992.

Patterson, James. *Grand Expectations: The United States, 1945–1974*. New York: Oxford University Press, 1996.

Perlstein, Rick. *Nixonland: The Rise of a President and the Fracturing of America*. New York: Scribner, 2008.

Pincus, Fred L., and Howard J. Ehrlich. "The New University Conference: A Study of Former Members." *Critical Sociology* 15 (1988): 145–147.

Polenberg, Richard. "Franklin Roosevelt and Civil Liberties: The Case of the Dies Committee." *Historian* 30 (1968): 165–178.

———. *War and Society: The United States, 1941–1945*. Westport, CT: Greenwood, 1972.

Poling, John D. "Standing Up for Gay Rights." *Chicago History* 33 (Spring 2005): 4–17.

Potter, Claire Bond. "Queer Hoover: Sex, Lies, and Political History." *Journal of the History of Sexuality* 15, no. 3 (September 2006): 355–381.

Poveda, Tony, Richard Gid Powers, Susan Rosenfeld, and Athan Theoharis, eds. *The FBI: A Comprehensive Reference Guide.* Phoenix, AZ: Oryx, 1999.

Powers, Richard Gid. *Broken: The Troubled Past and Uncertain Future of the FBI.* New York: Free Press, 2004.

———. *G-Men: Hoover's FBI in American Popular Culture.* Carbondale: Southern Illinois University Press, 1983.

———. *Secrecy and Power: The Life of J. Edgar Hoover.* New York: Free Press, 1987.

Rosenfeld, Seth. *Subversives: The FBI's War on Student Radicals and Reagan's Rise to Power.* New York: Farrar, Straus, and Giroux, 2012.

Schrecker, Ellen. *Many Are the Crimes: McCarthyism in America.* New York: Little, Brown, 1998.

Scott, Henry E. *Shocking True Story: The Rise and Fall of* Confidential, *"America's Most Scandalous Scandal Magazine."* New York: Pantheon, 2010.

Sears, James T. *Behind the Mask of the Mattachine: The Hal Call Chronicles and the Early Movement for Homosexual Emancipation.* New York: Harrington Park, 2006.

Steele, Richard W. "The Great Debate: Roosevelt, the Media, and the Coming of the War, 1940–1941." *Journal of American History* 71 (June 1984): 69–92.

Stein, Marc. *City of Sisterly and Brotherly Loves: Lesbian and Gay Philadelphia, 1945–1972.* Chicago: University of Chicago Press, 2000.

Stephan, Alexander. *"Communazis": FBI Surveillance of German Émigré Writers.* New Haven, CT: Yale University Press, 2000.

Stockham, Aaron J. "'I Have Never Cut His Budget and I Never Expect To': The House Appropriations Committee Role in Increasing the Federal Bureau of Investigation's Cold War Power." *Historian* 75, no. 3 (Fall 2013): 499–516.

Streitmatter, Rodger. *Unspeakable: The Rise of the Gay and Lesbian Press in America.* Boston, MA: Faber and Faber, 1995.

Strub, Whitney. "The Clearly Obscene and the Queerly Obscene: Heteronormativity and Obscenity in Cold War Los Angeles." *American Quarterly* 60, no. 2 (June 2008): 373–398.

———. *Obscenity Rules:* Roth v. United States *and the Long Struggle over Sexual Expression.* Lawrence: University Press of Kansas, 2013.

Strunk, Mary Elizabeth. *Wanted Women: An American Obsession in the Reign of J. Edgar Hoover.* Lawrence: University Press of Kansas, 2010.

Summers, Anthony. *Official and Confidential: The Secret Life of J. Edgar Hoover.* New York: Putnam, 1993.

Teal, Donn. *The Gay Militants: How Gay Liberation Began in America, 1969–1971.* New York: St. Martin's, 1971.

Theoharis, Athan. *Abuse of Power: How Cold War Surveillance and Secrecy Policy Shaped the Response to 9/11.* Philadelphia, PA: Temple University Press, 2011.

———. *Chasing Spies: How the FBI Failed in Counterintelligence but Promoted the Politics of McCarthyism in the Cold War Years.* Chicago: Ivan R. Dee, 2002.

———. *The FBI and American Democracy: A Brief Critical History.* Lawrence: University Press of Kansas, 2004.

———. "The FBI, the Roosevelt Administration, and the 'Subversive' Press." *Journalism History* 19 (Spring 1993): 3–10.

———. "How the FBI Gaybaited Stevenson." *Nation* (7 May 1990): 1, 635–636.

———. *J. Edgar Hoover, Sex, and Crime.* Chicago: Ivan R. Dee, 1995.

———. "Roosevelt and Truman on Yalta: The Origins of the Cold War." *Political Science Quarterly* 87 (June 1972): 210–241.

———. "Secrecy and Power: Unanticipated Problems in Researching FBI Files." *Political Science Quarterly* 119 (2004): 275–278.

———, and John Stuart Cox. *The Boss: J. Edgar Hoover and the Great American Inquisition.* Philadelphia, PA: Temple University Press, 1988.

Theoharis, Jeanne, and Athan Theoharis. *These Yet to Be United States: Civil Rights and Civil Liberties in America since 1945.* Toronto, ON: Wadsworth, 2003.

Thom, Cathleen, and Patrick Jung. "The Responsibilities Program of the FBI, 1951–1955." *Historian* 59, no. 2 (Winter 1997): 347–370.

Timmons, Stuart. *The Trouble with Harry Hay: Founder of the Modern Gay Movement.* Boston, MA: Alyson, 1990.

Tripp, C. A. *The Homosexual Matrix.* New York: McGraw-Hill, 1975.

Tropiano, Stephen. *The Prime-Time Closet: A History of Gays and Lesbians on TV.* New York: Applause Theater and Cinema Books, 2002.

Valelly, Rick. "The Conflicted Gay Pioneer." *American Prospect* (online), 8 October 2013.

Von Hoffman, Nicholas. *Citizen Cohn: The Life and Times of Roy Cohn.* New York: Bantam, 1988.

Washburn, Patrick S. "FDR versus His Own Attorney General: The Struggle over Sedition, 1941–1942." *Journalism Quarterly* 62 (Winter 1985): 717–724.

Weiner, Tim. *Enemies: A History of the FBI.* New York: Random House, 2012.

Weiss, Adrea. "Communism, Perversion, and Other Crimes against the State: The FBI Files of Klaus and Erika Mann." *GLQ: A Journal of Lesbian and Gay Studies* 7, no. 3 (2001): 459–481.

White, C. Todd. *Pre-Gay L.A.: A Social History of the Movement for Homosexual Rights.* Urbana: University of Illinois Press, 2009.

Index

Abbey Lithographers, 187
Abney, John, 336
Academy Awards of Washington, DC, 256
Adams, Sherman, 121
Adkins, Warren D. (pseud. John Richard
    Nichols, Jr.), 246, 263, 264
Advocate, 354
Advocates of Gay Action, 336
AIDS Coalition to Unleash Power
    (ACT-UP), 348, 350–351
Alcoholics Anonymous, 218, 221–222, 232
Alheim, Ronald, 337
Alien Detention Act (1798), 167
Allen, Frederick Lewis, 20
All in The Family, 300
Allott, Gordon, 189
Alsop, Joseph, xii, xiv, 148–151
Alsop, Stewart, 148, 149
Alternate University, 308, 319
Amarfio, Willie, 321
Amerasia, 70
American Civil Liberties Union (ACLU),
    44, 230, 233, 235, 267, 335
American Federation of Labor (AFL),
    100, 102, 132
American Youth for Democracy,
    171–172, 184
Anderson, Jack, 5, 293–294, 295–298,
    300–301
Andren, Peter, 337
Angie's Place (gay bar), 72
Annenberg, Moe, 43
Army Map Service, 238, 239, 243, 252
Arndt, Ernest Theodore, 81–82
Arnold, Ervin, 13–14, 15, 17
Arnold, Jeff, 338
Associated Press, 25
Avery, Chuck, 329

Baldwin, James, 286
Ballard, Ron, 315
Bamberger, Rose, 193
Bankhead, William, 38

Barkley, Alben, 45, 46, 47, 66
Barry, Frank, 115
Beardwood, Jack, 143
Beck, Louis C., 52–55, 57, 58–59, 60–61,
    61–63, 64, 377n51
Beekman, Herman, 45–48
Bell, Steve, 327
Belmont, Alan, 117, 122, 123, 129, 146, 147
Bentley, Elizabeth, 70
Bergstein, Marti, 338
Bevel, James, 321
Biddle, Francis, 43, 45, 48, 49, 50, 167
Birchard, Roy, 337
Bittman, Bill, 292
Black, Fred, 310
blackmail, xv
    criminal blackmail, 286–287
    and David Owen, 116
    and Faymonville, 53–54, 63
    fears during cold war, xii, 32, 69, 71,
        74, 81, 82, 109, 151, 159, 181, 266, 349,
        361, 363
    fears during Second World War, 31,
        32–33, 36, 65, 66, 68, 366
    and Hoey Committee, 92, 93
    and Hoover, 2, 5
    and Sumner Welles, 41, 69
    and Walter Jenkins, 274
    and Wherry Committee, 86
Black Panther Party (BPP), 303, 314, 317,
    318, 366
    GLF sympathy for, 308, 313, 331
    homophobia of, 319–320
    influence on GLF, 305, 315
Blick, Roy, 90, 96, 106, 147
    arrest of Carmel Offie, 98, 133
    estimates number of gays in State
        Department, 85
    FBI relationship, 83, 89, 141, 219, 230,
        233, 236, 248, 256
    and MSW, 236, 245
    and Wherry Committee, 85–86
Block, Martin, 161, 162, 175, 397n68

Boden, George, 48
Bohlen, Charles, xiii, xiv, 78, 127, 129, 145,
    151, 355, 362
    FBI report on, 131–141
    and Joseph Alsop, 149
Boozer, Mel, 349
Bradley University, 112, 116–117
Brewster, Ralph, 48–49, 50–51, 66
Bricker, Bill, 328–329
Bridges, Styles, 126, 136, 138, 139, 141
Brissette, Gerard, 160, 163, 395n33
Brock, Ray Benton, 135
Brosse, Jacques, 77, 128, 134, 140,
    390n204
Brown, Irving, 121
Brown, John, 314
Brown, Michael, 307, 315
Bryant, Anita, 344, 346, 348
Brydon, C. F., 349
Budenz, Louis, 184
Bullitt, William, 40, 41, 49, 66, 135
Bumblebee, Michael, 329
Bundy, McGeorge, 280–281
Burch, Charles, 334
Burch, Dean, 272, 273
Burns, James, 57, 62
Burns, Kenneth, 159, 160–161, 165
Busbey, Fred, 142, 145
Bush, George H. W., 351
Bush, George W., 350
Buttino, Frank, 352–358

Cafiero, Renee, 336
Call, Hal, 160, 164, 196, 396n37
Campbell, John, 336
Cannon, Howard, 288
Cardinale, Claudia, 283
Carlyle, Thomas, 161
Carmichael, Stokely, 303, 307
Carnegie-Mellon University, 323
Carpenter, Liz, 271
Carr, Frank, 91
Carter, Jimmy, 343–348
Casper, Joseph, 295
Central Intelligence Agency (CIA), xii, 94,
    247, 268
    and Carmel Offie, 99–100, 101–102,
        120, 121

and Charles Thayer, 98
and gay support group, 352
and Joseph Alsop, 149, 150
Chapin, Dwight, 294, 295
Chicago Daily News, 114
Choka, Andy, 269, 271, 274, 275
Christie, Joseph, 336
Citizens' Committee to Outlaw
    Entrapment, 158
Civiletti, Benjamin, 349
Civilian Conservation Corps (CCC),
    25, 26
Civil Rights Congress, 173, 219
Civil Service Commission (CSC), xv, 85,
    88, 142, 144, 151, 248, 341
    and Buell Dwight Huggins, 227, 230
    and Carmel Offie, 120
    and Carter's reforms, 346–347
    and FBI, 83–84, 89, 93, 95, 103, 105, 106,
        107, 146, 255–256, 265, 361
    and Frank Kameny, 238, 239, 242,
        405n75, 406n81
    MSW protests, 262, 265, 267–268
Clark, Ramsey, 289
Clarke, Elijah Hadn "Lige," 266
Clarke, Thurmond, 185–186
Cleveland, W. V., 274, 279
Clifford, Clark, 271, 273
Clinton, Bill, 3, 350, 352, 357, 358
Coates, Paul, 159, 160, 161–162, 165, 181,
    395n31
Cohn, Al, 50–51
Cohn, Roy, 3, 91, 122–123
    sexuality, 383n68
Colby, James, 233–234
Columbia University, 223, 323, 332
Come Out!, 313
Commission on Government Security, 229
Communist Party, 80, 98, 100, 148, 156,
    165, 166, 178, 179, 180, 182, 198, 216,
    220, 226, 246, 261, 300, 304, 311, 312,
    315, 320, 328, 361, 393n7, 396n41,
    397n64, 398n85, 417n49
    and Eric Julber, 184
    gays and COINTELPRO, 323
    and Mattachine, 154, 155, 159
    and ONE, 189
    and Welles, 51

See also Hay, Harry; Hull, Bob;
   Rowland, Chuck
Confidential (magazine), 114–115
Confidential File (TV show), 181
Congress for Racial Equality, 302, 318
Connors, Don, 112
Constanza, Margaret, 346, 348
Coolidge, Calvin, 29
Coors Beer Distributor, 329–330
Coplon, Judith, 80
Coronet (magazine), 28, 73–74
Cory, Donald Webster (pseud. Edward
   Sagarin), 217, 224, 244, 253, 254, 363
   book service, 194, 221
   and Homosexuals Anonymous,
      220, 222
   outed to FBI, 221
   view of "deviate," 218
Cotter, Francis, 219–220
Cotton, Norris, 288
Council for Repeal of Unjust Laws
   (Mattachine Society, Washington,
   DC), 228
Covell, Howard, 267
Covello, David, 336
Cox, Oscar, 46
Cronin, Father John, 87
Cummings, Homer, 30
Customs Bureau/Service, 313, 351–352
Cutler, Robert, 121

Daniels, Josephus, 14, 16
Darrow, Clarence, 19–20
Daughters of Bilitis (DoB), ix, xiii, 257,
   307, 319, 362, 363, 366
   FBI interest in, 195–198, 199, 225, 258–
      260, 409n134
   and Martha Shelly, 324
   origin, 193–195
Davidon, William, 311
David's Bar, 101
Davies, Joseph, 61–63
Davis, Angela, 315
Davis, Rennie, 325
de Dion, Al, 244, 245
DeLoach, Cartha, 98, 249, 250, 252, 255,
   276, 277
   and Abe Fortas, 288, 289–290

FBI liaison to LBJ, 270, 273–274, 275,
   278, 279–280, 282
   on Hoover's sexuality, 5–6
   and Jack Anderson, 293–294, 295
   and Jenkins incident, 270, 271, 273–274,
      275, 278
Democratic National Convention, 113, 311,
   321, 325–330, 334–337, 339, 341
Department of Justice, 17, 29, 30, 46, 48,
   66, 80, 100, 123, 124, 164, 185, 186,
   267, 292, 293
   Buttino case, 356, 357
   liaison with gay groups and civil
      liberties, 348, 349
   picketing of, 254
DeRiver, J. Paul, 74
Derry, Edward, 329
Dewees, Curtis, 244–245
Dickenson, Leonard, 171
Diercks, F. O., 239, 241
Dies, Martin, 70
Dirksen, Everett, 116–117, 288
Dole, Bob, 3
Donegan, Tom, 125
don't ask, don't tell (DADT) policy, 350
Dotterer, Harold, 143
Douglas, Paul, 288
Douglas, William O., 199, 293
Dowling, W. Randolph, 328
Drebin, Frank, 3
Dreyfus, Alfred, 130
Drum (magazine), 260–261
Dufty, William, 225–226
Dulles, Allen, 149, 150
Dulles, John Foster, 123, 125, 131, 135–136,
   137–139, 140, 141, 277
Duncan, Jack, 55, 57, 61–62, 63
Dunn, James C., 121
Dunne, Irene, 50

East Coast Homophile Organizations
   (ECHO), 211 (illus.), 255, 257, 258,
   363
East Village Other, 317
Edwards, Don, 356
Edwards, Leonard, 143
Egan, James, 126
Ehrlichman, John, 294, 295, 300

Eisenberg, Edward, 336
Eisenhower, Dwight D., x, xii, 98, 113, 121,
    146, 147, 151, 152, 242, 268, 293
    and Arthur Vandenberg, Jr., 118–119
    Bohlen nomination, 131, 135, 136
    executive order 10450, 129, 164–165, 366
    and FBI investigations, 277
    and Scott McLeod, 138
Ellis, Albert, 218
Ellison, Phillip Louis, 219–220, 222
Ernst, Morris, 44–45, 66–67
Escoffier, Jeffrey, 336
Evans, Arthur, 324, 331
Executive Order 10450, 129, 164

Fabricant, Joel, 317
Faymonville, Philip, xiv, 37, 55–64, 67,
    68, 79, 203 (caption), 360, 369n5,
    377n54, 378n65
    background of, 55–57
    and Cordell Hull, 42–43
    FBI investigation of, 51–52, 58–61
    and General Joseph Michela, 53–54,
    57–59, 61–63, 378n55
    presumed sexuality of, 59–60
    and Westbrook Pegler, 64
Federal Bureau of Investigation (FBI)
    administrative division, 41, 255, 262, 264
    administrative pages, 165, 191,
    396nn41–42, 398n79
    blind memos, 99, 103–104, 105, 107,
    108, 113, 123, 298
    COINTELPRO, xiii, 311, 313, 322, 323
    COMINFIL, 162, 312, 363
    Crime Records Division, 3, 5, 32, 33,
    41, 72, 83, 96, 98, 110, 111, 113, 120,
    153, 181, 184, 185, 204 (caption), 224,
    249, 250, 255, 260, 261, 270, 286
    Custodial Detention Program, 167–168
    destruction of records, 88, 96, 109, 199
    Domestic Intelligence Division, 5, 88,
    142, 189, 261
    do-not-contact list, 91
    educational campaigns, 67, 70, 110, 360
    FOIA, xi, xii, 36, 81, 111, 130, 151, 234,
    235, 351, 375n1, 395n31, 407n104,
    407n112, 409n135, 409n141
    FOIA Section, x, 82, 88

Identification Division, 83, 89, 95, 96,
    97, 102, 255, 270
image, xi, 77, 96, 116, 153, 281, 283, 347
Impersonation Desk, 261
indexing, 105
informants, xv, 27, 55, 60, 63, 91, 128,
    162, 163–164, 165, 166, 168, 169, 172,
    173, 175, 176, 177, 178, 180, 184, 186,
    187, 190, 191, 195, 196, 197, 219, 220,
    225, 226, 246, 248, 252, 253, 254, 255,
    256, 257, 279, 280, 282, 283, 284,
    286, 287, 289, 312, 313, 316, 317, 318,
    319, 320, 321, 322, 323, 324, 326, 327,
    328, 329, 337, 339, 340, 341, 365, 366,
    395n31, 396n37, 400n104
INLET, 311, 322
Key Activist Program, 322
laboratory, 23, 72, 82, 172
legal attachés, 126, 351
LGBT program, 358
liaisons, xv, 32, 51, 64, 77, 86, 93, 94,
    103, 104, 107, 108, 110, 142, 173, 176,
    180, 198, 203 (caption), 260, 270,
    288, 364
Liaison Section, 126, 138, 149, 255,
    256, 261
manuals, 312, 325
Media, PA, break-in, 311, 341
mental cards, 234
microphones (bugs), 58, 70, 101, 262,
    310, 322, 341, 364
Obscene File, 72, 285, 313, 315, 351, 352
Obscene Matter Desk, 185
Office of Professional Responsibility, 354
Official & Confidential File of J. Edgar
    Hoover, 113
pretext interviews, 168, 173, 187, 191, 364
Records Section, 105
research files, 32, 43, 35, 111, 366
Responsibilities Program, 87
Security Index, 168, 169, 170, 172, 173,
    174, 175, 178, 179, 180, 190, 191, 192
Sex Deviates File (*see* Sex Deviates File)
Sex Deviates Program (*see* Sex
    Deviates Program)
Special Correspondents' List, 127
Special Intelligence Service (SIS), 53
Special Inquiry Files, 295

wiretaps, 23, 58, 70, 172, 310, 311, 322, 341, 344, 364
Federal Employee Loyalty Program, 109, 110, 111, 141
    and Charles Bohlen, 138
    and Charles Thayer, 76, 77, 78, 79, 99, 122
    and Civil Service, 89
    difference between security investigation, 93, 106, 151
    Eisenhower expansion of, 129, 164, 229, 366
    and Ernest Theodore Arndt, 81
    and FBI role, 71
    Liaison-Loyalty Branch of FBI, 142, 189
    White House denial of records, 88, 122
Federal Security Agency (FSA), 141–145
Ferguson, Homer, 122, 123
Fifth Avenue Vietnam Peace Parade Committee, 307, 317, 417n49
Finlator, John, 77–78, 79, 112, 122, 123
Finley, Tom, 321
Finn, David, 160–161, 164, 176, 365, 395n29, 396n37
Flanagan, Francis "Frip," 87–91, 93–95, 106–107
Foggee, Charles, 27
Ford, Gerald, 293, 343
Foreign Intelligence Surveillance Act (FISA), 344
Forster, Rudolph, 39
Fortas, Abe, 213 (illus.), 270–273, 274, 276, 287–293, 364
Foster, William Z., 168
Fouchette, Louis, 245
Fouratt, Jim, 329, 337
Franks, Bobby, 18, 19
Freeh, Louis, 358
Freeman, David (pseud. Chuck Rowland)
    claims gays in FBI, 153, 181–182
    and FBI, 165, 182–183, 187, 396n41
    FBI identifies him as Rowland, 189–190
Friedan, Betty, 303, 304
Froines, John, 325
Frontline (TV show), 2
Frost, David, 344
Fulbright, William, 4

Gabrielson, Guy, 82–83
Garner, Richard, 338
Gates, Phyllis, 282
Gay Activists Alliance (GAA), 312, 325, 329, 330–342
    difference with GLF, 331–332
    and Ohio State University, 338–340
    and political conventions, 334–338
    tactics, 330–331, 332–333
Gay Flames (magazine), 313, 315
Gay Journal, 313
Gay Liberation Front (GLF), 215 (illus.), 302–330, 331, 332, 334, 335, 336, 337, 338, 339, 341, 350
    and Coors Brewing, 329–330
    development of name, 307–309
    difference with homophile movement, 302, 307–309
    dissolution of, 324–325
    FBI interest, 310–324, 324–330
    influences on, 302–305
    and informants, 302, 313, 316–319, 319–320, 323, 326, 328, 341
    and Key Activist Program, 322–323
    membership, 309–310
    and Nixon dirty tricks, 301
    and political conventions, 325–329
    Red Butterfly, 304, 314, 324
    and Stonewall Riot, 305–307
Gay Liberation Front Bulletin, 319
Gay Liberation Front Newsletter, 313, 314
Gay People's Alliance of Washington, DC, 336
Gay Power, 317
Gay Publishing Company, 258
Gay Scenes, 317
gender, perceptions of, xiii, xv, 107, 148, 358
    and 1920s, 21, 359
    and David I. Walsh, 45
    and Great Depression, 30–31, 359
    homophobia, 13
    and Hoover's sexuality, 1, 6
    and Newport Scandal, 13–14, 17
    and Philip Faymonville, 58, 67
    terminology, 12
Georgetown University, 238, 299
George Washington University, 108, 255, 275, 336

George W. Henry Foundation, 220–221
Gernreich, Rudi, 156
Gilbert, William M., 227, 231, 365, 403n37
Ginsberg, Allen, 307
GLF News, 313, 314
Goldberg, Arthur, 288
Goldwater, Barry, 272, 278
Goodpaster, Andrew, 147–148
Gouzenko, Igor, 70
Graham, Fred, 292
Grande, Mathew, 336
Gray, L. Patrick, 234, 297, 298, 327–328,
    329, 336, 337, 338, 341, 342
Great Depression, 10, 17, 18, 20, 21, 34, 35,
    36, 64
    sex-crime panic in, 27–31, 72, 359–360
    tramps and hobos, 25–26, 27
    See also gender, perceptions of
Greer, Will, 155
Gross, Alfred, 220–224, 365
Guerin, Robert, 143
Guthrie, James, 336

Haldeman, H. R., 294–295, 298–299
Harper, Mr., 121
Harriman, Averell, 120
Harrison, Gail, 345
Hart, Louis, 315
Hay, Harry, 154, 393n7
    Bachelors for Wallace, 155–156
    background, 155–156
    FBI and citizenship, 177
    FBI investigation of, as communist,
        166–171, 178, 180, 190–191
    founding Mattachine, 156–157, 173
    and HUAC, 178–180, 398n85
    as Mrs. Henry Hay, 165
    sought as FBI informant, 191–192
    view of gays as minority, 160
Hayden, Carl, 104
Haynes, Fred Orrin, 25, 26
Henderson, Lloyd W., 121
Henry, George W., 223. *See also* George W.
    Henry Foundation
Hickenlooper, Bourke, 288
Hill, Lister, 85
Hill, Milt, 113–114, 115

Hipsley, S. Preston, 104
Hiss, Alger, 70, 80, 87, 125, 138, 364
Hobby, Oveta Culp, 142–145, 207 (illus.).
    See also Federal Security Agency
Hoey, Clyde, 86–87
Hoey Committee, 87, 88, 91, 94, 95, 96,
    106–107, 221
    report of, 86
Hoffman, Janet (Viva), 284
Hoglund, Steve, 328
HOMEX (Compromise and Extortion
    of Homosexuals), 3, 286–287,
    364, 366
Homophiles of Penn State, 336
Homophobia, xv, 3, 6, 8, 13, 73, 156, 158,
    249, 305, 358–359, 361, 366, 393n7,
    418n58
Homosexual in America, The, 217, 218, 221,
    224, 244. *See also* Cory, Donald
    Webster; Sagarin, Edward
Homosexuals Anonymous, 217, 219, 220,
    221, 222, 223
Homosexuals Organized for Political
    Education, 336
Hooker, Evelyn, 224
Hoose, Jerry, 308
Hoover, Herbert, 29, 322
Hoover, J. Edgar, 204 (illus.), 214 (illus.)
    on Bohlen, 135, 136
    on Carmel Offie, 98–99, 120–121, 145
    on Charles Thayer, 79, 122
    death, 233, 235, 297, 298, 324, 327, 335,
        342, 343, 353, 364
    and Franklin D. Roosevelt, 30, 34, 39,
        40, 41, 43, 66, 322, 360, 363
    and gays, 31, 83, 90–91, 95, 246, 249,
        283, 286, 327
    and George Washington University, 108
    on Harry Hay, 169–170
    and Hoey Committee, 89, 90
    ingratiation of, 29–30, 360
    and Jack Anderson, 293–295, 296, 297
    and James Baldwin, 286
    on Jay Lovestone, 100
    and Joseph McCarthy, 91, 355
    publications/speeches, 28, 32, 34, 35,
        72–73, 74, 110, 111–112

and Richard Nixon, 291, 311, 312, 364
and Scott McLeod, 123–127, 138–139
sexuality of, 1–10, 182, 352
and Supreme Court, 293
values of, 76, 283, 358
and Walter Jenkins, 275–276, 277
and Welles, 40–41
Hopkins, Harry, 132
Hotel Diplomat, 320, 321
Hotel New Yorker, 259, 260, 409nn133–134
Hottel, Guy, 77, 78, 79, 98, 101, 102,
    115–116, 141
House Appropriations Committee, 81, 87,
    95, 96, 142
House Un-American Activities
    Committee (HUAC)
    and FBI, 71, 77, 87
    and Harry Hay, 178–180, 190, 191, 192,
        398n85
    and Mattachine Society, 159
    origins, 70
Howard, John, 336
"How to Handle a Federal Interrogation"
    (pamphlet), 257–258
Hruska, Roman, 288, 298
Hubbard, Elbert, 124
Hudson, Erastus, 14, 15, 17
Hudson, Rock, 281–283, 297, 350,
    399n91
Huggins, Buell Dwight, 404n43
    background, 227–228
    expelled from university for being
        gay, 227
    FBI investigation of, 229–233, 235,
        363, 365
    founds Washington Mattachine,
        228–229
    and Sex Deviates File, 234–235
    therapy, 227
Hull, B. D., 239
Hull, Bob, 154, 156, 160, 171–174, 396n41,
    397n64
Hull, Cordell, 37–38, 42, 43, 49, 50, 66
Humphrey, Hubert, 291, 294
Hunt, E. Howard, 292
Hunt, Judge, 158
Hunter, James, 85

Hunter, Karen (pseud. Harry Hay), 166
Huston, Harris, 81

Ickes, Harold, 147
"If You Are Arrested" (pamphlet), 258
Immigration and Naturalization Service,
    14, 177
International Broadcasting Division. *See*
    Voice of America

Jackson, Henry "Scoop," 301
Jackson, Robert, 167
Jameson, Ty, 328
Janus Society, 217, 257, 260
Jefferson, Thomas, 343–344
Jenkins, Marjorie, 269, 271, 272
Jenkins, Walter, 40, 212 (illus.), 269–280,
    287, 290, 363
Jennings, Dale
    arrested in LA, 157–158, 395n16
    brother-in-law as FBI informant, 187,
        189, 365, 400n104
    FBI investigation, 162–163, 175
    helps found Mattachine, 156
    leaves Mattachine for ONE,
        161–162
Johnson, Bob, 326
Johnson, Gail, 251
Johnson, Lady Bird, 272, 273
Johnson, Lyndon, xii, 118, 213 (illus.), 268,
    291, 293, 363
    exempts Hoover from mandatory
        retirement, 311
    and Jack Valenti, 279–280
    orders FBI checks of Cabinet,
        273–274
    orders FBI checks of Goldwater
        staff, 278
    orders FBI checks of staff, 277, 278,
        280–281
    orders FBI checks of White House
        entertainment, 278, 282
    and Walter Jenkins, 269, 270–275,
        276–277
Joint Chiefs of Staff, 151, 265, 266
Jones, Milton, 113, 153, 184, 186, 249–251,
    255–256, 261, 286

Joyce, Robert P., 121
Julber, Eric, 183–186, 189, 198–199

Kameny, Franklin Edward "Frank," 209
    (illus.), 210 (illus.), 211 (illus.),
    219, 252–255, 257, 261, 262, 265,
    267, 268, 277, 301, 315, 328, 346, 363,
    405n75
    Army Map Service, 238–244
    background of, 236–238
    formation of Mattachine Society of
      Washington, 244–246, 247–248
    meeting FBI official, 249–251
    suspects FBI investigation, 251–252
Karpis, Alvin, 296
Karpman, Benjamin, 240–241
Katzenberg, Bill, 308
Kelley, Clarence, 235
Kelley, William, 336
Kemper, Edward, 255
Kennan, George, 134
Kennedy, John F., 118, 253, 273, 353
Kennedy, Robert, 251–252, 253, 288
Kennedy, Ted, 288
Kent, Samuel, 15–16
Kent, Tyler, 52, 58
Kent State shooting, 322
Kepner, Jim, 159, 161
Kerr, Jean, 296
King, Martin Luther, Jr., 254, 302, 355
King, Robert, 250–251
King, William, 16
Kiniry, Richard, 336
Kirby, V. J., 104
Kirk, Alexander, 53, 77, 121
Kissinger, Henry, 294, 299–300
Klaus, Samuel, 43
Knights of the Clock, 154, 159
Korth, Fred, 248
Kuchel, Thomas, 288
Kunstler, William, 321

Ladd, D. Milton, 113, 120
    and Faymonville investigation,
      58, 60
    forwarding gay information while
      retired, 229
    and Francis Flanagan, 88, 89, 90

    testifies before Hoey Committee, 91–
      94, 106–107
Ladder, The, 195, 197, 260
Lait, Jack and Lee Mortimer, 75
Lambert, William (journalist), 291–292
Lambert, William (pseud. W. Dorr Legg),
    183–184, 187–188
Lamont, Chuck, 336
Lane, Arthur Bliss, 135
Langhorne, Henry, 336
Laughlin, Leo, 142–143
Lauritsen, John, 304, 310, 324
Lazero, Tim, 27
League, the, 217, 224
Lee, Robert Emmet, 81
Legg, W. Dorr, 399n102
    background, 159
    FBI investigation of, 187–189
    FBI learns identity, 186–187
    interviewed by FBI agents, 183–184
    leaves Mattachine for ONE, 161
    See also Lambert, William (pseud.
      W. Dorr Legg)
Lehrbas, Lloyd, 76–77
Leitsch, Dick, 307, 308
lend-lease, 37, 42, 51, 54, 55, 56, 57, 59, 62,
    63, 67
Leno, Jay, 3
Leopold, Nathan, and Richard Loeb,
    18–21
Levi, Edward, 343, 344
Levine, Isaac Don, 135
Levinson, Johnnie, 18
Levittan, Shirley, 333
Liberace, Wadziu Valentino, 3, 286, 364
Liberation News Service, 319
Lindbergh, Charles, 22, 23, 29, 43, 359
Lindsay, Eric, 237
Lindsay, John, 306, 318, 330, 331
Livingston, Dave, 328–329
Lodge, Henry Cabot, Jr., xiv, 98
Lonesome Cowboys (film), 283–286. *See
    also* Warhol, Andy
Los Angeles Mirror, 159, 161
Lourie, Donald, 129, 130
Louys, Pierre, 194
Lovestone, Jay, 100, 101, 102, 120, 121,
    135, 146

Lovett, Robert, 78
Lucas, Don, 160, 164, 396n37
Lyon, Phyllis, 193–194, 195, 197, 259

MacArthur, Douglas, II, 121
MacDonald, Eann (pseud. Harry Hay), 166
MacPhail, Paul, Jr., 338
Mafia, 5, 287, 305, 316, 317, 332
Major, Ralph, 28, 73–74
Mallard, William, 143
Malone, John, 330–331
Manford, Morty, 332–333
Mann, Steve, 329
Marcucci, Richard, 336
Marshall, George, 52
Martin, Del, 193–194, 195, 196, 197, 259
Mattachine Review, 188, 195, 196, 224, 225
Mattachine Society, 156–166, 170–171, 173,
        175–178, 180–182, 186, 188–199, 216–
        217, 224, 225, 228, 229, 236, 244, 260,
        362, 365, 396n37, 399n91
    FBI targeting of, 153–154, 159, 161–165,
        180–181, 182, 199
    and informants, 161, 162, 163–164, 165
    and Jennings's arrest, 157–159
    origin, 154–155, 156–157
    and Paul Coates, 159–161, 161–162
    philosophical shift, 159–161, 163–164
    responds to Hoover article, 111
    San Francisco insurgents, 160–161
    See also Hay, Harry; Hull, Bob;
        Rowland, Chuck
Mattachine Society of NY, 224–227,
        239, 307
    and Edward Sagarin (Donald Webster
        Cory), 218, 221
    FBI interest, 225–227
    origin, 217
Mattachine Society of Washington
        (MSW), 210 (illus.), 219, 227, 236,
        244, 245–257, 261–268
    advocacy efforts, 247–249, 261–267,
        267–268
    and ECHO, 257–258
    and FBI, 236, 239, 246–247, 249–251,
        253–256, 256–257
    founding, 236, 244–245, 248
    and informants, 246–247, 253, 254–255

picketing of, 254–255, 261–262, 265–267
and Robert Kennedy, 251–253
See also Kameny, Franklin Edward
    "Frank"; Nichols, John Richard, Jr.
Mattachine Society Washington, DC,
    227–235. *See also* Buell, Dwight
    Huggins
Mattson, Charles, 17, 33, 36, 67, 109, 200
    (illus.), 366, 373n11, 374n28
    FDR comments on, 24–25, 29–30
    and Hoover article after, 32, 67, 360
    kidnapping of and murder, 22–24
    media sensation, 27, 29
Maye, Michael, 332–333
Mayflower Hotel, 115–116
McCarran, Patrick, 71, 137, 138
McCarran rider, 71
McCarthy, Eugene, 288
McCarthy, Joseph, xiii, 3, 68, 79, 106, 107
    and Carmel Offie, 99–100, 102
    and Charles Bohlen, 135, 136–140
    and Charles Thayer, 99, 130
    and Hoover, 91, 122–123, 127, 296, 355
    and sexual deviance, 80–81, 96, 157,
        383n68
    and State Department, 79–80, 82, 85, 157
McCarthyism, xii, 80, 129, 131, 157, 159, 182,
        219, 267, 361
    conflation with Lavender Scare, 96
    Lavender Scare predating, 73
McClellan, John, 91, 93, 94
McCloskey, Pete, 301
McIntyre, Marvin, 42, 46
McLeod, Robert W. Scott, 123–127, 135–
        141, 146, 150
McMorray, Bob, 336
McMullen, Jay, 114
McNamara, Robert, 248
Melchiorre, Gene, 117
Metcalf, Erma, 295
Metropolitan Police Department
        (Washington, DC), 115, 270
    and FBI, 94, 110, 150, 230, 232, 264, 265,
        266, 267, 270
    morals squad, 83, 85, 133, 147, 219, 230,
        233, 245, 248
    and MSW, 245, 249, 256, 264, 265,
        266, 267

Michela, Joseph A., 55, 56, 60, 61, 62–63
    and resentment of Faymonville, 53–54,
    57–58, 59, 67, 378n55
Mickey's Grille (gay bar), 101
Miles, Sherman, 53
Miline, Paul, 336
Miller, Leo, 141, 142, 143
Miller, Patrick, 340
Minogue, Thomas, 223–224
Mitchell, John, 291, 292, 294, 314
Molotov, Vyacheslav, 70
Mondale, Walter, 344–346
Monroe, John, 1–2
Moral Majority, 347
morals charges, xi, 55, 59, 60, 64, 89, 98,
    99, 109, 114, 118, 129, 221, 226, 229,
    230, 270, 271, 280, 292, 366
Morford, Sam, 217, 224
Morrell, D. C., 252
Morse, George, 143
Motor Vehicle Theft Act, 82
Moyer, Lawson, 83–84
Moyers, Bill, 274, 275, 278
Mullender, Joseph, Jr., 186
Mundt, Karl, 77
Murphy, Edward, 287
Murphy, George, 288
Murphy, Michael, 337
Mutual Security Agency, 119–120

NAACP, 318, 348
Nabokoff, Dimitri, 133
Nabokoff, Nicholas, 77, 128, 133–134, 140,
    206 (illus.), 390n203
Nader, Ralph, 6
Naked Gun 33 1/3: The Final Insult
    (film), 3
Nathan, Harold, 23
National Archives, 32, 109, 110, 347,
    386n126
National Coalition of Gay
    Organizations, 336
National Gay Task Force, 348–349, 421n8
National Newsletter, 314
National Security Agency, 268, 352
Nazi Germany, 45, 48, 52, 56, 93, 261
Nease, Gordon, 98
New Era (1920s), 17, 20, 27, 359

New Left, 304, 307, 309, 311, 312, 319, 320,
    322, 323, 324, 327, 329, 337, 338, 341,
    342, 366
Newport Navy Base Scandal, 13–17
New University Conference, 338
New World Liberation Front, 329–330
New York City police, 118, 226, 266, 314
New York Herald Tribune, 76
New York Post, 2, 45, 47–48, 225
New York Times, 17, 24, 27, 135, 137, 138,
    265, 287, 292, 321
New York Transit Police, 226–227
New York University, 108
Nichols, John Richard, Sr. (FBI agent),
    209 (illus.), 244, 262–265, 363
    confronts son, 262
    FBI learns of his son, 262–263
    FBI punishment, 264–265
    learns of son's activism, 245–246
    tells FBI about son, 263–264, 363
Nichols, John Richard, Jr. (gay activist),
    210 (illus.), 211 (illus.), 265,
    266, 363
    background, 244, 245
    and father, 245–246
    FBI learns about, 262–264
    founding of MSW, 236
    and picketing, 261–262
Nichols, Louis, 2, 3, 32, 96, 120, 153, 180,
    189, 204 (illus.), 224
    and Adlai Stevenson, 113–115
    and Faymonville, 64
    and Henry Caboty Lodge, Jr., 98
    and Roy Cohn, 91, 122
    and Scott McLeod, 124, 125
    and Welles, 41
Nicholson, Donald, 76, 78
Nimitz, Chester, 117
Nixon, Richard, 268, 291–294, 298, 327,
    330, 343, 344, 363
    and Abe Fortas, 291–292, 293, 364
    and gay baiting, 298–299, 301, 364
    and GLF, 314, 318, 322, 325, 326
    and Hoover, 87, 291, 311, 312, 364
    and INLET, 311, 322
    and Jack Anderson, 296, 300–301
    and McCarthy, 136
    views on homosexuality, 299–301

Nkrumah, Kwame, 321
Norton, Clifford, 268

Obama, Barack, 358
O'Beirne, John W., 250–251, 407n105
O'Brien, John, 318
O'Connor, Daniel, 144
Offen, Hal, 337
Office of Naval Intelligence (ONI), 45, 46,
    52, 229–230
Office of Strategic Services (OSS), 5, 48,
    70, 78, 127
Offie, Carmel, 77, 127, 128, 129, 131, 140, 151
    arrest on morals charge, 98, 100, 158
    in Bohlen FBI report, 132–133
    and Charles Thayer, 98, 99
    and CIA, 99–100
    and FBI break-ins, 101
    FBI dissemination of information
        about, 120–122, 136
    FBI investigation of, 119–121, 145–147
    FBI surveillance of, 100–101
    and Jay Lovestone, 100, 101–102
    and McCarthy, 99–100
Ohio State Lantern, 338, 339
Ohio State University, 338–340
O'Leary, Jean, 348, 349
Olney, Warren, 192–193
Olsen, Dale, 399n91. *See also* White, Curtis
ONE, Inc., 189, 194, 195, 196, 216, 244
    FBI investigation of, 162, 175–176, 180,
        183, 199, 229, 362
    origin, 161
ONE (magazine), 7, 159, 165, 175, 188–189,
    189–190, 195, 196, 239, 365, 399n102,
    400n104, 400n112
    FBI investigation of, 161–163, 176–177,
        180–187, 192–193, 199, 362
    focus, 161
    mentions FBI, 153–154, 181–182, 225, 362
    name origin, 161
    and Supreme Court, 198–199, 216
Orth, Jeff, 339
Owen, David, 112–113, 116–118, 387n153
Owles, Jim, 331, 332, 337

Palmer, A. Mitchell, 14
Pan Graphic Press, 196

Parrish, Michael, 21
Pearson, Drew, 135, 140, 146, 293, 294,
    295, 296
Pegler, Westbrook, 64, 101–102
Pentagon, 54, 55, 56, 262, 265–266, 276
Perkins, Isham W., 81–82
Perrotta, Corona, 334
Perry, Willis, 119
Pestana, Frank, 179
Petrovich, Mike, 128
Peurifoy, John, 71, 76, 82
Pinkerton Detective Agency, 117–118
Pitts, Charles, 308
Pitts (Washington, DC, Morals Division
    officer), 133
Platky, Anita, 155, 167, 170, 191
PORNEX (pornography extortion),
    286–287
Porter, Ira W., 77, 127–128
Post Office, 39, 162, 165, 180, 184, 185, 186,
    188, 193, 228, 229–230, 232, 245, 260,
    261, 267, 277, 348, 364
Pratt, Harden de Valson, 42
Price, Frederick C., 173
Prindonoff, Eric, 79
Public Health Service, 85, 141, 142, 143, 144,
    227, 228

Quaker Emergency Committee, 221
Quigley (FBI liaison agent), 138–139, 140
Quinn, George, 295
Quinn, T. Vincent, 90
Quo Vadis (film), 223

Rankin, J. Lee, 199
Rat, The, 308, 315, 316, 319
Rauh, Joseph, 298
Reagan, Ronald, 347, 350
Reaugh, Ernie, 337
Reber, Samuel, 130–131
Red Butterfly, 304, 305, 310, 313, 314, 324.
    See also Gay Liberation Front;
    Lauritsen, John
Refugee Relief Act, 126
Reid, Ann Carll (pseud. Irma "Corky"
    Wolf), 189
Relsner, Christian, 27
Reno, Janet, 358

Republican National Committee, 272, 273, 274, 279
Republican National Convention, 325, 326, 327, 328, 334, 336, 338, 339, 341
Reyes, Tony, 162, 175–176, 400n107
Reynolds, Don, 121, 146
Rinta, Eugene, 81
Rivera, Sylvia (Tony), 334
Roach, Ralph, 126
Robert, Rankin, 128
Roberts, Ken, 337
Robinson, Marty, 331, 332
Rogers, William, 122, 123, 299
Rome, 97, 299, 300
Roosevelt, Franklin D., 31, 49, 50, 51, 56, 57, 58, 61, 62, 64, 65, 66–67, 69, 70–71, 76, 80, 131, 132, 148, 322, 360, 363
    and Hoover, 29–30, 33, 34, 40–41
    and Mattson kidnapping, 24–25, 29
    and Newport Scandal, 14, 16–17
    and Walsh, 43–44, 47
    and Welles, 37, 39, 40–42
Roosevelt, Theodore, 39
Rosen, Alex, 75, 76, 140–141
Rosenstiel, Susan, 3–4
Rowland, Chuck, 396n41
    and article mentioning FBI, 153, 181–183, 362
    background, 171
    cofounder of Mattachine, 154–155, 156, 160
    and Communist Party, 165, 171–175
    expelled from Communist Party, 173–174, 397n64
    FBI identifies him, 189–190
    leaves Mattachine for ONE, 161
    See also Freeman, David
Rubin, Jerry, 325
Rusk, Dean, 266

Sagarin, Edward, 217–219, 221–224. *See also* Cory, Donald Webster
San Francisco, 13, 59, 60, 111, 160, 163, 164, 191, 195–198, 216, 217, 224, 225, 228, 236, 237, 238, 239, 241, 242, 244, 258, 259, 282, 285, 300, 329, 330, 339, 344, 345, 396n37
San Francisco police, 237

Scarberry, Warren, 246–247, 248, 252, 253
Scheidt, Edward, 112–113
Schine, David, 383n68
Schmidt, Frederick, 145
Schuyler, Bruce, 247, 248, 249, 253
Scott, Bruce, 267, 268
Second World War, xiv, 5, 31, 44, 78, 80, 87, 90, 116, 122, 133, 148, 167, 171, 172, 188, 217, 220, 223, 236, 262, 276, 302, 367
    and concerns with gays, 31, 32, 34, 35, 36, 51, 65, 67–69, 71–72, 75, 98, 106, 154, 161, 360, 361, 362
Secret Service, 39, 147, 266, 267, 297, 317, 327, 349, 351
Segura, Tony, 217, 224
Senate Appropriations Committee, 90–91
Senate Foreign Relations Committee, 135, 139
Senate Internal Security Subcommittee (SISS), 71, 87, 102, 112
Sessions, William, 356
sex-crime panic, 20, 106, 110, 252
    during Great Depression, 25, 27–28, 29, 31, 32, 33, 65, 361
    during post-Second World War, 72, 73, 74, 95, 154, 157, 361
sex criminals/offenders, 176, 240, 280, 386n126, 397n68
    and cold war, 67, 71, 72, 73, 109, 111, 360, 366
    and Edward Sagarin, 218
    and First World War era, 16, 17
    and Great Depression, 24, 25, 28, 29, 31, 32, 33, 109, 110, 360, 366
Sex Deviates File, xii, xiv, 5, 31–32, 33, 67–68, 72, 109–112, 113, 131, 141, 153, 180, 181, 185, 204 (illus.), 224, 234, 249, 256, 257, 258, 260, 280, 281, 282, 283, 287, 297, 323, 329, 331, 333, 335, 351, 362, 374n28, 382n53, 388n166, 392n242, 408n129, 413n52, 418n66, 419n75
    destruction of, 31–32, 67, 151, 347
Sex Deviates Program, xii, xiv, 31–32, 78, 81, 92, 93, 118, 121, 146, 163, 176, 208 (illus.), 235, 255, 351, 355, 366, 405n75, 421n8

expansion of, 95–97
  first version (1950), 83, 87, 89, 94, 361
  second version (1951), 102–108
sexual psychopath laws, 72, 154, 240
Shelly, Martha, 305, 307, 308, 309, 317, 319, 320, 324
Shibley, George, 158, 175
Shtasel, Sana, 349
Sirgal, John, 318
Slater, Don, 161, 175–176
Smith, Walter Bedell, 121, 123, 125, 129, 138–140
Snider, Fred, 159, 162
Spalding, Sidney, 62
Spingarn, Stephen, 88, 90
Stack, Paul, 337
Stahl, O. Glenn, 242–243
Stalin, Josef, 56, 61, 69, 100, 135
Standley, William, 55, 56, 58
  resentment of Faymonville, 57, 61, 62, 64
State Department, 94, 97, 102, 134, 136, 140, 141, 146, 149, 150, 151, 157, 159, 177, 201 (illus.), 206 (illus.), 230, 262, 266
  during cold war, 71, 73
  under FDR, 37, 41, 51, 52, 53, 55, 56, 57, 65, 69
  gays in, 84, 85, 86, 87, 106, 112, 114, 132, 133
  and Joseph McCarthy, 81, 82, 99
  and VOA, 75, 76, 77, 78, 79, 80, 99, 134
State Department Security Division, 76, 77, 78, 79, 85, 86, 126, 133, 134, 230
Stegall, Mildred, 278, 282
Steffens, Lincoln, 63
Stevens, D. H., 185
Stevenson, Adlai, xii, xiii, xiv, 112–118, 204 (illus.), 205 (illus.)
  ex-wife of, 114–115
Stevenson, Coke, 288
Stone, Harry, 46, 47, 48
Stonewall riots, 215 (illus.), 304, 305–307, 316, 318
Strong, George, 51–52, 53, 55, 60, 61, 62, 64
Student Nonviolent Coordinating Committee (SNCC), 302, 304, 318

Students for a Democratic Society (SDS), 304, 308, 312, 322, 323
Sullivan, William, 214 (illus.), 274–275
Summerfield, Arthur, 113
Summers, Anthony, 2–6, 352
Sumner, Charles, 37
Surine, Don, 122, 135
Syriana Club (Washington, DC), 256

Tamm, Edward, 23, 25, 27, 51, 53, 54, 55, 57, 203 (illus.)
Tavenner, Frank, 179
Taylor, Elizabeth, 350
Thayer, Charles, xii, xiii, xiv, 80, 100, 112, 121, 127, 140, 145, 151, 206 (illus.)
  and Bohlen, 131
  and Carmel Offie, 98, 102
  FBI report on, 127–129
  and Joseph McCarthy, 99, 122–123
  loyalty investigation, 78, 79, 122, 129
  and Nicholas Nabokoff, 133–135
  security investigation, 77–78, 122, 123, 129
  sexuality, 77–78, 127–130
  start of FBI interest, 75–77
  in Yugoslavia, 79, 102
therapists, 4, 231, 365, 220–221
Third World Gay Revolutionaries, 309
Third World Gay Revolutionaries Preamble, 313
Thomas, Charles C., 74
Tillson, Dana, 356
Tolson, Clyde, 41, 75, 91, 97, 120, 124, 125, 180, 204 (illus.), 289, 294
  and Charles Thayer, 112
  and Hoover, 1, 4, 6–8, 89, 153, 182, 297
  on Lambert and Julber, 184
  on *ONE*, 153, 182
Tracy, Stanley J., 83, 89, 102, 255
  at George Washington University, 108
transients (hobos), 25, 26, 27, 34, 35, 359
Trotter, Les, 270
Truman, Harry, 80, 82, 83, 86, 97, 131, 169, 253, 268
  and Hoey Committee, 87–88, 107
  and Loyalty Program, 71, 164
  as new president, 69–70
  Second World War committee, 49, 90

Truman Committee, 49, 90
Turner, William, 6–7
Tydings, Millard, 81, 99

United Nations, 128, 262, 320, 323
United States Park Police, 230
United States Supreme Court, 213
    (caption), 286, 310
    and Abe Fortas, 270, 288, 289, 290,
        291–292, 293
    and Frank Kameny, 243–244
    and *ONE*, 185, 198–199, 216
    and Sex Deviates Program, 104
University of Illinois, Urbana, 227, 230,
    231, 234, 235, 365
University of Virginia, 337

Valenti, Jack, 274, 279–281, 282
Valeska, Lucia, 349
Vandenberg, Arthur, Jr., xii, xiv, 118–119,
    147, 150, 277, 393n261
Vanity Fair, 2
Vasbinder, Sue, 339
Veterans Benevolent Association, 154,
    217, 220
Vick, Allan, 336
Viereck, George Sylvester, 223
Vietnam War, xiii, 291, 292, 296, 304, 307,
    309, 313, 316, 322, 323
Voeller, Bruce, 348, 349
Voice of America (VOA), 79, 94, 99, 128,
    206 (illus.), 390n202
    hearings, 122–123
    and Nicholas Nabokoff, 133–134
    problems with FBI, 75–77
von Krafft-Ebing, Richard, 10

Waddington, James S., 150
Wald, Mark, 336
Wald, Patricia, 348–349
Walker, Frank, 39
Wallace, Henry, 156, 184
Walsh, David I., xiv, 37, 43–48, 66–67, 68,
    98, 202 (illus.), 360
Walsh, Frank, 142
Walsh, Thomas, 30
Wannall, Ray, 5

War Department (Defense Department),
    42, 44, 52, 85, 97, 98
Warhol, Andy, 283–286, 313, 363
Warner Brothers Studios, 49
Warren, Earl, 290
Washington Daily News, 271
Washington Herald, 30
"Washington Merry-Go-Round"
    (column), 146
Washington Park Police, 133
Washington Post, 143–144, 266, 271
Washington Star, 271
Washington-Times Herald, 64, 96
Watson, Edwin, 39, 50
Watson, Marvin, 282
Weaver, Bill, 307
Webster, William, 349–350
Welles, Sumner, xiv, 48, 65–66, 67, 68, 69,
    135, 201 (illus.), 360, 363, 375n14
    background, 37
    and Cordell Hull, 37, 42–43, 49
    FBI investigation, 39, 41–42, 43, 49–51
    Hoover's opinion of, 40–41
    and Senator Ralph Brewster, 48–49
    sexual improprieties of, 38–39, 41
Wereb, Stephen, 178–179
Westphal, Karl, 10
Weyerhaeuser, George, 22, 23
Wheeler, Burton, 40
Wherry, Kenneth, 84–85, 86, 100, 106
Wherry Committee, 86, 95, 96, 106
Wherry Report, 86
White, Curtis (pseud.), 181, 399n91. *See
    also* Olsen, Dale
White, Francis, 41
Whitehurst, Elmer, 104
Whiteside, Dale, 39
White Slave Trafficking Act, 146, 259, 366
Wiand, Burton, 143
Wiley, Alexander, 135–136, 180, 185
Willer, Shirley, 198, 259, 260, 409n133
Wilson, Stem (pseud.), 348–349
Wilson, Will, 291, 292
Winter, Ella, 63
Winterrowd, E. H., 225–226
Wolf, Irma "Corky," 189–190. *See also*
    Reid, Ann Carll

Wolfinger, Henry J., 109, 386n126
Wolfson, Louis, 289, 292
Wolfson Family Foundation, 289, 290, 291
women's liberation, 301, 303, 315, 320, 321
World Assembly of Youth, 320
World Federation of Democratic Youth, 320
Wynne, Claude, 337

Yalta Conference, 69–70, 80, 131, 132, 138
Yarger, Orval, 114–115

Yeagley, J. Walter, 123, 143, 144
Young, Philip, 144
Young, Roger, 349
Young Lords Party, 320, 323
Young Men's Christian Association
    (YMCA), 14, 15, 269, 271, 299, 410n2
Youth International Party (yippies), 305,
    320, 325